T0314086

GOING THE DISTANCE

GOING THE DISTANCE

*Eurasian Trade and the Rise of
the Business Corporation,
1400–1700*

RON HARRIS

PRINCETON UNIVERSITY PRESS

PRINCETON AND OXFORD

Library of Congress Cataloging-in-Publication Data

Names: Harris, Ron, 1960– author.
Title: Going the distance : Eurasian trade and the rise of the business corporation, 1400–1700 / Ron Harris.
Description: Princeton : Princeton University Press, 2019. | Series: Princeton economic history of the Western world | Includes bibliographical references and index.
Identifiers: LCCN 2019016740 | ISBN 9780691150772 (hardcover) | ISBN 9780691185804 (e-book)
Subjects: LCSH: Corporations—Europe—History. | Eurasia—Commerce—History. | Eurasia—Economic conditions.
Classification: LCC HD2844 .H37 2019 | DDC 382.095–dc23
LC record available at https://lccn.loc.gov/2019016740

British Library Cataloging-in-Publication Data is available

Editorial: Joe Jackson and Jacqueline Delaney
Production Editorial: Kathleen Cioffi
Text and Jacket Design: Lorraine Doneker
Production: Erin Suydam
Publicity: Nathalie Levine and Kate Farquhar-Thomson

Jacket image: Science History Images / Alamy

This book has been composed in Minion with Gotham for display

Printed on acid-free paper. ∞

Printed in the United States of America

1 3 5 7 9 10 8 6 4 2

For Hadas

CONTENTS

~ ~ ~

ACKNOWLEDGMENTS

~ ~ ~

This book was in the making for more than a decade. During that time, I delved into the history of civilizations, periods, and institutions that were new to me. I needed guiding through the historical literature, direction to sources, explanations about the details of institutions, and suggestions for theoretical frameworks. Joel Mokyr is the scholar to whom I owe the most. He is an ideal series editor, encouraging, motivating, and insisting on timely progress. He warned me of the consequences of becoming a dean, but once I assumed that office (which I held for five long yet rewarding years) he supported me and the book through the consequent protraction of the project. He was critical in the most insightful and productive way possible. He also wisely selected three anonymous referees who examined the manuscript from three distinct disciplinary and regional perspectives. I am grateful to these reviewers for their invaluable comments and suggestions. Over the years, I also benefited from the advice and assistance of numerous scholars with a wide range of expertise, ranging from Roman Egypt to Yuan China and from Armenian merchants in Amsterdam to Dutch merchants in Indonesia. Some of them introduced me to wholly new fields, while others provided a single important lead. Some provided comments in presentations of the various chapters at different stages of their writing. With others I had long exchanges and conversations. I am grateful to Gregory Ablavsky, Ran Abramitzky, Benito Arruñada, Sebouh Aslanian, Michal Biran, Ritu Birla, Peter Borschberg, Katherine Burke, Murat Cizakça, Mark Cohen, Robert Cooter, Albrecht Cordes, Giuseppe Dari-Mattiacci, Kent Deng, Rowan Dorin, Jorge Flores, David Faure, Lawrence Friedman, Mordechai Akiva Friedman, Oscar Gelderblom, Joshua Getzler, Stefania Gialdroni, Robert Gibbons, Francois Gipouloux, Jessica Goldberg, Yadira González de Lara, Avner Greif, Timothy Guinnane, Li Guo, Merav Haklai-Rotenberg, Valerie Hansen, Henry Hansmann, Pierre-Cyrille Hautcoeur, Richard Helmholz, Santhi Hejeebu, Phil Hoffman, Ella Jager, Matthijs de Jongh, Hassan Khalilieh, Amalia Kesler, Dan Klerman, Timur Kuran, Naomi Lamoreaux, Guy Laurie, David Lieberman, Ghislaine Lydon, Pius

Malekandathil, Neil Nathanel, Patrick O'Brien, Mihoko Oka, Şevket Pamuk, Om Prakash, David Powers, Dominic Rathbone, Himanshu Prabha Ray, Jean-Laurent Rosenthal, Youval Rotman, Tirthankar Roy, Billy K. L. So, Harry Scheiber, Peter Temin, Chris Tomlins, Francesca Trivellato, Sidney G. Tarrow, Dean Williamson, Gavin Wright, R. Bin Wong, Wen-hsin Yeh, Uri Yiftach, and Madeleine Zelin. Unfortunately, and fortunately, the list is too long to detail their individual contributions.

I was privileged to be part of the exceptional group of legal historians at Tel Aviv University's Faculty of Law. This collective, which is one of the largest, strongest, and most diverse groups of legal historians anywhere, supported me in so many ways. One could not hope for a more engaging and open-minded intellectual community of scholars than Leora Bilsky, José Brunner, Arye Edrei, Roy Kreitner, Shai Lavi, Assaf Likhovski, Doreen Lustig, Yifat Monnickendam, Lena Salaymeh, David Schorr, Elimelech Westreich, and Shay Wozner. I was fortunate enough to spend a year completing final revisions as a fellow at the Center for Advanced Study in the Behavioral Sciences (CASBS) in Stanford. My colleagues at Tel Aviv and cofellows in Stanford inspired me in many ways and broadened my horizons. I presented chapters of the book and the book framework as a whole in seminars, workshops, and conferences at various universities in Europe, Asia, and North America. The list of these is too long included here. I'll settle for mentioning only two: the six annual Eurasia Trajecto research network conferences, organized by Francois Gipouloux, and the day-long symposium on the book organized at Caltech by Jean-Laurent Rosenthal.

I benefited from the work of able and devoted research assistants on texts in languages I have not mastered and in archives and libraries I did not visit personally: Oded Abt, Roy Binkowicz, Rachele Hassan, Rachel Klagsbrun, Githa Markens, Marcelo Melnik, Einat Toledano, and Kriti Sharma. In addition, over the years I employed young and talented Tel Aviv Law School students as research assistants on this project: Shahar Avraham, Jonathan Bensoussan, Meshi Ben Naftali, Tom Binkowicz, Rotem Ernreich, Olga Frieshman, Mor Greif, Nathanel Habany, Maya Hay, Amit Itai, Avshlom Kasher, Hilit Orny, Oz Pinhas, Yoav Schori, Maayan Shelhav, Ido Tzang, Andrey Yagupolsky, Eyal Yaacoby, and Noga Zamir. In the early stages of the project, Gila Haimovic was an excellent editor, and in the final stages Amanda Dale conducted very high quality developmental and copyediting of the manuscript. The Israel Science Foundation (Grant #1128/11), the David Berg Foundation Institute for Law and History, and the Cegla Center for Interdisciplinary Research of the Law provided generous financial support.

My family traveled with me on the long, fascinating, and laborious intellectual (and at times also geographical) journeys during which this book was created. It could not have been written without the love, companionship, and endless patience and support of my spouse Hadas and my sons Yuval, Guy, Ido, and Dan.

NOTE ON THE USE OF CITY NAMES

~ ~ ~

Cities and other geographical places in Eurasia have been given many names over the years, in different languages, different eras, and due to different methods of transliteration. As a general rule, the most common contemporary name is used as the default in this book. Those other names are used in the text when they appear in contemporary records or in the secondary literature that is discussed directly in the text. In the list below, the name that is used as the default appears first, followed by other names mentioned in the text:

Batavia was the older European name for modern-day *Jakarta*.

Bombay was the older European name of *Mumbai*.

Cochin was the older European name of *Kochi*.

Fustat, also known as *Fostat*, *Al Fustat*, *Misr al-Fustat*, and *Fustat-Misr*, was the first capital of Egypt under early Muslim rule. Today, Fustat is part of Old Cairo.

Fuzhou was formerly romanized as *Foochow*.

Guangzhou was traditionally romanized as *Canton* and is now again named *Guangzhou*.

Madras was the older European name of *Chennai*.

Malacca is also known as *Melaka*.

Quanzhou was formerly called *Chinchew* (also spelled *Chinchu*). Old European works use the city's Arabic name, *Zayton*.

Samarkand is also known as *Samarqand*.

Turfan is also known as *Turpan* and *Tulufan*.

GOING THE DISTANCE

INTRODUCTION

~ ~ ~

Around the year 1400, long-distance oceanic and overland trade along the Eurasian landmass was still mostly conducted over short trajectories. Porcelain, making its way from China to the Middle East or Europe, changed hands many times in various ports in the South China Sea, the Indian Ocean, and the Arabian Sea and its gulfs. Silk and spices were exchanged between merchants in oases along the overland Silk Route. Merchants from several major regions of Eurasia—Chinese, Indian, Persian, Arab—and from a number of ethnic groups, such as Jews and Armenians, were major players in this high-value trade in tropical goods. Europeans were marginal to this commerce, buying their share of Asian goods at the Eastern Mediterranean entrepôts.

Business was generally conducted by sole traders or organized around small-scale enterprises: stationary and itinerant agents, family firms, small partnerships, and ethnic networks. But by 1700 the scene had changed completely. Goods were making their way directly from China, Japan, and the Indonesian archipelago to northwestern Europe. They were transported mostly by sea, across the Indian Ocean and around the Cape of Good Hope into the Atlantic. Trade was controlled by English and Dutch merchants, organized on a much larger scale and in an impersonal, organizational form: the joint-stock business corporation. Two such corporations, the English East India Company (EIC) and the Dutch East India Company (VOC), dominated the growing oceanic Eurasian trade.

In the fifteenth century there was no regular trade between Europe and Asia around the Cape of Good Hope. In the sixteenth century, following Vasco da Gama's discovery of the Cape Route (1497–98), 815 ships—most of them Portuguese and none operating on behalf of a business corporation—took this route on their way eastward to Asia. But in the seventeenth century, no fewer than 3,187 ships took the route, close to 95 percent of them operating on behalf of business corporations. Of these, 2,577 ships (80 percent of the total) were operated by the VOC and

EIC alone.[1] Dutch and English dominance in the long-distance trade gradually trickled down to intra-Asian trade and was manifested in the growing presence of European merchants residing in Indian Ocean ports. This is not to say the Asians were pushed out of trade altogether, but the longer the haul, the more likely it was to be handled by Europeans. Furthermore, the Europeans were the only merchants who connected Eurasia with the Americas (and their silver) across the Atlantic and the Pacific, thus creating a global commercial network for the first time in human history.

From another perspective, that of organizing business more generally, until around 1500 business enterprises throughout Eurasia were organized quite similarly in family firms, partnerships, and ethnic networks. Thereafter, Western Europe diverged. Its larger businesses—first in trade, then in finance, later in infrastructure and transportation, and later still in manufacturing—were organized in the form of business corporations, many of them with joint-stock capital. This new organizational form remained exclusively European for three hundred years before it slowly migrated to other parts of Eurasia and the globe.

Another, more abstract perspective identifies the shift from personal to impersonal exchange as a key developmental stage that was essential to the economic rise of Europe.[2] Personal exchange, or cooperation, was based on family, locality, or ethnic kinship ties. Impersonal exchange between strangers was traditionally confined to simple and instantaneous bartering or cash transactions. The shift in Western Europe from family firms and closed partnerships to the joint-stock corporation constituted more than just a switch from one organizational form to another. It was a shift from personal cooperation to impersonal cooperation. This shift amounts to what can be termed an organizational revolution.

RESEARCH QUESTIONS

The book addresses a wide set of research questions on the organization of trade as a whole and then zooms in on research questions that focus on the development of the joint-stock business corporation. The wider research questions are the following: Did the regions involved in pre-modern Eurasian trade use similar or different organizational forms for conducting their trade? To the extent that they used similar organizational forms, was this because each of them reached indigenously and independently similar organizational solutions to similar functions? Or did some of them import and transplant organizational forms that were developed in other regions? Or, alternatively, did differently configured organizational forms that were functional equivalents develop in different regions? To the extent that they did not adopt similar or equivalent organizational forms, why didn't organizational forms that proved to be efficient in one region migrate to and transplant in others?

The answer to these general questions with respect to the period from 1400 to 1600 in parts II and III of the book leads to a culmination and focusing of the research questions in part IV, on the joint-stock business corporation in the period around and after 1600. Why did the joint-stock business corporation emerge exclusively in Western Europe? This question can be separated into three subquestions: Why did this shift occur around 1600? Why in the context of long-distance trade? Why in England and the Dutch Republic and no other Western European countries? The last chapter of the book deals with two comparative questions: Why wasn't the European business corporation, if so effective in organizing long-distance trade, mimicked by other Eurasian regions for another three hundred years? Why did institutions that had some corporate-like features, and were used in other regions (e.g., family lineage, waqf, guild), not further evolve to compete successfully with the corporate-based European mercantile enterprises? While dealing with organizational development, the book will also address the question of how consequential these organizational developments were. Were these new organizational innovations (as opposed to technology, violence, or geography) a major cause of the rise to dominance of Western Europeans in long-distance Eurasian maritime trade?

To answer these questions, this book closely examines the role played by organizational forms in the transformation of Eurasian trade roughly between 1400 and 1700. Each of the three centuries examined here is distinct. The first, the fifteenth century, was one in which European merchants were not yet present in Asia. Asians organized their trade via family firms, merchant networks, and state-operated voyages, trading in high-value goods between China, India, and Arabia. The next century saw the arrival of the Portuguese from around the Cape, using their state apparatus to trade all the way to Cochin (Kochi) and Goa in India, Macao in China, and Nagasaki in Japan. In the third century examined, the seventeenth century, the Dutch and English arrived, organizing their entrepreneurial activities into corporations and taking over much of the long-distance trade with India and Indonesia.

A comparative perspective is essential in addressing the research questions posed by this book. It thus compares the organizational forms that were used in four major regions: China, India, the Middle East, and Western Europe. We have here a unique opportunity, a natural experiment, for a comparative institutional analysis, because all four regions were involved in the same kind of business activity—long-distance trade— within the same environment, the greater Indian Ocean.

ARGUMENT

The book's core arguments are made on two levels, the first being less ambitious and narrower in scope, the second being more ambitious and perhaps more challenging to substantiate. The first level of argument aims to explain the emergence of the business corporation in Western Europe and the shift to impersonal cooperation in the context of Dutch and English corporations. The second level aims to explain the rise to dominance of Western Europe, in general, and England and the Dutch Republic, in particular, in long-distance Eurasian trade and eventually global trade. The first level contributes to the history of business organizations, while the second contributes to the history of trade and of economic development.

The first-level argument is that the organizational design of the EIC and VOC, the first long-lasting joint-stock corporations, enabled for the first time in human history the formation of large-scale, multilateral, impersonal cooperation. More concretely, it enabled a huge amount of capital to be raised voluntarily from thousands of passive investors. In order for such large-scale, impersonal cooperation to be possible, credible commitment had to be conveyed on two levels of relationships. The first commitment needed was that of the ruler not to expropriate the newly pooled, tangible capital. Such a commitment could be credibly conveyed around 1600 only in England and the Dutch Republic due to the restrained characteristics of their governments, which we take here as exogenous. The second commitment needed was that of the entrepreneurs not to cheat or shirk the outside passive investors. The commitment devices designed for the VOC and EIC governance provided outsiders with a reasonable mix of participation in decision making, exit through the selling of shares, access to information, and share in the profits. Without such institutionalized and credible commitments, the outsiders would have refrained from investing with the new, strange, and impersonal institution known as the *business corporation*. The ability to convey credible commitment to strangers through the corporate form was a breakthrough on the way to impersonal investment and, ultimately, the modern economy. Impersonally pooled capital was used for regular voyages by numerous large and well-equipped ships on journeys that lasted several years. What is important for this line of argumentation is that the organizational revolution brought about around 1600 by the EIC and VOC in the context of long-distance trade was a turning point in the history of business organization. It formed the basis for the future use of the joint-stock business corporation in the financial, transportation, colonial, and even industrial revolutions.

The second-level (and more ambitious) argument makes claims with respect to a more immediate economic and political impact of the organizational revolution on English and Dutch maritime trade performance. It argues that shipping, navigation, warfare, and the motivation to resort to violence cannot fully explain the rise to dominance in long-distance trade by the English and Dutch. The new organizational form enabled the English and Dutch to deploy more capital, more ships, more voyages, and more agents than other organizational forms. The emergence of the joint-stock business corporation had significant impact on trade within the first decades of the seventeenth century. It had a longer-term bearing on the history of trade, and the globalization and imperialism that accompanied it.

The first level of argumentation (that is, the organizational level) can explain Europe's later, longer-term rise in the eighteenth and nineteenth centuries, when the model of the joint-stock business corporation, together with the supplementary stock market, played a major role in the financial, transportation, colonial, and industrial revolutions. The first-level argument does not have to assert that the emergence of the business corporation had immediate economic impact—that is, that Europeans took over long-distance Eurasian trade from Asians by the seventeenth century or that institutional factors, as distinct from technological or military factors, were crucial in the taking over of Eurasian trade by Europeans. Historians who believe that Europeans rose to dominance only in the nineteenth century, or who attribute their rise to the use of violence, may nevertheless be convinced by the argument on the first level. This level does not build on the validity of the second-level argument, while the second-level argument (pertaining to Eurasian trade) assumes the first-level argument to be correct.

A reader interested only in the first argument, about the birth and rise of the business corporation, cannot jump straight to part IV of the book. Parts II and III are essential for understanding the need for an organizational innovation. They explain the shortfalls of even the most successful premodern organizational forms: the family firm, the merchant network, and the ruler-owned enterprise. They uncover basic building blocks that were used for the configuration of the first business corporations. The differences between the organizational models of the VOC and EIC cannot be understood without realizing that they subsumed within the corporate entity earlier building blocks shaped by quite different histories. The fact that the business corporation did not migrate cannot be understood without an understanding of which earlier forms migrated and why. The uniqueness of the corporation as embedded in European religion and Anglo-Dutch political structure, and connected to their stock markets, can only be perceived in a comparative perspective. The success of the VOC and EIC cannot be explained without understanding the organizational crises of the Portuguese in Asia, the termination of Zheng He's maritime voyages, and the turn of attention of the Mughal, Ottoman, and Ming rulers from the ocean to the Eurasian landmass that created a window of opportunity. So even those interested solely in the business corporation will have to endure parts II and III.

The unfolding of the core arguments of the book has three meaningful byproducts. First, the book provides a survey—the first of its kind—of organizational forms used in Eurasian long-distance trade in this period and the way the various organizational forms dealt with these challenges. It is well known that Eurasia was a fertile ground for the migration of people, religions, technologies, and knowledge. The migration of institutions has not yet received its due attention. Secondly, the book offers an account—also the first of its kind—of the migration of trade organizations throughout Eurasia. In order to study the migration, and given the lack of an articulated theoretical framework for studying institutional migration, the book, finally, had to develop its own theoretical framework for the migration and, even more importantly, for the resistance to the migration of institutions, a theory that can be valuable in other contexts as well.

THEORY, METHODOLOGY, AND SOURCES

This study follows the evolution of institutions in the various regions along two paths: indigenous institutional evolution, stemming from interaction with the immediate environment, and the migration of institutions from other regions not part of the immediate environment. In order to be more precise in the analysis I will employ a typology of three types of institutions and ask which of these types fits each of the organizational forms studied and why. The first type of institution is the endemic institution that originated and expanded independently in various regions, on a local, indigenous, and evolutionary path. Institutions of this type will be referred to as "endogenous" institutions. The second type is that in which institutional developments took place mostly as a result of emulation, copying, transplantation, importation, and circulation from other regions (that is, following an evolutionary path of diffusion from region to region). Institutions of the second type will be referred to in this book as "migratory" institutions. The third type of institutions will be called "embedded" institutions. They have evolved along the path of indigenous evolution, yet, importantly for the typology offered here, they evolved historically only in one region and *not* in various regions independently, as was the case with endogenous institutions. In addition—and this is fundamental for the typology—they did not readily and rapidly circulate beyond the original domain, as is the case with migratory institutions. My use of types here does not assume that types are actual historical stages. The types are employed for analytical purposes, in order to identify the indigenous evolution of some organizational forms and the migration of others. I do not wish to argue for a historical reality in which distinct institutional types had actual existence in any essentialist sense.

As the book will show, relatively simple organizational forms (endogenous institutions such as the itinerant trader, traveling and stationed agents employed in bilateral relationships, small family firms, and general partnerships) developed locally and independently in various places along the Eurasian landmass.[3] More complex, and more socially and culturally embedded, migratory institutions (such as the *caravanserai*, the sea loan, and the *commenda* partnership) were established more rarely—as far as we can tell, in only one or two places—and spread around much of Eurasia by way of emulation, transplantation, and importation. The most complex and embedded institution used in Eurasian trade in early modern times, the corporation, originated in only one region, Western Europe, and was not imported for several centuries by any other region.

The shift from the prevalence of the endogenous organizational forms to the dominance of the migratory organizational forms is not historically chronological; even when migratory organizational forms followed endogenous organizational forms in time, the timing throughout the regions was not uniform. The shift was not well defined in time; it occurred, at least partly, before the period covered in this book. By contrast, the shift from migratory organizational forms to an embedded organizational form, the corporation, was sharp, and took place in a well-defined time and place: Western Europe around 1600. The ultimate embedded organizational form, the corporation, extended beyond family and ethnic networks, as it had to facilitate multilateral, impersonal cooperation. But once this was achieved, the new form allowed for the accumulation of capital, the spreading of risk, the flow of information, and the longevity of existence so important to Europe's Eurasian trade. Yet the corporation, which was more embedded in European civilization, also more vehemently resisted importation by other regions and civilizations.

Chapter 1 will present the literature on Eurasian trade, the geography of trade environment and the organizational challenges faced by long-distance trade. Chapter 2 will survey institutional and organizational theories that will be used for studying the statics and dynamics of the development of institutions in interaction with their environment. Chapters 3 through 5 examine the basic organizational building blocks—chapter 3 the more universal and endogenous organizational forms, their features and employment, chapters 4 and 5 the varying building blocks, those organizational forms that migrated and were usually available in some parts of Eurasia but not in others, and their migration paths. Chapters 6 through 8 study the biggest organizational forms of the precorporation era, complex forms that used the basic building blocks: the family firm, the merchant network, and the ruler-operated enterprise. Chapters 9 through 12 take the story into the corporate era, explaining both the emergence in England and the Dutch Republic, and the embeddedness and nonmigration of the business corporation.

In order to avoid an overly abstract and structural discussion, the book will present microstudies of several organizations that participated in Eurasian trade. These will examine the details of various organizational forms, from agency and loan contracts, to partnership agreements, to family firms, to merchant networks, to corporate charters. They will give the reader a sense of the available primary historical records and their content. They will also assist in understanding the functioning of the different organizational forms in real life, the individual merchants, the goods, the places, and the actual trade. By using a microstudy methodology, we can go deeper than a survey of the secondary literature would allow, and get a sense of the primary historical records—that is, a nuanced understanding of the period and its real persons and actual trade enterprises (as opposed to mere prototypes of organizational forms in the abstract). To be sure, the use of this methodology does not imply that I am a specialized historian in all the regions and time periods covered by the microstudies. The microstudies rely on the work of specialists who have mastered languages and archives that are beyond my capacities. The microstudies do not contribute to the specialized histories; rather, they are intended to serve the larger comparative project.

Cases will be selected on the basis of two main criteria. The first is the pertinence of the organization to Eurasian trade, either as representative of a wider phenomenon or as forming part of a turning point. The second is the availability of extensive enough primary sources to enable an analysis of the organizational details. In addition, to comprehend these sources (which are often fragmented and in ancient languages), sufficient secondary literature has to be available to provide transcripts and commentary, and preferably some historical analysis. This created a selection bias toward winners and hierarchical bureaucracies—in other words, toward Western Europe and, to a lesser extent, China. Thus, with respect to India and the Middle East, I had to be less selective in terms of the first selection criteria and settle for microstudies that were not ideal in terms of timing or centrality.

The chapters in parts II through IV of this book include microstudies of all the major organizational forms used in Eurasian trade, starting with contract, agency, and family firms and ethnic networks, continuing with partnerships and commendas, the political ruler, and ending with the corporation. The selected microstudies are also spread widely in terms of geography: from Quanzhou, Nanjing, and Turfan in China; to Lisbon, London, and Amsterdam in Europe; and, via the Java Sea, to Surat in India, Isfahan in Iran, Quseir-al-qadim and Cairo in Egypt, and Livorno in Italy.

Availability of data is a challenge because the standard sources on the history of trade, such as custom records, port dockets, artifacts found in archeological excavations, and travel narratives, rarely reveal enough about the organization of trade. The pattern of survival and preservation of records containing information about organizational details creates a bias in favor of European trade and organizations. The vast majority of surviving Eurasian trade records for the period 1500–1700 (located in archives in Lisbon, Amsterdam, and London) contain minute details of the organization of the *Estado da Índia*, the VOC, and the EIC, and only marginal trade information about their Asian counterparts. However, this book endeavors to offset this bias, at least in part. In the case of Asia, it draws on sources from earlier and later periods and on less conventional types of records, including papyri from the Egyptian desert; contracts from caves in Western China; archeological surveys of shipwrecks from the Sea of Java; genealogical records from a Chinese port; wills from a German family archive; the reflections of a Guajarati family firm in the VOC archive; letters from the Cairo Geniza; account books and powers of attorney from an Armenian monastery in Iran; contracts of the king of Portugal from the state archive in Lisbon; an official history of a Ming emperor; and incorporation charters issued by the queen of England and the Dutch States General. Such are the kinds of primary sources used in the microstudies.

PREEMPTION CONCERNING EUROCENTRISM

The mere asking of the question "Why was European civilization the birthplace of the corporation?" is likely to be critiqued as representing an assumption that the corporation is an efficient institution and a necessary stage in economic development, and that Europe should be praised for developing it. Indeed, the book as a whole may be criticized as Eurocentric because it asks a question that seems to take Europe as the yardstick. I would like to preempt this possible first impression. It *is* Eurocentric to an extent. But it is equally *not* Eurocentric, in a few important respects. As will become apparent, the Indian Ocean and the Silk Route are at the center of analysis. Much attention is devoted to Chinese, Indian, and Middle Eastern business organizations. The yardstick applied to address the research question "Why did corporations develop only in Europe?" is not, in fact, Europe or the European path of development. Rather, it is the Eurasian long-distance trade that predated the European arrival. It will be shown that the European business corporation was developed due to Europe's difficulties and not because of an inherent European advantage. Similarly, the other core research question—"How did different regions organize their long-distance Eurasian trade?"—does not use Europe as the yardstick.

Furthermore, the book is not Eurocentric in terms of the space devoted to each part of Eurasia. It surveys and analyzes trade organizations and their evolution, function, and effect in Eurasia as a whole. The timeframe of the book covers, consciously, a full century, 1400–1500, in which Europe was entirely absent from the scene. Much of the book is devoted to long-distance trade within the Indian Ocean and its peripheral seas, which was dominated by Asians—the Cape Route controlled by Europeans being the exception. Despite the scarcity of historical records dealing with much of Asia, significant effort was devoted to ensuring that the majority of the microstudies conducted are not about Europe. The book does not compare all the rest of Eurasia to Europe, but deliberately compares China, India, and the Middle East with each other. It acknowledges that non-European organizational forms (the family firm, the network, and other personally based forms) had their advantages and enabled trade to flourish for centuries. It also shows that much of the migration of knowledge, know-how, and technology, and even institutions, was *into* Europe, not *out of* Europe. The corporation was the exception.

PART I

~

The Context

Geography, Historiography, Theory

~ 1 ~

Environment and Trade

The expansion of trade from local to long-distance to Eurasian trade was a major challenge to merchants everywhere. Operators had to overcome tough and, at times, even hostile environments on the oceans, straits, deserts, and steppes. They had to match the supply of goods in one location to the demand in a faraway, climatically and culturally different location. But the rewards could be enormous. What were the challenges? What was the role of technology, determination, and institutions in overcoming the challenges? Which regions solved the problems earlier and reaped the payoffs? How did they do it? I will address these questions in this chapter, showing that institutions were crucial in overcoming such challenges. I will also explain how institutions have not received their due attention from scholars.

THE NONINSTITUTIONAL LITERATURE ON GLOBALIZATION OF TRADE

Long-distance Eurasian trade has received much attention from historians. But the details and evolution of its organization has not. The literature has dealt mostly with the trade itself and its social and economic ramifications, and only seldom with its organization. Let us examine four of the influential traditions in the earlier literature on Eurasian trade and on Europe's rise to a leading position in it.[1]

Those scholars interested in Smithian growth—that is, growth driven by the expansion and integration of markets and by specialization of different regions in the production of different goods based on relative advantage—view the expansion of long-distance trade as the perfect manifestation of this kind of growth. Findlay and O'Rourke offer the most authoritative study of actual exchanges (goods, prices, quantities) involved in Eurasian and global trade and the resulting level of integration of markets.[2] Their interest in the firms involved in trade derives exclusively from their desire to examine whether they had market monopoly. For the most part, Smithian scholars view the firms involved in trade merely as "black boxes." They are not interested in their organizational details.

For those approaching trade from a Marxist perspective, the main issue is capital accumulation. Marxist scholars are interested in the profits of merchants and corporations. Eurasian trade was a great opportunity for huge profits and capital accumulation. Wallerstein's *The Modern World-System* is a good example of such an analysis.[3] The modern world political-economic system was formed due to the expansion of European trade to the Atlantic, the Cape Route, and eventually the Pacific. It was distinguished from earlier empires by its reliance on trade rather than political and military power. The nascent capitalist centers of Europe took advantage of trade with peripheral parts of the globe and used the world system to accumulate capital and become the dominant force in the capitalist era. The organizational details of capitalist world trade did not receive much attention from these historians. But the outcome in terms of exploitation, capital accumulation, and dependency—the new world system—did. Janet Abu-Lughod's *Before European Hegemony: The World System A.D. 1250–1350* is a prime example of the analysis of Eurasian trade in this tradition for the period before the rise of the Europeans.[4]

Another strand in the literature is inspired by Braudel[5] and the *Annales* school. Braudel employed the concept of the *longue durée* that began historical analysis with the longest-lasting and slowest-changing elements and gradually moved on to faster-changing elements. The geographic environment was the starting point for this analysis. The next level of analysis was that of the slow-changing demography and agriculture. He then moved on to domestic manufacturing and retail, regional trade, and (at the top of the analytical framework) long-distance trade. He downplayed the importance of short-term political and military events. Long-distance trade has a unique place in his analysis because it was not routine. Uncertainties were high and, because of this, so were the potential profits. The dynamics of change, and particularly the rise of capitalism, can be identified only when reaching this level of analysis. Braudel's work on the Mediterranean and on the rise of capitalism inspired a line of research on the Indian Ocean, exemplified by, among other works, Chaudhuri's influential book *Trade and Civilisation in the Indian Ocean: An Economic History from the Rise of Islam to 1750.*[6]

The most relevant strand in the preinstitutional literature for our purposes is that inspired by Max Weber. Most specifically, the literature inspired by Weber's conception of rationalization is extensive. For Weber, rationalization involved the individual cost-benefit calculation; the wider, bureaucratic mode of operation of organizations; the organization of the legal system as a sphere separated from religion; and, in a more general sense, disenchantment. For us, the main issue is the development of highly rational and calculating capitalism, in which business accounting is a tool and profit maximization is an end. Weber-inspired studies of Eurasian trade are few and far between. Historian Niels Steensgaard's *The Asian Trade Revolution of the Seventeenth Century: The East India Companies and the Decline of the Caravan Trade* is the most prominent example.[7] This Weberian tradition is the most relevant for us because it is interested in looking into the "black box" of the firm and not only in its economic outputs. Steensgaard studied the different modes of calculability and operation of the Portuguese Estado da Índia (a state-owned enterprise), on the one hand, and the EIC and VOC (shareholder-owned enterprises), on the other. He analyzed how they managed their accounts, how they made decisions, and what objectives they were trying to achieve, and particularly what was the mix between profit-maximizing and power-maximizing objectives. The Weber-inspired academics were the noneconomist scholars whose studies of Eurasian trade went furthest in terms of understanding the firm's "black box." But they did not use new developments that were formulated in economics since the 1960s and ranged from theories of the firm and transaction costs to contract theory and agency theory. They understood that not all "black boxes" function the same but did not fully open the "black box" of the firm and examine its discrete components in order to better understand why.

THE OCEANIC ENVIRONMENT:
GEOGRAPHY AND WORLD SYSTEM

Janet Abu-Lughod persuasively portrays the world system that emerged in the period 1250–1350 as consisting of eight circuits. The Indian Ocean was composed of three interlocking circuits, each based on a subregion—namely, the South China Sea, the Bay of Bengal, and the Arabian Sea.[8] These were more than just distinct bodies of water. The geographical structure of the Indian Subcontinent and of Malaya and the monsoon regime made the passage from one circuit to another a more complicated matter than traveling within each circuit. In addition, each circuit was dominated by a different civilization and its main religion. The Arabian Sea (including many of its major Indian ports) was dominated by Islam, the Bay of Bengal by Hinduism (with some Buddhist presence), and the South China Sea by Chinese Confucian civilization. About two-thirds of world's population in 1400 lived along the Indian Ocean, of which 28 percent lived in India and 21 percent in China.[9] Four of the ten largest cities in 1500 were in China—Beijing, Hangzhou, Guangzhou (Canton), and Nanjing—and two of them were in India (Vijayanagar and Gaur).[10] The Indian Ocean was, according to Abu-Lughod, at the center of the world system.

Figure 1.1 shows the different regions of the world system. Europe was also part of the world system, albeit marginally and distantly so (only one of the ten largest cities, Paris, was located there). It was connected to the major centers of the system by land and sea.

The overland connections are known collectively as the Silk Route. They connected the major eastern Chinese cities, Beijing (Peking) and Hangzhou (Hangchow), with the Mediterranean and Black Sea ports of Aleppo, Caffa, and Constantinople through the Central Asian Steppes. The Indian Ocean trade with Europe could make use of two sea routes. The first was from the Arabian Sea to the Persian Gulf, the Mesopotamian rivers, and a final overland section through the deserts of modern-day Iraq and Syria to the Eastern Mediterranean ports. The second route was from the Arabian Sea to the Red Sea, overland to the Nile, and down to Alexandria on the Mediterranean coast. The Silk Route, Persian Gulf, and Red Sea were at the center of three additional circuits. Nearly 10

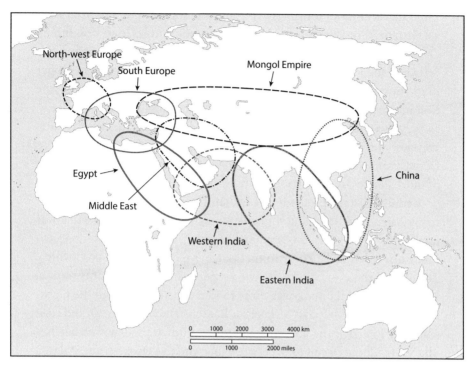

1.1. Circuits of the world system with names of regions. Source: adapted from "Thirteenth Century World System," https://commons.wikimedia.org/wiki/File:Archaic_globalization.svg.

percent of the world's population and three of the world's ten largest cities in the year 1500 (Cairo, Tabriz, and Constantinople) were located within these circuits.[11] The Mediterranean and Western Europe were at the center of the seventh and eighth circuits that completed Abu Lughod's world system. The Americas were not part of this system.

THE OCEANIC ENVIRONMENT

Pre-European Indian Ocean voyages, from Arabia to China, were considerably longer than any European or Mediterranean voyage.[12] The voyage from Fuzhou to Aden was about 5,450 nautical miles;[13] from Nanjing to Basra was about 6,330 nautical miles.[14] One of the longest routes of the Mediterranean trade, from Alexandria to Barcelona, is only about

1,480 nautical miles long.[15] A typical Baltic trade route, say from Amsterdam to Saint Petersburg, is just 1,280 nautical miles long.[16] So Indian Ocean shippers, navigators, and merchants were involved before the arrival of the Europeans with voyages that were four to six times longer than voyages experienced by the Europeans any time before 1492. The Colombian discovery voyages were a leap forward in European standards, as they were almost three times longer than Mediterranean or Baltic voyages, but were still short by Indian Ocean standards. The distance from Cádiz to Havana of about 3,980 nautical miles is still just 60 percent of the distance from China to Arabia.[17]

Medium-distance trade in the Indian Ocean was a challenge met by many Asian merchants and ship operators. It was on a timescale that was familiar to Europeans. The Arabian Sea circuit took four to five weeks to sail, from Aden or Hormuz to the Malabar Coast (Calicut or Cochin). The coastal route was a week or two longer than a cross-oceanic route.[18] The Bay of Bengal circuit was three to four weeks long, from the Coromandel Coast to Malacca (Melaka) or Banten/Batavia (Jakarta), and considerably longer if the coastal route up and down the bay was taken.[19] The South China circuit took between four and five weeks, from Malacca or Banten/Batavia to Guangzhou/Fuzhou (Foochow).[20] Most merchants were involved in short- or medium-distance trade that involved four- to six-week journeys, and not in the long-distance trade that stretched all the way from China to Arabia.

As will be shown, the longer the distance, the larger the price differences of goods, and the higher the potential payoffs. Yet the monsoon was a major disturbance on long Indian Ocean voyages, a factor not captured by nautical distances alone. The Arabian Sea and Bay of Bengal experienced two monsoon seasons each year: southwest monsoon (April or May through September) and northeast monsoon (October, November, or December through February, March, or April).[21] At the peak of the monsoon, ships could not sail either against or with the wind.[22] A ship had to reach a safe harbor before the Indian Ocean "closed" at the height of each monsoon. The ocean around India was considered to be totally closed for some ninety days every year, from June to August.[23] During each monsoon season, ships could sail with the wind but not against it.[24] For example, according to Ibn Majid's navigators' manual, written around 1490, just before the Portuguese arrival, ships could sail from Muscat to

Malabar between February 20 and April 11, before the peak of the southwest monsoon, and again from Aden to India between August 29 and September 18 to ensure safe arrival in India before the northeast monsoon.[25] The voyage from Malabar to Malacca had to leave by April 18 to avoid being hit by the southwest monsoon when crossing the Bay of Bengal. It had to leave by September 28 to avoid a frontal northeast monsoon before arriving in Malacca. A ship wishing to go all the way from the Arabian Peninsula to Malaya in the same year had a very narrow window of opportunity. It had to leave Muscat as soon as the sea opened in February and stop very briefly in a Malabar port in April. It could not do the same in the August–September eastward departure slot from Muscat because by the time it arrived in Malabar it was too late to depart for Malacca within the same year. The same problem was faced by those wishing to sail west from China. There was a narrow window of opportunity, less than two months every year (late December to mid-February), in which ships could cross both the Bay of Bengal and the Arabian Sea and make it all the way from Malacca or Sumatra to Aden or Hormuz. By the time ships from China could reach Malacca it was usually too late to depart to Aden, and the furthest they could aim for in that same year was along the coast to Bengal.[26]

The well-documented convoys of Zheng He's fleet took, on average, fifty-four days to cross the first circuit from Tai-p'ing Bay to Malacca, forty-four days to cross the second circuit from Malacca to Calicut, and thirty-four days to cross the Arabian Sea to Hormuz.[27] In theory, ignoring for now the effects of the monsoon and stopovers, a voyage from Hormuz to Liujiagang could take eighty-two days (about three months), and a voyage from Fuzhou to Hormuz could take 135 days (almost four and a half months).[28]

We can see from tables 1.1 and 1.2 the duration of the seventh voyage of Zheng He's fleet. The monsoon regime added to Indian Ocean trade three layers of complications that the mere nautical distances do not reflect. First, it prolonged travel time and, as a result, capital turnover time. Second, it narrowed the time windows for travel and thus condensed competition between merchants on both ends of each voyage. Third, it required merchants and shipmasters to achieve a high level of familiarity with changing sea and weather conditions and put outsiders to the regions, such as Western Europeans, at an initial disadvantage.

1.1. Itinerary of the Seventh Voyage of Zheng He's Fleet,
Sailing Westward from China

Origin	Departure date	Destination	Arrival date	Net sailing time
Wuhumen, Changle (Foochow)	January 12, 1432	Champa/Qhi Nhon/ Zhan City (modern-day Vietnam)	January 27, 1432	15 days
Champa	February 12, 1432	Surabaya, Java, Indonesia	March 7, 1432	24 days
Surabaya	July 13, 1432	Palembang, Srivijaya, Sumatra, Indonesia	July 24, 1432	11 days
Palembang	July 27, 1432	Malacca	August 3, 1432	7 days
Malacca	September 2, 1432	Semudera/Samudera (modern-day Aceh, Sumatra, Indonesia)	September 12, 1432	10 days
Semudera	November 2, 1432	Beruwala, Simhala (modern-day Sri Lanka)	November 28, 1432	26 days
Beruwala	December 2, 1432	Calicut	December 10, 1432	8 days
Calicut	December 14, 1432	Hormuz	January 17, 1433	34 days

Total net sailing time: 135 days (about 19 weeks). Total voyage time including stopovers: 372 days (about 53 weeks).

Sources: Hui and Xin (2011, pp. 212–214); Ma (1970 [1433], pp. 14–17); Dreyer (2007, pp. 150–155, 161).
Note: The table does not include Chinese destinations visited before Foochow.

The real leap forward for the Europeans in maritime trade took place with the first Cape Route voyages to India and beyond. While it took Columbus nine weeks to cross the Atlantic, it took Vasco da Gama about ten months to reach Calicut in India on his first voyage out of Lisbon.[29] The return journey was more than twelve months long.[30] The distance from Lisbon to Calicut around the Cape of Good Hope is 9,510 nautical miles. Ships going farther east in Asia, say to Singapore, traveled 10,730 nautical miles, and those going to Guangzhou went about 12,125 nautical miles.[31] A voyage from Europe to India was more than six times longer than the longest European or Mediterranean voyage and more than twice

**1.2. Itinerary of the Seventh Voyage of Zheng He's Fleet,
Sailing Eastward to China**

Origin	Departure date	Destination	Arrival date	Net sailing time
Hormuz	March 9, 1433	Calicut	March 31, 1433	22 days
Calicut	April 9, 1433	Semudera	April 25, 1433	16 days
Semudera	May 1, 1433	Malacca	May 9, 1433	8 days
Malacca	May 28, 1433	Champa	June 13, 1433	16 days
Champa	June 17, 1433	Liujiagang (modern-day Liuhe, Taicang, Jiangsu province, China)	July 7, 1433	20 days

Total net sailing time: 82 days (about 12 weeks). Total voyage time including stopovers: 120 days (about 17 weeks).

Source: Dreyer (2007, pp. 155, 160–161).
Note: The itinerary from Champa was not fully recorded by Ma Huan. Hence, we cannot determine whether Zheng He's fleet stopped somewhere between Champa and Beijing.

as long as the voyage across the Atlantic to Central America. A voyage to China was three times longer than a voyage to the Americas. It was twice as long as the longest voyages experienced by Asians in the Indian Ocean. The Europeans that arrived in the Indian Ocean around the Cape had to surmount huge challenges. The challenges this book is interested in are not those of discovering the Cape Route and sending a one-off voyage of a few ships around the Cape but that of establishing trade routes and repeat oceanic voyages. They had to be able to send repeated voyages to Indian Ocean ports, which were eight time more distant than their European and Mediterranean trade destinations, destinations in which they encountered well-versed Asians merchants. The challenge was organizational at least as much as it was navigational.

THE SILK ROUTE ENVIRONMENT

The term "Silk Route" does not refer to a single, well-defined road but rather was invented in the modern era to refer collectively to a variety of overland routes forming a network that allowed overland travel from China all the way to the Mediterranean.[32] The routes made use of the vast steppe that stretched north of the more fertile, agricultural, and densely populated lands of Eurasia that lay south of it, and bypassed rather than crossing them. It began in the hinterland of China and continued west through the Gansu Corridor (between the Gobi Desert and the Himalayan range). Then it flanked, from either north or south, the Taklimakan desert, reaching Kashgar, and then crossed the mountain passes south of Tian Shan mountains and north of the Pamir range of the Himalayas. The road continued to the steppes of Central Asia, the Iranian plateau, the Fertile Crescent, and the Mediterranean.[33] Traveling the main stretches of the Silk Route involved navigating open steppe or desert terrain, from one oasis to the next. A side branch took a northerly route in the Central Asian Steppe, bypassed the Caspian Sea from the north (Sarai), and continued via Tanais (on the Sea of Azov) to the Volga River and the Black Sea (Caffa).[34] Another connecting route went from the Indian subcontinent to the Silk Route in Central Asia via the Khyber Pass and Afghanistan.[35] Figures 1.2 and 1.3 show the different trajectories of the Silk Route.

The Silk Route had been used by traveling itinerant traders since antiquity. During certain periods in history it was used extensively, while at other times it fell out of favor. For our purposes, the more relevant era in the history of the Silk Route is the *Pax Mongolica* (the era just before the period examined in this book), in which the Mongols, following the conquests of Genghis Khan and his heirs, dominated practically all of it, both militarily and politically.[36] In this era, the thirteenth and fourteenth centuries, the Silk Route was safe from bandits and unpredictably expropriating rulers, and trade flourished.[37] Some historians argue that Silk Route trade declined as early as the fifteenth century. Others assert that it declined only in the seventeenth or even eighteenth century. The causes of decline are also debated by historians. Some attribute it to the dismantling of Mongolian rule in Asia, some to the Black Death, some to political crises in China, Central Asia, and Persia, and some to the rise of European Indian Ocean trade.[38] We do not have to take a position in these debates.

Historians know quite well the itineraries and travel times for the Silk Route. Famous travelers as such Marco Polo (1254–1324) and Ibn Battuta (1304–69) reported on their journeys along significant sections of the route.[39] According to an itinerary produced in or around 1340 by Francesco Balducci Pegolotti, a traveler needed about 270 days (net time) to

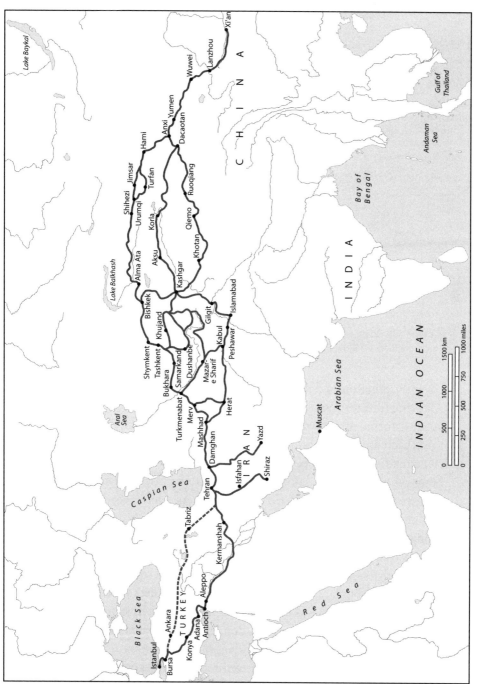

1.2. The Silk Route. Source: adapted from https://commons.wikimedia.org/wiki/File:Seidenstrasse_GMT.jpg.

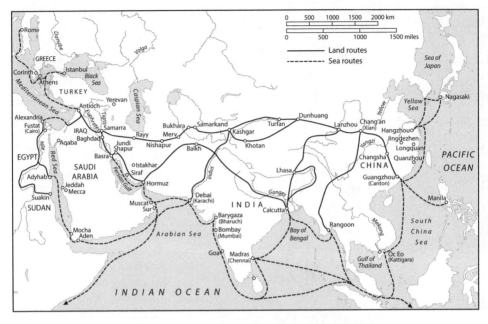

1.3. Map of the Silk Route and trade sea routes. Source: adapted from http://voices.national geographic.com/files/2012/09/silkroadmap-950x492.jpg.

cover the Silk Route all the way from Tana, on the Black Sea, to Peking.[40] Allowing time for rest and recovery and delays due to bad weather (such as sandstorms or snowstorms), one could expect eighteen months of travel each way.[41] Therefore, a full Silk Route trip, allowing time for trade, could take more than three years. These durations sound reasonable given other reports from the same era that mention a travel time of between eight and ten months from Crimea to Central Asia, and a year from China to Central Asia.[42] These reports reflected travel times during the Pax Mongolica, one of the periods characterized as having the safest journeys and best-equipped oases and infrastructures, caravanserais, garrisons, and postal services. Travel times in earlier and later periods must have been longer, involving more uncertainties. Regardless of the period in question, the journey was an overland passage that involved switching between many modes of transportation: ox wagon, camel wagon, camels, pack-ass, and riverboat.[43]

Transportation costs were not well recorded. Pegolotti is a unique source for these as well. He calculated the costs of a merchant with a caravan of between forty and sixty animals, supplies, and sixty accompanying men. Pegolotti estimated the total cost, including customs payment to Mongolian rulers, at about 3,500 golden florins.[44] A Florentine golden florin of the time contained 3.5 grams of gold.[45] Thus, the entire costs of the voyage totaled about 12.25 kilograms of gold. But goods transported on such a caravan could be sold for as much as 25,000 golden florins,[46] providing a huge profit margin. That said, it was unusual for goods to be carried by the same merchant all the way from Beijing to Tana. Due to the long distances involved, the time taken to complete a return trip, and linguistic and cultural barriers, it was much more typical for goods to change hands several times along the way, splitting both transportation costs and profits between the different merchants concerned.

GOODS TRADED

The literature on goods traded along Eurasia is substantial, but we need not rehearse it here. A very concise survey will convey a sense of what the organizational forms studied in this book were trading in, and also what the price gaps between the various goods were (and thus what profits from trade could be).

Tropical goods were in demand in temperate, cold climate regions from antiquity and were still in demand around our starting point (1400). The tropical goods in highest demand were spices such as pepper, nutmeg, clove, mace, cinnamon, ginger, and cardamom, among others. Spices were in high demand in the Mediterranean and Europe, a demand that was driven by their culinary and medicinal use and their conspicuous consumption as a status good.[47] Other tropical goods included coconut, fruits, sugar, ebony, ivory, precious gems, and incense. As we shall see when discussing the Muziris Papyrus, merchants in ancient Rome already exported these from India.[48] Arabs imported spices from the Malabar Coast of India before the end of the first millennium and reached even as far as the Indonesian islands.[49] Chinese of the Tang and Song dynasties era imported the tropical goods of Southeast Asia.[50] The Europeans, on arrival in the Indian Ocean, imported spices from Sri Lanka and the Malabar Coast of India. The Dutch also planted spices in plantations owned and operated by the VOC in the Moluccas, on the small Banda islands which they called, for this reason, the Spice Islands. Tropical goods were traded mostly via the Indian Ocean, to China through the Indonesian straits of Malacca and Sunda, to the Middle East and Europe through the Persian Gulf and the Red Sea, and later around the Cape of Good Hope.

More northerly, temperate, or dry countries, such as China, Persia, and European countries, exported agricultural products and raw materials typical of their climate. They also used their relative advantage and specialization in the manufacturing of silk products, carpets, and porcelain, and exported these finished products, which were often bulkier and could be transported only when their value-per-weight was high enough. They were typically exported as luxury and status goods to the upper classes of the importing society. The bulkier and lower in value the good was (grains, rice, and most timber, for example), the more likely it was to be consumed locally or to be shipped only short distances. Temperate countries' goods were traded both overland, traveling the Silk Route, and by sea, sailing the Indian Ocean and later the Atlantic via the Cape Route.

The Silk Route was used for trade in Chinese and Mediterranean and European goods but also for trading in tropical goods that arrived in China from Southeast Asia and made their way to Central Asia and beyond by land. The Silk Route, it is important to note, was used not only for long-distance trade but also for trade between the nomads of the steppes and China, Persia, and other adjacent countries. By the eighteenth century, its northern branches were used for trade between westward-expanding China and eastward-expanding Russia.[51] Nor was it used only for trade in silk, as its name might suggest, but also (in different periods and across varying distances) for trade in horses, slaves, weapons, furs, woolen cloth, carpets, tea, spices, medicinal herbs, silver, and gold.

Price differentials were the engine of long-distance trade, and a few examples will provide some helpful context. Economic historians Findlay and O'Rourke found that in the seventeenth century, pepper from India and the islands could be sold in Amsterdam for three or four times its price in Southeast Asia.[52] They quote an earlier figure from Godinho, according to which the gross margin between Malabar and Lisbon was 260 percent and the net margin 152 percent, after wastage and transport costs had been allowed for.

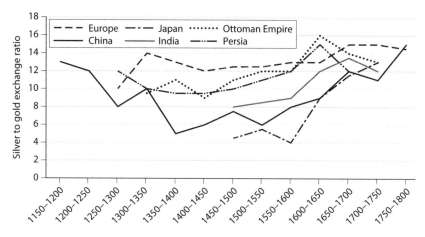

1.4. Number of weight units of silver to one weight unit of gold; exchange ratio in several locations, 1150–1800. Sources: von Glahn (1996); Flynn and Giráldez (2002); Pamuk (2000, pp. 46, 63, 136, 163); Floor and Clawson (2000); Chaudhuri (1968); Fragner (1986, p. 565).

Clove prices in Malacca were thirty times higher than in the Spice Islands or Moluccas, in India one hundred times higher, and in Lisbon as much as 240 times higher. Later, as trade developed, margins became narrower. In the seventeenth century, the markup from Southeast Asia to Amsterdam fluctuated between twenty-five times at its peak, fifteen times for several decades, and less than five times at its lowest. Nutmeg could be sold in London for 840 times its price in the Banda Islands.[53]

According to Lopez, the price of raw silk in Constantinople in the fourteenth century was three times its price in China.[54] Findlay and O'Rourke, drawing on work by Shiba, state that silk prices were forty times higher in Hsi Hsia (Southern Mongolia) than in Song China. A multiple of forty must have been unrepresentative; a multiple of three seems somewhat too low. But once raw silk production developed in Persia and Italy, price differences were likely to become narrower.

Silver price differences throughout Eurasia were considerable and had a fundamental global effect. They can best be measured by comparing the silver-to-gold conversion ratio. Figure 1.4 sets out this exchange ratio for the period 1150–1800. The vertical axis shows the number of weight units of silver that were exchanged for one weight unit of gold in each location over the period.

In 1400, the beginning of our period, the ratio was twelve in Europe, only six in China, and four and a half in Japan. In Europe, a merchant had to pay twelve units of silver for one unit of gold, while in China he could pay just six units of silver for the same amount of gold. Ratio differences were about the same a century later. The further east one traveled in 1500, the lower the ratio: twelve and a half in Europe, eleven in the Ottoman Empire, ten in Persia, eight and a half in India, six in China, and four in Japan. By 1700, prices had converged considerably, the ratios in the various years all being in the range of twelve to sixteen.

Rather than selling twenty-five units of American silver in Lisbon for two units of gold, a Portuguese merchant in the early sixteenth century could export them to Macao and sell them there for 4.16 units of gold. He could theoretically ship the gold back to Europe and buy fifty-two units of silver, travel back to China and buy 8.66 units of gold there, and so on. Silver price differences were a major force in long-distance trade. Silver had three functions. First, it was used for jewelry. Second, it was a medium of exchange, often in the form of minted coins. Finally, it was a means of storing value. Silver was a low-weight, high-value commodity easily transported long-distance, and it was essential for European merchants who had little else to offer their Asian trade counterparts. Silver was exported from the Spanish mines in the Americas to Europe, and from Europe (around the Cape) to India and China. Alternatively, it was directly exported from the Americas (via Acapulco and Manila) to China and from Japan to China.

Price differences made long-distance trade enormously profitable. Yet the trade was not without risks. The longer the distance, the higher the transportation costs and associated uncertainties—an issue to which we will turn later in this chapter and the next. Price differences were not constant, and fluctuations in price created market risks. The demand for luxury goods was not elastic. For example, pepper prices in Amsterdam fluctuated considerably and presented a general downward trend throughout the period of 1500 to 1700 due to imports from India and the Spice Islands. Interestingly, as Findlay and O'Rourke show, sugar prices did not fall. This divergence is explained by the fact that pepper was in good supply in Asia, for both Asian and European markets, whereas the supply of sugar produced in Brazil and the West Indies was constrained by shortages in labor force, settlers, and slaves.[55] Importation from Asia was subject to market risks that were different in nature from those linked to importation from the Americas. So the fact that pepper, other spices, and tropical goods in general were produced *by* Asians and *for* Asians, assured they would be in ample supply in Asia and, once transportation obstacles were overcome, also in Europe. So European merchants were in constant search of Asian goods that were not yet abundant in the European markets. They moved to importing porcelain and Chinaware, cotton, tea, pearls, coffee, indigo, and saltpeter, but market risks were still present despite the initially huge price gaps. The organization of trade had to take these risks into account, both by aiming at improving information flows as to market prices and by spreading risks. How was this accomplished? I analyze organizational challenges and solutions next.

THE ENVIRONMENTAL CHALLENGE TO TRADE INSTITUTIONS

Long-distance oceanic trade was the most challenging business activity to be organized in the premodern world. Merchants had to deal with risks associated with transportation, navigating their way through unfamiliar routes in the Indian Ocean and along the Silk Route. At sea, they had to confront risks such as storms, monsoons, reefs, and sandbars, and overland they contended with sandstorms, winter storms, and a lack of water and food supplies. They had to bear political and military risks such as those posed by pirates, land bandits, and hostile or unreliable foreign rulers, both en route and in the trade destinations, that could result in expropriation and even death. They had to assume market risks such as price fluctuations and lack of demand for exported goods. If they aimed at anything more than basic spot-barter transactions, they also had to identify common means of exchange and deal with credit risks and contract-enforcement risks.

In economic terms, long-distance Eurasian trade involved greater uncertainties than short-distance trade—the unforeseeable outcomes of oceanic currents and monsoons, pirates, inhospitable Asian rulers, and unknown market conditions. Often these uncertainties could not be quantified (even intuitively) into probabilities or converted into risk distributions. In more familiar trade routes, where uncertainties *could* be converted into calculable scenarios, they were at the high end of the spectrum of contemporary business risks. They were greater than investment risks in any domestic activity, such as retail, wholesale, crafts, or manufacturing, or in shorter-distance trade missions to more familiar destinations via more routine routes.

The simplest format for conducting business was that of a sole trader, an itinerant trader, carrying goods and walking, riding, or sailing to the chosen trade destination. The person involved in peddling was a lonely person living a tough life. He was subject to bodily risk, even the risk of death, and to travel and market risks. He had to act based only on his own acquired knowledge and information with respect to the trade, and could not spread or allocate risks.

To overcome such pitfalls, itinerant trader cooperation schemes were formed. These schemes will be described and analyzed in parts II through IV of the book—for now, only an initial introduction will be offered. Such schemes provided individual traders with a common infrastructure, such as ships carrying itinerant traders and their goods for a fee (freight ships) and caravanserais providing overland itinerant traders with shelter, food, and protection in return for payment. Agents were employed for specialization, to overcome cultural barriers and geographical spans, and for the spreading of risk. Loans and equity investment were sought by wealth-constraint merchants and also for motivations similar to those for the employment of agents. Merchants could cooperate on a wider scale in firms, partnerships, and networks in which they could provide each other with services based on mutuality, use the same infrastructure, and share market information.

The larger and more complex organizational forms solved the problems faced by the itinerant trader but generated a new set of problems. They required a leap in capital investment, as the merchants had to finance large ships, large crews, and a large quantity of high-value export goods. The merchants had to be able to provide this finance for a longer period of time, many months or even several years, depending on the route and distance traveled.

When employing others as agents, or investing together with others in partnerships, agency problems started to occur. The larger the multi-person trade enterprise, the higher the agency costs. Principals had to require bonds, monitor their agents, and take into account residual agency costs.[56] Information was a major problem for itinerant traders as well, as they had to learn about unfamiliar routes and markets. Larger enterprises encountered a different informational challenge because they employed agents. Investors and managers were separated from their agents by thousands of miles of oceans and steppes. Before the age of the telegraph, information could not travel faster than human beings. Agency problems within these enterprises were augmented by information asymmetries between principals and agents. Each of these more complex enterprises had to find ways to overcome the investment thresholds (by raising capital from more investors) as well as information asymmetries (by improving information flows and monitoring devices).

By being involved in cross-cultural, cross-jurisdictional international trade, these enterprises faced legal problems. They were subject to a multiplicity of legal systems. Often, they and their trade partners were subjected to different territorial, ethnic, or religious norms, and their trade partners enjoyed home bias in courts of law. In their direct dealings with foreign rulers, transactions were subjected to no third-party enforcement, meaning that such rulers could expropriate the property of foreign enterprises, goods, ships, and warehouses at will. Itinerant traders were at risk as long as they were on foreign soil, but the wealthier the foreign trade enterprise and the more permanent its facilities abroad, the more it was in danger of expropriation. The greater the foreign merchants perceived the threat of expropriation by the domestic ruler to be, the more likely they were to keep away from his ports in the first place, and the less likely it became for potentially beneficial trade to materialize. Yet the foreign ruler often was unable to credibly commit not to expropriate. The larger the organizational model that was adopted to overcome long-distance trade difficulties, and the more assets were pooled together, the more tempting it became for domestic rulers as well to expropriate the assets of the merchant enterprise. In order to offset the domestic expropriation threat, the domestic rulers had to find ways to credibly commit not to expropriate.

Long-distance international trade posed the greatest challenges for organizational design: organizations faced uncertainty, high risk, high investment threshold, shortage of reliable collateral, asymmetric information between traveling merchants and passive investors, augmented agency problems, concern over the protection of their property rights by foreign rulers, and more. Merchants from any region involved in long-distance trade in any environment faced a similar set of problems. Long-distance trade organizations were at the organizational cutting edge of the period 1400–1700. The particular challenges they faced were comparable in scale and ambition to those of organizing the Roman Catholic Church and independent cities in earlier centuries; canals in the eighteenth century; railways in the nineteenth century; the financial sector today; and planetary and intergalactic spacecraft voyages in the near future. This makes their study analogous to the study of the technological advances made in any of these periods. It is fascinating, illuminating, and beneficial in understanding both organizational evolution and the impact of organizations on economic change.

This book surveys the most demanding business activity of the premodern world, long-distance trade, in both its maritime and overland Eurasian environments. The trade organizations had to face the most challenging difficulties of any institutions of the time, and thus constituted the institutional vanguard of the premodern world. This book will focus on the organization of trade not only because this is the birthplace of the business corporation, but also because it can explain, no less than technology or the use of military power, the globalization of trade and the rise of Europe to a dominant role in Eurasian trade.

WHICH NONORGANIZATIONAL FACTORS COULD EXPLAIN EUROPE'S TRADE ASCENDANCY?

As stated in the introduction, this book makes two core arguments. While I will be quite satisfied with convincing readers with the first-level (organizational) core argument, which explains the emergence of the business corporation in Europe and the shift to impersonal cooperation in Western Europe, I nevertheless wish to make the extra effort of convincing at least some of my readers with the second-level core argument (concerning trade), namely that the organizational breakthrough explains the rise to dominance of Europe in long-distance Eurasian trade. To do this, I will first evaluate other explanations for Europe's rise to dominance in

Eurasian trade in the remainder of this chapter, in order to make space for my argument in the rest of the book.

The relatively recent literature that endeavors to explain the great divergence between Europe and Asia (and particularly China) is voluminous, as is the earlier literature on Europe's singularity, the European miracle, the rise of the West, Europe's hegemony, the wealth of nations, and the like.[57] And justly so. One cannot bypass these topics when trying to understand modern human history and present global inequality. Yet this divergence is relevant for our project only in a limited sense. The task here is not to understand divergence that occurred during the industrialization of Europe, its urbanization, the transportation revolution, or the financial revolution. I focus only on trade. Thus, the question at hand is as follows: Why did Europe, or some western parts of it, come to dominate long-distance Eurasian trade? As our timeframe is 1400–1700, we have to look at explanations for differences that were in place by the sixteenth century or the early seventeenth century. The literature that identifies a later divergence in the eighteenth or even nineteenth century is not relevant for us.

Let us now examine geography, technology, and politics, in that order, as possible explanations for Europe's ascendency to trade dominance. The less these factors convince us as sole or dominant explanations for the ascendance of European trade, the wider the scope for an organizational explanation. We will turn to geography first, as it can be dismissed easily. Geography could not be Western Europe's advantage. India was centrally located; Southeast Asia was strategically located on the passages from the Indian Ocean to the South China Sea; and the Arab Middle East had access to both the Mediterranean and the Indian Ocean. By contrast, Portugal, England, and the Low Countries were remote, even insulated, from the Eastern Mediterranean ports that connected with the Silk Route and the overland routes to the Red Sea and Persian Gulf. Their only locational advantage, which became apparent only after the discovery of America, was their relative proximity to the silver deposits of America which became, for them, an essential Eurasian trade good. In terms of geography they were, with this one exception, disadvantaged. Possibly they were so disadvantaged as to search for organizational innovation. I shall return at a later stage to geographical disadvantage as a possible explanation for the Dutch and English organizational revolution.

Shipping

Let us turn to technology: Did Western Europe enjoy a technological advantage that enabled mastery of the seas? The macroinventions associated with the British industrial revolution—the steam engine, the new spinning and weaving machines in the textile industry, and new coke-smelting techniques and more efficient furnaces in the iron industry—can explain the economic divergence of the late eighteenth and nineteenth centuries.[58] As Daniel Headrick convincingly demonstrated, in the nineteenth century European and American navies acquired steam-propelled ships, constructed from steel and armed with guns, that gave them unprecedented advantages over their Ottoman, Indian, and Chinese counterparts and enabled them to carry forward gunboat imperialism around the globe, from the Niger and the Nile to the Yangtze River, Tokyo Bay, and the Hawaiian Islands. European armies used machine guns in small colonial wars, resulting in killing fields from South Africa to Afghanistan.[59] But these are irrelevant for the historical puzzle at hand here. The root causes of this technological breakthrough, be they in demography, agricultural changes, or in the ideas of the Enlightenment—which encouraged empirical and experimental research, critical scientific and philosophical thinking, exchange of ideas, and accumulation of knowledge—are not to be found before the late seventeenth and eighteenth centuries.[60] Such late underlying causes of technological innovations cannot explain an earlier navigational advantage, such as it was, in the sixteenth and early seventeenth century. We have to zoom in from technology at large to the specific technologies relevant for us, shipbuilding and navigation, and to an earlier period, around the time the Europeans first arrived in the Indian Ocean, and compare the Western Europeans to Asians not in the abstract but rather in the context of functionality in the Indian Ocean environment.

Indigenous ships in the Indian Ocean, prior to the arrival of the Europeans, were built with several factors taken into account: the monsoon regime, the changing nature of coastline, and materials available for construction.[61] Different ships were used in the Arabian Sea and its branches—the Red Sea and Persian Gulf (the dhow), Sri Lanka and the Bay of Bengal (the single outrigger), Southeast Asia (the double outrigger), and the South China Sea (the junk).[62] Indian Ocean ship construction used mainly ropes, often coconut coir, rather than iron nails. Asians used indigenous wood, the most useful being Indian teak. The Chinese used nails and pine. The Chinese junk was undoubtedly the largest vessel used in the Indian Ocean before the arrival of the Europeans. Arguably, it was also the most technologically advanced. The flat bottom and the shallow draft of the typical junk made it ideal for sailing in shallow or estuarial waters. The steering mechanism of the Chinese ships was more scientifically developed than in those of Europe.[63]

Compared to these features, Western Europeans enjoyed no advantage in shipping technologies in the late Middle Ages. On the contrary, shipping technologies migrated westward—in the twelfth and thirteenth centuries with the Crusaders from the Eastern Mediterranean to Italy, and then in the fourteenth and fifteenth centuries from Genoa, following its decline, to Spain and Portugal.[64] The Iberians used these technologies and their carriers—famously Christopher Columbus—to sail down the coast of Africa and across the Atlantic. In these parts of the globe, their shipping technologies were far superior to indigenous technologies. But did these technologies provide them with any advantage when they first arrived in the Indian Ocean in 1498? The short answer is no. Their only salient advantage was that they used iron nails, which were not used in the Indian Ocean and which presumably made ships sturdier. But the Chinese and Arabs used iron nails too. And there were advantages in the Indian Ocean environment in the use of coconut coir, which was readily available and did not rust. Furthermore, by the beginning of the seventeenth century, many Indian ships used iron nails.[65] In terms of masts, rigs, sails, keels, and hulls, the Portuguese ships enjoyed no clear advantage in the Indian Ocean. On the contrary, whereas Asian ships were constructed to different designs in different localities to better fit the oceanic conditions, goods, and routes for which they were made, the Portuguese ships were uniform, made to endure the voyage in the Atlantic and around the Cape, with no adaptability to the unique conditions of the Arabian Sea, the water around Sri Lanka, or the Malacca Straits.[66]

Even in terms of sheer size, Chinese and Southeast Asian ships encountered by the Portuguese when they first arrived in Asia were much larger than their own. Vasco da Gama's flagship was 27 meters long. The crew of his four ships together was just 170 men. The early English and Dutch East India Companies ships were 30–50 meters long, carrying

150–500 tons and having crews of 50–150 men each. Just decades before the arrival of the Portuguese, Zheng He's fleets included, according to Chinese sources, huge "treasure-ships," the largest of them 140 meters long, having nine masts, carrying more than 1,250 tons of cargo and hundreds of crew members. There is an ongoing controversy as to the accuracy of the official reports of the sizes of the ships. However, even leaving aside those fleets, the reports of travelers from Marco Polo and Ibn Battuta to the first Portuguese in Asia, and archeological evidence from Chinese shipyards and South China Sea shipwrecks, suggest that there is ample evidence for Song and Ming's Chinese ships that were 50 to 100 meters long, having an average burden of 350–500 tons deadweight and even 1,000 tons for the largest ships, ones that could carry up to a thousand men. So even by the lowest estimate, Chinese ships of the period were considerably larger than sixteenth- and early-seventeenth-century European ships.[67]

From an early stage of their presence in Asia, the Portuguese used ships built in Asian shipyards to supplement the capacity of their fleets. They reached agreements with the local authorities and established major centers for shipping in Goa and Cochin. The natural result of this process was the integration of Asian shipping methods and materials with their European equivalents.[68] The European presence and shipbuilding in India created a two-sided learning process. Indians learned the effective use of nails from the Arabs, the Chinese, and the Portuguese, and, by the end of the sixteenth century, the majority of Indian vessels were built using iron nails. The English, arriving around 1600, had preferred to use some Indian methods for certain kinds of vessels. The use of planks that were not nailed to the frame of the boat but attached to each other by wooden ties was much cheaper and to some extent more effective than the European iron-nailing method. It was also easier to replace damaged planks with new ones this way, which naturally prolonged the longevity of the ships. The EIC shipyards adopted them in conjunction with nailing. Another feature that the Europeans adopted was the use of Asian teak. This material was found to afford the vessels much greater longevity. While the vessels made from European oak lasted between ten and twelve years, boats made of Asian teak could last between fifty and eighty years. This was obviously a very significant difference, leading all the Europeans (Portuguese, Dutch, and English) to transfer their dockyards to locations with easy access to teak—the Malabar Coast, Gujarat, and Burma. The cost saving achieved by transferring the dockyards to Asia was very significant. From a cost of RS54 per ton for a ship built in Europe, it was reduced to as little as RS27.[69] The extent of the exchange of shipping-construction technologies and materials between Europeans and Asians supports the arguments that Europeans did not enjoy any advantage at the first stage, that by the seventeenth century most ships were hybrid, and that shipping advantage cannot explain European dominance in the Indian Ocean.

Navigation

Navigationally, too, the Europeans enjoyed no marked advantage in the sixteenth or seventeenth centuries. All Eurasian navigators had reasonable methods for calculating latitudes by measuring the altitude of the North Star or the Southern Cross above the horizon with instruments such as the astrolabe, used in this period by Arabs, Indians, and Europeans, or the qianxingban, used by the Chinese. The more sophisticated sextant was invented by the Europeans only in the eighteenth century. The magnetic compass, which was first developed by the Chinese, was in use by the sixteenth century for directional bearing by all Eurasians. Neither Europeans nor Asians had any adequate way to precisely determine longitudes throughout our period, as the marine chronometer was invented only in the eighteenth century.

In other respects, the Asians had advantages. They were much more familiar with the monsoon regime—knowledge that was crucial for sailing across the Indian Ocean. They were also familiar with coastlines that were essential for littoral navigation and for approaching harbors and straits. They had sailing charts and maps at the ready that the Europeans still had to produce or obtain. An understanding of the nature of the seabed and of sea plants, fish, birds, and flotsam, and awareness of dangerous sandbanks, rocks, fog, or mist, were being employed by Asian navigators who had mastered them much more than the newcoming Europeans.[70] Despite the fact that Europeans had similar navigational instruments to those of the Asians, they nevertheless depended in their first few decades in the Indian Ocean on Arab and Indian pilots to guide their way across oceans to their intended landfall, through straits, and into ports. Conversely, Asians were able to navigate their ships independently throughout the Indian Ocean from the East African coast to the South China Sea. It is not known whether Asians aimed to search for lands beyond Africa. As much as they were motivated to do so, was their failure to find the way around the Cape of Good Hope due to navigational limits or other reasons? This question awaits a response.[71] To conclude, marine navigational know-how and technology were either endogenous or migratory and were available throughout Eurasia, and Europe's commercial expansion in the Indian Ocean cannot be explained by a navigational advantage.

Violence and Wars

Once the European nonmilitary technological and navigational superiority argument is questioned, an additional line of argumentation is offered: that Europe's rise to trade dominance resulted from its military technology and from the willingness and determination of its elites to resort to violence and force. The use of force in the *conquista* of the New World in the face of the pacified American Indians is regarded as the prime example of the European propensity for violence.[72] The skirmishes between the Portuguese and the Zamorin of Calicut shortly after the former's arrival in India and throughout the first decades of the sixteenth century is an Asian example. The intensified use of violence on the arrival of the Dutch and English in the early seventeenth century is given as another example. Other prime examples from this period include the fighting over Hormuz, which ended in its capture by the EIC and Persians from the hands of the Portuguese in 1622; the Amboyna massacre; and the 1623 torture and execution on Ambon Island (Maluku, Indonesia) of twenty English and Japanese men by agents of the Dutch VOC.[73]

Another sign of the introduction of violence by the Europeans into the Indian Ocean can be seen in the changing regime of law of the seas. It is often argued, albeit not well documented, that before the arrival of the Europeans the Indian Ocean was considered to be a free sea. Even the most powerful Asian rulers did not challenge the right of ships of any origin or ethnic group to sail the Ocean and trade freely.[74] The Portuguese, on arrival, wished to impose a new regime, according to which the Ocean was the domain of the King of Portugal, and any other ship had to obtain a license from the king to sail it. They wanted to apply a conception that was originally developed in the Eastern Mediterranean, and justified the domination of the high seas by rulers of superpowers. The difficulty for the Portuguese was that, in Roman law, the open sea could not be owned by anyone. The Romans regarded the Mediterranean, *mare nostrum*, as their internal sea and, by this, distinguished it from the open seas. It is difficult to determine whether this view was based on a sense of ownership, sovereignty, or jurisdiction over this sea. The Venetians and Genoese, who did not control all the shores of the Mediterranean, declared parts of it (such as the Adriatic) to be closed seas (*mare clausum*) to justify the imposition of their jurisdiction over them. In addition, they used a different rationale, introducing a distinction between ownership and jurisdiction. The Portuguese carried the same rationale to the Indian Ocean, declared it to be within their jurisdiction (though not owned by them), and imposed the *cartazes* licensing system. Non-Portuguese ships had to apply at a Portuguese port for a license to sail and trade, and to pay for that license. Unlicensed ships were subject to capture. On arrival in Asia, the Dutch developed, through the ingeniousness of Grotius, a competing sea law conception, that of *mare liberum*, according to which the ocean was free and could not be placed under the jurisdiction of any ruler. But this was not a concept of peace. Grotius was, after all, an attorney at the service of the VOC. He was hired by the VOC to justify the capture of Portuguese ships by the Dutch, most concretely the capture of the Santa Catarina in 1603 between present-day Singapore and Pengerang in Malaysia.[75]

European violence in Asia, it can be argued, was an extension of the frequent wars in Europe. European rulers fought many wars because political units in Europe in the passage from the Middle Ages to the early modern era were small, fragmented, and unstable. One line of argument in the literature emphasizes that Europe developed a strong state capacity to conduct wars. The British fiscal-naval nexus is a prime example of this capacity. The British were able to collect more taxes and borrow money on a large scale in the developing stock market—and thus build an empire. Eighteenth-century British expenditure was premodern in the sense that it was mainly military. But its size constantly grew until it reached a modern scale, enabling Britain to operate more ships and soldiers in more remote parts of the globe than in previous centuries and, most importantly, on a scale with which the French and other European fiscal systems, not to say Asian systems, could not compete.[76] The British navy rose to world dominance thanks to this state fiscal capacity. The number of navy ships Britain operated rose from one hundred in 1689 to 214 in 1815—that is, from smaller than the French navy to almost three times its size.[77] This literature cannot resolve our puzzle. Britain's fiscal revolution took place starting around 1689. Its navy grew rapidly only in the eighteenth century. This cannot explain superiority in Asia throughout the seventeenth century. The "early start" works better for explaining the rise to trade dominance of the Dutch Republic in the seventeenth century, as it began its fiscal revolution in the late sixteenth century. Portugal did not go through a fiscal revolution and nevertheless had a significant presence in the Indian Ocean in the sixteenth century. Furthermore, the direction of causation in this literature moves from expansion of the tax base through expansion of trade, to improvement of the tax collection apparatus, to a rise in taxation, to the design of credible commitment devices committing the ruler not to expropriate, to expansion of national debt, to naval power, and to empire building. But here we search for the causes behind the initial success in Asia, before trade-based taxation even picked up.

Another thread in the literature emphasizes the frequent wars in Europe as a booster for the development of Europe's military and naval technologies. These technologies were superior to those of other regions that were less violent and fought less frequently. The superiority of Europe's military and naval technology enabled it to expand its trade and eventually conquer the world. Between 1550 and 1600, principal European powers were at war 71 percent of the time; between 1600 and 1650 they were at war 66 percent of the time; and between 1650 and 1700, 54 percent of the time.[78] Applying a tournament model, Hoffman concludes that the anticipation of an approaching war pushed European rulers to adopt the best of the gunpowder technologies of the previous war and to try to innovate and improve beyond it. They were involved in large-scale learning-by-doing, generation after generation. The high frequency of wars pushed the pace of innovation.

It is not that Asians did not use violence in their conquests. Indeed, they used it to the utmost extent, as was the case with Genghis Khan and

Tamerlane. But in some Asian regions, political unification and stability lessened the intensity of rounds of war breaking out, as was the case in Japan; cutting-edge gunpowder technology proved ineffective in the fight against nomad enemies, as was the case in China; or there was low state capacity to tax and finance innovation, as was the case in the Ottoman Empire or Mughal India. Asians fought more on land than at sea. In the seventeenth century the armies of the Portuguese, Dutch, and English each experienced several defeats by Asians across all of Asia. The effective deployment of violence that we identify today with European territorial colonialism in Asia is based mostly on eighteenth- and nineteenth-century wars. As we are most interested in seafaring wars, let us examine the European ability to more effectively use guns on board ships as early as the sixteenth and seventeenth centuries.

Guns and Ships

Writing in 1965, Cipolla, relying on Panikkar, concluded: "In the course of the fifteenth century, European technology made noticeable progress and by 1498 'the armaments of the Portuguese ships was something totally unexpected and new in the Indian (and China) seas and gave an immediate advantage to the Portuguese.' European artillery was incomparably more powerful than any kind of cannon ever made in Asia."[79] Guns on sailing ships, according to Cipolla, explain European expansion in Asia. Because Western Europeans constructed ships for stormy Atlantic waters and weather, their vessels were sturdier and more stable and handled gunfire better than the narrower or shallower ships constructed in the Mediterranean or the Indian Ocean. The Europeans developed lighter, safer, and smaller bronze guns. They soon realized that these should be located not high up, atop the vessel, but rather as low as possible, on deck and even close to the waterline. This is still a widespread view.[80] But the fifty years that have passed since Cipolla's classic book have given rise to a more complex picture.

Both cannons and gunpowder were most likely invented in China, and it took them a while to migrate across Eurasia. However, by our period they had been adopted by Indians, Arabs, Ottomans, and Europeans. Until their defeat in the Battle of Lepanto in 1571, the Ottomans made advances westward in the Mediterranean at the expense of the European maritime leaders, the Venetians, Genoese, and their Latin allies. They were doing well against the Spanish fleet along the Moroccan coast even after Lepanto. It is argued that, on the Indian Ocean, when using sailing ships rather than galleys, the sixteenth-century Portuguese enjoyed a considerable advantage over the Ottomans—not due to superior guns or ships but due to their superior ability to operate cannons on deck.[81] But others argue, as we shall see in chapter 12, that the Ottomans actually won some of their maritime battles in the second quarter of the sixteenth century against the Portuguese in the Arabian Sea.[82]

As much as the Portuguese enjoyed an initial advantage, compared to Indians, in using guns on deck, new evidence suggests that the Indians learned from them. Indian merchants had cannons located on their ships but initially they provided insufficient room to operate them effectively. It took them some time to learn that they needed to give up some of their merchandise and devote more space to the effective use of the cannons; otherwise, that merchandise would be in danger.[83] Indian engineers also realized they had to build stronger hulls to be able to load more than a few guns on the ship. This probably spread the use of iron nails in gun-carrying ships.[84] By the early seventeenth century, local Indian vessels could carry enough arms to compete with the Europeans. Just as Europeans hired Asian pilots, so did Indian shipowners hire European gunners at first, to ensure proper operation of the guns. These gunners were important agents of transfer of knowledge to the locals.

Facing China, the European naval capabilities were even more constrained. Neither the Portuguese nor the Dutch made any significant inroads into mainland China in the sixteenth and seventeenth centuries. The Portuguese settlement in Macao was secured by the payment of annual tribute. Their trade with China was restricted only to the port of Macao. The Dutch presence was confined to the island of Taiwan. Even there they had to fortify themselves in two forts on a peninsula that was separated from the main island by a lagoon. The Dutch VOC lost in a maritime battle with the Ming navy in Liaoluo Bay off the coast of Fujian in 1632. They lost again in 1661 to the Ming loyalist Koxingam, who decided to invade Taiwan and make it his basis for fighting against the Qing dynasty. A recent analysis of the battle by Andrade shows that the Dutch did not enjoy a clear military or naval superiority over the Chinese. The Chinese had their own cannons, yet they also studied carefully every

European cannon they captured. They used handguns and experimented with muskets. Their troops were well trained and disciplined. Chinese junks were well adapted to the conditions of the South China Sea and to monsoons. They proved effective in the maritime battle. The Dutch ships and sailing techniques proved better only when sea conditions turned more similar to those of the Atlantic, particularly when sailing close to the wind in deep water. The only clear advantage of the Dutch was in constructing forts. They used European techniques that evolved over generations of wars and sieges.[85] But eventually the two forts yielded. All in all, in the only major wars between Chinese and Dutch in our period, the Dutch did not enjoy a clear technological or naval advantage and lost. The victory provided Koxinga and his sons, the Zheng family, with an opportunity to form a merchant enterprise that exceeded the VOC in terms of trade revenues.[86]

In short, the only clear advantage of the Europeans was their ability to effectively use guns from ships in maritime battles. Cipolla was mistaken—not due to lack of competence but rather due to the fact that studies of the Ottoman fleet in the Indian Ocean, of Indian and Chinese shipping and gun technology, and of technological exchange in India and China were not yet available.

To conclude, the following is now known: to begin with, Europeans did not enjoy any advantages in shipping or navigation technology over Asians; Asians had better-adapted ships and better knowledge of the Indian Ocean environment; and maritime technology traveled relatively easily because it was not deeply embedded in culture or civilization, so any technological advantage in this realm could be offset by a short technology-adoption timespan.

Let us assume that the Europeans enjoyed a technological advantage in the use of guns from sailing ships but not in shipbuilding or navigation technology. This is not an altogether unreasonable assumption. Yet to make a difference, the number of European ships with superior guns on board in the Indian Ocean had to be substantial. They had to be used in maritime battles, and their superior guns had to be the crucial factor in these clashes: the outcomes had to disrupt Asian merchant ships' voyages either by actually blocking trade routes or by having a deterrent effect throughout the Indian Ocean and the South China Sea. This had to occur at an early stage, before the trade dominance of the European merchants could be secured in other ways, such as by organizational means. Gunship superiority in the eighteenth century cannot explain what I am trying to explain in this book. At this stage I am not convinced that historical research can confirm that all of these requirements were met. I would like to encourage additional research by military historians and historians of technology into the nature of alleged European superiority in ship-gun technology. More specifically, two key questions are the following: Didn't Asians copy this technology? And could the Europeans make this technological advantage a decisive factor in securing their dominance in long-distance trade? As long as those other studies are not conclusive, the study of the evolution and migration of trade-organizational forms is worthwhile. It is worthwhile not only for understanding the emergence of the corporation—my first-level (less ambitious) argument—but particularly for addressing the second and more ambitious level of argumentation, of the impact of organizations (primarily the corporation) on Europe's ascendance in Eurasian trade.

Note that this book does not try to explain or appraise European colonization in Asia and the role of the EIC and the VOC in it. It does not hold violence to be a major factor in the early history of these companies or in their rise to long-distance trade dominance. It is likely to be critiqued for ignoring the deplorable later chapters in the history of the two companies.[87] The formal response to this critique is that the book focuses on trade, and the timeframe of the book ends in 1700. Much of the resort to effective use of military force and the territorial expansion of the two companies took place in the eighteenth and (with respect to the EIC) nineteenth centuries. It is this effective resort to violence and colonialism, which is widely known, that often anachronistically pictures the early history as a forerunner. The known violent European encounters in the Americas are also wrongly assumed to reflect realities in Asia as well. The early EIC and VOC were trade enterprises. The Europeans had no overwhelming naval or military advantages over Asian merchants and rulers. The idea of compelling Delhi or Beijing to yield to Dutch or English commercial or political demands would have been absurd in 1600. Until the late seventeenth century, their territorial rule was confined to a few spice islands and port towns.[88] They could not have ambitions to conquer large territories, establish colonies, or subordinate Asian rulers. In a way, the assertion that the Europeans were superpowers in Asia thanks to their naval technology and resolute violent policies is Eurocentric and goes against the grain of the thesis of late divergence.

By ruling out violence and other explanations, this book establishes the existence of a wide historiographical space that justifies the focus on the early history of the two companies as late-coming trade companies, and on their organizational challenges and solutions. By downplaying the role of violence in the seventeenth century, it does not preclude the possibility that the organizational innovations of the early seventeenth century enabled the next stage in the history of the companies, their turning into colonial enterprises in the eighteenth and nineteenth centuries, enterprises that relied on military might and exercised sovereign authority over a growing number of Asian people.

~ 2 ~

Theoretical Frameworks for Analyzing the Development of Institutions in Interaction with Their Environment

Why did specific trade institutions develop? Did they effectively resolve the long-distance trade problems faced by traders? How can we answer such questions in the absence of contemporary evidence as to the intentions of those jurists, politicians, and aldermen who shaped the institutions and the institutional experience of those traders who employed them? Theory can take us a long way. It cannot fully substitute for historical records. But it can offer tentative answers in historical contexts in which records are unavailable and contemporaries did not necessarily grasp the meaning and consequences of the institutions they employed. In this chapter I will outline the theoretical frameworks I have chosen to study the development of institutions and particularly of trade organizations. I will first discuss theories that are useful for static analysis, then examine theories that can be deployed for the dynamic development of institutions within their environment, and finally assert that the theoretical framework for the study of institutional migration is lacking. In chapter 4 I will present theoretical insights that can be gained from other fields and disciplines that can be useful for the study of the migration of institutions and particularly trade organizations. And lastly, in chapter 12 I will provide theoretical insights that can assist in understanding the resistance to the migration of institutions. This book is intended for diverse readership in terms of disciplines. Economic historians and corporate scholars can skip the parts of this chapter that they are familiar with.

What do I mean by institutions? The definitions of institutions in the various social science disciplines are numerous.[1] A famous definition among economists is that of Douglass North: "Institutions are the rules of the game in society, or more formally, are the human devised constraints that shape human interaction."[2] Another, more recent influential definition is that of Avner Greif: "An institution is a system of social factors that conjointly generate a regularity of behavior."[3]

The institutional context is composed of the rules and norms that shape long-distance traders' transactions. The rules and norms are manmade and not endowed by nature. But they are exogenous to the traders and not fully controlled, or subject to alteration, by them; and they are nonphysical, comprising not only tools or buildings. However, I believe institutions cannot be reduced to legal rules and social norms as such. Rather, they encompass the systems composed of the rules and norms, the individuals who are subject to them, the devices that motivate the individuals to follow the rules and norms, and the imposition of sanctions on those who deviate from the rules. The rules themselves can be spontaneously created or purposely and intentionally drafted—that is, they can be informal or formal. For instance, the rules that applied to institutions could be informal in several senses: they could be unwritten, vague, based on the allocation of nonmonetary benefits, based on unspecified, in-advance payoffs, or nonenforceable. Conversely, formal rules applying to institutions could mean "legal" in the positive sense that they were decreed by a sovereign state, or that they satisfied the criteria provided by the rules of recognition of a legal system even if not produced by a state (say, recognized communal customs). As this book does not set out to deal only with legal institutions, I need not enter into the old debate as to what, if at all, distinguishes legal rules from nonlegal or social norms.[4]

Some may judge that, because this book deals with ships, caravanserais, the Armenian merchant network, and Portuguese state-operated voyages, it is not a legal history book. I believe it is impossible to understand clearly legal-business organizational forms such as the commenda or the corporation without understanding the full organizational menu (be it formal or informal, legal, or social) that is, or could be, available in any region. This book covers not only the full span of organizational forms but also the full span of norms that create and govern them, from rulers' decrees and legislation, to the codes of learned Roman-law jurists, to religious codes, religious response, and religious court rulings in the three monotheistic religions, to unwritten merchant customs, merchant codes, and ethnic, clan, and family norms. The same applies to enforcement mechanisms and sanctions. The book covers institutions enforced by state courts, religious courts, merchant tribunals, and merchant practices. It covers sanctions ranging from capital punishment, expropriation, and ostracism out of a city or community to dismissal of agents, winding-up of partnerships, or refusal to conduct new business transactions with fellow merchants.

North distinguishes between organizations and institutions. The former, he argues, are players, while the latter are rules. This is not the sense in which this book analyzes organizations. North's organizations operate within an institutional framework and aim to promote their strategic goals, maximize profit, acquire political power, generate believers, and so on, within the institutional constraints exogenously imposed on them. In other words, rather than focusing on organizations in North's sense (such as the network of Armenian merchants with its hub in New Julfa and other similar examples I provide), this book examines the generic institutional structure of the merchant network, an institution. It focuses on the family firm of the Pu or the Fuggers not from North's perspective (that is, as specific organizations), but rather on the family firm as an institution, and not on the EIC as a specific organization but rather on the joint-stock business corporation as an institution. Specific organizations are examined in the relevant microstudies. But these serve us specifically in understanding institutional formation and transformation, which is the subject of the book as a whole.

The confusion between institutions and organizations might be amplified to readers by the fact that the subjects of the book are termed "business organizations." A business organization in this book is a group of people that collaborate to achieve certain commercial goals. The book studies the menu of business-organizational forms present in different regions between roughly 1400 and 1700. Its main research topic centers on the generic forms themselves, not the specific organizations that adopted them. I could thus use only the term "organizations," referring to generic organizational forms, such as the business corporation or the commenda. However, some readers might use the term "organizations" with respect to the itinerant trader, the ship, the caravanserai, ruler-operated enterprise, or the merchant network. Thus, I will use the term "organizations" with respect to the former, institutions with respect to the latter, and both terms interchangeably with respect to the full range. In addition, some of the theoretical literature I survey in this chapter and use in the rest of the book identifies itself as belonging to the new institutional school and uses the term institutions, while other work identifies itself as belonging to organizational economics or organizational studies more broadly.[5] In the theoretical discussions, I attempt to follow the terms used by each of the generators of the theory, another decision that led to the use of both terms.

STATIC INSTITUTIONAL ANALYSIS

Over the last three generations, the discipline of economics has gone a long way in turning its attention from markets, in which firms transact with other firms or with consumers, to hierarchies and institutions. It has also made significant progress toward studying internal relationships within the firm, based on an understanding that the law plays a constitutive role in transactions and firms. The theoretical approaches that have been developed since the 1960s include transaction cost economics (starting with Coase); theories of the firm (Coase; Jensen and Meckling; Hart);[6] property rights (Alchian and Demsetz);[7] contract and agency theory (Williamson; Macneil; Macaulay; Fama and Jensen; Ayres and Gertner);[8] information economics (Akerlof; Stiglitz; Spence);[9] and theories of limited liability (Easterbrook and Fischel);[10] of asset partitioning (Hansmann, Kraakman, and Squire);[11] and of corporate governance and finance (Bebchuk; Black; Rock).[12] The theoretical tools used for the static analysis of institutions are, by now, the standard tools offered by applied economics and law and economics. Theory can now bring much to the study of the functioning of institutions within their environment, the problems they face, and the impact they may have. In my static analysis of institutions and their function, I will use, sometimes explicitly but more often implicitly, familiar bodies of literature. I have no aspirations of methodological innovation, or to sharpen existing theoretical tools. My contribution is in applying familiar tools (which are usually applied only to modern organizational forms, and primarily to the publicly traded corporation) to the organizational forms used in premodern Eurasian trade—the traveling agent, the family firm, the partnership, the merchant network, and the early corporation.

DYNAMIC INSTITUTIONAL THEORIES

Douglass North and the consolidating historical new institutional economics (HNIE) school aimed to integrate dynamic institutional analysis, the analysis of how institutions evolve and change over time, into economic history and economic theory.[13] North famously attributed the rise of the West to its ability to design institutions that protected property rights, spread risks, monitored agents, and reduced transaction costs.

One can identify four stages in the turn of economists and economic historians to institutions, expressed in a series of models.[14] In the first stage, institutions, including legal institutions, were viewed as a precondition for the market. However, scholars still did not study the institutions themselves—they approached them simply as "firms," examining only their inputs and outputs, rather than how they were structured or managed. The focus of scholarly interest at this stage was still on markets and the impact of institutions on them. In the second stage, the question was around how institutions developed. The answer was that economic change, in the form, for example, of expanding markets or new technology, changed the incentive for creating and altering institutions. The assumption was that demand generated institutions. The third stage produced theoretical models that were structured similarly to second-stage models but added supply-side factors (political, legal, cultural) to demand-side economic factors.[15] Economists began to realize that the law and institutions were not supplied passively by the state on first demand. Demand for institutions was met only when the supply-side factors could produce them. In the fourth stage it was realized that the process was reciprocal, and that an ongoing interaction between the state, including its legal elements, and the market led to the emergence and evolution of institutions. The models aimed to account endogenously for both economic and legal change. Such models tried to illuminate the interaction

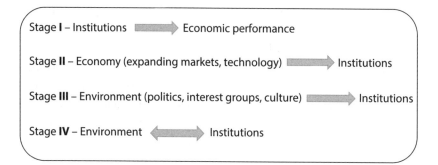

2.1. Stages of the study of institutions.

between institutions and their environment, beginning with the economic change, through its effect on the value of the legal institution (say, property rights) and its distributive effects on interest groups' gains and losses, through the state's legal and political process which involves transaction costs—at times change inhibiting—to the change in property rights and back to its effect on economic performance. Fourth-stage models of institutional change were developed and empirically examined by several new institutional economic historians, including North, Barzel, and Libecap in the 1990s.[16]

One might summarize graphically the development of the theory of institutions, and the causal direction of institutional evolution, since the 1970s, in four stages, as represented in figure 2.1. The arrows represent how economists and economic historians grasped the causation between institutions and the environment in each stage.

A good opportunity for spreading awareness of the importance of institutions was created with the awarding of the 1993 Nobel Prize to two of the dominant figures in the cliometric revolution (and in the practice of economic history in the four decades that followed): Robert Fogel and North.[17] Since the 1970s, ever-more powerful tools for studying how institutions emerged in interaction with their environment were developed. I will use these tools (which were not available for economic historians, legal historians, or global historians of trade before the 1970s) in my study of the dynamics of the evolution of endogenous institutions.

One useful example for the introduction of dynamics to the analysis of institutional change can be found in the theoretical insights of Paul David and Brian Arthur, who introduced the concept of path dependency into the theory of institutional change.[18] Before their contribution, a common assumption held that institutions will evolve in interaction with their environment in a path leading toward greater efficiency. David and Arthur each showed that, under specific circumstances, such as increasing returns and network effects, this might not be the case. The path dependence theory that was originally applied to the adoption of technology was later applied to institutions, including organizational forms. For example, Bebchuk and Roe claimed that path dependence dominated the development of modern corporations. They distinguished between two kinds of path dependence: structure driven and rule driven. The initial structure of ownership had a direct effect on the future ownership structure. Moreover, the initial structure of ownership had a secondary effect on legal rules, to create path dependence in the development of these rules. According to Bebchuk and Roe, the combination of these two sources of path dependence created divergence in organizational law and organizational structure among the world's advanced economies.[19]

Only a few of the institutional economists analyzed trade institutions; even fewer did so dynamically; and fewer still did so in the context of Eurasian (rather than European) trade. North, very generally and abstractly, talked about organizational innovations along three cost margins: those that increased the mobility of capital (methods for evading usury laws, bills of exchange, improved control of agents); those that lowered information costs (printed price lists, trade manuals); and those that spread risks (insurance, investment portfolio diversification).[20] Carlos and Nicholas and Jones and Ville debated the question of whether the seventeenth-century long-distance trading corporations constituted efficient mergers that mitigated agency problems and reduced transaction costs, or inefficient firms that were formed to rent seek and extract monopoly rent.[21] A couple of other studies, which interpreted the creation of the EIC as vertical integration, as horizontal integration, and as a means to deal with agency problems between the company at home and its factors and other servants in Asia, had their value.[22] Other studies analyzed trade institutions in Europe, the Mediterranean, and the Middle East.[23]

COMPARATIVE INSTITUTIONAL ANALYSIS

As noted in the previous section, economic theory is getting better at studying the relationship between institutions and the environment. It is not good at analyzing the transfer of institutional know-how, but comparative studies are a first step in this direction. New institutional economics was not comparative in its first stages, but recently several scholars working within this framework added a comparative perspective.[24] Their new question was the following: Why did one environment give rise to one set of institutions, while another environment gave rise to a different set? The comparison helped to isolate and identify the elements in each environment that molded its institutions.[25] Greif compared the different ways in which traders organized their activities in North Africa and Italy, and attributed the distinctions to societal differences between collectivist and individualist societies.[26] Kuran compared the development of institutions in the Islamic Middle East and in Europe. More recently Rubin compared these two regions, offering a different interpretation.[27] Pomeranz compared the economic development of China and Europe, and paid particular attention to the role of institutions.[28] More recently, Rosenthal and Wong placed a strong emphasis on institutions.[29] In particular, they analyzed the use of personal and informal contractual arrangements and networks in China, compared to more formal, legally based, and impersonal arrangements in Europe. Even more recently, Zhang compared the English mortgage to its Chinese functional equivalent. He showed why the differences in institutional details were created and how these differences had profound effect on the different tradeoff between economic growth and social equality.[30] Their work can be viewed as a fifth stage in the economic understanding of institutional evolution. Figure 2.2 presents graphically this fifth stage of the study of relationships between institutions and the environment. In this stage, a comparative dimension is added to the research to explain the development of different institutions in different contexts.

In stage V a comparative perspective is added, by comparing one set of institutions and its environment to another set of institutions and its (different) environment. The main aim in this stage is to explain different sets of institutions by differences in the environments or in the process

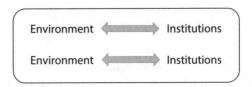

2.2. Stage V of the study of institutions—comparative studies.

of interaction with the environment (indicated by the bidirectional arrow). Stage IV reciprocal models of institutional evolution are assumed to operate also in stage V studies. The comparative studies of stage V are insightful, both methodologically and historically, and have set the agenda for my research in this book. They may call attention to differences between environments or to differences in the interaction mechanisms in the two regions. Yet these are also useful in studying endogenous institutions. Comparative studies do not incorporate the analysis of migration of institutions between environments. Thus, they are not useful for studying migratory institutions.

The identification of the distinctions between institutions in different environments calls us to address the next set of questions: Was each environment aware of the institutions developed in the other environment? For example, were the Italians aware of the Maghribi institutions, the Ottomans aware of the European institutions, or the Europeans aware of the Chinese institutions? If they were, did they consider importing them? If not, was this because these institutions did not fit well with the environment of the observing party? Or, in other words, was there a good reason *not* to import them because they could not efficiently solve the organizational problems of the region in question? Or was it the case that they *could* be efficient in solving problems in the second region but could not be imported because of path dependency, lock-in, switching costs, vested-interest opposition, religious objections, or the like? It is conceivable that an institution such as the informal network or the partnership was more efficient than formal and legal institutions, but by the time they ceased to be efficient, blocks were already in place preventing the importation of more formal and legal institutions such as the corporation. This book aims to integrate into its analysis these sets of issues, which deal with the migration of institutions, as visualized in the horizontal arrow in figure 2.3.[31]

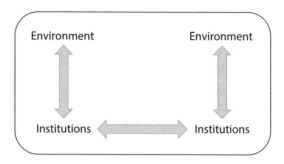

2.3. Stage VI—migration and transplantation of institutions.

Institutions that were connected by the horizontal arrow are migratory, according to the framework used in this book. Do we have institutional theories that provide insights for analyzing the horizontal arrow?

ECONOMETRIC STUDIES OF THE EFFECTS OF LEGAL/INSTITUTIONAL MIGRATION

Over the last decade and a half, a wave of high-impact studies by economists has focused on the effect of the migration of institutions. But, as we shall see, they are interested in the effect of the migration of institutions on economic development and not on the detailed design of institutions or on the causes of their migration.

The influential studies of La Porta, López de Silanes, Shleifer, and Vishny (hereafter LLSV) within the law and finance literature found that legal origins matter for economic performance. Stock market capitalization and economic growth are predicted by the legal origins and legal family of the current legal system. The family of legal systems to which a given legal system belongs determines the economic performance of the country in which that legal system functions. Systems whose modern law is a transplant of French law fare worst of all. Systems whose legal origin is German have better economic performance. Anglo-American systems lead to the best performance of all. The legal origins of most legal systems were determined by way of a transplantation of law from the European colonial power to their colonies in Asia, the Americas, and Africa. LLSV argued that, because the law was transplanted in most countries from the outside and involuntarily by colonial powers, the causation problem is resolved.[32] It is not the case that developed economies adopted common law; common-law countries became developed due to their legal origins. So, once econometric correlation is found between common-law legal origins and economic performance, the causation is from law to economic performance and not the other way around. The difference in economic outcomes is explained by the mechanisms of change that characterize each family of legal systems.[33] The case-law-based common law system responds faster to changes in economic needs than statute- or code-based civil law systems.

Acemoglu, Johnson, and Robinson (hereafter AJR), in another set of influential articles, tackled the causation problem in a different manner.[34] Their theory was that mortality rates among early Europeans (soldiers, bishops, and sailors) in various colonies around the globe determined the feasibility of establishing long-term settlements in these colonies and, in turn, the type of early institutions in the colonies. Through inertia, these mortality rates went on to shape present-day institutions that determine current economic performance. Colonies that could not be settled by Europeans (due to the mortality rates among the latter) developed extractive institutions. Colonies that were settled by Europeans developed European-like institutions that protected private property rights and provided checks and balances against government expropriation. The theory is well supported by the empirical findings: a high correlation was found between mortality rates and institutions, and between institutions and economic performance parameters such as income per capita. The mortality rate was exogenous to economic development. The correlations hold well when endowments and other variables are accounted for. The conclusion is that it was both legal and political institutions, mostly relating to the protection of property rights, that determined economic development. Institutions migrated with immigrants—not with colonial political power, as suggested by LLSV.

Neither LLSV nor AJR studied the actual migration of legal institutions and its causes. They relied on legal scholars, in general, and comparative lawyers, in particular, for their legal data. They did not follow the details of the migration of legal institutions, as do legal historians. Their analysis is confined to the context of European empires and the migration of European law in the European colonial period. This is a relatively simple context for the study of the migration of institutions by political and military force from the center of empires to their overseas colonies. These authors did not study the more complex context of migration, that of early modern Eurasia. But their conclusions are relevant for us in showing that (a) in their context, law and institutions mattered for economic performance, and (b) migration was common and made a difference.

THE LEGAL-TRANSPLANTS LITERATURE

If economic theory will not suffice, can we use legal theory of migration? The most relevant legal literature for our purposes is that of legal transplants. The study of the migration and expansion of Roman law and common law goes back to the nineteenth century. But the term *legal transplants* was coined only in the 1970s, by the comparative lawyer and legal historian Alan Watson.[35] The literature on legal transplants made a strong case for the assertion that considerable parts of the legal rules and legal institutions, in any given legal system, did not evolve indigenously, but rather were imported from other legal systems.[36] In the terms of the present book, the assertion is that many legal institutions are of the migratory type.

Historically, Roman law expanded throughout Europe and the Middle East with the Roman Empire. After its revival in the late Middle Ages, it was again received in much of Europe, with the notable exception of England. It then expanded to Latin America and other parts of the globe with the Spanish, Portuguese, Dutch, and French empires. English law migrated with the settlers to North America and Australia and was imposed in British colonies in Asia and Africa by colonial officials. French revolutionary law was exported throughout Europe, and the Napoleonic Code was imported by newly independent Latin American states and imposed on French colonies around the world.

The legal-transplants literature offers an appealing framework for the study of the migration of institutions. It predicts that transplantation is more likely in fields of law that are more universal, and less likely in fields that are more embedded in the local culture. It suggests that legal codes are more mobile than rules created by court decisions. It draws attention to the difference between forced transplantation of law by colonial powers and voluntary importation by sovereign states and, more generally, between transplantation "from above" and transplantation "from below" (that is, where domestic jurists voluntarily adopt the law of another jurisdiction). It points to the post-transplantation adjustment of the transplanted rules in each local environment and to a phenomenon termed "legal irritation," in which the transplant is rejected or forces the local law to reconfigure itself around it.[37]

If legal institutions can indeed migrate between environments, and historically migration was the norm, then the appearance of a specific institution in a given environment may result not only from the endogenous and reciprocal interaction between the environment and the evolving institution. It may be that the mechanisms of migration and transplantation, and reactions to them, affect the spread and evolution of migratory institutions to a significant extent that has so far been understudied.

The legal-transplants literature has two main shortcomings. The first is that it tends to be Eurocentric, studying mostly the expansion of European law. While it does follow its expansion also outside Europe, it has, so far, devoted less attention to the transplantation of non-European law. As a result, its methodologies were shaped in a manner tailored specifically for the study of the transplantation of European law. The same applies to the legal-origins and colonial-origins literature that builds upon it and that will be discussed in the next section. The second shortcoming is that it has not thus far paid much attention to legal-economic institutions, in general, and to institutions for the organization of trade, in particular. There are a few interesting exceptions, which were, unsurprisingly, studies by nonlawyers.[38] The lawyers' legal-transplants literature focused mainly on the transplantation of the main branches of civil law, contracts, torts, and property. Thus, once again, a methodology that is tailored to the study of trade organizations is less developed, and so are the narratives of their expansion.

CONCLUSION

What is the "takeaway" from this theoretical chapter? The proliferation of academic research activity over the last half a century in areas including transaction-cost economics, theories of the firm, property-rights theories, contract and agency theory, information economics, theories of limited liability, asset partitioning, and corporate governance and finance has revolutionized our ability to understand trade organizations. These theoretical tools and frameworks are particularly strong at analyzing the problems faced by traders in financing their trade, allocating risks and liabilities, monitoring agents, pooling assets, sharing profits, and gathering and disseminating information. They are also strong at evaluating the effectiveness of various institutional designs and identifying the means to mitigate such problems.

But these theories, which are at their best in static analysis, do not offer as much to the dynamic analysis of the formation and evolution of trade institutions. Here, Douglass North's school of historical institutional economics has more to offer. It primarily provides a framework for thinking about causal relationships between environments, markets, politics, and so on, and for the consideration of institutions. The framework hypothesizes how change in one realm affects the other realm. The dynamic theory is not as rigorous as the static theory, and it does not offer precise predictions. This is not a criticism; it is an observation resulting from the more complex, dynamic reality that this theory tries to explain. The main contribution of historical institutional theory to the present study lies in shaping the research agenda and focusing research questions. The economic and legal theory of institutional and legal migration is still in its infancy. The literature surveyed here will not be sufficiently instrumental for my needs. In chapter 4 I will try to offer an initial framework for the study of the migration of organizational forms. In chapter 12 I will offer an initial framework for the study of nonmigration, the embeddedness of institutions, and the resistance to migration.

Any historical study of Eurasian trade institutions undertaken before the 1960s and 1970s could not make use of the fundamental theoretical developments discussed in this chapter and is, in this respect, outdated. Any of the more recent studies that did not use insights from these theories missed a major opportunity. One of the main contributions of the present book is that it seizes the new opportunities offered by institutional economics and organizational theory and uses these theories to analyze the functioning of long-distance trade organizations.

PART II

~

Organizational Building Blocks

~ 3 ~

Universal Building Blocks

In this chapter I argue that a number of precursor institutions of the long-distance trade organization developed locally, independently, and endemically in many different places along the Eurasian landmass. There is often no direct and clear evidence for the endogenous origins of institutions. The endemic appearance of an institution without a clear pattern of migration, together with its relatively simple structure, supports identification of an endogenous institution. Endogenous institutions are often organic, as is the case with the itinerant trader or the family, or simple institutions that address basic functions, such as the loan, agency, or ship. They are to be found throughout Eurasia, and there is no historical evidence of a single historical origin for any of them or of a clear route of their migration. So, for our purposes, for now, I will classify them as endogenous organizational forms—as universal (in the Eurasian sense) building blocks.

I will present three basic forms of endogenous institutions: the individual itinerant trader; the basic bilateral relationships of loan and agency; and the ship as an organizational unit. This chapter includes three microstudies: the Roman-era trade document known as the Muziris Papyrus, which deals with loans and agents in the trade between Egypt and India; the Turfan contracts, which reflect the reality of itinerant traders along the Silk Route between the seventh and tenth centuries; and a microstudy of the ownership and operation of Indian Ocean ships.

ITINERANT TRADERS

Itinerant traders (named "peddlers" in the older European literature) were individual vendors who traveled around with their merchandise, selling it to end-consumers, to shopkeepers, or to other traders. Itinerant traders usually traveled on foot, carrying their wares, or by means of animal-drawn carts. Silk Route trade was often conducted by itinerant traders, each typically covering only segments of it.[1] The Turfan contracts, which will be analyzed later in this section, exemplify this. On some sea routes, itinerant traders traveled on boats or ships, as was the case with the hundreds of itinerant traders who boarded Chinese junks in the South China Sea.[2] The shipwrecks and ships studied in this section are the closest we can get to this reality.

The traditional European view of trade in Asia before the arrival of Europeans around 1500, most lucidly expressed by van Leur in his concept of the "small-scale peddling trade," was that it was of a primitive, small-scale nature, consisting mainly of lesser merchants, inexpensive goods, and watercraft designed only for coastal trips of short duration.[3] Meilink-Roelofsz argued that, on the contrary, a highly sophisticated system of trade existed in Asia long before the Europeans arrived. She pointed out that Arab, Persian, Indian, Chinese, and Javanese ships sailed long distances throughout the Indian Ocean and South China Sea.[4] On the other hand, trade by peddlers was very common in early modern Europe.[5]

FAMILY FIRMS

Families were involved in Eurasian trade in many places and times. Their involvement was manifested in various configurations. The family seems, at first glance, to be the basic organic unit of society and of business that mushroomed in every human civilization. The larger the extended family—say, a household of three generations and a few married couples, or even a family clan—the larger the scale of trade enterprise it could sustain. If family structures were different, so was the role they played in organizing business. Since the 1960s, social and demographic historians have argued that European families became nuclear before Europe industrialized and not because of industrialization. For our purposes it is important that the shift from extended to nuclear families occurred before the starting year of this book, 1400. The initial impetus was that of the Roman Catholic Church, which preached in favor of consensual rather than arranged marriage and against marriage with second and third cousins.

Then a social norm emerged that required the newly married couple to establish their own household—the so-called neolocal marriage. This, in turn, led to the need to save money for setting up a new house, marriage at a later age, and less universal marriage.[6] The nuclear family, being smaller, had to rely more on the market and less on intrafamily dealings, with respect to labor, capital and commodity supply, compared to the extended family.[7] The nuclear-family model was most widespread in the Low Countries and the British Island, had substantial presence in northwestern Europe at large and did not spread to Southern or Eastern Europe.

The uniqueness of northwestern European family structure can have two ramifications for the current book. First, it may reduce the scope and affect the type of merchant-family firms that could be created in nuclear-family societies compared to extended-family societies. Second, because nuclear families could internally supply less of their needs, they relied on markets more extensively. Thus, a demand for an organizational substitute for the family firm could appear in northwestern Europe, and could ultimately give rise to the business corporation. The first ramification, the effect on the evolution of family firms, is not as applicable for long-distance family firms as for other types of family firms. Long-distance family firms seem to have been at the very high end of the distribution of family firms in terms of their size. The European family firms that will be discussed in chapter 6 were urban, Italian, and south German and were sustained in our period by very rich families. We are not analyzing here rural, northwestern European, lower- and middle-echelon families that are the paradigmatic families of the literature on the nuclear family. The merchant families of Florence and Augsburg had larger households, strategic marriage and other marriage customs, and more extended family structures closer to those of regal and aristocratic families than to those of peasants and craftsmen.[8] The second ramification, the effect on the development of business corporations, will be discussed in part IV. In chapters 10 and 11 the focus will shift to England and the Dutch Republic, where the nuclear family was indeed more prevalent.[9] In chapter 12 I will examine the effect of the family on the development of corporate substitutes in the Middle East, India, and China.

I would like to propose here a basic categorization of family-related businesses and family firms. In most civilizations, family firms were not subject to a distinct or specific legal framework. Several legal realms could apply to such firms (though the firms did not actively select them), including family law, property law, agency law, and partnership law. Families regarded themselves as subject not only to law but also to social customs, norms, and sanctions. The categorization of family firms is not based on a legal distinction but rather on internal organization and scale.

The first category of family involvement in business, the patriarch-led family firm, is, in fact, comparable to sole proprietorship. In this category, the head of the family, the patriarch, functioned as the only member of the family involved in business activity, say, as an itinerant trader or a single merchant. The patriarch earned money in trade, to then be consumed by the family as a whole. The basic business entity was, therefore, the individual patriarch and not the family.

The second category, family partnership, includes families in which several family members worked for the same family enterprise, making collective decisions on behalf of the family, with a utility function of maximizing value (not necessarily monetary) for the family as a whole. Each individual was willing to sacrifice his own utility for that of the family as a whole. In a familial or a collective society, the individual did not view himself as the utility or profit maximizer. In his trade, he used the resources of the family as a whole and earned money for the family as a whole. It is often asserted that there was a high level of trust among family members, and that cheating and monitoring within families in traditional societies were minimal. Such families did not separate their personal assets from their business assets. The family served as the coordinator of its various members engaged in trade.

The third category, family enterprise, featured as a platform for more extended enterprises that includes nonfamily members. Such family-based firms were more like large partnerships, in two respects. First, enterprise involved nonfamily members in key positions that often entitled them to a share in the profits. Second, their formation was not merely spontaneous or organic, but rather involved some design and agreement. This kind of family firm could be the basis for a multinational or cross-cultural entity or a component in a wider ethnic merchant network. In chapter 6 I will deal with three mega family enterprises.

LOANS AND AGENTS

A step up from the itinerant trader among endogenous institutions is the bilateral contract. At the organizational level, long-distance maritime trade could, in the abstract, use three basic bilateral contractual forms: the loan, the agency, and the partnership. The loan was based on ex ante, agreed-upon payment for the use of capital. The loan allowed a wealth-constrained traveling merchant, even an itinerant trader, to finance his business. The agency was based on ex ante, agreed-upon payment for labor. Agency allowed a wealthier merchant to engage in trade without actually assuming the hard labor and high personal risks of traveling long-distance. The partnership was based on ex post splitting of profits (the upside) or losses (the downside). Partnership could be capital based, labor based, or both. It allowed two or more individuals not only to share investment and risk but also to divide labor. Agency and the loan were most likely endogenous organizational forms. The partnership is, for me, an organizational form that is likely to be endogenous but cannot at this stage of the research be affirmed as endogenous or migratory.

Microstudy: Loans and Agents in the Muziris Papyrus

TRADE BETWEEN THE ROMAN EMPIRE AND INDIA

Merchants in the Mediterranean and India began trading with each other by ancient Greek and Roman times.[10] As Greek and Roman mariners learned how to cope with the monsoon, more of the trade was diverted from overland routes across the Syrian desert, Mesopotamia, and the Iranian plateau, to the maritime Red Sea and Indian Ocean route.[11] This route typically began in the Mediterranean in the port of Alexandria, and continued from there up the Nile to Koptos, across the desert on camel caravans to the Red Sea ports Myos Hormos or Berenike, and down across the Red Sea into the Indian Ocean.[12] Trade destinations included the East African coast, the Malabar coast of Southern India, Sri Lanka, and possibly destinations further east. Trade goods imported to the Roman

Empire included luxury items (such as silk, pearls, and ivory), spices, incense, and exotic goods.[13]

Not much is known about the organization of the trade between Egypt and India in Roman times. Roman law is obviously well documented in legal texts of various sorts, notably the *Corpus Juris Civilis*. Trade practices in the Indian Ocean routes are sketchily known from surviving manuscripts.[14] Actual organizational documents are practically unavailable, with the rare exception of the Muziris Papyrus, around which this microstudy was constructed.

But why should we devote the first microstudy in a book whose formal starting point is 1400 to a papyrus of the second century CE? The answer is that it adds an important dimension to our knowledge of the organizational practices of Eurasian trade in antiquity and is, in fact, the best available source on the contractual practices of merchants trading between the Middle East and India from antiquity to the early Middle Ages, up to the era of the Cairo Geniza (on which one of our microstudies will rely), almost a millennium later. The microstudy deals with basic Roman-era building blocks, such as the loan and the agency agreement, that endured and were present in Europe and the Middle East well into the second millennium CE. The microstudy is also important because it shows how trade could be organized in a stable political environment, when infrastructure was dense and the economy relatively developed.

The Muziris Papyrus

The Muziris Papyrus, named after a port on the Malabar Coast of India, is also known as the Vienna Papyrus because it was purchased in 1980 by the Austrian National Archive from an antiques merchant. Its exact place of origin in Egypt is unknown. It is written in Greek, and has been dated to the mid-second century CE. A transcript was first published in 1985, and it has been republished, translated, and annotated several times since.[15]

The papyrus contains incomplete texts on both its sides. Its reverse side (verso) contains an account of goods shipped from India to Egypt on a single voyage of the ship *Hermapollon*. It calculates values and customs payments based on weight and prices. The goods that could be identified in the one column that was sufficiently preserved include sixty containers of Gangetic nard (a fragrance), ivory tusks, and ivory fragments. Much of the list was not preserved, and the exact calculation of the prices is not clear.[16] The total weight of the shipment is calculated at nearly 4,000 kg, and its value in Alexandrian prices after taxes, according to one calculation, was nearly 7 million drachmas, a huge amount, equal to that needed to buy a luxury estate in Roman Italy at the time.

The front side (recto) of the papyrus looks like a contract. Due to its importance for the present microstudy, which focuses on organizational-legal aspects of the trade, I will provide its text in full. I use Rathbone's transcription and English translation from 2000, with Morelli's amendments (marked with *) from 2011, as published by Grønlund Evers in 2017:

The Muziris Papyrus (SB XVIII, 13167)

Recto, column ii (column one being lost)

――] your other administrators or managers, and on agreement(?)

I will give(?)] to your trustworthy camel-driver [――] (?) for the conduct*

of the journey up] to Koptos; and I will convey (the goods) through the desert under guard and protection

up to the] public tax-receiving warehouses at Koptos, and

I will] place them under the [authority] and seal of yourself, or of your administrators or whichever

one of them is present, until their loading at the river; and I will load them

at the requi]red time onto a safe ship on the river; and I will convey them down

to the warehouse for receiving the quarter-tax [at Alex]andria, and

likewise] will place them under the authority and seal of yourself or your men.

All the payments out of my own pocket from now to collection of the quarter-tax, and of(?) the*

desert tran[sport] and the carrying-charges of the river-workers and the other incidental(?)

exp[ens]es [――] on occurrence of the date for repayment specified in

the contracts of lo[an] for (the trip to) Muziris, if I do not
then] duly discharge the aforesaid loan in my name, that then
you] and your administrators or managers are to have the option and
com[plete] authority, if you so choose, to carry out execution without
notifica]tion or summons to judgement, to possess and own the
afore[said] security and pay the quarter-tax, to convey the
three] parts which will be left where you choose and to sell or use them
as security
and] to transfer them to another person, if you so choose, and to deal
with the
items of the security in whatsoever way you choose, and to buy them
for yourself at the
price current at the time, and to subtract and reckon in what falls due
on account of the aforesai]d loan, on terms that the responsibility for
what falls due
lies] with you and your administrators or managers and we are free
from
accus[at]ion in every respect, and that the surplus or shortfall from the
capital
goes] to me the borrower and giver of sec[urity——[17]

The papyrus's fragmented nature, with the top and bottom missing, as
well as some unintelligible words in the remaining text, has given rise to
a variety of annotations, glosses, gap fillings, and interpretations.

Due to its uniqueness and its fragmented text, the Muziris Papyrus
was the topic of a heated controversy involving several notable historians
of Greco-Roman Egypt.[18] The debate regarding the contract on the recto
raised several issues. Geographically, some argued that it covered the
entire route from Muziris to Alexandria, while others asserted that it
dealt only with the overland route from the Red Sea port to Alexandria.
Some argued that it was drafted in India and some that it was drafted in
Egypt. Some held that it was in the legal format of a sea loan, while others
claimed it was an ordinary loan agreement. There were at least three
distinct identifications of the parties involved. The first, that one party
was a financier and the other a merchant; the second, that both parties
were merchants; and the third, that one party was a merchant and the
other an agent of another merchant. There was also a debate as to who
was the active—initiating—party, and disagreement as to which assets

were used as security in the transaction. Lastly, there was a debate as to whether the text is of an individualized contract, whose parties' names are missing due to the missing top and bottom, or a boilerplate, a standard template in its original form that bears no names of parties.

THE APPLICABLE LAW

The dating of the Muziris Papyrus—well into the Roman period, yet before the formal Romanization of provincial law—and its use of the Greek language suggest that it was drafted in the shadow of Greek law, not Roman (or demotic) law. However, we do not know the identity of the parties to the agreement (or the intended parties, if the document was a template). Nor can we preclude the possibility that the segment visible in the papyrus was only part of a transaction or a network that went beyond Alexandria to Rome or another part of the empire in which Roman law dominated, or that the parties to the agreement (or at least the financing party) were Roman citizens. Hence, we cannot rule out the possibility that the drafters envisioned Roman law to be the background law of the agreement. That said, the question of which law applied to the Muziris Papyrus—Greek or Roman or a mixture of the two—is pertinent only inasmuch as the applicable rules in the two sets of laws were different.

In the Greco-Roman period, the organization of long-distance maritime trade could, in the abstract, use three different organizational forms: the loan, the agency, and the partnership.[19] The basic contractual category in Greek and Roman law that could apply to the employment of agents in trade was the *mandatum*.[20] The *mandatum* was a gratuitous consensual contract between a mandator and mandatary, according to which the latter would act on behalf of the former. It was used for commercial transactions such as personal security, suretyship, or guarantee. It is thought of by scholars as the Roman equivalent of agency. Another framework, applicable to the relationships between ship owners, ship captains, and third parties, is that of the *actio exercitoria*.

Loans could rely on the *stipulatio* contract or the *mutuum* contract. The *stipulatio* was a contract recognized by Greek and Roman law "by the uttering of formal words [*verbis*]."[21] There were two loan contracts created by the transfer of an object (a *res*, hence termed "re" or "real" contracts): *mutuum* and *commodatum*. *Mutuum* is the loan of something whose use requires its consumption (such as money), and *commodatum* is the loan of an object that is not to be consumed (and thus not relevant for our purpose here).[22] The *mutuum* was traditionally a gratuitous loan that could not bear interest, and, as such, was not very useful for financing business activity. In order to charge interest and make the loan feasible, the parties had to resort to the more formal *stipulatio*.

The Sea Loan

As both Athenian and Roman maritime law recognized a separate category of maritime loans, it is not essential to determine which of the two applied to the Muziris Papyrus. In Athenian law the loan was termed *nautikòn dáneisma* and in Roman law *faenus nauticum*.[23] These loans were distinct from regular loans in two major respects. First, they were not subject to strict usury restrictions, and permitted higher interest to be charged, reflecting the level of risk. Second, they provided the ability to separate the allocation of different risks to the various parties. The sea risk, loss of ship or goods at sea, was allocated to the lender, while the business risk, market price fluctuations, was held by the borrower. More specifically, in the case of loss of the ship or goods on the way in the open sea, either due to drowning or to capture by pirates, the borrower was discharged of the debt.

Sea loans were commonly used in the Greek regions of the Eastern Mediterranean.[24] The sea loan documented fixed rates of interest and allocated the risk of shipwrecking, while security for repayment could be placed on either the goods, the ship itself, or real estate back home.[25] The question of whether the loan referred to in the Muziris text was a sea loan cannot be fully resolved because the formal legal Greek or Roman term was not expressly mentioned in the preserved parts of the papyrus. Still, most scholars believe that it was.

The legal-financial device mentioned explicitly on the recto of the Muziris Papyrus is a loan. The surviving sections of the text refer to "loan agreements" and twice to "the aforementioned loan." The "I" party was the borrower. The "you" party was the lender. The Muziris Papyrus could, at first sight, be viewed as a loan agreement, most likely a sea-loan agreement (*faenus nauticum*), as it mentions an agreement made in Muziris (and Muziris could only be reached by sea). But a more careful reading suggests that it could also be an additional agreement appended to an earlier sea-loan agreement made in Muziris. If this is the case, and the text refers to the Red Sea to Alexandria segment—an overland (and down-river) trajectory—then it is possible that either the earlier sea loan was converted to a regular loan or that the sea loan applied to the journey as a whole.

AGENCY

The agreement does not declare itself to be an agency or an employment agreement. Yet one party, the "I," makes repeated references to instructions given to him by the other party, the "you." Note here the elements I have underlined:

> I will give(?)] to your trustworthy camel-driver [——] (?) for the conduct of the journey up] to Koptos; and I will convey (the goods) through the desert under guard and protection up to the] public tax-receiving warehouses at Koptos, and [I will] place them under the [authority] and seal of yourself, or of your administrators or whichever one of them is present, until their loading at the river; and I will load them [at the requi]red time onto a safe ship on the river; and I will convey them down to the warehouse for receiving the quarter-tax [at Alex]andria . . . [26]

The text is, in fact, saying that the "I" has been given instructions by the "you." It includes a set of five operational instructions, covering the entire span from the Red Sea port to Alexandria. Furthermore, the last paragraph of the surviving text lists expenses that had to be accounted for. Expenses are typically reimbursed to the agents (or partners) and not to borrowers, as the latter are responsible for their own expenses.

In addition, the text reflects the wide use of agents in the India trade. The phrase "your administrator" (or, in Casson's translation, "your agent") appears four times in the short text; the phrase "your manager," three times; and "your camel-driver" and "your men" appear once each. One of the parties to the agreement, the stationed party, the "you," seems to have agents spread throughout the trade route, in the Red Sea port, in

Koptos, and in Alexandria. But the text is not an agency contract with respect to those agents who are not parties to it. It only acknowledges, and preserves as historical evidence, their existence.

Partnership

The basic Roman law category that could apply to partnership was the *societas*.[27] The partnership form of business organization is not referred to in the text. Yet one of only a handful of other records that refer to the trade with "the spice-bearing lands," possibly India, mentions a consortium. That papyrus, dated to the Ptolemaic period, records a contract between a consortium of five merchants and a financier, in which the consortium borrowed money in the form of a sea loan to finance a voyage. This arrangement can, in fact, be understood as a partnership of five merchants that borrowed money.[28]

Boilerplate

Rathbone suggests that the papyrus contains a master contract, a boilerplate, a template—not an agreement between named parties.[29] What supports such a conclusion? There are no party names and no signatures or seals. There are no specified sums, interest rates, goods, or dates. There is not even any reference by name to the Red Sea port, only to Muziris, Koptos, and Alexandria: origin, destination, and unavoidable hub, respectively. It is possible, albeit not very likely, that some of the absent specifications were lost due to the damages to the papyrus (the top and bottom parts being missing and the edges damaged). It is possible that some of the missing specifications were assumed to be completed according to well-known merchant practices. It is unlikely that the missing details result from neglect or unskilled drafting. The basic structure and drafting seem to be quite formal, legal, and detailed. This is not a hastily drafted text written at a brief meeting. But the scribing, on the other hand, is sloppy, including grammatical and syntax errors, and could possibly have been copied in haste from a master form.

These indications increase the likelihood that the recto side of the Muziris Papyrus was not an individual contract but rather a template that could be filled in with different names, sums, and dates. Rathbone suggests that it should be understood as representing a system in which the financier is the repeat player and the initiating party, and the traveler—an agent or a service provider—was different in each use of the template. The "you" party is the drafter. The contractual terms clearly favor him. It is likely that the "you" party was a financier in Alexandria and was, in fact, the first to take action, approaching traveling merchants on his own initiative and asking them to accept his boilerplate contract. These merchants could be viewed as his agents. They could be seen as counterparts to whom he granted sea loans. The financier selected experienced and reputable traveling merchants, provided them with funding and instructions, signed them up to the template contract that was preserved in the Muziris Papyrus, and sent them to India. This view of the financier as the initiating party is supported by the fact, clearly stated in the papyrus, that he had agents and managers in the Red Sea port and in Koptos, and camel drivers linking the two. A passive investor was unlikely to have such an infrastructure.

The Papyrus in a Merchant-Network Context

Understanding the Muziris Papyrus as a standard-form contract used by an active financier fits other contemporary evidence about merchants and the trade infrastructure in Egypt and its Red Sea ports. The author of *Periplus Maris Erythraei* represents himself as a Greek-speaking merchant based in Egypt with first-hand experience in India and East Africa trade.[30] Inscriptions and archeological evidence from the upper Nile Valley, along the desert routes, and from the Red Sea ports suggest the existence of wealthy merchants, bearing respectable Roman and Greek names, involved in trade coming from the Red Sea and the Indian Ocean. Notable evidence of such wealthy merchant families can be found in the Archive of Nicanor, which contains a group of *ostraca* found in Koptos, dated between 6 CE and 62 CE. These are receipts for transport services provided by Nicanor and his family or partner, by camel, between Koptos and Myos Hormos and Berenike, on the instruction of various people. The name of one of the recipients of the services mentioned in the archive also appears in an inscription dedicating a temple in Koptos in his honor. Another important figure mentioned in the archive is known to have been a member of a rich Jewish family in Alexandria. The multiple appearances of these names indicate that these were repeat merchants—most likely also professional and wealthy merchants like Nicanor. An inscription from a temple at Medamoud, in the Nile Valley, is dedicated to two female Red Sea merchants. An inscription in Latin found on the desert road between the Red Sea and the Nile alludes to a merchant who is also mentioned by Pliny in his *Naturalis Historia* as being connected with trade to Sri Lanka and elsewhere, as the Red Sea port's tax farmer. The accumulated evidence suggest that Nicanor and his partners were not unique, and that numerous merchants and agents were involved in the trade along the Red Sea to the Nile route.[31] It is quite likely that on either side of the system—the financier or the traveling party—a consortium could be formed, though our specific papyrus does not provide evidence of this.

It is also likely that some of the capital invested in the India trade came from as far away as Rome.[32] There is a growing sense among historians of the Roman economy that the expansion of the Roman Empire into the Greek Eastern Mediterranean after 30 BCE led to Roman investment in eastern trade. By the first and second centuries CE, Roman tax farmers and other contractors, Roman soldiers and veterans, the imperial family, and Rome's wealthier elite began investing directly and actively in eastern trade.[33] Alongside investors, a pool of willing and able agents was formed. Some of them were freedmen; some were slaves; some had an Egyptian social and cultural background, and some Greek. The identity of the agents depended both on the background of the investors and on the tasks that the former were expected to perform. The trade in Asiatic goods combined with the trade in grains originating in Egypt, creating a combination of Greek and Roman merchant networks that traded between Alexandria and Rome.[34]

CONCLUSION

The Muziris Papyrus captured only a snippet of an ongoing enterprise, in which the merchant actively managed and repeatedly transacted with employees, agents, and itinerant merchants, based on a standard contract. In addition to agency and loans, it also used options and security in assets.

One can infer that merchants based in Egypt repeatedly transacted with India. They actively managed mercantile enterprises. They borrowed and lent capital and hired employees, agents, and itinerant merchants. They possibly used standard-form contractual templates in their trade. Their transactions were complex and included elements such as options, non-recourse loans, and security in assets. One can conclude, based on the Muziris Papyrus and contextual evidence, that by the second century CE, a legally and financially sophisticated trade network connecting Egypt and Rome with India was in operation. Wealth was ample, markets within the Empire were well integrated, the legal system was effective and developed, and entrepreneurs were sophisticated. Large-scale trade would have been feasible and profitable.

Such networks as the one glimpsed at here declined with the decline and ultimate demise of the Roman Empire and the weakening of the Byzantine Empire holding in Egypt.[35] Indeed, evidence of the renewal of trade with India was only found in the Cairo Geniza, pertaining to the tenth through twelfth centuries CE, and of shorter-distance Red Sea trade in Quseir al-Qadim records that documented thirteenth-century Arab merchants.[36] The level of sophistication of the Geniza merchants' trade seems to have been much lower than that associated with the second century CE, as reflected in the Muziris Papyrus. There is no evidence of an extensive trade infrastructure along the Nile or across the desert; no evidence of the use of sophisticated contractual and financial instruments; no evidence of the use of boilerplates; and no evidence of drawing investments from further afield through intermediaries or consortia.

It is remarkable to note that, as we shall see in chapter 4, the sea loan, which was renowned in the Greco-Roman world, was not available to Geniza-era Jewish and Muslim merchants. One notable contractual design that was used by the Geniza traders but not available to their Greco-Roman predecessors was, as we shall see in the next chapter and its microstudies, the commenda. The joint-stock business corporation, which came to dominate Europe's trade with India in the seventeenth century, is also conspicuously absent from the history of Roman India trade. There were associations with some corporate features in Roman law and in the Roman Empire. But these were used for public or semipublic purposes—for example, the *collegium*—and were not financed based on joint stock.[37] I will turn to the corporation and its medieval origins in chapter 9.

Microstudy: Silk Route Oases, Sogdian
Itinerant Traders, and Turfan Contracts

A good case study of the organization of trade along the Silk Route can be based on the Turfan contracts. This case study will show a harsher and more secluded trade environment than the one exposed by the Muziris Papyrus, and a much more rudimentary level of organizational solutions.

The preservation of a large number of contracts makes this an appealing case study. A total of 280 contracts were excavated, together with numerous other documents, mostly between 1959 and 1975, from burial complexes in the Turfan (in today's Xinjiang Uyghur Autonomous Region, modern China's most westerly region). A further 280 contracts were found in a cave for the deposit of sutras in Dunhuang (in today's northwestern Gansu province of China).[38] Both places were on what we now call the Silk Route. The Turfan contracts are mostly from the seventh and eighth centuries, while the Dunhuang contracts are mostly from the ninth and tenth centuries. The period of these contracts is helpful for my purposes because it reflects the organizational form used before the migration of organizational practices from Western Asia with the advance of Islam late in the first millennium, and with the establishment of Pax Mongolica that connected east and west early in the second millennium.

Figure 3.1 shows the segment of the Silk Route between the oases of Turfan and Dunhuang. Turfan was the first major oasis encountered by travelers on the Silk Route coming from Central Asia.[39] Between around 640 and the decline of the Tang dynasty in 907, Turfan was controlled by Tang China.[40] Dunhuang was some 800 km further east.[41] The distance from Dunhuang to the Tang Capital of Chang'an (Xi'an) was about 1,800 km.

At first sight, the Dunhuang contracts and the Turfan contracts deal mostly with domestic issues such as share cropping, family matters, work contracts, and the like. Less than 15 percent of each group of contracts deal with trade and exchange. Table 3.1 shows how many texts were found in Dunhuang, and classifies them by two factors. One is the subject of the documents, such as loans, division of family property, and trade contracts. The other is the document form: contracts, copy exercises, or

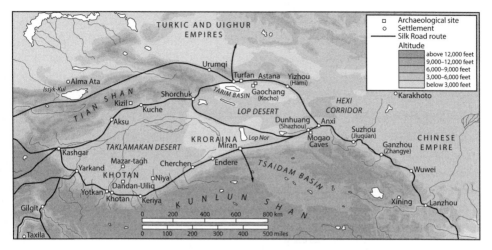

3.1. The Silk Route—Turfan to Dunhuang. Source: Maps in Minutes, 2003.

document compilations from templates. Table 3.2 presents contracts from Turfan divided into two different eras (pre-Gaochang and Gaochang, Tang dynasty).

The subjects of many of these contracts also included domestic property, agricultural land, and residences. Only the remainder involved movables such as livestock, slaves, and goods—not high-value luxury goods, in the main. Some of the loan or labor contracts could also be related to trade. But here, too, many of the contracts related to loans for consumption, for the construction of local sites, or for domestic labor.[42] The low percentage of longer-distance trade-related contracts may be explained by the low volume of trade in that era, by the oral nature of trade transactions, by the coincidental survival of only nontrade documents, or by the fact that, although both oases were on the Silk Route, most of their population did not deal with trade. What was found were the kinds of domestic contracts that were required by law to be put in writing.[43]

The Turfan contracts, all in Chinese, whether involving Sogdians or not, were quite elaborate. The typical template included the following: names of parties, date, detailed description of the objects of transaction (silk, silver, land, etc.), nature of transaction (sale, exchange, loan), reason for transaction or loan (in some contracts), price or interest rate, mode of payment, actions to be taken in the case of breach of contract, guarantor

3.1. Number of Contracts Found in Dunhuang, Classified by Subject and Type of Contract

	Trade	Unclear	Loans	Tenancy	Hiring of services*	Misc.	Testa-ments	Division of family property	Divorce of wives	Emanci-pation of slaves	Model docu-ment compila-tions	Total
Contracts (including drafts)	19	32	60	8	17	4	4	3	1	1	0	149
Copy exercises	12	20	17	3	35	0	1	1	1	0	0	88
From model document compilations	2	0	0	0	6	0	7	3	8	6	14	46
Total	115		77	11	58	4	12	7	10	7	14	283

Source: Yamamoto and Ikeda (1986, p. 14).

* Hiring of services includes contract work (both indenture and adoption).

3.2. The Turfan Contracts

	Trade and exchange	Loans	Rent	Share-cropping	Hiring of services*	Misc.	Total
Pre-Gaochang and Gaochang	17	24	6	35	9	17	108
Tang Dynasty	25	35	5	75	21	12	173
Total	42	59	11	110	30	29	281

Source: Yamamoto and Ikeda (1986, p. 10).
* Hiring of services includes contract work (both indenture and adoption).

of payment (in a few contracts), number of copies and their intended whereabouts, scribe (not always present), signatures or finger marks of parties, and names and signatures or fingermarks of witnesses.[44] These were contracts at an ex ante fixed price, not contracts for sharing profits or risks or for joint ventures. In them, one cannot identify anything that resembles a partnership contract, a commenda contract, or an agency contract. They show none of the sophistication of the Muziris Papyrus and the networks that it exemplifies.

Turfan was one of the oasis cities in which Sogdian trade diasporas took residence.[45] The Sogdians' homelands were in Transoxiana—in western Turkestan (modern-day Uzbekistan, Tajikistan, southern Kyrgyzstan, and southwest Kazakhstan). Their prominent cities were Bukhara and Samarkand (Samarqand), and they spoke an Iranian dialect. The Sogdians were dominant among the groups of merchants using the Silk Route.[46] Contracts involving Sogdians in Turfan could be identified based on names or the label "merchant western barbarian" attached to their names. Contracts involving Sogdian parties were quite likely to be connected to the Silk Route trade. These contracts seem to be the most promising in terms of capturing long-distance trade and its organizational forms. About one-fifth of the sale documents found in Turfan involved a Sogdian buyer or seller.

It can be inferred from the contracts and other associated trade documents that some of the Sogdians had a place of residence in Turfan or China, suggesting that they were members of the Sogdian diaspora, whereas others were foreigners who presumably arrived via the Silk Route to trade with locals. Some of them were involved in short-distance trade covering a few hundred kilometers; others traded between China's borderlands (Dunhuang) and its capital Chang'an, about 1,800 km away; and some traveled all the way from Sogdiana to Turfan or Chang'an, the distance to the latter being 3,750 km.[47] The Sogdians were involved more often than others in trading high-value goods such as gold, silver, ammonium chloride, silk, and incense. They used camels, horses, mules, and donkeys for transportation, and the caravan size varied considerably, between just a few itinerant traders traveling together to much larger groups when traveling longer distances in hostile bandit regions.[48]

As far as historian Jonathan Skaff, who studied Sogdians in Turfan, could infer from the surviving documents, these larger caravans were also made up of independent itinerant traders. De la Vaissière, the leading historian of Sogdian traders, concluded—based on the available sources, not only in Turfan but all the way from Byzantium and Persia, through Sogdiana and India, to China—that Sogdians used simple forms of commercial organization and based their business activity on the family unit.[49]

Historian Valerie Hansen provides fascinating evidence of the dispute-resolution system surrounding these contracts. She was able to reconstruct a dispute based on nine documents found in the Astana graveyard in Turfan.[50] On both sides of the paper were records, affidavits, and testimonies regarding the dispute. Eventually, the documents were discarded and later reused for making funerary garments. They were preserved in that state, thanks to the dry Turfan weather, for more than a thousand years, before being recovered and pieced together (with some gaps) by archaeologists and reconstructed and interpreted by Hansen. The disputed transaction involved a loan of 275 bolts of silk from a Sogdian merchant to a Chinese merchant in the year 670 CE in a small location along the road to Central Asia, hundreds of kilometers west of Turfan. Details are scant, but this may have been a loan for the purpose of sale or a consignment agreement. What we do know is that thereafter, the Sogdian continued to another small location, some 300 km to the south, with an additional two hundred silk bolts, saddles, bows and arrows, and cloth, carried by two camels, four cattle, and a donkey. He never arrived, probably killed en route by bandits. In 674 CE, his brother, presumably as his inheritor, sued the Chinese merchant for the recovery of the loan in 674 CE. The Sogdian's copy of the contract disappeared. The merchant's copy was never presented, for obvious reasons. The Turfan court accepted the account of two Sogdian traders who testified to being witnesses to the contract, as a substitute for a written contract. The ability of the brother of a foreign merchant to enforce a contract whose written copies had disappeared is impressive. The contract itself, which did not survive but can be reconstructed based on the litigation documents, is similar to those discussed earlier. It is a contract for the loan of goods, not money. Interest must have been in kind as well, at a rate higher than the official interest rate of 6 percent per month. Though Hansen refers to the two parties as partners, there are no partnership features in the legal sense in the contract. There is no sharing of investment, labor, profits, risks, or losses. Strictly speaking, the two parties can be viewed as business associates, not partners. The loan was not secured. There was no notarial or public registry of contracts.

Though the concept of peddler trade (as it was termed then) has been dismissed by historians of Asia in recent years, currently there is no evidence, either in the Turfan contracts and related documents or in Sogdian sources, that in the seventh or eighth century CE trade along the Silk Route was anything but peddler trade.[51] "Peddler" in this context means an itinerant traveling trader who carried his own goods with him. The trade was based on sale, exchange, and loan contracts. But the loan contracts, such as the one reported by Hansen, indicate that at least some of the itinerant traders did not only trade on their own wealth. Rather, they borrowed money or goods and leveraged their trade (as did the Chinese trader in this case). Loan finance, bearing fixed, in-advance interest, was used. But there is no evidence that other types of contracts and ventures, such as partnership, commenda, or even commissioned agency contracts, in which profits were shared, were in use. It may be fruitful for future scholars to follow the use of organizational forms along the Silk Route in the following centuries, when Arabs and Mongolians met in China and the Middle East, on land and at sea.[52]

A single itinerant merchant traveling by himself with two camels and disappearing along the way to an oasis in Central Asia is the example we draw from this microstudy. The general picture we get from the Turfan microstudy is that Silk Route trade was on a much lower scale and shorter spans of distance and was much less sophisticated than the Alexandria to Muziris trade. Was this the case because the Turfan trade was overland trade, whereas Muziris a mostly maritime trade? Or was this the case because the Muziris micro study captures a trade at the heyday of a great empire, whereas the Turfan trade captures a trade at the margins of an empire that did not have trade or territorial ambitions? Or is the difference just a result of biases in the preserved sources? For now, the popular imagining of endless caravans, composed of hundreds if not thousands of camels, traveling along the Silk Road, presumably relying on well-developed infrastructure, is not yet supported by the historical records. Does it represent a later reality, say, at the heyday of the Pax Mongolica? I will return to the Silk Route and its caravanserai in chapter 4.

THE SHIP AS AN ORGANIZATIONAL UNIT

Trade using ships was universal in the Eurasia of our period. But shipping technologies differed, depending on the region. Different masts, rigs, decks, sails, nails, arms, and navigation systems were used by shipbuilders, captains, and crews in different regions. Their tonnage was different. Their ability to cross open oceans was different. But their function was quite similar. They carried merchants and goods from port to port. How were ships organized? Who owned, financed, controlled, and operated shipped goods, and who traveled as passengers on ships in the Indian Ocean? A ship could be owned by a single wealthy person or family. It could be owned jointly—in joint ownership, a syndicate, a partnership, or in the form of part-ownership. These modes were different with respect to decision-making mechanisms and exit options. A prototypical joint-ownership or syndicate was a passive ownership of assets. A partnership involved joint active management as well. A part-ownership differed from partnership in the lock-in feature—it allowed each of the owners to sell his share to outsiders without dissolving the ship partnership.

The owners of the ship could operate it as part of their mercantile business, using it to transport their own goods and servants at their own risk. They could charter it fully to others. They could operate it as freight-service providers to itinerant traders, family firms, or merchants and their traveling agents. Each model of ship ownership could be matched with a variety of models of ship operation. The ship is an endogenous institution in the sense that its organizational structure was similar in various parts and ports of the Indian Ocean, and the similarity is not known to be the result of copying. The case of the Indian Ocean ship to be presented in this section provides us with a glimpse of the organization of various ships, mostly Arab ships (as evidence survived mostly for such vessels).

Microstudy: The Indian Ocean Arab Ship

Unfortunately, but not surprisingly, the organization of the most typical ships is the least documented. I will provide here a description of a typical Arab-owned Indian Ocean ship using four sources: the excavations of a shipwreck discovered near the cost of Java in 1998;[53] the Geniza records;[54] the records found in Quseir-al-Qadim;[55] and the detailed report on Arab ships captured by the VOC in Malacca.[56]

The shipwreck discovered in 1998 by an Indonesian sea-cucumber diver less than two nautical miles off the shore of Belitung Island, northeast of Sumatra, Indonesia,[57] turned out to be of great importance in both marine archaeology and Eurasian trade history. The ship was dated by most archaeologists to the ninth century CE.[58] Based on an analysis of construction methods and materials, the ship probably originated from either the Persian or Arabian side of the Persian Gulf.[59] It was clearly carrying Chinese ceramics, and therefore it is the earliest evidence ever found of direct maritime trade between the Middle East and China.[60] According to the archaeological findings, the ship underwent a process of refurbishment or even reconstruction in Southeast Asia, to fix damage caused along the way.[61] The ship's estimated length was 18 m,[62] and its cargo weighed about 25 metric tons.[63] Some sixty thousand pieces of Chinese ceramics, mostly bowls and some jars, were recovered (making the estimated original cargo before breakage about seventy thousand pieces).[64] Ceramics were by far the ship's main cargo. Not much is known about the crew. Human remains were not found, but the nature of the personal equipment and coins retrieved from the wreck suggests the presence of Chinese, Indonesians, and Middle Eastern merchants or crew members.[65] A small quantity of nonceramic and general trade goods (not intended for personal use), such as gilt silver and Chinese bronze mirrors, may suggest that crew members were involved in private trade, and were perhaps even given permission for private trade as a substitute for wages.[66]

The size of the ship, the value of the cargo, and the length and riskiness of the voyage may suggest that the vessel and its cargo were not owned by a single wealthy merchant.[67] It is more likely that it was used to transport freight purchased by several merchants, either stationed in China or the Middle East or traveling on board. Unfortunately, the archeologists who investigated this shipwreck have not yet addressed the question of the ownership of the cargo. Such a task is daunting due to the fact that no packaging or shipment documents were preserved. But the method of packaging in jars, bales, and compounds might provide some clues. This would be a valuable research question for marine archeologists to investigate.

Chronologically, the next significant sources on the organization of Arab ships are to be found in the Cairo Geniza. Most shipowners mentioned in Geniza documents were individuals. Many were Muslim, and some were Jewish. The Geniza refers to fewer than a handful of cases in which ships were owned in partnership by two individuals. One notable example pertains to a letter, sent c. 1130,[68] describing a partnership between Madmun, the Jewish *nagid* (political head) of Yemen, and Bilal, the governor of Aden, for the construction and fitting out of a ship that would sail from Aden to the island of Ceylon (modern-day Sri Lanka). It is remarkable that, in Geniza–Indian Ocean ship-ownership, there is no trace of the part-ownership system that appeared in Italy in the twelfth and thirteenth centuries, which allowed the pooling together of funds and the spreading of risks.[69]

In addition to an owner and a captain, a ship usually had a *nakhuda*. The term *nakhuda* appears seventy-five times in the Geniza documents collected in the India Book.[70] Though its use is not always consistent, and this gave rise to a controversy among historians, the more recent common wisdom holds that the nakhuda performs a function distinct from those of the owner and the captain, pertaining to the person in charge of mercantile and financial activities. To elaborate, the nakhuda decided on matters concerning destinations, length of stay in ports, accepting freight and passengers and collecting their fares, which goods to throw overboard in emergencies, dealings with local rulers, and the like. It makes sense that the nakhuda consulted the captain on maritime issues. In some cases, the owner or captain was also the nakhuda. This is one of the causes of confusion among historians. But in most cases, the sedentary owner employed the traveling nakhuda and a captain. Though the word *nakhuda* was originally of Persian etymology; the function was used widely in Arab shipping and later also in Indian shipping. Very tellingly, this was a unique Indian Ocean profession unparalleled in the Mediterranean.[71]

The many examples in the Geniza correspondence of merchants traveling on ships they did not own provide clear evidence of a separation between the ownership of ships and the activity of merchants. On board most Arab ships were traveling merchants distinct from the owner. The position of the nakhuda as a coordinator between the shipowner, the captain, and the merchants facilitated this separation. Furthermore, the existence of nakhudas on board enabled the shipment of unaccompanied freight. A merchant wishing to import or export goods aboard a ship had the choice to entrust them either to one of the traveling merchants or the nakhuda.[72] A letter sent by Khalf b. Isaac in Aden to Abraham Ben Yiju in India, shortly after 1138, mentions iron sent from India with one nakhuda, small items sent with another nakhuda, betel nuts sent with a slave agent of a merchant, and pepper and iron entrusted to a Muslim merchant, who split them and sent them in two separate boats owned by an Indian (one with his slave and the other apparently in the care of an unknown merchant or nakhuda).[73] A merchant, either traveling or entrusting goods to other merchants or a nakhuda, could hire a space on deck to store his bales, baskets, jars, and the like, or full compartments. A traveling merchant could hire a cabin or just sleep on a mattress on top of his goods. Before departure, a ship's captain would prepare a *satmi*, a list of all passengers and cargo on board.[74] The Geniza documents reflect a flourishing commerce that did not rely on itinerant traders, traveling merchants, or traveling agents, making extensive use of Arab ships and the services offered by their owners and crew and on board.

The hundreds of paper fragments uncovered since 1978 in archeological excavations at the "Sheikh's House" in Quseir al-qadim, a Red Sea port in Egypt, provide a wealth of information for the study of Red Sea commerce and the economic history of Islamic Egypt.[75] These paper fragments form a kind of a private working "archive" (not a store of discarded documents, as was the Geniza) used for the activities and operations of a family's shipping business on the Red Sea shore during the late Ayyubid and early Mamluk dynasties.[76] The documents and letters from the "Sheikh's House" are mostly business letters, shipping notes, and account records written in Arabic that detail the business transactions undertaken by a certain Sheikh Abū Muffarrij and his son Abū Isḥāq Ibrāhīm as they participated in the Red Sea–Nile Valley trade (mostly 1200–1250 CE, about a century later than the core of the Geniza documents).[77] From the Quseir documents it can be discerned that the main commodity traded by the Sheikh's family was grain,[78] presumably intended to feed the *Haramein*, the two holy cities of Mecca and Medina, across the Red Sea. Numerous other items are identified in the shipping notes, such as cooking oil, baked goods, and nuts, in large enough quantities to suggest commercial use, and vegetables and other perishables that were probably for local consumption.[79] Unlike Geniza trade, this trade was relatively short-distance and low-value in nature. Unfortunately, the documents are in a worse state of preservation than the Geniza documents, and their reconstruction and analysis are still at a preliminary stage.[80] Their main advantages over the Geniza documents, from the perspective of this microstudy, are that they deal directly with Muslim merchants and ships and cover a later period. These documents reflect the mercantile practice of using Arab ships to send accompanied and unaccompanied goods on board ships that were not owned by Sheikh Abū Muffarrij, his suppliers, or his clients. For example, see the following letter from agents to their principal in Quseir:

> In the name of God, the Merciful, the Compassionate. From 'Abd Abu al-Sa'ada ibn Ridwan and Ibn Kilan. We are writing to inform Shaykh Abu Mufarrij—may God prolong his strength, lead his enemies astray, and assure him success with regard to his gentleness and contracts!—and report to him—may God make him successful!—that we have sent to you, to be accompanied by Majli the porter, three and a half loads and a wayba [of wheat? . . .]. So [you,] the Master would profitably receive [this shipment . . .]. To the shore of Quseir, and to be delivered [to] Abu Mufarrij al-'Abawi [?]—may God prolong his happiness! Peace.[81]

The trade in which the sheikh was involved utilized preexisting ships and purchased freight services that offered connections between Red Sea ports and markets. In some cases, suppliers traveled personally with the goods, and in other cases their employees or agents traveled with the goods. In some cases, freight services were used, and the goods were not accompanied by either the suppliers or by the sheikh (or their employees

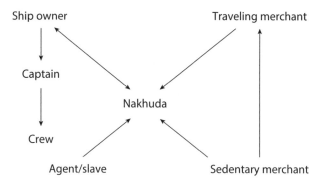

3.2. Interaction between a ship's personnel.

or agents). The commercial letters and shipping notes preserved in the "Sheikh's House" were a major device for conducting the trade, as they contained orders, notices about shipments, and bills that facilitated the flow of goods that were not always personally accompanied by either of the parties.[82]

Another snapshot of shipping practices in the Indian Ocean is provided by a contract of freight, the type of contract that was not preserved in any of the aforementioned sources. This is a much later contract, involving a ship belonging to the Surat shipowner and merchant Abdul Ghafur. This 1704 contract was acquired by the VOC when it captured the ship, and was subsequently kept in the company's archive.[83] It was made between Aga Muhammad Sadik, presumably a merchant, and Muhammad Husain, the nakhuda of the vessel *Fez Ressan*, owned by Ghafur. It set rates for the freight of different commodities: 2 percent for gold and silver; 4 percent for vermilion; 5 percent for copper and saltpeter, lacquerware, and fine porcelain; and 8 percent for rough porcelain.[84] One may argue that it does not represent earlier Arab practices. But it is the best we have, and its general context resembles the Geniza context. Earlier Indian Ocean freight contracts may have been simpler or may have been made orally. But there is no reason to believe that they were radically different.

Figure 3.2 shows the common interactions between the ship's personnel. The microstudy of the Indian Ocean Arab ship demonstrates that ships were not merely means of transportation. They were also means of organization. Capital, labor, maritime know-how, and trade know-how met on board ships. Shipowners and stationary merchants provided capital; captains and their crews provided maritime navigation and ship operation skills; itinerant merchants and traveling agents provided trade know-how; and nakhudas coordinated them all. The presence of the freight ship and the nakhuda reduced the barriers to entry into Indian Ocean maritime trade. It allowed merchants who could not own ships to travel the ocean. It allowed merchants to stay home and send traveling agents across the ocean. The nakhuda made the Indian Ocean freight ship more accessible and effective than ships in Eurasian regions that did not adopt the nakhuda as an organizational device, such as northwestern Europe. However, the freight ship by itself did not form a network, did not enhance the flow of information, and did not offer agent monitoring device.

CONCLUSION

This chapter presented five examples of endogenous institutions (the most basic being the itinerant trader, followed by the family firm, the bilateral agreements of loan and agency, and the ship), which could each take several forms. Three microstudies, those of the Muziris Papyrus, the Turfan contracts, and the Indian Ocean ship, were used to exemplify the actual functioning of some of these forms. The microstudies convey the sense of how isolated, subject to fears from storms and bandits, and un-informed about states of markets and whereabouts of agents and family members merchants could be in the huge spans of the Indian Ocean and the Silk Route. In the coming chapters and microstudies, I will analyze organizational forms that used these building blocks in larger-scale or-ganizational forms that mitigated some of the limitations of these simple and discrete building blocks.

~ 4 ~

Varying Organizational Building Blocks

Organizational forms were not the only human constructions that migrated in Eurasia. Religions migrated. Buddhism traveled out of India and into Sri Lanka, Southeast Asia, China, Japan, Korea, and Central Asia. Generally speaking, this migration began in the third century BCE and reached its zenith by the eighth and ninth centuries CE.[1] Islam migrated from Arabia, reaching Spain by the early eighth century, India in the eighth and ninth centuries, and Indonesia in the thirteenth and fourteenth centuries.[2] Scientific knowledge migrated. Three key mathematical innovations—the numeral system, the use of zeros as placeholders, and the use of zero as a number—were first developed in India and then migrated within the Islamic world and beyond it to Europe.[3] Practical know-how migrated. The domestication of plants and animals and their use in agriculture migrated from the Middle East. Writing seems to have followed, having its origins in Mesopotamia some time before 3000 BCE and migrating to Egypt and possibly also to China.[4] Technological inventions migrated. Printing, gunpowder, and the compass are notable examples of Chinese inventions that migrated to the Middle East and Europe. The three were singled out by Francis Bacon as the most important migrations of innovations, ones that transformed literature, knowledge dissemination, warfare, and navigation.[5]

This chapter and the next examine the second type of organizational form identified in this book, migratory institutions. In these chapters we will analyze more complex, and somewhat more socially and culturally embedded, organizational forms than the ones discussed in the previous chapter: the sea loan, the *funduq* and caravanserai, and the commenda.

These were invented, as far as we can tell, in only one or two places in Eurasia each, and spread around other regions of Eurasia by way of importation or imposition.

How should we study the origins and migration of these organizational forms? The baseline of migration as a frequent and common occurrence with respect to know-how, technology, religion, and other human creations makes the scarcity of the treatment of migration of institutions and organizational forms by legal and economic theory a perplexing phenomenon. It warrants studies of the migration of legal-economic institutions, in general, and of long-distance trade organizational forms, in particular. As we have seen in chapter 2, theory in the disciplines of economics and of law does not take us far enough in providing a rigorous theoretical framework for the study of the migration of institutions. I have searched for implicit theoretical insights from the literature on the migration of specific human practices, techniques, and technologies, with emphasis on Eurasian migration.[6] The insights I will now present are thus derived from disciplines as varied as genetics, archeology, linguistics, and the history of science and technology.

METHODOLOGIES FOR STUDYING MIGRATION

Tracking Migratory Routes and Timings

The ability or inability to find evidence for a plausible migratory route between two appearances can be used to support the argument for migration or of independent and unrelated inventions. The Americas were practically detached from Europe, Africa, and Asia, for several millennia. Thus one can argue quite conclusively that the domestication of plants and animals; the inventions of writing, modes of transportation, and technologies; and religious and political organization took place independently in Eurasia, Africa, and the Americas. A major migration of domesticated crops and animals did take place starting in 1492, when the means to reach the Americas on a regular basis, on board ships across the Atlantic, was discovered. An era known as the "Columbian Exchange" began.[7] The Columbian Exchange involved the migration of cows, chickens, horses, and many other animals to the New World; and of the turkey, llama, alpaca, and a few other animals to the Old World. It involved the migration of corn, cocoa, the tomato, the pineapple, the potato, and many other fruits and vegetables to the Old World; and of rice, coffee, the cucumber, wheat, the watermelon, and other goods in the opposite direction. It also entailed the traveling of germs and other causes of disease both ways. This exchange had a major effect on the economies of both continental landmasses.[8] The outbreak of massive migration after 1492 demonstrates the obstacles to migration before 1492, a combination of geography and human limitations. The "insurmountable" nature of geographic barriers was, in fact, not static, but rather a function of human technology, know-how, and ambition. The timing of its lifting and the ensuing route of migration are clearly trackable.

Multiple sequential observations of the migrant along a known Eurasian route support migration. The absence of a plausible migration route or of timely observations along a route weakens the argument for migration. It is well established that writing was invented independently in Mesopotamia (around 3200 BCE) and in Mesoamerica (around 500 CE). These origins are known to be distinct and independent because of the detachment of the Americas from Eurasia in the relevant period. Focusing on Eurasia: Did the Mesopotamian writing system migrate all the way to China, or was the Chinese writing system independently invented? The oldest evidence for Chinese writing is from around 1300 BCE, but with possible precursors. It featured unique local signs and some unique principles. One could track the trajectory of writing that began in Sumer, four thousand miles west of China's urban centers, before 3000 BCE and traveled east to the Indus Valley, 2,600 miles west of China, where it had existed since around 2200 BCE. But no early writing systems are known from the area between the Indus Valley and China. Theoretically, writing that migrated 1,400 miles in eight hundred years could have migrated another 2,600 miles in nine hundred years. But there is no evidence of writing anywhere between the Indus Valley and China between 2200 and 1300 BCE.[9] On the other hand, there is evidence that Chinese writing became the basis of other forms of writing in East and Southeast Asia, and the main vehicle for the transmission of Chinese culture throughout these regions. So a study of actual or plausible migration routes and timings assists us in determining common or separate origins of organizational forms.

Identifying Gradual or Abrupt Origins

A gradual development from rudimentary origins to a more elaborated or well-functioning stage can indicate independent origins, whereas an abrupt appearance of an advanced knowledge, technology, or organization supports a migration. Another example in the realm of the origins of writing is illustrative here. Egyptian hieroglyphics are assumed by some researchers to have been invented independently, but the alternative position of idea diffusion is more plausible. Egypt lay only eight hundred miles west of Sumer, with which Egypt had trade contacts. No evidence of the gradual development of hieroglyphs has been found, even though Egypt's dry climate would have been favorable for preserving earlier experiments in writing, and despite the fact that the similarly dry climate of Sumer has yielded abundant evidence of the gradual development of Sumerian writing over several centuries.[10] So one can conclude that the Egyptian writing system was not endogenous but rather migratory based on its abrupt recorded start. The same method can be applied to organizational forms.

Material and Textual Evidence

One might think that migration of physical artifacts or migrations that left material evidence can be investigated more systematically. Remains of organisms found in archeological excavations can take researchers a long way in studying the domestication of plants and animals. But physical evidence doesn't address some of the more interesting questions. Did one early farmer learn how to domesticate a specific species of animal or plant by looking at the practices of the next farmer? In this method, know-how traveled, according to the famous saying, at the pace of one mile per year. Or did farmers acquire the animals from their neighbors after domestication, without learning themselves how to domesticate them? These questions cannot easily be answered by resort to DNA evidence and analysis.

Taking the example of writing systems, these left abundant material evidence, such as inscriptions that included numerous signs with an assortment of minute details. Taken together, the multiplicity of observations and the abundance of data allow researchers to identify steps in the genealogy of a single system of writing and divergence between systems of writing within the same family. But the role of human agents cannot be fully exposed based on such evidence. It is definitely the case that the study of the migration of organizational forms, some of which were designed orally and some in written documents that only rarely were preserved until the present, is very challenging compared to the study of the migrations that did leave material traces. But it is not the case that the study of the migration of domestication, the writing system, or the compass is easy, while that of the commenda or the sea loan is hopeless.

Morphological Similarities

When studying organizations, one often tackles the following question: Does similarity between forms arise from migration and emulation or from similar environmental challenges and similar functions? Morphological comparisons, aimed at determining common origins, are more valuable when the subjects under study are constructed from numerous comparable components. The level of detail that is available at the DNA level is the most a researcher can hope for at this stage. Genetic methodologies, and particularly the analysis of mitochondrial DNA (mtDNA), allow researchers to follow plant and animal domestication paths and timeframes very accurately. For instance, old debates about the mono- or multi-origins of the domestication of plants, cattle, and boar are now settled by the application of new research methods developed in the last two decades, relying on the analysis of modern and ancient mtDNA sequences.[11] Comparisons of hieroglyphs, alphabets, and numeric systems provide a wide basis for conclusions as to similarities, evolution, and common origins. The organizational forms studied in this chapter are far from being as detailed. Yet we can use details in comparing the organizational details of different manifestations of the commenda or the caravanserai.

Abstract or Detailed Nature of Migration

A significant complication in investigating migration is that what migrated was not necessarily the full detailed organizational form but only more abstract ideas. The investigation thus should account for the possibility of migration at various levels of detail or abstraction. The example of domestication is instructive. Know-how could migrate in the form of the movement of actual plants, seeds or domesticated animals. It could migrate on the level of learning how to domesticate specific plants and animals. It could migrate on the level of the abstract idea of a shift from hunting and gathering to societies based on domestication and agriculture (a transition known as the "Neolithic Revolution"). What could have migrated was not the know-how of domestication of specific grains or cattle, which could often not adjust to different longitudes, soils, or continents, but the abstract idea that human beings can shift from a nomadic hunting-and-gathering mode of survival to a mode of agriculture-based settlements. Human beings learned the more general notion that different dietary needs can be provided by domesticating plants and animals from different families, as available in different regions. The variation in types of cereals, pulses, fibers, roots, and melons domesticated in different parts of the globe is not conclusive evidence of the multiple independent origins of the Neolithic Revolution.[12] The example of writing systems is analogous. Similarity in form is telling, but only for the migration of actual signs and letters from region to region. The absence of morphological similarity between the writing systems of Mesopotamia and Egypt does not disprove copying of the more abstract idea of using graphic forms to record oral language in general or of what became its dominant form, phonetic representation. While the differences between Egyptian hieroglyphs and Sumerian cuneiform writing are evident, some scholars have argued that Egypt borrowed from Sumer not simply the abstract idea of writing but also logography, phonography, and linearity with sequencing.[13] We have to look for the migration of abstract ideas such as the sharing of investment or the splitting of profits or allocation of risks to a second or third party, and not necessarily the detailed organizational form.

Migration of the Structure or the Function

The fact that the same knowledge or technology was used in different places does not necessarily mean that it was being used for the same function. Shipping, in general, and navigation in the open seas, in particular, were a universal challenge. Every nation that wished to cross the oceans for exploration, trade, or war faced similar difficulties. The compass, as we know it today, relies on a natural feature that can be applied anywhere on earth, the magnetic poles, and served a universal function in navigation, indicating geographical position and desired direction. One could put forward a hypothesis that the compass was invented for that purpose and yielded itself for migration because of this. Yet this was clearly not the case. The compass was used in China for feng shui and fortune-telling purposes long before it was used for navigation.[14] Similarly, gunpowder was used for fireworks before it was used for fighting. Both became attractive migration subjects only when used for their later function. Astronomical observations were used in China to determine whether the state of heaven was harmonious, in Islam to determine the time of prayers and fasts, and in Europe (among some observers at least) to predict the movement of planets. The printing block was used in China mostly by the state and for official purposes, but in Europe mostly by private printers and for private purposes. The numerals and the zero were originally formed in India; they were adopted by Arabs and Chinese mostly for use in mathematics. Only the Europeans used them widely in business accounting.

We shall see that the same applies to business organization. The family performed a different business function in different regions. The commenda was used in some places for maritime trade and in others for overland trade. The guild and the partnership were used in some places for manufacturing and in others for trade. To determine common or separate origins, we should not only take into account the possibility of similar function. We also have to explain how a technology or an organization change function in transition.

Conclusion

The review of methodologies used for the investigation of the migration of practical know-how, technologies, science, and mathematics equips us with a few important methodological tools for the study of organizational forms. When turning to the study of the migration of the sea loan, the caravanserai, and the commenda, we should look for plausible migration routes and evidence on timings, morphological similarities and gradual or abrupt origins. We should also be aware of the fact that the migration can occur in different levels of detailed configurations or abstract ideas and that the migrating institution can change function between contexts. The next important component in the development of a richer theoretical model for the migration of organizational forms is defining the environments and agents that facilitate migration. Before doing this, I will hint at two additional components of the model that will be elucidated in the next stages of the development of the argument: the transformation of the organizational form during migration and the resistance to migration at the receiving end. The migration of the sea loan, the funduq/khan/caravanserai, and ultimately the commenda will exhibit transformation. Our most important example of resistance is that of the business corporation, which made it an ultimate, embedded institution.

WHAT FACILITATES MIGRATION?

Geography and physical separation were the most obvious obstacles to migration in the premodern world. One does not have to resort to high theory to grasp the basic factors that affect the extent and speed of migration. Geographical proximity is an obvious factor. Proximity is not measured by distance alone, but also by ease of access, given geography, modes of transportation, and knowledge of the routes and the destinations and availability of carrying agents.

Agents carry with them practices, know-how, tools, religious beliefs, ideas, stories, scripts, maps, and manuals. I will next identify migratory agents that have the potential to be relevant for the migration of institutions. I will examine the potential and actual role of empires, migrant populations, religion, travelers, and cross-cultural hubs in the migration of law and legal-economic institutions. The most relevant agents for institutional migration, the merchants themselves (whom I view as endogenous to the migration process), will also be discussed as I examine the migratory organizational forms themselves.

Availability of Institutional Carrying Agents

EMPIRES

Empires are the paradigmatic agents for the migration of law in the legal transplant literature. They achieve this through wars, conquests, and the exercise of political sovereignty. From its modest beginnings in the form of the Twelve Tables in a tiny town in the central-western region of the Italian peninsula, classical Roman law was carried by the Roman Empire to much of ancient Europe, the Middle East, and North Africa. The Holy Roman Empire was a key driver in the reception of Roman law in late medieval Central Europe. The conquistadors of the Spanish Empire carried their Roman canon law to Latin America. The British Empire carried its common law overseas. These are relatively well-studied instances of European law transferred by empires.

Islamic law was carried by the Arab and Ottoman Empires into their conquered lands in the Middle East, southeastern Europe, Persia, and Central Asia. The legal migration enabled by the vast expansion of the Mongol Empire, and its heirs throughout Asia, is less well studied. The Mongol Empire expanded very rapidly from its homeland. Beginning with Genghis Khan in 1206, conquering much of Central Asia in the 1210s and 1220s and Iran and parts of Eastern Europe in the following decades, and had its zenith with the conquest of Bagdad in 1258.[15] The Pax Mongolica that followed it enabled a flow of ideas, technologies, and institutions eastward from China to Central Asia, Persia, and beyond, and westward from the centers of Islam to China.[16] So the Mongol Empire did not facilitate the migration of Mongol civilization but rather that of other civilizations—and in both directions.

The Crusaders could have carried European law to the Holy Land and the rest of the Middle East. But empires can also do the reverse. They can carry the law of newly annexed provinces to the center or create the political stability that enables the carrying of bodies of law, of the kinds we are interested in, by merchants over long distances. Thus, the Crusaders could have carried Islamic institutions to Europe or facilitated Italian merchants' ability to carry them. By bringing about the Pax Mongolica, the Mongols facilitated the carrying of law along the Silk Route all the way from Eastern Europe and the Middle East to China, or in the other direction. We shall return to such potential migration agents in the following chapters.

Migrant Populations and Travelers

The massive population migrations in Eurasia ended long before our period. The first was the migration of early humans out of Africa and into Asia and beyond.[17] Second was the migration of Germanic and Slavic tribes from Asia into Eastern and eventually Western Europe, known as the "Migration Period," which coincided with the fall of the Roman Empire. The three major migrations in the early modern age were those of Europeans (and their African slaves) across the Atlantic to the Americas, of Russians into Western and Central Asia, and of Chinese to Central and Southeast Asia.[18] The migration to America is clearly connected to the migration of law, partly within the confines of empires and partly beyond, partly carried by political organs and partly as human capital and knowledge of the migrants. Thus the agents that carried the common law to North American were not only empires but also migrant populations.

There are additional minor migrations that bear directly on the potential migration of law in our period. These include the migration of Arabs (and Islam) to South and Southeast Asia, the migration of Jews to Asia, possibly after the destruction of the First or the Second Temple and particularly after their expulsion from Spain, and the migration of Armenians from their historic homeland to Persia and then further east in Asia and to Europe.

Travelers can be placed at the end of the spectrum of migrations in terms of scale. European travelers, such as Marco Polo (1254–1324), arrived in Asia starting in the thirteenth century.[19] Jesuit missionaries, such as Matteo Ricci (1552–1610), arrived in East Asia in the sixteenth century, and brought selective knowledge about Europe and its science to China and Japan.[20] European merchants and conquerors arrived in the Indian Ocean and South and East Asia in growing numbers in the sixteenth and seventeenth centuries, bringing with them various elements of European civilizations.

Migration, as we have seen, can take place within empires or across political boundaries. The early stages of mass migration—migration on a small scale or within small ethnic groups—often constitute trade diasporas. Such are the examples of the Chinese trade diasporas in Central and Southeast Asia and the Jewish and the Armenian diasporas in Asia and Europe. Law is often carried from the center to the diaspora or between diasporas. Human migration and the migration of religions are interconnected.

EXPANSION OF RELIGIONS

Several religions expanded over large territories in our period or in the preceding centuries, when some of our institutions were already in place. Zoroastrianism, which was pushed out of Iran by Islam, expanded to Central Asia, where it took hold among Sogdian traders and Turkish tribes, and to China and India, where Parsi merchant communities were formed.[21] Manichaeism traveled a somewhat similar route from Iran to Central Asia and China, due to the same pressure by Islam. After the Assyrian Church of the East split from the Byzantine Orthodox Church, Nestorian Christianity spread from Constantinople to Persia, Central Asia, China, Mongolia, and Korea before declining rapidly in the fourteenth century with the waning of the Mongol Empire. The Indian branch survived on the Malabar Coast; its members were considered to be the lost Saint Thomas Christians by the first European Christians to arrive there via the Cape Route, around 1500.[22] Catholic missionary Christianity arrived in Asia with the first ships taking the same route. Confucianism expanded with Chinese migrants to Central and Southeast Asia.

Buddhism made its first excursions out of India as early as the first century CE. It made initial inroads in China, particularly among foreigners and merchants, in the fourth century. In the period between 600 and 1000 CE, it spread to Southeast Asia and the Central Asian oases. Eventually a mass conversion to Buddhism took place in China. The main Buddhist sites were located in northern India. Pilgrimage to them prompted a constant movement of pilgrims, monks, and missionaries between China and India.[23] The fact that Buddhism achieved such a strong hold among merchants also facilitated the flow of knowledge and commercial practices in the Buddhist networks on the south-north axis across the Himalayas and the west-east network between Central Asia, China, and Southeast Asia.

The most important religious expansion for our purposes is that of Islam. Its territorial scope was vast, and its timing was closest to this book's early modern timeframe. But, even more significantly, in Islam, theology and law are interwoven. As a result, the expansion of the religion was more likely to carry with it both law and institutions. Islam expanded within a generation of its founding from Arabia to the Levant (Syria, Iraq, and Egypt). By 750, the Umayyad Caliphate had expanded to Iran, Armenia, and Transoxiana in Central Asia, to the Indus Valley, and to the Maghreb (North Africa) and the Iberian Peninsula. The Muslims penetrated Sicily in 827 and held it until 1061–72. The Delhi Sultanate, the first significant Islamic political presence in India, was established in 1206, and ruled until the establishment of Mughal Empire in 1526. Muslim merchants first arrived in Indonesia in the eleventh century, but mass conversion did not begin before the thirteenth century in Sumatra and the following century in Java; Islamic states came to dominate most of these islands only in the sixteenth century. Similar expansion took place in the Malay Peninsula, including in Malacca and in the southern Philippines.[24]

Islam served as an agent of legal migration not only through outward expansion but also internally, among Muslims. During the *haj* to Mecca and back home, pilgrims from different places met and shared religious, legal, and practical knowledge of topics such as trading and business. By teaching Islamic law, religious higher education institutions, *madrasas* (such as the Al-Azhar University in Cairo and Al-Nizamiyya in Baghdad), became knowledge centers and hence disseminated legal knowledge throughout the Muslim world.

Cross-Cultural Hubs

Port cities, particularly entrepôts, were important sites of cross-cultural exchange, not only of goods but also of trade know-how, including how to design institutions that would support and enhance trade. Port cities could be viewed as endogenous to trade. Hubs were formed by merchants, who relied on the preexistence of trade. But hubs were also created by geography and politics, and can even be viewed as being created by earlier merchants—and so taken as given by later merchants. The hubs surveyed in this section were mostly in place by the year 1400, the starting point of this book. I will therefore classify them as exogenous for my expositional purposes and thus introduce them in this methodological chapter rather than in the following substantive chapters.

The huge dimensions of the Indian Ocean, in its wider sense that encompasses all the seas and gulfs from the Red Sea to the South China Sea, prevented most merchants from traveling its full length. Each merchant traveled a segment to a major port, and there met merchants from other regions, who came from other directions and traveled other segments. The geography of the Indian Ocean, comprising several seas connected to each other by straits or other essential passages such as capes, gave several ports a singular locational position. The topography of many coastlines of the Indian Ocean isolated port cities from the hinterland and from centers of land-based political power. On the other hand, these port cities were more easily reached by sea and composed part of a maritime network.

The major Indian Ocean entrepôt cities included Aden; Yemen (just off the Bab-el-Mandeb Strait's exit from the Red Sea to the Arabian Sea); Hormuz (an island on the Bab-el-Mandeb Strait that connected the Persian Gulf to the Arabian Sea); and Malacca (on the Malaysian Peninsula's southern coast, in the straits that connected the Bay of Bengal and the South China Sea). Other ports that were strategically located for trade included Cochin (on the Malabar Coast of Southern India); Gale (on the southwestern tip of Sri Lanka); Hội An (on the central coast of Vietnam); Ayutthaya (at the confluence of three rivers just North of Bangkok, Thailand); and Quanzhou (on the shore of the Taiwan Strait in Fujian Province, China). Somewhat later, toward the end of the period covered by this book (1700) and beyond it, additional ports became prominent and a few new ones were built, including Guangzhou and Hong Kong on the delta of the Pearl River in Southern China; Singapore (an island at the southern tip of the Malay Peninsula); Batavia in Java; Shanghai; Bombay (Mumbai); and Calcutta.

What is important for our purposes is the fact that such cities enjoyed relative political autonomy, either formally or due to lax control, had significant diasporic communities of foreign merchants, and played a role as entrepôts in the long-distance Eurasian trade routes and networks. As historian Craig Lockard notes: "In many of the ports merchants became a more powerful group in local politics. The populations of these ports were cosmopolitan, a mix of local people and outsiders from diverse backgrounds who were open to the outside world and accepting of cultural differences."[25] Though port cities shared many such common characteristics, each had its unique ethnic mix and position in the network.

Let us begin with Malacca. Lockard provides the following description of this important hub:

> By the later 1400s the port probably had some 50,000 to 100,000 people and was Southeast Asia's largest city. Like many entrepôts, Melaka was famously cosmopolitan, attracting trading ships from many lands and at least 15,000 foreign merchants speaking some eighty-four languages in temporary or permanent residence. These came from all over the Indian Ocean basin and Indonesia but also included Vietnamese, Chams, Okinawans, Japanese, and Muslim Filipinos (some perhaps of Chinese ancestry). The sultan appointed four merchants, usually including one Chinese, from the leading expatriate communities to the post of *shahbandar* (harbormaster), charged with supervising trade and presenting visiting merchants to the prime minister. This ethnic diversity, the centrality of free trade, and the prominence of foreign residents has prompted some historians to refer to Melaka as one of the world's first globalized cities—its streets as cosmopolitan as those of any city in the world today.[26]

Hormuz was a barren island, strategically located not far from the coast at the entrance of the Persian Gulf. From about 1100 until the Portuguese arrival, Hormuz was the seat of a dynasty of princes, who originated from Oman.[27] It relied on supplies of water and food from the mainland and from nearby islands. It gradually rose from the position of a regional port to that of the jewel in the crown of the Western Indian Ocean trade network. It was visited by many of the better-known European and Islamic travelers (including Ibn Battuta and Marco Polo).[28] It provided tribute to the Yuan emperors, as part of the Chinese tributary system, and was visited by a couple of Zheng He's fleets.[29] Abd-al-Razzāq Samarqandī (1413–82), a Persian historian, described Hormuz in 1442 as a major emporium, frequented by merchants from all over Eurasia.[30] He notes that: "During the trading season there were people from all over the world in Hormuz . . . 'You would find here Persians, Arabs, Ethiopians, Armenians, Tatars, Turks, Mores, Italians, Frenchmen, Germans, English, Poles, and other Europeans . . . .' "[31] The permanent population of Hormuz was composed of Muslims, mostly Persians, Hindus from Sind and Cambia, and Jews. From the early sixteenth century, the Portuguese controlled the island, making it a key component of their Asian empire.[32] The Portuguese population of Hormuz grew considerably during the century. In this period, other Europeans settled in larger numbers, as did Armenians, Greeks, and Spanish-speaking Jews coming from Spain via Constantinople and Aleppo. Fifty-four ships arrived in Hormuz annually, from India alone, circa 1620.[33] The goods were later distributed by smaller local ships to ports across the Persian Gulf, notably Basra, and from there to the overland routes. Niels Steensgaard considers Hormuz the prime example of the shift from itinerant trader to corporate-based trade, and describes the town's atmosphere as "cosmopolitan."[34] In 1622, Hormuz was captured from the Portuguese by a joint Persian-EIC fleet.[35] It never regained its position and was replaced by the mainland port of Bandar Abbās, which was less cosmopolitan in atmosphere.

Aden was a hub on the very western edge of the Indian Ocean. It was located at the entrance of the Red Sea, just as Hormuz was located at the entrance to the Persian Gulf. Foreign traders came to Aden from all directions, including Persia, India, Somalia, Ethiopia, the Red Sea, and even China. It played a prominent role in the trade of Jewish merchants from Cairo and North Africa with India, as is evident from the Geniza records.[36]

According to Ibn Battuta, large vessels arrived at its harbor from Cambay, Tana, Qulan, Kalkout, and other Indian ports.[37] Zheng He also visited Aden, sailing all the way from China.[38] Merchants from Egypt and India established themselves there, while its indigenous inhabitants were traders, fishermen, and porters. "All the spices destined for Maghreb and Europe passed through customs in Aden. . . . It was here that the exchange of Oriental and European goods took place," note Bouchon and Lombard.[39] Aden was similar to Hormuz in several respects, although its cosmopolitan mix included more Arabs and Jews and fewer Persians and Central Asians than Hormuz, which was just off the coast of Persia. There is ample evidence of its cosmopolitan character from as early as the eleventh century,[40] long before the arrival of the Portuguese.

Turning east from Malacca, we can take Quanzhou in China as a prime example of a South China Sea port. The Chinese of the Song dynasty opened their ports to the merchants, priests, and travelers of other Indian Ocean regions with which they were in religious, tributary, and commercial contact. Quanzhou, due to its location and its political openness, was the focus of a cultural and economic exchange between China and the societies of the Indian Ocean littoral. Gradually, a permanent presence of diasporic communities of foreign residents developed.[41] We can say conclusively that there was a resident community of Muslims in Song Quanzhou with roots extending back certainly to the early eleventh century and very likely into the preceding century. Indian merchants, mostly Hindu, established a presence in the South China ports even earlier in history. It is recorded that, during the Song dynasty (in the 980s), a monk from India purchased land in the southern suburbs of Quanzhou.[42] The Mongol Yuan dynasty empowered foreign merchants, particularly Muslims, as a means of weakening the political power of Han Chinese. This made a large influx of Muslims from the Middle East possible, and provided unprecedented mobility for them, both within China, beyond Quanzhou and Guangzhou, and between China and their home countries, thus significantly altering the nature of the communities and their diasporic identity.[43] The collapse of the Yuan dynasty marked the end of the Muslim community of Quanzhou. In 1365, the Han Chinese governor of Fujian crushed a rebellion of local Muslim leaders during the transition (the Ispah Rebellion), massacred many of the Arab and Persian merchants, and transferred his loyalty to the Ming dynasty.[44]

While in the Atlantic, the Americas were altogether separated from Europe, and the Mediterranean was in some periods sharply divided into Christian and Muslim spheres, the Indian Ocean was quite cosmopolitan. Cosmopolitan port cities, the locus of cross-cultural interactions, rose and fell with political circumstances. But in any given period a few cosmopolitan port cities existed. These cities had different ethnic mixes, although most of them included Arabs, Persians, Indians, Southeast Asians, and Chinese, and, after 1500, also Europeans. These ports were places of learning about religions, cultures, and technologies, in which linguistic and other types of hybrids were formed. They were the place in which business practices and institutions could cross cultural, legal, and political boundaries.

THE MIGRATION OF TRADE ORGANIZATIONS

Migratory organizational forms are dissimilar from one another. They are distinct in their functions, and they have different origins and paths of migration. I focus here on three organizational forms: the sea loan, the funduq/caravanserai, and the commenda. The sea loan migrated from the Mediterranean to Latin Europe and eventually, via the Cape Route, to East Asia, but not to Islamic regions. The funduq/caravanserai migrated from the Middle East to Islamic North Africa and Central Asia but not to Christian Europe. The commenda migrated throughout Eurasia. By comparing the migration paths of the three important institutions, one can learn much about the factors and agents that shape migration paths and those that impede and block migration.[45]

The approach of this chapter is to use three key organizational forms rather than to offer a comprehensive survey of all migratory organizational forms. Some organizational forms, such as the general partnership or the joint ownership of ships, are more complex than typical endogenous institutions and are likely to be migratory. One could also study the migration pattern of the bill of exchange, letter of credit, bill of lading, charter party, general average, premium marine insurance, or supercargo, to mention but a few additional examples. The study of these is definitely warranted. I did not study them only because of space constraints, because of the scarcity of the historical evidence and historical literature on their early history and possible migration, and because the three institutions I selected represent three regional patterns of migrations I want to demonstrate. All of them merit thorough, primary-source-based historical studies on a variety of Eurasian regions in the future, before definite assertions about their origins and migration can be made.

As I devote the whole of chapter 6 to the commenda, I will provide here only a brief sketch of its essence and migration, to provide readers of chapter 5 with a sense of direction vis-à-vis the full map of three paths. The commenda is an agreement (in modern terminology, a "bilateral limited partnership" agreement) between an investor and a traveling merchant. It is a relatively complex nexus of contracts that deals with employment, agency, finance, risks, and more. The commenda developed mostly along the second line of institutional development, migration from one region to another. It originated, as far as one can tell based on surviving records, in one place—Arabia, or, more generally, the Middle East. It migrated east, to Persia, India, the Indonesian archipelago, and possibly also to China, and west to Italy and the western Mediterranean, Central and Western Europe, the Baltic, and possibly also to England.[46]

The commenda is the prototypical migratory institution. The business corporation is an embedded institution in the terms of this book. A good and enlightening example for the factors that created the contrast between migratory organizational forms and embedded organizational forms is that which compares the commenda with the corporation. This contrast is one of the main themes of the second half of the book.

THE SEA LOAN

Loans as means of financing trade are quite universal and, as such, are endogenous organizational forms. The sea loan is a specific and compound configuration of the loan. This form originated in antiquity and reemerged with the revival of trade in Italy, but it was not accepted by Islamic law. This section will follow its unique path of spatial diffusion and contrast it with the different paths of the funduq and the commenda.

As we have learned from the Muziris microstudy, both Athenian and Roman maritime law recognized a separate category of loan contract applicable to the financing of sea voyages. In Athenian law, this was the *nautikòn dáneion*.[47] In Roman law, the category of *faenus nauticum* was applicable to maritime loans.[48] These loans were distinct from land loans in two major respects. First was the rate of interest. Unlike gratuitous loan contracts such as the *mutuum*, the maritime loan allowed the charging of interest. Unlike other forms of nongratuitous loans, such as the *stipulatio*, it was not subject to strict usury restrictions and permitted the charging of higher interest due to risk. A second distinction was the ability to separately allocate different risks to the various parties. The sea risk was allocated to the lender, while the business risk was held by the borrower. As we saw earlier, in the case of loss of the ship or goods at sea, either due to natural causes or to piracy, the borrower was discharged of the debt.

Sea loans were commonly used in Athens in the fourth century BCE. There is some evidence they might also have been operative in the commerce of the Phoenician merchant kings of the Levantine coast as early as the second millennium BCE.[49] So, they were a product of early Greco-Roman antiquity and possibly even of the ancient Middle Eastern civilizations. Whatever the case may be, Demosthenes's speeches include references to some twenty such loans. They were mostly used for financing voyages from Athens to various ports, some as far off as Sicily or the Black Sea. A traveling merchant with limited wealth, or wishing to spread risk or leverage, would borrow money from another party—such as a wealthier person, an older person who did not wish to travel, a nonmerchant, or a syndicate of several individuals—to fund the purchase of a ship or goods, or both, for a single or return voyage. While some scholars viewed Athenian sea loans as having fixed formulae or templates, more recently others, notably Cohen, identify a significant level of flexibility and modularity in drafting sea loans, one that was able to meet the conditions of diverse voyages and the risk-taking inclinations, wealth constraints, and business preferences of the parties. Risk of sea loss could be allocated to either party; interest was fixed based on level of sea risk given the season and destination; security could be created in either the goods, the ship itself, or real estate back home; moral hazard was dealt with in several ways; minimum equity investment by the borrowers was sometimes required; different monitoring devices could be agreed upon; and loans could be provided by individuals or syndicates.[50]

While there is ample evidence for the use of sea loans in fourth-century-BCE Athens, mainly in literary sources, the evidence for their use in later periods is scanter. A papyrus dated from the Ptolemaic period records a contract between a consortium of five merchants and a financier in which the consortium borrowed money in the form of a sea loan to finance a voyage to "the spice-bearing lands."[51] In addition, the Muziris Papyrus is most likely a sea loan, which deals with financing trade between Muziris on the Malabar Coast of India and Alexandria, Egypt.[52] It is the clearest evidence of the use of the sea loan in the heyday of the Roman Empire. In Rome itself, the main evidence is found in juristic sources, notably in the Justinian Digest.

The remarkable similarity between the forms of contracts used in the trade of the Mediterranean in periods separated by half a millennium raises the question of whether the sea loan of twelfth-century Genoa, Venice, and other Italian towns was independently invented in the late Middle Ages in the face of similar environmental and business challenges, or whether the awakening of trade in the western Mediterranean made use of the device that was used frequently in Greco-Roman antiquity and was last captured and preserved in the sixth-century Justinian Code and Digest.

This continuation argument can be substantiated based on two grounds. First, the sea loan was known to the Byzantines and reflected in Eastern Mediterranean legal codes such as the Rhodian Sea Law (*Nomos Rhodion Nautikos*) maritime regulations, compiled probably between 600 and 800 CE, and the Basilica, a collection of laws completed ca. 892 CE in Constantinople.[53] Second, the Italian maritime cities, such as Venice and Genoa, had strong political ties and conducted considerable trade with Constantinople, from the time of their very origin as medieval commercial centers.[54] There are numerous examples of sea-loan contracts providing funds for trade with Constantinople, Syria, North Africa, and Egypt in the second half of the twelfth century.[55] Thus, it seems probable that there exists a direct historical connection between the Roman and the medieval Italian forms of the sea loan, through the medium of the Byzantine Empire.[56] Yet it is interesting to note that the term *faenus nauticum*, which was employed in Roman times, was never used in the Genoese contracts. Instead, the term *mutuum* was used—which in Roman law was traditionally a gratuitous terrestrial loan—to implicitly deny the usurious character of the contract.

The sea loan reemerged as a mode of organizing trade and by the middle of the twelfth century it was widely used. The interest rate on sea loans, which reflected also the sea risk premium, was 25–33 percent for western Mediterranean round trips, and as high as 40–100 percent for voyages to the Levant. The expected profits were high enough to justify this. Two variations emerged out of the ordinary sea loan. The first was the bottomry, a loan secured by the ship itself. The second was the respondentia (*respondência* in Portuguese), a loan secured by the goods. In the latter, the loan had to be repaid even if the ship sunk, as long as the goods were salvaged. The splitting of the sea loan into variations allowed more flexibility in matching lenders and borrowers, in using loans for different purposes relating to the same voyage, and in allocating risks more precisely.[57] The heyday of the Italian sea loan was short. By the second quarter of the thirteenth century, it was rarely used. It was gradually replaced by other organizational forms, notably the commenda, to which we will turn in the next chapter.

Being so common in the legal codes and practices of the Greco-Roman and Byzantine Eastern Mediterranean, and such a popular mode of organizing and financing overseas trade in Italy, one might speculate that the sea loan must have made its way also to the Islamic Middle East. Islamic law was influenced in its formative period by the preexisting Greco-Roman, Byzantine, and other laws of the Middle East. Upon arrival on the shores of the Mediterranean, Islamic law faced new challenges in relation to maritime laws, not least because Islamic maritime law was not as developed as Greco-Roman law. But eventually it did follow many forms and rules found in the Rhodian Sea Law. This is evident from an eleventh-century Islamic treatise on the law of the sea, *Kitāb Akriyat al-sufun*, which was discussed by Udovitch.[58] One could expect Islam to be exposed to the sea loan at some stage, but it was not discussed in that treatise. The existing literature on early Islamic law asserts that the sea loan was not recognized in other Islamic sources either. Hassan Khalilieh concludes that documentary and legal materials on the use of the sea loan by Muslims are few and far between.[59]

Because the sea loan was not imported into Islamic civilization, its ability to travel east into the Indian Ocean or to travel the Silk Route east toward India and China was blocked. Things changed with the arrival of the Portuguese in Asia. Sailing around the Cape of Good Hope, they took with them the sea loan.[60] The Portuguese, like the Spaniards, were familiar with the Italian sea loan. They used sea loans on the margins of their ruler-centered Asian Empire, to which we will turn in the next part. Private Portuguese merchants financed their trade by borrowing money in the form of sea loans both in Europe and in Asia. In Asia, they used the sea loan in the Macau–Nagasaki trade route, in both its variations: the bottomry loans and the *respondência*. They used it for borrowing money from Japanese investors–importers.[61] The main evidence for the use of the sea loan on that route is from the early seventeenth century. The Japanese lenders most likely learned of the sea loan, and its risk-shifting feature, from the Portuguese borrowers.

The migration path of the sea loan was unique in that, unlike the funduq or the commenda, it did not travel in the Islamic civilization. Fascinatingly, while the sea loan did not make its way eastward with Islam as did the commenda, it bypassed the Islamic parts of Asia via the Cape Route and, with the Europeans, reached the very far end of it, Japan.

What can explain this unique migration path that resulted from Islam's resistance to the sea loan? The explanation that immediately comes to mind is Islam's prohibition of usury. Several verses in the Quran condemned *ribā* (literally, "increase") in commerce, and a hadith reports Prophet Muhammad's objection to interest-charging.[62] Most Islamic legal scholars, including leading Hanafi and Shafi'i jurists, have interpreted the Quranic verses as prohibiting any interest on loans.[63] Ways were developed over the years in order to bypass or and evade the prohibition. They often used *hiyal*, a term that refers to fictions used to avoid compliance without a violation of the Islamic legal prohibition. Two famous *hiyal* used to avoid the usury ban are the double sale in which the difference between the two sell prices embodied the interest and loan payable in another currency in which the exchange rate embodies the interest.[64] Yet bypasses are not relevant for my concern here. Bypasses changed the form of the legal and organizational arrangement. I am trying to explain why the sea loan as such was adopted in the Islamic Middle East and not whether there were ways to bypass the usury prohibition and grant interest-bearing loans that were different from the sea loan.

But Islam was not exceptional in this sense. Christianity was also not fond of lending at interest. In order to determine that differences in content or in timing of usury law in Islam and Christianity can nevertheless explain the rejection of the sea loan by Islam, but not by Christianity, let's examine the development of usury prohibition in Christianity. Based on various verses in the Old Testament early Christianity had negative moral views on interest lending. In the fourth century, the rhetoric evolved into law when the First Ecumenical Council of Nicaea (325 CE), as well as regional Councils and Synods, prohibited clergymen from engaging in usury.[65] But there was not legal prohibition at this stage on interest bearing loans between laypersons. Thus there was not religion rejection of the sea loan.

In 540, Justinian the Great, the Byzantine Emperor (527–65) who codified Roman law in the *Corpus Juris Civilis*, approved of maritime loans because they had been a custom for so long. He permitted higher interest on maritime loans than on other kinds of loans, presumably because they involved higher risks.[66] Byzantine and Eastern Mediterranean maritime codification and legislation from the sixth to the ninth century—which was based on Greco-Roman law and maritime practices, for example the Rhodian Sea Law and the *Ecloga*—approved of sea loans.[67]

As the theological split between Roman Catholicism and Orthodox Christianity widened in the eighth and ninth centuries, the attitudes of the two churches to usury and to sea loans began to diverge as well. The Third Council of the Lateran (1179) held in Rome prohibited usury altogether and usurers were sanctioned very harshly in the denial of sacraments and of proper burial, invalidation of wills, amounting practically excommunication of the usurers.[68] By the thirteenth century, the harsh counterattack on usurious loans by the church had intensified, and the use of the sea loan declined during the papacy of Pope Gregory IX (1227–41).[69] The campaign against usury was led by the Franciscan and Dominican orders.[70] It culminated at the Council of Vienne (1311–12), which decreed excommunication for all "magistrates, rulers, consuls, judges, lawyers, and similar officials" who "draw up statutes" permitting usury or "knowingly decide that usury may be paid."[71] The Roman Catholic Church proved less forthcoming on the separation between interest and risk premium than the Byzantine Church. Western Christianity was tolerant of the sea loan only within a short timespan from the revival of maritime trade in the Italian cities until the theological response that mounted attack on usury in general and sea loan in particular. The higher level of commercial activity and the growing resort to loan finance in

Italy may have made the issue of usury more acute and more controversial at that specific time and place.

The difference that emerged between Christian Orthodox—Byzantine and the Roman Catholic—and the Italian attitude to usury is explained by their different attitude to Roman Law. The Byzantines accommodated the Justinian code and Roman law more generally. With them they accepted their permissive approach towards some interest rates on some types of loans. In eleventh- to thirteenth-century Italy the status of Roman Law was contested by the Roman Catholic Church and by canon law. The differences between the practices in Western Christianity and Eastern Christianity were not as stark as they were in religious doctrine. Some Italian and southern French maritime cities ignored the new religious prohibition and continued the Roman Law distinction between permitted interest and forbidden usury until the early fourteenth century, and in some cases even afterwards. The Church objected these permissive lay rules but was only able to partially enforce its prohibition on usurious commercial loans. It is not yet known to what extent the decline of the use of sea loans in Italy can be attributed to the new religion prohibition as distinct from organizational and economic explanations.

In conclusion, the explanation for the difference between reception of the sea loan in Christianity and its rejection in Islam is that Christianity in the East did not view sea loans as usurious and Christianity in the West began prohibiting commercial interest-bearing loans only late in the twelfth century. Islam on the other hand prohibits interest bearing loans from its very beginning in the seventh century.

But how did Islamic civilizations, during periods in which they flourished economically and commercially and were in contact with Christian and Jewish law, manage without the sea loan?[72] One potential hypothesis is that they did not—that they contracted around the prohibition, disguising interest as price. Or that they, in fact, used sea loan contracts, but these did not survive. Much of what we know about the use of the sea loan in Italy is based on notarial depositories of contracts which have no parallel in the Middle East. So the preceding observations could be erroneous. Assuming that the sea loan indeed was *not* used by Muslims, I will offer three explanations for why this might have been so.

First, Islamic trade was initially mostly overland: in Arabia, to Central Asia and the Silk Route, across the Sahara. Maritime trade was a relative latecomer. The sea risk component of the sea loan could not be applied in the same way in camel caravans, in which losses were not all-or-nothing and the causes of damage were not always observable and verifiable. By the time the organizational demands of Muslim maritime merchants became acute, Islamic law had already rejected the sea loan.

A second, supplementary, explanation is that the commenda was available to Islamic merchants, as will be shown in chapter 5, from the dawn of Islam. Whenever maritime merchants needed external capital, they resorted to the commenda; being an equity-investment and profit-sharing institution, it was not subject to the prohibition on usury. The commenda became available to Christian merchants only a few centuries later.

A third possible explanation, not fully aligned with the previous ones, is that Islamic law prohibited usury only among Muslims. There is evidence for the borrowing of money, even in the form of sea loans, from Christian and Jewish moneylenders.[73] The existence of large Christian and Jewish communities in the Middle East made sea loans available to Muslim merchants without violating the usury prohibition of their religion.

There was no stark difference between the content and the enforcement of usury prohibition in medieval Islam and Christianity. The heyday of the sea loan in Latin Christianity, unlike in Eastern Christianity, was short-lived. The intensified theological attack on it galvanized in the decretal *naviganti* issued by Pope Gregory IX in 1234, which condemned sea loan interest as usurious.[74] The rationale for the *naviganti* was that, in a sea loan, if the ship arrived safely, the creditor would receive a profit, regardless of the business outcome or whether the debtor gained or lost. Sea loans were not considered true partnerships because a partnership demands that all risk of loss be borne jointly, whereas in sea loans the lenders transferred most of the responsibility to the borrowers.[75] By the middle of the thirteenth century it was barely used.[76]

Did Jewish law recognize the sea loan? Can we learn anything from its attitude to the sea loan about the differences between Christian and Islamic law? Babylonian Talmud prohibited usury.[77] Until the early eleventh century, there were no rules or cases discussing sea loans.[78] The earliest known post-Talmudic case to explicitly address sea loans was that of twelfth-century French Rabbi Meir ben Isaac (also known as Rabbi Meir MiCarcasson).[79] Ben Isaac, who lived in Carcassonne, not far from the Mediterranean port of Narbonne in southern France, permitted sea loans in his Halachic book *Sefer HaEzer*. Ben Isaac's great-grandson, Ishtori Haparchi (Isaac HaKohen Ben Moses, 1280–1355), who grew up in Provence and was expelled to Spain and eventually migrated to North Africa, agreed with Ben Isaac's ruling.[80] However, other rabbis in later generations ruled otherwise. For example, Ribash (Rabbi Issac ben Sheset Perfet, 1326–1408) addressed sea loans in a *responsum* written after 1388 to Rabbi Moshe Gabbai: ". . . it seems clear that it is prohibited for a Jew to lend his fellow Jew a gold dinar, worth 20 dinars upon the security of a ship going overseas, and that he [the debtor] should give him 24 dinars [in return], when she [the ship] returns [safely], because this is a loan and he [the debtor] stipulates a specific amount of interest to him."[81] Yet, Ribash approved the "current custom" among merchants and mariners to pay for insuring the goods on a ship, apparently approving third-party insurance and not insurance as part of a loan agreement.[82] One could speculate that Jews in Christian societies who approved of the sea loan recognized it, while Jews who lived in Muslim societies that rejected it refused to approve it. But the observations are too sporadic for us to establish a conclusive argument.

The sea loan migrated for centuries widely and freely throughout the Mediterranean and the Middle East. The formulation of prohibition on usury by Christianity, Judaism, and Islam roughly between 200–700 CE had a major impact on its migration route. All three religions prohibited usury, yet they treated the sea loan differently. These differences resulted from different demand patterns, different histories, and different substitute institutions.

THE FUNDUQ, KHAN, AND CARAVANSERAI

Inns that hosted traveling merchants were known by different names in different periods and regions: *pandocheion, funduq, fondaco, khan, caravanserai, leggia, wakala,* and *ribat*. Yet, according to most accounts, most of them shared a common origin, exhibited similar features, and had a continuous two-millennia-long genealogy. As such, they should be viewed as migratory institutions for the purposes of the present book. Why institutions? In the material sense they were just buildings that could be viewed as subjects for architectural history. But they performed a very important function in long-distance trade. They provided accommodation, protection, food, water, and supplies to traveling traders and their riding animals. They were important hubs of information. They were marketplaces. They served rulers for customs and tax-collection purposes. A network of such inns along the Silk Route allowed private itinerant traders to overcome the entry barriers to engaging in long-distance trade. Without such institutions to provide services even to individual low-means traders, the entry barriers for this overland trade would have been much higher, allowing only states or large associations to enter. The inns in town played another crucial role as sites for cross-cultural transactions and exchanges. They hosted foreign merchants and provided a place for them to transact with locals.

The study of the migration of these inns is particularly useful for our purposes because they left much more significant physical remnants than our other migratory institution, the commenda and the sea loan. Methodological tools applicable to the study of the migration of domestic animals and writing, such as archeological excavations (discussed in the methodological sections of this book), are relevant here as well. We can draw on the physical survey of some 2,500 observations of such inns, some of them well preserved, many reconstructed by archeologists and architects, scattered throughout Eurasia, often dated precisely, and often referenced in inscriptions and travelers' accounts and on the excellent study by Olivia Constable on the migration of the funduq.

The Greek word *pandocheion* literally means "accepting all comers." This institution, which provided paid lodging, was only one among different types of hostelry available to travelers in the classical and late antique world.[83] It was mentioned by Demosthenes (384–322 BCE) and in Jewish and early Christian texts (including Luke's gospel). Archeological and epigraphic evidence of the pandocheion is available from fourth- to sixth-century CE Byzantine Syria, particularly from sites around Antioch.

When the Arabs took control of the Byzantine cities in the near east, many of their institutions were absorbed into the Muslim context, including the pandocheion.[84] By the eighth and ninth centuries CE, a mention of a Muslim institution named *funduq* appeared in the Arab texts.[85] The oldest surviving inscription bearing the term is from the late ninth century. It was etymologically close to the Greek *pandocheion*, to the Hebrew *pundaq*, and to similar Syriac and Aramaic words. Its structure was similar, though not identical, to that of earlier Byzantine pandocheions, and it fulfilled similar functions. Its early appearances are from Umayyad Syria, around Palmyra. All these matches support Constable's conclusion that the Arab funduq is a descendant of the Byzantine pandocheion.[86]

Over the next two centuries, the funduq spread from the Eastern Mediterranean, westward. One could find the funduq in Egypt (Cairo/Fustat,[87] Alexandria), the Maghreb (as far as Fez and Marrakesh), Spain (Granada, Cordoba, Toledo), and Sicily (Palermo).[88] In the Eastern Mediterranean, the term used by contemporaries gradually switched between the eleventh and thirteenth centuries from *funduq* to *khan*. Initially, the same institution, the very same building, was referred to by some contemporary observers as *funduq* and by others as *khan*. The switch could possibly be attributed to the migration of Turkic-speaking Seljuk and Ottoman tribes to Anatolia. Urban khans maintained the features of funduqs. But after defeating the Mongols and Crusaders, the Ayyubid dynasty began constructing khans also along the caravan roads leading east, connecting to the Silk Route.

The roadside khans were different from urban khans and funduqs (the term still being in use at that time in North Africa and Spain). While urban khans were more often owned by private individuals and waqfs, the khans along the caravan routes were constructed and owned by rulers. While the same town usually had several khans, roadside khans were constructed a day's travel (20–40 km) apart. While urban khans often catered for merchants dealing with specific goods, roadside ones catered to the needs of all travelers, including officials, pilgrims, and traders of all sorts. Rural khans tended to be larger, fortified, and locked at night.[89]

Ibn Hawqal offers a classic description of the role of urban funduqs as commercial spaces in Nishapur in Persia in the 970s: "Funduqs where the merchants lodge and do commercial business, and there are places in them for buying and selling. Each funduq is known for the particular variety of merchandise predominantly brought there."[90] There were funduqs that handled goods of high quality (silk, for example), while the trade in other funduqs focused on staples and more basic commodities such as grain, fruits, salt, and such like.[91]

Just as the funduq and khan were not always clearly distinct from one another, neither were the caravanserai and the khan. The earliest evidence

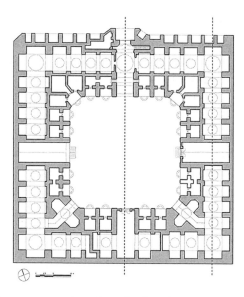

4.1. Floorplan of a caravanserai from the Safavid era (1501–1736) in Karaj, Iran.
Source: photo by Babak Gholizadeh, "Carvansara Plan," https://en.wikipedia.org
/wiki/File:Carvansara_plan.png.

of buildings called caravanserais is from Iran and dates to the eleventh–
twelfth centuries. The Persian *kārvānsarā* is a compound word combining
kārvān (derives from the word *karban* which means "one who protects
trade") with *sara* (palace, building with enclosed courts), to which the
Turkish suffix *-yi* is added.[92]

Caravanserai buildings varied in size. Figure 4.1 shows a sample floorplan of a caravanserai. Ribat-i Karim, in Northwestern Iran, has all the
attributes of later caravanserais: fortified exterior, single monumental
entrance, large internal courtyard framed by arcades, a central well, stables
on the diagonal, and individual "cells" to accommodate travelers, distributed behind the arcades.[93] Fortified buildings appeared in Central Asia
from the tenth century onward. Seljuk caravanserais appeared in Anatolia
from the twelfth century onward. The Saljuk caravanserais in Anatolia
served as symbols of the empire's administrative and economic power.[94]

The main function of the caravanserai, like the roadside khan, was to
provide protection and accommodation. They provided an opportunity
to renew water and food supplies, cooking facilities and a fireplace,
bathing services, and houses for prayer like temples or mosques.[95] Beyond immediate travel necessities they facilitated trade by providing

opportunity to buy local products, particularly in urban locations, to meet merchant travelers from other regions and exchange goods and information with them.[96] On a more general level the caravanserai created the exchange of cultures, languages and ideas by providing a platform for social and cultural interaction among travelers.[97]

There were many variations to this simple formula, in different periods and regions. Most caravanserais had to have room to store merchandise. Larger caravanserais usually had at least one resident porter, whose task was to maintain order and be responsible for security.[98] Some caravanserais had small garrison. During the Mamluk and Ottoman eras and possibly in other periods and regions in which central government had more capacity caravanserais also served as a poll station for collecting taxes and for administrative control.[99] In some regions they served official travelers and postal services.

Hillenbrand classifies three groups of urban caravanserais: those with an open courtyard and an emphasis on the provision of accommodation and stabling; those with an open courtyard, limited accommodation and stabling, and an emphasis on trading facilities; and those consisting of a building of more modest dimensions with a fully closed roof, providing accommodation only for merchants and travelers, not for their animals.[100] Constable compares funduqs with caravanserais and holds that the latter, in urban locations, functioned in very similar ways to the former.[101]

It is surprising how little is known about the organization, ownership and the finance of the construction and operation of caravanserais. It is hard to tell whether this results from lack of historical records or from the interests of historians. Some caravanserais were established by rulers or local administrations. Other caravanserais were established and owned by local individuals and families or endowed as waqf by wealthy persons. There are reports of caravanserai that offered free services and others that charged use fees. The motivation for constructing caravanserai was the encouragement of trade or alternatively the monitoring of travelers and collection of taxes from them, or both. It seems as though defense against external enemies or generation of profits from fees were not leading motivation.[102]

The caravanserai expanded eastward from Iran well into Central Asia, to the Tian Shan mountain passages and Taklamakan Desert oases and the frontiers of China, and into Afghanistan and the borders of India.[103]

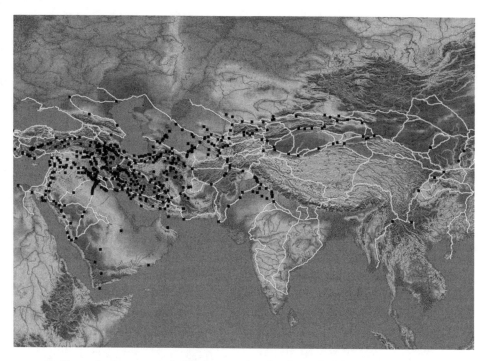

4.2. Network of caravanserais (black squares) and trade roads (white lines) in Eurasia. Data from P. Lebigre and E. Thomopoulos, EVCAU. Source: reprinted from UNESCO, www.unesco.org/culture/dialogue/eastwest/caravan/countries.htm by permission of EVCAU Laboratory.

A network of funduqs, khans, and caravanserais ultimately stretched from Iberia to South and East Asia, allowing merchants to travel overland by caravans throughout Eurasia and by ships to port towns across the Mediterranean. Figure 4.2 shows the vast network of caravanserais and trade roads in Eurasia.

Figure 4.3 shows one of the most eastern caravanserais, the Tash Rabat, in modern-day eastern Kyrgyzstan. It is located at an altitude of 3,200 m, and served Silk Route caravans stopping on their way to cross a Tian Shan mountain pass, en route to Kashgar, around the edge of the Taklamakan Desert, to Turfan and into China. This stone caravanserai is dated to the fifteenth century, with possible older construction going back to the tenth century.

The importation of the funduq by the Latin world was made possible by means of a particularly intriguing three-stage process. The Europeans

4.3. The Tash Rabat caravanserai.

first used funduqs in the Eastern Mediterranean, then conquered funduqs during the Crusades, and lastly emulated them in Europe. The revival of maritime commerce in the Mediterranean resulted in European merchants, initially mostly Italians, visiting Muslim cities in the Eastern Mediterranean and North Africa. When looking for places to lodge and transact, Europeans became aware of the funduq. The earliest reference to European merchants' residence in Egypt comes from the late tenth century.[104] By the twelfth century, the funduqs in major Islamic towns began serving the needs of a broader cross-cultural clientele and not only Muslims.[105] The existence of funduqs in the Middle East and their absence in Europe created a disparity; Europeans were able to frequent Islamic ports while European ports were much less frequently visited by Muslim merchants.[106]

The second stage in the introduction of the funduq to Europeans was by the conquest of Islamic lands by Christians in Spain, Southern Italy

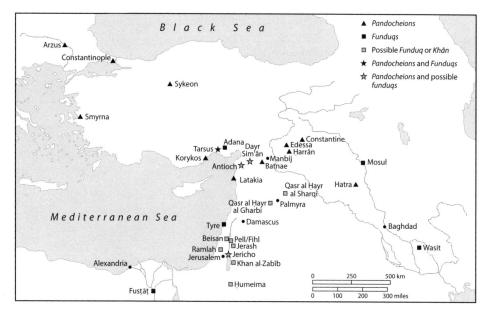

4.4. Distribution of the pandocheions and funduqs in the Eastern Mediterranean (second to tenth centuries). Source: Constable (2003, p. 12).

and Sicily, and Palestine and the Levant, by the eleventh–thirteenth centuries. Cities that housed many funduqs were conquered during the Reconquista and the Crusades. These funduqs maintained the same structure and function under Christian rulers. Europeans called this preexisting hostelry *fundicum* in Latin, or *fondaco* in Italian. The two maps in figures 4.4 and 4.5, in Constable's masterly representation, demonstrate the process vividly.

Figure 4.4 shows how a Greco-Byzantine institution was transformed into the Arab institution by the tenth century. The process was centered in the area around Antioch. The second map, figure 4.5, shows how the Islamic funduqs were taken over by Europeans and converted into fondacos in the tenth to fifteenth centuries. This process was unfolding along the shore from Alexandria, through Jaffa, Acre, and Beirut to Antioch and Aleppo. A similar process took place in Spain and (in a less well-documented way) in Sicily.[107]

The fondaco only appears in documents referring to Europe from the middle of the twelfth century. Funduqs converted into fondacos are found

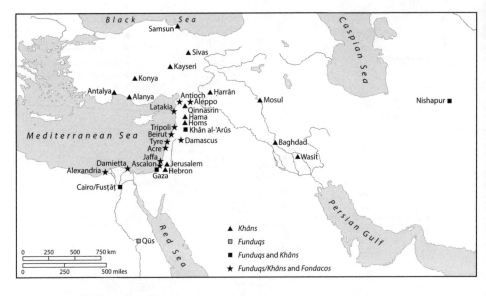

4.5. Distribution of funduqs, fondacos, and khans in the eastern Islamic Mediterranean (tenth to fifteenth centuries). Source: Constable (2003, p. 69).

initially in Sicily and Iberia. They gradually migrated northward, from southern Spain to Barcelona, Montpelier, and Marseille, and from Sicily to Naples, Florence, Venice, and Genoa. By the thirteenth century there were many versions of the word *fundaq/fondaco* in Latin and other southern European languages. Although European fundacos shared many characteristics with fundacos in Muslim cities, not all of the fondaco's functions were necessary in Western Europe. The regulated residential aspect, one of the main characteristics of the fondaco in the Muslim world, was not much needed in European cities that had separate local hostelries and no cross-cultural trade. These new European fondacos all shared a purely commercial and fiscal utility. Residential fondacos were often short-lived in Christian Europe, appearing only briefly during the twelfth and thirteenth centuries. Special buildings used by foreign merchants already existed by then and were not generally called fondacos, they were referred to as houses (*domus*), hostels (*hospitia*), or increasingly, by the fourteenth and fifteenth centuries, as *loggias*.[108] So Europe embarked on a distinct path of institutional configuration in which commercial fondacos were used only for storing and taxing goods and not for accommodating people. In the fourteenth century, in many locations the fondaco ceased to be a separate building and became part of a larger complex or structure. By that time, fondacos in many Italian cities were frequently connected with banking, lending, and accounting. They bore some resemblance to the Muslim funduq but also assumed new identities and roles. They occupied new fiscal niches and served as state warehouses, storage facilities, and spaces for private business affairs.[109]

Why did the nonurban caravanserai not migrate to Europe? The answer is, mainly for geographical reasons. The caravanserai served functions that were most needed in long desert and steppe roads, such as those in Arabia, the Middle East, Persia, and Central Asia. Why did the funduq— as an institution that combines lodging and commercial services—not migrate into Christian Europe? The explanation here is partly on the demand side and partly on the supply side. The funduq offered solutions to problems related to cross-cultural and interreligious trade. For reasons that are exogenous to our discussion, there were many more Christian traders in the Islamic Middle East than Muslim traders in Christian Europe. The Christian traders needed lodging and religious services, and, at the same time, the Muslim rulers wanted to separate them from the Muslim population of their towns and to regulate them. On the supply side, lodging solutions for travelers evolved in Northern Europe separately from commercial functions. By the time the combined Islamic solution arrived in Southern Europe, the Europeans, with a few exceptions, took only the term and the commercial functions of the funduq, and supplied the accommodation needed through their indigenous hostels and lodges.[110]

Venice is a singular exception that supports this explanation. The Fondaco dei Tedeschi was constructed in 1228 for German (and other Imperial) merchants, integrating several functions including a warehouse, a market, and restricted living quarters. It maintained its residential function for centuries. Why? The Venetians imposed this because they wanted to regulate and monitor the German merchants; they were similar in this sense to the Muslim rulers that required Latin merchants to reside in funduqs. Why only the Venetians? Quite simply, because they could. Genoa and Milan tried and failed. In western Italy, when city authorities became too strict or demanding, the foreign merchants moved on to the next city, say from Milan to Genoa, or from Genoa to Marseille, Pisa, or

Livorno. Venice had a singular location as the only access for German merchants crossing the Alps through the Brenner Pass and wishing to reach the Adriatic, the Byzantine Empire, and the Levant. The Germans could not bypass it and had to abide by its demands.[111] The Fondaco dei Turchi, constructed in 1381, is a rare case in which Muslim merchants resided in a European port, and in which commercial and residential functions were combined, as they were in the funduq. Ironically, Venice had a funduq to accommodate Muslims. The Venetian authorities re-quired—in 1516 and, before that, in 1252—that Jews, initially of Italian and German origins and later also of Sephardic origins, reside and trade in a confined quarter of the city. By this, the first Jewish Ghetto in Europe was created. The explanation of the Muslim and Jewish residential cum commercial confinement is possibly the same as with the Germans. But Venice was the exception in Latin Europe.

CONCLUSION

The migration paths of the sea loan and the funduq were distinct. The sea loan has its origins in Phoenician and Greek practices, and was inte-grated into Roman law. It survived the acceptance of Christianity, de-spite its hostility to usury, as the official religion of the Roman Empire. It was commonly used by merchants in late medieval Italian port cities. It was not accepted by Islam because it was considered usurious. It made its way to East Asia with the early European merchants traveling around the Cape.

The funduq/khan/caravanserai was an institution that began in the Greece of antiquity, made its way in adapted forms to the Byzantine Em-pire, the Arab Middle East, to the Islamic Maghreb and Iberia, to Anatolia and Persia, to Central Asia, and only in a transformed and restricted way to Latin Europe. The funduq/khan/caravanserai offered solutions to the problems related to long-distance trade—solutions that were not unique to only one location or culture but were rather quite universal. As a result, it traveled widely. Yet it encountered both obstacles and resistance that were of different levels and natures in different parts of Eurasia.

The fact that the funduq and the sea loan originated in the Eastern Mediterranean and coexisted in that region for a while did not lead to similar migration routes throughout Eurasia. Resistance to the importation of institutions could lead to repulsion and rejection. The sea loan was rejected by Islam for theological reasons. The funduq was not imported by Latin Europe. Objection to an institution could lead to mutations and efforts to hide the foreign or objectionable origins and to fit the institution into preexisting institutional configurations. Such was the pattern of migration and transmutation of the commenda, to which we now turn in chapter 5.

~ 5 ~

The Commenda

The commenda is regarded as a very important institution that played a major role in the commercial revolution of the Middle Ages and in the transition to capitalism.[1] Under various terms and in several variations, it appeared in the early modern era in many regions and trade destinations throughout Eurasia.[2] It is a prime example of a migratory institution—that is, one that was developed in one place (or two at the most) and migrated through much of Eurasia.

This chapter discusses the characteristics of the commenda, its origins, and its migration. This survey of the migration of the commenda synthesizes the discrete bodies of literature that discuss the appearances of the commenda in various regions of Eurasia. The Italian commenda has been intensely studied for more than a century now. The Islamic commenda has been a popular topic of study for the last half century. Other appearances escaped historians' attention until recently or have even been neglected altogether. The isolated study of each appearance of the commenda narrowed historians' perspective and led to several major shortcomings. First, its widespread appearance was not fully perceived. Putting the appearances side by side enhances the notion that the commenda was the ultimate migratory institution. Second, the methods developed in examining each of the appearances were not applied to other appearances, as a result of which the study of each case applied a limited set of methodologies and theoretical tools. Third, the question of migration was either investigated with respect to one migration move (Islam to Italy, Italy to the Baltic) or not investigated at all. This limited the ability to identify additional links and repeated patterns. It also limited the application of methodologies, confining the examination to a morphological comparison of organizational features and inference from them, irrespective of whether the given appearance was independently developed or copied. This chapter aims at overcoming these limits.

THE FEATURES OF A PROTOTYPICAL COMMENDA

While it is common wisdom among historians that the commenda was widely used in late medieval and early modern trade and was essential for the economic development of the Middle East and Europe, its features are not well understood. Many historians are familiar with the fact that it was a contract between two parties, an investor and a traveling trader, and that the two split the profit at the end of the voyage. But issues such as the liability of either party, the discretion of the traveler, the accounting of profits, and the relationships with third parties are often skimmed over or, worse, misconstrued. The legal categorization of the commenda is also not clear to many. Is it a partnership, an agency contract, a loan, or a sui generis contract? Before answering these questions, one has to understand the structure of the available sources on the commenda and the level of understanding of its features that these sources allow.

The nature of the surviving sources makes it possible to provide a thick and inclusive description of the commenda and its legal features only in the Islamic context. The surviving Arab-Islamic sources on the commenda are mostly legal treatises from the late eighth century to the eleventh century.[3] They discuss various ramifications of problems relating to the functioning of the commenda, based possibly on both actual examples and hypotheticals. This literature provides responses to a wide array of legal inquiries. It is of a highly juristic quality and provides refined analytical insights, but it does not deal with abstractions, rationales, or theories.

The surviving Jewish records on the commenda are to be found almost exclusively in the Cairo Geniza repository, and date from the eleventh to thirteenth centuries. These were mainly merchants' letters that reflect the everyday use of the commenda. The records contain very few legal materials and just a few responses and reports on rabbinical court decisions. In addition, the code of Maimonides, *Mishneh Torah*, written between 1170 and 1180, has references to the commenda as a gentiles' partnership. As the commenda was not integrated into Jewish law, the Jewish sources, written in the Middle East, can at most add a perspective to the understanding of Islamic commenda.[4]

Surviving Christian-Latin records are either contracts or, more often, records of the existence of commenda contracts, as were often preserved in an abbreviated form in notarial and municipal archives. Though the information preserved was mostly of practices and not law, it is extensive. Altogether, thousands of contracts and recordings of contracts survived in major Italian towns from the twelfth to fourteenth centuries.[5]

The basic commenda was a bilateral contract involving only two parties, the sedentary investing party and the traveling agent, who would follow the itinerary of his principal. The commenda was an equity-investment contract, specifying investments and payoffs. The investing party provided capital in the form of goods and cash (used for the purchase of the trade goods and for travel-related costs), and was entitled to a share of the profit. The traveling party typically did not invest capital. The commenda was also a labor contract with the traveling party investing labor, expertise, information, contacts, and bodily risk. The profits of the commenda were split between the two parties.[6]

The investor conveyed capital (in Islam, in cash only; in the Latin world, in goods as well) to a separate pool of assets. The traveling merchant was granted control over the pool and traveled with it to a faraway port or market. The traveling party was thus geographically separated from the investing party and did not work under his direct instructions or supervision. The investor could not fully predict, ex ante, the circumstances, opportunities, or risks. He provided the traveler with a pool of assets, subject to business instructions that were considered, in legal terms, a power of attorney or a mandate.[7] In the Islamic Hanafi school this mandate was discretionary. It could be as wide and permissive as "Act with it as you see fit." It could limit destinations or goods. In other words, in Hanafi law, the mandate was, by default, wide and could be opted out of in favor of a more restrictive one. In the Maliki school, by contrast, the scope of the mandate was strict and confined to buying and selling goods for cash. As far as we can tell from the work of Udovitch, this definition of the scope of the mandate was binding and not only offered as the default.[8]

Could the traveler impose increased risks on the investor to increase his own payoff? He could sell on credit to third parties. But could he also borrow from third parties to increase the volume of his trade? He could borrow, but only as long as he did not borrow beyond the value of the assets and as long as he kept the assets. He could not leverage based on investors' capital to increase his own payoff. He could go to riskier markets or buy riskier goods. But these actions could be prevented by a restrictive mandate (as long as its infringements could be effectively monitored).

Who was liable for what in a commenda? It has been argued that the investing party was a limited partner, similar to the limited partner of a limited partnership or a shareholder in a limited corporation; however, as far as I can tell, this was not the contemporary conceptualization. The investor was not liable vis-à-vis third parties beyond the capital originally invested. This resulted, first, from the fact that his existence or identity was often not known. Second, it resulted from the remoteness between him and the third party. The third and most significant reason is that the traveling merchant was not allowed to leverage. Without leverage (and without tort liability), no exposure to liability beyond the investment of the investing party could be formed. He risked losing his investment, but not his other assets, which often constituted great wealth. The commenda contract may be conceptualized as creating a new pool of assets, a fund, separated from that of either party.[9] Creditors of the commenda could reach its pool of assets, but not the investing party's private pool of assets.

What was the liability of the traveling trader? That party could lose his own investment in the commenda, in the form of his labor, and expertise. But he was not personally liable for the loss of the commenda capital as long as he did not breach his duties or act beyond his mandate. If he traveled to an unauthorized port, borrowed and leveraged, or intentionally caused damage to the goods, the traveling party become personally liable for the loss of the investment. But the traveler was not liable for any routine loss. Internally, the traveling party would be liable toward the investing party only when he acted outside the scope of his agreed mandate or breached his fiduciary duties by not acting according to common merchant customs and practices. The sea risk was borne by the investor. This was similar to a sea loan. The business risk for the invested capital was also borne by the investor.[10] And this was *not* the case in a sea loan.

A key feature of the commenda was the use of a separate pool of assets. The pool was created when the investor transferred money to the commenda account and the traveler assumed control over that money.[11] As mentioned earlier, in Islam, only money and not goods (the distinctions between the two being drawn by the jurists) could be deposited into the account. The capital of the commenda was now conceptually separated from both the assets of the investor and the personal assets of the traveler. The traveler applied it to trade according to the mandate. Related expenses were attributed to the commenda account. On the termination of the commenda, the original capital invested was returned to the investor, expenses deducted from the balance, and the remaining sum split between the two parties, typically under Islam in a fifty-fifty split, though deviation was possible based on the level of investment or experience of the traveling party. The creation of a separate pool of assets had ramifications not only for liability, as mentioned, but also for accounting techniques. The commenda could barely function in an oral society. Written accounts were essential when expenses were numerous and spread over time.

The duration of the commenda was also affected by the creation of a separate pool of assets. A commenda could last for just a single voyage, as was often the case early in its history. But it could also last for several years. Two basic courses of action could be followed. In one, the commenda would terminate and a similar commenda between the two parties, subject to the same terms, would succeed it. In the other, the two parties could split profits from time to time, after settling accounts, without the original capital investment being repaid and without terminating the commenda.[12]

Figure 5.1 shows the structure of the commenda partnership, including the separate pool of assets and the parties involved, as discussed here.

The commenda appeared in different places and times, in several variations:

1. Profit splitting appeared in different variants. In Islam, the common scheme split the profits fifty-fifty. A common arrangement in Italy was 75 percent to the investing partner and 25 percent to the traveling partner, but other splitting arrangements, including two-thirds to one-third, and so forth, were also used.

2. The common commenda involved investment only by the sedentary party, but an important Italian variant, according to Raymond and Lopez, was one in which the traveling party also invested money, which affected the

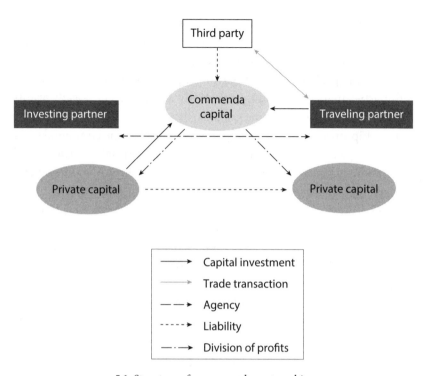

5.1. Structure of a commenda partnership.

splitting of profits.[13] The first variant is often termed a "bilateral" commenda and the second a "multilateral" commenda.

3. The traveling party could, if not prohibited, create a second commenda in which he placed all or part of the goods in the hands of a third person who traveled to an even more distant market. The traveling party of the first commenda became the investing party of the second. This variant was recognized both in Italy and in Islam.

4. The commenda could be established not only with respect to distinct goods but also a share in a pool of goods or in a ship.

5. The two-party commenda could form part of a complex multilateral system. For example, a single traveling party could pool together goods from numerous investing parties into a commenda, offering all concerned the benefits of economy of scale.

6. Conversely, an investing party could split his investment among several traveling parties[14] to spread his risk.[15]

The commenda is not an employment or a loan contract, as the payoffs are not determined ex ante but rather ex post. It is an equity investment. The traveler does not receive a predetermined wage or interest but rather a share in the profits. It is not a partnership, either. It is not the case that both parties manage the enterprise jointly and represent it as its agents in relation to outsiders. Some consider it a predecessor of the limited partnership, an asymmetric, multilateral contract.[16] The commenda was a more complex institution than one may grasp at first sight. It determined the relationship between parties on several levels, including investment, agency, managerial control, risk allocation, profit allocation, and the creation of a separate pool of assets. Hence, it should be viewed, in modern terms, as a nexus of contracts for equity investments as well as a template or standard-form contract. When selecting the commenda, the parties established a fixed and detailed contract containing only a few default rules that could be tailored to their needs. They selected a well-developed and detailed form of business organization.

To sum up, the commenda combined several functions within a single legal-economic institution. It provided an opportunity for efficiency gains compared to standard agency and loan contracts. It allowed the formulation of tailor-made incentivization schemes for traveling agents. It was also an outlet for risk-prone passive investors. It allowed landowners who were keen to invest in risky projects while protecting their family fortune to limit their liability. It enabled young merchants with limited funds to cross the overseas trade threshold and to leverage their business. The single commenda contract not only brought several contracts together, but it was itself also part of a complex web of contracts. Each of the parties to that contract could be, and often was, a party to other commenda contracts. Thanks to this configuration, the commenda could serve as a risk-spreading institution and an invaluable building block in mercantile networks.

THE ORIGINS OF THE COMMENDA: ISLAMIC *QIRAD* AND *MUDARABA*

The first well-documented appearance of the commenda in fully fledged form was in early Islamic Arabia.[17] Why there, of all places? Two answers have been offered: one, that it was indigenously Arabian and resulted from the unique needs of the cross-desert incense caravan trade; and two, that it represented just a further step in the development of earlier Byzantine and Middle Eastern organizational forms, as used in Mecca and reflected in early Islamic texts. A third possible view, that the commenda was developed for the first time by Islamic jurists, is not held by many historians.

With the expansion of the Islamic commenda, it was named differently in different regions and by different schools: *mudaraba, qirad,* or *muqarada*.[18] From its origins in the Arabian Peninsula, the commenda traveled, with conquerors, religious leaders, legal scholars, and merchants, both west and east. It traveled with rapidly expanding Islam during the Umayyad Caliphate to Iraq and Syria, to Palestine and Egypt, and to the Maghreb.[19] But it is important to note that the basic features of the commenda were similar in all major schools of early Muslim law.[20] This stands in sharp contrast to the variations between the major schools, Hanafi on the one hand and Maliki and Shafii on the other, with respect to general partnerships. The uniformity of the commenda throughout Islam can support the "single origins" hypothesis. The differences between the schools with respect to the general partnership lend support to its classification as an endogenous institution with multiple origins. The legal texts on partnership written in the second half of the eighth century include a well-developed discussion of complex aspects of the commenda.[21] The level of sophistication is clearly evident from the discussion of its features in the previous section, which is mostly based on the Islamic sources of that period. This can lend support to the assertion that the commenda had earlier origins and that it was already well developed when it was first dealt with by Islamic jurisprudence.

With regard to the question of where the commenda originated, the first answer, offered by Udovitch, writing in the 1960s and 1970s, claimed that it was, in fact, in use in the long-distance caravan trade of the Arabian Peninsula and its surroundings before the rise of Islam, but was captured in texts only with the development of Islamic law.[22] It was not explicitly mentioned, as such, in the Quran. However, according to Udovitch, the later prophetic and legal texts reflected pre-Islamic and early Islamic reality. Numerous early Muslim traditions attribute its use to the Prophet himself. The Prophet, before his prophethood, traveled to Syria to trade there in goods given to him by Khadijah, his wife-to-be.[23] According to tradition, the Prophet was the traveling partner and Khadijah the investing partner in this commenda-like partnership. Other traditions view the dealings with merchandise of two sons of Caliph 'Umar (634–44) upon returning from Iraq to Medina as involving commenda. We are further told that the third caliph, Uthman (644–56), used to invest his money in the form of a qirad on the basis of half profit for himself and half profit for the agent. Whether or not these anecdotes are historically authentic, Malik and his contemporaries in the latter half of the eighth century certainly believed them to be true.[24] It is also clear without any doubt that, whatever its earlier history, by the second half of the eighth century the commenda was used and distinctly conceptualized in the Islamic Middle East. It operated there at least two hundred years, possibly even four hundred years, before its first appearance in the Italian cities.

This answer, namely, that the commenda was developed indigenously in Arabia, was questioned by other historians. One alternative line of research casts doubt on the uniqueness of Arabian caravan trade and suggested searching for origins of the commenda in the caravan trade of the larger commercial hubs of the Middle East. Another line suggested that we should look at a wider context, the sources of influence on Islamic law in general, sources in Greco-Roman, Byzantine, Jewish, and Sassanid law.

Our sources for the pre-Islamic Jāhilīyah period, in which the northern Arabians had no system of writing, are limited to traditions, legends, proverbs, and, above all, to poems, none of which, however, was committed to the written form before the second and third centuries after the Hijrah, two or four hundred years after the events they were supposed to record.[25] Based on these limited sources, historians concluded that the Arabia trade was in high-value luxury items from Yemen (incense and spices) and, by way of the Yemen, from India and beyond (precious metals and stones, dyes, silks, and spices). According to some scholars, such as Crone[26] and Bulliet,[27] contrary to this common belief, Mecca, the birthplace of the Islamic commenda, was not on any major trading routes, and its trade was not a transit trade but was mostly for local consumption. They claim that the trade of Arabia as a whole was not particularly developed compared to that of the Fertile Crescent, the Middle East, or Central Asia. In a nutshell, Crone rejects the view of earlier scholars of Mecca as a center of trade, for three main reasons: first, the location of

Mecca; second, the fact that Mecca is a barren place; and third, the problem of available commodities. Mecca was away from the main incense routes, at the edge of the peninsula and not on a natural oasis. Crone added: "Neither the incense trade nor the transit trade survived long enough for the Meccans to inherit them, and there was no such thing as Mecca trade in incense, spices, and foreign luxury."[28] Crone's work was criticized by later historians. Donner asserted that Mecca *did* rise to a position of great importance in Arabia during the sixth century. This was partly the result of the skill with which the Meccan tribe of Quraysh organized a network of trade contacts spreading over the whole peninsula, and partly a result of the presence there of an important religious shrine and pilgrimage center, a Haram.[29] The question at hand for us, though, is not whether Mecca was a local center of trade or an international trade center. It is whether trade in Arabia more generally created the functional need for the development of the qirad-commenda.

One possible pre-Islamic Arabian source of qirad was the *ilaf* agreement noticed in passing by Udovitch. *Ilaf* agreements were formed by the leaders of the Quraysh tribe of Mecca with other tribes through whose territories Quraysh merchants had to pass on their way to the fertile lands of Syria and Iraq. The *ilaf* agreement set up the basis for a share in trade profit for the heads of these tribes and apparently for the employment of the men of the tribes as escorts of the Quraysh caravans.[30] It has some resemblance to the qirad. One party invests in trade; the other provides a service (or extorts protection fees). But there are clear differences, the most noticeable being that the *ilaf* is a deal between collectives and not individuals. This explanation could well fit a historical view, such as Donner's, according to which trade in sixth-century Arabia was not exceptionally developed. Nevertheless, according to Donner, the Quraysh did have a unique role in the development of the commenda.

As the leading centers of the caravan trade networks were Palmyra and Petra, and not Mecca, historians may search for the origins of the commenda there. Both Petra and Palmyra maintained standing armies primarily to protect caravans and caravan station from robbers. The rise of the Palmyrene caravan trade appears to have been closely linked with the city's ability to protect routes from bands of roving bandits. Both the Nabataean and Palmyrene armies were made up of cavalry soldiers riding camels and horses. In addition to official protection, armed private escorts were sometimes hired.[31] "At Palmyra, caravans were often financed by one or more wealthy merchants or, in the case of a particularly large caravan, by the city itself. This pattern of finance and organization of caravans was apparent in the period before the Islamic conquest. In addition to very wealthy investors, middle class townspeople also invested in caravan enterprises."[32] There is no evidence for the use of the commenda, or a precursor of the commenda, in the organization of Nabataean and Palmyrene caravans. Yet not much is known about their organization, and thus little that is useful for us can be inferred.

According to several historians, early Islamic law and legal institutions at large were inspired by older Middle Eastern legal systems: the Greco-Roman and Byzantine, the Jewish, and the Sassanid systems.[33] So the roots of the commenda might be found in any one of these. Indeed, the qirad has some similarity to earlier institutions, the Jewish *isqa* and the Byzantine *chreokoinonia*. But, as demonstrated by Udovitch, there are also dissimilarities that make the hypotheses of direct influence questionable.[34]

The main purpose of this survey of the deliberations among historians on the origins of the commenda is not to settle the long-standing debate and reach a single and unequivocal conclusion. The main purpose is to learn what the most promising methods for approaching the question are, which environments foster the development of such institutions, and which factors can impact their migration. But as I cannot resist the temptation to provide my take on the issue, I would say that I am more convinced by the argument that the Islamic commenda did develop out of earlier Middle Eastern institutional building blocks. This explanation seems to me to be more likely than the uniqueness of the needs of the Arabian caravan trade. But the sophistication of Islamic jurisprudence and the expansion of Islamic trade networks from Iberia to Central Asia contributed to the high level of sophistication of the Islamic commenda.

THE ITALIAN COMMENDA: INDEPENDENTLY DEVELOPED OR A TRANSPLANT?

Late-nineteenth-century European historians such as Weber asserted that the commenda had its roots in Roman law, made its early appearance in vulgar Roman law of the early Middle Ages, and became widespread with

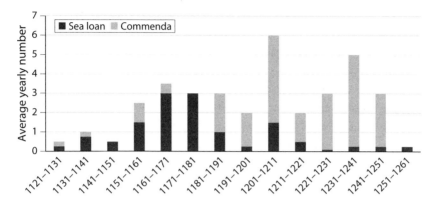

5.2. Documented sea loans and commenda contracts and their distribution over time in Venice. Source: González de Lara (2008, p. 253).

the revival of trade in tenth- and eleventh-century Italy.[35] But later studies of Italy acknowledge that there are only a few vague hints at the existence of the commenda, in law or practice, before the First Crusade (1096–99). The earliest mention of the term *collegantia*, the Venetian vernacular for *commenda*, was a brief reference in 976.[36] Two *collegantia* contracts from 1072 and 1073 Venice are the earliest surviving commenda contracts from Latin Europe.[37] A Pisan municipal act of 1156 is the first to mention the term *commenda* as such. The earliest surviving contracts from Genoa are dated 1163. By the second half of the twelfth century, the commenda was widely used throughout Italy.[38]

The dominance of the commenda in the revival of Italian commerce is reinforced by several recent quantitative studies, such as those of González de Lara, Williamson, and Van Doosselaere. González de Lara counted sea loan and commenda contracts documented in Venetian notarial registers for the period 1121–61, as shown in figure 5.2.

She also found evidence for one sea loan and eleven commenda contracts for the previous century: 1021–1120. In addition, there are thirty-eight contracts that could not be classified with certainty and hence do not appear in this figure.[39]

Dean Williamson, in a parallel study of Venice, found that the set of contracts he located for the years 1278–1400 comprised in excess of 777 commenda contracts, 119 pooling contracts, and 805 debt contracts. Important destinations included Palatia (formerly Miletus), the principal port of the Turkish emirate of Menteshe on the Anatolian Peninsula (289 contracts), and Theologo (formerly Ephesus) the principal port of the Turkish Beylik of Aydin (forty-seven contracts). Egypt (Alexandria or Damietta), Rhodes, and Cyprus show up in 123, 104, and 120 contracts, respectively. Most other contracts involve trade with islands in the Aegean. A smaller and earlier sample identified by Williamson found that of the 122 documents (contracts and receipts) for the period 1190–1220, some seventy-eight were commenda (fifty-two unilateral and twenty-six bilateral) and forty-four were for debt.[40]

In a comprehensive study of Genoa, Van Doosselaere found that 93 percent of the commercial ties recorded in a huge sample (6,764 out of 7,221 ties) collected for the years 1154–1300 were of the commenda form.[41] We have to bear in mind that Van Doosselaere could observe only ties that were recorded in writing and kept with notaries. Organizational forms that did not require registration with the municipality or with a notary, and those that were often not even recorded in writing at all (say, simple employment or agency contracts or partnerships), were not included in Van Doosselaere's dataset. Thus, the existence of commendas in 93 percent of the ties refers only to the percentage in the subset of ties that were formalized in written and preserved documents. The aforementioned figures undoubtedly do not cover all commenda contracts formed in Italy, as many contemporary Venetian and Genoan contracts did not survive in the notarial and municipal records, and as we know less about commenda contracts concluded in less well-studied Italian cities.

The debate over the Italian commenda's origins has raged for decades. Most historians of the Middle East believe that it was imported to Italy from there. They rely on timing, the fact that the origins of the qirad predated the commenda by at least two centuries, and on the basic morphological similarity. They refer to the fact that commenda contracts were first used by Italians on trade routes to the Eastern Mediterranean around the time of the First and Second Crusades. This suggests that encounters with Muslims in the Levant were the link through which the Italians learned about the commenda.[42] The wider context, the routes and timing of the expansion of the funduq from the Middle East to the Latin world around the same time and through similar contacts, can also be used as a support.[43] The migration of other business practices, such as the bill of exchange and bookkeeping, followed a similar course.[44] The examples

5.1. Differences between the Qirad and the Commenda

Feature	Islamic qirad	Italian commenda
Type of investment	Coins only	Coins or goods
Investing parties	Unilateral	Unilateral or bilateral
Split of profits	Usually 50%–50%, but flexible	Usually 75%–25%
Duration	Could be for a set term	One voyage
Use	Terrestrial and maritime	Maritime

presented in the methodological chapter (the compass, the Indian/Arab numerals, and the printing press) all show migration of knowledge from the east (either from China or India via the Arab Middle East or originating in Islam) to Europe.[45]

Most Italian historians of previous generations believed that the Italian commenda developed independently and indigenously in Italy. Notable historians of European Mediterranean trade agree that the Islamic qirad can be found in a commercial manual published in Damascus in the late ninth or tenth century, some two centuries before its first mention in Italy.[46] But they argue that the Italian commenda appeared with the rising Italian port cities, due to their growing mercantile needs, claiming that it was based on earlier Roman building blocks.[47] Those who favor independent Italian origins stress differences rather than similarities between the qirad and the commenda: the commenda was used only for maritime trade, while the qirad was used also for terrestrial trade; the commenda was used as a one-voyage, one-venture contract, whereas the qirad was created for a term of years; the split of profits in the commenda was fixed (or at least subject to a rarely altered default), while in the qirad it was flexible and negotiable; and investment in a commenda could be in goods or coins, while in the qirad it was only in coinage.[48] Table 5.1 highlights some of the differences between the Islamic qirad and the Italian commenda.

The differences between the Italian and Arabian commenda may seem significant when table 5.1, which is based on earlier scholarship, is placed at the center of the discussion. Yet more recently, a synthesis was advanced by younger Italian historians. Favali asserts that when the commenda is compared to the pre-Islamic and early Islamic qirad, the differences are insignificant.[49] At first sight this is odd. How could the Italians imitate an institution, the pre-Islamic qirad, that had disappeared in the Middle East three centuries earlier? There are two ways to explain this. The first is that the commenda was, in fact, imported to Italy earlier than was believed, but no historical traces were preserved from its early history. The second is that, even though high Islamic legal texts intended to Islamize and modify the pre-Islamic qirad, the practices of using qirad did not change until the period in which the Italians learned about the qirad in action. Given the fact that the sources preserved for Islam are mostly of law in the books, and for Italy they are mostly of law in action, neither of Favali's reconciliations can be ruled out. Meanwhile, Mignone's reconciliation suggests several historical roots for the commenda.[50] The qirad was not invented in a vacuum. It was influenced by earlier Mesopotamian, Greek, and Roman institutions, such as the sea loan. The Italians were exposed to the qirad in the eleventh century, but at the time were also well aware of the Byzantine *creokoinonía,* of the Roman *foenus nauticum,* and of *societas.* So Mignone hypothesizes that the Italian commenda is an interbreeding of the qirad with earlier Roman and Eastern Mediterranean institutions that were preserved by the Byzantine Empire. The fact that the commenda first appeared in Venice, which was under strong Byzantine influence, supports this thesis.

I would like to suggest another reconciling interpretation. Rather than understanding eleventh- or twelfth-century Italian jurists' references to the Roman labor-capital partnership (*societas*) and the Roman maritime loan (*nauticum fenus*) as references to the historical Roman origins of the commenda, one can interpret them as an apprehensive attempt to fit a new institution into preexisting schemes. The commenda, whether its origin was in Arabia or in Italian mercantile practices, did not fit the schemes of Roman law as embodied in the *Corpus Juris Civilis.* Prior to the rediscovery of the *Corpus Juris Civilis* in Italy around 1070, and the establishment of the first European university in Bologna in 1088, the mismatch between the commenda (which made its first recorded appearance, either as independent or an imported institution, in Venice in the tenth century) and Roman law was not apparent and did not trouble anyone.

But the revival of Roman law as a dominant source (next to cannon law) of learned law, and the growing popularity of the commenda in the very same period and the very same Italian towns, led to a dissonance. In other words, the creation of a new institution, the commenda, from below, by merchants, or alternatively, the importation of an Arab institution, a transplant—the qirad—created challenges and irritations to the well-settled classifications and categories of Roman law. Jurists reconceptualized it so it would better fit Roman law schemes. But this was a reconceptualization on an academic level that should not confuse historians; it had nothing to do with the actual historical origins of the institution itself. Nor did this reconceptualization have much bearing on the functioning of the commenda in the hands of merchants.

I do not intend to resolve here this decades-old debate. It is likely that the commenda was not invented from scratch in Italy of the tenth and eleventh centuries. It was either based on older legal building blocks found in Italy or on the importation of an Islamic institution from the Levant (or Sicily). It is also likely that the Islamic commenda was not invented from scratch in Arabia in the seventh or eighth century, but rather was formed there based on pre-Islamic practices in Arabia, or provincial Roman law and, in turn, on Greco-Roman or even Phoenician, Israelite, Egyptian, and Mesopotamian building blocks that had existed around the Eastern Mediterranean since antiquity. It does not make much of a difference, for the purposes of the current book, whether those Eastern Mediterranean building blocks influenced Islam and the Latin world in parallel and independently, or whether they first influenced Islam and only later (via Islam) influenced Italy. From the perspective of Crete, whether its origins were in Italy or Arabia made a significant difference. But contemplated from Samarkand or Guangzhou, or even from Hamburg or London, the question of whether the origins of the commenda was in the eastern or western part of the Eastern Mediterranean basin was not of great significance. In other words, when examined from the perspective of Eurasia as a whole, the commenda seems to have relatively confined and singular origins.

Now that we have traced the history of the sea loan and the commenda, we can display in figure 5.3 the main maritime contractual forms developed by different regions in the Eastern Mediterranean throughout an-

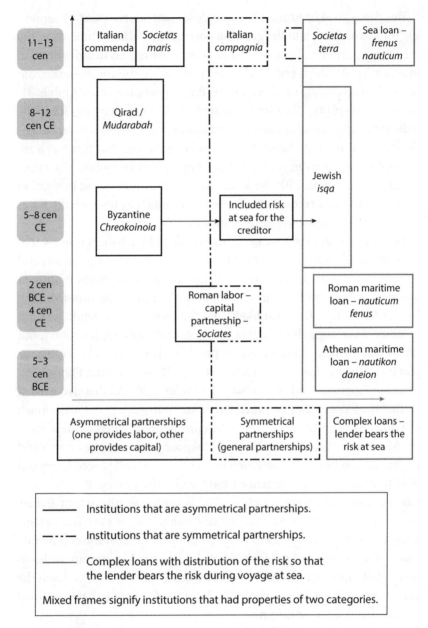

5.3. Organizational forms in the Mediterranean—antiquity to the Middle Ages.

tiquity and the Middle Ages. It shows the evolution of contracts with similar characteristics from ancient Athens to Italy of the Middle Ages, demonstrating the prevalence of their being migratory institutions used in maritime trade.

What is most important for our purposes is that the commenda was not invented independently and indigenously in a large number of localities. It had a single environment of origins in terms of building blocks, and one (or at most two) occurrences of actual invention. The migration of the commenda from Italy further west, to other port cities in the Latin Mediterranean, such as Marseille, Montpelier, Narbonne, and Barcelona, is a direct continuation of its expansion in Italy itself, and is well documented.[51] Its migration north, across the Alps, to the Atlantic and Baltic ports, is less well documented and more in debate.

THE HANSEATIC COMMENDA: A *SONDERWEG*?

In the Hanseatic ports, notably Lübeck and Hamburg, around 1250, there existed a form of sea-trade organization known as the *Widerlegung*. In this form, a merchant received capital from a partner, possibly added his own means to it, traded abroad with the capital, and, following his return, shared the profits with the partner.[52] Did the Hanseatic towns copy the Italian commenda or develop a similar organization independently?

One school of thought argues that the fact that an organizational form similar to that of the commenda of the High Middle Ages of the Latin Mediterranean ports appeared about 150 or 200 years later in the Hanseatic towns suggests emulation.[53] It makes sense, according to this argument, that the organizational know-how made the 1,300 km trail within 150–200 years, given the cross-Alpine passes and the commercial connections.[54]

Another school of thought, led by Levin Goldschmidt in the nineteenth century (followed by his pupils, Willy Silberschmidt and Paul Rehme), asserted that Hanseatic trade law developed independently from the Mediterranean, but since it encountered similar maritime trade problems, it also developed similar solutions.[55] This theory was applied by Silberschmidt, who classified the Hanseatic organizational forms as parallel to the Italian commenda, *societas maris,* and so on.[56]

Cordes more recently offered a third compelling interpretation. His method first carefully compared the Italian commenda to the contract forms that were common in the Hanseatic towns. These contracts were similar in many respects. In the south as well as in the north, there were two partners with clear and separate roles: one was a mere investor (*Kapitalgeber*) who gave his money or goods to the other, the capital bearer (*Kapitalführer*), who combined it with his own means for a business trip overseas. The participation ratio was certainly different. In Genoa, the investor provided two-thirds, and the capital bearer only one-third. As a result, a clause about repayment of the capital invested before splitting of the profits was needed. In Lübeck, on the other hand, final profits were to be halved.[57] Here there was no need to calculate the reimbursement of the contribution in advance; rather, the entire final capital was simply halved.[58]

In the commenda, the investor kept three-quarters of the profit and the capital bearer only a quarter. From there, together with the arrangement of the *societas maris*, a system was formed, which can be best inferred from the decisive keywords *quartum proficui*: the capital bearer was entitled to this "quarter of the profit" for his trade activities. The remaining three-quarters was divided according to the capital ratio. In the commenda, three-quarters was paid to the investor; in the *societas maris*, he kept two-thirds according to his contribution, and the remaining third went to the capital bearer. In total, therefore, he kept half of the profit.[59]

In the Hanseatic case, the profit was halved between the two partners. The difference between that and the commenda was explained by previous scholars as resulting from differences in the environment.[60] The voyage across the Baltic and North Sea was more dangerous than that across the Mediterranean, and therefore the share of the traveling party—the capital bearer—was larger than that in the Mediterranean case. Yet this explanation, Cordes argues, does not fit the rules that apply to the *Widerlegung*. There, the capital bearer also kept half of the profit, even if he not only carried the burdens of the trip but also contributed half of the capital.[61] In Lübeck, the custom was to divide the profit in two equal parts, regardless of the relative capital investment and work contribution.[62] The idea of division based on shares in capital investment is not foreign to Lübeck law, but it comes to fruition only in cases of loss. Profits are shared equally.[63]

Essentially, there are two principles of profit sharing, namely either by headcount or by capital share. Only when applying the capital-share principle, as did the Italians, did the problem of how to appraise the investments, costs, and profits of the capital bearer arise.[64] Cordes concludes that the early Hanseatic contracts were based on the first principle and not on the second, Italian, principle. The Italian commenda principles could not be imported and applied by the Hansa merchants because they, unlike the Italians, did not use writing. The first surviving Hanseatic contracts were concluded at the beginning of the fourteenth century. Among the oldest written legal documents in the Hanseatic region, they appear at the end of the oral epoch, in the transition to written law and written business records.[65] The development of writing and computation skills in the second half of the fourteenth century, together with the transition to the German language, was the basis for advancing to more complex and flexible structures of contracts.[66] The *Widerlegung*, with its markedly simple structure, clearly originated from an oral business culture. The principle of dividing the profit of a trade enterprise in accordance with headcount fits well the practice of conducting business in the pre-writing era. It is a principle that does not necessitate writing or written computation.[67]

The transition to writing led to the almost complete loss of the two formative characteristics of the earlier Hanseatic contract forms, namely the one-sided capital-bearing form and the profit-halving form. The profit-sharing form was now more commonly oriented toward capital-investment proportions. The work portion of the capital bearer, as before, was not considered in the profit sharing.[68] The stationed merchant could manage his businesses from his office, using the written word, and soon developed capabilities to handle more complicated contracts, with the help of documents and trade journals. This tendency is already evident in the earliest debt registers and becomes more marked from around 1400 onward. Nevertheless, the old *Widerlegung* was not discarded, but was adapted with the flexibility and imagination that the new written medium brought. To all appearances, it was this flexibility that made it unnecessary to borrow the trade techniques of the Mediterranean.[69] In table 5.2, we can see how the profit-sharing system of the commenda and *societas maris* differs from that of the Hanseatic region shown in table 5.3.

5.2. Comparison of the Commenda and the *Societas Maris*

Latin Mediterranean	Commenda		Societas maris	
	Investor	Capital-bearer	Investor	Capital-bearer
Capital share (estimated at 3/4)	1 (× 3/4)	—	2/3 (× 3/4)	1/3 (× 3/4)
Work portion (estimated at the quartum proficui, 1/4)	—	1 (× 1/4)	—	1 (× 1/4)
profit share	3/4	1/4	1/2	1/2

Source: Cordes (1997, p. 142).

Therefore, Cordes shows, the Hanseatic commercial organization was not originally based on the north Italian system of commenda and *societas maris*. Similarities in some features resulted from similar environments and challenges, not from the actual importation of an Italian institution.[70] The main difference, the profit-sharing principle, resulted from differences in writing technologies, the Italians being literate and the Hanseatic exclusively conducting their business orally until a much later period.[71] Because of these differences, even if the Italian influence had reached the Hansa in the twelfth or thirteenth century, it could not have been transplanted and adopted there when it first arrived. By the second half of the fourteenth century, the profit-sharing principle of the *Widerlegung* was gradually revised due to the introduction of writing and accounting practices. At a later stage, Cordes acknowledges, the Hanseatic partnership law of the early fifteenth century was modernized by Dutch as well as Italian influences.[72] Cordes offers a complex narrative on this. Initially there was an independent Hanseatic path of development that fitted the oral nature of transactions. The path was then driven by the introduction of writing technology into commerce. This path, which lasted for several centuries, diverged from that of the Italians. Later, after the introduction of writing in the Baltic cities, the Hanseatic merchants emulated the Italian forms, and the two paths converged. Cordes concludes that his case is a criticism not only of the mainstream literature on the origins and migration of the commenda, but also of the wider literature on the

5.3. Comparison of Hanseatic Contracts

Hanseatic region	Rheme's *Sendegutgeschäft*		*Widerlegung*	
	Investor	Capital-bearer	Investor	Capital-bearer
Capital share	1	—	For example: 1/2 or 8/9	For example: 1/2 or 1/9
Work portion	—	1	—	1
Profit share	Halving the profit [*Geweinnhalbierung*]			

Source: Cordes (1997, p. 145).

development of mercantile law, which argues that, in the Middle Ages, there was a uniform European merchant law.[73]

ENGLAND: A COMMON-LAW COMMENDA?

There is some controversy over whether the commenda ever reached England. Legal historians—Postan, for instance—argue that it contradicted basic concepts of common law and even customary law, and that the common law developed substitutes for this institution.[74] Some English historians, notably Holdsworth, Plucknett, and Rogers, argue that even though the English did not use a distinct name for the commenda, they in fact used and recognized contracts similar in content to those of the commenda by the late thirteenth century.[75] Some fourteenth- and fifteenth-century yearbook cases indeed refer to transactions between parties that have profit-sharing elements in them. It is likely that these were commenda contracts because at least one of them was between Italian merchants (who often used this form of contract), because of the asymmetry in the inputs of the parties (one providing only capital and one only labor), and because they were retrospectively identified as such by notable historians. However, these transactions were litigated within the framework of the common-law writ of account that gave rise only to disputes between partners, not to disputes between partners and third parties. As a result, it is not possible to determine clearly whether these transactions involved the commenda or general partnerships.[76] The fact that we cannot determine whether common-law courts enforced the commenda may indicate either that they were rejected in England or that their acceptance was obscured by the process of fitting them to common-law forms of action and terminologies.

JEWISH MERCHANTS OF CAIRO: ISQA OR QIRAD?

Turning back east, the commenda—in its Islamic form, the qirad—appears frequently in the Cairo Geniza records, which contain correspondence and contracts dealing with the overseas trade of Cairo Jews. These reflect the wide use these merchants made of the Muslim commenda (qirad or *mudaraba*), termed in Hebrew *qirad al-goym* (qirad of gentiles), as distinct from the Jewish partnership (*qirad betorat isqa*). Goitein, the leading historian of the Geniza, concludes that the Muslim commenda was in much more frequent use in the maritime trade of these Jewish merchants than the Jewish partnership or *isqa*. The earliest appearances of the commenda in the Geniza are from the first decades of the eleventh century in some of the oldest documents preserved, fitting the claim that the origins of the commenda are Muslim. The commenda was used in contracts with both Jewish and Muslim partners, and disputes were resolved according to the relevant Muslim law.[77]

The reception of the qirad by Jews in Cairo and beyond occurred in a unique manner, unlike any other covered in this chapter. The qirad was not made part of Jewish law. But it was not rejected by it either. Apparently, Jewish community leaders (*Geonim*) and rabbis did not want Jewish merchants who found the qirad to be an appealing organizational form to desert Jewish courts altogether and opt for Muslim law and courts of law.[78] Jewish law responded to the concern in a manner that would be termed today as "legal pluralist."[79] Jewish merchants adopted it as part of their business practices. When Jewish judges were presented with disputes involving a qirad, they were responsive and accepted them for consideration. Jewish rabbis, the authors of *responsa*, dealt with the difficulties that ensued from such a mix of an Islamic institution and Jewish litigation. Eventually, the codification of Maimonides synthesized and integrated the qirad into the wider system. But it was integrated as a foreign, Muslim, institution whose norms were taken not from the Jewish *Halacha* but rather from the Islamic *Sharia*. In conflicts-of-law terms, Jewish merchants were given the option to choose a Jewish forum with a Jewish organizational forms, although they could also choose a Jewish forum with a Muslim organizational forms.[80] The hope was that this would decrease the choice of Muslim forums, which was often made not for the sake of the forum but rather for the sake of the Muslim institution that was considered more in tune with current merchants' needs.

The Geniza merchants used the commenda primarily in their Mediterranean trade, but they also used it when trading with India via Aden.[81] The Geniza records are thus revealing as to its migration to the trade destinations of these merchants. They carried it not only westward to North Africa, and possibly also to Spain and Sicily, but also eastward to Aden and India. They were agents of migration, perhaps serving as the exporters of this institution to India. Most historians believe that their reality represents the Muslim reality as well, about which we simply lack records. There is no reason to believe that Jewish merchants used the Muslims' qirad in India and their fellow Muslims did not. We even know that Jewish merchants were partners with Muslims in India trade. One could infer quite safely that Muslim traders traveling from Cairo, and other Middle Eastern cities such as Baghdad and Basra, also used the qirad as an organizational form. Thus, the number of agents carrying the commenda to India and beyond was much larger than the number of Jewish merchants traveling the route.

ARMENIA: ISLAMIC OR LATIN COMMENDA?

An alternative route to the oceanic one for the migration of the commenda eastward was along the overland Silk Route to Armenia and Central Asia. It is now well documented that the commenda was a central organizational form used by New Julfa Armenians in the seventeenth and eighteenth centuries. Dozens of commenda contracts from the seventeenth century were deposited in New Julfa archives. The Armenian law code of Astrakhan, written in the 1760s, devoted fifty-eight articles to it. The Armenian commenda is an unequal partnership contract between a master (*agha*), usually a *khwaja* (a rich and powerful merchant) residing in New Julfa, and an agent (factor, *ĕnker*).[82] It is accordingly termed *ĕnkerut`iwn*. The standard ratio of profit sharing in the unilateral commenda is three-quarters of the profits to the master (apart from his initial investment) and one-quarter to the agent; however, there are documented contracts of a two-thirds–one-third distribution, possibly in accordance with the agent's experience—on the basis that the greater the experience, the larger the share of the profits.[83] The bilateral version of the contract involved investment by the traveling agent as well. This version of the commenda contract was less standardized than the unilateral form, and several versions of profit divisions existed—even up to a fifty-fifty split.[84] The contract was typically open-ended and could last anywhere from a few years to ten or more years, after which the *ĕnker* would return home to New Julfa with the profits meticulously accounted for in ledgers and ready for splitting.

In light of the striking similarities, it is surprising that the resemblance of the Armenian partnership to the commenda was first identified, by Khachikian, only in 1988.[85] By now, it is commonly accepted among historians that Armenian merchants used the commenda as a prime organizational form. This late discovery suggests that additional unidentified commenda further east in Eurasia may still await discovery.

Khachikian called attention to the similarity of features to those of the Venetian commenda. She speculated that the link between Venice and the Armenians was the Armenian Kingdom in Cilicia (1080–1375) on the southeastern shores of Asia Minor, which had strong political ties to the Latin crusaders and was Venice's major maritime partner in the Eastern Mediterranean in the twelfth century. At that stage, the Venetians already used the commenda in their maritime trade. From Cilicia, familiarity with the commenda reached the Armenian homeland. With Shah Abbas's expulsion of the Armenians from Julfa in 1604, it also reached New Julfa.

Herzig, in a 1991 dissertation and subsequent publications, suggested a different origin: the Islamic qirad/*mudaraba*.[86] Herzig used morphological similarities, etymology, and the wider context to support his conclusion. He noted that, in some of its characteristics, the Armenian *ĕnkerut`iwn* resembled the Arab form more than the Italian form of commenda. Armenians, like Arabs, used it in overland terrestrial trade as well as maritime trade, while the Italian commenda was used only in maritime trade. It was made for a duration of years and not for just a single voyage like the Italian commenda. The Persian terms *muzarbay* and *muzarabat*, which are similar to the Arabic *mudharaba*, were also used by the Armenians. Lastly, Herzig argues that for centuries, the Armenians lived in Armenia and in New Julfa within Islamic cultures, the Arab Caliphates, the Ottoman Empire, and the Safavid dynasty, and even though they held to their religion, culturally they borrowed from their neighbors in many fields. At a minimum, even if the Armenians learned of the commenda initially from the Venetians, in the following century they were likely to absorb influences from the Islamic *mudharaba*.

Aslanian, in his 2007 dissertation and 2011 book, revisited the question of origins. He concluded that the paucity of records on Armenian mercantile practices in the thirteenth through sixteenth centuries, before the establishment of New Julfa, prevents one from reaching a clear conclusion as to the origins of the Armenian commenda. Some two to four centuries of its early history are missing, and, without these, any conclusion is tentative. The current state of research allows no more than speculation. While he was reluctant to make statements as to its origins, Aslanian acknowledges the existence and popularity of commenda among New Julfa Armenians.[87]

CENTRAL ASIA AND MONGOLIA: ORTOY ASSOCIATIONS

The similarity between the *ortoy* and the commenda is apparent: two partners, one investing the money or goods and the two splitting the profits. The ortoy relationship was eventually to become the model for ties between nomadic rulers and Central Asian merchants.[88] By the thirteenth century, the *ortag*, which had spread rapidly with the Mongolian expansion, was a commercial institution widely used from Persia to China. Was the *ortoy* an incarnation of the commenda, or did it merely share functional similarities with it? Interestingly, to date, the study of the history of the ortoy, with just a few exceptions, has been separated from the study of the history of the commenda.[89] I will connect the two bodies of literature in the following paragraphs.

The Mongol ortoy was composed of two parties. One was a wealthy person, a member of the Mongol elite, from among the nobility, landlords, or, in the case of Yuan China, even a prince or the emperor himself. The other party was an experienced and reputable merchant, often central Asian Muslim or Uighur. The ortoy was used in a context different from that of the commenda, in that one party was the ruler or a member of his elite and the function was partly political.

According to de la Vaissière, in the early stages of the Mongol empire the ortoy played a dual role of maintaining diplomatic relations, in the form of tribute missions, and engaging in trade activities. Merchandise transferred to the Mongol regime as tribute was handed over to ortoy merchants to be employed as capital in trade. In this way, tribute from other countries or taxes on occupied territories became capital for ortoy merchants, who traded in these commodities on behalf of their Mongol partners.[90] Gradually, the relationship was transformed from tribute based to commercially based.

The wealthy party entrusted, invested, or lent capital (depending on the interpretation), often in the form of silver, to the traveling party. The merchant traveled with the silver or converted it to exportable goods, and returned from the west with imported goods. On his return, profits were split. According to some sources, 70 percent of the revenue was to be reserved for the investor from among the Mongol elite; the remaining 30 percent was reserved for the ortoy.[91] The ortoy was a one-venture contract.

In 1218, Genghis Khan ordered his family members and commanders (*noyan*) to each choose eligible non-Mongol clients (merchants from Bukhara, Khorazm, and Otrar), supply them with capital, promise them tax exemption, and send them together as a trade party to the realm of the Sultanate of Khorazm, then ruling Central Asia and Iran. These Central Asian merchants kept the Mongol rulers supplied with clothing, grain, and other provisions. Following Genghis Khan's precedent, his successors encouraged foreign merchants from further afield, whether Hansa traders entering Russia or Indians from Lahore going to Central Asia, to take advantage of similar privileges.

The model of the ortoy traveled with the expansion of the Mongol Empire to Central Asia, Iran, and the Middle East. It was used with the fragmentation of the Mongol Empire after 1259 in the separate khanates that succeeded it. The Persian historian and vizier Rashid al-Din (1247–1318), who lived in Ilkhanate-ruled Iran, invested a major part of his wealth (some 32.5 million of his 35-million-dinar fortune) in a large wholesale undertaking. He writes: "The greater part of the money I gave to trustworthy merchants and they conduct their trade with this money, and I have written down their names in my account book." Rashid al-Din kept long, detailed lists of goods, mostly textiles but also leather and fur goods, and so on, which he received from the merchants.[92]

After Möngke Khan's 1258 conquest of Baghdad, he appointed a Khorazmian client, Ali Ba'atur, the overseer (*darughachi*) of the city, with special oversight of the ortoy—a move designed to restrict their use. However, his brother Hüle'ü (his successor in the Ilkhanate after his death in 1259), and Hüle'ü's son, Abagha Khan (1265–81), ignored Möngke Khan's restrictive regulations and ordered their officials not to interfere with ortoy in any way, leaving ortoq commerce free to flourish once again. As the Mongols did not enforce the Islamic prohibition of usury, many with no mercantile background, often Jews and Assyrian Christians, flocked to borrow money, buy rare items (*tangsuqs*), and form ortoy.[93] Persian and Armenian sources mention examples of merchants from modern-day Syria and Iraq, Umek (Asil) and Simeon, who worked for Mongol princes in ortoy.[94]

One could argue that the ortoy originated in Mongolia and migrated westward with the expansion of the Mongol Empire. But linguistic etymological studies indicate the contrary. The *ortag, ortoq, urtaq* (*ortey* in the plural), or ortoy [95] is a term that appears in slight variations in Persian, Turkic, Uighur, and Mongolian. Its literal meaning is merchant or merchant partner. The origin of the term *ortoy* goes back at least to the sixth-century Turkic languages. The term appears in several ninth-through-eleventh-century Uyghur sources describing the Turkic trade networks across Central Asia. By the eleventh century, *ortoq* meant commercial partners who pooled their capital and shared their profits according to agreed percentages. This reconstruction supports the thesis that the origins of the term *ortay* are most likely Persian or Turkic and that it had migrated eastward to Mongolia and China by the twelfth or thirteenth century, and not westward.[96] In terms of timing, the *ortay* is not mentioned in Mongolian or Chinese sources before the arrival of the Mongols in Central Asia. One possibility is that the origin of the ortoy is to be found in an indigenous Central Asian institution that was based on Turkic steppe practices and needs. Another possibility is that the profit-sharing version of the ortay was introduced to a preexisting Persian or Turkic institution by Islamic merchants or jurists who were already familiar with the qirad.[97] If indeed there is solid evidence for the existence of the ortoy in sixth-century Central Asia, before the arrival of Islam, then the independent-origins thesis is more convincing. In any case, it is unlikely that the ortoy was originally a Mongol organizational form that migrated to Central Asia only with the Mongol expansion.

INDIA

According to Das Gupta, commenda contracts, in which the principal and the agents split the profits and allocated the risk, were quite common among Indian maritime merchants.[98] Chaudhuri also believes, based on scattered evidence, that commenda contracts were used in Indian Oceanic trade.[99] The form could have been copied from Arab or Jewish merchants arriving in India or imported by Muslim Gujarati merchants trading with Persia and Arabia or making the pilgrimage to Mecca.

The commenda was also used by sedentary merchants using traveling agents in India's overland trade.[100] It was used in the trade of Multani, Marwari, and Khatri merchants with Isfahan and other Persian cities, with Bokhara, Samarkand, and other central Asian cities, and with Astrakhan and even Moscow. These merchants—Hindu, Jain, and Muslims—often traded on the same routes as the Armenian merchants of New Julfa. Much of the evidence for the use of the commenda by Indian merchants on these routes is from the eighteenth century. Earlier records did not survive. But it is likely that the use of the commenda in these regions was centuries old by then and was not copied from the Europeans but rather from the Islamic commenda.[101]

Commenda contracts were also used by European traders when they reached Asia, using the Cape Route, in the sixteenth century. Portuguese merchants funded by commenda contracts sailed on board Crown ships taking the Crown routes (*carreiras*) to Asia.[102] The commenda was also used by the first Dutch traders who arrived in the Indian Ocean shortly before 1600, and served as the basis for precompanies that initiated the first Dutch voyages to Asia. It follows that those Indian merchants who were not exposed to it via Arab and Persian merchants, say, those originating in the Bay of Bengal ports, could learn about the commenda from European merchants.

THE EAST INDIES

The migration of the maritime commenda further east is not well documented in surviving records. The reconstruction of this migration involves significant methodological problems, as discussed in chapter 4. In his travel book written in around 1510, Tomé Pires, one of the first Portuguese to arrive in Indonesia, provided a first-hand impression of local trade practices before the disruptive arrival of the Europeans.[103] He reported on a practice of splitting profits and risks between merchants and junk-ship owners. The leading historians of the early modern Indonesian trade view this and other records as evidence of the use of the commenda in the trade between India and Indonesia, in interisland trade, and even in trade with China.[104] They also mention Chinese merchants investing in commenda and foreigners using commenda in Chinese port towns. This may be the last missing link in the migration of the commenda from Arabia to China. But contemporary reports of the prevalence of the commenda in Java and Sumatra may reflect European-centered perceptions rather than the nature of actual Asian practices.

CHINA: ORTOY MEETS QIRAD?

There is preliminary evidence of the use of joint-venture transactions in China's maritime trade as early as the Song dynasty (960–1279). Yoshinobu identifies them as commenda and *societas maris*–type transactions. Billy So, more cautiously, labels them joint ventures, but draws attention to the similarity to the commenda. Both find evidence, in twelfth- and thirteenth-century sources (including, interestingly, in mathematical treatises), of investment in shipping, both for fixed interest and for a share of the profits.[105] The latter contractual form is akin to that of the commenda. It is possible that Persian and Arab merchants used the Middle Eastern commenda, the qirad, in their voyages to the Indian Ocean and beyond it to the South China Sea. It is not inconceivable that diasporic

Arab and Persian merchants and agents in Chinese ports used it as well, possibly even with Chinese merchants as the other party. International entrepôts such as Quanzhou and Guangzhou, having thousands of Middle Eastern residents for generations since the arrival of the first merchants in the eighth and ninth centuries, were likely to be familiar with the commenda even before the arrival of the Mongols in China's southern ports.[106] Recent research on the tributary system during the Song period shows that the Song Chinese government cooperated with foreign west Asian merchants who acted as official envoys of tributary missions from Dashi (Arabia or the Persian Gulf) to the Song court. According to Masaki Mukai, overseas traders from these countries found it profitable to carry out tributary missions that afforded them special treatment by the government, including exemption from taxes on other merchandise they carried for their own separate trade purposes.[107]

The earliest known Chinese reference to the ortoy dates to 1237, during Ogodei's reign (1229–41). It refers to two Southern Song envoys testifying to the Mongolian ruling house's practice of entrusting Muslim merchants with silver to earn interest on it. In 1253 there appears the first record of a government agency in charge of ortoy activities. The *ortay* took hold in China with the Mongols, who defeated the Song dynasty and took control of China as a whole as the Yuan dynasty (1279–1368). Chinese Yuan records refer to the ortoy in the overland Silk Route trade with Muslim traders from Bukhara and other places in Central Asia. These ortoy associations were chiefly composed of Muslims and Uighurs, who maintained trade relations linking China, through overland and maritime routes, with inner Asia, Western-Central Asia, and Persia.[108] After the defeat of the Southern Song dynasty and the takeover of the major maritime ports by the Yuan dynasty, the ortoy made its way into maritime trade. The *Yuan Dynastic History* contains the following passage, dated 1284: "The [Yuan] government itself, providing ships and capital to selected individuals to go abroad to trade for sundry goods. As for the profits so obtained, the government, calculating on the basis of ten parts, took as its [share] seven [parts], whereas the traders received three [parts]."[109]

The Muslim merchants played a vital role in Chinese foreign trade. A large part of the Yuan dynasty's tax and customs income depended on their commercial activity, and therefore the Mongol regime granted them privileges to help sustain their activities. Their mercantile activities were carried out to a great extent through their participation in the ortoy.[110] Ortoy merchants received loans in the form of silver from the Mongol regime and members of the Mongol elite, which enabled them to finance the trade caravans and engage in moneylending at exorbitant rates.[111] Some 70 percent of the revenue was to be reserved for the government and the remaining 30 percent for the ortoy.[112] During certain periods, members of the imperial family accumulated great profits from investing with the ortoy merchant-moneylenders. At other times, some of them accumulated large debts to ortoy merchants.[113]

The Yuan government's reliance on members of the *semu* class and, more specifically, the Muslim merchants, was particularly salient in Southern Fujian, where the Muslims held many key administrative posts in the local government. Posts connected with the lucrative maritime trade had been highly sought after by officials since the Tang era (608–917) and even earlier. A growing number of officials were involved with this trade during the late Song and early Yuan periods. These posts offered many opportunities to accumulate private assets and, whether directly or indirectly, to personally engage in foreign trade. This trade in Yuan times was carried out mainly by ortoy merchant associations.[114]

The regulations aimed at tighter government control over ortoy activities were much more vigorously developed during Kublai's reign. This regulatory impulse was further enhanced with the occupation of Southern Song and its incorporation into the Yuan Empire. The reorganized Office of Maritime Affairs of Quanzhou (*quanfusi*) was responsible for the Crown Treasure and the capital of the royal family and its closest dependents. It invested in maritime trade activity, among other things, which produced sizeable profits, and from then on it supervised the entrusting of imperial funds to ortoy merchants.[115] Pu Shougeng (ca. 1230 to ca. 1297) and his ancestors, who are the subject of an elaborated microstudy to be presented in the next part of the book, held key offices in maritime and customs affairs and political roles in Quanzhou and beyond and were heavily involved in ortoy trade. According to H. F. Schurmann, this "indicated the leading role which the ortaq mercantile interests were beginning to play in maritime commerce after the occupation of South China."[116] The Quanzhou bureau turned the city to the primary residence of most ortoy households involved in maritime trade.[117] Pu Shougeng and his successors were ideally located to take advantage of the ortoy system. In his official position, he took an active role in overseas missions for the Mongols, but at the same time he was utilizing his connections with the Mongols to expand his own personal trade network to Southeast Asia, Malacca, Java, and beyond. His foreign origins made it easier for him to communicate with foreign merchants and employ them as ortoy agents.[118]

Less than two decades after Kublai's death, the government's control over the ortoy started to decline. By 1311, the Office of Maritime Affairs (*quanfusi*) was closed down. On the one hand, this signified the weakening of the central-control characteristic of Kublai's reign. However, it did not signal the end of the practice of entrusting imperial government funds to ortoy merchants. In fact, after the Office of Maritime Affairs was abolished, the ortoy merchants were relatively free of restrictions and controls. This most likely generated potential tensions between the central bureaucracy and the growing power of merchants in the remote port cities. Some scholars claim that the late Yuan economic crisis was a result of the inability of the post-Kublai court to distinguish between a governmental budget and an imperial family budget. This confusion led to a scenario in which the debts owed by members of the Mongolian ruling house to ortoy merchants were erroneously viewed as governmental debts, rather than personal ones.[119]

In summary, a few historians argue that joint ventures that look like the commenda were used by diasporic Persian and Arab merchants in the major cosmopolitan port cities of Southern China during the Song dynasty. Chinese merchants could possibly be parties to such commenda. There is solid evidence that the Mongols carried the ortoy with them from Central Asia to Mongolia, and from there into China with the conquest. While the commenda was a contract between two private parties, the ortoy was a contract between the ruler, or an office holder appointed by the ruler, and a foreign private party. The commenda better fitted the characteristics of Song maritime trade, which was mostly private and relied on cooperation between Han Chinese and foreigners. The ortoy better fitted the characteristics of the Yuan trade, in which Han Chinese were banned from being involved, merchants of foreign origins were integrated into the domestic system, and the rulers and their supporters played an important role. So it is likely that the commenda and the ortoy, two variations of equity partnership, were used in the same port cities in different times, and possibly even simultaneously.

CONCLUSION

The commenda was much more than a simple profit-sharing contract. It was a complex cluster of contracts that was not likely to have been invented casually and endemically. Our three microstudies of merchant networks—of Cairo, New Julfa, and Livorno—that will be analyzed in chapter 7, demonstrate that the commenda, as complex as it was, should not be analyzed in isolation from its wider business context. It was one of several organizational building blocks, which included family firms, sea loans and regular loans, and salaried and commission agents. It could not be effective in an informational vacuum—institutions had to support and enhance the flow of information. Lastly, a legal framework was needed for creating the rules that would complete the rudimentary commenda contracts and adjudicate the disputes. The invention of the commenda relied on the emergence of a written culture among not only jurists but also the merchants themselves. Written documents provided the legal framework, were the medium for conveying instructions, were used as evidentiary devices in cases of dispute, enhanced information flows, and, last but not least, were essential in settling the quite complicated accounts between the parties.

The development, spread, and ultimate decline of the commenda was affected by three kinds of processes. One was the transfer of cross-regional know-how. This process involved learning about the commenda, its concept, its legal and contractual features, and its uses from the original region and legal system in which it was first developed or from cultural and legal intermediaries. The second was the instrumental responses. The law responded to the changing needs of merchants that resulted from changes in the trade environment. Exogenous changes, such as wars, the Black Death, or the opening up of new markets, affected the selection of the commenda by merchants, its intensity of use, and its spatial spread; and these, in turn, affected the selection and drafting of contractual terms and the legal framework that constituted the commenda and settled disputes regarding it. The third was internal and autonomous legal dynamics.

In some cases, the law developed within its own logic rather than in interaction with its social and economic context. When the same commenda was introduced in different legal systems, these systems received, rejected, or modified the commenda accordingly, depending on their jurisprudence, their canons of interpretation, and their conventions.

The institutional economic analysis of the benefits and costs of the commenda is still in its infancy. The following discussion is thus preliminary and tentative. The commenda was a good platform for matching capital and labor. It seems to have been a particularly good organizational form for heterogeneous parties, say, an older investor and a younger traveler, a wealthy person and a person with wealth constraints, a risk-averse person with a person willing to bear more risk, or a person with know-how and a person lacking such know-how. The utility of the commenda was not only due to the asymmetry inherent in the investment—capital on the one hand and labor on the other; it was also due to the different forms of liabilities imposed on the two parties, the different role they had in managerial decision making, and the different payoffs.

A more homogenous set of parties was likely to lead to a choice of a general partnership, in which all partners had symmetrical positions, in terms of management, liabilities, payoffs, and often (but not always) investment. A commenda could be used to govern a personal collaboration or an impersonal collaboration. When collaboration was very personal, say, between father and son or between siblings, they often preferred to organize their business activity within an informal family firm, subject only to family law, marriage, inheritance, and adoption, but not to commercial law, which was more voluntary, more at arm's length, and more conducive to third-party enforcement. But to function efficiently, a commenda required a supporting institutional infrastructure, mainly because of the asymmetry in information between the investor and the traveler. The traveler conducted the commenda's business in destinations that were remote from the investor, who would often be unaware of the scant means of communication, unstable maritime routes, political crises, market fluctuations, and so on, encountered by the traveler. Payoffs were directly affected by each of these uncertainties. The monitoring of commenda traveling parties, being an equity venture in which net profits were shared, was more sensitive to information flows than the monitoring of debtors in debt contracts. The payoff in debt contracts was known in advance: principal plus ex ante agreed interest. A creditor had to make sure that his debtor would not abscond or pretend to be insolvent. But he did not have to follow his accounts or determine exactly how much he earned or spent.

Pioneering studies by Yadira González de Lara and Dean Williamson on the choice between commenda and sea loan by Venetian merchants roughly conform to these theoretical insights.[120] The extent of information asymmetry, resulting from the speed and quality of the flow of information, affected the choice. The further away a node was in a mercantile network (say, a Black Sea or a Levant port, compared to a Sicilian or Aegean port), the younger the network and the newer the destination, and the lower the frequency of voyages to that destination, the more likely it was that sea loan would be selected rather than a commenda. Wars, the Black Death, and other such large-scale interruptions led to an increase in the percentage of sea loans taken out, and a decrease in the percentage of commenda. The better the state institutional support for information-flows—say, by organizing annual convoys, employing state registering clerks on ship boards, or establishing *fondacos* in which all commenda traveling agents had to reside, store goods, and conduct business—the more likely it was for the commenda to be selected. In a pioneering study of commercial agreements in Genoa, Van Doosselaere found that the commenda was used in the relatively riskier maritime eastern trade and not in the less risky overland northern trade. It was employed mostly between occasional partners and not as part of repeated matching. Commenda partners were drawn from a diverse range of social and political groups.[121] Van Doosselaere, as a sociologist, was more interested in the effect of social stratification and shifts in the political power than in business risks and information flows. But his findings do not sit neatly alongside those of González de Lara and Williamson. Theirs suggest that a shift from debt to equity finance occurred with the improvement in information flows. His suggest that a shift from equity to debt finance took place with regularization of trade. The discrepancy can be reconciled in that the two sets of findings report a different phase—in the case of González de Lara and Williamson, the early stages of the commercial revolution, and in the case of Van Doosselaere, its later part. Differences in locality, Genoa compared to Venice, or methodology, can also explain the differences in findings.

It is important to note that the studies available so far provide only a partial look at the use of the commenda in Eurasian trade. The well-studied cases of Venice and Genoa refer only to a short segment of the Eurasian trade network, at the far-western end. It is not necessarily the case that what could be concluded based on these examples applies to more central segments. The Maghribi network is a case study of a small group of merchants, which does not necessarily represent other contemporary networks. The Armenian and Livorno networks are from a late period in the history of the commenda, when it functioned in the shadow of the corporations. We are missing studies, and most probably preserved records, of Arab merchants centered in the Middle East and trading with India and the Indonesian archipelago, of Persian merchants trading by sea with China, and of Central Asian Islamized merchants using the Silk Route. This absence affects not only our historical understanding but also the development of the theoretical framework that is currently available for the analysis of the environments in which the commenda was selected over debt finance and over the employment of waged and commissioned agents.

The commenda seems to capture the middle range of the spectrum in three somewhat related dimensions. When parties are personally close enough, as with immediate family or other kin, they do not need the commenda. If they have no common basis—either reputational, religious, or ethnic—for forming trust, they will not be able to use it. When information flows are meager, the parties cannot use what information exists. If there is full transparency, the investor does not need a traveling equity partner. When trade is sufficiently routine, the commenda is not needed. But when risks are very high, the commenda will not be formed either. For these reasons, it is not surprising that the commenda as a central trade institution rose and declined with the advance of maritime trade in the Mediterranean and in Eurasia more generally, and that its heyday was between the tenth and fifteenth centuries.

Once established, it spread from the Eastern Mediterranean throughout Eurasia, making it the prime migratory institution and a crucial institutional component in some segments of Eurasian long-distance trade for more than half a millennium. But it became outmoded when enterprises owned and operated by Chinese and Portuguese rulers developed in the sixteenth century, and even more so when English and Dutch corporate-based enterprises developed in the seventeenth century.

The commenda was, as far as historians can currently tell, an innovation that arose once or, at most, twice. In one version or another, the commenda migrated from its place of origin, in Arabia or the Eastern Mediterranean, or Central Asia, according to various accounts, to almost all other regions in Eurasia. It migrated to the Levant, North Africa, Mesopotamia, and Persia. It migrated to Venice and other Italian towns, to other Mediterranean ports of the Latin West, to the Hanseatic ports, to England, and to the Low Countries. It migrated to India, the Indonesian archipelagos, and China, and to Armenia, Central Asia, and Mongolia. The agents of migration were diverse: conquerors (Arabs, Crusaders, Mongols), merchants (Venetian, Maghrebi, Arab), travelers, missionaries, and possibly others. Figure 5.4 shows the far-reaching migration of the commenda from its place of origin throughout Eurasia.

The reception of the transplanted commenda created different responses in different legal systems. In Arabia, the reception of a pre-Islamic institution necessitated its integration into Islamic historical narratives and legal schools. In Italy, its transplantation had to overcome resistance by Roman law and had to be fit into Roman law schemes. In the Baltic ports, it had to survive the transition from oral to written law and from oral to written business practices. In England, it had to adjust to the contours of common law. Jewish law recognized it as an Islamic institution that could be litigated in rabbinical courts. In Armenia, it blended Christian and Islamic traditions. In Mongolia and Yuan China, it was converted from a private instrument into a public tool in the hands of the rulers. The wide array of receptions, in different legal systems, religions, and political regimes, provides an exceptional opportunity to observe and analyze the myriad responses to the transplantation of the very same institution.

At first sight, the reader may surmise that, despite the imitation of the institution itself, there were different terms used to denote the commenda in different part of Eurasia, showing no common etymological origins. One of the common outcomes of contact between people using different languages is lexical borrowing—the loan of an individual word or words from one language to another.[122] Need is one of the most obvious reasons for borrowing words. If a culture acquires a new technology, new technical concepts, or reference to foreign locations, for instance, the easiest thing to do is to borrow the foreign word together with the new foreign technology or concept. But this is not what happened with the commenda.

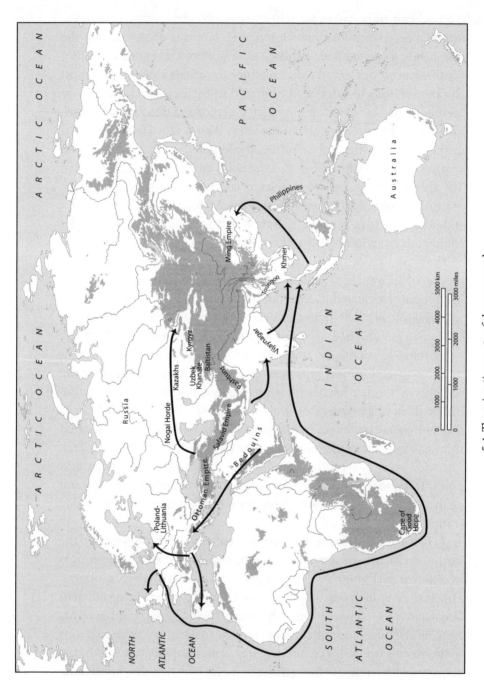

5.4. The migration route of the commenda.

While some words are not borrowed because of structural linguistic differences, others, explain linguists, are not borrowed because of cultural, religious, or political objections.[123] Some linguists term the opposition to loanwords "language nationalism" or "language purism."[124] This may explain the different etymology of the commenda in Italian and in Armenian, compared to the Arabic origins. Admittedly, the theory is not fully determinative. In some contexts, loanwords are commonly found, while in others they are rare, and the theory seems to support either scenario. For example, as we saw in the previous chapter, the term *fondaco* in Italian is borrowed from the term *funduq* in Arabic. What can explain the difference between the funduq and the qirad, the former becoming a loanword (with some modification of the function), while the latter did not? The funduq itself is a modified loanword from the Greek and Byzantine *pandocheion*. This modification made its pronunciation sound less Arabic and more cosmopolitan to the Italians. In addition, the function of the fondaco was to attract travelers, particularly foreign travelers, and the similarity to the funduq helped make it appealing to foreigners familiar with the latter.[125] Lastly, Stefania Gialdroni suggests that it was important for the Italians of the time, who were involved in the revival of Roman law, to use Roman-law terminology for the commenda to convey its compatibility with Roman law. She argues that it could be expected that in the city of Pisa, of all Italian cities—one that preserved an old manuscript of Justinian's digest and had a self-image as "new Rome"—the Arab organizational form was dressed with a Roman name: *commenda*.[126] She points to possible Byzantine connotations of the word *collegantia* that was used by the Venetians, and Roman connotation of the term *commenda* used by the Pisans. Note that this analysis does not fully account for why different terms were in use in different Italian cities and in different schools of Islamic jurisprudence. Linguists are encouraged to study the roots of these differences. I will expand on the resistance to migration of organizations in chapter 12.

The commenda emerges from this account of its migration as the ultimate migratory institution. It is hard to think of another trade organization that was sophisticated and complex enough to have only one or two historical origins but nevertheless migrated throughout Eurasia. The commenda is our ultimate example thanks to (a) its unique pattern of diffusion and (b) its dominant role in early modern Eurasian trade, serving as a key building block of many merchant networks, in Cairo, Venice, Genoa, Marseille, Amsterdam, Lübeck, New Julfa, Cochin, and Malacca.

The cases of the sea loan, the funduq, and the commenda demonstrate the three diverse patterns of institutional migration. The sea loan migrated from the ancient Levant to Greece, to Rome, to the Byzantine Empire, and to the Latin cities of Southern Europe. It was rejected by Islam as usurious, and did not make its way into the Arab Middle East and North Africa, nor to Persia, Central Asia, or India. The funduq was developed in the Islamic Middle East, based on small-scale earlier origins. It was carried with Islamic trade into Central Asia, India, and the borders of China, and to Anatolia, the Maghreb, and Spain. It was not adopted, as such, by Christian Europe. The commenda migrated into all of these realms, from China and India all the way to Northern Europe. What is the explanation for the different patterns of spatial migration of these three important institutions? Demands for different institutional solutions, based on differences between regions practicing maritime trade and overland trade, and based on different geographical locations throughout Eurasia, can explain much. Differences in attitudes to preexisting cultures and religions, to foreign-born institutions, to trade, and to usurious interest can take us a long way in understanding the willingness to import institutions into different civilizations. Contingent historical factors played their role in each of the patterns of diffusion. We will return to the ramifications of the three migration patterns for the theory of institutional migration in the conclusion of the book.

The migration of the sea loan, the funduq, and the commenda, and the big migratory picture beyond institutions, augments the puzzle: Why do we have embedded institutions at all? Why, of all the organizational forms studied in this book, did the corporation not migrate? In the big picture, Europe was much more of an importer than an exporter of technologies and organizational forms until 1500. Why did the cutting-edge organizational innovation—the corporation—not originate in China, India, or the Middle East, as did so many scientific, mathematical, and technological innovations? The development of the ultimate trade organization, the corporation, in West Europe, and its failure to migrate eastward, is the exception that requires explanation. Part IV of the book will be devoted to such an explanation.

PART III

~

Long-Distance Trade Enterprises on the Eve of the Organizational Revolution

~ 6 ~

Family Firms in Three Regions

This chapter deals with the examples taken from the uppermost end of the size spectrum of family firms. The purpose of this chapter is twofold. First, it aims to show that family firms were an important organizational form even in long-distance trade, and could reach large magnitudes. Second, it reveals the weaknesses and limitations of this organizational form, which the business corporation aimed to overcome.

The chapter is based on three microstudies, each taken from a different region in Eurasia and each representing a different version of the family firm. The families of Abdul Ghafur and Virji Vora, of sixteenth- and seventeenth-century Gujarat, with which we will deal in the first microstudy, were the organizational basis of major enterprises. They owned a large number of ships; and they employed many workers in various capacities, from factors and merchants to nakhudas, sailors, and soldiers, to bookkeepers and storekeepers. The Pu lineage of thirteenth-century Fujian in Southeast China, the second microstudy of this section, is somewhat distinct from the Gujarati cases in two senses: first, because the organization of Chinese family lineages became more formal and elaborated as time progressed; and second, because the Pu lineage also relied on holding public positions in the Yuan dynasty state apparatus, and on the institutional platforms provided by the state, to organize and expand its business enterprise. The last microstudy in this chapter is that of the Fugger family firm. Here again, family structures became more formal, but in a different way. The Fuggers, like other early modern Italian and German family firms, relied on partnerships and syndicates to expand their geographical reach and collaborate with outsiders to the family. Like the Pu, they were connected to rulers, but not as office holders but rather as major lenders.

MICROSTUDY: GUJARATI MERCHANTS' FAMILY FIRMS—VIRJI VORA AND MULLA ABDUL GHAFUR

The view of Asian overseas traders as being of the peddler variety is, as mentioned earlier, more than half a century old, originating with J. C. van Leur in his 1955 classic *Indonesian Trade and Society*.[1] However, subsequent research indicated that some of India's leading merchants were as far from the peddler or itinerant trader as one can imagine. The dearth of historical records has long impeded historians' ability to fully portray Indian merchant firms. What could be said about such firms was mostly based on European records and, as a result, was biased toward viewing Indian firms as secondary to the European corporations and as collaborating with them. Over the years, the histories of a few individual Indian merchants were reconstructed using these European records. Two Surat merchants, Virji Vora and Mulla Abdul Ghafur, and their families, are the best-documented and possibly the largest Gujarati merchants of their eras.[2] They were everything that van Leur's peddlers were not. In this section, I will describe the findings of microstudies I conducted on these two firms. This microstudy shows how family firms that did not rely on state support could trade over much of the span of the Indian Ocean. It also reveals the vulnerability of family firms that did not rely on a wider mercantile network, state support, or corporate entity platform.

Virji Vora must have been born sometime between 1590 and 1600. The first recorded mention of Vora is found in an English document of 1619.[3] These records do not indicate when he actually began his business career or what the state of his family business was before he rose to prominence.[4] He was, according to more recent studies, Jain by religion, not Muslim as was previously believed.[5] He was based in Surat—the major Mughal port in Gujarat since its annexation to the Mughal Empire in 1576, frequented by Europeans and other foreign merchants. He bought opium and cotton from local merchants and exchanged these for pepper in Southern India or in the Spice Islands. He was also involved in the clove, turmeric, and cardamom trade, and transacted with the English and Dutch for coral, quicksilver, lead, and other European commodities. On various occasions, he monopolized the market for pepper, either operating alone or by forming a syndicate. He sometimes traded with the

English, on other occasions competed with them, and on yet other occasions was involved in private, unauthorized (rather than company) trade with the EIC factors.[6] Vora lent huge amounts of money to locals, Mughals, and Europeans. Since the English and Dutch companies had little to offer the Indian markets in terms of European goods, they were compelled to borrow large sums to finance the purchase of Indian goods.[7] He is mentioned in European sources as involved with goods or credit transactions in 1619, 1630, 1633, 1648, 1654, 1661, 1669, and other years.[8]

He developed a large organizational network with branches throughout India, in Baroda, Broach, Ahmadabad, Burhanpur, Golconda, Agra, and the Deccan and Malabar Coasts. His agents were prepared to supply goods to all Indian ports not controlled by the Portuguese.[9] He also established branches in port towns of the Persian Gulf, Red Sea, and Southeast Asian countries. A significant number of brokers, clerks, accountants, and other personnel worked in his service, and he was reported to have amassed RS8 million and several ships in his lifetime.[10]

He suffered losses in the 1664 and 1670 Maratha raids of Surat, in which much of his property was looted. There is no mention of him after 1670, but it is known that his grandson, Nanchand, traded with the English after 1670. A reference to the Boras brothers in the memoirs of the French factor in Surat in the years 1681–86 is viewed by Varadarajan as a reference to Vora and his brother.[11] But this could be a reference to his sons. What we do know for sure is that Virji Vora himself was a major merchant and banker. It is not known whether a significant family firm survived a generational transfer.[12]

Mulla Abdul Ghafur was another Gujarat merchant operating on a large scale. He was active in the era that followed Vora's. He too had his central place of business in Surat, having arrived there in around 1670, young and poor, of Bohra Ismāʿīlī Muslim origins. Ghafur traded in the Red Sea, Persian Gulf, and Arabian Sea. His hub in the Western Indian Ocean was in Mocha, Yemen, where he had a large mansion and several warehouses. His nakhudas would stay at the mansion during the season and sometimes all year round to supervise the sales of his merchandise. He used his wealth to achieve political power, and enjoyed exemptions at customs and other privileges.[13]

Two famous episodes demonstrate the extent of his firm. Due to previous attacks by European interlopers and private traders (or, as the

Indians would have it, pirates), the Mughal ruler requested the VOC to provide an escort (using its Dutch vessels) to Indian ships. This escort brought about the preserving of the story of the "fleet of Hindustan" for the 1701 VOC records, and enabled its reconstruction by Das Gupta. Abdul Ghafur owned eight of the nineteen ships on the 1701 convoy. His nakhudas were the most influential next to royal Mughal nakhudas. The convoy sailed to Aden, Mocha, and Jedda. The Jedda leg was pursued mostly for pilgrimage purposes as this was the Red Sea port serving Mecca. Spices, sugar, and a few other goods were brought from India and exchanged mostly for coffee.[14]

The second episode took place in 1704–5, when the Dutch at Malacca detained three ships from Surat. Two were owned by Parsi merchants and one by Ghafur. Ghafur's ship had sailed to Malacca from Manila. He was able to send a new nakhuda, more able or trustworthy, pay off the Dutch, repair the ship, and sail it back to Surat with his goods as well as other passengers and their merchandise.[15] Within five years, Ghafur's ships and nakhudas were involved in trade eastward all the way to Manila, with Malacca serving as a regional hub, and westward all the way to Jedda, with Mocha serving as a regional hub hosting the permanent presence of Ghafur's agents.

Hence, by the mid-1680s, Ghafur had made his initial fortune, probably in Red Sea trade. He also combined ship ownership with trade. In a survey conducted by the Dutch, he owned seventeen out of Surat's 112 ships (the second-largest owner had just five).[16] His family—known as the Mullas—was recorded in the Dutch shipping records as owning ships between 1707 and 1736 (when the annual lists come to an end), eighteen years after Ghafur's death. Altogether, the list mentions thirty-four Mulla family ships, the largest weighing four hundred tons and carrying twenty-five guns. By the time of his death in 1718, Ghafur had accumulated RS8.5 million in addition to the ships and land he owned.[17]

Since Abdul Ghafur had no son, his death led to a major dispute on the issue of succession. The local administration, executing the imperial orders, confiscated all his property. After ceaseless lobbying and political maneuvering, Abdul Hai successfully established himself as an adopted son of Ghafur and regained possession of the enterprise. Soon after, however, Abdul Hai died, and his son, Mulla Muhammad Ali, took over the enterprise. Thus, the family firm survived an intergenerational transfer.

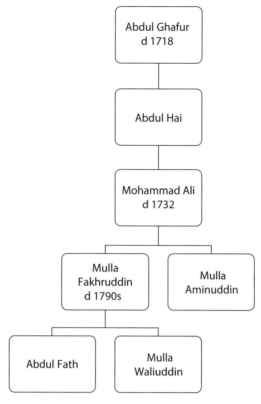

6.1. The succession of Abdul Ghafur. Source: Ghulam Nadri, "The Maritime Merchants of Surat: A Long-term Perspective, *Journal of the Economic and Social History of the Orient* 50, nos. 2/3 (2007): 235–58.

Figure 6.1 shows family genealogy and the succession of the Abdul Ghafur enterprise to his adopted son, Abdul Hai, and through the different generations.

Both the enterprises were based on the individual ownership and management of Virji Vora and Mulla Abdul Ghafur, respectively. They are not known to have been partnerships and did not separate business from family assets and affairs. Both merchants were active for around fifty years, and their businesses survived in family hands for a while longer. The combined business activity of the two families spanned from 1619 to at least 1736. They were both merchants and shipowners, and Vora, at least, was also a banker to other merchants and to European corporations. They both traded east and west, covering the entire span from Malacca to Mocha and beyond. They employed brokers, nakhudas, and agents in various ports in India, Arabia, and elsewhere in the Indian Ocean. They were both involved in politics but were not major political figures. We know little about the organization and management of their firms. We do not know what the scope of the mandate granted to the agents was, how they received their instructions from Surat, what their compensation and incentive structure was, or how were they monitored. There is no indication of a formal, legal organizational structure used by either Vora or Ghafur. They solved risk-spreading problems by being wealthy enough to spread their wealth among numerous fully owned ships, operating in different ports and markets, and dealing with a variety of goods. It is not clear from the available historical evidence, however, how they crossed their initial wealth constraints in a manner that allowed them to move beyond a single ship that subjected their entire wealth to unspread risks, and progress to a multiple-ship and multiple-destination firm that spread risks. To the best of my knowledge, owning small shares in several ships was not an available option in India. The ultimate scale and scope of their firms, as much as they can be ascertained from the surviving records, are no smaller than those of the largest Italian or German family firms of early modern Europe. They were independent from the European corporations and acted as free agents, making their independent decisions, often manipulating rather than obeying the Europeans, and maximizing their own wealth.

MICROSTUDY: THE RISE AND FALL OF THE PU LINEAGE

The Pu lineage is distinct from that of the Guajarati merchants in several important respects, justifying a full microstudy.[18] The Pu were not a loose family firm. Unlike the Guajarati families, they were closely and formally connected to the Chinese state. They used the uniquely Chinese family lineage, at a time at which it began to acquire corporate features, as an organizationally well-defined platform for their business enterprise. Unlike the Gujarati firms, they did not do business in the shadow of and in collaboration with European trade corporations.

The Pu lineage was closely related to the foreign maritime-merchant community of the international port city of Quanzhou. The most celebrated ancestor of the Pu lineage was the famous merchant official Pu Shougeng, who held important government posts during the late Song and early Yuan dynasties. According to most scholars, Pu Shougeng's ancestors, merchants of Arabic or Persian origin, settled in Southeast Asia in around the tenth century.[19] Pu is popularly believed to be a transliteration of the Arab name *abu* ("father of") to Chinese. During the eleventh century, they moved to the city of Guangzhou in Southeast China. In the thirteenth century, Pu Shougeng's father immigrated with his family to Quanzhou. Due to its location as a leading port on the shore of the Taiwan straits in Fujian Province and its political openness, a permanent presence of diasporic communities of foreign residents developed in the city during the Tang and Song dynasties. Pu Shougeng and his brother Pu Shoucheng occupied a number of official administrative and military positions and established close relations with scholars and local officials. In 1274, toward the end of the Song dynasty, he received the office of commissioner of maritime affairs of Quanzhou, the consequence of an expanding influence of foreign merchants. His titles were an approval of the expanding influence of foreign merchants in the late Song period, of his private militia consisting of thousands of men, and of his effective control of maritime trade at Quanzhou. Pu Shougeng leveraged his political and naval power to further enlarge his private family enterprise.[20] Pu Shougeng's wealth was enormous and his private residence covered a huge portion of Quanzhou's foreign settlement.[21]

In 1276, Hangzhou (the capital of Southern Song) succumbed to the Mongol forces, which by then had already conquered Northern China. The center of Song resistance, headed by one of the Song princes, shifted to Fujian and ultimately was confined the city of Quanzhou. Initially Pu Shougeng aligned with the retreating Song dynasty and the local Han Chinese elite.[22] According to some sources the retreating Song army commanders confiscated Pu Shougeng's entire fleet and property as part of their preparations to resist the Mongols in Quanzhou. In his rage, Pu Shougeng decided to side with the Mongols.[23] He prevented the Song allies from gaining control of the city and, while awaiting the arrival of the Mongols, massacred dozens of Song imperial clansmen who resided in the city.[24]

Following the overthrow of the Song dynasty, the social, political, and economic structure of Quanzhou was transformed. Foreign merchants became increasingly powerful and enjoyed unprecedented dominance over the city's finances and administration. Pu Shougeng was repaid generously by the new Yuan regime, which bestowed high official positions on him.

Merchants such as the Pu family—foreigners in origin, who had lived in China for several generations and had undergone a process of social and cultural assimilation—depended during the Song era on the support of local Han elite. Under a foreign dynasty, the Yuan, they were granted an even higher status and more favorable conditions than ever before, not only because they supported the Yuan takeover but also because they, like the Yuan, were of foreign origin. Soon after the surrender of Quanzhou, Emperor Kublai Khan made special efforts to revive the foreign trade relations so crucial to the region's economy. In 1278 he "commanded Pu Shougeng and other officials in Fujian province, that as the foreign peoples of the south-eastern islands are filled with the most loyal devotion to the righteous cause of our nation, they should make the traders going to those islands proclaim to the foreign peoples our gracious intention that, if they come, they would be cordially treated and allowed to travel and trade anywhere in our country as they please."[25] This order may, in fact, have been a license to send his private ships, or to invest in ortoys with foreign merchants, in profitable maritime trade.[26] Shortly after, several Southeast Asian countries reestablished trade relations with South China ports.[27] Pu Shougeng also continued to play a crucial role in maritime military activities. In 1280, he was ordered by the emperor to build two hundred warships that would constitute part of the huge fleet of six hundred ships for the intended invasion to Japan.[28] In the following years and until 1297, he was appointed to a series of key positions and enjoyed a flourishing military and political career, which established his hegemony over Quanzhou's affairs.[29]

Pu Shougeng's long career and his widespread connections solidified the position of his whole family, which became one of the most powerful lineages on the South China Coast during most of the Yuan period. His eldest son, Pu Shiwen, was appointed immediately after the Mongol takeover as pacification commissioner, a lieutenant-general for the army, and a customs commissioner for the Fujian Coast. In 1297, he succeeded his father as governor of Fujian.[30] His second son, Pu Shisi, was assigned to the post of historiographer of the Hanlin Academy (the imperial academy) in 1284. His third son, Pu Junwen, was a renowned scholar celebrated for his literary achievements. In 1296, he was appointed a secretary to the prime minister. In 1307, he was ordered to prepare the imperial edict recognizing Confucius as the "Greatest Sage of Fullest Sanctity."[31]

Pu Shougeng's eldest grandson, Pu Chongmo was appointed a commissioner of one of the provincial governments. He married a Han Chinese woman from the Yang family of Dongshi town, to the southeast of Quanzhou, and they had two sons.[32] A Quanzhou foreign Muslim named Fo Lian, who married a Pu woman, owned a large trade fleet of over eighty vessels.[33]

Thanks to the foreign merchants' special status in that period, many local Han sought their company and were even inclined to adopt their religion and marry into their families. By doing so, they hoped to be classified as belonging to the caste of the Central and West Asian foreigners (*semuren*) and thus benefit from the privileges bestowed by the Yuan on that caste. The Su family provides an interesting example of this phenomenon.[34] In the early Song period, the Su family held great power and influence in Southern Fujian. Following the Yuan takeover, they moved from the city to rural areas west of Quanzhou, and lost all their assets and status. Only one family branch managed to maintain its status, and its members remained, for the most part, influential landowners. The founding ancestor of this branch was Su Tangshe, who returned to Quanzhou, married an Arab Muslim, converted to Islam himself, and even changed his name to Ahemo, the Chinese transliteration of the Arabic name Ahmed. His sons and two of his grandsons also married Muslim women of the Pu family. In 1351, at the time of Su Tangshe's death, he owned lands, groves, and a formidable fortune. This suggests that the recovery of that branch of the Su family can be attributed to their involvement in maritime trade and their association with the influential Pu lineage.[35]

The support Pu Shougeng lent to the Mongols is believed to have caused the harsh fate of his descendants after the fall of the Yuan dynasty and the rise of the Ming dynasty. Until recent decades, the widely accepted narrative recounted that, after the Ming takeover, most members of the Pu family were forced to emigrate from Quanzhou to remote rural areas, where they adopted the local religions and customs and, in some cases, even had to conceal their identity.[36] However, researchers have recently encountered increasing evidence showing that the Pu family's close ties with the Mongol regime were already severed during the late Yuan era. In the last decades of the Yuan regime, the central government's hold over the peripheral areas gradually weakened, and many rebellions broke out across the empire, including the Fujian Province. The Muslim dominance in Quanzhou reached its abrupt end shortly before the fall of the Yuan dynasty, following a violent and destructive uprising by the local garrison, composed mainly of members of the city's West Asian community. It began in 1352 when several popular uprisings broke out in the area of Quanzhou. In an attempt to cope with the rebellions, the central government organized thousands of Quanzhou's foreign residents into military units. But in 1357 the Persian garrison itself, headed by two of the Persian merchant leaders in Quanzhou, rose in rebellion (the Ispah Rebellion, 1357–66). Encountering little resistance, they managed to gain control over the Quanzhou Prefecture. During the next five years, the Persian militia enjoyed regional hegemony and, taking advantage of the central government's weakness, easily managed to take over additional territories north of Quanzhou, including the provincial capital of Fuzhou.[37] The second phase of the rebellion began in 1362. Nawuna, presumably a Persian who married a daughter of the Pu family and who also inherited the position of commissioner of maritime affairs, ousted the leader of the southern faction of the rebellion and took his place as the acting ruler of the city of Quanzhou. The Ispah rebellion was eventually quashed in 1366 by a combined force of the provincial army and a strong militia of local Han Chinese families.

Those years of political revolt and military turmoil elicited a great deal of resentment toward the foreigners of Quanzhou, but especially toward those who were considered responsible for the bloody events. After the final defeat by the Chinese forces, the Pu lineage, now linked to Nawuna, suffered the anger and resentment of the local population. Thousands of the foreign Arab and Persian merchants were massacred when the uprising was crushed, and their graves desecrated. The decade of devastating fighting took a heavy toll on the economic and political status of Quanzhou. During that time, the Muslims exerted strict control over maritime trade, imposing restrictions and relentlessly harassing the local Chinese elite. During the rebellion, and in its aftermath, many wealthy merchants, both Chinese and foreign, chose to move to other regions in China and thus diminished the local wealth reserves even more. The detachment of

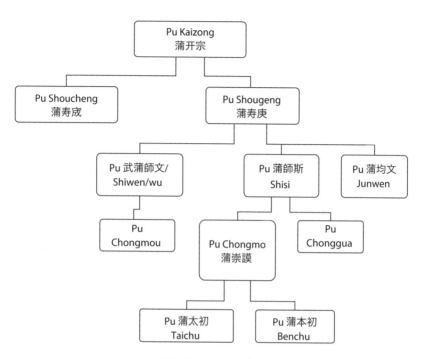

6.2. Pu lineage genealogy.

the port of Quanzhou from the internal commercial system resulted in a sharp decline of its importance and volume of activity.[38] Thus, the end of the Ispah rebellion also brought about the final demise of the Pu hegemony over political and economic affairs in Fujian.[39] In fact, it changed the rules of the game of long-distance trade in the Indian Ocean as a whole. The diasporic, community-based network and the ortoy had to be replaced by different organizational schemes in order for the trade to continue. Figure 6.2 shows the Pu lineage in Quanzhou through five generations, from Pu Shougeng's father to his great-grandson.

To conclude, despite the fact that the Pu were not a typical Chinese lineage, they serve as a good microstudy. Their history and genealogy are referred to in a wide array of sources because of their exceptional historical role in the transition from Song to Yuan. The history of this lineage demonstrates the important role played by lineage in organizing trade in China: the lineage was the platform used by the family firm. The lineage exercised ancestral worship, created and preserved genealogical manuscripts, and jointly owned common family halls, shrines, and burial grounds. Marriage, invention of fictitious common ancestors, and adoption were used strategically for business purposes. The lineage allowed resources to be pooled together and ensured the longevity of the enterprise. The Pu lineage was active too early to benefit from the greater flexibility of lineage formation that developed during the Ming dynasty into what some historians call the "contractual lineages."[40] Nevertheless, the Pu lineage operated a continuous trade enterprise from the tenth or eleventh century all the way to the second half of the fourteenth century. The duration of the family business was longer than that of any of the Gujarati, Italian, or German family firms I survey in the following microstudies. In fact, it survived longer than any Indian, Middle Eastern, or European family I encountered in the literature. Chinese lineages were more formally structured than European or Middle Eastern families. The Pu family's accumulated wealth and number of ships also seem to be larger than those of any known non-Chinese family firm.

The story of the Pu lineage also demonstrates nicely the interweaving between state, family, and business in China. The state was an additional platform, alongside lineage, upon which families were able to develop their business aspirations. Ties to the state were a mixed bag. When times were good, the family business flourished thanks such ties, getting business, privileges, and protection from the state; but when times were bad, the family could fall from power—just as the reigning dynasty could.[41] The Pu lineage was particularly sensitive to political upheavals, as it was of foreign origin. But its case also demonstrates the blurring over time of the distinctions between locals and a merchants' diaspora.[42] Han lineages strategically intermarried with the Pu in their Yuan dynasty heyday. After the fall of the Yuan, the Pu, who lost favor, strategically intermarried with local Han lineages. Members of the Pu lineage, notably Pu Shougeng, held official positions and played important roles in domestic politics. They accumulated and deployed their social capital and economic capital interchangeably in the private and public spheres. Looked at from the perspective of the rulers of China, official positions in Chinese ports were used, at times, to regulate merchants, of local or foreign origin, and at times to legitimize the private maritime trade of local elites which could not be effectively contained by the central government. So the holding of office was the amalgamation of the state and the family lineage that safeguarded the longevity of the family firm. But it was also an Achilles' heel of family lineages. Officeholding family lineages were left vulnerable if unable to maintain good relationships with the declining dynasty during the problematic stage at which it tended to become more expropriative and less rewarding—or when they had to decide if and when to tactically switch allegiance from a collapsing dynasty to the ascending dynasty that appeared likely to succeed it. Maintaining an alliance with a dynasty that eventually collapsed, or forging an alternative alliance with a contending dynasty that ultimately did not prevail, could prove catastrophic for the family. The Pu were able to make the transition from Song to Yuan but not the transition from Yuan to Ming. Aligning with a rising political power, timely detachment from a losing political horse, and good relations with reigning rulers were important for any large family firm. It was particularly important to the Pu family and its likes in China because they not only relied on the state as a supporter, and feared it as potential expropriator, but also used state platforms such as official positions to consolidate the family enterprise and property and facilitate cross-generational longevity. Their relationship with rulers was different from that of the Surrat family firms, which did not rely on Mughal office holding as a key organizational component, and from the Fugger firm, which was vulnerable not due to office holding but rather due to semiforced loans that they extended to rulers. The Pu indeed enjoyed an impressive longevity of some three centuries but faced their ultimate demise not long before Zheng He's voyages.

MICROSTUDY: THE FUGGER FAMILY— INTERNATIONAL MERCANTILE BANKERS

The microstudy of the Fugger family adds to what we have learned from the two previous microstudies of family firms due to its timing and location. It was located in west-central Europe just in the period in which the first Europeans sailed directly to Asia around the Cape. It operated in parallel to and in conjunction with the Portuguese. The Fugger family firm was the organizational model that the first English and Dutch who aimed at oceanic trade with Asia were aware of and decided not to adopt.

Any study of the innovation that led to the formation of the EIC and VOC not presenting the Fugger firm as the alternative will be deficient.

The first traceable member of the Fugger family was Johann Fugger, a farmer from a small village called Graben, near Augsburg, in southern Germany. According to municipal records, he settled in Augsburg in 1367 and entered the weaving business. Augsburg was located at the intersection of routes leading to the Rhein and Danube valleys, on the one hand, and routes across the Alps to Italy, on the other. Augsburg produced large quantities of woven goods, cloth, and textiles. It was made a Free Imperial City in 1276. All of these factors made Augsburg a major trading center and an attractive city for the young Fugger. He benefited from the city's independent status and, through marriage, he became a citizen there, which emancipated him from his feudal restrictions. In the last quarter of the fourteenth century, he expanded his business to include fifty weaving looms and a few horse-drawn carriages, with which his employees carried his goods to fairs throughout southern Germany. After a successful career that combined manufacturing and trade, he died in 1408, leaving two sons, Andreas (1394–1457) and Jakob (1398–1469). His two heirs greatly extended the business they inherited, to include trade in spices, silk, and woolen goods with Venice.[43]

The third-generation Fuggers were split into two branches, the Fuggers of the Roe Deer (Andreas's sons Lukas and Hans) and the Fuggers of the Lily (Jakob's sons Ulrich, Georg, Markus, and Jakob II). The most prominent of the third-generation Fuggers was Jakob Fugger II (1459–1525), also known as Jakob the Rich, of the Lily branch of the family. Jakob II, the tenth son of the family, aspired to become a cleric, and studied Latin. Upon the sudden death of two of his brothers, he was called to join the family business. Initially, he was its representative in Nuremberg and then in Venice. From 1477, he was the Fugger firm's factor and agent in Venice. His office was in the Fondaco dei Tedeschi, the living quarters of the city's German fondaco.[44] He developed the Fuggers' role in trade in Asian goods considerably. The Venetians imported these goods from the Levant, Egypt, and the Black Sea. The third-generation Fuggers exploited Augsburg's location to carry these Asian goods across the Alps into southern Germany and beyond. Jakob learned the double-entry bookkeeping system and the Arab numerals in Venice. He combined his new knowledge with the use of Latin as the transregional language in Europe, and, with the different branches of his family's firm across Central Europe, expanded the family business. In 1484, he moved to Innsbruck and became involved in the mining industry in Tyrol and the goldsmithing and minting business. Within three generations, the realm of activity of the Fuggers had expanded from Augsburg to Nurnberg, Ulm, and Frankfurt, to Venice and Innsbruck, to Hamburg and Lübeck, to Paris, London, Madrid, and Lisbon, and to Cracow, Warsaw, and Riga. Jakob Fugger's Lisbon agent, Markus Zimmermann, was involved in sending ships to India in 1503 and possibly 1506.[45] But gradually the German merchants were relegated by the Portuguese king to playing the secondary roles of providing copper and silver and of distributing, in Northern European markets, pepper and other spices imported by the Portuguese from India to Lisbon, instead of playing the primary role of sending ships to Asia.[46]

As Jakob II had no children, in 1510 he entered into partnership with his nephews, under the trading name of Jakob Fugger & Nephews. Initially he retained control of the firm and trained his nephews to be able to take the lead in the future.[47] In a testament written shortly before his death in December 1525, he bequeathed his entire business to his nephews, Georg's sons, with management powers assigned to Anton Fugger (1493–1560), Georg's third son. During Anton Fugger's term as the executive partner (1526–60), the firm reached the zenith of its wealth and political influence. By 1546, the Fugger firm's working capital had reached 5 million guilders, compared to the 2 million guilders the firm had inherited from Jakob II in 1525, making it the largest-ever firm in Europe to date. Anton, like Jakob II before him, encountered difficulties in attracting his nephews to play an active role in the new firm, Anton Fugger & Nephews. When he grew older, and as his sons were too young to take over the business, Anton became anxious about the future of the firm he had directed for thirty years, and approached his nephews one by one to convince them to take over the executive director's position. In the end, his elder son Markus (1529–97) and his nephew Hans Jakob (1516–76), Raymund's son, took over joint management of the firm.[48]

In 1574, the Fugger lineage split along family branch lines into separate northern and southern spheres of activity. Philipp Eduard Fugger (1546–1618) and Octavian Secundus Fugger (1549–1600), of the seventh generation, the sons of Georg Fugger II, decided to enter the expanding trade with India via the Cape Route. They moved their activity westward to the

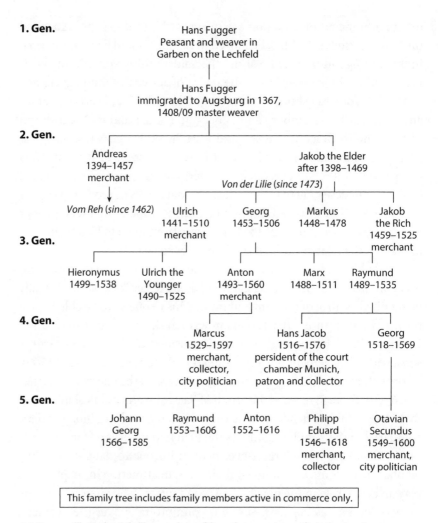

6.3. Fugger ("von der Lilie") genealogy, fifteenth to seventeenth centuries. Source: Häberlein (2012, pp. x–xi).

Atlantic due to the crisis of the eastward Levant-Venice-Augsburg trade in Asian goods. As Portugal dominated this route, they set up factories in Madrid and Lisbon and eventually Goa under the firm known as Georg Fugger's Heirs. The 1585 Asia Contract, a contract for sending ships and goods from Europe to Asia and back, was signed between King Philip II of Spain (and from 1581 also king of Portugal as Philip I), on behalf of Portugal, and the Italian merchants and financiers Giovanni Battista

Rovellasca and Giraldo (Gerhard) Paris. The Welser Company joined in and took five-twelfths of the contract from Rovellasca and Paris, further allocating three-twelfths to Georg Fugger's Heirs. Thus, the Fuggers ended up with 25 percent in the syndicate that won the five-year 1585 Asia contract. In 1591, they took a 7/32 share in the two-year Europa Contract, the contract for distributing Asian goods in Europe, at the request of Philip II, the king of Spain and Portugal.[49] Theirs was the most direct and intensive involvement of any of the Fugger firms in Eurasian oceanic trade.

Figure 6.3 shows the Fugger family genealogy, with a focus on the "Fugger of the Lily" branch, and the different splits in this branch through eight generations.

How was the Fugger family firm organized? A single answer cannot be offered for a firm that was in existence for more than two centuries. But we can identify the organizational features that will allow us to compare it to the Chinese Pu and Indian Vora and Ghafur family firms.

To analyze the Fuggers' organizational form, let us first step back in time to the Italian banking and merchant companies of earlier centuries. An in-depth analysis of these firms is outside the scope of this book, as they only marginally dealt with Eurasian trade and were active in a period that predated our starting point. We are interested here only in their possible influence on the organizational model of the Fugger firms. The Alberghi clans of thirteenth- and fourteenth-century Genoa; the Bardi, Peruzzi, and Acciaiuoli of fourteenth-century Florence; and the Medici of the fifteenth century, who expanded from Florence, were prime examples of the Italian family-based merchant banking firms. The number of partners in the Bardi firm ranged between eleven and sixteen in the period 1310–30. They employed 346 factors between 1310 and 1345,[50] and were the largest European family firm of their time. Sapori explained that they evolved in three stages: first, as a family establishing a business; then, taking on additional equity partners from the outside, often employees and agents; and third, leveraging by drawing deposits from outsiders and investing this debt capital in lending to rulers and in other banking activities.[51] They had a head office in Florence and branches in Venice, Rome, Milan, Avignon, Geneva, Bruges, and London.

How were these large Italian firms organized? At the core of each of these firms was the family itself, with the senior family members seen as partners. Factors and agents were either younger family members or paid employees. The entity as a whole could be seen as a general partnership, a *compagnia*. The partnership was for a specific term, ranging from just a few years to twenty-one years.[52] The fourteenth-century Florentine companies had a centralized organizational form, so business was done within one partnership. The fifteenth-century Medici firm was different. It was decentralized and organized into a network of partnerships. Each partnership was composed of a senior member from the Florence headquarters, the agent (either a member of the family or a nonmember) representing the Medici's banking and mercantile enterprises in a major town, and in some cases also more junior factors and employees in that town. Additional partnerships were formed for the manufacturing enterprises, silk manufacturing, and cloth manufacturing. This decentralized model was based on the lessons learned from the collapse of the fourteenth-century firms. The idea was to separate pools of assets and accounts to prevent the failure of the entire firm due to the insolvency of one branch, and to allow better monitoring of the business of each branch and enterprise.[53] Padgett termed these organizational forms "partnership systems."[54] Hunt termed them "quasi-permanent multiple partnerships."[55]

Johann Fugger settled in Augsburg two decades after the bankruptcy of the Bardi and Peruzzi companies in 1345, and the business activities of the early Fugger firms overlapped chronologically for about a century with those of the Medici Company. Though its headquarters were based across the Alps, the Fugger firm had senior agents in various Italian towns. Did it follow the Italian merchant banks' organizational model, in its centralized or decentralized version? To the best of my knowledge, this question has not, to date, been explored in full, either in terms of organizational similarities or in terms of identifying actual organizational learning.

Let us examine, based on the available secondary sources, two episodes in the history of the Fugger firms that shed light on its organizational challenges, the first from the early sixteenth century and the second from the late sixteenth century. The first revolves around Jakob the Rich's firm (1480–1525).[56] After the death of Jacob the Elder (a third-generation Fugger) in 1469, the Fugger family estate was held in joint ownership, termed *Ganerbschaft* in old German inheritance law, by his sons and heirs. *Ganerbschaften* were typically established to keep the primary family property, such as a castle or a palace, as one undivided residence, allowing the heirs to cohabit side-by-side in different residential wings while using common facilities. This inheritance institution was admittedly not very well adapted to the inheritance of an active mercantile family firm. In around 1480, the brothers formed a partnership by verbal agreement for running their family operation. Due to the expansion of their range of mining activities, and with the addition of outside partners, a formal written partnership agreement was concluded in 1494. Jakob the Rich, the youngest brother, was the lead partner and manager. The Fuggers did not follow joint management, as *Ganerbschaft* might suggest, nor primogeniture inheritance by the eldest son, as was the case in England and other parts of Europe, nor egalitarian inheritance, as was the case under Islam. They opted to use partnership contracts and testacy by wills to pragmatically transfer the firm's control to able businesspersons.

Upon the deaths of his older brothers Ulrich (1510) and Georg (1506), Jakob paid their widows their due share in the partnership's equity. To attract younger members of the family to the firm, he offered a partnership to their sons and his nephews Ulrich II, Hieronymus, Raymund, and Anton (fifth-generation Fuggers). The written agreement with the nephews was concluded in 1512 and was extended several times until Jakob's death in 1525. According to these agreements, partners had to devote their labor and capital exclusively to the firm. The capital investment was locked into the firm for the duration of the partnership. It was distributed with retained profits at the end of the partnership term, typically six years. But the practice was to renew the agreement and lock-in the original investment and profits for a further six years. During the life of the partnership, partners were entitled to a salary. They were also entitled to withdraw some money for personal needs, subject to the approval of the managing director, to maintaining sufficient liquidity in the firm, and to the deduction of the withdrawn sum from the partner's share at dissolution. Management powers were increasingly concentrated, from one contract to the next, in the hands of Jakob. For example, while his brothers had the power to act as agents of the firm and bind it in transactions, according to the 1494 agreement, this authority was no longer granted to his nephews in the 1512 agreement. Their powers were similar to those of senior employees but with shares in the equity. By 1494, the name of the firm was Ulrich Fugger of Augsburg and Brothers. In 1512 it was changed to Jakob Fugger and Brothers' Sons [Nephews], to reflect the shift in control.

Next to control, capital lock-in, and the borderline between business and private assets, intergenerational transfer was the other major organizational concern. Upon the death of partners, their share was bought out by paying it to their widows. Alternatively, when a partner's share was inherited by his sons (for example, when the wife died first or children inherited by will), only sons that were willing and suitable to work for the firm could retain their portion of the partnership share held by the estate. Sons who went on to careers in politics or the clergy were also bought out with sums paid in installments over a period of three years, so as not to harm liquidity. The death of partners was handled swiftly upon Georg's and Ulrich I's deaths. One could not be a passive partner. So fourth- and fifth-generation Fuggers who did not become merchants—for example, Georg's son Marx, who was a cathedral provost—were not made partners.

The gravest threat to the firm's longevity was the death of a managing partner. The transition from Jakob the Elder to Jakob the Rich was not swift. The former died in 1469; the latter assumed full management and control only in 1512. In the meantime, the firm went through a joint-ownership stage, an unwritten-partnership stage, and a written-partnership stage with three, formally equal managing partners. How could a family firm of this magnitude and complexity of business avoid the same instability in the next expected transition, upon Jakob the Rich's death? Though Jakob had been married since 1498, he had no children, and this, counterintuitively, eased the transfer of centralized control. He could design the intergenerational transitions in his wills of 1521 and 1525 without being concerned over feuds between his sons or the need to buy any of them out. By the time Jakob the Rich died, on December 30, 1525, at the age of sixty-six, he was extraordinarily rich. The inventory of his estate revealed assets totaling 3,000,058 Rhenish florins (guilders) and liabilities amounting to 867,797 guilders, resulting in a net value of about 2.1 million guilders. The Fugger firm and its assets were bequeathed to his nephews, Raymund and Anton Fugger, the latter to be given control in case of deadlock.

The second episode takes us half a century past the death of Jakob to the seventh-generation *Georg Fuggerische Erben* (Heirs of Georg Fugger firm). This was a partnership between Georg's three sons that was active between 1574 and 1600.[57] The available sources on the organizational details of this partnership are more limited, but despite this, I selected this episode because in this firm the Fuggers' involvement in Eurasian trade was at its height. The name of the enterprise suggests that it originated around the inheritance of an active firm by several brothers who held it as a joint property, as was the case with the original Fugger firm of the previous episode, and with other southern German trade companies. The absence of formal partnership contracts makes it impossible to make clear statements regarding the legal structure of the company,[58] hence one has to infer it from accounts and letters. Three brothers, Philipp Eduard (1546–1618), Octavian Secundus (1549–1600), and Raymund III (1553–1606), seem to have been the partners in terms of investment and sharing of profits. Philipp Eduard and Octavian Secundus signed all agreements and contracts together. Correspondence was always written on behalf of the two of them.[59] Thus, they seemed to have controlled the firm with equal rights as the two managing directors. They had centralized headquarters with competences and tasks that enabled the tight and consistent control of the various branches. Accounts of the firm as a whole were kept by the chief accountant at its headquarters in Augsburg, and it had agents in Hamburg, Cologne, Frankfurt am Main, and Venice. During its participation in the Asia Contract, it also had a factor in Goa, and, during its participation in the Europe pepper contracts, agents were also based in Lübeck, Amsterdam, Middelburg, and Antwerp.[60] It was a globalizing yet centralized family firm. In terms of the level of centralization, it resembled the model of the earlier Italian firms, such as the Peruzzi and Bardi firms—not the decentralized "partnership system" model of the later Medici firm.

It is not clear whether there was a separation between the private property of the partners and the firm's capital. Some accounts and balance sheets include only business-related capital, while others include all the wealth of the partners, including also immovable property and what looks like private wealth.[61] It is likely that, while the partners recognized the firm as a separate pool of assets for their internal affairs, such as calculations of investments and division of profits, this did not affect liabilities toward third parties. Each partner was separately and jointly liable for the debts of the company. In modern terms they had unlimited liability.

The Fugger family firm was a success story. It was established in 1367 and was still in active business in 1591 and beyond. It survived six generations and five intergenerational transfers, and was the largest enterprise in Europe in the middle of the sixteenth century. It allied with kings and emperors. It had branches all over Europe. It was involved in manufacturing, the mining trade, and banking in a manner that created synergies and allowed diversification. It was able to shift its trade in Asian goods from full reliance on Venice and the overland routes to a focus on Lisbon and the oceanic route. It was able to provide the kings of Portugal with silver that was the only European good in high demand in India, with credit that funded the *Carreira da Índia* (the voyages to India), and with a distribution network in Europe for Indian pepper and spices.[62]

But its organizational form was problematic in several senses. Note that the problems analyzed here were identified based on organizational theory and on historical reality, not on explicit and documented statements by the Fuggers. Intergenerational transfers were a repeated major concern. Capable and motivated managing directors were in short supply. This was partly the case because heirs preferred a leisurely aristocratic or religious life over the life of agents in trade destinations. Splits between family lines lead to divisions of enterprise and, at times, to competition and rivalries. The Fuggers were not able to separate their private wealth from the company's business capital—they remained personally liable for business debts. Business failures were a major concern for German merchant-cum-banking firms. There were at least sixty-three business bankruptcies in Augsburg alone between 1529 and 1580, including two within the Fugger family.[63] Business failure could result from the default of a ruler who borrowed heavily from the firm, or from the materialization of trade and market risks. Public finance and private business were conducted within the same Fugger family firm, subjecting the latter to the less calculable risks of the former. While the Pu were vulnerable to political upheavals due to their reliance on office holding, the Fuggers were vulnerable due to their large-scale lending to rulers. The lack of separation between business and private assets must have also been a major concern for the Fuggers. Family members who inherited fortunes may have preferred to keep their windfall at a safe distance rather than investing it in business and its associated liabilities, to secure a more leisurely and respectable aristocratic lifestyle. The Fuggers depended on family assets and ploughed back profits. They did not draw equity capital from outsiders. If more capital or wider risk-spreading were necessary, they collaborated in syndicates with other family firms, such as the Welsers. They had no access to an impersonal equity stock market. While the Fugger network in Europe was well placed, a network in Asia (beyond Goa) was never fully formed. The Fuggers relied on other commercial intermediaries or political rulers, initially the Venetians and later the Portuguese, to gain access to Asian goods. They did not form a network of branches and factories in Asia. This must have been beyond their capital, labor, and management capabilities. The Portuguese state and the English and Dutch corporations to which we will soon turn did have such capacities.

CONCLUSION

In the period covered in this book, large-scale family firms could be found in India, China, and Europe. In all three regions, family firms were involved in long-distance trade, and all shared a common core: the family itself. Often the firms combined trade with banking or, less often, with manufacturing or mining. In addition to the general challenges of the trade environment, they faced similar family-related challenges: relationships within the family itself and intergenerational transfer. Yet there is no reason to presume that the Pu, Voras, or Fuggers learned from each other how to organize their family firms and deal with such challenges.

In China, family lineage created a protocorporate framework. The holding of state official positions provided a stable platform for longevity and for security from expropriation by the state. The Pu relied on traditional Chinese lineage as the basis of their business. They attached their enterprise to the office of commissioner of maritime affairs of the port city of Quanzhou.

In organizing their firms, the Fuggers relied on the Roman and continental European legal institution of the *compagnia*. In Europe, there were no institutions of family lineage. Thus, achieving longevity and intergenerational transfers of large trade enterprises was more challenging. The relationship with the state was less stable due to the multiplicity of small political entities and frequent wars. Rich families and enterprises such as that of the Fuggers were pressed to provide loans to rulers. This made for good business when the borrowing ruler won the war and paid back the principal plus high interest—but it was catastrophic for the fate of the family firm when that ruler lost the war. As there was no asset partitioning between private family assets, banking assets, and long-distance trade assets, family firms such as that of the Fuggers were vulnerable to sovereign-debt failure and consequently to business bankruptcy. Chinese solutions could not be imported to Europe because of differences in family structure, in the religious base, and in the characteristics and scope of the political state.

We know less about the Indian family firms, their organization, legal status, management, and longevity, due to scarcity of records. The Gujarati families did not rely on either Chinese-like or European-like supporting institutions. But they could lean on the European corporations, the EIC and VOC, and, to a lesser extent, on the Mughal rulers, for business infrastructure and longevity.

As much as family firms evolved to suit their particular trade challenges and political and social environment, they eventually encountered inherent outer limits. They were sensitive to intergenerational transfer problems, to asset partitioning, and to state expropriation. The Pu lineage disintegrated with the collapse of the Yuan dynasty. The largest European trading-cum-banking family firms, such as the Fuggers, were particularly vulnerable to bankruptcy due to the frequency of religious wars during the sixteenth and seventeenth centuries.

The family-firm model of organization was not able to maintain long-lasting, large-scale, financially stable enterprises that could cover the full geographical span between Europe, India, and China. The organizational limitations of the family firm, even in its most developed form, called for the search for new institutional solutions. Commenda-based networks, to which we will turn next, were able to cover much of Eurasia. But they did not rely on impersonal cooperation and did not enjoy longevity. Ruler-owned enterprises, most notably the Estado da Índia or Zheng He's voyages, which relied on state taxation and state borrowing, will also be examined here. A new institutional solution, the joint-stock business corporation, to which we will turn later, was sought out to make the leap into oceanic Eurasian trade. And, as we shall see in the last part of the book, the corporation offered longevity, a widespread investor base, asset partitioning between private and business assets, and stronger political lobbying that could make rulers' commitments to it more credible and thus shield its shareholders from expropriation.

Merchant Networks

Merchant networks were relatively complex organizational forms that combined several building blocks. A prototypical network had members who belonged to the same town or region, ethnic group or religion. The place of origins of the members often served as the hub of the network. The hub served not only as a place of residence of nontrading family members, but also as a meeting place, marketplace, and center of information flows for traveling and diasporic members, and a place in which norms were generated and adjusted and disputes settled. The nodes of the network were located in ports and other market cities. Some network members resided in these nodes either permanently or temporarily as young merchants; others visited them as itinerant merchants. Various organizational building blocks could be used in networks, family firms, regular loans, sea loans, employment of salaried or commissioned agents, partnerships, commenda, and more. The legal framework could be based on customary or religious law of the ethnic group or on the law of the general civilization within which the group was living. Universal building blocks were available to all Eurasian networks. But varying building blocks were not available uniformly to all networks. The sea loan or the commenda, being legal building blocks, were adopted in Latin Europe or in the Islamic Middle East only if they were received by the law of the ethnic group of the network, if they were received by the general civilization in which the group operated, and if the ethnic group did not oppose these blocks (as was the case with Jewish law and the commenda). Caravanserais were a building block only for networks that were involved in overland trade within their territories of expansion. The sanctions could be legal, but as the ethnic group usually did not enjoy sovereignty or autonomy, the sensations were more typically reputational, religious, or social.

The three microstudies in this chapter offer real-life examples of merchant networks in operation. The Cairo-based Jewish merchants' network, whose records (from the tenth through twelfth centuries) were preserved in the Geniza—the first microstudy in this chapter—represents, in its India segments, a simple and thin network. Next, the Armenian network centered in New Julfa (from the seventeenth through eighteenth centuries) represents the epitome of the merchant network in its most sophisticated, elaborated, and expanded form. This network began its expansion before the corporations rose to dominant position, but as the corporations expanded the network had to adjust to their presence and was able to free-ride their Cape Route voyages. Finally, the Sephardic Jewish network based in Livorno (eighteenth century) exemplifies the marginalization of the network in the shadow of the corporation. Taken together, these three microstudies provide us with a taste of some episodes in the rise and decline of merchant networks.

MICROSTUDY: THE JEWISH MAGHRIBI MERCHANT NETWORK (CAIRO–ADEN–INDIA)

The microstudy based on the Cairo Geniza provides a unique opportunity to study in detail the organization of long-distance trade of Jewish merchants based mostly in Cairo trading with India. The exceptionality of the records preserved in this collection makes it the best available source on the organization of trade, Muslim as well as Jewish, in many centuries.[1] It allows us a comparison of the organizational forms and infrastructures of India trade in the era of the Roman Empire with that of the medieval Islamic era. It is also the last available opportunity for a comprehensive microstudy of a merchant network before the arrival of Europeans in Asia.

The Cairo Geniza is a collection of some 210,000 Jewish manuscript fragments found in the late nineteenth century in the sacred manuscripts storeroom (*geniza*) of the Ben Ezra Synagogue in Cairo. Jews were obliged to store any manuscript containing any of the names of God in the Geniza.

Thus, the Geniza contains Jewish religious texts such as biblical, Talmudic, and later rabbinic works. In addition, it houses many secular documents that were stored because they were likely to include God's name even just as a courtesy blessing. The collection provides a detailed picture of the social, economic, and cultural life of Jews in the North African and Eastern Mediterranean regions, and even in Yemen, especially during the eleventh to thirteenth centuries. As Goitein and others have shown, the Cairo Geniza contains a treasure trove of merchants' correspondence, contracts, and dispute-resolution records. The merchants' records show they were involved in trade in the Mediterranean, Middle East, and India.

The Cairo Geniza contains an unparalleled collection of documents referring to the trade between the Middle East and India. More than 450 such documents, which are now dispersed throughout various libraries and archives around the globe, were already identified, dated, completed, glossed, and edited thanks to the painstaking work of Goitein, Friedman, and other historians. Fortunately for this book, a long-standing project of publishing and analyzing the Geniza records relating to the Indian Ocean trade was recently completed. Goitein worked on the project, albeit with interruptions, from the 1950s through to his death in 1985. Thereafter, his former student Mordechai Akiva Friedman took over. A book in English, covering the more significant documents, was published in 2008, and a more comprehensive publication of documents in Hebrew is underway, the first four volumes having been published in 2009–13. The India Book collection contains correspondence, commercial lists, bills and the like, and legal records. This corpus allows historians to reconstruct a rich description of the trade in the period 1090–1150.[2]

Certainly, the Geniza has its limitations. Only those documents that ended up in Cairo reached the Geniza. Only those documents that, according to the Jewish religious decree, were prohibited from being destroyed because they mentioned the name of God were stored in the Geniza. Only those documents that survived in the Geniza underneath the synagogue in a readable state for some eight hundred years are accessible.[3] But despite these limitations, this repository surpasses, with respect to institutional and legal issues, any other repository of Eurasian trade documentation for the period before the Portuguese arrival in the Indian Ocean. Its inclusion here is therefore justified, even though it predates this book's timeframe by two hundred to three hundred years.

The Cairo Hub and Its Spokes

Much of the literature based on the Geniza deals with Mediterranean trade, but in the Geniza-based microstudy I present here I focus on trade with India. The India trade headed overland from Cairo to the Red Sea, sailing to its exit and to nearby Aden, from Aden along the Arabian Sea coast or across the ocean to Indian ports, mostly along the Malabar Coast (notably Kulam), and occasionally further north in Konkan (for example, Mangalore) or Gujarat (Tana, Nahrwara). Goods heading east included textiles and clothing, ornaments made of silver, glass and brass, carpets, and paper. Goods returning west included spices, aromatics, iron, silk, pearls, Chinese porcelain, and ivory.[4]

Cairo-Fustat served as a major hub of the trade network. From there, many traders, including Maghribi merchants (originally from northwest Africa), initiated and financed trips to India. Agents were initially employed in Cairo, reported to principals there, settled their accounts, received their payment, and were ultimately dismissed there.[5] In Cairo, disputes were resolved by the Jewish rabbinical court.[6] From Cairo, goods imported from India were reexported to the Eastern Mediterranean, North Africa (the Maghreb), and Southern Europe (Sicily and Spain). The pivotal position of Cairo is exemplified by the fact that not a single business letter referring to trade going directly from a place southeast of Egypt to a Mediterranean destination was found in the Geniza. Goitein and Friedman believe that this did not represent merely a preservation bias but rather stemmed from the fact that Cairo was the terminus of the India trade.[7] Figure 7.1 shows Cairo as the central hub of the Maghribi network. The network spreads from Cairo eastward to India, the Eastern Mediterranean, North Africa, and Southern Europe.

Aden was the secondary hub, where shipping segments ended and most ships from Egypt and India terminated their voyage. There are almost no records in the Geniza for ships going all the way from Egypt to India.[8] The Geniza documents reveal the pivotal role of Aden, not only in providing ships with safe shelter, food, and water, but also as a place for striking deals, storing goods, building and hiring ships, collecting customs, supervising agents, gathering information, and settling disputes. Many of the services were provided by prominent members of the Jewish

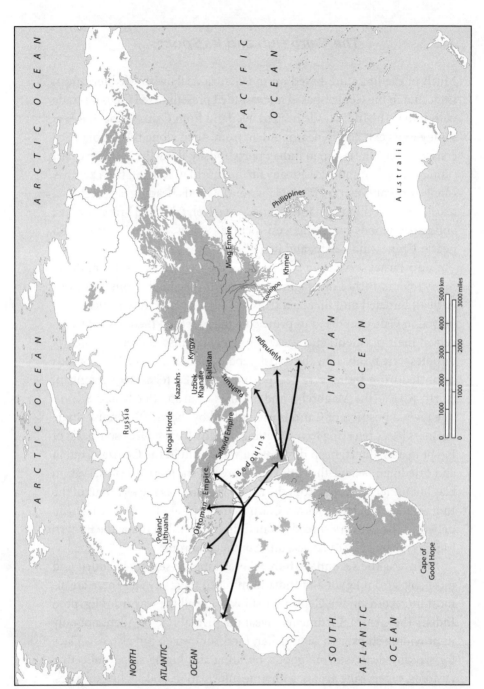

7.1. The Maghribi network.

community of Aden. The *nagid*, the head of the Jewish community, represented the community and the Jewish merchants vis-à-vis the political authority, and settled disputes among merchants. The *wakil al-tujjar* (in Hebrew, *pequīd ha-soharīm*) was a representative of the traveling merchants in Aden.[9]

The Organizational Menu

I will begin by surveying what is known about business organization in this era, based on the wider and better-studied Mediterranean trade corpus of documents. I will then proceed to the documents that deal specifically with India trade. At the center of Mediterranean trade were extended families. These often comprised three generations who lived together or as nearby as possible. Family members often shared living expenses and revenues, showing a high level of trust in each other.[10] They often acted as a single unified party in dealing and contracting with outsiders and in accepting liabilities.[11] Family members resided temporarily in trade destinations or traveled back and forth between Cairo and such destinations. Family-based networks were extended and enhanced by the bringing in of nonfamily members. Such inclusion, in the case of the Geniza era, was encouraged mainly to add labor force rather than capital. Nonfamily members were employed as fixed-payment agents, commission agents, commenda agent-partners, and (though rarely) as full partners or partners financed through sea loans.[12]

A distinctive and remarkable arrangement that appears in the Geniza records is that of "formal friendships," as this relationship was labeled by Goitein, the don of Geniza studies, or "informal business cooperation," as labeled by Udovitch, also a leading historian of the Geniza.[13] Following Greif, the recent literature devotes much attention to this arrangement and debates its nature.[14] The formal friendship is a framework within which reciprocal agency services were provided by the two parties to each other. Each of the parties provided trade services to the other, typically receiving goods to sell, with a request to buy others in exchange. The reciprocity was nonpecuniary. However, in the long run, the services provided by the two parties were expected to be balanced off. The relationship was considered informal in the sense that the parties did not conclude a written contract.[15] But most other forms of agency and partnership were also not created by a written agreement but rather by letters or verbal understanding. The friendship was also less formal in the sense that the consideration for each service performed was not fixed or monetized. However, as Goldberg recently showed, the law regulated some aspects of the relationship, and some kinds of disputes among the parties could be brought to courts of law.[16] All scholars agree that formal friendships were the most popular form of employing agents. In Goldberg's sample, 67 percent of all agency services used this form.[17]

Was India trade organized using the same organizational forms, with roughly the same regularity? The organization of India trade was not studied as systematically, and no quantitative study of the use of organizational forms in this context is available. Yet the gathering, annotation, and publication of India trade documents in the recent volumes of Goitein and Friedman allow us to achieve a better sense than ever before of the organization of that trade. Let me start by presenting three particular merchants who figure prominently in Geniza documents; I will then outline what is known about Indian Ocean shipping; and lastly, I will offer a few concrete examples from the documents. Joseph Lebdi exemplifies a traveling merchant; Abraham Ben Yiju exemplifies a merchant based in India (where he resided for seventeen years); and Madmun b. Hasan b. Bundâr exemplifies a merchant based in the transit hub of Aden.[18]

Lebdi traveled from Libya via Cairo to Gujarat, India, making his documented journey between 1094 and 1097. He most probably made additional journeys before and after. We know best about this particular journey because of the ensuing litigation.[19] He carried a combination of his own goods, goods in partnership, and goods as an agent for Jekuthiel al-Hakim of Fustat and other merchants. He also carried instructions from merchants to buy certain goods in India. In Aden, he transacted in some of the goods and assumed additional tasks. In India, he handled some of the goods personally, and some through a local broker. Some of the goods bought he sent with other merchants traveling back to Aden, and some he carried himself on his return in the second season. The subsequent litigation resulted from the loss of goods at sea on the way back. In that litigation, no written contract was presented for any of his agency or partnership relationships.[20] The relationships behind all these forms were agreed upon orally.

Elsewhere, Ben Yiju arrived in India from Tunisia, via Cairo and Aden, in 1132 and stayed there until 1149.[21] From India, mostly from Mangalore, he sent merchandise such as pepper, spices, betel nuts, and iron to merchants in Aden and Cairo. From Aden he received gold and goods to be sold in India, in exchange with traveling merchants. His relationships with merchants in Aden and Cairo took the form of friendship (formal or not), partnership, and commissioned agency.[22]

The third of our prominent merchants was Madmun the Nagid of Yemen, who, in addition to his trade activities, was the political head of the Jewish community in Aden in 1140–51, representative of the merchants (*wakil al-tujjar*), and superintendent of the harbor.[23] His family is believed to have migrated to Aden from Persia. He had marriage ties to the representative of merchants in Cairo and to other Mediterranean merchants, and was involved in India trade by employing agents, entering partnerships, and owning ships. The Geniza preserved many letters he sent to Ben Yiju in India with requests and instructions regarding merchandise he wished to buy or sell.[24] He also had frequent correspondence with Cairo merchants. His three sons also entered the trade and traveled to India.[25]

Two differences between Mediterranean trade and India trade from the perspective of Jewish merchants centered in Cairo in the era of the Geniza are the ability to resort to existing infrastructures unique to Indian Ocean trade and the absence of a significant and permanent Jewish diaspora in India. A full survey of Indian Ocean shipping and trade infrastructure is beyond the scope of this microstudy.[26] It is enough to say that small and midsize merchants could rely on a preexisting infrastructure to transport their goods. For example, a merchant could make his way from Egypt to India with his goods, without owning a ship. He could also send unaccompanied goods—in the care of the nakhuda, on board ship, and in the care of the representative of larger merchants, in port. The ship managed by a nakhuda was an organizational form unique to the Indian Ocean. Representatives of merchants, similar to the aforementioned Aden representative, were not present in all Mediterranean ports.[27] On the other hand, there were not many Jewish merchants in Malabar or Gujarat (Ben Yiju being a notable exception). The two differences taken together made formal friendships less relevant in India trade, made paid-commission agents and commenda agents more relevant, and made the sending of unaccompanied goods to agents staying temporarily in India more feasible.

The Geniza records that relate to India trade do not contain many partnership or commenda contracts. Most of the evidence on the existence of such agreements is taken from correspondence and court-litigation records. Let us examine a few specific examples.

Examples Relating to Traveling Itinerant Traders and Agents

A letter from Amram B. Joseph in Alexandria to Naharay b. Nissim in Cairo, sent around 1094–96, requested his assistance in locating his sister's husband, Abu 'l-Faraj Nissim, and goods sent by him from India:

> He [Abu 'l-Faraj Nissim] wrote to us in his letter, that he sent 1¼ manns [of] old camphor to Aden to Sheik Abu Ali Hasan b. Bundar and asked that he sell it and send us [Nissim's family in Alexandria] the proceeds. He]Nissim] knew that the camphor reached him [Hasan in Aden] but did not know whether he sent it to us [in Alexandria] or not. The latter dated two years ago, and we trusted God that the proceeds will reach us with Jews arriving from Aden.[28]

The letter goes on to list at least three Jews who had recently arrived from Aden but carried no news or money from Nissim. Amram begs on behalf of his sister that Nahary, the highest Jewish religious authority in Cairo, exercise his authority and press Hasan, the representative of merchants in Aden, to respond to the repeated enquiries and provide information regarding the whereabouts of Nissim in India and the fate of the money sent by him. It is not necessary to follow this story to its end. The section suffices to demonstrate the extent to which information asymmetries were huge, travel times long, and risks high. This is probably a typical case for a low-means trader, an itinerant trader,[29] traveling to India, relying on Aden as a hub, on domestic shipping, and on favors from other traveling itinerant traders or agents in sending back information and small quantities (in this case 30 kg or so) of high-value goods. His wife back home lived in extreme uncertainty, having no income for family subsistence, not knowing whether she was now a widow, and pinning all her hopes on receiving news from occasional travelers. This trade was experienced by lone itinerant traders and their worried families.

An example of the use of correspondence as a means of instructing and empowering agents in India can be found in the following letter, written by Joseph b. Abraham in Aden around 1136–39, and sent to Abraham Ben Yiju in India:

> I have sent it, my lord, to you, its weight exactly 160 pounds. And it is fine arsenic. Please make an effort my lord, to sell it all, as you are graciously accustomed to do, for whatever price God apportions as livelihood. With the proceeds purchase for me, your servant, a small quantity of iron, if available, and cardamom, and if you can, a little borax, or whatever you consider proper. For one who is present sees what is not seen by one who is absent. Send it to me on the first ship traveling to Aden. And you, my lord, are free of liability. And if you my lord, have an opportunity to come, bring it with you, God willing.[30]

This letter contains additional references, including the following: instructions regarding other goods; five presents "in return for some of your services"; a request to search for an absconding commenda agent of Joseph who may have fled to Ceylon; a recommendation on an Egyptian merchant who was a newcomer to India; and a letter to be forwarded to another merchant in India. Based on the correspondence as a whole, it seems that the relationship between Joseph and Abraham was in the nature of a formal friendship, perhaps with some elements of commissioned agency, but did not resemble a partnership or commenda. This sort of relationship was possible because of the unique position of Ben Yiju, who, unlike most other Jewish merchants, did not travel back and forth but rather lived in India for seventeen years.[31] The letter acknowledges a significant information asymmetry between Aden (not to say Cairo) and India. As a result, the principal empowers the agent with discretion as to price and even goods and modes of transportation.

Examples of a Commenda and a Partnership

The Islamic commenda was familiar to those Middle Eastern and North African Jews who lived among Muslims. They made use of it in their long-distance trade. But they did not import it into Jewish law. Their use was selective, in some forms of transactions with some partners. Let us turn now to examples of the use of the two basic kinds of partnerships. The first is unmistakably a commenda:

> Buy from me now and write and sign and deliver this to Joseph Lebdi, and be this note his evidence . . . that I received from him goods, and was satisfied by them, because I believe that I can profit from them, and the price of all the goods is 460 fine Egyptian Dinars, so that I will take them and travel to the state of [Yemen, India, Maghreb] and other states as I see fit, and as becomes possible, in the form of merchant commenda, and buy and sell, and upon returning safely, whatever God provides, Lebdi will receive ¾, and will bear no liability for damage on sea or on land . . . and I will receive ¼ of the profit alone. . . .[32]

This late eleventh-century document, written in Fustat, is the only example in the India book for a commenda contract,[33] specifically a unilateral contract in which the traveling partner did not make any investment. Profits were split 75 percent and 25 percent, accordingly. It was drafted as a declaration made by the traveling partner, confirming receipt of the goods and the terms of the partnership. It was deposited with the Fustat scribe, presumably as notarial evidence.

For a general partnership, see, for example, the evidence presented before court in Cairo in 1099:

> I remember having been together with Mr. Salomon and his brother Joseph, the Son of Mr. David Lebdi, in al-Mahdiyya.[34] They were both in one room, and all their merchandise was in both their hands [was dealt-with by them as common property]. I asked each of them separately about their relationship. Each of them answered: "we gave each other full power over all we have."[35]

Thereafter, one brother, Salomon, traveled to Spain, and the other, Joseph, to India. Salomon, taking the shorter and ostensibly less dangerous leg, ended up drowning in the Mediterranean. This is one of the rare examples of partnerships, documented in the Geniza, between brothers and other close relatives. Solomon's son David eventually sued Joseph for not splitting the profits of the India trip with him and his family. In the litigation that followed in the Fustat court, Joseph was forced to take the following oath, as well as providing an inventory:

> Joseph b. David—may he rest in Eden!—will swear, on behalf of David, the son of his brother Solomon—may he rest in Eden!—that he never cheated his father Solomon in any transaction, partnership, commenda, inheritance, or other dealings from when any such commenda, or transaction had been concluded between them until now.[36]

Taking this oath, itself a disgrace to a respectable merchant, was meant to prove that Joseph did not conceal the profits made in the India trade from his brother's family. It was assumed that such profits had to be shared in full with his brother's heirs.

The concrete examples presented in this microstudy demonstrate the network that stretched from the Maghreb via Cairo and via Aden to India. The network was founded on family and ethnic grouping. Its expansion was based on ethnic diaspora; on formal friendships, agents, commenda, and partnership contracts; and on low-density information flows. It was held together by legal and customary rules and on dispute-resolution institutions that aimed at mediation. The existence of a network facilitated the ability of individuals, families, bilateral agency and commenda relationships, and partnerships to conduct longer-distance trade in a more efficient manner. But the network's coverage and density were limited. The network did not construct its own infrastructure in terms of shipping, communication, and defense. It had to rely on the services of outsiders for networking. Itinerant agents on the ocean or in India were often left to take care of themselves in isolation, and their whereabouts and fate were unknown to those who stayed behind in Cairo. The volume of trade that the network could facilitate was small.

MICROSTUDY: THE ARMENIAN NETWORK— FROM NEW JULFA TO MANILA AND LONDON

We now turn to a microstudy of a merchant network that is centrally located, both spatially and temporally, for the purpose of this book. Its hub was closer to the middle of Eurasia than any other microstudy, and its origins lay just past the halfway point of the period covered by the book (1400–1700). This microstudy presents a diasporic merchant network in its most developed form.

Since its foundation in 1604–5 CE, following Shah Abbas I's deportation of Armenians from Old Julfa (in today's Azerbaijan), New Julfa (a suburb of Isfahan, in today's Iran) had been the hub of the Armenian mercantile network.[37] Armenian merchants from Old Julfa formed trade diasporas in Goa, Surat, and Agra in the second half of the sixteenth century, and merchants from New Julfa formed settlements in Bombay, Madras (modern-day Chennai), Calcutta, Guangzhou, Manila, and other ports in South and East Asia in the seventeenth century. They settled in Venice and Livorno in the sixteenth century, and in Izmir, Marseille, Amsterdam, Paris, and London in the seventeenth century. They formed merchant diasporas in Aleppo and Basra in the sixteenth century and in Astrakhan, Kazan, and Moscow in the seventeenth century. New Julfa became the hub of the Armenian Eurasian merchant network, with spokes going east, north, and west (see figure 7.2).[38]

Historical sources on Armenian merchants are abundant compared to sources on other ethnic groups and merchant networks.[39] The largest repositories of Armenian manuscripts can be found in Venice, Moscow, and London, where Armenian merchant families settled and some of their correspondence and account books were preserved. Records were also kept in the archives of the European merchant corporations, notably those of the EIC, and in Armenian historical centers in Yerevan and Jerusalem.[40] Other important sources include the Astrakhan Code of Law, which reflects commercial norms and organizational practices in the 1760s, and the archive of the Holy Savior Cathedral (also known as the *Vanak*—the monastery) in New Julfa. The latter archive, which houses a wealth of commercial documents, contracts, accounts, bills, powers of attorney, and dispute settlements, has not been used extensively by historians of trade until recently. The focus of the microstudy on the New Julfa hub and the start date of 1604 are an artifact of the sources. It is likely that Armenian merchant networks existed before that date, with a hub in Julfa or elsewhere; we simply lack comparable sources on such networks.

An Oxford University dissertation by Herzig (1991) was, until recently, the most comprehensive study of the organization and business of the

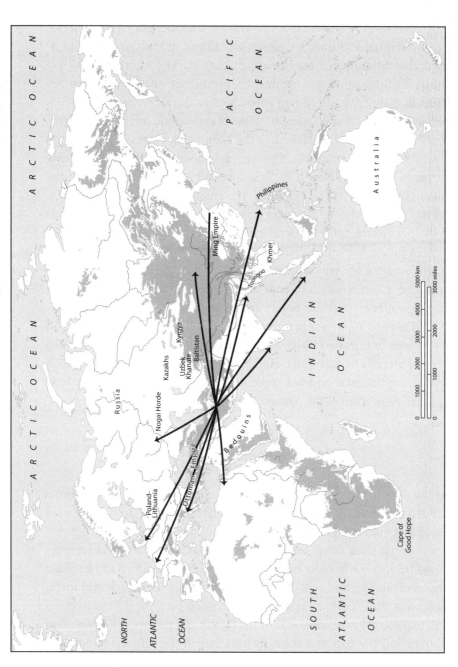

7.2. The Armenian network.

New Julfa–based Armenian network.[41] A book published in 2011 by Aslanian, based on a Columbia University PhD dissertation (2007), serves as a substantial addition.[42] Aslanian was able to use the Holy Savior Cathedral archive much more extensively than Herzig. Another important source he drew upon was commercial correspondence between Armenians in New Julfa and Indian cities, held in the archives of the EIC. A particularly remarkable source is a trove of eighteenth-century documents discovered recently by Aslanian in the National Archives in London.[43] It consists of approximately 1,700 mercantile documents, including many letters to traders in New Julfa. It was seized by the British navy in the Indian Ocean in 1748 on board an Armenian freighter, the Santa Catharina. Both Herzig and Aslanian translated and reproduced commenda and other contracts for the benefit of historians unable to read the handwritten Julfan Armenian dialect.

The sources on Armenian merchants are unique in their wealth and coverage, a combination of contracts, powers of attorney, release bills, correspondence, account books and ledgers, and a contemporary law code. They are important because of the pivotal role played by Armenian merchants in Eurasian trade, and the fact that many of the documents pertain directly to that trade. Herzig's and Aslanian's works, along with some complementary studies, serve as an excellent basis for a microstudy of the organization of the Armenian network.[44]

The Family Firm

At the core of the Armenian network were family firms.[45] These firms resided originally in New Julfa, and were based on patriarchal extended families. Often two generations were active in business. In each generation, several sons, often between three and six, were the active international traders, while older members of the family remained in New Julfa and oversaw the business. Younger members traveled back and forth, east, west, and north, or resided for extended periods of time in ports and markets. The business side of the family and the personal side often overlapped. The patriarchal family took care of the wife and children of traveling members, with marriage arranged according to business needs. Churches and residential houses were constructed using the profits of the family firms. Custom, as reflected in the Astrakhan code, governed the allocation of profits, authority, liabilities, and inheritance within each family. The family provided continuity for many generations.[46]

The Khwaja Minasian family firm, studied by Aslanian and Herzig, was active in New Julfa from the 1660s to 1747. It had family members and agents in various ports in India and in Malacca and Manila, and business activities in Mocha and Ethiopia. At one point, its patriarch owned eight ships.[47]

The Sceriman/Shahrimanian family firm moved from Old to New Julfa in 1605, and was still recorded as active in the 1740s. Aslanian was able to construct a twelve-generation genealogical tree for this family. In its heyday, family members resided in Venice, Moscow, Amsterdam, Izmir, and Livorno. The firm employed fifty servants in its New Julfa offices and a hundred agents, in addition to family members in these locations, as well as in Surat, Goa, Madras, Aleppo, Istanbul, Astrakhan, Saint Petersburg, Vienna, and Cádiz.[48]

The Commenda

Family firms extended their networks beyond kin by adding commenda agents, either as traveling agents or as resident agents at the network's spokes. They also used, albeit only rarely, commissioned agents, representatives, and general partnerships.[49] The Armenians used the commenda in its most advanced form.[50] Both the unilateral commenda, in which only the partner who stayed behind invested capital, and the bilateral commenda, in which the traveling partner also invested capital, were in use.

The following is an example, taken from Aslanian, of a typical unilateral commenda, signed also by twelve witnesses:

In the name of God

With the Will of the Omnipotent Jesus Christ
I, Hovanjan son of Marcar, became a commenda agent of Khwaja Sarukhan of Baghesh and received from him a capital sum of two thousand four hundred marchils half of which makes one thousand two hundred marchils which is equal to one hundred and fifty six tomans. Whatever

profit God grants Khwaja Sarukhan shall take two shares, and I Hovanjan shall take one share. Done in Livorno. This document was written in the year 1108 [or 1659 of the Gregorian calendar] on the 25th day of the month of July. Good and evil belong to God. This is my handwriting.[51]

Table 7.1, taken from Herzig, demonstrates that even the unilateral commenda was used in a variety of formats. As can be seen from the table, the party investing in a single contract could consist of several investors jointly. The traveling agents' party could also include several agents entrusted by the same contract. This is a relatively advanced form in the sense that the contract was used not only as a two-party agreement but also in a multiparty version that is closer to the modern limited partnership. Profits were split in a negotiable and flexible way, not dictated by law or custom, and fixed in a range of 22–35 percent of the profits to the traveling party.[52]

Bilateral commendas, in which the traveling agent also invested capital, were more complex, and required contracts that would deal with additional dimensions. This is an example of a bilateral commenda:

> I Marcos, son of Gaspar, became a commenda agent in Saidabad and received a capital sum of six thousand eight hundred freshly minted Arcot siccas from my master Sethagha, son of the deceased Mukel, and I Marcos added my own investment of one thousand five hundred freshly minted Arcot rupees. The two totals amount to eight thousand three hundred Arcot rupees half of which makes 4,150 which, with the help of God, I shall take and conduct trade with or put to work in whatever manner. Whatever profits the benevolent God shall grant, five thousand one hundred rupees of the profit granted by God along with his 6,800 capital sum, I shall hand over to my master Sethagha and I Marcos shall take the profits from 3,200 along with my investment of one thousand five hundred rupees. May the Lord God bring us good and not evil. Whatever happens will depend on our luck, and success will rest with God. I shall return without any excuses to my master or to his appointed representative the capital sum that he has given along with the profit granted by God at whatever place that he may request it. My master Sethagha gave the above sum from his capital account. We wrote two [copies] of this commenda contract with the same contents. I Marcos sealed one and gave it to my master Sethagha, and Sethagha sealed the other and gave it to me Marcos. The end.[53]

7.1. Examples of Unilateral Commenda Contracts

	Date	Place	No. of investors	No. of agents	Capital in tumans	Profit split
Khach'ikyan, Shahvelu	1712	Isfahan	3	3	90	75:25
H1D, 67	1682	Isfahan	2	1	250	75:25
PNJ, I, 161	1719	Julfa	3	1	600	78:22
NJHV, 124	1711	Astrakhan	?	1	660	67:33
ASVA, 30th Hamira 95	1711	Hugli	1	1	210	67:33
ASVA, 1st Nadar 79	1694	Isfahan	1	2	480	75:25
BLL 1047. f. 249	1736	Madras	1	1	210	67:33
BLL 1047, f. 157	1714	Julfa (?)	1	1	630	71:29

Source: Herzig (1991, p. 216).

This commenda contract was most likely signed in Saidabad, an Armenian suburb of Murshidabad (the capital of Bengal during the Mughal rule), between 1737 and 1746. It was followed by eleven signatures of witnesses and persons who confirmed that the copy corresponded to the original. This is a relatively simple bilateral commenda. The traveling agent invested 1,500 sicca rupees (Bengali rupees). The financier invested RS6,800. The total pool thus contained RS8,300. It was agreed that, at the end of the investment period, each party would receive his own investment, and profits would be split as follows: RS5,100 to the investors and RS3,200 to the traveling agents. Thus, because the traveling agent made part of the initial investment (18.08 percent of it), his share of the profits—38.55 percent—was higher than in unilateral commenda contracts. The traveling agent received a share of the profit as a return on his labor and another share as a return on his financial investment. In some contracts, a third category of investment was a "deposit" made by the investor, which could be withdrawn before the termination of the commenda and in that case would bear interest rather than yield a share of the profits. This was a sort of debt finance rather than equity finance.

Table 7.2, again drawn from Herzig, demonstrates the range of uses of the bilateral commenda contract. Traveling agents invested between 4.2 percent and 27 percent of the total investment. Their share of the profits ranged from 30 percent to 50 percent. A deposit was used in one-third of the contracts.

7.2. Examples of the Uses of the Bilateral Commenda Contract

	Year	Place	Investor's capital	Agent's capital	Deposit	Total	Agent's capital as % of total	Profit split
1	1731	Rasht	900	300	0	1,200	25.0	50:50
2	1742	Saidabad	510	40	80	630	6.3	67:33
3	1744	Julfa	1,100	100	300	1,500	6.6	67:33
4	1740	Bengal	345	15	0	360	4.2	64:36
5	1744	Saidabad	340	75	0	415	18.0	61:39
6	1741	Madras	375	50	60	485	10.3	64:36
7	1736	Calcutta	300	70	0	370	19.0	61:39
8	1741	Bengal	300	20	0	320	6.7	70:30
9	1712	Tabriz	5.1	1.9	0	7	27.0	50:50

Source: Herzig (1991, p. 221).

As we have seen, some of the unilateral commenda contracts had more than one traveling party or more than one investing party.[54] The same sedentary investors were parties to several commenda contracts, and the same traveling agents took money in the commenda from more than one investor, allowing for simultaneous risk-spreading and pooling of resources. New Julfa Armenians almost exclusively employed other New Julfans as commenda agents. Often the wealthier families extended the span of their networks by employing agents from families with more limited resources within their community.

Norms and Dispute Resolution

There were detailed rules in the Armenian law books, such as the Astrakhan code, that governed commenda relationships and other organizational forms. And there were dispute resolution tribunals that applied the rules. The relative autonomy of New Julfa enabled the functioning of the Assembly of Merchants as a tribunal for settling disputes among Armenian merchants.[55] A chief occupation of the assembly was dealing with disputes over commenda contracts. There were also portable tribunals that settled disputes among the Julfans in the diasporas.[56] Aslanian provides a detailed description of the use of correspondence and couriers as means of enhancing the flow of information. Information flow was an important element in managing trade, adjusting supply, setting prices, deciding where to send commenda agents, and the like. But it also played a crucial role in the monitoring of traveling agents and the verification of breaches of duty. After all, by itself, the legal code had limited value in the absence of verifiable information on breaches. The network's structure, based on a single hub, enhanced monitoring, as information from all agents and all ports and markets arrived at the same place and could be cross-checked. Furthermore, the fact that family members of the traveling agents were supported by the sedentary investors and their families had a dual effect in that they also served as security for the return of the agent. Furthermore, a cheating agent could not use the stolen money to support his family, as the financier would notice the increase in their standard of living. In addition, in the event of cheating, the sanction could involve a social component such as ostracism of the family in the form of a ban on entering churches or on marrying off children.[57]

The reliance on fellow New Julfa Armenians was, at the same time, a strength and a weakness of the network. A strength, because communal relationships between the family of the investor and the traveling agents in New Julfa ensured higher levels of transparency, trust, and social enforcement. A weakness, because the system could not be extended on the same foundations beyond the size and locations of the New Julfan diasporas. The Armenian New Julfa network, with its basic hub-and-spokes structure and its reliance on agency and partnership relationships, was no different organizationally from the Jewish Cairo network. But it expanded further; it employed agents in a more intensive and orderly way; the circulation of goods and flow of information through its hub was faster; and it relied more heavily on the commenda. It was the ultimate Eurasian trade network (at least among those for which records have survived and been studied). Its expansion beyond the geographical scope of the Geniza network was made possible by the overall development of Eurasian trade. The trade expanded with Islam and the network of caravanserai that Muslims constructed across Eurasia. It further expanded with the Pax Mongolica and its positive effect on silk route and maritime trade. Later it expanded with the Europeans' arrival in the Indian Ocean (via the Cape Route). All of these developments provided the Armenians with state-based (Portuguese) and corporation-based (English and Dutch) infrastructures.

MICROSTUDY: THE SEPHARDIC JEWISH NETWORK—LIVORNO TO ALEPPO AND GOA

Our third and final merchant network microstudy represents the post-heyday phase. This network operated in the shadow of the big merchant corporations. It used their oceanic freight services. Its agents, unlike the Armenian agents, were mostly stationed and commissioned rather than itinerant and commenda agents.

In its heyday, between the late sixteenth and late eighteenth centuries, Livorno, a port city in Tuscany on the coast of the Tyrrhenian Sea, was one of the largest distribution ports in the Mediterranean, linking the Italian peninsula with Northern Europe and the Ottoman Empire, and competing successfully with Venice and Marseille. It offered merchants a facilitative political and legal environment by declaring military neutrality, eliminating import and export customs, and providing good shipping and storage facilities, and it was hospitable to foreign merchants and religions, unlike many other port cities.[58] These features made Livorno an attractive port town for English, French, Dutch, Jewish, and Armenian merchants, among others.

The Jews were expelled from Spain in 1492 and from Portugal in 1497, with most migrating to North Africa, the Ottoman Empire, and Italy. Of those who were formally converted and became "New Christians," some migrated away from the hold of the Inquisition to the overseas empires of Spain and Portugal in Asia and the Americas. By 1550, Jews had settled in Venice and Florence. They gradually spread to other towns in Tuscany, and, in around 1593, the first Sephardic Jews settled in Livorno and constructed its first synagogue. In the second half of the seventeenth century and in the eighteenth century, the Jewish community of Livorno numbered in the range of 1,500 to 4,000, representing 10–13 percent of the town's population.[59] The Sephardic community of Livorno and the other Sephardic communities of the Mediterranean, the Ottoman Empire, and the Iberian empires all feature in this case study.

In her book, Francesca Trivellato provides us with an excellent study of the business practices and network of Sephardic Jews in Livorno. Her study focuses on two families, the Ergas and the Silveras, and their business partnership. She was able to construct the genealogy of the families going back to Lisbon of the first half of the sixteenth century and forward to the late eighteenth century, when family members resided in many major cities in Europe and the Middle East.[60] Trivellato reconstructed the history of the two families, their partnership, their commercial network, and the Jewish community of Livorno as a whole, based on detailed records that allowed her to provide a thick description of their organizational practices. Her main sources were the business letters of Ergas and Silvera, which number 13,670 for the years 1704–46 and are kept in the Florence State Archive. In addition, she used powers of attorney and other legal documents preserved in the Livorno and other city archives, court records from litigation in which the partnership was involved, and the records of the Jewish community relating to marriages, deaths, and other family issues.

The Ergas and Silvera network stretched east to the Ottoman Empire, with Aleppo as the hub in the Levant, and Alexandria, Smyrna, Acre, and Cyprus as important additional destinations. From Aleppo they imported chintz, raw silk, and spices. The network stretched west to Europe, with Amsterdam, London, and Marseilleas the leading destinations. From there, local woolen cloth and goods from the Americas were imported to Livorno, mostly for reexport to the Levant. The Western Europe-Livorno-Aleppo axis was a classic Eurasian trade route. Aleppo was the endpoint for caravans arriving from Baghdad and Basra and carrying Persian and Indian goods such as spices, silk, cotton textiles, and indigo.[61] Another important axis was the Livorno-Lisbon-Goa route, which gave the partnership direct oceanic access to the Indian Ocean markets. Via Lisbon, the partnership exported Mediterranean corals to Goa, which were bartered there for Indian diamonds. Livorno was thus a hub of both the more traditional overland trade and the newer oceanic trade between Europe and Asia. A good sense of the network can be gained by viewing the geographic dispersal of the destinations of the Ergas and Silvera letters, as depicted in figure 7.3. Figure 7.4 shows the network's path from Livorno to the different destinations in Europe and Asia.

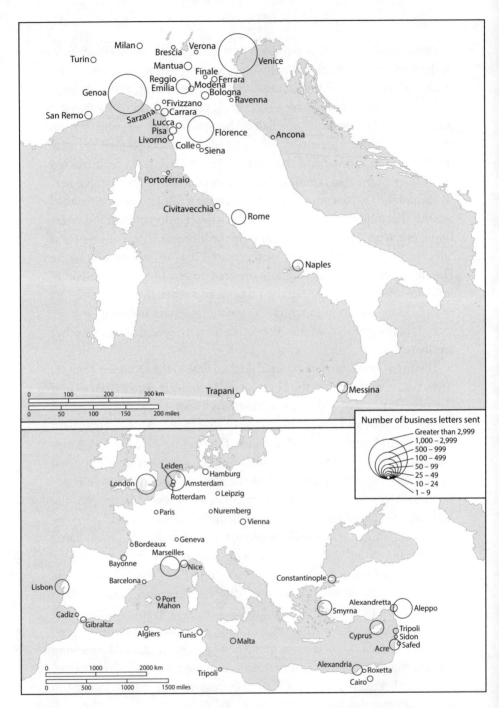

Milan
Turin
Brescia
Verona
Venice
Mantua
Finale
Reggio
Emilia
Modena
Ferrara
Genoa
Bologna
Ravenna
Fivizzano
San Remo
Sarzana
Carrara
Lucca
Pisa
Florence
Ancona
Livorno
Colle
Siena
Portoferraio
Civitavecchia
Rome
Naples
Trapani
Messina

0   100   200   300 km
0   50   100   150   200 miles

Leiden
Hamburg
London
Amsterdam
Rotterdam
Leipzig
Paris
Nuremberg
Vienna
Bordeaux
Geneva
Marseilles
Bayonne
Nice
Lisbon
Barcelona
Constantinople
Port
Mahon
Alexandretta
Aleppo
Cadiz
Smyrna
Gibraltar
Algiers
Tunis
Cyprus
Tripoli
Sidon
Malta
Acre
Safed
Alexandria
Roxetta
Tripoli
Cairo

0   1000   2000 km
0   500   1000   1500 miles

Number of business letters sent
Greater than 2,999
1,000 – 2,999
500 – 999
100 – 499
50 – 99
25 – 49
10 – 24
1 – 9

7.3. Destinations of the Ergas and Silvera letters, 1704–46. Source: Trivellato (2009, p. 197).

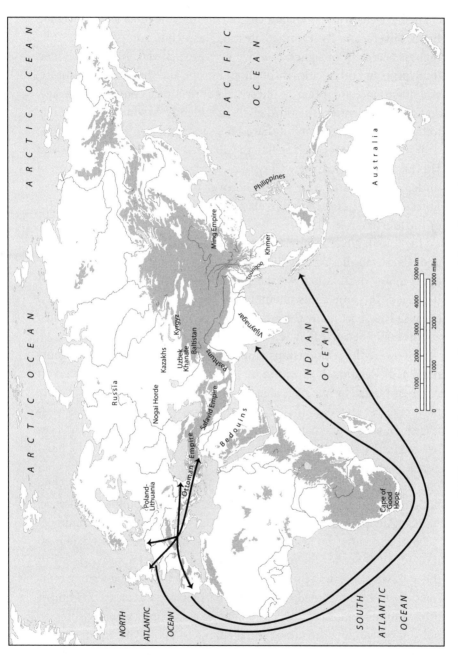

7.4. Livorno Sephardic network, seventeenth to eighteenth centuries.

Who were the members of the Livorno network of Sephardic merchants? Trivellato identifies four circles. The first, the inner circle, included Ergas, Silvera, and their immediate kin. The second comprised the "Portuguese Nation," Portuguese Jews who were expelled from Spain, resided in Livorno and other cities throughout Europe and the Ottoman Empire, and maintained their family and social connections, common language, and cultural identity. The third circle included Jews who did not belong to the Portuguese nation but shared the same religion. The fourth circle comprised non-Jews such as Italian Christian merchants in Lisbon and Hindu agents in Goa. New Christians, former Jews who had converted under pressure and were spread all over the Iberian empires in Asia, Europe, and America, could be classified as belonging to either the third or the fourth circle.

The fourth circle is where cross-cultural trade took place. The Ergas and Silvera families were willing to employ the most qualified worker or agent in any destination, irrespective of the circle to which that person belonged. In some cases, members of the inner circle were preferred because they best knew the business of the firm and its various agents, and not only because they were kin and, as such, could be trusted.

How were the relationships among the partners and with the agents regulated? Relationships within the inner circle were typically based on family, arranged by marriage alliances, family firms, and unlimited family partnerships. The main tool used for forming the partnership was marriage.[62] David Silvera married Esther Ergas in 1705. Additional marriages between the families in later generations further strengthened the partnership. Members of both families also married members of other Sephardic merchant families in Livorno. The network was expanded by both marriage and migration to other Sephardic communities in Florence, Venice, Aleppo, Constantinople, Bordeaux, Amsterdam, and London.[63]

No contract for the Ergas-Silvera partnership has been found, and no indirect evidence for the existence of such a contract appears in any of the archives surveyed. Thus, Trivellato believes that such a written contract was never concluded, and that the partnership was based on implicit or oral understandings.[64] Occasionally—for example, when wishing to opt out of the default rule of equal shares to all partners in profit—a *fraterna* contract could be drawn up. The *compagnia* partnership (commonly used by the large Italian merchant-cum-banking firms, such as the Medici and Dantini and the Fuggers and Welsers, as holding companies controlling their branch companies) was rarely used by the Sephardic Jews of Livorno.[65]

The Livorno Jews also very rarely used the commenda or the newer and more sophisticated version, the *accomandite* (which allowed a multilateral contract, a term of existence, and flexible sharing of profits), to contract with their agents. Trivellato reached this finding by examining the *accomandite* register in the merchant court of Florence for the period 1632–1777, identifying a couple of rare examples. In 1717, Jacob Ergas formed a commenda with his three sons, Samuel, David, and Raphael. He entrusted twenty thousand Spanish dollar coins to them, presumably as his traveling agents. He must have formalized this relationship because his sons were litigious, as apparent from contemporary court records. Another example is that of a commenda-like contract between two brothers and their nephew, in which each invested a third of the capital, was entitled to a third of the profits, and was subject to a third of the liability.[66] Altogether, Trivellato identified some twenty *accomandite* contracts between Livorno Jewish merchants in the period 1670–1764.[67] Commenda contracts between Jews and Christians appeared in the 1770s in small numbers.

Most agents were commissioned agents. They were employed informally, either orally or based on business correspondence, but not on written—and definitely not notarized—contracts. Powers of attorney were used, but they were not meant to be employed as enforcement tools. Specific powers of attorney that appointed agents to perform well-defined tasks were also used as notarized certificates for the property rights of the principal in the property held by the agent. The certificates were applied to third parties, not to the agent. General powers of attorney were sometimes used to appoint commissioned agents or legal representatives. For the former, informal means such as letters were more commonly used. One particularly interesting finding of Trivellato's study is that agency disputes were not litigated in courts. Thus, powers of attorney were not used because of their evidentiary status.[68] Trivellato finds no evidence of the use of more formal legal tools in the agency relationships in the third and fourth circles, that is, with non-Sephardic Jews and with Hindu and Christian agents.

Trivellato follows Mark Granovetter's typology of "strong ties" within networks and "weak ties" in the outer circles that provided the scope to expand the network beyond its core domain, in our case cross-culturally beyond ethnic boundaries, to innovate and explore new markets and business opportunities.[69] As the outer-circle agents did not share religious, ethnic, or community bonds with their principles, the basis of this relationship was a repeated interaction and multilateral reputation mechanism, not a third-party dispute resolution or shared community norms and social and religious sanctions.[70] Monitoring was based on the flow of information in commercial and social correspondence. A language and literacy had to be shared by the corresponding parties. Trivellato follows anthropologist Marshall Sahlins in categorizing the level of reciprocity among partners or between principals and agents. This level is socially rather than legally based. The relationship in the inner circle, the family partnership, is classified as "general reciprocity" because it was based on mutual liability for which there were no limits in time, quantity, or quality. In the second circle, that of other Sephardic Jews, the relationship is classified as one of "balanced reciprocity" because each transaction is expected to be commensurate with future transactions in the other direction, within a finite period of time. Presumably, in the outer circles, there was immediate reciprocity.[71]

The Livorno-based network, particularly in its eighteenth-century phase, represents the post-heyday period of the merchant network. Agents were mostly commissioned and stationed. They could be so because the network relied on familiar destinations in which diasporas regularly resided, on well-established shipping and freight services, on a rapid flow of correspondence-based information, and on decreasing business- and transportation-related risks. All of these were achieved in the late seventeenth and eighteenth centuries, by the business corporations, the VOC and EIC, for their own benefit and that of their allies in the Eurasian trade such as the Livorno-based network.

CONCLUSION

After the dismantling of Greco-Roman state infrastructures and dense trade networks (that were reflected in the Muziris Papyrus), the revival of trade late in the first millennium CE involved the recreation of trade networks. The case of the Maghribi merchants trading with India is situated in this revival and recreation stage. It is characterized by a new and distant destination, low frequency of interactions, and no state infrastructure. The main supporting element in the flow of information conducive to trade itself and to agency and partnership relations among members of the network was the structure of the network, which included two informational hubs, a central one in Cairo and a secondary one in Aden. This is an example of a network in its very early stages of development.

The case of New Julfa Armenian merchants demonstrates the network organizational form at its height, both in terms of components and in terms of geographical expansion. It was a relatively close-knit ethnic-based network; it was a single hub through which all transactions had to pass; it featured cross-reporting between commenda and other agents of different investors; it had a strong legal enforcement tribunal in New Julfa; and it was characterized by relatively well-established trade destinations and frequent trips. And, interestingly, it enjoyed support from an external institution that fostered the flow of information, the newly established EIC and VOC, to which I will turn in the next part of the book.

The Sephardic Jews of Livorno relied on waged and commissioned agents. By their time, the eighteenth century, trade was routinized to a level at which the advantages of commenda were not sufficiently relevant anymore. Itinerant merchants were replaced by stationed agents, who did not have to physically carry goods with them (goods could be shipped to them using business corporations and commercial freight lines). The full-fledged merchant network was no longer the essential institution for dealing with the high risk and information asymmetry associated with long-distance trade. The network could survive in enclaves, in the shadow of corporations, in symbiosis with them and on their margins.

Trade by Rulers and States

Many premodern rulers aimed at assembling a mighty military force, wining wars against other rulers and against domestic challengers, and collecting taxes in sums that would assure sufficient finance for their armies so that these would actually win wars. Many rulers had no immediate commercial ambitions. I will survey here two notable exceptions, the mercantile endeavors of early Ming China and sixteenth-century Portugal. The two were radically different. The Chinese state was based on Confucian ideology, on extensive learned bureaucracy, on a worldview of being the Middle Kingdom, and on its huge geographic scale and huge population. In these important senses and others, it was singular. As we shall see in the first microstudy, in many eras the Chinese Empire had no ambitions with respect to overseas trade, and in others it allowed either foreign or local merchants to trade but was not involved in trade directly. The microstudy involves a significant exception in the realm of commercial endeavor, led by the emperor. Portugal was a small and young kingdom on the margins of the Iberian Peninsula. Its state capacity was limited, but its exposure to seafaring was significant due to its location on the coast of the Atlantic Ocean. As we shall see in the second microstudy, the Portuguese king aimed at forming a mercantile enterprise. In this chapter we will examine the formation, weaknesses, and demise of these two ruler-owned trade enterprises.

MICROSTUDY: ZHENG HE'S VOYAGES

Between 1405 and 1433, seven voyages, each involving a fleet of dozens of ships and thousands of personnel, sailed from China to the Indian

Ocean. The first six voyages were initiated by the Yongle emperor, and the seventh and last voyage by the Xuande emperor.[1] They were headed by Zheng He, a Muslim eunuch who reached senior positions in the Imperial Court and was appointed admiral of each of the voyages. The vessels chosen for the journey, known as treasure ships, were constructed in the royal shipyards in Nanjing, the Ming capital. The officers, crews, soldiers, and servicemen were drafted and appointed by the emperor himself.[2]

They were by far the largest fleets of the period covered in this book. They surpassed the European flotillas sent by states, merchants, and business corporations to Asia or America by an order of magnitude. The Chinese voyages to the Indian Ocean, in the early Ming dynasty era, are the prime example, in our period, of a state-financed and state-operated long-distance trade enterprise.

The sources on Zheng He's voyages are quite abundant, comprising official histories of the Ming emperors, journey memoirs and accounts by some of the officers on board, and inscriptions on monuments in China and elsewhere. Zheng He's reports themselves are missing. There are disagreements within the primary sources and in the historiography with respect to some of the details (dates, destinations, routes, number and size of ships, and so on), which are not to be resolved here.[3] Unfortunately, the sources refer only sketchily to organizational issues, which are our main concern. The details on the magnitude of the voyage, numbers of ships, ship size, and crew size outlined in the case study presented here should all be approached with caution, as some historians believe they were either technologically impossible or included literary exaggerations. But the general scope of this enterprise and its public nature can hardly be disputed.

We will focus in this case study on the first voyage, which is the best reported and was the hardest to organize, given its starting point. Though the emperor demanded that coastal provinces supply ships for his service, it seems the bulk of the ships for the first voyage of the fleet were built in the imperial capital, Nanjing, in the imperial treasure-ship dockyards near Longjiang on the Yangtze River. Thousands of craftsmen throughout the country were drafted, by imperial decrees, for the task.[4] The number of ships in the first voyage was reported to be 317, of which sixty-two were large treasure ships. Of these, four were huge wood junks measuring approximately 120 m in length and 50 m in width. Included in the fleet were ships some 100 m in length that carried nothing but horses; water ships that carried fresh water for the crew; and troop carriers, supply ships, and war ships for offensive and defensive needs. The large treasure ships were loaded with Chinese goods to trade and deliver as gifts during the voyage.[5]

The men on board were reported to number 27,870.[6] At the head of the fleet was Zheng He. His seventy senior officers were all court eunuchs, seven of whom held the title of grand director and served as ambassadors and commanders. Their ten-highest assistants held the title of junior director. Different submissions to different countries were led by eunuch directors. Below the eunuchs in the hierarchy were 302 military officers, who held the standard ranks found throughout the Ming military estab-lishment: two regional military commissioners, ninety-three guard com-manders, 104 battalion commanders, and 103 company commanders. The crew also comprised guard judges and battalion judges, together with 190 civilian specialists, including 180 medical personnel who ranked alongside (and were rewarded on the same scale as) squad leaders and common soldiers. The other civilians were an official from the ministry of finance (who presumably performed the role of chief purser for the fleet), two secretaries, two protocol officers from the Court of the State Ceremonial that was in charge of the reception of foreign tributary envoys in the capital, and an astrologer with four assistants. The eunuch directors, military officers, and civilian specialists numbered 562. The rank and file numbered 26,803, including petty officers, courageous troops or "braves," exceptionally strong soldiers named "official soldiers," supernumeraries, civilian boatmen, buyers, and clerks.[7] Figure 8.1 shows the structure of command of the fleet.

The voyage used cutting-edge contemporary marine and navigational technology. The fleet utilized the compass for navigation and determined latitude by monitoring the North Star (Polaris) in the Northern Hemi-sphere and the Southern Cross in the Southern Hemisphere. Graduated sticks of incense were burned to measure travel time.[8] The ships of the Treasure Fleet communicated with one another through the use of flags, lanterns, bells, carrier pigeons, gongs, and banners.

The voyages all made their way through the South China Sea, Southeast Asia, and the Indonesian archipelago, crossed the Bay of Bengal, and arrived at Calicut on the Malabar Coast of Southern India. From there,

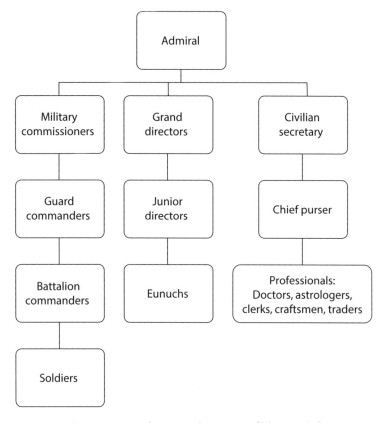

8.1. Organization and command structure of Zheng He's fleet.

some of the voyages continued to Hormuz and the Persian Gulf, some to Aden and the Red Sea, and some to the East African coast. In figure 8.2 we can observe these routes. In terms of size, intensity, and even distances covered, these voyages dwarf the first European voyages to the Atlantic and Indian Oceans. The Iberian exploratory fleets of Columbus, da Gama, and Magellan included just three or four ships, 20–30 m long, with a crew of between 100 and 250. Later Portuguese voyages to India included between five and twenty ships. The magnitude of the Chinese voyages, even when discounting for exaggerations in the reports, is of a different order.

Why did the Yongle emperor undertake this ambitious maritime project? Several explanations have been offered by scholars. The first is that

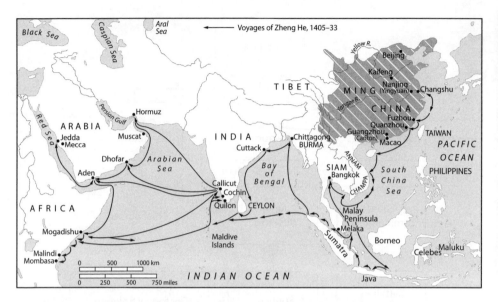

8.2. Voyages of Zheng He, 1405–33. Source: reprinted from J. Ding, C. J. Shi, and A. Weintrit, "An Important Point on the Way to Sailing History: Zheng Navigates to the Western Ocean," *TransNav: The International Journal of Shipping and Maritime Safety* 1, no. 3 (2007): 285–93.

he wished to reestablish the regional tribute system, upon assuming power, in a bid to legitimize his reign, which was obtained by force.[9] Insofar as this was the sole motive, it is not clear why this emperor entered a maritime enterprise on such an unprecedented scale. Another explanation is that he reacted to the expansion of Tamerlane's empire in Central Asia. Here again, as in the case of reestablishing the tribute system, military concerns and political rivalries mixed with the need to divert long-distance trade from the overland Silk Route (which was controlled by Tamerlane) to the bypassing oceanic routes. A third possible explanation is that he wished to reverse the Yuan dynasty's trade policy. The Mongols discriminated against ethnic Han Chinese, put obstacles in place to impede their ability to participate in maritime trade, and, on the other hand, invited foreign merchants, particularly Arabs, to reside in Chinese port cities and take over the trade. The Ming dynasty aimed to put the Han Chinese back in control of overseas trade. A fourth possible explanation is that the Yongle emperor wanted to expand overseas trade because this could be an easily collected kind of taxation, a free lunch that would not be resented by the propertied elites. Why did the emperor not do so by permitting private Chinese merchants to trade on more favorable terms? Possibly the Yongle emperor preferred to operate on a grander scale and in a more centrally controlled manner, at least in the first stages of restoring Chinese trade.

Could the Chinese voyages be considered long-distance trade voyages, comparable to others we have examined in this book? Or were these imperial projects executed as state naval expeditions? Are we not perhaps comparing Chinese apples to European oranges, so to speak? The Chinese voyages were indeed involved in international relations and the enhancing of China's dominant political position, reflected in the tribute system. The organization we examine in this case study is a not-for-profit entity, but so were the Portuguese projects in Asia, as was (at least in part) the Dutch VOC's enterprise in Asia. They all combined political and commercial considerations. Not one of them was a fully rational profit calculator, in the Weberian sense. The imperial Zheng He organization we examine in this case study was a premodern redistributive institution that mixed protection and business expenses and revenues, and not a modern corporation that invested in protection only if it was profitable to do so. But Zheng He's voyages traded. The trade and the tribute intermingled, as they usually did for China.[10]

The historical sources describe many examples in which Zheng He's fleet took part in trade. His men were trading porcelains and silks for spices and copper coins on Java and had a bartering ritual in Calicut with Indian brokers that sometimes lasted up to three months. The first two voyages had reestablished China's trade links in Southeast Asia and promised a steady importation of foreign goods. Malacca was also a valued trading partner to the Chinese, and one of the purposes of the third voyage was to keep it in check. On future expeditions to Malacca, Zheng He even establish guarded storage facilities for goods to be stored in before the journey home. The emperor later became interested in the prospect of trading with the wealthy commercial hub of Hormuz and bringing back exotic treasures for his new palace—he therefore gave the officers of the fleet coins to obtain goods. The Chinese eagerly traded their porcelains and silks for Hormuz's precious gems, woolens and carpets. There, as well as in Calicut, Zheng He probably met merchants from the East African city-states of Mogadishu, Brawa, and Malindi whom he persuaded to return with him to China and pay tribute to the emperor. In the Maldives, Zheng He and his men purchased ambergris and shells.

They received a warm welcome by the sultan of Aden, and only those with "precious things" were permitted to trade with them. The Chinese bartered their goods with the exotic gems and animals. In Jidda and Dhufar the Chinese exchanged silks and porcelains for local goods and drugs.[11] Zheng He's recruitment of 180 physicians and pharmacists who served on the fleet, more than would have been necessary to take care of sick men on board, indicates that he was interested in the search for medicines. This conclusion is coherent with the shortage of foreign medicinal herbs in China at that time, which was due to the former emperor's restrictive trade policy. A report shows that silver pieces that were brought on the third voyage were examined in front of the envoys who had brought them, and then, in the following day, were handed over to the ministry of revenue. As much as China wanted to hold to a self-sufficiency policy, it had to give up the import of tropical and exotic goods into China. But even as much as it was willing to do this, giving up the possibility of importing medicinal herbs and silver could be particularly damaging.

Though the persons on board ships were all imperial servants and not private merchants, there is indication of clear separation between tributes that were designated exclusively for the emperor, such as a giraffe bestowed by the sultan of Aden, and trade goods that were intended for exploring commercial potential and for sale in China.[12] It might be fair to conclude that there was a kind of overdetermination by which the voyages were simultaneously diplomatic displays, military exercises, and trading ventures, and can be regarded as the emperor's attempt to reconcile China's need for maritime trade with the desire to outflank private channels of trade.[13]

How did the maritime-voyage project solve the organizational problems typical of long-distance trade? The funding was achieved through taxation. Manpower, for the shipyards and the fleet itself, was achieved through mandatory conscription. Agency problems were solved by the use of administrative and military hierarchies. In particular, eunuchs were used as the long hand of the emperor to lead the fleets and supervise the military and civil apparatuses. The idea was that eunuchs, who grew up in the imperial court and had no intergenerational concerns, were less self-interested and more loyal to the emperor than other administrators.[14] In addition, commanders on board were given the sovereign power of punishing disobedient crew members and even executing them. The size and wealth of the Chinese state and its well-developed tax collection and administrative systems supported a well-funded, well-manned, and well-run enterprise that produced seven voyages comprising dozens of ships and thousands of crew members each, for one-way distances of 10,000 km and more. The state provided the legal-institutional platform to ensure longevity of the enterprise—twenty-eight years from first to last voyage.

So why did China dismantle this state-operated commercial-cum-political enterprise after 1433? This question is often asked in the "What if . . . ?" sense (that is, if China had not withdrawn from this maritime enterprise, Chinese ships might have reached Europe or discovered America before European expansion). A few explanations were offered by historians for the termination of China's grand oceanic voyages. The death of the Yongle emperor is one possible explanation. After his death in 1424, just one final voyage took place. Yongle's successors may not have suffered from similar legitimation problems to those of the early Ming emperors. Thus, they did not have to show off their might in maritime voyages. The geopolitical position of China changed with the decline of the Timurid Empire after the death of Tamerlane in 1405.[15] The need to bypass Central Asia by sea therefore diminished. On the socioeconomic level, the tax burdens on society created a backlash. Those who paid the costs did not benefit from the political or business gains of the voyages; hence they opposed them. The administrative apparatus that executed the voyages, with eunuchs at its core, lost power and cohesion. The emperor's trust in the eunuchs, in the face of growing antagonism and criticism by the competing Confucian scholarly and administrative elite, therefore dwindled.[16] This enterprise suffered the downsides of state-owned enterprise as well as the advantages. The downside is that change of rulers, administrative and tax issues, and geopolitical fluctuations that have nothing to do with the profitability of a trade project diverted attention and resources away from this project.

This case study does not categorically prove that the state-owned and state-operated long-distance trade enterprise was unsustainable. We can conclude that a state-owned enterprise had its drawbacks. With sufficient political will and support, an effective and loyal enough state apparatus, a large and stable enough tax base, and realistic ambitions in terms of fleet size, Ming China could possibly have carried on the project. We can realize, though, why a small state such as Portugal, with a limited tax base, administration, and state capacity, could find it hard to sustain such a state-owned enterprise. With this insight, let us turn to the microstudy of Portugal.

MICROSTUDY: THE SIXTEENTH-CENTURY PORTUGUESE PUBLIC-PRIVATE ASIATIC VENTURES

The Portuguese were the first Europeans to attain direct access to Asian markets and goods via the oceanic Cape Route, rather than through intermediaries in the Levant or via the overland Silk Route. In 1497–98, Vasco da Gama not only discovered the route around the Cape for the Europeans, but he was also the first European to arrive at East African ports and the first to cross the Indian Ocean with three ships (*Sao Gabriel*, *Sao Rafael*, and *Bérrio*) to Southern India. En route, his flotilla navigated twice for ninety days on the open ocean without sight of any coastline. This achievement was a continuation of a long Portuguese maritime and navigational tradition. Da Gama was sent on his mission by King Manuel I. He commanded a fleet of crown ships and was expected to follow the king's instructions and promote state policy.[17] In 1500, King Manuel sent another fleet of thirteen ships and at least 1,200 men. Common wisdom views the unfolding of events in the following decade as the formation of a state-based Portuguese empire in Asia, which served as a platform for Portuguese Eurasian trade. In 1499, Manuel assumed the title "The Lord of the Conquest, Navigation and Commerce of Ethiopia, Arabia, Persia, and India." In 1505, the Estado da Índia was declared and Francisco d'Almeida was appointed the first viceroy. Cochin, followed by Goa, became the capital of the Asiatic empire. The king initiated annual voyages to India, the Carreira da Índia, on ships owned by him and commanded by his captains. By 1510, as many as 151 ships had departed Lisbon on the Carreira da Índia on their way to Asia. The royal Casa da Índia was formed to house goods imported from India and control their distribution in Portugal and Europe.[18] A network of factories, soon to be transformed into forts, was constructed in East Africa, the Arabian Sea, the western coast of India, Malacca, and Moluccas. These were manned by officials, soldiers, merchants, and clergy, and connected by inter-Asian state *carreiras*. The inter-Asian trade was based on a growing number of Portuguese royal ships stationed in the Indian Ocean. To the extent that one can separate rhetoric from real aims, it appears the motivation for building this huge empire came from a mix of political, religious, military, and trade objectives.

This notion of the Portuguese presence in Asia as an empire-cum-enterprise that was state owned and state operated is sustained by historians observing it from the perspective of the Asians, say, Indians on the Coromandel Coast, to whom all European Christians (be they state officials or private merchants) looked the same.[19] It is also sustained from the perspective of historians who contrast the Portuguese century in Asia, the sixteenth century, with the Anglo-Dutch century, the seventeenth century, in which corporations were the dominant organization of European Cape Route trade.[20] Yet historians who focus on internal political and social tensions in sixteenth-century Portugal, say, between the king and his court and the landed nobility and gentry, view the enterprise as less homogenous.[21] From the perspective of merchants, particularly foreign merchants such as South Germans and Italians, the enterprise looked more private and less Portuguese.[22] The state-centered image is based more on intentions and declarations than on facts on the ground.

The Portuguese state aspired to directly own the annual voyage on the route from Asian ports (mostly Cochin and then Goa) to Lisbon via the Cape Route, the Carreira da Índia and the end-ports, and factories in Asia. It aimed to monopolize the trade upon arrival in the Estado da Índia in Lisbon and distribute it in European markets. It also aimed at monopolizing the Indian Ocean trade by enforcing the *cartazes* licensing system on local merchants, which allowed trade only subject to fee-based licensing from the Crown. But in fact, sixteenth-century Portuguese trade was far from being fully dominated by the state. King Manuel's inability, from the very start, to finance his Asian ambitions based on Portugal's tax system compelled him to allow the participation of private merchants, many of them German and Italian. In addition, he relied on the supply of German copper and silver, which were the European commodities that attracted the highest demand in India. The basic domestic political tension that challenged the Crown's exclusive dominance of the Asian enterprise was between the Crown, the nobility, and the gentry (*fidalgo*)—and, to a lesser extent, Portuguese merchants, who wished to manage the Asian enterprise as a decentralized entity, just as they wished the Portuguese state to be feudal and decentralized rather than absolute. The first European century in the Indian Ocean is marked by the repeated failure of Portugal to base its enterprise on a centralized state apparatus and public finance, and on a constant process of trial and error in which different configurations of public-private partnerships were tested.[23]

Private Merchants in the Voyages of 1500–1510

The first chapter in the Portuguese microstudy is taken from the first decade of the Portuguese Asian enterprise. The need to rely on private finance was evident for the first time just three years after the discovery of the trade route. King Manuel I issued an order in June 1500 allowing the Portuguese, as well as foreigners residing in Portugal, to participate in the Malabar trade, providing and fitting out their own ships.[24] Though Portuguese merchants and noblemen were among the potential investors in trade with India, much of the private capital that could be invested in India trade was that of Italian merchants, who made their fortune in the Levant trade and aimed to invest in the competing Cape Route trade as well, and German merchants, who made fortunes in copper and silver mining and in banking.

The cooperation between these merchants and the Portuguese state was not based on well-defined institutional and legal frameworks. These merchants were neither subjects of the king nor residents of his realm. Thus, they could initially decide autonomously whether to bring their wealth to Portugal (and face expropriation by the king) or invest it in Asian trade (beyond the reach of the Portuguese king) and face the risk of expropriation by Asian rulers. This is a classic "credible commitment" problem. The Portuguese king needed capital from the Italian and German merchants. They, in turn, were pursuing the lucrative Cape Route business opportunities that, in the early sixteenth century, could only be offered by this king. But they were not certain they could trust him not to expropriate later on. Hence, before investing, the German and Italian merchants negotiated the terms of the deal with the king, through correspondence and agents.

The voyage commanded by Pedro Álvares Cabral left Lisbon on March 9, 1500, with thirteen ships, ten of which were on the account of the Crown, the remaining three belonging to different syndicates of Portuguese noblemen and Italian financiers.[25] The Florentine merchant Marchioni fitted out a ship in the 1500 fleet and imported spices from Malabar. The same Marchioni formed a consortium of merchants that owned and operated two of the four ships sent to India in 1501. He sent another ship in the 1502 voyage, in partnership with the king, splitting the returning spice cargo fifty-fifty.[26] In the following two decades, most of the voyages included privately owned ships next to Crown ships.[27] The deal was that those who sent their ships to India were bound to entrust one-fourth of the commodities to the king on their return.[28]

The negotiation and agreement between the German merchants and the king are relatively well documented, not only in Portuguese but also in German archives, and are well researched. Thus, the agreement can be used as a case study for our purposes. The ultimate agreement between the Portuguese king and the group of German merchants was fixed in grants of privileges, or rather charters of privileges, given to merchants of a specific foreign nation, city, or family or to specific individuals or consortia.[29]

In December 1502, three Germans (Lukas Rem and Scipio Lowenstein, led by Simon Seitz), acting as representative agents of Anton Welser, Konrad Vöhlin, and their Augsburg fellows and other German merchants, made their way from Germany via Antwerp to Lisbon to negotiate the terms for the participation of the German merchant financiers in the next India voyage. King Manuel was favorable, possibly because they carried the blessing of the Holy Roman Emperor Maximilian I, who was his nephew, and possibly because of Manuel's need for German money, copper, and silver. On February 13, 1503, they attained a contract that granted them privileges, according to which all German merchants were permitted to join their ships in the *carreira* voyages to India, sell and purchase goods in Portugal and its territories in Asia, reside in Lisbon, and sell goods imported from Asia outside Portugal. They received immunity from searches, arbitrary taxation, and expropriation. In return they had to pay customs to the Crown.[30] In addition, they were expected to establish branch offices in Lisbon, appoint an agent to represent them in their dealings with the king, and invest a minimum of 10,000 ducats each in the trade. Furthermore, they had to place their ships under the command of the admiral of the Portuguese fleet and, in Asia, obey the instructions of the royal factors. The privileges were initially requested and negotiated with the king by the Welsers. The Fuggers were quick to grasp the importance of this treaty and therefore sent Markus Zimmermann to be their representative in Lisbon.[31] It was he who negotiated (in October 1503) what was probably an annex to the February treaty, pertaining mainly to jurisdictional matters.[32] The merchant families of Grossenprott and Höchstetter, from Augsburg, as well as the Nuremberg houses of Imhof and Hirschvogel, seem to have soon followed.[33] Once granted, the privileges applied to all German merchants who met the minimum investment requirement. The grants were formally a unilateral charter and not a contract or a treaty; they provided a framework, not an actual project.

The privileges were followed in August 1504 by a specific contract that Lukas Rem signed with King Manuel on behalf of the German merchants. It was agreed by the parties that, on the next voyage to Cochin (due the following year), the Germans, together with Italian merchants, would be allowed to send three ships as part of the fifteen-ship royal *carreira*. They were allowed to send their own agents to buy spices, under the supervision of royal factor. The spices had to be deposited at the Casa da Índia in Lisbon, and 30 percent was to be deducted as customs duty to the Crown before the remainder could be sold. Based on this contract, a consortium was formed between several South German and Italian merchant families. The Italians, headed by Bartolomeo Marchioni, a Florentine merchant, invested 29,400 cruzados. Among the Germans, the Welsers invested 20,000 cruzados; the Fuggers, 4,000; the Höchstetters, 4,000; the Grossenprott, 3,000; the Imhof, 3,000; and the Hirschvogel, 2,000.[34] Three ships laden with silver, copper, bullion, and coins, headed by three German factors, joined the *carreira*, commanded by the newly appointed viceroy Alameda. The ships departed for India in March 1505, anchored in Cochin and other ports along the coast of western India, and returned safely to Portugal in November 1506 loaded with 13,800 quintals (1,380 tons) of spices. The profit on the voyage, after deduction of the buying price, transport costs, and the Crown's 30 percent customs, was estimated to be in the range of 150–397.7 percent.[35]

This successful voyage of the German-Italian syndicate could not serve as a model in the long run, for a variety of reasons. It was a one-shot venture. Every new venture had to be renegotiated with the king and among the merchants, bringing with it the resulting disagreements and transaction costs. Risk was not well spread among voyages. In 1506, the king prohibited private merchants from sending ships to India but, shortly thereafter, the prohibition was partially abolished.[36] When, in the next voyage, that of 1506, two of the three participating German ships sunk, the investors in that voyage took significant losses, and the fact that this framework did not spread risks over time became apparent.[37] The relationship with the king was not based on a commitment that could be enforced on him by third parties or by internal commitment devices. When Manuel realized that the cartel's imports were driving the price of spices in Europe down, to his detriment, he first prohibited the release of private merchant spices from Casa da Índia without his permission and then set up a minimum price below which the merchants could not sell their pepper and spices. This was, at the very least, a unilateral alteration of contractual terms and can even be seen as expropriation of private property.

The king was quite unpredictable in his actions, and his granting of favorable terms to foreign merchants was dependent on his mood and surrounding circumstances. Thus, for instance, in early 1504, before granting the aforementioned privileges, he refused the request of the Welsers to participate in the fleet of that year.[38] In 1504, the king renewed this order, whose basic conditions were that the private merchants should pay to the Crown the one-fourth-and-5-percent share (*quarto e vintena*) on their return.[39] In 1506, the king issued an order prohibiting private merchants from equipping and sending ships to India, since he wanted to take up the entire trade in the name of the Crown. However, he was unsuccessful in his ambition. The private merchants continued to take part in the trade as usual, and the regulation was partially withdrawn.[40] In 1510, while giving certain privileges to private merchants traveling to India, the king made it clear that they should not deal in spices, drugs, sealing wax, dyes, indigo, or benzoin, making these part of the Crown monopoly.[41] This fluctuation in his attitude toward the participation of foreign and/or private merchants in Indian trade created uncertainty as to the longevity of the enterprises and syndicates, and the long-term value of investment in trade. Francisco Corvinelli commanded his own ship in the Portuguese fleet to India in 1509. He was appointed royal agent for purchasing spices for the king in India. The 1510 fleet was largely staffed and financed by the House of Sernigi and commanded by de Vasconcelos.[42]

Various Forms of Private Trade around the Middle of the Sixteenth Century

The Crown allowed private merchants, be they Portuguese or foreigners, to ship goods from Asia to Portugal via the Cape on Crown ships. This paid service allowed private merchants who did not have the capital needed for sending a full ship, or did not want to risk a full ship and its goods, to take part in the newly initiated oceanic trade with Asia. In 1510, the king granted certain privileges to the officials going to India, but prohibited them from trading in spices, drugs, sealing wax, dyes, indigo, or benzoin. Similarly, copper, silver, and gold were declared to be goods under royal monopoly. But he permitted them to trade in any other commodities such as seed pearls, precious stones, cloth of all sorts, musk, amber, porcelain, and other sorts of goods. The king also issued an order in 1518 prohibiting every Portuguese Christian from purchasing or selling pepper on the Malabar Coast. The *Ordenação da Índia* issued at Evora on September 8, 1520, expressly named the commodities reserved for the Crown and imposed strict punishment on anyone found trading in the following items: pepper, cloves, ginger, cinnamon, mace, nutmeg, sealing wax, silk, and tincal (borax).[43] Thus, a division was formed over time between the core goods—pepper and spices, for which the king wished to maintain Crown monopoly—and other goods, which could be traded by private individuals.

Another way in which the Portuguese Crown promoted private-public collaboration was by means of permits issued to the officials, to send a defined quantity of spices purchased at their cost, but transshipped to Lisbon free of freight charges. The difference between this category and the former lies in the identity of the goods carrier—a private trader or a state official. The quantity of spices permitted to be taken to Portugal varied according the status of the officials and the privileges they were able to secure from the Crown. The commodities taken by the officials under such permits were called, in general, *liberdades da Índia*. The officials were normally expected to pay to the king the *vintena* (one-twentieth) and *quarto* (one-quarter) of the quantities on arrival at Casa da Índia, and this amounted altogether to 28.75 percent of the total.[44] The officials at the Casa da Índia were required to deduct the duties and other shares due to the king according to the specific authorizations issued to various officials when the commodities reached Lisbon. A part of their salary was withheld for such permits, which saved the king the trouble of paying the officials in full. In addition, the permits for private trade incentivized officials to invest effort in developing trade destinations and exploring market opportunities. The private trade thus served as an additional source of revenue for the Crown. Lastly, it reduced the motivation of officials to involve themselves in illegal trade and smuggling. Yet, the counter concern was that officials would prefer their private trade over Crown trade.[45]

Beginning as early as the period of Afonso de Albuquerque (1509–15), the intra-Asian trade of the Portuguese was considerably larger in value and substantially more lucrative than the trade between Cochin and Goa and Lisbon. While a large part of the profit in the intercontinental trade went to the Portuguese Crown, which controlled the Carreira da Índia, the profit from the intra-Asian trade accrued overwhelmingly to private individuals.[46]

An important branch of Asian trade that the Crown initially monopolized for itself was the spice trade with the Moluccas. However, from the very beginning, the monopoly was rather loose, with crew members of the royal ships being allowed private participation. In addition, rights were also granted to select state officials to engage in a limited amount of trade in the "forbidden" goods. On occasions, a shortage of resources also obliged the Crown to permit private traders and private ships to participate. Thus, in 1523, a cargo of cloves was loaded in Ternate on private ships because the royal factory did not have the resources to buy it. This was repeated two years later because the factory did not have a Crown ship with adequate capacity. There were also cases, as in 1524 and 1536, when private Portuguese traders managed to violate the royal monopoly by paying more for the cloves than the Crown factor was willing to pay. All these problems persuaded the Crown, in 1539, to formally declare the trade in cloves and nutmeg free, subject only to the condition that anybody dealing in these spices would be obliged to provide one-third of the quantity bought to the Crown factors at cost price.[47] The

Crown participated in several other branches of inter-Asian trade—mostly those linking Malacca to the Bay of Bengal, but also, marginally, in the Western Indian Ocean—as a "merchant among merchants," the others being Portuguese traders, Asian traders, and Portuguese renegades and their descendants of mixed origins. The Crown even formed occasional partnerships with traders of either group. In the 1530s and 1540s, changes in both the nature and the scale of Crown involvement in this trade were discernible, with Crown shipping increasingly giving way to private shipping. Around the middle of the century, of the seven or eight ships that sailed each year from Malacca to Coromandel, only one belonged to the Crown. Also, even on voyages operated with Crown shipping, the investment of Crown capital in the cargo was on the decline and they were increasingly converted into some kind of a freight service. The captain of the vessel received free freight space, which he normally rented out.[48]

The Asia and Europa Contracts of 1575–91

In 1575, King Sebastian I, who faced financial constraints at home and political complications in India, decided to outsource the spice trade, which had been a Crown monopoly for some time, to private merchants.[49] This was the first time the king had delegated the entire procurement of pepper in Asia to private interests; no earlier monarch had seriously contemplated a contract of such scope. The idea was to hand over the decision-making in business matters to experts and to hedge the risks. The king's aides designed two separate agreements, known as the Asia Contract and the Europa Contract, and auctioned them to German, Italian, and Portuguese merchants.[50] The Asia Contract involved purchasing spices from India and shipping them to Lisbon. According to the terms, a certain amount of pepper had to be bought for a certain price in India and delivered to the king's warehouses in Lisbon. There, the king sold half of it for a fixed price to the contractors, who could then sell the pepper on their own account. These later agreements were called the Europa Contracts, and included the right to distribute and sell spices in Europe. King Sebastian was already planning, and raising funds for, his fatal campaign in North Africa, and the contracts promised quick profits to finance the project.

The 1575–80 Contracts

Konrad Rott, a relatively unknown merchant from Augsburg, not a member of any of the well-known merchant firms, successfully bid for both the Europa and Asia Contracts.[51] The Europa Contract stipulated that Rott had to buy 12,000 quintals of pepper in the first year and 20,000 thereafter, at 34 ducats per quintal. He was to distribute and sell the spices throughout Europe and profit from the margin between the buy and sell prices. In addition, he was to stand surety for a loan to Portugal of several hundred thousand cruzados at a moderate interest rate. This loan would be repaid in pepper deliveries in the last years of the contract.[52] The Europa Contract was for five years. He was unsuccessful in his attempt to form a syndicate and sell a share in the contract to any German merchant and, in April 1576, ended up selling three-eighths to the Bardi Company of Florence.[53]

The Habsburgs auctioned another category of contract, the Asia Contract. A consortium was to build and fit out the five ships bound for India each year. The contractors were paid a flat sum of 50,000 cruzados for each ship.[54] The Asia Contract, concluded in 1578, obliged Rott to import to Portugal 20,000 quintals of pepper and specific smaller quantities of other spices. He was to buy the spices in India at a fixed price at his own expense, ship them to Portugal, again at his own expense and risk, and deliver them to the Casa da Índia warehouse in Lisbon at a mutually agreed price.

By 1578, Rott was thus able to combine the two contracts, allowing him to control the full span of the spice trade. But the combination was such that it required exceptionally high investment, on the one hand, while, on the other, allocating almost all of the risks to Rott without enabling him to reap the upside in full. He was able to share the burden with additional merchants by dividing the project into thirty shares, selling ten of them to Portuguese merchants and seven and a half to Italian merchants. Yet his share in the contracts was still too big and his exposure to risks beyond his wealth. The political instability in Portugal, which led to the unification with Spain under the Habsburgs, also contributed to his financial downfall. His enterprise suffered a liquidity crisis in 1580 and duly went bankrupt.[55]

The 1580 Contract

In 1580, following Rott's bankruptcy, Giovanni Rovallesca, an Italian merchant from Milan, took over Rott's Asia Contract. Rovallesca appointed some German agents and made use of the networks created by Rott.[56] He was obliged to send 150,000 quintals of pepper from India to Lisbon over the course of five years. Each year the agents were supposed to purchase in India a total of 30,000 quintals of pepper—15,000 for their own account and 15,000 for the king's account in consideration for the contract. To purchase pepper over the five-year term, the consortium was required to transfer in total 1.2 million cruzados to Goa. The contractors were free to sell their half of the pepper as they chose, in the European markets. The king made it a practice to sell his half, the 15,000 quintals, to the Rott-Rovallesca consortium at 32 cruzados per quintal. By allowing the same consortium to ship and buy all 30,000 quintals of pepper that made their way to Europe, the king, in fact, awarded the contractors the exclusive European distribution of Portuguese pepper. Rovallesca's contract was backed by Italians and by the Spanish branch of the Fuggers.[57]

The 1585/6–91 Contract

After the expiration of Rovallesca's contract in 1585, King Philip (reigning since 1581 over both Spain and Portugal) was in dire need of cash,[58] and tendered the Asia Contract once again. In December 1585, a new Asia Contract was concluded with Gerhard Paris of Aachen, who served as representative of Rovallesca. According to this contract, the contractors were to equip five ships annually for a period of six years (1586–91) heading for India and Malacca (in some years, five vessels to India and another to Malacca). The holders of the Asia Contract had to send 170,000 cruzados annually for the purchase of 30,000 quintals of pepper and deliver it to the Casa da Índia. Again, they had to pay 24,000 cruzados each year to the king for the sea-going vessels that would be used for the contract trade.[59] The contractors could also send their own agents to India to conduct the trade.[60] For their maintenance, the holders of the contract were allowed to take, free of duty, 450 quintals of spices (cinnamon, cloves, and such) and sell them in Europe. The price for purchasing pepper from India was fixed at 5⅔ cruzados, whereas the pepper taken to Casa da Índia was to be sold at 12 cruzados per quintal. They might receive an additional 4 cruzados for the freight and transshipping costs.[61] The Casa sold the pepper to the European contractors at prices negotiated each year in Lisbon. The European distributors included, besides the Fuggers and Welsers, several investors who were not parties to the Asia Contract. The consortium marketed pepper through a network of correspondents in Hamburg, Lübeck, Middelburg, Amsterdam, Leghorn, and Venice. By not awarding the European distributorship to the group holding the Asia Contract, the king took on the risk of pepper price fluctuations in Europe, bargaining in Lisbon for a high price.[62]

The contract, in reality, shielded the contractors from market fluctuations in pepper as they bought and sold it at fixed prices. Thus, in effect, they provided the Crown with freight services. They were obliged as part of the bid to maintain a volume of shipping as expected by the Crown. This was defined by the number of ships they were required to pay for to be sent annually, by the value of bullion they had to take to Asia, and by the weight of pepper they had to transport back to Portugal. The contractors were to profit by capturing part of the price arbitrage of pepper and by using the same ships to import other spices into Portugal, acquiring the profits (or losses) on these spices in full. The Crown's profit was made on the price difference between the buy price in India and the sell price in Lisbon (to the contractors of the Europa Contract or directly to the market), minus the freight cost (6⅓ cruzados). The Crown was saved from the need to operate the Carreira da Índia as a public enterprise. The Portuguese Cape trade and shipping had always depended on private participation and financing, but never before had private merchants assumed so many functions formerly performed by royal officials and almost the entire financial burden of the Carreira da Índia.[63]

Rovallesca—either because of wealth constraints or some level of risk aversion—did not want to assume the investment and risk in full, preferring to form a syndicate and share them with other investors. Markus and Mathäus Welser and Company bought five out of the twelve shares (41⅔ percent) of the Asia Contract. Octavian and Philipp Edward Fugger then bought three out of the five acquired by Welser, ending up with 25 percent (three out of twelve shares) in the contract as a whole and leaving the Welsers with two shares (16⅔ percent).[64] Rovallesca kept 58⅓ percent of the contract (seven out of twelve shares) to himself.[65]

On the European side, the king was ready to sell 30,000 quintals of pepper annually to the Venetians at the rate of 30 ducats per quintal, which was much lower than the price to the previous European contractors (36–38 ducats). Nevertheless, neither Venetian merchants nor merchants from any other Italian city agreed to buy this European contract, as they could purchase pepper in the Levant for a lower price.[66]

The Italian-German syndicate could not supply the promised 30,000 quintals to Lisbon in a single year. Due to private traders diverting pepper from India to other parts of Asia and to Eastern Mediterranean routes, it was difficult for the agents of the contractors to achieve this amount in India. International circumstances also had an effect. Syndicate merchants' ships were increasingly looted by English and Dutch corsairs. In addition, following the fall of Antwerp to the Spaniards in 1585, Amsterdam became the center of the European spice trade.[67]

The Habsburg king, now uniting Spain and Portugal, wanted to achieve control over the pepper trade by reorganizing its administration and introducing a centralizing program. The spice trade and the Casa da Índia were put under the auspices of his council. These changes were intended to take back the pepper trade for the Iberians once the Asia Contract with the Italians and Germans ended in 1591.[68]

Conclusion

Throughout the sixteenth century, the Portuguese Crown struggled with maintaining its full monopoly over the Cape Route–Eurasian trade and its control of the nascent Asian Empire. The Crown's tax base in Portugal and its tax-collection apparatus could not provide the required funding, hence the king had to seek private finance, often outside Portugal. Part of the funding was in the form of loans, and part of it was in kind—in ships. This amounted to the outsourcing of operations hitherto performed by the Crown to foreign merchants. Various organizational models were tried over the century. They involved contracts between the state and family-based merchant firms or consortia of merchants, in which shares were allocated to the firms.

There were a few avenues for private trade initiative and public-private collaboration. The first was that of allowing private vessels to join the Carreira da Índia on its way from Lisbon to Asia around the Cape. The second was to allow private merchants to ship freights (some goods, but not the core spices and pepper) on Crown ships from Asia to Portugal. The third was to permit state officials to conduct private trade alongside their official duties, and bring back the goods they bought, in chests on board Crown ships, as part of their remuneration package.[69] A fourth avenue was the inter-Asian trade in which private merchants were allowed to trade on some routes or in some commodities. A fifth and related avenue was the permission granted to private merchants to engage in privateering in the Indian Ocean.

The building blocks used in the Portuguese enterprises were traditional: states (or rather crowns) and families. Both provided some degree of longevity. The basic issue of contract enforcement, for contracts between the Crown and the family firms, was not solved in any innovative way. The Crown could not credibly commit *not* to breach its contracts. Reputation was the key informal enforcement mechanism. Interactions were repeated—every year during the period of the 1500s voyages, and every five years in the Europa and Asia Contracts of the 1570s and 1580s. There was a limit to the Portuguese Crown's ability to breach contracts with the Fuggers and their like without paying a prohibitive reputational price. In a way, the Crown's contracting with foreign merchant houses was another device that supported performance. The Crown could not expropriate Italian or German assets back in their hometowns, nor extort them beyond the stake they had at any given time in Portugal.

This Portuguese microstudy demonstrates the differences between Portuguese and Chinese trade. China, having a huge tax base and an extensive administration, could support, at least for several decades, maritime enterprise on the scale of Zheng He's voyages. The Portuguese

Crown found it difficult to finance even a few ships per year in its Asia voyages. It also demonstrates the differences between Portugal and England and the Dutch Republic. Portugal lacked the kind of private wealth that could invest in such an enterprise. It also lacked the institutional design that would allow the Crown to credibly commit not to breach contracts and not to expropriate the investment of domestic or foreign merchants. English and Dutch merchants, possibly after observing Portuguese organizational experiments, may have concluded that Portugal was unable to identify a stable and successful organizational model and realized that they had to be innovative in organizing their own emerging trade.

Does the Portuguese case show that a country could dominate long-distance oceanic trade without undergoing an organizational revolution, or that it could not? Were skilled oceanic navigation, accurate guns on board ships, and determination to use violence sufficient for achieving a long-term dominance? The decade with the highest number of Portuguese ships taking the Cape Route was the 1500s, with 151 ships. The lowest was the 1680s, with only 19 ships. But part of this decline is attributed to competition by the business corporations. The question is really about a counterfactual seventeenth century in which there were no EIC and VOC. It is hard to say what that might have looked like. We cannot know whether Portugal (and the Iberian Habsburg union) could have overcome its repeated organizational crises or whether another European ruler with stronger state capacity would have organized a more effective ruler-owned trade enterprise so as to achieve Eurasian trade dominance.

PART IV

~

The Corporation Transformed

The Era of Impersonal Cooperation

~ 9 ~

The Origins of the Business Corporation

One institution, the business corporation, and two companies, the Dutch East India Company (VOC) and the English East India Company (EIC), form the basis of part IV, the last part of this book. In fact, in this part of the book we will come to understand why and how the corporation was transformed into a business corporation.

What is a corporation? A widely shared modern legal definition of the corporation is as follows: an artificial person or legal entity created by or under the authority of the laws of a state, composed of an association of numerous individuals, having a legal personality and legal existence distinct from that of its several members, and which is, by the same authority, vested with the capacity of continuous succession, irrespective of death of members or changes in its membership, either in perpetuity or for a limited term of years, and of acting as a unit in matters relating to the common purpose of the association, such as buying, selling and owning property, contracting with others, suing or being sued in court.[1] As we shall see, this definition could sound familiar to Edward Coke (1552–1634) in England, Hugo Grotius (1583–1645) in the Dutch Republic, and contemporary jurists in much of the rest of Europe in the early seventeenth century.

What is a "business corporation"? The following seven characteristics are in my view the core characteristics of the business corporation: (1) a separate legal personality, which provides longevity and corporate ownership of property; (2) a collective decision-making mechanism which includes delegated centralized management; (3) joint-stock equity finance; (4) lock-in of the investment; (5) transferability of the interest (decision-making and profits) in the corporation; (6) protection from expropriation by the ruler/state; and (7) asset partitioning, which includes two elements—protection of private assets of shareholders from creditors of the corporation and protection of corporate assets from the creditors of shareholders.[2] Some may include in the definition a profit-maximization purpose, but for me this is not a unique feature of the business corporation, but rather a feature of business firms in all types of organizational forms. This seven-characteristic definition of the business corporation would have been incomprehensible for jurists in 1600.

I will now trace the appearance and the attachment to the corporate form of a number of organizational characteristics (shown in table 9.1). The first two attributes could be found centuries before 1600 in religious and municipal corporations. Attributes three through six were attached to the corporate form for the first time around the year 1600 as part of the design and early evolution of the first two joint-stock business corporations, the EIC and the VOC. Attribute seven, which is now considered as one of the cornerstones of the business corporation, was developed only after our period and outside the context of trade.

To be clear, I do not argue that features three through six appeared out of the blue in 1600. My argument is that one cannot understand the innovation and leap forward of 1600 without understanding the earlier history of the organization of Eurasian trade. Earlier developments in the organization of trade are important in three respects. First, some of the attributes that were attached to the corporate entity around 1600, notably joint-stock finance and transferable shares, had earlier history in other organizational forms. The cliché that all Western European commercial practices had Italian origins is valid in this case as well, but with qualifications. Second, the shortfalls of organizing long-distance trade in ruler-owned enterprises, family firms, and merchant networks convinced the English and Dutch that it was necessary to innovate in order to make up for being latecomers entering the scene from the very far end of Eurasia. Third, on the more conceptual level, the earlier experience called their attention to the issues that had to be dealt with by the new and innovative organizational form—namely, agency problems, risk mitigation, and information flows.

My argument is that the years around 1600 constitute an organizational revolution. This revolution was constituted by identifying the organiza-

9.1. Attributes of the Business Corporation

Attribute	Detailed description	Historical origins
1 Separate legal personality; longevity	Legal entity separated from the legal personality and capacities of its members, capable of owning property, contracting, suing in courts, receiving privileges.	12th–13th centuries: Roman Catholic Church.
2 Governance; collective decision making	Centralized management. Some powers delegated from members to directors or managers. Other powers exercised by members voting in meetings. Some information disseminated from central administration to members in order for decision-making to be effective.	12th–13th centuries: Roman Catholic Church. 14th–16th centuries: municipal corporations, guilds, regulated corporations.
3 Joint-stock equity finance	Pooling together of investment, the returns on which were based on profit or loss.	In noncorporate business context: general partnerships, commenda. In state debt context: Roman societas publicanorum and late Middle Ages Casa di San Giorgio. In corporate context: around 1600.
4 Lock-in of investment	Individuals could not withdraw for term of years or until dissolution.	Around 1600.
5 Transferability of interest	Transferability of shares could be done without dissolution of the entity. In stronger form, shares could be transferred without consent of other members or directors; in strongest form, shares could be transferred in stock market.	Around 1600.
6 Protection from expropriation by ruler	Agreement between incorporators and ruler in the form of charter, or general protection from expropriation in the form of rule of law and constitutional rights.	Weak form with initial Crown chartering. Stronger form around 1600.
7 Asset partitioning	Creditors of members could not access corporate assets (entity shielding); creditors of corporation could not access members' assets (limited liability). In the weaker form, creditors could access as subordinate creditors or only at dissolution.	In weak form: Roman times. In strongest form: 18th–19th centuries.

tional challenges of Eurasian trade, recognizing the pitfalls of earlier organizational forms, by making use of a uniquely European public-law organization—the corporation, with its legal personality and governance structure, attaching to it financial and business attributes that were developed in the context of trade—joint-stock equity investment and transferable shares, and creating by this intermingling two additional features—lock-in of capital and a sufficient level of protection from expropriation.

So the innovation with respect to attributes three through six was that they were attached for the first time to the corporate form and compounded with each other. The various attributes could not be fully separated from each other. They supported and enhanced each other. For example, the lock-in of capital relied on legal personality and longevity. The delegated governance structure of the corporation had to undergo changes when it was applied to equity investment. Attributes three through six were unfamiliar to the greatest English jurist of the time, Edward Coke, and his contemporaries as corporate attributes.[3]

This chapter follows the early history of the corporation and examines how the corporation acquired attributes one and two, which were familiar to Coke and his contemporaries. Chapters 10 and 11 will analyze the transformation of the corporate form of organization into what could be termed the "joint-stock business corporation" or, in short form, the "business corporation" with the establishment and configuration of the EIC and VOC in the early seventeenth century. In this period attributes three through six first appeared. Attribute seven was still irrelevant at the time and was developed only in subsequent centuries, when business corporations were increasingly funded by long-term debt finance and were subjected to liquidation due to insolvency. While from a legal perspective it may seem that these chapters of the book deal with the emergence of four new and important attributes of the business corporation, from an economics perspective the formation of the EIC and VOC is an even more dramatic transformation from personally to impersonally based organizational form.

Part IV as a whole explains why European corporations were transformed around 1600 from public entities into joint-stock, for-profit entities, why this occurred in Northwest Europe and not elsewhere in Europe, and why corporations were so suitable for long-distance trade that they rapidly took control of the Cape Route and rose to dominance in Eurasian trade as a whole, at the expense of family firms, merchant networks, and ruler-operated enterprises. Chapter 12 focuses on the question of why the corporation was the ultimate embedded institution—in other words, why China, India, and the Ottoman Empire did not develop similar corporate like entities, and why they did not imitate the European corporate form before the late nineteenth century.

THE ORIGINS OF THE CORPORATION

A long-standing debate surrounds the early history of the corporation. I identify four different approaches in the historiography of the corporation. The first, which views the corporation as a Roman jurists' invention, was advanced by legal scholars and historians of Roman law, such as Duff.[4] They interpreted Roman legal texts and the *Corpus Juris Civilis* as containing evidence for the existence of a corporate conception in classical Roman law. Recently, Malmendier suggested that the *societas publicanorum*, a society of government leaseholders, was the earliest predecessor of the modern corporation. Yet this institution, which appeared in the fifth century BCE and reached its height during the republic, was not reflected in later legal texts such as the *Corpus Juris Civilis*.[5] More recently, Abatino, Dari-Mattiacci, and Perotti identified another Roman institution, the *peculium*, as another possible forerunner of the corporation. The *peculium* provided de facto depersonalization by making a nonlegal person the fulcrum of the business: the slave. This format exhibited all the distinctive features of modern corporations, including asset partitioning, thereby providing a functional equivalent of the modern corporate form.[6] Even if the identification of corporate features in the *societas publicanorum* or the *peculium* is widely accepted by scholars, these institutions, which might be relevant for understanding Roman economy and may offer an interesting alternative to the corporation, had no direct continuation into the High Middle Ages.

The second approach in the historiography of the corporation argues that it is a product of eleventh- through thirteenth-century revivers of Roman legal scholarship in the newly established European universities. According to that view, the glossators and commentators, the interpreters of Justinian Code, read into a few scattered statements by Roman jurists a coherent legal concept unrecognized by contemporaries. They may have done so either as a scholastic exercise or in order to serve the new needs of their age.[7] Specifically, they may have responded to their changing environment in which associations such as independent cities, universities, colleges, and guilds were gaining importance. These associations needed an institutional platform for owning property, setting autonomous governance structures, resolving disputes, and the like that the corporation provided. The Roman-law jurists, working in medieval Italian universities, clothed Roman law for this need.

The third approach views the corporation as originating in medieval Germanic tribal traditions. It points to the communal spirit of German tribes as evidence of a corporate ideology. This view was advanced by German nationalists, notably von Gierke, in the late nineteenth century.[8] Unlike Roman law and the Southern European Latin culture, which were individualistic in their orientation, the basic Germanic orientation was toward the group, the association, and the fellowship. This view lost support with the discrediting of German nationalism and of Gierke's historical analysis.

The fourth approach considers the corporation an invention of the church and canon law.[9] Harold Berman is the most influential proponent of this approach.[10] He relies on the work of historians of the late medieval Roman Catholic Church, notably Brian Tierney.[11] Several controversies that shook the Catholic Church between the eleventh and fifteenth centuries—including over investiture (the conflict between the emperor and the pope), conciliarism (the conflict between the College of Cardinals and the pope), and the Papal Schism (the split between claimants in Avignon and Rome to be the true pope)—were often argued in corporate terms. The issues at stake included the following: Who appoints the pope? Who appoints bishops? Does the pope have to consult or seek the approval of the council? Where did the authority and ownership of property rest when the seat of a pope, a bishop, or an abbot became vacant? Did the pope or Council of Bishops have the ultimate authority? Was the church a corporation?

We do not have to enter here into the detailed history of the Catholic Church or the exact positions in the various debates. What is important for our purposes is that the corporate features were developed within these controversies in order to resolve organizational difficulties within the Roman Catholic Church. Several of the features related to internal governance: election of office holders by consent of the governed through majority decision-making subject to set rules of quorum requirement and discussion and voting procedure; representativeness of the whole body by office holders through delegation of legal authority to act and bind; and the jurisdiction of the collective body to issue bylaws that will govern internal affairs and settle disputes. Based on these governance rules the collective body became entitled to own property, to convey property to third parties, and to litigate disputes with such third parties. The existence of these collective bodies was not confined to a single human lifetime. Issues of inheritance and cross-generational transfer of property were alleviated by the longevity of existence of the collective entity. This was a big advantage in a Church in which celibacy was required of monks and clergymen, and hereditary transmission of titles and property was not an option. These working tools for running collective bodies were used by the full range of ecclesiastical offices and organizations, from the papacy and bishopry to the monastery, fraternity, and religious order.

Once corporate practices, such as corporate ownership of property, collective decision-making, and group litigation started to take place in the context of the Church, they were gradually legalized and formalized in canon law. The question of how to reconcile the evolving canon-law conceptualization of the corporation with older Roman-law texts and concepts had to be addressed next. The glossators and commentators reread Roman-law texts, doctrines, and institutions in line with newly developed medieval canon law theory. It is likely that canon law and Roman-law concepts and theories of the corporation coevolved. After all, to take just two examples, Irnerius (1050–1125 or thereafter), the founder of the Glossators School at the University of Bologna, was involved in an investiture controversy, and Pope Innocent IV (1195–1254) taught canon law at the same University of Bologna before his ascendance to the papal throne. At this point the boundaries between arguments based on Roman or canon origins of the corporation are blurred. We don't need, for our ultimate purposes, to determine whether corporate ideas were originally Roman, were creatively read into Roman texts by medieval Roman-law jurists, or were formulated anew by canon-law jurists.

The emerging law of corporations became the constitutional law of the late medieval Roman Catholic Church as a whole and of its various subunits. Some historians view the corporate features of the corporation as important in turning the Roman Catholic Church into the large business enterprise that it was in late medieval Europe.[12] Others offer less ambitious and more detailed study of one Catholic religious order, the Jesuits. The Jesuits had headquarters in Rome, connections in universities throughout Europe, and missions and agents in Japan, China, India, and the Americas. The corporate structure of the order allowed it to circulate information globally, instruct and monitor agents, own property and finance its activities.[13] The corporation served the objective of providing the Church with autonomy and separating the constitution of the church from that of territorial rulers. The theological-legal-philosophical conceptualization of the Church on the one hand and of secular rulers and their territorial states, on the other hand, diverged.[14]

Can this divergence explain Europe's singularity in developing the concept of the corporation as a separate legal entity and ultimately developing the business corporation? Why did the Roman Catholic Church, out of all the organized religions, need such a legal–constitutional conceptual framework? Two factors played an important role. While several major religions were an integral part of the apparatus of states, a prime example being Confucianism and the early Eastern Orthodox Church, the Catholic Church aspired to separate itself from the emperor and other secular rulers.[15] Although several major religions were decentralized, notably Hinduism, Buddhism, Judaism, and in many respects also Islam, the Roman Catholic Church was fully centralized and hierarchical. The combination of these two factors made it quite singular. Another layer of the explanation, beyond the singularity of the Church is Roman law. The combination of the practice of having collective bodies within the Church with the learned tradition of Roman law, as manifested in the Justinian Code and in the revival of its study and interpretation in the first universities that were formed in Italy, made the corporate conception as developed in late medieval Europe particularly legal and elaborated. Roman law and the Roman Catholic Church were the breeding ground of the corporation and created the preconditions for its transformation into the business corporation.

THE EUROPEAN CORPORATION: FROM CHURCH TO MUNICIPAL TO TRADE

By the fifteenth and early sixteenth centuries, the corporation was already well established as an important organizational and constitutional platform in Europe well beyond the Church. It was uniquely European, having been employed for several centuries to ecclesiastical ends. However, the use of the corporate form had already expanded from spiritual to secular functions. It was increasingly used in the municipal context. Cities in some regions of Europe assumed a level of independence and autonomy from popes and emperors and from the rural feudal system. They found the corporation to provide a good platform for organizing municipal governance and city-based economic activities such as craft guilds, merchant guilds, livery companies, regulated companies, and educational endeavors such as universities and colleges. Guilds—the most significant, late-medieval economically active corporations—had considerable social, fraternal, ritual, and even religious elements. They served as fellowships or brotherhoods that controlled and ritualized whole aspects of their members' lives.[16] They were total institutions in the sociological sense of administering most aspects of the members' lives, not passive investment tools, and they disciplined their members accordingly, applying social and religious norms and sanctions. Membership was determined by status and not contract. In modern terms, guilds were not aimed at profit maximization but rather were conceived as regulatory orders, performing public or semipublic duties. It is conceivable that these functions of the corporation were positive spillover from the development of those ideas in the context of the Church. Had the church not developed the corporate form, these municipal organizations, towns, colleges, and guilds would have undoubtedly taken a different organizational path, either by obtaining less autonomy and independence or by basing such an autonomy on different organizational platforms and characteristics.

The characteristics of the city-based corporation became, with time, quite stable. It had a legal entity separate from that of its members. Its legal personality secured longevity. It did not terminate with the death of any one individual: it was potentially perpetual and subject to dissolution only in a strictly defined manner. A corporation could own and convey land, albeit at times with restrictions. It did not have to litigate by listing all of its members' names, but could sue and be sued, for better or for worse, in its separate corporate personality. It could make bylaws to govern its internal affairs. As a legal entity, a corporation could acquire additional franchises, liberties, and exemptions from the state, usually in the incorporating charter or act itself.[17]

The first five centuries in the history of the European corporation can be divided into three periods. As with most periodization, this one isn't neat. Yet the rough scheme is of a first period in which the corporation was conceptualized and used for legitimizing and organizing various elements within the Roman Catholic Church and was used for the constitutional and practical purposes of the Church. In the second period the corporate concept spilled from religious to secular contexts and was used by municipalities and other urban organizations, such as guilds and universities, in order to address their governance needs and consolidate their autonomy vis-à-vis popes and emperors. England, with its more centralized monarchy, was the first to enter the third period. In that period the Crown monopolized to itself the privilege of creating corporations and used the corporate form as one of its tools for policy promotion, income generation, and control. Entities that viewed themselves as corporations formed in the second period were reincorporated by charters in the third period in order to assert and demonstrate the Crown's monopoly on incorporation.

As can be seen from table 9.2, most corporations formed in England by royal charters in the third phase were universities, colleges, schools, livery companies, and craft companies, some of them reincorporations of craft guilds. The reincorporation of preexisting municipalities and ecclesiastical companies was politically sensitive due to the tensions between the Crown and such entities, and as a result only a few of these were reincorporated by royal charters. The business of chartering trading companies was small relative to the whole business of chartering.

Prior to the sixteenth century, a number of groups of merchants in England, such as the Merchants of the Staple and the early Merchant Adventurers, traded with nearby continental ports, but these were associations of individual traders that usually had no formal corporate charter.

9.2. Incorporation by Royal Charter in England to 1700

Field of activity/years	To 1500	1501– 1550	1551– 1600	1601– 1650	1651– 1700	Total
Universities and colleges	12	5	7	6	0	30
Livery and manufac- turing companies	18	5	7	28	14	72
Municipal	1	0	0	0	0	1
Ecclesiastical	1	2	1	1	0	5
Professional and scientific	0	2	2	0	3	7
Schools	0	6	25	2	1	34
Hospitals	0	2	4	1	0	7
Charities	0	1	1	2	2	6
Overseas Trade	0	0	5	1	3	9
Colonial	0	0	0	4	1	5
Water Supply	0	0	0	1	0	1
Banks	0	0	0	0	1	1
Total	32	23	52	46	25	178

Source: https://privycouncil.independent.gov.uk/royal-charters/chartered-bodies/.

They operated overseas on the basis of a license or a franchise.[18] In the sixteenth century, the regulated corporation gradually replaced the merchant guild in the organization of English trade with Western European ports. The Spanish Company, whose trade also covered Portugal, was chartered in 1577; the Eastland Company, for trading in the Baltic Sea and Scandinavia, was chartered in 1579;[19] and the French Company was chartered in 1609. The territorial monopoly of the Merchant Adventurers, which were first licensed in 1407 and again in 1505 and 1546, was extended in 1564 to include, in addition to Flanders, the Low Countries and parts of Germany.[20]

These corporations were referred to by historians as *regulated* because they regulated the trade of their members. The regulated corporation (also called the "regulated company") was, in fact, a descendant of the merchant guild. The term *corporation* rather than *guild* was used with respect to these sixteenth-century organizations in order to emphasize that they, unlike the earlier guilds, were formed by way of a charter of incorporation issued by the English Crown. The guilds, as ancient associations, acquired their legitimization from the voluntary association of their members from time immemorial, or from establishment by municipalities. The formalization of the guild into the corporation was important for legitimizing the Crown's claim to monopoly over the creation of new corporations and its authority to regulate their activities.

As will be seen in figure 9.3, the trade in regulated companies took place at the level of the members/merchants, not at the level of the corporation. Members invested their own capital, provided their own labor, assumed the risk, and either collected profits or bore losses. Members had to keep the trade regulations issued by the company. Regulated companies collected membership fees, annual payments, and duties on imported and exported goods. Money collected in this way was used to provide facilities and services for individual members, such as factories, embassies and consulates, and convoys. Thus, while each member traded separately, bearing investment and risk on his own account, some of the infrastructure was held in common.

The dominance of regulated corporations over England's trade with Western Europe is one of the explanations for the marginalization of the commenda in England. Scott, the author of a seminal three-volume book on the early history of joint companies, explains that in order to be an active merchant trading with ports within a corporate trade monopoly, one had to be a member of the relevant regulated corporation. Young and ambitious itinerant agents could not offer their service on commenda basis because they were not members or apprentices of the regulated corporation.[21] Another explanation that was offered by legal historians, and discussed in chapter 5 above, is that the commenda was rejected in England because it did not fit English common law's forms of action. In any case, as we shall see below, a divergence occurred between England and the Dutch Republic. In England, the business corporation evolved as a transformation of the regulated corporation that was combined with joint-stock finance, while in the Dutch Republic the business corporation evolved as a syndicate of commenda partnerships that was combined with a corporate entity.

JOINT-STOCK EQUITY INVESTMENT

Attributes one and two, legal personality and collective decision-making, were an inherent part of the corporation long before 1600. Attribute three of the business corporation, equity investment, could definitely be found in use before 1600 (or 1553) but with no connection to the corporate entity. Transferable shares were used in Italy in the context of public finance and colonial undertakings. The *compera* was a financial scheme initiated in Genoa and mimicked by other Italian cities, in which money was lent to the city-state by a consortium of well-to-do residents with interest paid in return. Repayment and interest were secured by specific sources of tax income. The shares in the consortium became transferable over time. The *maona* for the colonization of the island of Chios and the *Casa di San Giorgio* built on the *compera* involved an additional activity, the delegation of one of the city's main sovereign activities, the running of overseas colonies, to the *compera-maona*.[22] These schemes relied on taxation, performed a relatively routine administrative activity (not trade), and in fact had characteristic more like those of transferable city bonds than equity shares in an enterprise.

General partnership, commenda contracts, and ship part-ownership were equity-funded organizational forms. These organizational forms pooled together equity investment from several persons. The partners/part owners shared investment in the business activity in return for sharing the profit if such would materialize, or losses if such occurred. We have seen in chapter 6, family firms such as the Medici and Fugger used equity investment in enterprises that grew in scope and complexity and drew equity partners from outside the family. Their organizational form, which was originally based on the *compagnia* partnership, is referred to by some business historians in its complex form as *quasi-permanent multiple partnerships*. In chapter 7 we analyzed microstudies of merchant networks in which equity investment was made through partnerships and commenda. But neither of these organizational forms use the corporation as a platform.

An important step in the direction of attaching the corporation to commenda and ship part-ownership equity investment can be found in the Dutch Republic of the late sixteenth century. In the seven years that predated the formation of the VOC (1595–1602), the Asian ambitions of the Dutch were channeled into newly formed business entities, later referred to as *voorcompagnieën* or precompanies, meaning the precursors of the VOC. An analysis of these organizations is essential for understanding the mix between continuity from the organizational forms discussed in previous parts of this book and change as reflected in the organization of the VOC. They are also imperative in emphasizing the organizational differences between the VOC and the EIC. The first of these precompanies was formed in Amsterdam by nine merchants in 1594,[23] and was named the *Compagnie van Verre* (Far Lands Company). Each of the entrepreneurial merchants invested his own money and, in addition, raised investments from others. Altogether, fl.290,000 was raised to purchase and equip four ships for the long and dangerous trip to Asia. The active entrepreneurs, known as the *bewindhebbers,* determined the business plan and received commissions for extra efforts, while passive investors, the *participanten,* were entitled only to a share of the profits based on the sums they had each contributed. They invested through active partners who, supposedly, represented them. The first trip, to Bantam in Java and back, took about two years. One of the ships and nearly two-thirds of the crew were lost, and the voyage was not a commercial success. But it served as a model for several additional companies that were formed in Amsterdam and other cities in the Netherlands; and the mere fact that Dutch ships had proceeded directly to the East and had returned with spices roused national enthusiasm. Altogether, sixteen voyages, composed of sixty-six ships in total, were sent by companies from various cities in the southern and northern Netherlands within this seven-year period, using the precompany model.[24]

The precompanies were a cross between share partnerships in ships and multilateral commenda. In various European ports, ownership of ships was divided into shares, often 1/16, 1/32, or 1/64. This organizational form was known in England as part ownership in ships. The share was in the body of the ship itself, not in the goods or in the business activity. The division into shares was intended to spread risk and allow diversification of investment in ships.[25] Investors could purchase small shares in a variety of vessels sailing to different destinations and exposed to unrelated risks. They could sell their shares in a ship in a secondary market for such ship shares without dissolving the partnership. Secondary markets in ship shares were quite active in major Dutch ports,[26] as the capital of the ship was physically locked in, but the shares in it were tradable.[27] As shareholders were not liable to losses beyond their investment, they could be quite passive. Such partnerships were recognized and regulated by the leading maritime codes of Europe and by regulations of the Dutch cities.

The precompanies, unlike ship ownerships, were asymmetric in the sense that they had two classes of partners. In commenda, passive or sedentary investors entrusted sums of money to itinerant or otherwise active merchants. The precompanies were based—conceptually and, most likely, historically—on the commenda. They were partnerships in the trade business and not in the ships themselves. According to one historical interpretation, they were a syndicate or a joint venture of several commenda contracts or limited partnerships, each of which was composed of an active merchant and his passive investors. According to another interpretation, each precompany was a partnership (not a syndicate of partnerships) comprising several active and several passive partners. Figures 9.1 and 9.2 illustrate these interpretations. Figure 9.1 shows how the structure of a precompany was based on the commenda, while figure 9.2 illustrates that the structure of a precompany was a limited partnership.

The precompany looks like an advanced phase in the path of evolution of the medieval European commenda. The commenda started as a two-party agency agreement, evolved into a multilateral commenda, devel-

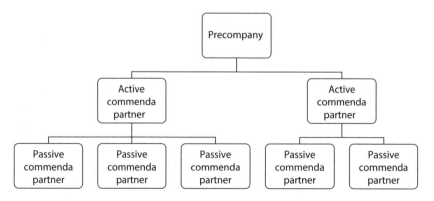

9.1. The precompany as a syndicate of commendas.

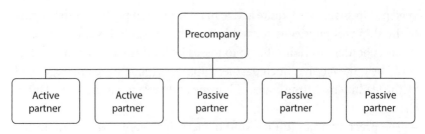

9.2. The precompany as a limited partnership.

oped further into a silent or dormant or limited partnership (known in Germany as the *stille Gesellschaft*), and finally became a syndicate of such partnerships in the Dutch precompanies.

In England in the sixteenth century, voyages of exploration, plunder, and trade in the Atlantic and beyond were financed mostly in the form of joint ventures. Such voyages included privateering in the Caribbean, voyages along the African coast for trade and slave capture, explorations in search for the Northwest Passage and Northeast Passage to Asia. Earlier and smaller voyages were organized by a handful of part owners using their own ship. As the number of investors increased, the share of each investment was not necessarily equal. Accounts of expenses, revenues and profits had to be kept. A typical scheme for the distribution of profits in a privateering venture in the second half of the sixteenth century was 15 percent to the lord admiral and queen as license fees and taxes, and of the remainder a third went to the ship's part owners, a third to the crew, and a third to the joint-stock investors in the ships' goods.[28] Expeditions along the West African coast were also organized by groups of investors who shared costs and profits. The first voyages consisted of only five senior partners. With time, the number of ships, the required capital, and number of investors grew. The 1564 Merchant Adventurers for Guinea was composed of three ships. It consisted of five senior partners, but each of these had "under" him additional investors who shared the investments and profits.[29] For practical reasons, the number of senior partners was only five, so that not all partners would have to contract with the queen and hire the ships. The first Frobisher voyage of 1576, also known as "The Adventurers to the Discovery of the North-West Passage," was a syndicate of eighteen investors. Four of the investors invested £100 each, five investors £50 each, and nine investors £25 each. This investment was made for a single voyage.[30] These joint ventures terminated at the end of each voyage. A new venture with new investors had to be formed for the next voyage. These ventures did not rely on the corporate form, had no longevity beyond a single voyage, and the stakes in each of them were not traded during the voyage. They were joint ventures, not business corporations.

MILL, MINE, AND WATER SUPPLY COMPANIES: THE FIRST BUSINESS CORPORATIONS?

In a classic 1953 book, Germain Sicard argued that that the grain watermills of late medieval Toulouse were the origins of the business corporations. Thanks to the survival of an extensive collection of records on the activities of the mills in the archives of Toulouse, Sicard was able to reconstruct the organization and activities of the mills. He came to the conclusion that the mills of Bazacle and Château Narbonnais on the Garonne river in Toulouse acquired, as they evolved, particularly between the thirteenth and fifteenth centuries, most of the organizational characteristics we associate today with the business corporation. He concludes by arguing that "these companies can be summarized in the following manner: the division of capital into salable shares, the shareholders' participation in the profits and losses in proportion to their share, and the administration, by elected delegates, of a company that was endowed with the rights of a distinct juridical person."[31] Sicard's work is admirable and illuminating, and the institutions he studies are fascinating and quite complex. I endorse his assertion that they were closer in their nature to business corporations than the Italian *maones*, *compres*, and Casa di San Giorgio, which, as discussed above, involved public functions such as management of city debt or city colonies, and whose shareholders were creditors and not equity investors. But I beg to differ with those (I am not certain that Sicard would fully agree with them) who view the mills as the first modern business corporations or as an essential phase in the development of the business corporation. They differ in some important respects from the English and Dutch East India Companies to which we are about to turn. The cooperation they promoted was between neighbors, not strangers.[32] Their shares were not traded in impersonal stock exchanges. They were private, but their main purpose was not to maximize profits for shareholders but rather to provide services to the community and, in the process, to distribute accumulated profits. They did not deal with agency problems, information flows, or the spreading of particularly high risks. They were not formalized by learned jurists and canonic legal texts of the time as corporate entities. There was no attempt to integrate them into the categories, concepts, and interpretations of Roman law or canon law.[33] In all these respects they were different from the East India companies.

The mill companies were, in my view, on the general historical path followed also by mining companies that could be found in various parts of Europe, including Sweden, Germany, and England, and water supply companies, such as London's New River Company, rather than the path of long-distance trade companies. The common feature of this path is that in terms of its business activities, physical real estates were of central importance: mines, aqueducts, and mills. The organizational form of each of the three is likely to have its historical origins in property law. There is an element of joint ownership of property. They still had some remnants of older feudal structures and terms. The shares were usually designated by a friction of the total ownership—say, 1/64—and not by sum of money invested. What makes these forms more complex than mere joint ownership are primarily two elements. First, the shares in their ownership could be sold and transferred by means other than inheritance and without dissolving the entity (unlike partnership in which change of members resulted in disolussion and reestablishment). Second, members were expected to contribute capital based on needs and were entitled to get a share in the profits once there was no need to retain these for the continued operation of the facility. The English mining companies were based on the cost book system of accounting, which is somewhat analogous to the mills' accounts. The system was based on the ability to call for additional investment from shareholders when additional construction or maintenance was needed.[34]

Part ownership of ships, a model that was used in various ports in Europe, was an organizational form with some resemblance to mill, mine, and water supply companies. It was also built around a single physical asset. Yet, ownership of ships involved a riskier, less routine, and less local activity. While part ownership can be viewed as being on a similar developmental path as the other physical assets based organizational forms, the long-distance trade joint-stock corporations was radically different and did not share the same developmental path.

THE FIRST JOINT-STOCK TRADE CORPORATIONS

Toward the end of the sixteenth century, English long-distance trade to the eastern edges of Europe, Russia, and the Levant was redesigned in a new and experimental organizational form: the joint-stock corporation. Unlike the regulated corporation, the joint-stock corporation traded in only one joint account. This meant that members shared not only overhead but all business outcomes of the corporation—that is, all profits and losses. Unlike joint ventures, these companies had a continued existence beyond a single voyage, often because of the need to make more permanent investments in Russia and the Levant. This existence was anchored on the corporation.

Figure 9.3 compares the structure and hierarchy of a joint-stock corporation to those of a regulated corporation. The blue bidirectional arrows show where the trade took place in each case.

The first of these was the Russia Company (also known as the Muscovy Company), founded in 1553 and chartered in 1555.[35] Its ambitions included the discovery of the maritime Northeast Passage to Asia and the reaching of Asian markets overland via Russia. But eventually its main business centered on whaling and the fur trade. The Levant Company (Turkey Company) was formed in 1581 for trade with Turkey and the Eastern Mediterranean.[36] The Levant Company traded in Asian goods. But its business patterns were outdated. Its merchants relied on Venetians and Arabs to carry the Asian goods to the Eastern Mediterranean and did not go themselves all the way to India or China. The two companies did not confront the new institutional challenges posed by the opening of longer-distance trade routes following the discovery of the Cape Route in 1497, but they did face the business challenge posed by the mass oceanic importation of Indian spices and pepper by the Portuguese to the European markets.

The experiment of both corporations with the use of joint-stock capital finance was not very successful. The initial investment in the joint-stock capital of the Russia Company covered neither the high expenses of

Joint-stock corporation

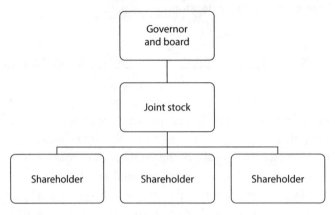

Regulated corporation

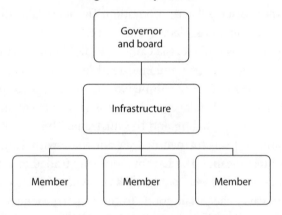

9.3. The structure and hierarchy of a joint-stock corporation vs. a regulated corporation. In a regulated corporation, trade transactions with third parties take place at the
level of the members; in the joint-stock corporation, they take place at the level of the
corporation and the joint stock.

establishing the new trade nor the losses of ships and cargoes. In later
years, more calls were made upon shares, with no dividends in sight. As
a result, in 1586, the company was financially restructured under the
same legal form, but using short-term rather than longer-term capital,
and it was organized in several separate accounts, each for a period of

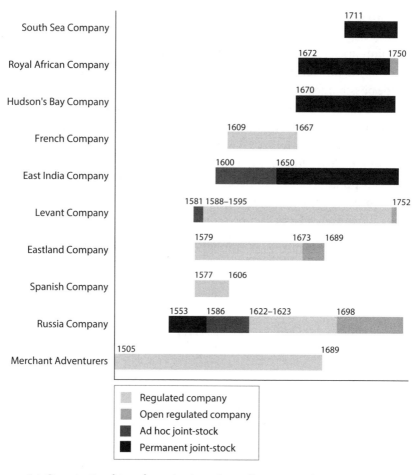

9.4. Organizational transformation in major trading corporations, 1505–1750.

one to three years. We shall see that this technique was adopted by the EIC a decade and a half later. This change stemmed from the difficulty in collecting from the original shareholders.[37] By 1622–23, this process had been taken one step further, and the separate accounts were replaced by individual accounts. With this step, the Russia Company was in fact reorganized into a regulated corporation.[38] The financial structure of the Levant Company was debated as the charter expired in 1588. The merchants opposing joint-stock trade had the upper hand, and the new charter of 1592 incorporated the Levant as a closed, regulated company with high admission fees.[39] There were a handful of other enterprises that experimented with joint-stock finance, in some cases in tandem with

Crown corporate charters. But these companies were experimental, relatively small, and often short-lived, and they could not be clearly classified as joint-stock corporations rather than mere joint ventures. Importantly, most of them were active in the Atlantic and did not engage in the new trade possibilities—or the accompanying organizational challenges—that opened up after the discovery of the Cape Route to Asia.[40]

So, as can be seen in figure 9.4, by 1599, the joint-stock company model had failed to prove itself as a good way to raise funding, to manage trade, and to establish a long-lasting enterprise. The quantum leap of the business corporation—which involved the raising of joint-stock capital on an unprecedented scale, relying on more sophisticated financial design on a longer-term basis—came only with the formation of the EIC and VOC, in 1600 and 1602, respectively. It is to the changing trade environment, the two East India Companies, and the institutional quantum leap that we now turn.

THE DUTCH AND ENGLISH: LATECOMERS TO EURASIAN TRADE

The direct Portuguese trade with Asia, which amounted to buying spices, tropical commodities, and other Asian goods at source, put English and Dutch traders at a disadvantage. These traders traditionally bought spices and other Asiatic goods from the Venetians or at the Mediterranean entrepôts that served as the western terminals of the overland Silk Route and of the maritime Red Sea and Persian Gulf routes. Now that these routes were bypassed by the Portuguese, they had to buy the goods from the Portuguese in Europe at higher prices. The Portuguese dominance also extended to controlling the network that distributed, in cooperation with Italian and German merchants, Asian goods, particularly spices, in Europe. The English Levant and Russian companies found it hard to secure an ample supply of Asian goods at the western ends of these routes in the Ottoman Empire and on the Volga. The Dutch, who had so far focused their maritime attention on the Baltic and the Atlantic, also wanted their share of the growing Euro-Asiatic trade. In the closing decades of the sixteenth century, there were already signs of a weakening of the Iberians' (now in the form of the Spanish-Portuguese Habsburg kingdom) control of the sea routes to Asia. These were manifested in the defeat of the Spanish Armada at the hands of the English, the advance of the Dutch Revolt, and the repeated organizational crises of the Portuguese ruler-owned Asiatic trade enterprise—the Estado da Índia.[41]

The EIC and the VOC were incorporated by state charter in 1600 and 1602, respectively. They were involved in similar business activities, namely, oceanic trade in high-value goods between Europe and Asia, via the Cape Route.[42] Both were organized as joint-stock corporations, with huge capital and hundreds of shareholders. The formation of the companies occurred at a crucial juncture in the history of business organizations and stock markets. The two entities were significantly larger, in terms of capital and number of shareholders, than any earlier merchant company in England or the Dutch Republic. They were larger than any other Eurasian trade enterprise in history, with the exception of the Portuguese king's Estado da Índia and the Chinese state-operated, commercial-cum-political enterprise headed by Zheng He. They remained the largest business corporations in Europe for the next two centuries and served as the basis for the formation of the British and Dutch Empires.[43]

What can explain the emergence of corporations in England and the Dutch Republic, out of all the European countries? The first explanation that comes to mind is Protestantism. Weber attributed the rise of capitalism to the Protestant ethic. But as we will see, Protestantism played no role in the singularity of the organizational models used in England and the Dutch Republic. The English and the Dutch were located at the very far end of Eurasia, hence their shipping and trade costs and information-obtaining costs were the highest, and their turnover time was the longest. Given their latitude, the goods they could offer (sheep wool and Atlantic cod) were least in demand in Asia. They were the last to enter the trade and thus had to be able to cross significant entry barriers in the form of competitors and knowledge. They could not rely on rulers to fund their enterprise, either by way of taxes, as did the Chinese, or by a combination of taxes and sovereign borrowing, as did the Portuguese.

The challenges faced by Northwestern European merchants in their efforts to enter Eurasian trade could not be resolved using vehicles such as a single, self-financing investor, a two-party investment contract, cooperation within a small and closed group of family and kin, or any other personally based association. Voyages to Asia were all-or-nothing undertakings. Insurance was still in its early stages of development in London, due to the rudimentary insurance infrastructure with respect to legal framework, dispute resolution institutions, organization of underwriters, and information flows. Infrastructure in Amsterdam was only a bit more enabling. No insurance underwriting was available for Asian voyages because they operated under uncertainties, most of which not even convertible to measurable risks and priceable premiums. Similarly, large-scale loans were unavailable, and were not even subject to security in the ships or goods because interest rates were either unpriceable or usurious.[44] The English and Dutch adventurers had to break through the frontiers of well-established Eurasian organizational forms. The challenges could only be met by designing a multilateral institution that would pool together capital from a larger group of equity investors, based on impersonal cooperation. As the investment was mainly in working capital, ships, crews, and goods in remote seas, no significant collateral could be offered to creditors. The extreme business environment made it more difficult to align the interests of entrepreneurial equity holders and passive debt investors. What they needed was a multilateral institution that could provide a good platform for equity investment, longevity, and capital lock-in. The business corporation was invented to meet this need. It was invented by adding four features—joint-stock, lock-in, transferability of shares, and protection from expropriation—to the corporate platform, turning it into a joint-stock corporation.

~10~

The Dutch East India Company

This chapter and the next are devoted to microstudies of the two companies I believe mark not just a decisive organizational revolution but a turning point in history—namely, the VOC and the EIC. I will begin with the microstudy of the Dutch VOC, despite the fact that it was established two years after the English EIC, because it constituted an incomplete transition from ruler-owned enterprise to business corporation. Its closer connection with state objectives and state elites places it somewhere on the continuum that leads from the Portuguese ruler-owned enterprise to the EIC.

MICROSTUDY: THE ORGANIZATION OF THE VOC

The Dutch ambitions in Asia have to be understood in their wider historical context: the Dutch Revolt against Catholic Spain; the struggle for independence of the northern Netherlands; the competition with the Portuguese—who, since 1580, had been ruled by the Spanish Habsburgs—over naval mastery in the Atlantic and oceanic trade routes; the migration of skilled and wealthy protestants from the southern Netherlands; and the rise to economic and political power of the protestant urban middle classes—particularly shippers and merchants in Holland and Zeeland, and particularly in Amsterdam.[1]

The intense competition between the city-based precompanies in the years 1595–1602 had the effect of raising prices in Asian markets and lowering the price of Asian goods in Dutch and other European markets. The intense competition was also wasteful in terms of the multiple investments in infrastructure made by the various precompanies. In a bid to achieve monopoly prices, at least in the Netherlands, to save in infrastructure costs, and to coordinate the struggle against the Portuguese and the English, six city-based precompanies (from Amsterdam, Delft, Rotterdam, Enkhuizen, Middelburg, and Hoorn) unified into a single cartel, the United East India Company (the VOC) in 1602.[2] One cannot rule out the possibility that the motivation for the unification was also political. That the unification was driven by statesmen wishing to strengthen the Dutch Republic vis-à-vis Portugal or England, or the Dutch federal government at the expense of city or provincial government. The question of whether the unification of the precompanies into a single VOC was driven primarily by merchants and investors or primarily by federal-level politicians still awaits a fuller analysis.

THE CHARTER

The VOC was formed on the basis of these earlier business entities, and was chartered on March 20, 1602, by the States-General, the federal assembly of the Dutch Republic. The chartering was an outcome of negotiations between the active partners of the precompanies then in existence, representatives of the cities and provinces, and representatives of the States-General. The charter can be viewed as creating a syndicate of precompanies. It can be viewed as formal horizontal merger of six city-based companies into a single company. The preamble of the charter emphasized the company's private, or at least semiprivate, character and its goal of profit maximization:

> We saw it fit to invite the administrators of the aforementioned companies to meet with us and to propose that it would not only be honorable, important and profitable for the United Netherlands but also for those who had commenced such commendable trade and were shareholders in it that these companies unite, and that by the creation of a single fixed and defined entity and by a common order and policy, the aforementioned trade be maintained, carried out and expanded to the benefit of all those inhabitants of the United Netherlands who wished to be partner to it.[3]

The charter fixed the existence of the company and its financial structure:

The United Company shall last for twenty-one consecutive years provided that there is a general audit every ten years. After ten years have elapsed, anyone may withdraw from the Company and take his capital with him.[4]

It is noteworthy that two levels were addressed in these sections of the charter: the corporate longevity level and the capital lock-in level. Although this charter, unlike that of the EIC, does not allude to the creation of a corporation in so many words, in fact it creates an entity separated from the state and separated from human beings that can own property, transact, and hold privileges from the state.[5] Furthermore, the charter contains a permission to issue a public offering of shares, grants all residents of the Netherlands the right to subscribe to such shares, and locks in the capital so raised for a period of ten years—a long duration, yet half the longevity of the corporate entity:

All of the inhabitants of these United Netherland shall be allowed to be shareholders in this company and to do so with as small or as great an amount as they see fit. . . . In the months that follow, the inhabitants of this land shall be kept informed of developments by means of public posters pasted in those places where they are usually pasted. As from the approaching 1 April, they will be admitted into this company and the moneys that they wish to invest may be paid in three installments [in 1603, 1604, and 1605].[6]

THE JOINT STOCK

Each city-based VOC Chamber opened its own joint-stock share-subscription counter and its share registry following the issuing of the charter. The active members of the VOC, those who were active partners in the precompanies, led the marketing of shares and opened subscription offices. Information about the new company, the lucrative Asian trade, and government support was circulated in various ways. By the last week of August 1602, mania had erupted. Altogether, 6,424,588 guilders was raised across all six chambers, as shown in table 10.1. The table also notes the number of subscribers in the Amsterdam and Middelburg chambers, and calculates the average value of an individual share (in guilders).

10.1. VOC Share Offering, 1602: Capital and Subscribers

Chamber	Capital(in guilders)	No. of subscribers	Average value of individual share(in guilders)
Amsterdam	3,679,915	1,143	3,220
Middelburg	1,300,405	264	4,926
Enkhuizen	540,000	n/a	n/a
Delft	469,400	n/a	n/a
Hoorn	266,868	n/a	n/a
Rotterdam	173,000	n/a	n/a
Total:	6,424,588	1,815[1]	3,540[2]

[1] Estimated, based on the total capital subscribed divided by the average sum of investment of each shareholder in the Chambers of Amsterdam and Middleburg.
[2] Calculated.

The number of subscribers in Amsterdam was 1,143 and in Zeeland (Middleburg), 264.[7] One can make a guess that, assuming the ratio of capital to shareholders in other chambers was similar, the number of shareholders in the VOC as a whole was approximately 1,815. The capital and the number of investors were by far higher than in any previous Dutch enterprise or in the recently established EIC, or in any other known Eurasian trade enterprise.

It is very likely that some of the money came through social networks. But the number of investors, the fact that many of them came from professions that were not connected to trade, and the wide geographical area from which investors came suggest that they were quite heterogeneous.[8] It seems that many investors decided to place their money with an anonymous company—on the basis of business plans—and not with familiar faces. This was a major shift from personal to impersonal cooperation—from a local *bewindhebber* attracting a few passive investors in a commenda-like relationship in a precompany, to a united VOC with approximately seventy *bewindhebbers*, about 1,800 shareholders, and a capital of nearly 6.5 million guilders coming from six cities and beyond them.

The initial public offering of shares was not accompanied by additional offerings. Bear in mind the original capital of 6,424,588 guilders: ninety years later, in 1693, it was still 6,440,200 guilders, the slight increase resulting from technical adjustments. The initial capital was still locked in. The company's activities and investments throughout the century were financed through retained profits and loans, and not through the raising of additional equity.

The first profits account was set to be conducted after ten years. Investors were allowed to withdraw their capital, principal, and profits from the company at that exit point but not before, and their full exit was dependent on raising capital from the new investors in a second joint stock. The investors in the first joint stock were not allowed to simply strip and divide the VOC assets at the end of any voyage, and not even in 1612. Shareholders were not entitled to accounts at the end of each voyage, which meant they were not entitled to information or dividend, the latter being at the discretion of the active shareholders.[9] In fact, dividends were distributed only once in the first ten years, in 1610, and even then they were in kind (spices) and not in cash.

THE GOVERNANCE STRUCTURE

The VOC governance structure reflected the fact that it was a merger of preexisting precompanies. It had six city-based chambers. Each chamber had two classes of VOC shareholders: *bewindhebbers* and *participanten*. As in the precompanies, the VOC *bewindhebbers* had the status of directors/governors and took an active role in management of the chamber; the VOC *participanten* were not allowed to take part in decision-making.[10] The *bewindhebbers* of each chamber met regularly to discuss managerial issues, while there was no general meeting of all the shareholders, either on the chamber or corporate level, and thus *participanten* had no access to information and no voting rights.

Each chamber had an Assembly of Directors (with between seven and twenty members, based on size as decreed by the VOC charter) and various offices and services, such as an audit office, treasury, warehouses, and shipyard. The VOC had a central management function, the board known as the *Heeren XVII* (the Seventeen Directors), which was in charge of general policy.[11] These directors operated in assembly and through committees, and were assisted by a lawyer. Only chamber governors were

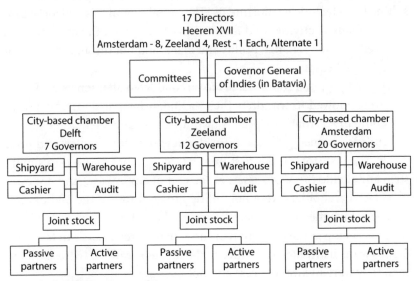

10.1. Organizational structure of the VOC. Source: Gaastra (1991, pp. 150, 160).

eligible to serve as VOC directors. As can be seen from figure 10.1, the management structure of the VOC reflects both the fact that it was a merger of preexisting companies and that it was oligarchic, having two classes of shareholders.

THE VOC AND THE STATE

The VOC was granted several privileges by the state. The most important of these was a territorial trade monopoly:

> No person regardless of constitution or capacity save those of the afore-mentioned Company as constituted within these United Provinces shall be permitted to sail east of the Cape of Good Hope or beyond the Straits of Magellan for the next twenty-one years. . . . Infringement thereof shall be punishable by confiscation of ships and goods. . . . Officials of the afore-

mentioned Company shall be permitted to enter into commitments and draw up contracts with the rulers . . . in the name of the State General of the United Netherlands.[12]

The VOC was also granted sovereign powers within its monopoly territory:

They may also build fortifications, and secure places, appoint governors, armed forces, officers of law . . . in order to retain the place and keep good order, as well as jointly maintain police and justice so as to promote trade.[13]

Furthermore, it received a commitment not to have its assets, be they ships of goods, expropriated either through taxation or conscription.

The spices, Chinese silk, and cotton cloth that this Company shall bring back from the East Indies shall not be taxed more than they are now, neither upon entry nor upon departure. Unless the Company gives its permission, none of the ships, weapons or ammunition that belong to the Company shall be used in the service of the country.[14]

The charter can thus be viewed as an agreement between the Dutch Republic and the group of directors and investors in the newly formed company on the privileges, rights, and obligations of the VOC. One concern of investors was that the state would take advantage of the readily available, pooled-together assets and would be able to expropriate some of them. Was charter a credible commitment by the republic not to expropriate?[15]

The success of the VOC was important to the government. The VOC promoted the policy aims of the Dutch Republic by expanding Dutch influence into the Indian Ocean and by diminishing the political and naval power of Iberian and English competitors.[16] It did so at no expense to the government. The Asia policy of the Dutch Republic did not have to be funded through tax collection. On the contrary—if profitable, it could generate additional revenues for the Republic.

In the Dutch Republic, unlike in England or Portugal, the state and the merchants did not comprise clearly distinct entities or interests negotiating with each other. The state was not dominated by the Crown and its court, by the nobility, or by landed classes more generally.[17] The balance of political power in the Dutch Republic had moved toward mercantile interests before the chartering of the VOC. This was so partly because of the level of urbanization, partly because of the resentment toward pro-Spanish landed groups, partly because of the federal structure of the republic, and partly because of the dominant position of Amsterdam and its merchants in the politics of the province of Holland.[18]

The federal government facilitated the formation of the VOC by co-ordinating among the city-based groups of merchants and city-based precompanies, supporting them in forming a horizontal merger and by granting them a monopoly.[19] This move was a sign of government commitment to the enterprise. It also indicated potential monopoly rents—a fact that acted as a device for attracting investors. The federal government colluded with the active promoters to ignite interest in the company and optimism about its prospects. To summarize, in the Dutch Republic the federal structure of the state, the overlap between political power and economic power, and the political will to expand trade all helped ensure that the VOC's assets would not be expropriated by the state and that its charter would not be repealed unilaterally. These factors—not the rule of law, as was the case in England—made the VOC charter a credible commitment device.

THE LOCK-IN OF CAPITAL

Why did the insiders want to lock in the external investors of the VOC? Past investors in trade were used to investing in one voyage at a time in commenda, joint ventures, and precompanies. The shift from a single voyage to a long-term enterprise was motivated by the need for longer-term capital that would support several voyages. As the insiders were not certain that the outsiders would voluntarily agree to invest their money for such a long period, given the uncertainties involved, they decided to shift to involuntary lock-in. Whether this was a move planned in advance or a decision that was reached only down the road as problems arose is a question that deserves further investigation. The mechanism that had performed quite well in the earlier period, that of per-voyage partnerships and precompanies, was based on repeat investment transactions and on the reputation of the managers. It could not survive the transition into a long-lasting enterprise. The VOC was not formed for a single voyage but as a perpetual enterprise. The intention was to send annual voyages to Asia and maintain permanent agencies and warehouses—fortified, if needed—in India and Indonesia. For this reason, its charter incorporated a new and separate legal entity that would exist for at least twenty-one years. Further, the charter created joint-stock capital—that is, capital generated by the investment of numerous individuals in a common pool of capital, which would exist for ten years and would not be easily dissolved even at that stage. The VOC was formed to assure continuity, from voyage to voyage, in the flow of commodities between Asia and Europe; to coordinate among competing Dutch city-based companies; and to overcome Portuguese and English competition. It was an endgame. Once capital was locked in, maintaining a reputation with investors in the primary market was not essential. The rules of the game between insiders and outside investors could be changed unilaterally ex post.

The government played, according to my interpretation, a softer, unnoticed role in the lock-in. After luring investors to invest in the company, it locked them in. The VOC charter issued by the federal government locked in the invested equity capital for ten years. As it turned out, during these years the passive investors did not receive financial accounts, and, even at the end of the first joint stock, the accounts they received were partial and unaudited.[20] As we have seen, they took no part in corporate management. They were paid dividends for the first time only in 1610, and, even then, in spices and not cash. In 1612 they were locked in again, involuntarily, for the remaining duration of the charter and the corporation.

Despite the preexistence of a stock market, in which city, province, and Dutch Republic bonds were traded, the VOC did not simply raise equity capital on a purely voluntary basis in that market. Initially, its promoters also used the networks and reputation that served the pre-companies, with the support of the state. More than this, they wanted to raise capital for a relatively long term, without deterring outside investors. But the VOC promoters did not reveal this intention in full. In fact, they changed the rules retroactively. The state was willing to issue a charter that did not disclose in full the disempowerment of the passive investors; the state assisted the insiders to lure the passive investors; and eventually the state was willing to legitimize the change in the rules of the game and the lock-in of the passive investors.[21]

The intention to move from repeat-game to endgame was obscured by the insiders. Passive investors were asked to put in their money in annual installments over a four-year period. These installments may have conveyed to the passive investors that it was "business as usual" despite the formation of the VOC, and that they were still investing on a per-voyage basis, as in the precompanies. In fact, they could not withdraw their money at the end of every voyage or even every year. Further, once they had subscribed, they were legally obliged to pay all four installments in full, irrespective of the performance of the VOC.

As described earlier, even when the VOC was doing well and making profits, its dividend policy was very restrictive. The active shareholders retained control of the joint-stock capital of the VOC through the city chambers and the Heeren XVII for a period of no less than ten years. They offered passive investors no voting rights, no information on trade, no account of profits, and thus no share in control. The active shareholders used their positions as both merchants and city magistrates to exercise political influence on provincial and federal governments and to unilaterally lock in the external investors by way of the charter. They could (and, in fact, did) lock in the passive investors again at the end of the ten-year period by using their political clout to amend the terms of the original charter and extend the duration of the holding together of the joint-stock capital.

Once locked in, the passive investors became agitated. In addition to expressing dissatisfaction with their legal status, many of them were also disconcerted at the realization that the VOC did not aim only at maximizing profits and returns. The VOC was also being used by the financial-political elite to promote the military, religious, and political aims of the republic and the provinces.[22] For example, it financed armed ships to attack the Spanish-Portuguese fleet in the Indian Ocean and capture territorial strongholds. The passive investors began to sense that profits were compromised at the expense of political aims. Investment in territorial strongholds and in war could be interpreted as intending to promote longer-term profits and not necessarily as nonbusiness investment. But for the passive investors, it was another indication that they were not going to see any return anytime soon and that the lock-in left them powerless.

It was not easy for them to organize their protest. In time, however, they came together to challenge their lack of voice, information, and dividends. Following protests by Isaac Le Maire and a short selling of shares that led to a drop in the share price, in 1610 the company distributed the first in-kind dividend,[23] in the form of spices. The 1612 dividend was in pepper and nutmeg, with only 7.5 percent awarded in cash. The dividend in spices advantaged the active investors, who, as merchants, could accumulate stock and had better access to the market, as Gelderblom, Jonker, and their coauthors showed. The demand of the passive investors to participate in management was avoided throughout the first joint stock, and, even in 1612, the state assisted the active shareholders to delay and eventually refuse the demand.[24] On these two fronts, the passive investors did not achieve much; however, they were more successful with the exit option.

THE VOC AND THE STOCK MARKET

The Dutch revolt against the Habsburg Empire that began in 1568 placed new demands on Dutch public finance.[25] By 1574, the public debt of Holland, by far the largest (and best-documented) province, stood at 1.4 million guilders. By 1600, it had reached nearly 5 million guilders,[26] and the figure kept rising throughout the seventeenth century.[27] Much of the borrowing was from lenders with close ties to the state, and some of it was forced on involuntary lenders. The province facilitated the creation of a secondary market in its bonds to allow liquidity for its coerced creditors. In turn, the secondary market in bonds made use of the well-developed Amsterdam commodities marketplace, with its regularly published (since 1583) price list and institutions designed to facilitate information flow and transaction-cost reduction. By the end of the sixteenth century, Amsterdam, the dominant city in Holland and in the federation as a whole, was an active marketplace for commodities, freight, insurance, foreign currencies, and government bonds.[28]

There appears not to have been any significant trading in shares of precompanies, probably for three main reasons: the precompanies were limited in time to one venture; the number of members of each was small; and they were personally connected and unwilling to include outsiders. The VOC was a much larger and more impersonal enterprise. Its shares were not bearers' shares, and no share certificate was issued to holders.[29] Thus, no physical asset could be conveyed to share purchasers by private

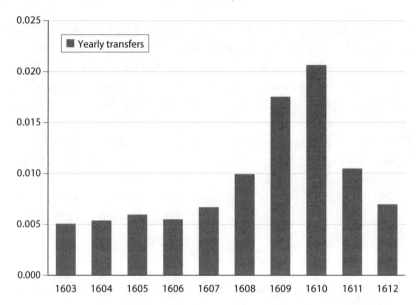

10.2. Yearly transfers of shares of the Amsterdam Chamber of the VOC, calculated as a percentage of the total stock of capital, 1603–12. Source: Gelderblom and Jonker (2004, p. 656).

contract. However, its charter included a clause that allowed transfer by registration of the transfer in the VOC books in the presence of two directors and payment of a small fee. Shortly after the formation of the VOC, its shares were also traded in the various city chambers. The Amsterdam *Beurs* building was built in 1611, shortly after the establishment of the Bank of Amsterdam (*Wisselbank*) in 1609. The Tulip Mania of 1636–37 manifested the sophistication and centrality of the Amsterdam markets.[30] Thus, while passive shareholders of the VOC had no voting rights, in contrast to the shareholders of the EIC, and their initial investment was locked in for ten years, they were soon able to exit the company by selling their shares.

An important study by Gelderblom and Jonker convincingly documented the volume of Amsterdam Chamber VOC shares traded in the years 1603–12.[31] Roughly 0.5 percent to 1.5 percent of the shares were traded every month. Nearly 33 percent of the shares changed hands in the first decade (see figure 10.2). The Amsterdam stock market became sophisticated, with full-time brokers, a meeting place, and several nonspot transactional designs.[32] Figure 10.2 presents the yearly transfers of shares of the Amsterdam Chamber of the VOC between 1603 and 1612. The numbers on the vertical axis indicate the percentage of the transfers from the total stock of capital.

The exit option through the sale of shares in the secondary market was introduced because of the need to offset the lock-in of capital for decades, given the nature of business in long-distance Cape Route Eurasian trade. The option was exercised with growing frequency by passive investors, partly offsetting the oligarchic and cooperation-damaging effects of the other institutional features of the VOC.

THE VOC IN ASIA

The company's charter was renewed in 1622 and then again on several occasions during the seventeenth century and beyond. The monopoly was extended as part of the extended charter.[33] By 1610, some seventy-six ships had been sent by the VOC to Asia around the Cape, and 117 were sent in the following decade. Altogether, an unprecedented number of 1,770 ships were sent eastward by the VOC during the seventeenth century.[34] The VOC was able to beat the Portuguese, at sea and on shore, to conquer many of their factories and forts—including Malacca, Hormuz at the entrance to the Persian Gulf, Galle in Sri Lanka, Quilon and Cochin on the Malabar Coast, Southern India, and parts of the Spice Islands (Moluccas)—and to establish its presence from the Cape of Good Hope and the Persian Gulf to Formosa and Japan. Batavia in Java became the headquarters of the VOC in Asia. It was the hub of Dutch inter-Asian trade and the informational hub of their entire Indian Ocean and Cape Route business.[35] The Governors General and the Council of the Indies (*Raad van Indië*) managed the Asian affairs from there, receiving instructions from, and reporting to, the Heeren XVII in Amsterdam. Figure 10.3 shows the hierarchy of the Dutch colonial administration in Asia.

While the VOC managed its Asian affairs through a centralized hub, in the case of the EIC, as we shall see, each factory collected information about affairs in its respective region and reported directly to the headquarters in London. Information that flowed to Batavia from all over Asia allowed the Governor General and his staff to cross-check information arriving from various agents, enabling better monitoring. Jan Pieterszoon

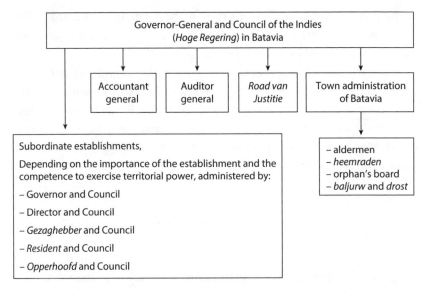

10.3. Hierarchy of the Dutch colonial administration in Asia. Source: http://www
.tanap.net/content/voc/appendices/voc_asia.htm.

Coen, the founder of Batavia, was the ultimate centralizing governor general (1618–23 and 1627–29). But Batavia monopolized and controlled information flows to Amsterdam in a manner that made it harder for the headquarters and the seventeen directors to effectively monitor the senior agents in Batavia. The EIC model created a different way of trading off between fast information flow and control of agents in Asia by headquarters in Europe, so that in the EIC there was no central hub in Asia that collected, verified, and processed all information about the state of affairs in Asia. All such communications had to arrive at the London hub, which was many months of travel away. This physical distance affected information flows, monitoring of agents, and business outcomes. Figure 10.4 shows the trade routes and the commodities traded by the VOC in the seventeenth century. It gives a sense of the magnitude of the VOC-based Dutch mercantile empire in Asia at its height, after the victories in the second and third Anglo-Dutch Wars.

The VOC rose to the position of the leading player in the Cape Route trade of spices and silver, sending more than 230 ships per decade eastward in each of the last four decades of the seventeenth century. It also

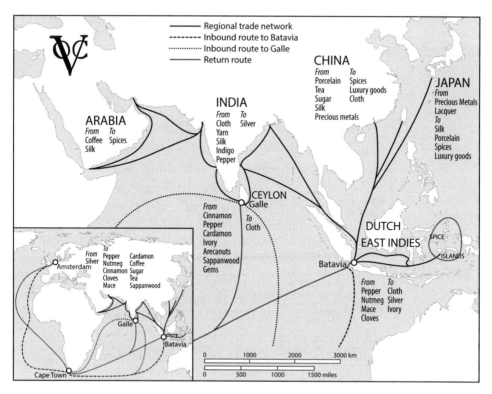

10.4. Trade routes and commodities traded by the Dutch East India Company in the seventeenth century. Source: reprinted from Jean-Paul Rodrigue, *The Geography of Transport Systems*, 4th ed. (London: Routledge, 2017).

became a major protagonist in the Indian Ocean trade of silk, porcelain, cloth, and precious metals, with a presence in Japan, China, Taiwan, the Spice Islands, Java, Sri Lanka, and India, among other locations.[36]

CONCLUSION

What can explain this extraordinary business accomplishment? On first reflection it is not clear why the outside investors were willing to buy an inferior class of shares in the VOC. Why did they invest without receiving in return voting rights, information, or at least a better defined right to dividends? The VOC possibly relied on three methods for raising initial capital: social networks, prior business reputation, and government inducement and support.

So the VOC was a transitional organizational form, between involuntary and voluntary, personal and impersonal. Indeed, it was a business corporation and not a state-owned enterprise, one that raised capital in the open market and not by way of taxation. But investors were not fully informed, and the rules of the game were changed by political means ex post. On the other hand, passive investors in the VOC were eventually given an option to exit the corporation by selling their shares in a functioning stock market. The VOC was not as redistributive an organization as the Estado da Índia, but neither was it as profit-maximizing a business corporation as the EIC. It promoted business ends but also political ones. Its managers and directors, its active investors, overlapped with the Dutch Republic's political elite and partially even with the state apparatus.

The VOC was an endemic Dutch model of the business corporation. It was created using a building block that was present elsewhere in Europe, including in England: the corporation. But it included another building block that was not present in England: joint equity investment in the form of the Dutch precompany, which in turn was based on the commenda and ship part-ownership. Though formed just two years after the EIC, the VOC did not mimic it. The Dutch model resulted from the federal political structure of the Dutch Republic, the history of Dutch maritime trade, and the resulting role of merchants in Dutch politics. The VOC was therefore an embedded organizational form according to our typology.

The VOC did not represent, at its inception, a full shift from personal to impersonal collaboration. But as it continued to evolve, and as investment through the secondary stock market became the norm, the VOC gradually became more impersonal. Nor did it represent full detachment between the state and the corporation. In the first decade of the VOC, the republic and the corporation insiders worked hand in hand to attract and capture outside investors. But with the passing of time, the lock-in was eased, information and dividends were distributed, and the voice of the passive investors became more influential. Having analyzed this transitional organizational form, which takes us half the way into the organizational revolution, we now turn to the EIC, which completed it.

~ 11 ~

The English East India Company

The English only belatedly and slowly developed an interest in Cape Route trade with the Indian Ocean. In the second half of the sixteenth century, English merchants settled for importing Asian goods via Russia by way of the Russia Company or via the Eastern Mediterranean by way of the Levant Company. English explorers, such as Martin Forbisher and John Davis, devoted much of their attention to discovering the Northwest and Northeast Passages to India, which they never found. Only a few sporadic attempts to reach Asia through the Pacific Ocean—by Francis Drake (1577–80) and Thomas Cavendish (1586–88)—and a single attempt to send merchant ships to Asian markets around the Cape of Good Hope—led by James Lancaster (1591)—were made before the end of the sixteenth century. By the close of the sixteenth century, conditions for direct English trade with the East Indies were created. First, the victory over the Spanish Armada in 1588 made sailing routes south on the Atlantic and past the Cape of Good Hope more accessible to English ships. Second, the exclusion of English merchants (unlike Italian or German merchants) from sharing in the Portuguese East Indies trade became a concern for the English. Third, the formation of the precompanies and the growing Dutch activities in Asia in the closing decade of the sixteenth century alarmed those English merchants with Asian interests. The English learned a double lesson: that the Iberians were not invincible and that the Dutch soon would be.

MICROSTUDY: ORGANIZING THE EIC

In September 1599, a group of London merchants held a number of meetings that, we now know, turned out to be the founding meetings of the EIC. The group was dominated by members of the Levant Company, who felt it was crucial for them to enter the oceanic trade with Asia now that the Dutch precompanies had joined the Portuguese in using the Cape Route to the Indian Ocean markets. No written records of the deliberations on the design of the financial-organizational form of the EIC survived. It is not clear that any were produced at the time. Matters may have been discussed orally and informally before the first formal meeting and before the initiation of minute-taking.[1] The promoters (the intended inner circle of members) decided to work on two parallel tracks—one for obtaining a royal charter that would incorporate them as a corporate entity and permit them to enter trade with new territories, and the other for raising equity capital for voyages to the East Indies from a large number of passive investors. By employing this dual track, the promoters of the EIC coupled the familiar legal structure of the corporation with the less familiar element of joint stock. Let us now discuss each of these tracks.[2]

THE CHARTER TRACK

The promoters set up a committee that negotiated with the Privy Council for a charter of incorporation, customs privileges, license to export specie, monopoly, and possible political and military support. In October 1599, the talks failed because Queen Elizabeth I was negotiating a peace treaty in the ongoing Anglo-Spanish War with Philip III, the new king of Spain, and believed that by granting the charter she would hinder the relationship with her new potential ally. But deterioration of relations with Spain and further Dutch successes ultimately convinced Elizabeth to grant the charter to the EIC, which she did the following year, on December 31, 1600.[3] But she promised no investment or naval support. The company, unlike the Portuguese Estado da Índia and the Dutch VOC, was very much on its own. The first part of the charter is quoted verbatim here, with a few omissions, to give a sense of its style (the bold font is my emphasis):

Charter granted by Queen Elizabeth to the East India Company.

Dated the 31st December, in the 43rd year of Her Reign. Anno Domini, 1600.

ELIZABETH, by the Grace of God, Queen of England, France, and Ireland, Defender of the Faith, &c. To all our Officers, Ministers, and Subjects, and to all other People, as well within this our Realm of England as elsewhere, under our Obedience and Jurisdiction, or otherwise, unto whom these our Letters Patents shall be seen, showed, or read, greeting.

Whereas [the 218 named] Petitioners unto us, for our Royal Assent and Licence to be granted unto them, that they, at their own Adventures, Costs, and Charges, as well for the Honour of this our Realm of England, as for the Increase of our Navigation, and Advancement of Trade of Merchandize, within our said Realms and the Dominions of the same, might adventure and set forth one or more Voyages, with convenient Number of Ships and Pinnaces, by way of Traffic and Merchandize to the East-Indies, in the Countries and Parts of Asia and Africa, and to as many of the Islands, Ports and Cities, Towns and Places, thereabouts, as where Trade and Traffic may by all likelihood be discovered, established or had . . . greatly tendering the Honour of our Nation, the Wealth of our People, and the Encouragement of them, and others of our loving Subjects in their good Enterprizes, for the Increase of our Navigation, and **the Advancement of lawful Traffick to the Benefit of our Common Wealth** . . .

Do give and grant unto our said loving Subjects, before in these Presents expressly named, that they and every of them from henceforth be, and shall be **one Body Corporate and Politick**, in Deed and in Name, by the Name of The **Governor and Company of Merchants of London, Trading into the East- Indies** . . . we do order, make, ordain, constitute, establish and declare, by these Presents, and that by the same Name of Governor and Company of Merchants of London, Trading into the East-Indies, they shall have **Succession**, and that they and their Successors . . . **purchase, receive, possess, enjoy and retain lands. Rents, Privileges, Liberties,**

Jurisdictions, Franchises and Hereditaments of whatsoever Kind, Nature, and Quality so ever they be, to them and their Successors . . . And that they . . . **may plead and be impleaded, answer and be answered, defend and be defended, in whatsoever Courts** and Places . . . as any other, our liege People of this our Realm of England . . . And . . . may have a common Seal, to serve for all the Causes and Business of them and their Successors.[4]

In contemporary constitutional terms, incorporation was considered an essential component of the monarch's exclusive and voluntary prerogative to create and grant dignities, jurisdictions, liberties, exemptions, and, in this case, franchises (monopolies and corporations).[5] This authorization was normally given in the form of charters or letters patent. The law of corporations was classified by contemporaries as part of the Law of the King, the core of the English constitution. From a formalistic legal perspective, the new EIC had a charter and a legal status similar to that of regulated corporations, municipal corporations, the corporate bodies of the Universities of Oxford and Cambridge, the Royal Society, the Society of Antiquaries, and the craft-guild-like livery companies of the City of London. The charter and incorporation track of the EIC was a continuation of a tradition that was longer and more developed than the Dutch corporate tradition. The corporation was the centerpiece around which the EIC was organized, unlike the VOC, which was organized around its joint stock.

Its most distinct attribute, as evident in the charter text, was that it was incorporated as "one body corporate and politik," a separate legal entity. It had a full set of legal capacities and privileges: to own land, litigate in court, and hold franchises—such as monopoly. The charter did not refer to the limitation of liability of members of the corporation. The modern doctrine of limited liability had not yet emerged; the company did not rely on debt finance, and no conflict of interest between equity holders and creditors was in sight. Some degree of asset partitioning was evident from the fact that the company was a separate legal entity, and no indication was given as to the right of creditors of its members to dissolve it or withdraw any of its assets.

The EIC was incorporated in its first charter for a period of fifteen years, ending on December 31, 1614. For the same duration, the EIC was granted an exclusive trade monopoly for "all the Islands, Ports, Havens,

Cities, Creeks, Towns and Places of Asia, Africa, and America, or any of them, beyond the Cape of Bona Esperanza [Good Hope] to the Straights of Magellan." The monopoly meant that other subjects of Elizabeth could not trade with that part of the globe without EIC's permission. In the second charter, granted in 1609, James I decreed that the EIC should "for ever be, and shall be one body corporate and politick"[6] and enjoy all the aforementioned privileges of incorporation indefinitely, making the corporate body and the monopoly perpetual, subject to recall with three years' notice. This did not make the joint stock perpetual, as we will see shortly.

THE JOINT-STOCK TRACK

The high working-capital threshold needed for entering the oceanic Asian trade was beyond the means of any individual or small group of individuals. Even those with sufficient wealth, such as members of the landed aristocracy, did not have enough liquid assets. The high risks involved in such a project could deter risk-averse investors from investing a considerable share of their liquid capital in it. The exceptionally high capital needs of oceanic trade, coupled with the level of risk involved, made it necessary to raise small amounts of money from a large number of investors, including outside sources. Thus, individual investors, family firms, partnerships, and even the regulated company were unsuitable for this new and demanding task. Equity investment rather than loan capital was needed.

The second track, that of raising joint-stock capital, was where the innovative organizational action, so to speak, was going to take place. The first recorded meeting of the EIC promoters, on September 22, 1599, was devoted to advancing this solution and inviting potential investors to commit. A list of subscribers was prepared, noting the names of the 132 individuals, who signed for total capital of over £30,000. Individual sums varied between £100 and £3,000, with £200 being the most common sum. By the time the charter was granted (on December 31, 1600), there were 218 chartered members, presumably all subscribers.[7] This was the first and last formal encounter of the two tracks. All investors up to that point were listed in the charter. Further subscriptions were accepted up to the departure of the first voyage (on February 13, 1601),[8] and by then the total number of subscribers had reached 232, and the total capital had risen to £68,937.[9]

It is important to note that, while the basic financial structure of the EIC was set before its charter of incorporation was granted, the charter did not reflect this structure. It was practically identical in content to the charters of contemporary regulated corporations. Its 218 members were not referred to as shareholders. This later gave rise to dual terminology, referring to members of the corporation as *brethren*, *at freedom* or *at liberty*, and to shareholders in the stock of any voyage as *adventurers*. The charter did not grant different privileges to subscribers of different sums and did not relate to matters such as the issuing of further shares, additional calls on shares, dividend payments, or the like. It was taken for granted by the members that profits on the initial investment would be divided, based on the share of each adventurer in the joint stock, as was the practice in joint ventures and partnerships. But it was also taken for granted that each adventurer would have one vote in the General Court, irrespective of the amount subscribed. This was a concept taken from the model of the corporation, in which each member had one vote.

The real challenge for the promoters of the EIC, because of the exit option at the end of each voyage, was not to convince investors to subscribe £68,373 for the initial voyage, substantial as that sum was by contemporary standards, but rather to draw additional investment to the joint stock of each subsequent voyage. The court minutes of the EIC in its first few years demonstrate that it devoted more time to attracting outside investors than to the charter or to any other business matter. The minutes are full of calls to raise more capital and send more ships, goods, and silver, due to requests from agents in Asia, and to match the large number of ships sent annually by the major rival and competitor, the VOC.

The raising of additional capital beyond the first voyage was accomplished through separate accounts, which were not mentioned in the charter. A new account was formed for each voyage to Asia, and members could decide whether, and how much, to invest in each one. Expenses at home and abroad relating to a specific voyage were recorded in the relevant account. At the end of the voyage, the proceeds from the sale of the imported goods, less expenses on exported silver and goods, shipping,

11.1. Capital Invested in Each of the EIC Voyages

Year	Voyage	Capital in £	Profit in %
1601	1st	68,373	Combined with 2nd voyage
1603	2nd	60,450	95
1606	3rd	53,500	Combined with 5th voyage
1607	4th	33,000	Total loss
1608	5th	13,700	234
1609	6th	80,163	122
1610	7th	15,634	218
1611	8th	55,947	211
1611	9th	19,614	160
1611	10th	46,092	148
1611	11th	10,669	230
1612	12th	7,142	134
Total		£464,284	

Source: Chaudhuri (1965, p. 209).

wages, and bonuses, were divided pro rata among the investors in that voyage. As the investment was mainly in working capital, liquidation of the account was, theoretically, not overly problematic. Whatever fixed capital was left, mostly in the form of surviving ships, was sold to the next voyage and transferred to the next account. But, due to a range of factors (the use of company ships in Asia for the freighting of goods pertaining to more than one voyage, the mixing of goods from different voyages in a factory or warehouse, and accounting complications), the joint stocks of two voyages (the first and second; the third and fifth) would occasionally be merged.

Almost £400,000 was raised in the years 1603–12 for voyages two through twelve, about six times the initial investment. The promoters of the EIC, and later its directors, were preoccupied with raising equity capital from a large group of passive equity investors. Altogether, £464,284 was invested in twelve joint stocks, used for twelve voyages, within just thirteen years. This was an unparalleled sum in English history.[10] Table 11.1 details the capital (in pounds) invested in each of the EIC voyages, together with their profits and losses.

11.2. Number of Members/Investors in Each EIC List

List	Year	Number of members /adventurers
First meeting	1599	132
First charter	1600	218
First voyage	1601	232
Third voyage	1607	208
Fourth voyage	1608	56
Second charter	1609	275

Sources: Shaw (1887 [1774]) ; Harris (2005), database of EIC Charters; Calendar of State Papers, Colonial, East Indies 1515–1634, 5 vols., London, 1892 (Court minutes, correspondence); The Register of Letters of the Governour and Company of Merchants of London Trading into the East Indies, 1600–1619, London, 1843.

Achieving such a high level of investment required the circle of outside investors to be widened. This widening was not reflected in the charter, which still listed only the 218 original members. Table 11.2 details the number of members or investors in EIC charters and voyages. My entire database, covering all lists of members and shareholders from the first meeting (1599) to the second charter (1609) contains 410 names.[11] Rabb's list, covering the period to 1630, includes 1,318 names of EIC onetime shareholders.[12] The EIC had fewer than the 1,800 or so initial 1602 investors of the VOC, but was still larger than any other Eurasian trade enterprise surveyed in this book.

Insiders had to maintain their reputation when managing the EIC, its voyages, its business, and its distribution of profits, and nurture the relationship with outside investors so they would invest repeatedly in the ongoing voyages. I recorded in the database the names of investors from each of the joint-stock subscription lists so as to identify repeat investment. Table 11.3 details how many people who invested in an EIC voyage subsequently repeated, investing in the following voyages or in the second charter.

We can observe from table 11.3 that 156 of the 232 investors in the first joint stock reinvested in the third, while 181 of the 208 investors in the third joint stock were listed in the second charter. But only forty of the 232 investors in the first joint stock invested in the fourth. This empirical observation, combined with theoretical insights, suggests that the

11.3. Repeat Investors in the EIC

First appearance	Voyage 1	Voyage 3	Voyage 4	Charter 2
Total in voyage/charter	232	208	56	275
Repeated appearance in later voyage/charter				
Voyage 3	156	-	-	-
Voyage 4	40	49	-	-
Charter 2	172	181	53	-

Source: Author's database.

outside investors made deliberated decisions (based on risk propensity, wealth constraints, other investment options, and available information—which was imperfect) on whether to reinvest or not. But this is a hypothesis that requires further research to be well established.

Not only the mere size and the expansion of the investing group but also its diversity support my claim that the EIC represented a breakthrough to impersonal cooperation. K. N. Chaudhuri, the leading historian of the seventeenth-century EIC, provided the first hint. He wrote: "From the very beginning of its trade the East India Company operated as an outlet of investment. It thus drew its capital from a heterogeneous body of investors who can be classified broadly into two groups."[13] Chaudhuri identified the first group as that of City merchants who invested large sums, were actively involved in administering the company, and were often directly involved in trade by buying goods from the company and selling them at home or reexporting them to the Continent. The second group was of passive investors who came from several other social groups. Chaudhuri correctly noted that the EIC had insiders and outsiders.[14] He did not, however, identify the problem of cooperation between the two groups as a dominant factor in the institutional design, and did not analyze how the institutional design of the EIC enhanced cooperation.

The socioeconomic background of the shareholders in the EIC cannot be identified easily in historical records. Membership in other corporations is well recorded. Let us first examine in which other corporations EIC members were involved (table 11.4). Levant merchants were at the core of the EIC group—the insiders. At least twenty-three of the 132 present at the first EIC promoters' meeting in September 1599 were Levant

Company merchants, and seven of the fifteen directors appointed at that meeting were also Levant merchants. The first governor and seven of the twenty-four original chartered committee members were Levant merchants. Levant Company members provided 25–33 percent of the capital invested in the first, third, and fourth voyages.[15] The Venice Company, established in 1583, was a predecessor of the Levant Company. Its members were involved in a pioneering voyage to the Indian Ocean and became the core of the Levant Company. Of the five former Venice Company members who joined the EIC, four became EIC directors in 1600. The insiders also included members of the Russia Company. Of the twenty-four original EIC directors, five were members of the Russia Company. In addition, a few captains, navigators, and explorers who had been involved in searching for routes to Asia (in circumnavigation and in predatory privateering of the Portuguese Asian trade in previous years) can also be viewed as insiders. Some of the key figures in this active group of promoters were Thomas Smythe, Paul Bannyng, Thomas Cordell, Thomas and Robert Middleton, and James Lancaster.[16] These insiders evaluated the EIC's financial needs and selected the institutional design that would attract a larger group of passive investors into the new and evolving enterprise.

Potential passive investors in the EIC, the outsiders, could come from a wider circle and a variety of social and professional groups. They included members of the gentry and the aristocracy who were willing to undertake moderately speculative investments in the Asian trade, as they would, within a few years, in North American and Irish settlement and plantations. They included English merchants who were involved in the traditional large-scale wool- and cloth-based trade with Europe—the active members of the Eastland, Spanish, and, particularly, Merchant Adventurers–regulated corporations. Other potential external investors came from among London's well-established manufacturers, retailers, and artisans: tailors and mercers, skinners and drapers, goldsmiths and ironmongers.[17] Members of all three groups could not devote much personal attention to the Asian trade but would consider diversifying their limited fortunes within an appropriate institutional framework.

Table 11.5 shows the percentage of merchants and nonmerchant shareholders in various corporations. Note that the table presents membership only in long-lasting overseas trading companies. As can be seen from

11.4. Number of EIC Members Who Were Also Members of Other Corporations

Corporation in which EIC members participated		Number of EIC members						
Corporation goal	Corporation name	First meeting 1599	First charter 1600	First voyage 1601	Third voyage 1607	Second voyage 1608	Second charter 1609	Total
Asian trade	Levant	46	75	73	68	23	80	107
	Muscovy	19	20	19	18	6	20	31
	Venice	4	5	2	1	0	3	5
	Eastland	10	11	14	16	4	14	20
	French	32	43	47	46	13	61	73
European trade = regulated	Staple	1	1	1	1	0	1	2
	New merchant	6	13	17	20	10	24	26
	Merchant	25	34	38	32	7	35	46
	Spanish	58	75	73	70	18	88	117
Discovery and privateering	North-West	28	68	71	74	28	94	100
	Baffin	1	4	4	3	1	4	4
	Frobisher & Fenton	2	4	3	1	0	5	5
	Hudson	3	7	6	6	4	9	9

Source: Author's database.

**11.5. Percentage of Merchants and Nonmerchant
Shareholders in Various Companies**

Company	Type	Number of members	Percentage of merchants in the company	Percentage of merchant knights in the company	Percentage of non-merchants in the company
Merchant adventurers	Regulated	269	91	8.6	0.4
Eastland	Regulated	197	93.4	6.1	0.5
Levant	Regulated	572	92.1	6.2	1.7
Spanish	Regulated	1096	94.2	4.2	2.6
French	Regulated	548	93.8	3.3	2.9
Muscovy (Russia)	Joint Stock	211	78.7	14.2	7.1
East India	Joint Stock	1318	80.6	5.0	14.4

Source: Rabb (1967, p. 104).

table 11.5, while only 0.4 percent (Merchant Adventurers) to 2.9 percent (French Company) of the members of the various regulated companies were nonmerchants, the latter accounted for 14.4 percent of the members of the EIC. This indicates that at least this difference can be attributed to outside passive investors. But, in fact, some of the merchants were also outsiders—such as those who traded actively with nearby European destinations and invested passively in India trade.

In 1613, a first, longer-term joint stock was raised, for a period of eight years. A second joint-stock was raised in 1617 for fifteen years, even though the first was due to dissolve only four years later. A third joint-stock was raised in 1632 for ten years. Capital was separately raised in 1628, 1629, and 1630 for three Persian voyages, while the second joint-stock was still in effect. In 1641, an attempt was made to form general stock. In 1651, the various pending joint-stocks of the company were integrated into one permanent stock.[18] To sum up, experiments were made using both ad hoc capital and capital for a term of years, and at times the former was more profitable than the latter. Additional capital was sometimes raised by issuing new shares to new members, at other times by calling on existing shares, and in some cases through short-term loans rather than raising additional equity. In some circumstances, the entire capital, if not lost, was divided at the end of a voyage; in others, capital was divided up to the amount of the initial investments, while profits were reinvested for future use; and in yet others only the profits were divided, while the initial investment was retained by the company until the end of the joint-stock term. One can even find evidence of several models coexisting simultaneously. Yet, toward the middle of the seventeenth century, a general pattern of development can be identified within the EIC: from ad hoc per-voyage capital (one to three years, invested in specific ships), to capital for limited duration (eight to fifteen years), and finally to permanent and continuous capital.

The total capital of the EIC grew steadily over time, with only a few fluctuations. As mentioned, the capital for the first voyage of 1601 was £68,000; the capital of the first joint stock of 1613 was £418,000; and the general permanent stock of the company was £370,000 in 1657, £740,000 in 1682, and £1,488,000 in 1693. In 1709, after the "old" EIC and a "new" East India Company competed for a few years, they merged into a single firm, the United Company of Merchants of England Trading to the East Indies, which had a stock of as much as £3,163,000. The EIC capital reached an all-time high of £6,000,000 in 1794. Throughout most of the seventeenth century, the EIC was the largest joint-stock company in England (in capital) and second in Europe only to the VOC. By the eighteenth century, the EIC was second in capital only to the Bank of England and had overtaken the VOC to become the largest trading corporation in the world.[19]

The charter did not envision the joint-stock finance in general, nor the creation of a separate account for each voyage. Interestingly, the promoters of the EIC did not view the charter as preventing or constraining the development of the corporation as a joint-stock corporation. Pairing the financial tool of joint venture like equity investment in joint stock with the legal concept of the corporation represented a major innovation. However, this innovation created a whole new set of problems and gaps that had to be dealt with. From the start, the promoters of the company were determined to finance it with joint stock, but they do not seem to have asked the state for permission for such a move. While the charter created an organizational platform for the joint stock, it did not create any overlap between the organizational structure and the financial structure. The result was discrepancies between initial membership and future membership, and between financial rights and management rights. It took most of the seventeenth century to close these gaps, via a lengthy process of learning-by-doing and modification of both the joint stock and the charter.

GOVERNANCE STRUCTURE AND VOICE

The general governance structure of the EIC was indistinct from that of many earlier corporations. The charter of incorporation defined the basic governance structure of the EIC, which included a governor, a deputy governor, a committee of twenty-four—also called the Court of Committees (and after 1709, the Court of Directors), and a General Court. In fact, the full official name of the EIC (until 1709) was The Governor and Company of Merchants of London Trading into the East-Indies. The General Court was composed of all members of the company.

Initially, every member, regardless of his status or level of investment in the joint stock, had one vote in the General Court. The court convened at least once a year, in the first week of July, and elected the governor, the deputy, and the committees. The General Court was empowered by the charter to remove the governor or any of the members of the committees from office on the grounds of "not demanding themselves well in their said office."[20] Committees (directors) of the EIC, unlike those of the VOC, could come from among all members, were nominated for only one year, and could be removed from office.

For the governance structure of the EIC, see figure 11.1. The EIC's governance structure was more centralized than that of the VOC, as it had no organs, similar to the Dutch "six chambers," on the city level. England was not a federal state and London was its center of political and economic gravity. The EIC had only central organs that were all based in London.

The EIC, unlike the VOC, had only one class of member. Votes in the General Court, whether to vote-in the Committees (Board of Directors) or for any other kind of decision among members, were all based on the 1600 charter that set the one-vote-per-member rule. As a new organizational form, the young EIC was unprecedented—democratic, represen-

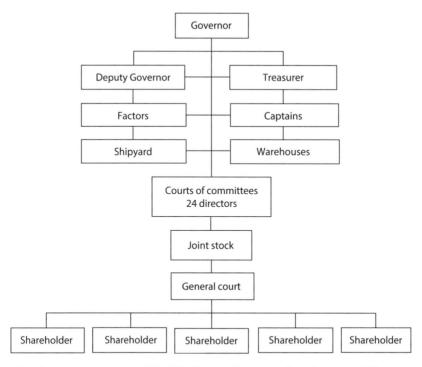

11.1. Governance structure of the EIC. Source: Shaw (1887 [1774], pp. 1–15) (discussing the EIC 1600 charter).

tative, and egalitarian, unlike the oligarchic VOC.[21] This principle was also followed by the traditional voting scheme in corporations, regulated companies, colleges, cities, guilds, and the like. It did not take into account what was going on at the same time on the second track, that of raising capital and forming joint stock. In other words, the sum invested as a share in the joint stock did not affect voting rights.

Gradually, the strict equality of members the EIC voting model altered toward a scheme that allocated votes based on investment, as we know it today. The 1609 charter granted one vote for every five hundred shares,[22] making this the minimum holding to qualify for voting. In practice, most of those who passed this threshold had one vote, or two at most.[23] The 1609 change may have been made to convince those shareholders who did not subscribe to any voyage beyond the first (in which the standard subscription was £240) to invest further to secure a vote. This arrangement was retained in the 1661 charter.[24] The 1693 charter established a capped system of one vote for every thousand shares up to a maximum of ten votes for holders of ten thousand shares or above. In the 1698 charter, a scaled method was established: one vote for holders of £500 in shares and above; two votes for holders of £1,000 and above; three votes for holders of £2,000 and above; four votes for holders of £3,000 and above; and a maximum of five votes for holders of any amount over £4,000. A minimum of £2,000 in shares was set as qualification for directorship.[25] This process obviously strengthened the influence of large shareholders in directors' appointments and in management affairs.[26]

The charter authorized the EIC to make bylaws that further detailed the structure and function of the three basic organs. For example, the bylaws ordered that a General Court be summoned whenever ships arrived from the Indies and that the Court of Committees be called upon receipt of letters from the Indies.[27] In addition, nonmembers were not permitted to attend meetings of the General Court (and speakers would be bareheaded, would address no one but the Governor, and would not interrupt the speeches of others).[28] The Court of Committees was to execute the orders of the General Court with respect to the sale of imported goods and the purchase of provisions and merchandise. Every task within the power of the committees was to be performed by at least two of its members, not by a single individual. Such tasks could not be assigned to others and were to be performed personally by committee members only. The governor was given the responsibility of summoning the courts and executing their orders. Accountability to the General Court was not abstract but established through detailed procedures.

The charter, together with the bylaws, created a participatory framework for managing the EIC. Participation was embodied not only in the structure of the organs of the EIC but also in the procedures that determined its functioning. Dates and circumstances of meetings and elections were prescribed in advance in these constitutive documents. The institutional design forced collective decision-making: insiders' proposals could not achieve a majority without the support of a large number of outsiders, as the latter enjoyed equal voting rights. This participatory governance structure, which ensured a voice for all shareholders, was not only provided for in the charter and bylaws—it successfully functioned in the early years of the company, when members were active, regularly attended general meetings, asked questions, and voted.

INFORMATION FLOWS

The level and quality of information about Asian trade held by EIC members and potential investors varied. Levant and Russia Company members were already involved in importing Asian goods to England from the entrepôts of the Persian Gulf and Red Sea, maritime routes, and the overland Silk Routes in Russia and the Eastern Mediterranean. They had access to information about goods, markets, and risks. By contrast, merchants who were members of the Spanish Company or the Eastland Company were one step removed from the sources of information. Merchant adventurers and French Company members possessed even less information. Both of these groups had experience in overseas trade, but they did not deal with Asian goods or markets. Aristocrats, landed gentry, London manufacturers, and artisans had the least access to information of all the collectives.

Insiders possessed information on the supply and demand for Asian goods.[29] They were better able to appreciate the risks involved, and they were willing to be actively involved in the running and management of the new enterprise. Outsiders naturally had less information than insiders. They did not view the EIC as a place of employment but rather as a relatively passive investment, hence they could not invest much time or resources in monitoring the insiders.

This information asymmetry proved to be a major challenge in terms of achieving cooperation. To entice outsiders, the insiders could not rely only on presenting the general prospects of oceanic trade with Asia or on promising a fair share of the profits. They had to credibly commit to provide information that would reduce the asymmetry, and they had to provide tools for acting on the information. An institutional innovation was required to enable this and to successfully raise huge amounts of capital from outsiders, and the EIC delivered this. While outsiders were willing to explore new investment opportunities, particularly ones with high expected returns, they could not have done so had the EIC not been designed to protect their interests. As investment by outsiders is indicative of an organization's ability to facilitate effective impersonal cooperation, the fact that the EIC embodied cooperation-enhancing attributes is, in itself, supportive evidence for the insufficiency of *personal* cooperation.

Though this may seem a tautological argument, it is not, as long as no other explanation for these attributes is offered.

The governance and financial structure of the EIC therefore induced information flows. The need to draw members into investing in subsequent voyages, beyond the first voyage and joint stock, compelled the insiders to provide them with information. The need to arrive at majority decisions with respect to major business decisions made the provision of information a precondition for voting. The EIC bylaws paid much attention to the preparation and auditing of accounts and their presentation to the General Court.[30] Further, the governance structure created a variety of opportunities for the informal flow of information. The two company courts served as hubs, at which information arriving from agents in Asia, from those en route to and from Asia, and from insiders in London, was shared with outsiders. The physical presence, at regular intervals, of all members and shareholders in one location, helped reduce informational asymmetry. Mandatory disclosure of information, provision of information as part of the decision-making dynamics, and informal gathering of information at meetings all ensured a continual flow of information from insiders to outsiders. Obviously, not every piece of information was verifiable, not all participants received it at once, and asymmetry did not disappear altogether. But one should look at the quality of information flows comparatively. The flow of information to EIC outsiders was considerably greater in both quantity and reliability than that to the Italian and German lenders of the Estado da Índia or to the passive shareholders of the VOC.[31] The more impersonal and voluntary the cooperation in an institution, the more information had to be provided to outsiders, so as to protect their investment, allow them to exercise their voice effectively, and monitor risk levels, accounts, and dividends.

LIQUIDITY AND THE EXIT OPTION

Exit options for EIC members were not mentioned in the charter of incorporation. The charter only envisioned hereditary transfer of membership from father to son, as in guilds and regulated corporations. It did not view the membership interest in any corporation, including the EIC, as commodified or freely transferable. However, the joint-stock financial structure, coupled with the corporate structure, de facto permitted exit. One means of exit was by collecting the principal and dividend paid at the end of a voyage and refraining from reinvesting in the next one. The second was by selling the share in any given joint stock while that stock was still active. The first category of exit was available only at the end of any given voyage, and the second at any point at which a buyer could be found.

Thus, members of the EIC were given a unique exit option not available in the VOC or in later English companies. Membership in the EIC, in fact, amounted to an option to invest in any of the future voyages. Some did, while others did not. In this sense, the corporation included potential, though not necessarily actual, investors. While potential investors had a voice in the majority-based decision to undertake a new voyage and raise more money, those who opted not to subscribe for a specific voyage could not share in its profits. Contributions to each of the first twelve voyages were made by different individuals, all supposedly members of the corporation. Membership allowed potential investors to receive first-hand information about the outcome of past voyages, the status of ongoing voyages, and the prospects and business plans of future ones. They were given the opportunity to exit by deciding whether or not to participate in emerging business opportunities. Hence, the more viable exit route at this stage in the history of the EIC involved opting out of an undesirable voyage rather than exiting the corporation altogether.

One intriguing outcome of the per-voyage stock and of the exit option at the end of each voyage was the creation of a framework for repeat transactions. The outsiders were not locked in for a long period of time, and cooperation had to be reestablished separately for each voyage. The repeated interaction effectively allowed outsiders to evaluate and reevaluate the performance and reliability of the insiders. Normally, reputation mechanisms function either in a repeat-transactions context, in which the sanction for breach is the loss of future transactions, or in a personal-exchange context, in which the sanction for breach is a social sanction within a network. The unique structure of the EIC compensated for the shift from network-based cooperation to impersonal cooperation by structuring the investment of outsiders in the form of repeat transactions. This organizational model provided the insiders with an opportunity to accumulate a positive reputation and secure impersonal passive investment for the longer term. In this sense it was somewhat similar to the Dutch precompanies, not to the VOC.

The second category of exit was not a trivial matter, for two reasons. First, the charter of the EIC did not recognize unrestricted transfer of membership. In practice, this meant that while a member could transact with a new entrant and promise to convey to him his right to dividend, principal, and profit in full, he could not transfer membership privileges or the right to vote and receive information, unless approved by the EIC court. In the first few years, the court did not always grant approval speedily.

To exit the initial investment in an ongoing voyage, a member had to match with a buyer and sell to that buyer his share in a specific pending joint stock. He had to do this without the aid of a functioning market or prestructured, low-cost transactions. Networks based on family connections could assist in matching sellers of EIC shares with buyers. But this was not an adequate solution for the widely held and impersonal corporation the EIC turned out to be.

The selling of shares was facilitated to a certain extent by the EIC's institutional structure, through which the corporation served as a focal point for sellers and buyers. In the general meeting, potential buyers could locate a seller, acquire information on the proper price of the shares by learning about the state of affairs in Asia, and derive some sense of the market price of the good in question. These meetings functioned more like annual fairs than modern capital markets, in which shares of various corporations are traded.

To acquire a sense of the frequency of transactions and the liquidity of the nascent share market, I have constructed a database, the first of its kind, of transactions in EIC shares. It is based on reports in the EIC minutes on transactions presented for approval in the EIC court. From 1601 until the introduction of the new EIC charter in 1609, I identified a hundred transactions altogether. Figure 11.2 offers a visual representation of the data. The vertical axis on the left and the grey columns represent the total transaction amount in pounds. The vertical axis on the right and the black dots represent the number of transactions. For example, in 1607, the number of transactions was forty-seven.

Taking into account that the EIC minutes for the period 1604–6 were lost and that 1600 and 1609 were not full years, the annual average can

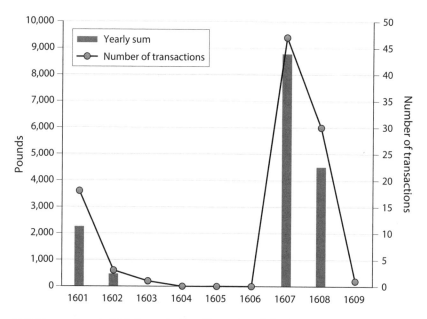

11.2. Transactions in EIC shares. Source: Harris (2005) database, based on *Calendar of State Papers, Colonial, East Indies 1515–1634*, 5 vols., London, 1892.

be extrapolated to be around forty transactions. This number is high for an environment that was devoid of a functioning stock market. Still, liquidity was limited.

If a transaction could not materialize, either for lack of approval or for failure to match with a buyer, the investor had to hold his share until the end of the voyage, in the hope that it would be successful and that there would be a final settlement of accounts for the voyage. Thus, the more viable exit option at this stage in the history of the EIC still involved opting out of a specific voyage rather than exiting the corporation altogether.

With free access to an effective stock market, the liquidity of VOC shares was higher than that of EIC shares. Nevertheless, I assert that the liquidity of EIC shares was higher than any historians, economists, or legal scholars have hitherto attributed to it (or have attributed, in fact, to any English business corporation existing before 1688). A market in stock developed in London only in the late seventeenth century. Throughout much of that century, the shares of the EIC were traded in company meetings, on a personal basis, or by ad hoc matching. The number of transactions in EIC shares began to increase after the Restoration, from an annual average of forty-four in 1661–63 to an annual average of 655 in 1688.[32] After the Glorious Revolution, things changed more dramatically. A market in government debt emerged. In the 1690s, a handful of corporate shares—the EIC, the Bank of England, the Royal African Company, and the Hudson's Bay Company—"free rode" the government bond boom and were traded together with commodities, insurance policies, foreign currencies, and government stocks (bonds, in modern terms) on the Royal Exchange.[33] The formation of the Bank of England contributed to the trade in bonds and shares. Around 1700, as the halls of the Royal Exchange became overcrowded, some brokers moved their activities across the street to coffee houses in Exchange Alley.[34] With the South Sea boom of 1720, a larger number of companies, mostly short-lived, made use of the English stock market.[35] In 1773, new premises were built by the stockbrokers in Sweeting's Alley behind the Royal Exchange and named the Stock Exchange. The development of an active government bond market, market liquidity for corporate shares, and stock market infrastructure in England came much slower and later, with a lag of a century or so, than those of the Dutch. In the Amsterdam *Beurs*, as we have seen, public bonds were traded as early as the late sixteenth century, and VOC shares were traded starting in 1602. By 1700, both London and Amsterdam had stock exchanges unparalleled anywhere else in Eurasia (with the possible exception of Paris).

The EIC's capital needs were fundamentally different from those of English merchants trading with Europe. The problems faced by the EIC were not of investing in infrastructure in the form of forts, ports, warehouses, and the like, as some scholars mistakenly assume.[36] What the new enterprise needed was primarily working rather than fixed capital—a fact that influenced its organizational design.

The EIC was designed organizationally as it was (coupling a corporation with a per-voyage equity financial investment) to facilitate cooperation between insiders and outsiders. To expand beyond personally based social networks, a repeated transactions-based reputation mechanism was designed in the form of per-voyage joint stock. The EIC offered external investors voice and information on a level far higher than in the VOC, in an attempt to attract their involvement and thus offset the lack of liquidity in the absence of an effective market for shares in England in 1600. The EIC was designed in a manner that would allow its members an exit option despite the lack of a preexisting stock market. This option had to be formulated in an unusual way, unfamiliar to modern scholars who view exit through the market as the standard route.[37] The large number of actual investors in the EIC, and their diverse social origins, are the best evidence to suggest that impersonal cooperation was achieved and that the EIC was able to break through the glass ceiling of traditional, personally based, and network-based cooperation.

CREDIBLE COMMITMENT

The charter details the exchange between Elizabeth I and the investors. The Crown provided monopoly, incorporation, and enforcement of the monopoly against interlopers, possibly naval support, and political backing. The merchants, on the other hand, provided resources in various ways, including upfront cash and future custom and tax payments, promotion of the Crown's foreign policy, and ships for the navy in times of war.[38] As we have seen, the charter also specified the deal between insiders and outside investors in which the former were to provide voice, information, and an exit option in return for capital invested in the EIC. But was the charter just a piece of paper that could be revoked at will by the Crown? Or was it a binding and enforceable agreement between the Crown and a group of merchants, and an agreement between insiders and outsiders within the EIC? Could the investors trust the Crown not to expropriate their investment once pooled together?

The same problem that North and Weingast identified with respect to the Crown's commitment to repaying debts also applied to its commitment to respecting charters.[39] The Crown, as long as it remained an absolute sovereign, could do whatever it wished. It had no constitutional or institutional devices by which to credibly restrain itself, in the present, from taking a particular course of action in the future. The Crown could revoke a charter at will, issue a new, competing charter, or refuse to enforce privileges granted in a charter. Similarly, the insiders could approach the Crown and request a change in the institutional rules of the game in their favor, at the expense of the outsiders, as did the directors of the

VOC. There was no third-party enforcer of the agreement.[40] This is a classic "credible commitment" problem. The Crown, as a sovereign exercising prerogative authority, could backtrack and revoke commitments. Thus, it could not credibly commit *not* to revoke. The charters would therefore lose their value, and the market for charters would be doomed to collapse altogether.

The evolution of "credible commitment" devices in England in the period 1558–1640 is therefore impressive. Although in doctrinal constitutional law, the granting of charters was still within the prerogative of the Crown, in fact parliament and the judiciary became highly influential institutions in the charter-granting arena. Parliament protested unilateral decisions by the Crown to grant charters (particularly monopolistic ones) or to revoke them. Gradually, case by case, the common-law courts began to review the validity and scope of charters issued by the Crown. New constitutional ideas, developed in public discourse relating to the clashes between the Crown and parliament and the judiciary, constrained the Crown's prerogative. These new ideas were mixed by shrewd jurists with old narratives and memories, in a bid to give them apparently ancient origins and thus render them entrenched and unalterable. The Crown had to take into account the vested interests of both the charter grantees and their competitors, because these interest groups had access to parliament and the courts of law, and had the option of refraining from doing business altogether or seeking alternatives overseas. In short, the Crown became constrained by reputational mechanisms, institutional devices, the consolidation of an independent judiciary, and new constitutional ideas. All of these constraints amounted to a gradual shift from an absolute monarchy to a nascent rule-of-law monarchy.[41]

Indeed, in some cases the Crown's overall ability to grant charters actually weakened. With respect to some of the activities for which the Crown wished to grant charters and monopolies, the outcome was an inability to grant or commit to them, because parliament or the judiciary could override its decision. With respect to other grants, uncertainty as to the validity of the charters grew. At the end of the period, when England deteriorated into full-blown civil war, Charles I obviously could not uphold his commitments, and thereafter the Commonwealth had to decide which to preserve. However, the test of commitment devices is not whether they hold up through a revolution, but rather whether they endure during the normal life of a regime. After all, even modern liberal democracies are neither fully committed nor fully credible. They often have to pay a reputational and political price for this, but so did Elizabeth I, James I, and Charles I when revoking their charters.

The argument made here is relative, not absolute, on several levels. It is not absolute because I cannot offer a counterfactual or a historical English state that presented fully credible commitments or was altogether predatory, against which to compare the late Tudor and early Stuart states. There is no benchmark to which the level of chartering activity in the period 1558–1640 could be compared, to infer from this the level of credibility of the English state. The Crown was better able in this period to convey credible commitment with respect to charters than to loans; this is because the use of charters had a longer history that, over the generations, facilitated the development of legal and institutional constraints. And it was able to convey greater credible commitment than in the past because of the general constitutional developments of the period, which strengthened the status of parliament and the common law. The English Crown could also convey commitments that were more credible than those of other European countries because of its judicially developed constitutional doctrines and the balance of powers between merchants and the state. A business corporation of the magnitude and longevity of the EIC could only be formed in a political system in which a space was created that was safely beyond the sovereign's ability to breach his past commitment, repeal the charter, and expropriate the pooled property of the chartered corporation. Such a space had to be protected by credible means from the sovereign's freedom to disregard it at will. As we just saw, England was such a state. The Dutch Republic was also such a state, as we saw in chapter 10, but this is due to its different configuration, its federal structure, and the dominance of merchants in its politics. Other European and Asian states were not such structures.

THE EIC IN ASIA

How did the EIC make use of its organizational innovation and the capital it successfully raised? Above all, it sent ships around the Cape to Asia—seventeen in its first decade and seventy-seven in the second decade

(1611–20). The following decades witnessed fluctuations in the range of 58–134 ships per decade. The total for the seventeenth century was 807 ships going eastbound around the Cape.

As early as the first voyage of the EIC, in 1602, some factors were left behind in Bantam, and in this way the first EIC factory in Asia was established. The second voyage was instructed to go there to bring home goods bought by the factors of the first voyage who were stationed there. In 1607, the third voyage was instructed first to go to Mocha and Aden, and to Surat in India, before going on to Bantam and other Indonesian destinations. Later voyages frequented additional ports in the Persian Gulf, in Eastern India, in Southeast Asia, and in the Indonesian archipelago. By 1613, Surat had become the major EIC factory in western India. The presence of resident EIC employees in Indian Ocean ports gave rise to a private trade by these employees. The private trade provided these employees with supplemental income and even made the more entrepreneurial of them wealthy people. But it was not detrimental to the company. As Erikson recently established, the private trade enhanced the flow of useful information to the company, expanded its trade network and encouraged entrepreneurial behavior of company agents.[42]

The increased autonomy of agents in Asia and the growing decentralization did not go by without reaction. In 1614, an attempt was made by the EIC board to appoint a factor-general for the entire Asian trade and to authorize this person to organize and supervise four regional factories. This attempt at rationalization and centralization, similar to the way the VOC was organized around Batavia, did not last. Bantam and Surat became the two main EIC trading centers in Asia. In addition, factories were established in other ports and market towns, from Yemen and the Persian Gulf, through various parts of the Indian subcontinent, to Indonesia. At some point, the chief factors at both Bantam and Surat were raised to the status of presidents, and councils were established alongside them. Growing Dutch pressure drove the English out of Bantam in 1682, with the result that the Indian subcontinent became its center of activity. Bombay, acquired from the Portuguese in 1661, gradually became the EIC administrative headquarters in western India. By the end of the seventeenth century, Madras, acquired in 1639, became the company's major trading center on the Coromandel Coast and in Southern India in general. By the 1680s, Calcutta had emerged as the company's center for the growing Bengal and Central India trade. All three fort cities, Bombay, Madras, and Calcutta, were raised to the status of presidencies in the eighteenth century.[43] In 1772, the president of Fort William–Calcutta was made governor-general, with some seniority over the other presidents.

This chapter and the book as a whole do not set out to explain British imperialism in India, Dutch imperialism in Indonesia, or Europe's imperial expansion more generally. The book deliberately ends in 1700, before imperialism really took hold. The present and the previous chapters focus on the era in which the EIC and the VOC were primarily trade enterprises. Their territorial presence in Asia was subsidiary to their trade objectives. In the seventeenth century, the EIC conquered and purchased a few strategic positions that served as factories and ports in the trade enterprises. Its territorial and colonial ambitions in India really took off in the First and Second Carnatic Wars (1746–48, 1749–54) and the Seven Years' War (1754–63), in which it fought the French in India and intervened in the war of succession for the throne of the Nizam of Hyderabad. After the loss of the North American colonies in the American War of Independence (1775–83), the Second British Empire was built around India. Even those scholars, notably Stern, who view the EIC as acquiring the characteristic of a territorial colonial power, exercising jurisdiction over locals and demonstrating sovereignty and governance early in its history, do not attribute such powers to the EIC before Cromwell granted it a charter in 1657 to govern the Atlantic island of Saint Helena (an important stopover on the way to the Cape) and the move of the company's factory from Mughal Surat to Bombay once this was granted to it in a charter of Charles II in 1668.[44] I am sympathetic to Stern's argument that territorial concerns became more prominent as early as the 1668 Charter of Bombay rather than by the 1757 Battle of Plassey, as common wisdom held. But even the earlier date is late enough to justify the analysis of the first seventy years of the EIC in terms of trade and finance. In its first decades, the EIC was preoccupied with raising capital and conducting trade, and its institutional design addressed these concerns above all. But the important historical phenomena of colonialism and imperialism are beyond the scope of this study.

COMPARING THE VOC TO THE EIC

The VOC and the EIC were totally different from any other entity that predated them in human history, but they did have much in common with each other—not least, in my view, three very important underlying characteristics. First, they endeavored to undertake the most challenging, risky, and complicated business activity contemporaries could imagine: the longest-distance trade possible on the globe, carrying American silver through Europe around Africa to southern and eastern Africa, and bringing back Asian goods in return. In this respect, the English and Dutch were challenged a little more than the Portuguese and far more than any other enterprise or ruler. Second, they pooled together resources on a level beyond the means of any individual or family and beyond the reach of any social network. The VOC and EIC were both based on outside investment, and brought about the transformation from personal to impersonal cooperation. Third, they were separate from the ruler and from the state apparatus. They were formed in an intermediate space between the state and the family, in which associations of individuals and families could freely exist. England and the Dutch Republic were singular in providing the preconditions for the creation of such a protected space that would, to some degree or other, be resilient to state expropriation of the property and capital accumulated by such associations. In short, the two corporations had several striking similarities, which are summed up in table 11.6. But the two institutions were different in their organizational details, which are best demonstrated in the attributes of their shares (see table 11.7).

According to my analysis, these differences result from several factors. The first and most important is the position of merchants in society and in politics, followed by the federal structure of the judiciary and the presence of a stock market. The Dutch Republic was dominated by merchants who had accumulated substantial wealth before the beginning of Asian trade, and additional wealth during the existence of the precompanies—and these increased their political influence. Merchants in the Dutch Republic enjoyed political influence, not only because of their absolute wealth compared to that of landowning classes, but also because the political and constitutional structure of the republic, a federation, was

11.6. Similarity of Basic Features, EIC and VOC

	EIC	VOC
Mode of formation	State charter	State charter
Year of formation	1600	1602
Business	Eurasian trade: silver for spices and silk	Eurasian trade: silver for spices and silk
Monopoly	Cape of Good Hope to Straits of Magellan	Cape of Good Hope to Straits of Magellan
Duration of incorporation	15 years	21 years
Features	Joint-stock capital, shares, centralized management	Joint-stock capital, shares, centralized management

11.7. Attributes of EIC and VOC Shares

	EIC	VOC
Classes	1	2 (Active = *bewindhebbers*, Passive = *participanten*)
Voice	One vote for each shareholder	One vote for each active shareholder. No voting rights for those with passive shares
Dividends	Principal and profit at end of each voyage	Discretionary (in practice minimal)
Information	Accounts and trade news	No information to passive shareholders
Exit	Subject to approval	Subject to registration at VOC books
Liability	Not defined	Not defined

favorable to them. The aristocracy was divided throughout the various provinces, while merchants were concentrated in several strategically positioned cities and particularly in Amsterdam. In England, a unitary political system, the Crown and parliament, although located in London, were dominated by the nationwide landowning classes. It took the merchant classes at least another century to gain substantial political power.

In the Dutch Republic, the active shareholders used their positions as both merchants and city magistrates, in Amsterdam and other cities, to exercise political influence on provincial and federal governments and to unilaterally lock-in the external investors by way of the charter. The VOC can be viewed as closer in its relationship to the state than that of the EIC to the Portuguese Estado da Índia. Because of the overlap between the merchant elite and the political elite, the VOC enjoyed more state support. At the same time, however, it was also more willing to advance the political goals of the Dutch Republic at the expense of pure business goals. Admittedly, the two could not easily be distinguished from each other. It could be viewed as a dual private-public enterprise, more private than the Estado yet more public than the EIC. Organizationally, it had much more in common with the EIC than with the Estado. In this sense, I accept Steensgaard's view that if one has to draw a clear distinction, it is more accurate to view the Estado as a distributive enterprise and the EIC and VOC as revolutionary, profit-maximizing enterprises. The distinction is confirmed by the existence of joint-stock and equity investment by outside passive investors and the expectation of the investors to receive a share in the profits.

The VOC could continue the lock-in of the capital of passive shareholders because an exit option through the secondary market was made available. A bond market was in place in the Dutch republic by the late sixteenth century, and the trade in VOC shares could take advantage of its infrastructure. In England, the bond market developed about a century later, after the Glorious Revolution. The early seventeenth-century EIC could not offer exit through a secondary share market. It could not conceive a long-term lock-in of external equity finance and instead had to offer exit at the end of each voyage. In addition, the EIC had to offer more voice through greater decision-making rights, in return for the constrained-exit option. As a result, the EIC governance structure was less oligarchic and hierarchical, and more voluntary, democratic, and participatory than that of the VOC.

The two corporations provided investors with an opportunity to diversify their investment. The opportunity was created by the fact that, unlike regulated corporations that required their members to be involved nearly full time in trade, the corporations allowed passivity. Unlike commenda investment or even part ownership of ships, which required a high threshold for entering the investment, investment in the corporations could be done with small sums as well. Investors could hold a port-

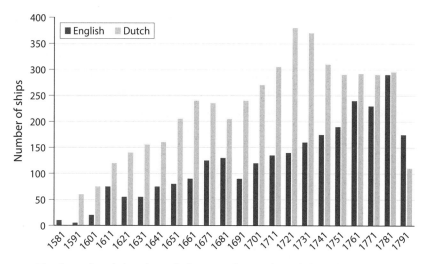

11.3. Numbers of English and Dutch ships traveling eastbound along the Cape Route.
Source: de Vries (2003).

folio of investments in which the risky investment in VOC or EIC was
only part of the portfolio. In the Dutch republic this investment could be
made side by side with investment in government and city bonds, investment in shares of ships involved in European trade and fishing, and investment in real estate. The only other significant investment in corporate
shares was in the West India Company. In England, a few decades into
the seventeenth century the diversification could be done to investment
in the shares of other corporations as well, including domestic, colonial,
and trade corporations.[45]

Of the two leading companies, the VOC seemed to do better in the
short run. It raised more capital, had more members, and sent more ships.
For the numbers of English and Dutch ships traveling eastbound along
the Cape Route, see figure 11.3. In terms of number of eastbound ships,
the English matched the Dutch only in the last two decades of the eighteenth century.

The two companies were by far the largest business enterprises of their
time in Europe. They were able to raise joint-stock capital on an immense
scale, unparalleled by earlier enterprises—with the exception of the Fugger family firm, the richest firm in Europe of the previous century and
the bankers of choice for European rulers.

Table 11.8 compares the capital raised by the English EIC in its first twelve voyages, 1601–12 (taken from table 11.1), the capital subscribed by the Dutch EIC in its first charter (1602) and paid in four installments (taken from table 10.1), and the wealth of the largest family enterprise of the previous century, the Jakob Fugger the Rich family firm (based on his estate inventory following his death in 1525, and taken from the text of the microstudy in chapter 6, starting on page 174). The magnitude of their capital is compared on the basis of exchange rates between coins and silver weight or silver equivalent of the relevant coins. The capital of the VOC is expressed in guilders, that of the English EIC in pounds, and that of the Fugger inheritance in florins.[46] The average exchange rate between pound and guilder in the period 1603–10 was 10.553. The florin was presumably a money of account of the Habsburg Empire that was equivalent to one guilder, which was the money of account in the Netherlands.[47] The silver price/equivalent in the Netherlands in 1602 (for the VOC) was 11.17 g of silver per guilder; in England in the period 1601–12 for the EIC it was 0.4640 g of silver per English penny; and the price of silver in the Netherlands (in the absence of prices for Augsburg) in 1527 for the Fugger family firm was 18.8 g of silver per guilder.[48]

In nominal exchange values, the VOC was the largest of the three companies; the EIC was second; and the Fuggers were a distant third at a ratio of roughly 64:49:21, and in nominal silver values at ratio of 72:52:40. However, it is important to remember that the passage of three-quarters of a century between the Fugger observation and the VOC and EIC observations coincided with the height of the European price revolution. While the Fugger family firm's capital in 1525 equaled the purchasing power of 40,044 kg of silver, by 1610 this capital would have equated to the purchasing power of only 22,812 kg of silver, due to the fall in the purchasing power of silver in Europe.[49] This perspective would make its scope even smaller compared to the VOC and EIC. But assuming that the Fugger fortune was not held in silver but rather in goods for the next seventy-five years, then its 1525 value would have to be inflated to calculate its value in real terms in around 1610. Pfister calculates the annual cost of a consumer basket in Augsburg (where the Fugger family firm headquarters were located). The cost of the basket in 1525 was around 150 g of silver, while by 1610 it had gone up to around 450—an increase of approximately 300 percent.[50] Others, using different baskets

11.8. Comparing the Capital of the Fugger Family Firm, the English East India Company, and the Dutch East India Company

	Fugger family firm	English East India Company (EIC)	Dutch East India Company (VOC)
Capital in local currency	2,130,000 florins	464,284 pounds	6,424,588 guilders
Capital in guilders (based on exchange rate)	2,130,000 guilders	4,899,589 guilders	6,424,588 guilders
Capital equivalent in kg of silver (based on current silver prices)	40,044	51,703	71,763

Sources: Allen (n.d.); van Zanden (n.d.); Ehrenberg (1928, pp. 17, 87–89, 94); Harris (forthcoming, p. 25); Denzel (2010, p. 64); McCusker (1978, pp. 42–45, 52, 55); Häberlein (2012); de Vries and van der Woude (1997, p. 85); Posthumus (1964, vol. 1, p. 107; vol. 2, pp. 46–48).

and methods, reported price increases of comparable magnitude for other parts of Western Europe and Britain.[51] So adjustment of the Fugger firm's 1525 value, in line with consumer goods inflation up to 1610, raises its value to about 8.5 million guilders—making it larger than that of either the VOC or EIC.

EAST INDIA COMPANIES ELSEWHERE IN EUROPE

Was the corporate organizational form more efficient than other forms, such as ruler-owned enterprises or family firms? What could be the yardsticks for dealing with this question? Comparing profitability or even transportation costs is not feasible when it comes to comparing such varied regions as China, India, and Europe of the seventeenth century. The best form of data to which we have access is ship count. It is available in the most comprehensive manner for only one route—but this, the Cape Route, is really telling. Within a short span of years, ships operated by companies dominated the Cape Route. In the second decade of the seventeenth century, the VOC and EIC together sent 194 ships past the Cape to Asia, while Portugal sent only sixty-six ships. In the third decade of the century, they sent 199 ships compared to sixty, respectively, and the rising trend in both the number and size of VOC and EIC Cape Route

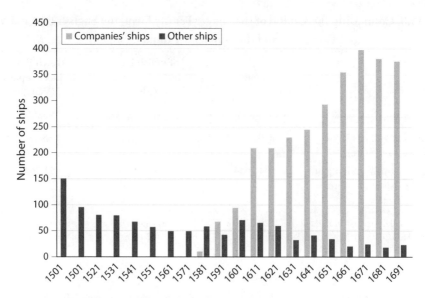

11.4. The shift from ruler-operated ships to corporation-operated ships on the seventeenth-century Cape Route. Source: de Vries (2003).

ships (and decline in Portuguese ship numbers) continued throughout the seventeenth century. To the best of my knowledge, there is no record of any Asian ship sailing the Cape Route on its way to Europe in the seventeenth century; European corporations dominated oceanic Eurasian trade in that era. The evidence for this is conclusive. The question of whether European corporations dominated long-distance intra-Asian trade in the same century is justly debated. It is unlikely that European corporations dominated short-distance maritime trade in the South China Sea or the Bay of Bengal. Figure 11.4 provides a visualization of the number of ships going past the Cape on their way to the Far East. According to the figure, Portuguese ships dominated the Cape Route until 1581, while the VOC and EIC dominated the Cape Route from 1610. The figure also shows the peak decade in terms of number of ships for the Portuguese was the 1500s (with 150 ships), whereas for the VOC and EIC it was the 1670s (with almost four hundred ships).[52]

Was the business corporation a migratory institution within Europe? The corporate form migrated within the confines of Western Europe in the seventeenth century.[53] The corporate form was used for organization of Eurasian trade in other European countries as well in the seventeenth and eighteenth centuries. Yet most of the other companies, with the exception of the EIC and VOC, were small in scale, short-lived, or both. Let us examine the other East India companies formed in Europe in the seventeenth and early eighteenth centuries.

The Portuguese organized their trade in the sixteenth and early seventeenth centuries to be state-owned, public-private enterprises. The 1628 incorporation of the Portuguese East India Company (*Compendia do commercial da Índia*) was a third attempt at incorporation, following failures in 1587 and 1619. This was just one more experiment by the Portuguese to reorganize their trade, one of many over the previous century and a quarter. Their shift to the corporate form was a reaction to the organizational crises and the decline in trade and shipping in the face of successful competition in the early seventeenth century from the expanding VOC and EIC. In 1628, the Crown issued two foundational documents, the *altar* and the *regiment* (taken together, these were roughly equivalent to a charter). The company was incorporated for twelve years. The Crown took it upon itself to invest 1.5 million cruzados in the venture. Part of the investment was in kind, in the form of ships. King Philip III granted the company monopoly over the main Asian goods, including pepper, cinnamon, coral, and ebony. He committed not to withdraw his share of the profits before the end of the twelve-year term, nor to intervene in the management of the company. These privileges and commitments were meant to make the Portuguese company attractive to private investors, yet it was unsuccessful in raising sufficient capital from outsiders. Most of the capital, about 80 percent, was eventually invested by the Crown, and much of the rest was invested by other public bodies such as towns and villages. The company was never fully separate from the state, its capital, its aims, or its personnel. Ultimately, it was unable to attract enough private investors and was dissolved five years into its twelve-year term, in 1633.

What can explain the Portuguese failure? They used the same building blocks as the Dutch and English—so one could attribute the ultimate failure to factors that have nothing to do with organizational issues. The English and Dutch may have had better technologies, more successful economies, and stronger navies. But I cannot fully isolate organizational concerns from these factors, and I would like to contribute to the discussion by offering an institutional explanation. My hypothesis is that the

Portuguese Crown could not credibly commit not to expropriate outside investors. Expropriation did not have to be outright taking; it could take the form of prioritizing political over business considerations. It could take the form of assessing the Crown's in-kind investment above its market value, or favoring the Crown when it came to dividend distribution. It could take the form of competition by the Crown, restrictions imposed on certain company activities, or new taxation. The Portuguese Crown functioned free of institutional restraints that would prevent it from expropriating. When dealing with syndicates of the leading Italian and German merchant and banking firms of the sixteenth century, of the caliber of the Welsers, Fuggers, and the like, the Crown was subject to threats of severe sanctions for breaching the Asia or Europa contracts. But investment by numerous Iberian individuals in the open market was very different from investment by a well-organized syndicate of wealthy foreign merchants and bankers. Such individuals would not invest without credible commitment. The absence of devices that could be used to credibly commit led to low investment; and that low investment by private individuals led to an enterprise that sent only thirteen ships to Asia and dissolved within five years.

Elsewhere, France had experience with the corporate form since 1604. Three short-lived and unsuccessful companies for trade with Asia were formed in 1604, 1615, and 1626. A somewhat more successful company was set up in 1642 and renewed in 1652, but it seems not to have been active beyond the island of Madagascar. The most significant French company, *Compagnie des Indus Orientals*, was planned by Jean-Baptiste Colbert and chartered by King Louis XIV in 1664 for fifty years, with monopoly for trading between the Cape of Good Hope and the Straits of Magellan. It resulted from the fusion of three earlier companies, the *Compagnie de Chine*, the *Compagnie d'Orient*, and the *Compagnie de Madagascar*. It too was influenced by the models of the VOC and EIC. But before long, the state assumed influence over the affairs of the company at the expense of the shareholders.[54] The government initiated the company, while the king set the capital, personally contributed one-fifth of the capital, decided on the distribution of dividends, and forced shareholders to make additional payments on shares. The French East India Company established factories in today's Réunion and Mauritius in the Eastern Indian Ocean and in Pondicherry in Southern India. The French sent only sixty ships around the Cape in the period 1600–1660, while the French Company was able to send between thirty and forty per decade for the rest of the century. This was much more than in the earlier period but only one-fourth of what the EIC sent and one-eighth of the number of VOC ships going east. The French East India Company was dissolved in 1723.

The company was, at most, a joint private-public enterprise like its Portuguese counterpart. In the French case as well, the Crown was too absolutist and unconstrainable and was not able to credibly commit to private equity investors. There was no space separating Crown and state in which private business corporations could develop.

The Danish East India Company (*Dansk Østindisk Kompagni*, or OK) was established in 1616 and lasted until 1650.[55] It was initiated by two Dutch immigrants from Rotterdam, its design influenced by the VOC model and its governance structure oligarchic. In 1625, the Aulic Council of the Holy Roman Empire, whose seat was in the Habsburg Court in Vienna, began an initiative to form an East India Company. It negotiated with the Hanseatic cities and with the king of Spain. The proposed company was inspired by the models of both the EIC and VOC. But the endeavor was terminated in 1629 with the closure of the Hanseatic Diet.[56] Meanwhile, the Brandenburg Company, established in 1682, was Dutch dominated, despite its Prussian base, and ended up being more involved in Africa than in Asia.[57] It was succeeded in 1752 by the Emden Company, which traded primarily with Guangzhou in China. The Ostend Company was chartered in 1722 by the Habsburg King Charles VI. It was an Austrian-Flemish trading company for trade with the East and West Indies, and its capital was raised mostly from merchants in Antwerp and Ghent. It sent out twenty-one ships before suspending its activity in 1731 due to British political pressure. The Swedish East India Company (SEIC) was established in 1731 by a Scottish merchant, a former supercargo for the Ostend Company who wished to take advantage of the vacuum created by its liquidation. The base of the SEIC was in Gothenburg, and all incoming and outgoing ships had to go through that port. It traded mostly with Chinese goods, primarily tea.

These companies followed either the EIC or the VOC model. Some of the companies—the Portuguese and French—were formed in absolutist states in which the king was highly involved, expropriation was immanent, and companies were not really separate from the ruler (and did not flourish). Some of the companies—the Danish, Brandenburg, Ostend, and Swedish—were mainly platforms for groups of interlopers from Britain, the Dutch Republic, and Denmark. They were operating in the eighteenth-century environment of well-known routes and markets and routinized trade, in which the corporation was more of a rent-seeking, monopolistic enterprise than an efficient enterprise using the joint-stock corporation form to cross entry barriers and engage in a trade otherwise inaccessible to individuals.

It seems as though various East India companies in different parts of Western Europe were not invented independently again and again from scratch, based on a similar building block (the corporation) and similar business needs. Knowledge about the formation and the success of the VOC and EIC circulated around. Just as immigrants carried with them technology, in our context they also conveyed know-how.[58] Itinerant Dutch, in particular, were involved in some of the other European companies. The charters of companies such as the Danish and Portuguese organizations include phrases that suggest the drafters had in their possession the charter of the VOC, and possibly that of the EIC as well. The plurality and proximity of political entities and the competition between them created fertile ground in Europe for copying institutional innovations. But knowledge and even willingness to import do not ensure successful transplantation.

CONCLUSION

The corporate form served as the constitutional basis of the Catholic Church wherever this prevailed. Orthodox Eastern Europe was not accustomed to it, but the newly reformed Protestant parts of Western and Central Europe were. East India corporations were formed throughout Western Europe, yet in some of these countries the joint-stock business corporation was a success story, while in others it was rejected or did not function well. To the extent that we refer only to *well-functioning* business corporations, then, even in Europe, the business corporation was confined for a long time to England and the Dutch Republic. Both countries were, by then, Protestant. Despite the temptation to explain this by Weber's Protestant-ethic thesis, such an account does not hold.[59]

My argument is that the relevant difference between England and the Dutch Republic, on the one hand, and Portugal and France, on the other, was not in the newly introduced Protestantism and the work ethic, devotion, and calling that its theology entailed. Rather, the relevant difference was in the political structure. In England and the Dutch Republic, the ruler (or state) was constrained and therefore could not do as it wished. There could be an indirect causal relationship between the Protestant Reformation and the divergence in terms of state constraints and credibility, but these did not go through theology to business ethics and motivation but rather through politics, to credible commitment devices, to the creation of pools of assets in business corporations. In Portugal and France, the ruler could expropriate the pool of assets created by the investment of private individuals in joint-stock companies. In England, a nascent rule of law allowed the Crown to credibly commit not to expropriate. In the Dutch Republic, a combination of federal political structure and the central role of merchants in the political elite made expropriation impossible.

We began this part of the book with three questions: Why did corporations develop only in Europe, and why, within Europe, in its northwestern corner? Why were European corporations transformed in around 1600 from public entities to joint-stock, for-profit entities? And why were corporations so well suited to long-distance trade as to rapidly take control of the Cape Route and rise to dominance in Eurasia trade as a whole, at the expense of organizational forms such as family firms and merchant networks?

We now have most of the pieces of these puzzles. Corporations developed in Europe because of the unique needs of the Roman Catholic Church, which sought to separate itself from secular territorial rulers and maintain a hierarchical structure. They were used for organizing joint-stock, for-profit enterprises when Western Europeans aspired to enter long-distance trade with Asia and particularly when European merchants entered Cape Route oceanic trade with Asia, without reliance on platforms provided by rulers and states. They could best thrive in England and the Dutch Republic because, in these countries, a space was created between the state and individuals in which corporate entities could fully develop and flourish. In both of these countries, the state could credibly commit not to unilaterally revoke the charter of incorporation and not to expropriate the merchants and investors.

The corporations, and in particular the EIC and VOC, became dominant in the Cape Route trade because they could raise more capital from more people than any other organizational form but the ruler himself. Unlike the ruler, joint-stock corporations were rational in the sense of accounting for business activities separately from other activities such as waging European wars. They were more focused on making the highest possible profits for their equity investors (or at least some of them). They could not raise the required capital through taxation, as could the Portuguese or the Chinese. Their size and span afforded them huge informational advantage over family firms and partnerships. As these large corporations employed many agents, they had to deal with more agency problems. But the information flows and crossflows within these firms could presumably improve monitoring of agents by the headquarters in London or Amsterdam and the VOC Asian headquarter in Batavia. The expansion and success of these firms suggest that, on the whole, informational advantages, with respect to the business itself and with respect to the monitoring of agents, offset the new agency problems created in the transition from personal to impersonal enterprises.

~ 12 ~

Why Did the Corporation Only Evolve in Europe?

This chapter resolves another important historical conundrum: Why did the business corporations not migrate from Europe to the Middle East, India, and China in the three centuries between their first introduction in Europe, around 1600, and their eventual colonial (or informally colonial) forced introduction in Asia in the late nineteenth century? And why did business corporations not develop indigenously in the rest of Eurasia? The answer to these questions can be illuminated by considering three further subquestions: Was there demand in Asia for long-distance trade institutions of large magnitude, such as the business corporation? Was this demand supplied by organizational forms other than the corporation, which were its functional substitutes? What were the obstacles and resistance to the development or migration of the corporation in the Middle East, India, and China? Let us first examine what theories and methodologies we can utilize in order to address these questions.

THEORIES OF RESISTANCE TO MIGRATION: INTERCONNECTIVITY AND EMBEDDEDNESS

The literature on institutional evolution either ignores migration altogether or assumes that contact and interaction are a necessary and sufficient precondition for institutional migration. In chapter 2 we surveyed the theoretical frameworks for analyzing the endogenous evolution of institutions. In chapter 4 we advanced the framework for analyzing the migration of institutions. A major conclusion of this chapter and of the book as a whole is that understanding the obstacles and resistance to migration is crucial for understanding the diverse spread of different trade organizations.

Let us start by defining the conditions under which we should view nonmigration as resulting from resistance to migration. When observing differences in institutions between economies and regions, we should distinguish between four basic states of affairs. In the first state of affairs, the two analyzed regions present different demand for institutions, say, urban and rural societies, or economies that are self-sufficient and economies that are involved in overseas trades, or economies that are involved only in overland trade and those that are involved in maritime trade. This state of affairs is not relevant for us, as we are choosing to focus on regions that were involved in quite similar activity: maritime and overland long-distance Eurasian trade.

The second state of affairs is one in which the demand for organizational solutions is similar; the organizational forms used are different; and there is no knowledge or awareness in either region of the organizational forms used in the other. While the Maya of Mesoamerica benefited from a writing system, they were not and could not have been (given the combination of geography and technology) aware of the Mesopotamian writing system. This second state of affairs was possible in Eurasia only for a limited duration. By the period discussed in this book, 1400–1700, and with respect to long-distance trade, organizational knowledge eventually circulated throughout Eurasia with merchants and through interactions in hubs.

In the third scenario, the demand for institutions is also similar. In this third state of affairs, the same demand was fulfilled by different yet functionally equivalent institutions. The organizational forms in the different regions could be equally efficient in meeting the demands. In our trade context, if the corporation had full functional equivalents in other regions, possibly in the form of the Islamic *waqf* or the Chinese family clan, then the demand for trade organizations could be met by a different organizational supply. I identified the trade-related features offered by the business corporation and examined their performance in different institutions across other regions. If the demand was supplied by functionally equivalent organizations, then the issue is not resistance to migration. Economic performance is not affected. The same level of economic activity is achieved by resort to substitute organizations. In this chapter we will have to preclude this possible state of affairs. Before labeling the business corporation an embedded institution that follows the fourth scenario—that is, one that developed in only one region and did not migrate beyond it despite the existence of unsupplied demand for it in other regions, we should consider whether other organizational forms found in China, India, or the Middle East were its functional equivalents.

In the fourth scenario, there are similar institutional demands as well, but functionally equivalent institutions do not replace each other, thus the domestic institutions in one region are less efficient than those of the other region. There is knowledge and awareness of the existence of more efficient institutions in the other region, but there are blockages and resistance that nevertheless prevent them from simply being copied. The fourth state of affairs is the only one in which true embedded institutions are manifested. The ultimate embedded trade organizational form is the corporation. The rest of this section aims at identifying and distilling the causes of having embedded institutions rather than only migratory institutions. I will use contexts such as technology and mathematics to identify the causes of resistance to migration.

Differences in the environment can prevent migration even when needs are similar. To explain this notion let us take the simple example of nutrition and plant domestication. Within each geographical region, migration of plants was likely, whereas *across* regions it was not. The same functional needs, say, for basic nutrition, could be met by functionally equivalent plants or animals, without the actual migration of either. Each region had to find a solution to similar natural human dietary needs. They each found a different solution. Jared Diamond, a leading multidisciplinary researcher of indigenous development and migration, surveyed major crop domestication around the globe. He found that different plants were domesticated in different regions. Plants that were domesticated in the Fertile Crescent could not be transferred to the Americas because of the detachment between the continents. But neither could plants be carried to China, India, or Ethiopia, despite human contacts, because of the differences in the environment, climate, and soil. The same functional need to provide carbohydrates and calories was met by domesticating different plants in different regions: wheat in Western Asia, rice in China, teff (*Eragrostis tef*) and finger millet in Ethiopia, quinoa in the Andes, and corn in Mesoamerica.[1] This could be achieved either by learning about the concept of domestication or independently developing the same concept. We see, then, that it is sometimes easier to develop functional equivalents than to import plants, technologies, or organizational forms from a different environment or a different region.

The more complex the institution, the less likely it is to migrate wholesale. Writing systems demonstrate this. They include many symbols, often with fine details. The hieroglyphic Egyptian writing system is quite different from the cuneiform Sumerian system. The Sumerian system, which contained many hundreds of signs, could not immigrate to Egypt wholesale. Simpler writing systems, such as the Phoenician script, which contained only twenty-two letters, could travel more easily. The Hebrew, Greek, Latin, and Arabic scripts are minor mutations of it, all having roughly the same number of letters.[2] The ten-digit Indian-Arabic numerals traveled more widely through Eurasia than the Roman numerals or Chinese numerals. Food recipes are another example. Simple dishes such as *dal bhat* (rice with lentils) could migrate more easily than more complex dishes such as *mansaf*, whose preparation required, in addition to rice, the availability of lamb, yogurt, vegetables, herbs and spices, a pot, a large tray, and knowledge of the recipe.[3] In another example, while the basic idea of using wood and sails in ships was common throughout the Indian Ocean, the detailed design of ships was different in different regions. This was partly due to differences in the availability of raw materials and in sea conditions, but was also partly because copying the full details was more complicated. The same may apply to institutions. As we shall see, simpler institutions, such as the sea loan and the commenda, traveled more widely than the more organizationally complex corporation.

The more the importation of new technology or institutions threatened the existing political order, the more likely it was that their migration would be opposed and blocked by vested interests or the ruler. The printing block is an example of an innovation that could threaten both political rulers and religious orthodoxies, as it enhanced the circulation of ideas. The use of paper money could also challenge the control of political rulers over specie. The corporation could also pose a threat to rulers, as it offered the possibility of organizing religious or business entities that were separate from, and independent of, the state.

The more an institution or an organizational form is complemented by or interdependent with other institutions in that civilization, the less likely it is to migrate. Understanding the complementarity between innovations is crucial for understanding the migration of technologies as well as institutions. Domestication of plants was part of a wider Neolithic Revolution that transformed nomadic societies into sedentary societies. The zero and the Indian numerals are somewhat interdependent. So are the cannon and gunpowder. The business corporation was interconnected with the stock exchange.

Let us examine and sharpen these intuitions by examining the development of printing, its interplay with paper money and the political resistance to the importation of either or both. Printing was known in China by around the second century CE. By then, the Chinese had the three elements necessary for printing: paper, ink, and surfaces bearing texts. Block-printed books were first produced in China before 800 CE, and large-scale block-printing began in the tenth century. There is no dispute that paper money was used in China well before it arrived in Europe. The first time there is a significant reference to paper banknotes is during the reign of Tang emperor Hien Tsung (Xianzong, 805–20 CE). It appears that a severe shortage of copper led the emperor to invent this new form of money as a replacement. The Mongol empire adopted the paper money of China as a means to standardize the use of money throughout Asia. It traveled as far west as their Persia-centered Ilkhanate, which adopted paper money in 1295 for a short time.[4] The extensive issue of paper money in China caused hyperinflation, and after 1455 there is no further mention of the existence of paper money in circulation.[5]

Marco Polo brought knowledge of the use of paper money to Europe. On his return to Genoa in the late thirteenth century, Polo described the use of paper currency throughout Kublai Khan's empire.[6] The first clear description of printing that was made available to Europeans was in Rashid-al-Din Hamadani's *Compendium of Chronicles* (also known as *History of the World*), published in Persia very early in the fourteenth century and soon thereafter translated and circulated in Europe.[7]

Despite being exposed to both print and paper money through cultural brokers, Western Europe did not adopt either in its first encounter with them in the fourteenth century. It was not until the fifteenth century that

Europe was ready for printing, taking advantage of the small number of letters in its alphabet compared with the thousands of signs in Chinese. The modern printing press was invented by Johannes Gutenberg in Mainz, Germany, around 1440. Gutenberg produced the world's first movable-type printed book in 1456. Subsequently, although Europe already knew of the use of paper money in China, two centuries elapsed between the introduction of printing in Europe and the production of the first printed banknotes in Europe.[8]

The first issue of banknotes in Europe, by a Swedish bank in 1661, occurred eight hundred years after banknotes were first used in China, about two hundred years after their use in China stopped, and more than 350 years after their use in China was first reported in Europe.[9] Due to a currency shortage in the British colonies in North America, they turned to paper money with great enthusiasm in the late seventeenth century.[10] However, until the nineteenth century, coins remained the main currency in Europe and North America.

Let us return to the printing press. Despite the fact that China was the first to develop this technology, at least four centuries before the Gutenberg press, China made slower progress in the actual printing of books. In Europe, the printing press was in use in 110 towns within thirty years and in 236 towns within fifty years of its first introduction. The number of books printed in Europe in the eighteenth century is estimated at one billion. Most printing was done by private firms.[11] The multiplicity of political units in Europe prevented rulers who objected to the practice from effectively blocking its expansion, while its late arrival ensured the adoption of the more advanced moveable-print technology. In China, though book production expanded, it did so more slowly. It is estimated that the number of new book titles printed in late Ming China, nearly fifty annually, was still forty times lower than the number of new titles in Western Europe of the same period. The dominant technology remained block printing, while movable-font printing remained marginal. This, in part, resulted from the Chinese writing system that, due to having thousands of signs, was much less suitable for the movable press than the European twenty-six-letter alphabet.[12] The economics of the Chinese block-print technique, unlike the European moveable-print technique, lent itself to a large run of a small number of titles, often Confucian texts and state-sponsored titles, as favored by Chinese rulers.[13]

Some scholars argue that block printing was also invented independently in the Arab world in the ninth or tenth century. Others speculate that it arrived there from China. Either way, it persisted until no later than the fourteenth century and disappeared without leaving a significant trace.[14] When the printing press expanded in fifteenth-century Europe, the Ottoman sultan resisted its introduction in the Ottoman Empire. The motive for the resistance was a combination of theological and political concerns and the opposition of the manuscript-copiers interest group. Books were initially introduced by Sephardic Jews, Carmelites, and Armenians.[15] The expansion of the movable printing press in Arabic script really took place only in the nineteenth century; only then did printed books become available to the Arab and Ottoman subjects of the Ottoman Empire at large.[16]

This example demonstrates that in some cases the importation of an institutional innovation, such as paper money, is preconditioned on the importation and application of a technological innovation, such as the printing press, which was initially only remotely connected to it. There is a complementarity between different technologies, and between technologies and institutions, which affects migration patterns. But while the production of paper money relied on print technology, the demand for paper money was not simultaneous with the demand for print. Demand for the former was created only when other means of payment, currency and specie, were not effective. Printing technology, like our ultimate embedded institution, the corporation, touched a sensitive nerve among both religious and political authorities, which were concerned over the possible dissemination of heretical ideas, and thus encountered opposition in some civilizations. Also, paper money is related to sovereign power, and its introduction may be facilitated or objected to by rulers. But the opposition to the movable printing press and paper money was far from being uniform throughout Eurasia. The different timing and different level of opposition to the two inventions deeply affected migration patterns. This example clearly demonstrates that knowledge of the technology or of the institution, and the potential demand for it due to the efficiency gains that the printed book and paper money could offer, did not lead to the reception and adoption of either or both in tandem, due to political or religious opposition. Note that, due to complementarity between the printing press and paper money, opposition to the printing press prevented the importation of paper money even to civilizations that did not resist paper money, as such. The movable printing press and paper money thus remained embedded institutions–cum-technologies for several centuries because they were socially embedded and interconnected, and faced vested interests that opposed them. In the present project, interdependence appears in the interconnectivity between the corporate form, the stock exchange, and the politically credible commitment in the formation of the business corporation in Western Europe and its absence in other regions of Eurasia.

WHY WERE CORPORATIONS ABSENT IN THE ISLAMIC MIDDLE EAST?

Demand

The geographical challenges for the organization of long-distance trade, in terms of travel distances and maritime and overland accessibility, were less pronounced in the Middle East than in Europe or China. The Middle East was more conveniently located with access to the Mediterranean, the Indian Ocean, and the Silk Route. It was not as conveniently located as littoral India, which had immediate ocean access and was more centrally located. Middle Eastern traders had to go overland to the Red Sea or Persian Gulf and then sail through the Straits of Bab-el-Mandeb or Hormuz, which were at times blocked. But thanks to their location they did not need to go around the Cape of Good Hope, as did the Europeans. The optimal scale of Middle Eastern (and Indian) trade enterprises was smaller than that of European trade firms because of their proximity to the Asian markets.

Under the Umayyad Caliphate (661–750 CE), the trade of Islamic merchants expanded from a small-scale regional incense trade between Yemen and the Eastern Mediterranean to a large-scale trade stretching throughout the Middle East and beyond. The Abbasid Caliphate (750–1258) moved its capital to Baghdad and the main routes taken by its merchants to the Persian Gulf and Central Asia. The conquest of Baghdad by the Mongols in 1258 caused, according to most historians, the decline in the Arabs' use of the trade route leading from the Mediterranean to

Baghdad, Basra, Hormuz, and the Indian Ocean.[17] The Red Sea route rose at its expense. The Fatimid dynasty (909–1171), the Ayyubid dynasty (1171–1250 in Egypt), and the Mamluk Sultanate (1250–1517), whose center of gravity was in Egypt, served as the basis for traders active in the Red Sea and the Indian Ocean and connecting to the Mediterranean (such as the Geniza merchants). The Seljuk Empire (1037–1194) and its offspring, the Sultanate of Rum (1077–1307), provided their merchants with convenient overland connections to Central Asia and India.[18]

Generally speaking, Middle Eastern rulers refrained from direct involvement in Eurasian trade. They did not construct or equip ships, did not send armies or navies, and did not employ agents or traders to serve them. The support of these rulers for private merchants was mostly indirect, by allowing them access to maritime and overland Western ends of the Eurasian trade route. Another important role of the political rulers of the Middle East was in blocking the access of European merchants to Eurasian trade routes. Italian merchants were dominant in the Eastern Mediterranean, despite experiencing fluctuations in trade volume due to political and military upheavals, for example, before, during, and after the Crusades. In buoyant periods they could buy Asian goods in Antioch, Aleppo, Acre, or Alexandria, but their access to points further east, on the Silk Route and the Indian Ocean, was sporadic. Before the arrival of the Portuguese, the political rulers in the Middle East in fact provided Arab and Persian private merchants, through political means, with exclusivity of access to these Eurasian overland and maritime routes from the West. One exception in which the rulers played a direct and significant role is that of the sixteenth-century Ottoman Empire, to which we will turn shortly.

Private Arab and Persian merchants had traveled eastward throughout the history of Islam. Indeed, as we saw earlier, one could find Arab and Persian private merchants in large numbers in India, Indonesia, and Tang and Song China.[19] There are sporadic reports of a group of Jewish merchants, the Radhanites, according to which they traded over long routes, stretching from Western Europe to China. Their place of origin was probably in the Abbasid Caliphate and their heyday in the ninth and tenth centuries.[20] The Karimi merchants seem to have been the leading Middle Eastern long-distance merchants in the late Middle Ages.[21] They traveled with goods between Cairo (and possibly also other Middle Eastern cities) and Aden, the Malabar Coast of India, and even China. They specialized in the spice trade, but may have dealt with other goods as well. Their period of operation was between the twelfth and fifteenth centuries. The unifying characteristics of the Karimis are debated among historians. Some argue they were members of an ethnic group or a clan; others believe that any great merchant, any wealthy merchant, or any merchant trading in Asian goods was called a Karimi. Their form of organization is also debated. Some believe they united to form convoys to India; some view them as a guild or corporation (though providing no analysis of corporate features and no supporting evidence), others as sharing the same funduqs (for example, in Alexandria, Fustat, and Aden), and others still as wealthy individual merchants having no common organizational infrastructure and fiercely competing with each other. But there is a consensus among the handful of historians who have studied them that they were private merchants, self-financed entrepreneurs, not operating on behalf of the Ayyubid or Mamluk rulers of Egypt, and not even connected to the state as large landlords or tax farmers.[22]

The Ottoman Sultanate, which began as a small western Anatolian principality in 1299, became the ruler of the Middle East and an empire stretching from the gates of Vienna to Algiers and to Basra, Mecca, and Aden during the reigns of Selim I (1512–20) and Suleiman the Magnificent (1520–66). The Ottoman naval expeditions in the Indian Ocean in the sixteenth century were an exception in the history of Middle Eastern trade with Asia, which in most other periods was initiated by private merchants. This was not a case in which trade followed religion or immigration or led the way, but rather one in which the political flag set the pace and direction of events. The full scale of Ottoman state-run involvement in the Indian Ocean was only recently reconstructed by Giancarlo Casale, who wove together primary sources found in Ottoman and Portuguese archives.[23] After annexing Egypt in 1517, the Ottomans expanded further south to Mecca and Medina, Aden and Mocha in Yemen, and the East African coast. They also expanded to Baghdad, Basra, and the Persian Gulf coast. Suleiman, who commanded a large fleet in the Mediterranean, began constructing a fleet in Suez to serve his Red Sea and Indian Ocean ambitions. For the next several decades, Suez was the basis of what was initially called the Red Sea Fleet and was later known as the Indian Ocean Fleet. In 1538, a fleet of some ninety galleys sailed to India. Other naval expeditions left Suez in 1546 and 1548, with the aim of regaining control of the Red Sea from the Portuguese. The 1548 fleet recaptured Aden, captured Muscat, and gained control of Oman. It fought the Portuguese navy and the garrison of Hormuz, but was unable to fully capture the city. It captured Bahrain, and finally reached the Ottoman port of Basra. On its way back to the Red Sea, it became engaged in skirmishes with the Portuguese navy, lost ships, and ended up fleeing to India. A smaller fleet operating out of Mocha was able to capture several Portuguese merchant ships in various locations between Diu in Gujarat India and the East African coast. In parallel to their naval activity, the Ottomans also used diplomacy, trying to ally with Muslim rulers all the way to Aceh in Indonesia, encourage the operation of Ottoman merchant ships in small contingencies, and send small exploratory and cartographic expeditions.

The Ottoman state-operated maritime presence in the Indian Ocean subsided toward the end of the sixteenth century. One explanation for this was the Portuguese navy's superiority in ships, guns, navigation, and maritime tactics. This is not a fully convincing justification. The Ottomans did quite well; they sailed freely in the Sea of Arabia, and in some skirmishes they sunk and captured Portuguese ships. In others they lost only due to bad luck.[24] Another explanation is that the European faction in the sultan's court won over the Asian faction, and the Ottomans decided to invest their state military and financial recourses in the Balkans and Central Europe rather than in the Indian Ocean. The second explanation, in other words, is that the Ottomans did not want to be involved in Eurasian maritime trade. The first is that they wanted to be involved but failed militarily to support their trade. Either way, just as the Chinese rulers retreated from the Indian Ocean prior to the arrival of the Portuguese, the Ottomans retreated from the Indian Ocean shortly before the arrival of the English and Dutch corporations. One could not argue that the corporations were necessarily better organized for the task of long-distance maritime trade than were rulers of empires.

Cities, Guilds, Universities: The Building Blocks of the Corporation

To answer this question with respect to the sixteenth or seventeenth century, one has to go back in time and look for building blocks of the corporation in the earlier organizational history of the Middle East. The

Middle Easterners did not search for new constitutional frameworks for organizing their religion, cities, guilds, and universities, as did the Europeans in the late Middle Ages. The fact that religion was not separate from the state, that cities were not autonomous enclaves within states, and that higher education was not conducted independently of state and religious organizational frameworks reduced the demand for new organizational forms.

In Islam, neither cities nor schools were in search of innovative organizational forms. Cities were neither independent political units nor even distinct subunits of governance. The Greek city-state tradition evaporated in the Middle East before the rise of Islam. Territory-based provinces that comprised both cities and rural areas were the administrative units. As much as there was some level of internal organization in cities, it was initiated from above as a means to more effectively extract taxes from city dwellers. City councils were organized by caliphs and sultans with the purpose of achieving collective responsibility of city elders for tax payment, not as self-governing juridical or political institutions.[25] The most important point for our purposes is that Islamic cities did not develop corporate institutions, and they did not need to.

A similar analysis applies for guilds. Islamic merchants and craftsmen were much less organized than their late medieval European counterparts. With time, Islamic merchant and craftsmen organizations slowly evolved. But in the period relevant for us, the couple of centuries before the development of the first Western European merchant corporations, Islamic merchant and craft associations had no distinct corporate features.[26] The same was true of religious schools, such as madrasas. In the early Islamic centuries, these were often state owned. When their independence grew, they relied on the waqf, to which we will soon turn, as their organizational platform.[27]

Overall, the lack of demand for autonomous and complex organizational forms for cities, madrasas, and guilds in the Islamic Middle East reduced the demand for institutional innovation in these realms. This is not to suggest that Islamic cities, guilds, or madrasas were not vibrant. They definitely were, in the heyday of Islam. Were they the focal point of innovation, as European cities arguably were? Or were they unconducive to economic development? This debate is not for me to resolve here. What is important for my argument is that, due to their organizational structure, no demand formed for developing protocorporate or corporate institutions in late medieval Islam. The notion of corporate personality did not develop in Islam.[28] The city, the university, and the guild were, along with the Catholic Church, the breeding ground of the Southern and Western European corporation. As a legal entity detached from individuals, the corporation was not recognized in Islamic legal texts; nor was it used in Arab civilizations for semipublic purposes. The fact that corporations were not developed in Islam in the semipublic context curtailed their development in the business context in the early modern period.

The Waqf

The Islamic waqf is relevant for our discussion in several ways, as highlighted by Timur Kuran. Some argue that the waqf was a quasi corporation. Others argue that, though different from the corporation in its features and structure, it was a functional substitute for the corporation, at least in the latter's semipublic fields of activity. Did the waqf serve as the corporation's functional equivalent in long-distance trade as well? Did it facilitate long-distance trade in ways that were different from that of the corporation? Is it perhaps relevant for us because it hindered the development of the corporation in Islam?

Characteristics

A waqf was created under Islamic law by a founder—a Muslim who endowed land or other immovable property. The act of endowment separated the waqf property from the founder's privately owned property, granted its ownership to God, and defined the consumption of its usufruct perpetually.[29] The purpose of the foundation of the waqf had to be considered charitable or pious, not profit making, and the property given to it was, in principle, inalienable. The waqf's purpose was advanced by enjoyment of the property itself (albeit in a manner that would not consume it) or of the income generated by utilization of the property. A caretaker (*mutawalli*)—or trustee, if we use trust analogy—was initially appointed by the founder, and in future generations according to the founder's instructions. The caretaker's role was to oversee the waqf's property, implement the purpose of the waqf, and make sure that the waqf's beneficiaries received their share of the usufruct.[30]

What was the legal status of the waqf's property? The beneficiaries were not the owners of the property; similarly, the caretaker held it in trust but did not own it. The common interpretation in the Hanafi school of Islamic law was that the property was not owned by anyone; it was God's property, as long as it remained waqf property. Though some modern scholars argue that the waqf was a separate, property-owning legal entity, this view is not grounded in history and is rejected by most scholars.[31]

The waqf is classified into two groups, depending on the purpose for which its revenue is applied: *waqf ahli* (family *waqf*) and *waqf khayri* (charitable endowment). In the family waqf, the revenue is devoted to the descendants of the founder.[32] In the charitable waqf, the revenue is devoted to the expansion and maintenance of public institutions. Another classification of the institution is the distinction between *land* waqf and *cash* waqf. The land waqf is more passive. The cash waqf can also be utilized to fund projects considered beneficial for society. The endowed cash can be invested or loaned out to earn income, and target projects are financed by earned income.[33]

History

Philanthropic endowments, possibly forerunners of the waqf, have a history considerably older than Islam, and it is very likely that Islam was influenced by somewhat similar institution in earlier civilizations, such as ancient Mesopotamia, Greece, Rome, the Byzantine Empire, or Sassanid Persia.[34] It is generally accepted that the waqf did not exist in pre-Islamic Arabian law. The Quran makes no explicit mention of the concept of the waqf.[35] The waqf in its Islamic form appeared about a century after the birth of Islam, in the middle of the eighth century, and increasingly came into use in the ninth through twelfth centuries.

Function

The waqf was used, as we have seen, for two basic purposes, private and charitable. The founder of the waqf could entrust its management to whomsoever he chose, including his offspring. The founder of a family waqf could stipulate that its caretaker (*mutawalli*) would earn a handsome salary, could appoint himself as the first *mutawalli*, and, in that capacity, could hire his relatives as salaried employees of the waqf. He could channel much of his family's wealth to the waqf and devote its resources to enhancing his and his family's financial well-being and security. The foremost use of the private waqf was for bypassing the rigid rules of Islamic inheritance law that considerably restricted the testator's discretion, limited the bequests to one third of the estate, and required equal division of the rest of the estate between legal heirs. The waqf provided flexibility in intergenerational transfer of wealth, allowing property to be held in one pool (rather than having it dissolved over time into ever-diminishing pools of assets), achieving the equivalent of primogeniture.[36] This kind of private use also enabled the founder to use the waqf to shield property from taxation and expropriation.

Over time, the waqf was also increasingly used for its second major role, semipublic purposes, and for the provision of public goods, such as the building and running of mosques, hospitals, bathhouses, religious schools (madrasas and *zawiyas*), and other social and charitable services.[37] As we have seen, it was used for the construction and maintenance of khans and caravanserais that served the Silk Route and other trade routes.[38] The waqf was the legal organizational form that supported these essential infrastructures that, in turn, facilitated overland Eurasian trade.

Though the waqf did not embody all the characteristics of the corporation, the two did have some features in common. The waqf allowed the holding of a separate pool of assets, implying both perpetual holding of property and a degree of entity shielding of the assets from creditors of the beneficiaries. It enabled the separation of ownership from control and the employment of agents. Its formation, like the chartering of a corporation, was a device for credible commitment by the ruler not to expropriate its property. However, it did not constitute a property-owning institution in a fuller sense that includes full transferability of that property. It did not provide governance or decision-making bodies, and its activities, more than those of a corporation, were constrained by the "dead hand" of its creator. There were practical ways to circumvent the creator's instruction, but the legality of these practices was questionable. A waqf could not expressly assume profit-making business purposes, and the interests in a waqf could not be traded in a stock market or otherwise. Ultimately, then, the waqf did not provide a full substitute for the corporation.

MIGRATION

The waqf spread from its place of origin in the Middle East. It was used not only by Arabs, but also by Iranians, Turks, Slavic Muslims, and even non-Muslim minorities in these regions.[39] By the twelfth century it had arrived in India. Even Hindus picked up the terminology and used it to describe their own endowments.[40]

The origin of the English trust has long been a subject of debate between legal historians. Early and fragmented evidence for the usage of the predecessor of the trust, called the use, as a means of evading taxation appears in the thirteenth century, with more considerable evidence accumulating for the fourteenth century. Most scholars debated whether the origins of the trust could be found in Roman law, Germanic law, a combination of the two, or the unique circumstances of feudal Norman England.[41] More recently, several scholars have pointed out that the waqf and the trust share similarities in terms of function and form, and have speculated that the origin of the English trust can be found in the concept of the waqf.[42] The period during which the trust first showed up in England corresponds with the height of popularity and usage of the family waqf in the Middle East. The English trust resembles the family waqf, not the charitable endowment for the provision of semipublic services. This resemblance could be explained by the timing of the alleged link between the waqf and the trust, which existed before charitable waqfs were widely used.

Three possible geographical links have been suggested for the migration of the waqf to Europe and eventually to England: via Spain, via Sicily, and via the Holy Land. In Spain, Christian and Muslim civilizations neighbored and, in some regions, even coexisted during the long Reconquista. This was an opportunity for learning about Islamic practices, including that of the waqf. Sicily can be regarded as a link because it was invaded by Normans, just as was England in the relevant period. The Normans of Sicily could have learned about the waqf from the Fatimid, because the island was ruled by Muslims for more than two centuries before the Norman conquest, and knowledge of the trust could have been transferred to England by the Normans. A third possible link is the Crusaders. Franciscan friars returning from the Crusades in the thirteenth century were looking for a means to commit to a life without property. At the same time, they wanted to maintain collective property, at the command of their order. The Templars feature in another version of this third link.[43] Whatever the linkage, it has to account for the fact that the idea of the waqf was planted in England while entirely skipping continental Europe.

The resolution of this dispute about the origins of the trust is beyond the scope of the present book. What is of particular interest for us are the parallels between this debate and that surrounding the origins of the Italian commenda.[44] Though the two debates unfolded entirely separately, both the timing and geography of the migration and the methodology for trying to identify the origins and links (morphological similarities, timing, agents) are analogous in both cases. The difference is that the commenda was transplanted on the continent, in civil law jurisdictions, while the waqf was transplanted in England, a common law jurisdiction. The debates would definitely benefit from conversation with each other.

In sum, the waqf was a migratory institution, apparently in modified form, within Islamic civilization—and was, to a debatable extent, also beyond it. Its pattern of migration was somewhat similar to that of the funduq, more limited than that of the commenda (which reached all of Europe to the Baltics and China), and, in a way, diametrically opposite to that of the sea loan.

Institutional Dynamics

The basic business-organizational unit in the Islamic Middle East was the family. This form is to be found in the records of Quseir al-Qadim, a Red Sea Port in Egypt. It is to be found in the Cairo Geniza records, which reflect Jewish practices but are believed by most scholars to reflect the surrounding Muslim practices as well.[45] Both of these sources were surveyed in previous chapters as part of our case studies. Kuran argued that the communal and family-oriented vision of early Islam disfavored the introduction of larger and more formal social and organizational forms.

Larger impersonal entities could end in factionalism of the kind that is unlikely to emerge in family- and tribe-based entities. Furthermore, demand for an institution that would serve large-scale business enterprises did not develop, because inheritance and partnership law splintered business entities in the Islamic Middle East into small economic and social fragments. Atomistic enterprises were unable to act collectively to lobby political and legal elites to introduce corporate forms of organization.[46]

When the need arose to exceed the boundaries of the family, say, to enable long-distance travel, to avoid physical risk, or to cross cultural and linguistic barriers, the family employed commissioned agents, usually in destination ports, and commenda agents, usually as itinerant agents. Muslim merchants usually traded within their own capital; they did not borrow money in the form of sea loans, due to the strict Islamic prohibition on usury. In Indian Ocean trade, Middle Eastern merchants could also make use of the services of nakhuda—the person, distinct from the captain, in charge of goods and mercantile and financial activities on board ship. This institution, unique to the Indian Ocean, allowed merchants to freight unaccompanied goods. In overland trade, Middle Eastern traders, many of them itinerant traders, could benefit from a well-spread chain of funduqs, khans, and caravanserais stretching from Spain and North Africa to Central Asia and beyond. These buildings-cum-institutions were owned and operated in many locations by waqfs.

The direct involvement of rulers in the Eurasian trade of Middle Easterners was very rare, with the exception of the sixteenth-century Ottomans. This could be explained by the political friction in the region. It could also be explained by the geographical accessibility and by the low financial entry barriers. Individuals and families could trade without the need to resort to state support.

What can explain the fact the corporation did not develop in the Middle East? The first explanation is that there was simply no demand for the corporate form. Family-based organization, expanded by agents, commenda, and the like enabled trade to flourish for many centuries.[47] The second possible explanation is that there was demand but no supply. Islam as a religion was not organized separately from rulers and states, and did not develop a separate constitution for its religious institutions. Islamic law did not recognize corporate entities. No corporate building blocks were formed within Islamic law because cities, academic institutions, and guilds were not independent from rulers and territorial administration. Islamic rulers were not willing to open up a space between their sovereign powers, on the one hand, and society, on the other, in which institutions separated from both the state and the family could exist for long durations without the threat of expropriation by the state.[48]

A third potential explanation, related to the second, is that as much as there was demand, it was met by institutional supply, but the supply set Islam on a path that did not lead to the corporate form. When demand for organizing activities with semipublic purposes first emerged in Islamic civilization, it was supplied by the waqf because the waqf, introduced early in the history of Islamic civilization, was already available. There was no need to invent a new corporate form. The waqf was gradually adapted from private, family purposes to charitable and semipublic purposes. Because of this, no demand emerged in the Islamic Middle East for indigenously developing or importing the corporation to organize activities promoting such business purposes. By using the waqf for semi-public purposes, Middle Eastern Muslims did not have to encounter the absence of the corporation until the early modern era. However, the structure of the waqf had rigidities that prevented it from being adapted to adequately match the full scale of semipublic institutions.[49]

Institutional responses to changing demand were different in different regions. When the need arose, the waqf was not suited to for-profit business purposes. The Chinese family lineage was more amenable to adaptation for business ends than was the waqf. It was increasingly used for business purposes, including maritime trade, by the time of the Ming dynasty. Parallels between the waqf and the trust are striking. The trust, which was debatably an offspring of the waqf, was initially designed for dealing, in the context of the family, with the holding of land and its intergenerational transfer. When the need arose to use the trust for holding intangible property and for organizing for-profit businesses, the adaptation process was slow and painful. It was in progress by the middle of the nineteenth century, but by then the corporation had bypassed it. So the similar path of the waqf and the trust proved to show less flexibility than the paths of the corporation and family lineage. The reasons for the different level of flexibility of different institutions are partly inherent to the institutional configuration of features, and are partly a result of the interaction with outside pressures for change and resistance to change.

The discussions in this book provide initial explanations. But much more can be achieved once the question is on the research agenda.

Although demand for a new institution for business and trade purposes did appear by the seventeenth and eighteenth centuries, the people of the Middle East were already locked in to the waqf path. The waqf had an early start compared to the corporation. As a result, by the time the corporation emerged in Europe and became available for importation to the Arab-Islamic civilization, much of the institutional demand by semipublic organizations was already supplied by the waqf. This is a path-dependency explanation.[50]

Up until the sixteenth century, Middle Easterners did well with their organizational menu. In the sixteenth century, the Ottomans were still neck and neck with the Portuguese in the Western Indian Ocean. The usefulness of the corporation to long-distance Eurasian trade was demonstrated by the VOC and the EIC only in the seventeenth century. Even then, there was only slow appreciation of the contribution of institutional factors to northwestern European success. Even when Arab and other Middle Eastern merchants recognized the advantages of the corporation, they could not introduce it without some support from the political and legal elite. By the time the advantages of the corporation were fully appreciated by wider circles of merchants and by rulers, European corporations already dominated Eurasian trade. It took the Ottomans two more centuries to fully appreciate the need for the corporate form and to overcome political and legal resistance to it. The first predominantly Muslim-owned joint-stock company in the Ottoman Empire was formed by Sultan Abdülmecid in Istanbul in 1851.[51] It was based on the European model, not on adaptation of an Islamic institution. Only then did the corporation migrate into the Middle East region.

WHY NO CORPORATIONS IN INDIA?

Corporations were introduced to India only very late, in 1866, as a colonial transplant from Britain.[52] Why was the corporation not developed indigenously in India before the arrival of Europeans? Why did the Indians not copy the model of the European corporation once they witnessed the success in India of the EIC and VOC, starting in 1600?

India was the most advantageously located of the four major regions discussed in this book. To use Abu-Lughod's words, it was "on the way to everywhere."[53] Its ports were on the Arabian Sea and the Bay of Bengal. Its merchants did not have to sail for more than one season to reach Persia, Arabia, or East Africa, or, going the other way, the Indonesian archipelago or Southeast Asia. Their access to the Indian Ocean did not depend on political circumstances outside of India. They could not be blocked in the Middle East, as were the Europeans, or in Red Sea and Persian Gulf straits, as were the Arabs. India's central location and easy access also had the reverse effect, making its ports accessible to foreign merchants.

In addition, because of its tropical location, Southern India was an exporter of goods that could not be produced in the other three major regions of Eurasia. Spices, particularly pepper, attracted maritime merchants from more northern locations such as the Middle East and China. Middle Eastern merchants sold spices in their own markets and also served as intermediaries in the supply of pepper and spices to Europe.[54] India was less of an importer because much of its consumption could be grown and produced somewhere in the Indian subcontinent. Indian merchants were only rarely to be found in China, while Arabs and Chinese were often recorded in India. After the fall of the Song dynasty and the takeover of Southern China by the Yuan dynasty, Chinese merchants were restricted from traveling to India, and Arabs rose to dominance in the Indian maritime trade. Abu-Lughod asserts that wealth, rather than poverty, kept India from playing a more active role in the world trade system.[55] These two reasons made the Indians' need to develop long-distance maritime trade superfluous in some eras, along with the organizational capabilities related to it.

The more powerful Indian political entities of our period, the Delhi Sultanate and the Mughal Empire, were centered in the plains of Northern India. They had strong familial, cultural, and religious connections with Turkic, Persian, Mongol, and Timurid dynasties in Central Asia. They were not oriented toward the Indian Ocean and were only marginally interested in maritime trade. To the extent they were interested in maritime trade, this was confined to activity in the ports of Gujarat, notably Surat, after its annexation in 1573, and to a lesser extent the ports of Bengal, after its annexation in 1576.[56] Delhi, the Punjab, and Sind were connected to Afghanistan, Central Asia, and Persia via overland routes, some of them connecting to the east-west Silk Route. The overland trade was conducted by private merchants, some peddling, some employing agents and commenda partners, and relied on diaspora communities and on social networks.[57]

South Indian Hindu rulers were more oriented toward oceanic maritime trade. But, by our period, they lacked the political power, economic resources, and motivation to be involved in long-distance overseas trade on a large scale. A notable earlier exception is that of the Tamil Chola dynasty. In the eleventh century, its kings launched naval expeditions from their Coromandel Coast ports to Sri Lanka, the Maldives, Burma, the Malay Peninsula, and Sumatra. The evidence for these expeditions in inscriptions is so sporadic and indirect that a few historians doubt they ever occurred. But recently some support was found for Indian presence in Southeast Asia in archeological findings from the region and in the Chinese sources. Among those who assert the expeditions did take place, a few argue that these were merely political and military expeditions, but most view them as commercially motivated.[58] They were the Cholas' attempt at the Indian Ocean trade, a response to the arrival of merchants from Song China and Fatimid Egypt in Southern India.[59]

The absence of control or direct involvement by territorial rulers and the low entry barriers allowed individual merchants and family firms to engage in maritime trade. The family firms of Virji Vora and Mulla Abdul Ghafur, already discussed in the chapter on the family firm, are good examples of the upper end of these organizational forms.[60]

Did Indian civilization develop indigenously more complex organizational forms such as guilds and corporations? This debate goes back to Weber, who argued that the caste, the basic Indian societal organizational structure (which was based on Hindu religion), determined social position and occupation, and left no space for voluntary associations. Weber's argument has since been disproved by sociologists who today view the caste as varying considerably over time and space, as applying to non-Hindus, and as creating primarily endogamous groups and a sense of affinity that did not predetermine occupation.[61]

The more recent literature recognizes the existence of endogenous guilds in medieval India. Names such as the *Nanadesi* guild, the *Manigramam* guild, and the *Five Hundred Lords of Ayyavolu* guild are often mentioned in the literature.[62] But there is no consensus as to the organizational structure of Indian merchant guilds. Some view them as a means for rulers to collect taxes from merchants. Others view them as basic informal communal units, either connected or unconnected to the family clan or the caste.[63] Scholars infer, based on fragments from ancient Hindu texts and inscriptions, that Indian merchant associations exhibited features similar to those of European guilds. These included formation based on a charter from the ruler, self-regulation, and corporate entity.

Davis found evidence for corporate groups in the ancient Dharma-śāstra.[64] Khanna holds the *sreni* to be an Indian corporate form that existed from ancient times to the Islamic invasion.[65] The *sreni* organized craftsmen and merchants in the Indian subcontinent, and was an association of persons rather than capital or property. Each *sreni* organized an identified branch in a defined locality, and was similar in some respects to the European guild. Khanna claimed that the *sreni* was, in fact, a predecessor of the business corporation,[66] but there is no evidence that it was actually used for the same range of functions as the corporation. Other scholars do not attribute such features or even an important role to the *sreni*. The texts and inscriptions often refer to donations and dedications to temples, and it is argued that one cannot read too much into them in terms of guild- or corporate-like organizational features of the donating community or association. According to Arasaratnam, the concept of joint stock was being used in some forms already in the merchant guilds of the fourteenth through sixteenth centuries. The fall of the Vijayanagara empire, under which the guilds had flourished, led to the destruction of the institution, leaving individual merchants operating on their own.[67]

As the European investment in Indian trade increased during the seventeenth century, trade expanded and became more routine and more closely linked to the needs of European markets. There was a trend of Indian merchants grouping into joint-stock companies that were inspired by the older organizational form to manage the supply of textiles to the Europeans.[68] Brennig indicates that these partnerships were not indigenous and were established as an effort on the part of the Europeans to improve the trade. This constituted an attempted transplantation of a European commercial institution.[69]

We can learn from Lucassen, De Moor, and van Zanden regarding significant differences between European and Indian guilds that might explain why the latter did not evolve into corporations. European guilds were permanent, in time achieving corporate entity, and were city-based organizations of individuals with similar occupations that were recognized (eventually by way of charters) by political rulers. One of their main purposes was to defend and maintain trade monopoly rights. They played a central role in influencing European urban politics, culture, society, and economy.[70] Indian guilds arguably did not exhibit such characteristics; they were neither based on a corporate governance structure nor on a commitment in the form of a charter issued by a ruler.

The current state of research does not support a conclusion that India developed an organizational form that was a functional equivalent to the business corporation or a form that was on a developmental path to becoming similar, in its features, to the European corporation. There was no Indian equivalent to the Chinese family lineage or the Islamic waqf. This can be explained by the absence of pressure to take institutions to new frontiers. Due to India's location and limited demand for imported goods, trade could be conducted perfectly well by family firms. Exports were dominated in the first centuries of the second millennium by the Arabs and Chinese, and after 1500 by the Portuguese, all of whom had access to Indian ports. Chinese and Western Europeans had to stretch their institutional barriers when searching for tropical goods from a starting point in the western Atlantic and China. To conclude, the Indians did not have the impetus to develop the corporation, because they were entirely well positioned and well served without it.

WHY NO CORPORATIONS IN CHINA?

The Demand Side

China, a huge and prosperous economy, was in most respects self-sufficient and did not rely heavily on the importation of goods. It imported spices, pepper, and a few other tropical goods from the Indonesian archipelago and Southeast Asia more broadly. It imported silver from wherever it could source it, primarily Japan and the Americas (via Europe or Manila).[71] It could export a variety of goods, from silk to porcelain. But in most periods, the central rulers of China were able to provide subsistence to their subjects based on availability of goods within their own empire.

When contacting foreign countries, either for political patronage or for their goods, the Chinese emperors often decided that international exchange of goods would take the tributary format, based on rituals and political format, rather than using the market-mediated, for-profit format.[72] They could decide how to share the tributary system to allow luxury goods into China and provide the opportunity for added profits for those wishing to export from China.

The Song rulers further developed an institution that had originated in the Tang era for that purpose, the Office of Maritime Affairs, headed by a high-ranking government official. The office was in charge of managing China's connections with other countries—receiving foreign tribute missions, checking incoming merchandise, assessing its value, and charging a customs tax. The government had the right of first refusal on merchandise, and private merchants could only buy what the government passed on. Only the foreign merchants who went through this official process were allowed to trade freely along the Chinese coast, and only the handful of ports in which such an office was established could be frequented by foreign merchants. The Office of Maritime Affairs was also in charge of purchasing all the Chinese products to sell them collectively to the foreign merchants. Quanzhou, in Fujian; Hangzhou, in the Yangtze River Delta; and Guangzhou, on the Pearl River in the South, are prime examples of port cities with such offices serving as hubs of long-distance trade. Foreign tribute missions began to frequent these ports in Song times.

In addition to the official missions, the Chinese rulers encouraged the development of international maritime trade. Foreign ships began frequenting these ports in growing numbers. Most foreign merchants who came to Quanzhou and Guangzhou originated in Srivijaya kingdom (Java) and Champa (Vietnam). However, ships also arrived from more distant locations, such as India, Persia, and the Arab world. Over time, significant diaspora Muslim communities settled in these ports, serving as agents and brokers of foreign maritime merchants. The foreigners in the port cities of Southeast China settled for the most part in designated neighborhoods known as *fanfang*.[73]

Non-Han dynasties, notably the Yuan, not only encouraged foreigners in China, but prohibited the Chinese from going abroad. They did so to weaken the economic and political power of Han Chinese merchants, preferring to ally with foreigners. There was a significant inflow of Muslims to China in Yuan times, overland from the territories in the west conquered by the Mongols, and on ships, as privileged merchants. Muslims dominated both overland and maritime trade during the Yuan, curtailing the development of Chinese long-distance trade institutions.

When China made its own leap into trading around the Bay of Bengal and the Arabian Sea, led by Zheng He in the early Ming period (early fifteenth century), it was the state, not individual merchants or merchant organizations, that served as the organizer of these massive long-ranging voyages.[74] Thereafter, the Ming rulers reversed their foreign and mercantile policy, turning to one of closure and isolation and denying Chinese merchants free access to overseas markets. Whatever the demand for foreign goods, and whatever the political attitude toward foreign trade, the location of China at the far eastern flank of Eurasia required Chinese merchants on export trips to travel long distances.

The Supply Side

THE CHINESE STATE

The population of the Chinese state was larger than that of all the European states put together. Portugal had a population of about one million at the beginning of our period,[75] the Netherlands just over two million, and England around three million,[76] compared to a Chinese population of nearly ninety million.[77] The tax base of China was also of a different magnitude, as was its civil-service- and examinations-based bureaucracy. The two features together created a significant state capacity to impose taxation, pool together resources, and make use of tax revenue.[78]

Thus, China had the viable option of conducting its long-distance trade based on the supply of capital, staff, and organizational structure by the ruler. And indeed, as we have seen, it used this ability for financing and organizing the huge voyages of Zheng He, which went as far as the Western Indian Ocean.[79] But the reliance on a capable state platform did not relieve the Chinese enterprise of all problems. The magnitude of its aspirations was such that even tax-based finance created backlashes. The involvement of the emperor and his senior court eunuch led to the mixing of business and political motivations, aims, and accounts. The Chinese ruler operated trade-cum-tributary voyages led by Zheng He—like the Portuguese ruler-operated Carreira da Índia—were redistributive and nonrational, in Steensgard's (and Weber's and Polanyi's) terms. They engaged in trade but were neither profit maximizers nor shareholder owned.

The presence of a bureaucratic state overshadowed the private sector. Smaller partnerships, major family firms, and even lineage corporations could rely on state-provided infrastructures. At times, as the case of the Pu lineage demonstrates, there was a strong symbiosis between the state and the family framework. The same person could serve, at the same time, as head of the Office of Maritime Affairs *and* as manager of the family business, the two functions being inseparable.[80]

THE CHINESE FAMILY LINEAGE ORGANIZATION

The Chinese kinship organization, sometimes called the lineage corporation, is considered by some historians, anthropologists, and even legal scholars as the Chinese variant of the corporation.[81] According to a second version, it was a Chinese functional equivalent of the European business corporation—equivalent in function but not in form. Was the lineage corporation an endogenous institution based on the universally available extended family or a unique institution embedded in Chinese civilization?

Lineage is a fundamental element of Chinese society. Extended families, comprising more than one generation of adults, were common in many civilizations. The lineage was a more complex societal form than the extended family found in other societies. Ever since Freedman called attention to lineage in 1958, it has been considered by anthropologists, sociologists, and historians as a cornerstone of Chinese society.[82] To understand it, we need to concisely survey the history and attributes of lineage.

There is a historiographical debate as to whether lineage developed organically and gradually, from below, out of the family structure, or was invented from above as part of the neo-Confucian revival, as a means for the court and the civil servants to monitor and control rural society in the provinces and to marginalize Buddhism. In theory, individuals on the same genealogical patrilineal line who maintained significant social relationships were considered members of the same lineage. Members of the same lineage usually lived near each other, in the same community, village, or set of villages. But some social historians and anthropologists argue that lineages were constructed in retrospect to include kin and nonkin alike. They show that family genealogies were invented to establish common ancestral origins for families with similar surnames, for the purpose of promoting solidarity and maintaining public order.[83]

Whichever way lineages were formed, the core bond of a lineage was ancestral worship, which was rooted in Buddhism, Taoism, and earlier protoreligions. What followed was a prototypical organizational and financial form of the lineage.[84] All members of the lineage, and only the members, worshipped the same ancestors. Ancestor worship took place on lower levels as well, in the family, the branch, and the sublineage. However, the lineage-level worship was the most important because it represented the widest circle connected to the same ancient ancestor. The worship ceremony involved gathering in ancestral halls, admission of the ancestor's spirit tablet, making sacrifices, and other rituals. The construction and maintenance of ancestral halls was funded by credit associations, which raised money in the form of donations or in some cases by charging for services.

Individual families contributed the money, and credit associations pooled it together, but who would own the newly created pool once invested in real property? The assets of the lineage (ancestral halls, temples, genealogical lists, and other resources needed for worship) were built and held by the lineage. Some anthropologists (Cohen, for example) refer to this property as *corporate property* and to the lineage as a *corporate entity*.[85] Historians, more cautious when using Western legal terminology outside Europe, and lawyers, more aware of the legal features of corporations, term them *lineage estates* or *lineage trusts*. In any case, the lineage organization held property separately from individuals and families.

Initially, the only common property held by lineages was related to ancestral halls. With the passage of time, income-generating land was also held, followed by more movable, liquid, and intangible assets accumulated in the lineage's pool of common assets. Gradually, the lineage organization assumed political, military, charitable, and educational functions in addition to the traditional religious and social functions. In the economic context, the lineage was first used in support of agriculture and as a sort of mutual insurance. Wealthier lineages that held more liquid common property gradually became active also in manufacturing and trade.[86]

In recent decades, several historians studied the family lineage as a framework for organizing business. I will begin by showing how it was used to organize production, and then move to trade. Zelin, one of the pioneers of the field, studied long-lasting salt production firms such as Fu-Rong salt yard in Zigong, in Sichuan, between the late eighteenth century and the early twentieth century.[87] She shows that lineage trusts were explicitly formed as a way to pool together and incorporate business property and separate it from household property and from daily consumption, even though the language of formation was that of ritual and ancestor worship. Here, all members of the households who invested in the salt well (the heart of the salt yard development project) and their subsequent descendants became shareholders in the trust. Profits, after subtracting for business expenses and a rough calculation that we can identify as depreciation, were distributed annually among the shareholders. While lineage trusts, as such, continued to be based on membership in the lineage, which was determined by birth or marriage and was closed to outsiders, they bought and sold salt-manufacturing shares and developed portfolios that included both wholly owned family firms and shares in a variety of nonkin ventures.

Pomeranz studied the Yutang Company, a maker of soy sauce, pickled vegetables, and various specialty foods in Jining, a Grand Canal port in southwestern Shandong province, in the period 1779–1956.[88] He showed how a lineage-based family firm was able to function throughout several generations, developing large-scale production and operation while allowing the lineage to maintain its status and remain firmly established in officialdom and the landed elite.

Billy So, in his examination of the case of two lineages of different standing in South Fukien, takes us to maritime trade and concludes that reliance on a cohesive and wealthy lineage provided an enormous advantage. Merchants coming from such lineages could raise capital for maritime ventures within the lineage. They were also considered more credible by outside equity investors, joint venture partners, and creditors. These outside investors could turn to the lineage for mediation and compensation in case of failure or dispute. Merchants from respectable lineages were more determined to protect their reputation; a merchant from an eminent lineage was much less likely to flee the homeland, leave behind unpaid debts, and settle elsewhere.[89] The family lineage lowered the risk of investment by outsiders in the maritime venture and lowered the financial costs; and it was gradually transformed into an institution that provided an infrastructure for individual merchants.

Faure studied the relationship between lineage and business in the Pearl River Delta and particularly the Guangzhou region. He documents the use of contractual instruments, lineage trusts, and shareholding in the eighteenth century as tools used by the lineage framework for business purposes.[90] McDermott studied Huizhou, also located in the Pearl River Delta but in Guangdong province. He shows how institutions emerged out of older lineages, such as ancestral halls and credit associations of commercial partnerships, in the form of what he identifies as commenda-like contracts, agency partnerships, and joint-share partnerships. The merchants studied by McDermott took two older forms: lineage forms, on the one hand, and partnership forms, on the other, blending them together from the late Ming era. According to McDermott's analysis, the lineage provided solutions to business organization problems such as the longevity and management of assets that were pooled together. He did not identify limitation of liability of the partners or a resort to a formal market in shares.[91]

The connection between lineage and economic activity is manifested in different ways in all of these studies. It varied over time, between regions, and across sectors. I would like to tentatively suggest that it could take place on three levels. The first was that of the association between members of the lineage, based on the fact that they were kin and relatives. Their bonding took place without any resort to the lineage's evolving institutional structure. On this level we observe an informal association much like those of any traditional extended family. The second level was reliance on credit associations—a reliance on preexisting pools of assets that were jointly owned by members of the lineage. At this level we see mutual activity on the borderline between charity and business. The third was a reliance on a common pool of assets owned by the lineage itself as quasi-corporate property. Business-related property was owned by the lineage. The lineage allowed, it is argued, not only the owning of common property, but also the formation of a concentrated locus of management, the appointment of agents, and the division of profits. For our needs, the third level of connection between the lineage and economic activity is the most relevant. The literature does not always clearly distinguish between this and the second level. More needs to be understood about the relationship, and further studies are likely to clarify it.

The institution of the family lineage was used in economic contexts to promote cooperation, pool assets, spread risks, concentrate the management function into the hands of a few, split profits, and marginalize nonproductive family members.[92] Zhenman indicates that these objectives were achieved by a combination of lineage-shaping strategies, including marriage alliances, adoption, family naming, the invention of common ancestors, the disjointing of a branch from a lineage, and the conferring of property to the lineage's ancestral estate.[93] He argues that by the Ming era, some of the richer and more active lineages were transformed into what he terms "contractual lineages" that were based on common interests rather than on agnatic links. They actively used all these strategies, thus allowing more flexibility in deviating from traditional lineages, and they were based on providing investment in return for a share in the profits and control. Such shares experienced commoditization, and eventually they could be bought and sold. By Qing times, the organization of share-based lineages, and their trust property, had become sufficiently sophisticated to allow their use in large-scale business enterprises.

To conclude, the lineage-based business enterprise was a uniquely Chinese institution. It developed within the specific Chinese context of ancestral worship and Confucian social order. It was embedded in Chinese culture, society and state, and as such could not be imported by other civilizations. It can be viewed as an organizational form that was embedded in Chinese civilization and developed on a parallel path to that of the corporation, which was embedded in European civilization. The lineage had a partial functional overlap with the corporation, with functions spanning from family and religion to business. The corporation's functions spanned from religion and political organization to business.

In some of their functions, lineages resembled European guilds and regulated corporations, but they were still considerably different from the European joint-stock business corporations that started to play a role in Eurasian trade around 1600. They did not raise equity investment from outsiders on impersonal stock markets. They could not be created over-night by a charter, but rather evolved gradually. Lineage-based enterprises were not totally separated from their members, in terms of liabilities, as were business corporations in Europe. They could not make use of a complimentary stock market. In terms of function, they did not take part in maritime trade over long distances and for long durations, as did the EIC and the VOC. When it came to the organization of early modern long-distance trade, the corporation had an advantage in both timing and dynamics. It appeared first, evolved faster, and took over long-distance trade shortly after 1600, before the lineage was even fully up to the task.

Conclusion

Why did China not develop the corporation per se? And why did it not import it in the seventeenth century, when the advantages of the EIC and VOC in large-scale, long-distance trade had become apparent? Note that the corporate form was introduced in China for the first time only in 1904, via the Companies Act, as part of the late Qing reforms.[94] So the second question, put more precisely, is as follows: Why did China not import the European corporation for three hundred years? A response to this question is not yet available in the literature, and I can only offer preliminary and tentative hypotheses. When Chinese maritime trade expanded in Song times (960–1279), the lineage institution was not well adapted to commercial uses. Song-dynasty maritime ventures relied on more basic forms of cooperation, such as loans, joint ownership of ships or goods, partnerships, and commendas. There was no demand in China for lineage-based maritime enterprises during the Yuan dynasty (1279–1368), as the Mongol dynasty preferred to rely on foreign merchants. There was no demand either during the early Ming years (1368–1433) for lineage-based maritime enterprises, because the state led the way, with Zheng He's state-funded and state-controlled maritime expeditions. In the following decades, the emperor objected to any further involvement in maritime adventures. Thus, in the centuries before the development of business corporations in Europe, there was no strong or lasting pressure to transform the lineage organization into an institution for maritime trade. By the time the lineage had evolved into a sufficiently flexible and contractual form, supportive of the conduct of business within its organizational framework, and could potentially serve as a substitute for the European business corporation, the European merchant corporations in the Indian Ocean and South China Sea had become substantial and detrimental to Chinese maritime trade.

In China, the family lineage organization gradually evolved into an institution that could function for new business purposes. China was not locked into a dead-end course of development. It evolved along its own evolutionary path, which was different from the European, Islamic, and Indian trajectories. Its family lineage was intrinsically flexible and adaptable. I cannot tell whether, at a later stage, this path could enable the quantum leap to impersonal cooperation between insiders and outside investors. This was achieved, as we have seen, by the European corporation. Exogenous shocks and the taking-over of much of Eurasia's long-distance trade by Europeans prevented the transformation of the family lineage into the institution of an impersonal cooperation. Thus, we cannot tell whether it had the potential for such a leap.[95]

Was China likely to develop corporation-like organizational forms? In other words, was China likely to develop trade organizations along the corporation path, rather than along the family lineage path? The Chinese environment was not supportive of the organizational model of the corporation. As we have seen, the precondition for there being a need for the corporation in the realm of religion was that the religion was detached from the state (all states), and that its apparatus was centralized and hierarchical. Such a religion required its own constitutional structure, and this could be provided by the corporation as an independent and hierarchical form of organization. But, in the case of China, Confucianism was intertwined with the state and its administration and public order. In China, the ruler could not credibly commit not to expropriate corporations even if they were to be formed somehow. There was no conception of rule of law similar to the common law and ancient constitution conception formed in England. There was no significant counterbalance to the ruler in the form of a well-organized mercantile elite that relied on city- and province-based political entities, as in the Dutch Republic. Nor was there any nascent stock market, as the ruler did not rely on borrowing on a voluntary basis from the public, in the form of bonds, as a partial substitute for taxation. What is more, the emperor could not rely on bond finance because he could not credibly commit not to expropriate the bonds. There was no space between the state and the family. As much as there any was such space to begin with, it was filled by the family lineage system, leaving no room for corporations.

CONCLUSION

~ ~ ~

Institutional Migration and the Corporation

It was not only practices, techniques, technologies, scientific knowledge, and religious beliefs (which have received the attention of the historical literature) that migrated across Eurasia. The migration of organizational models in Eurasia was pervasive, and it too deserves scholarly attention. Long-distance trade posed universal problems faced by all Eurasian regions. When solutions to the organizational problems were simple, they were achieved indigenously and were endemic. Such was the case with basic employment of agents, basic trade loans, and the combining of resources in operating ships. All of these forms are endogenous organizational forms within the analytical framework offered in this book.

When either problems or solutions were more complex, organizational solutions were imported if available. The agents of the migration of organizational forms were many and varied: migrating populations, expanding religions, conquering empires, and, most prominently, merchants themselves. Merchants met on board ships, in markets, and particularly in multicultural hubs, such as the port cities of Aden, Hormuz, Malacca, and Quanzhou. Indeed, organizational forms migrated. The commenda, the sea loan, the caravanserai, and the khan all migrated. Within our framework, they were migratory organizational forms. But migration did not happen mimetically. Alterations and modifications arose either because of variations in the demand for institutional solutions or because of constraints and resistance on the supply side. The overland commenda was somewhat different from the maritime commenda. The funduq in a large city, such as Damascus, was different from a caravanserai in a desert oasis on the way from Samarkand to Kashgar. The supply-side constraints caused additional differences. The different timing of the introduction of theology-based usury laws in Islam and Christianity shaped the reception pattern of the sea loans. The need to fit the commenda, which was first of all a merchant practice, to the larger legal framework created differences in details and rationales between the Middle East, in which it had to fit Islamic law, and Italy, in which it had to fit Roman law.

The major obstacles to the migrations of organizational forms were not the lack of contacts, knowledge, or opportunities. They were antagonism and resistance. The corporation was an embedded organizational form not simply because it was unknown or underappreciated in China, India, or the Ottoman Empire, but because it did not fit well with the religion and polity of these regions. Moreover, the corporation was not effective without complementary institutions. It could thrive only alongside a state that could credibly commit not to expropriate its asset pools and revenues, as was uniquely the case in England and the Dutch Republic. It could attract outside investors only because these investors were offered an outlet, an exit option, through a stock market. A business corporation unaccompanied by a preexisting bond market, as was the case in the Dutch Republic, or an emerging share market, as was the case in England, was a different and less attractive form of organization.

I offer here not only an account of the migration of trade organizations but also (as a byproduct) a contribution to the theory and methodology of studying the migration of institutions. The theoretical insights gained from this study are fundamentally different from the conventional insights gained from the legal history literature that studies the transplantation of Roman law and common law. Here we see less political and colonial imposition. Here we see migration of individual institutions and not of legal systems wholesale. Here the importation is conducted often from below, by merchants, and not top-down by rulers or jurists. Here we are dealing with the interplay between legal and nonlegal migration. So the insights gained here are an important addition to the theory of legal transplants and of the migration of economic institutions. They underline the need to stress the following factors in the theory of transplantation and migration of law and institutions: (a) the possibility that importation takes place on the level of abstract concepts rather than the full set of rules and organizational details; (b) the omnipresent role of resistance to importation and the need to fit the imported institution into a wider legal and institutional framework; and (c) the importance of paying attention to the complementarity between institutions and the fact that migration detaches some complementarities and creates new ones.

The interplay between family, religion, and ruler—three key components of every premodern society—was the major factor in shaping the pattern of migration of the various organizational forms that were analyzed in this book. This interplay determined the resistance of regions and civilizations outside Europe to the importation and transplantation of the business corporation.

THE CORPORATION AND IMPERSONAL COOPERATION

Before 1600, business organizations relied on personal familiarity between their members, either based on family ties, shared locality, or common ethnicity. Family firms were involved in substantial and quite sophisticated long-distance trade. Using either the lineage or the partnership as an organizing core, such firms conducted large-scale, long-distance trade from bases in Florence, Augsburg, Cairo, Surat, and Quanzhou, among other cities. They relied on family members and used marriage as a tool for extending outward and forming strategic partnerships. They employed agents, sometimes as partners, to further extend their reach. But family-based enterprises had their limits. They could hardly go beyond the family.

Merchant networks, another important precorporate organizational form, were usually structured with a hub and spokes. Typically, older and wealthier individual merchants, and the wives and children of younger traveling merchants, resided in the hub. The younger members of the core families and more distant relatives from the same ethnic or religious group served as itinerant agents traveling back and forth between the hub and the spokes, or were employed as stationed agents in spokes. The hub was where funding for the trade came from, a place for information exchange, for hiring agents and for dispute resolution. The networks were not as cohesive as the family firm. Networks were ruled and disciplined by merchant norms and enforcing tribunals. The boundaries of the networks were fixed by the size and scattering of the ethnic group. Networks as such were not able to be involved in cross-cultural trade.

By contrast, ruler-owned enterprises *could* go beyond the confines of the family and ethnic group and achieve a Eurasian span. Rulers could finance their trade using their sovereign powers of taxation, and could use personnel of the state apparatus, such as admirals, viceroys, ambassadors, administrators, and eunuchs, to manage and control such enterprises. They could use conscripts as employees and soldiers. They did not account for business expenses and profits separately from military and political ones. State-owned enterprises often mingled business and political aims and did not necessarily aim at maximizing monetary profits. They were in a sense impersonal, but unlike the business corporation, they were not voluntary, rational, profit-maximizing entities but rather impersonal entities that were coercive, irrational and redistributive. This was their downside. State-based trade enterprises were seen in fifteenth-century Ming China and sixteenth-century Portugal. However, neither enterprise lasted very long, and by the seventeenth century they no longer played a significant role in long-distance Eurasian trade.

The shift to impersonal, voluntary cooperation was achieved by using the corporation as a platform for advancing business purposes. The European corporation developed neither in the environment of the family nor in the environment of states and rulers. It developed in a religious environment. The exceptional circumstances that existed in the Roman Catholic Church served as the incubator for the corporation. As a religion, Roman Catholicism was hierarchical, on the one hand, and detached from any lay political ruler or state apparatus, on the other. The Church developed the corporation as the core of its constitution to organize decision-making and property ownership within the Church, from the level of abbot and monastery to that of pope and council. A nonhierarchical religion did not need a formal constitutional organizational form. A religion that, theologically and organizationally, was not separate from the state did not need a constitutional structure separate from that of the state. Neither would it serve as a good incubator for the corporation.

After the corporation was developed within the Catholic Church in the eleventh through thirteenth centuries, it was later used for other purposes as well, including the organization of colleges and universities, schools and hospitals, guilds, and cities. It was available "off the shelf" by the time the English and Dutch were looking for platforms for organizing their Cape Route trade, around the year 1600. The corporate charter provided longevity, a property-owning entity, and a governance structure. The corporate form was useful once the entrepreneurs realized that the family or the ruler could not provide the full solution and that a space was available between the family and the ruler in which corporations could function without concern over imminent expropriation or revocation. Such a space became available only when rulers could credibly commit to avoid expropriation and revocation. In the seventeenth century, among all European rulers, only the rulers of England and the Dutch Republic could credibly make this commitment.

The corporate entity was coupled by English and Dutch entrepreneurs with the financial scheme of joint-stock equity investment. The Dutch built upon experience with commenda and ship shares, while the English built on experience with joint ventures. The two together, when designed appropriately and used in a supportive environment, allowed the matching of outside passive investors with insiders, merchants, and managers and the pooling-together of immense working capital. The outsiders received a voice, an exit option, and information that assured them reasonable protection and a fair share in the profits.

The combination for the first time of the features of joint-stock equity finance, lock-in of investment, transferability of interest, and protection from expropriation by ruler with the older corporate features of separate legal personality, longevity, and concentrated governance amounted to an organizational revolution. The first business corporations, the EIC and VOC, achieved longevity of existence, concentration of management powers, employment of multiple agents and employees, legal standing in transactions and in court litigation, and tradeable equity investment by thousands of passive investors (though not limitation of shareholder liability in the modern sense). The corporations were able to use this longevity, together with the equity-capital-pooling and capital lock-in (the VOC achieved all this by 1602; the EIC by 1612) to maintain a long-term presence in Asia and undertake frequent voyages to Asia around the Cape.

The corporation constituted both a vertical integration, by having all the segments of trade within one firm, and a horizontal merger, by having all merchants from the same country operating in Asia within that firm.

The benefits of having such giant corporations, rather than smaller firms organized as commenda, partnerships, or family firms, lay not only, or primarily, in capturing monopoly rent, as many historians believe. The main advantage in having a single business corporation with ships, factories, and agents all over Eurasia was *informational*. The headquarters of the EIC and VOC had access to better information about markets in Asia and Europe, prices, goods, routes (and the risks involved in them), agents (and their loyalty and performance), and competitors (anywhere from Japan and China to Europe) than any earlier long-distance trade enterprise before them. They used this information to make better informed business decisions. They used the information to better monitor agents throughout Eurasia. Finally, they shared the information with outside investors in their home countries to ensure the latter's willingness to invest and to lock-in their investment.

We should bear in mind that the switch to impersonal relationships based on the corporate form did not only have advantages over the use of personal relationships as the basis of organizing business. Rosenthal and Wong showed, when discussing the parallel distinction between formal and informal enforcement of contracts, that neither is inherently superior.[1] In some environments, personally and informally based organization of trade works better than impersonally and formally based organization. Rosenthal and Wong predict that, when transactions are frequent enough, reputation mechanisms will work. When the distance between parties is large enough to be outside each other's court jurisdiction, court-based enforcement is less effective than social enforcement. So when courts cannot be used and reputation works, personally based cooperation will perform better. These were the conditions under which Chinese trade with Southeast Asia was conducted and this is why personally based organizations functioned so well there.

But when distances are large and transactions infrequent, as was the case for Europeans trading with Asia—or could have been the case for the Chinese, had they discovered the Cape Route first—here Rosenthal and Wong predict that neither formal nor informal organization will work, and transactions will be in cash only. But would they be conducted by itinerant traders? Itinerant traders could never access the capital and information required to overcome the huge entry barriers. The corporation solved the problem by facilitating impersonal cooperation in the home base, which resolved agency problems between the home base and the remote-destination markets. Once the EIC and VOC agents were in an Asian port for a long duration, they transacted frequently and over short distances in local markets with local merchants.

Greif and Tabellini argue that the kin-based clan and the voluntary-agreement-based corporation developed as the dominant forms in China and Europe, respectively. The clan was held together by moral commitments and personal interactions, and the corporation by common interests, generalized morality, and legal enforcement. Each had relative advantages and disadvantages compared to the other. The clan offered lower intragroup enforcement costs. The corporation offered scalability and economy of scale. Which of them gave rise to less corruption and less inequality is still a matter for future investigation.[2]

Masten and Prüfer show that communities and courts were complementary in the sense that they supported cooperation for different kinds of transactions due to the heterogeneity of transactors and transactions. But while communities supplemented courts, courts crowded out communities. These authors demonstrate how their model explains the rise and decline of merchant law in Europe and the persistence of communal enforcement in China and India.[3]

The scholarship on the tradeoffs between personal and impersonal collaboration is still in its early stages of development. An assertion that impersonal organizations are more efficient than personally based organizations, and necessarily represent progress, is too crude. The analysis of the relative advantages of each can be undertaken on several levels: that of the type of sanctions (legal, reputational, or social); that of the type of applicable rules (legal rules or communal norms); that of the identity of the adjudicators (professional judges or community leaders, such as leaders of the ethnic group, elders of the marketplace, or religious authorities); and the basic unit bearing rights and liabilities (individuals, families, clans, tribes, or local communities). I find that the distinction between informal and formal, unlike the distinction between personal and impersonal, is ambiguous and analytically unhelpful, if not confusing. What is clear is that the story of the design of the first impersonally based form of organization, the business corporation, represented a turning point in Western Europe's involvement in long-distance Eurasian trade. In Europe, long-distance trade was the first sector, but definitely not the last, to shift to impersonal cooperation. It was followed by the late seventeenth century by water supply, banks, and insurance corporations, in the eighteenth century by river navigation, roads, and canal construction, and in the nineteenth century by railway, gas lighting, and industrial corporations. By 1740, at least twenty-four joint-stock companies were in existence in England, of which only seven were overseas trade corporations. By 1760, 28 percent of the capital in the business sectors was invested in joint-stock corporations. By 1810, 90 million pounds (7 billion pounds in 2019 prices) were invested in joint-stock enterprises.[4]

But one should not conclude from this that every shift from personally to impersonally based cooperation is necessarily progressive and represents a shift from a less efficient to a more efficient organizational solution. Impersonal cooperation has its own costs and other downsides. Different business activities in different societies in different periods may have different optimal organizational designs. But more theoretical refinements and historical studies are due. The organizational revolution enabled the transition to impersonal cooperation, which in turn was crucial for English and Dutch dominance in Eurasian trade in the seventeenth and eighteenth centuries.

THE CORPORATION AND EURASIAN TRADE

Was the corporate form the only institutional solution for organizing long-distance trade? In short: no. Families and rulers could go a long way. As we have seen, the Ming emperor, with Zheng He on his side, was able to send political and commercial voyages all the way to East Africa. The Portuguese king, at times with funding from the Fuggers and other Italian and German family firms, was able to send voyages around the Cape and establish a presence in the Indian Ocean. By the eighteenth century, when the business corporations got into territorial governance and colonialism, they gradually integrated into the state, and trade became only a side activity for them as well. By the late eighteenth century and the nineteenth century, as long-distance trade became more routine, risks were reduced and information-flows enhanced; smaller merchant houses, family firms, and partnerships could cross the entry barriers, enter long-distance Eurasian trade, and operate on lower agency costs and greater adaptability than the giant East India Corporations, as Adam Smith asserted.

Before and after the seventeenth century, families and states did go a long way in organizing and facilitating long-distance Eurasian trade. But in the crucial seventeenth century, corporations were by far the ultimate organizational solution to the challenges this type of trade posed. Even in the seventeenth century, the Atlantic trade did not depend on the corporate form. The Spaniards, ever since the days of Columbus, had organized their Atlantic trade based on the massive involvement of rulers, and on licensing and private merchants, and not on widespread impersonal collaboration in the form of joint-stock corporations.[5] This can be explained by the shorter distances and lower risks involved in Atlantic trade compared to Asian trade and by the inability of the Spanish Crown, due to the political and legal structure of the king's reign, to credibly commit not to expropriate corporations. The same applies to the British in the Atlantic. Their few Atlantic-bound corporations existed for the purpose of settlement rather than trade, and were short-lived.[6] The "Manila Galleons" were voyages of trade ships traveling the longest continuous commercial route of the time (longer than the Cape Route trade). Each year between 1565 and 1815, usually one ship, but sometimes more, sailed between Manila in the Philippines and Acapulco in Mexico.[7] The ships sailing from Manila carried luxury goods from the Far East such as silks, porcelain, and jewelry. The galleons sailing west to Manila carried mainly silver that was used to pay for the Asian goods and as the annual Crown subsidy to the Philippine colony. The ships also carried soldiers for the garrison at Manila, missionary priests, civilians, and administrative personnel. We must await further research on the organization of the galleons to understand how they could operate for such a long period without resorting to the corporate form. So the argument of this book is not totally global but rather Eurasian. It is about the Cape Route and the Indian Ocean (and the Silk Route). But this is where the challenges were gravest and where long-distance trade was most significant in the period 1400–1700. Indeed, as time passed, plantation- and slave-based Atlantic trade became more significant, but an analysis of the organization of Atlantic trade is beyond the scope of this book. The role of England and the Dutch Republic in Eurasian trade could not have been the same had they not been able to generate the organizational revolution that the design of the joint-stock business corporation epitomized.

Was the path that led from the Roman Catholic Church to the joint-stock corporation the only path to impersonally based organization of long-distance trade? Could any of the other paths have led at a later stage to impersonally based organization of trade? In other words, could any of the other paths have broken through the glass ceiling of the personally based cooperation?

The most promising candidate to do so was the Chinese family lineage, which gradually became centered less on organic family relationships than on contractual arrangements. It grew larger, and became involved in for-profit business, including overseas trade. But it did not cross the dividing line into impersonal relations. It did not turn to hundreds and thousands of outside investors, either through private placement or through a nascent stock market. So one can only extrapolate based on the path the family lineage followed until the sixteenth century, and speculate as to its possible transformation in a counterfactual later world in which European corporations did not gain dominance in long-distance Eurasian trade. By the eighteenth century, it was too late for Chinese merchants to dominate trade in the face of the European corporations, and too late for China to develop its own functional equivalent to the European joint-stock business corporation, in the form of the family lineage.

The core argument that runs through this book has a more ambitious version and a less ambitious version. The more ambitious (second-level) argument is that the corporate form explains the trade dominance of the English and Dutch. The less ambitious (first-level) argument is that, even if other factors—such as technology or the use of violence—explain trade dominance, the design of the joint-stock business corporation in the context of trade nevertheless explains the shift to impersonally based institutions.

This book argues that sixteenth-century Europeans, particularly the Portuguese, relying on the state, did not design a good institutional framework for conducting Cape Route trade with Asia. Seventeenth-century Europeans, led by the Dutch and the English, designed an institutional framework that suited their environmental challenges well and facilitated long-distance trade between Europe and Asia. By the eighteenth century things have changed again, Europeans exceedingly used state-power and violence; the corporations relied on state granted trade monopoly and gradually turned into territorial-colonial entities.

The corporation successfully carried the English and the Dutch through the seventeenth century. According to the more ambitious version of my core argument, this made a huge difference in terms of their share of Eurasian long-distance trade vis-à-vis the Portuguese, Spaniards, and French and vis-à-vis the Ottomans, Indians, and Chinese. It was not navigation or warfare technology or willingness to use violence that gave the Dutch and English a clear advantage over all competitors. It was their organization, in the form of the joint-stock business corporation, that was their distinct and winning feature.

I do not wish to explain European trade and colonial dominance in Asia in the eighteenth and nineteenth centuries exclusively by way of the emergence of the corporation in 1600–1602. By the eighteenth-century, European rulers had advantages compared to other rulers, in the ability to finance and deploy large armies and navies, to resort to violence rather than diplomacy, to systematically win wars against Asian rulers, and to form territorial empires. By the nineteenth century, they had advantages in the manufacturing of industrial goods, in shipping technologies, in weapons, and in means of communication that altered the balance of trade in their favor. By the later part of the period, the French, Germans, and other European countries also got their share of the trade. The second-level argument aims at explaining the rise of the EIC and VOC to dominance in long-distance trade on the Cape Route in the seventeenth century. It does not attempt to expalin trade monopoly and colonialism in the eighteenth century.

And yet, one can analogize the organizational revolution of the early seventeenth century that was manifested in the design of the EIC and VOC to the financial revolution of the late seventeenth and early eighteenth centuries. Just as institutional and constitutional innovations that amounted to the financial revolution boosted the development of the British fiscal-military state of the eighteenth century and ultimately the rapid expansion of the British Empire, so did the organizational innovations that enabled the formation of impersonally based joint-stock business corporations—the organizational revolution boosted the rise of Britain and the Dutch Republic to dominance in Cape Route shipping, in Eurasian trade, and in the global trade system as a whole in the seventeenth century. Was the organizational revolution a precondition to the financial revolution, to the fiscal-military state, and to the British Empire? Possibly.

The less ambitious version of my core argument, the first-level argument, does not set out to explain the great divergence in per capita GDP and in growth rates, as significant as that divergence was after 1700. It focuses on the organizational transformation and not on its effect on the economy. I can only contirbute to the divergence debate by showing that the organizational solution shaped in England and the Dutch Republic in around 1600 to solve specific problems related to long-distance Cape Route trade—the joint-stock company, based on impersonal cooperation—turned out to be very useful in totally different contexts between the late seventeenth and mid-nineteenth centuries. It was used for organizing banks and insurance companies, canals and railroads, and eventually even industrial firms. It developed in tandem with the stock market, which also took its first developmental steps in the context of long-distance trade corporations. The business corporation was still an exclusively European organizational form during the financial revolution, transportation revolution, and industrial revolution.

Of course, some may not be convinced by the more ambitious (second-level) argument—that organizational factors determined the rise of English and Dutch Eurasian trade dominance in the seventeenth century—asserting instead that technology and violence had more determinative weight. The understanding of the early-seventeenth-century organizational revolution is nevertheless relevant for debates on the Great Divergence. It was this phenomenon, after all, that marked the formative period of the organizational form that was later critical in the financial, colonial, transportation, and industrial transformations of Western Europe in the eighteenth and nineteenth centuries.

NOTES

~ ~ ~

INTRODUCTION

1. de Vries, Jan. 2003. "Connecting Europe and Asia."

2. Greif, Avner. 2000. "The Fundamental Problem of Exchange." Greif, Avner. 2008. "Commitment, Coercion and Markets."

3. Note that the very basic institutions are not really multiparty business organizations. They are single individuals or two-party agreements, but for consistency I will refer to them as "organizational forms" as well.

CHAPTER 1. ENVIRONMENT AND TRADE

1. The literature on Eurasian trade, like any other body of literature, cannot be neatly pigeonholed. Good historians are often influenced by various schools and write within more than one line of research. The categorization of this literature into four traditions is thus an inevitable simplification.

2. Findlay, Ronald and Kevin O'Rourke. 2007. *Power and Plenty.*

3. Wallerstein, Immanuel. 2011 [1974, 1980, 1989, 2011]. *The Modern World-System.*

4. Abu-Lughod, Janet. 1991. *Before European Hegemony.*

5. Braudel, Fernand. 1981. *The Structures of Everyday Life.* Braudel, Fernand. 1982. *The Wheels of Commerce.* Braudel, Fernand. 1985. *The Perspective of the World.*

6. Chaudhuri, Kirti. 1985. *Trade and Civilisation in the Indian Ocean.*

7. Steensgaard, Niels. 1974. *The Asian Trade Revolution of the Seventeenth Century.* Steensgaard is also influenced by Karl Polanyi and his book, *The Great Transformation.* He views the Portuguese Estado da Índia as a premarket institution. It is a redistributive trade institution in the sense that, in it, trade was being conducted by the ruler and then redistributed to the members of Portuguese society. Society was separated from the market. The East India companies, on the other hand, acted *with* society and market.

8. Abu-Lughod, Janet. 1991. *Before European Hegemony.*

9. McEvedy, Colin and Richard Jones. 1978. *Atlas of World Population History.*

10. Chandler, Tertius. 1987. *Four Thousand Years of Urban Growth.*

11. McEvedy, Colin and Richard Jones. 1978. *Atlas of World Population History.* Chandler, Tertius. 1987. *Four Thousand Years of Urban Growth.*

12. Here and throughout the book I describe places using their most common contemporary name. For other names see note on city names, p. xiii.

13. "Distance Between Ports." 2001. http://msi.nga.mil/NGAPortal/MSI.portal?_nfpb=true&_st=&_pageLabel=msi_portal_page_62&pubCode=0005. pp. 2, 35. "Sea-Distances." www.sea-distances.org.

14. "Sea-Distances." www.sea-distances.org.

15. "Distance Between Ports." 2001. http://msi.nga.mil/NGAPortal/MSI.portal ?_nfpb=true&_st=&_pageLabel=msi_portal_page_62&pubCode=0005. pp. 3, 10.

16. The distance between Amsterdam and Saint Petersburg is drawn from www .searoutefinder.com.

17. "Sea-Distances." www.sea-distances.org. Columbus, Christopher. 1906 [1492–93]. "Journal of the First Voyage of Columbus." pp. 90–91, 109–10.

18. The journey from Hormuz/Bandar Abas to the Malabar Coast took between three-and-a-half and four weeks via the cross-oceanic route, compared to four to six weeks via the coastal route. The journey west from the Malabar Coast took five weeks via the cross-oceanic route, compared to four to six weeks via the coastal route. Mathew, Kuzhippalli. 1983. *Portuguese Trade with India.* p. 146. Ibn Battuta covered the distance from Calicut to a post on the south Arabic coast in one lunar month (twenty-eight to thirty days), with a favoring wind. Agius, Dionisius. 2002. "Classifying Vessel Types." p. 146.

19. Mathew, Kuzhippalli. 1983. *Portuguese Trade with India.* p. 147. Willetts, William. 1964. "The Maritime Adventures of Grand Eunuch Ho." p. 30.

20. Willetts, William. 1964. "The Maritime Adventures of Grand Eunuch Ho." pp. 28, 30. Shankar, D., et al. 2002. "The Monsoon Currents in the North Indian Ocean."

21. Shankar, D. et al. 2002. "The Monsoon Currents in the North Indian Ocean." p. 64. Amrith, Sunil. 2013. *Crossing the Bay of Bengal.* p. 10. Agius, Dionisius. 2005. *Seafaring in the Arabian Gulf.* p. 193.

22. Agius, Dionisius. 2005. *Seafaring in the Arabian Gulf.* p. 193.

23. Ibid. p. 193.

24. Ibid. p. 193.

25. Ahmad Ibn Majid (born around 1430 and died sometime after 1500) was an Arabian navigator and cartographer. His most valuable work for navigators was a navigators' manual dated to 1490, called *Kitab al-Fawa'id fi uṣūlʿilm al-bahr wa ʿl-qawāʿid* ["Book of lessons on the foundation of the sea and navigation" or "The book of useful information on the principles and rules of navigation"]. An English translation of this book is available in Tibbetts, G. R. 1971. *Arab Navigation in the Indian Ocean.* On the book and Ibn Majid, see Maqbul Sayyid, Ahmad. 2008. "Ibn Mājid." Glick, Thomas. 2014. "Ibn Majid, Ahmad." p. 252.

26. Chaudhuri, Kirti. 1985. *Trade and Civilisation in the Indian Ocean.* pp. 121–137. Abu-Lughod, Janet. 1991. *Before European Hegemony.* pp. 251–260.

27. Simkin, Colin. 1968. *The Traditional Trade of Asia.*

28. The itinerary of the seventh voyage undertaken by Zheng He's (also spelled Cheng Ho and originally named Ma He) (Down to the Western Ocean) was preserved, and is presented in table 1.1. Hui, Deng and Li Xin. 2011. "The Asian Monsoons and Zheng He's Voyages." p. 207. Dreyer, Edward. 2007. *Zheng He: China and the Oceans.* p. 150.

29. According to a journal of the first voyage of Vasco da Gama, he left Rostello, Portugal on July 8, 1497 and arrived Calicut on May 20, 1498, making a journey time of ten months. da Gama, Vasco. 1989 [1497–1499]. *First Voyage of Vasco da Gama.* pp. 1, 48.

30. Da Gama left Calicut on August 23, 1498 and arrived in Lisbon on August 29 (or September 8, 1499 depending on the source), a journey time of twelve-and-a-half months. Ibid. pp. 73, 94–95.

31. "Sailing Directions." 2011. https://msi.nga.mil/MSISiteContent/StaticFiles/NAV _PUBS/SD/Pub161/Pub161bk.pdf. pp. 20–22, 44, 57, 103.

32. de la Vaissière, Étienne. 2005. *Sogdian traders*. p. 1.

33. Wild, Oliver. 1992. "The Silk Road." http://www.ess.uci.edu/~oliver/silk.html.

34. Sarai (also transcribed as Saray) was the capital city of the Mongol kingdom (Golden Horde). Sarai is located in present-day Russia. Tana or Tanais is a medieval trading city on the Sea of Azov, near the modern city of Azov, Russia. Kaffa or Caffa was the ancient name of modern-day Feodosia (Feodosiya) or Theodosia. Arnold, Guy. 2000. *World Strategic Highways*. p. 261. Cohen, Sarai. 2008. "Sarai." p. 3452. "Feodosiya." 2014. http://www.britannica.com/place/Feodosiya.

35. Kaw, Mushtaq. 2011. "Restoring India's Links with Central Asia across Kashmir." pp. 179–181.

36. Beckwith, Christopher. 2009. *Empires of the Silk Road*. p. 183.

37. Rossabi, Morris. 1993. "The Decline of the Central Asian Caravan Trade." p. 356.

38. Beckwith, Christopher. 2009. *Empires of the Silk Road*. Starr, Frederick. 2013. *Lost Enlightenment: Central Asia's Golden Age*. Liu, Xinru. 2010. *The Silk Road in World History*. Rossabi, Morris. 1993. "The Decline of the Central Asian Caravan Trade."

39. Ibn Batuta, Muhammad. 1829 [ca. 1355]. *The Travels of Ibn Batuta*. Chapters 12–15. Polo, Marco. 1903 [circa 1300]. *The Venetian*. Vols. 1 and 2.

40. Francesco Balducci Pegolotti was a Florentine merchant in the service of the Bradi Company. In around 1340, Pegolotti wrote "La pratica della mercatura," a merchant handbook and one of the most complete itineraries. Pegolotti mentioned the distances between cities along the Silk Route, making it possible to calculate the overall distance. Pegolotti, Francesco. 1936 [ca. 1340]. "La pratica della mercature." pp. xiii, xiv, xv, xvii, xxv, 21. Pegolotti, Francesco. 2010 [ca. 1340]. "Notices of the Land Route to Cathay."

41. Rossabi, Morris. 1993. "The Decline of the Central Asian Caravan Trade." p. 356.

42. Ibid. pp. 352–360. Findlay, Ronald and Kevin O'Rourke. 2007. *Power and Plenty*. pp. 101–108.

43. Rossabi, Morris. 1993. "The Decline of the Central Asian Caravan Trade." p. 356.

44. Ibid. pp. 356–357.

45. Einaudi, Luca. 2013. "Florins and Ducats." http://www.histecon.magd.cam.ac.uk /coins_april2013.html.

46. Rossabi, Morris. 1993. "The Decline of the Central Asian Caravan Trade." pp. 356–357.

47. Freedman, Paul. 2008. *Out of the East*.

48. McLaughlin, Raoul. 2010. *Rome and the Distant East*. pp. 44, 142, 143, 153. Scammell, Geoffrey. 1981. *The World Encompassed*. pp. 10–102. Nutmeg, mace and clove were imported from Spice Islands. See Vaucher, Jean. 2014. "History of European–Asian trade." http://www.iro.umontreal.ca/~vaucher/Genealogy/Documents/Asia/European Exploration.html.

49. An Arabic source from 851 named "Akhbar al-Sin wa-al-Hind" (Notes on China and India) describes the route from the Persian Gulf to the Malabar Coast. See Hourani, George. 1995. *Arab Seafaring in the Indian Ocean*. Regarding Indonesia, see Flecker, Michael. 2011. "A Ninth-Century Arab or Indian Shipwreck in Indonesia."

50. Sen, Tansen. 2003. *Buddhism, Diplomacy, and Trade*. p. 209.

51. Millward, James. 2013. *The Silk Road*. p. 38.

52. Findlay, Ronald and Kevin O'Rourke. 2007. *Power and Plenty*. pp. 156, 208.

53. Ibid. p. 179.

54. Lopez, Robert Sabatino. 1952. "China Silk in Europe in the Yuan Period."

55. Findlay, Ronald and Kevin O'Rourke. 2007. *Power and Plenty*. p. 225.

56. Jensen, Michael and William Meckling. 1976. "Theory of the Firm."

57. See, for example: Landes, David. 1998. *The Wealth and Poverty of Nations*. McNeill, William. 1991. *The Rise of the West*. Jones, Eric. 2003. *The European Miracle*. North, Douglass C. and Robert Paul Thomas. 1973. *The Rise of the Western World*. Mokyr, Joel. 2005. *Gifts of Athena*. Pomeranz, Kenneth. 2000. *The Great Divergence*. Abu-Lughod, Janet. 1991. *Before European Hegemony*.

58. Mokyr, Joel. 2009. *The Enlightened Economy*. pp. 124–144.

59. Headrick, Daniel. 2010. *Power over Peoples*.

60. Mokyr, Joel. 2005. *Gifts of Athena*.

61. Devendra, Somasiri. 2002. "Pre-Modern Sri Lankan Ships." p. 132.

62. See, for example: Hourani, George. 1995. *Arab Seafaring in the Indian Ocean*. pp. 89, 150. Casson, Lionel. 1980. "Rome's Trade with the East." pp. 23–24. Alpers, Edward. 2014. *The Indian Ocean in World History*. p. 38. Bulliet, Richard, et al. 2015. *The Earth and Its Peoples*. Cunliffe, Barry. 2015. *The Birth of Eurasia*. p. 387. Risso, Patricia. 1995. *Merchants And Faith*. p. 27. This is a simplified survey. There were other types of ships and local variations, and there were overlaps.

63. Shiba, Yoshinobu. 1970. *Commerce and Society in Sung China*. Chaudhuri, Kirti. 1985. *Trade and Civilisation in the Indian Ocean*. p. 156.

64. Ellacott, Samuel. 1954. *The Story of Ships*. pp. 16–17.

65. Arasaratnam, Sinnappah. 1994. *Maritime India in the Seventeenth Century*. p. 250.

66. Chaudhuri, Kirti. 1985. *Trade and Civilisation in the Indian Ocean*. p.140. Risso, Patricia. 1995. *Merchants and Faith*. pp. 77–83.

67. Manguin, Pierre-Yves. 1993. "Trading ships of the South China Sea."; Chang, Kuei-Sheng. 1974. "Maritime Scene in China at the Dawn of Great European Discoveries." See also the microstudies of the respective enterprises bellow for additional references.

68. Arasaratnam, Sinnappah. 1994. *Maritime India in the Seventeenth Century*. p. 248.

69. Ibid. pp. 250–258.

70. Chaudhuri, Kirti. 1985. *Trade and Civilisation in the Indian Ocean*. p. 125.

71. Menzies, Gavin. 2002. *The Year China Discovered the World*. This is a pseudohistorical book that claims that the Chinese did reach the Atlantic and America. However, many historians dismiss this claim as baseless. For example, Finlay, Robert. 2004. "How Not to (Re)Write World History."

72. Elliott, John. 2006. *Empires of the Atlantic World*. Part 1 ("Occupation"). pp. 3–144.

73. Israel, Jonathan. 1998. *The Dutch Republic*. pp. 318–327. Andrews, Kenneth. 1985. *Trade, Plunder, and Settlement*. pp. 256–279. Steensgaard, Niels. 1974. *The Asian Trade Revolution of the Seventeenth Century*.

74. Anand, R. P. 1983. *Origin and Development of the Law of the Sea*. p. 20, 34.

75. Borschberg, Peter. 2011. *Grotius, Portuguese, and Free Trade*. pp. 40–77. Benton, Lauren. 2010. *A Search for Sovereignty*. pp. 120–148.

76. Dickson, Peter. 1967. *The Financial Revolution in England*. O'Brien, Patrick. 1988. "The Political Economy of British Taxation." Brewer, John. 1989. *The Sinews of Power*.

77. Kennedy, Paul. 1987. *The Rise and Fall of the Great Powers*. Ferguson, Niall. 2001. *The Cash Nexus*.

78. Hoffman, Philip. 2012. "Why Was It Europeans Who Conquered the World?" Hoffman, Philip. 2015. *Why Did Europe Conquer the World?*

79. Cipolla, Carlo. 1965. *Guns, Sails, and Empires.* p. 107.

80. Gat, Azar. 2006. *War in Human Civilization.* pp. 482–484. Kennedy, Paul. 1987. *The Rise and Fall of the Great Powers.* pp. 24–25. Rodger, Nicholas. 2001. "Guns and Sails in the First Phase of English Colonization."

81. Chaudhuri, Kirti. 1985. *Trade and Civilisation in the Indian Ocean.* p. 151.

82. Casale, Giancarlo. 2010. *The Ottoman Age of Exploration.* For further discussion, see chap. 12, p. 331.

83. Arasaratnam, Sinnappah. 1994. *Maritime India in the Seventeenth Century.* p. 249.

84. Ibid. p. 248.

85. Andrade, Tonio. 2011. *Lost Colony.*

86. Hang, Xing. 2016. *Conflict and Commerce in Maritime East Asia.*

87. Ironically this critique is not in line with the critique of the book as being Eurocentric. When focusing on European colonization one is Eurocentric at least to some extent.

88. Recent studies emphasize the colonial characteristics of the EIC and VOC. While I endorse these studies, I argue that the crucial issue is timing. Stern acknowledges that the first EIC territorial holdings were St. Helena in 1657 and Bombay in 1668, more than half a century after the trade enterprise was established. Stern, Philip. 2011. *The Company-State.* pp. 19–40. De Zwart acknowledges that the tiny Banda Islands in the Moluccas archipelago were the only plantation colonies formed in the first fifty years of the VOC. This was done when the VOC failed by 1621 to secure ample supply of nutmeg through contractual market transactions and in the 1650s, when it used violence and formed plantations in order to secure the supply of clove. The colonization in Java, Ceylon and the Cape was a slower process that began well into the seventeenth century and continued gradually through the eighteenth century. See De Zwart, Pim. 2016. *Globalization and the Colonial Origins of the Great Divergence.* pp. 62–70, 202–206.

CHAPTER 2. THEORETICAL FRAMEWORKS FOR ANALYZING THE DEVELOPMENT OF INSTITUTIONS IN INTERACTION WITH THEIR ENVIRONMENT

1. Hodgson, Geoffrey. 2006. "What Are Institutions?" Ostrom, Elinor. 2005. *Understanding Institutional Diversity.* Granovetter, Mark. 1985. "The Problem of Embeddedness." Williamson, Oliver. 1985. *The Economic Intstitutions of Capitalism.*

2. North, Douglass C. 1990. *Institutions, Institutional Change and Economic Performance.* p. 3.

3. Greif, Avner. 2006. *Lessons from Medieval Trade.* p. 30.

4. Hart, Herbert. 1961. *The Concept of Law.* Dworkin, Ronald. 1977. *Taking Rights Seriously.* Shapiro, Scott. 2007. "The "Hart-Dworkin" Debate."

5. The International Society for New Institutional Economics has recently changed its name to the Society for Institutional and Organizational Economics. This is just another indication for the growing convergence and for the overlap in the use of both terms.

6. Coase, Ronald. 1937. "The Nature of the Firm." Coase, Ronald. 1960. "The Problem of Social Cost." Jensen, Michael and William Meckling. 1976. "Theory of the Firm." Hart, Oliver. 1989. "An Economist's Perspective on the Theory of the Firm."

7. Alchian, Armen and Harold Demsetz. 1973. "The Property Right Paradigm."

8. Williamson, Oliver. 1979. "Transaction-Cost Economics." Macneil, Ian. 1978. "Contracts: Adjustment of Long-Term Economic Relations." Macaulay, Stewart. 1963. "Non-Contractual Relations in Business." Fama, Eugene and Michael Jensen. 1983. "Agency Problems and Residual Claims." Ayres, Ian and Robert Gertner. 1989. "Filling Gaps in Incomplete Contracts."

9. Akerlof, George. 1970. "The Market for Lemons." Stiglitz, Joseph and Bruce Greenwald. 1986. "Externalities in Economies with Imperfect Information and Incomplete Markets." Spence, Michael. 1973. "Job Market Signaling."

10. Easterbrook, Frank H. and Daniel R. Fischel. 1996. *The Economic Structure of Corporate Law.*

11. Hansmann, Henry, et al. 2006. "Law and the Rise of the Firm."

12. Bebchuk, Arye Lucian and Mark J. Roe. 1999. "Path Dependence in Corporate Ownership." Gilson, Ronald J. and Bernard S. Black. 1995. *The Law and Finance of Corporate Acquisitions.* Gilson, Ronald J. and Bernard S. Black. 2003. *2003–2004 Supplement.* Kahan, Marcel and Edward B. Rock. 2007. "Hedge Funds in Corporate Governance and Corporate Control."

13. North, Douglass C. 1990. *Institutions, Institutional Change and Economic Performance.*

14. Harris, Ron. 2003. "The Encounters of Economic History and Legal History."

15. Alchian, Armen A. and Harold Demsetz. 1973. "The Property Right Paradigm." This was based on an address to the 1972 annual meeting of the EHA and a call for empirical historical studies that would enrich the "speculative theory" (their own work included). See North, Douglass C. and Robert Paul Thomas. 1973. *The Rise of the Western World.* Libecap, Gary. 1978. "Economic Variables and the Development of the Law." Eggertsson, Thráinn. 1990. *Economic Behavior and Institutions.* pp. 247–262. For a comprehensive survey of examples for works representing the different stages in the study of economic history of law, see Klerman, Daniel M. 2018. "Quantitative Legal History."

16. North, Douglass C. 1990. *Institutions, Institutional Change and Economic Performance.* Barzel, Yoram. 1997. *Economic Analysis of Property Rights.* Libecap, Gary. 1989. *Contracting for Property Rights.* Alston, Lee J., et al. 1996. "The Determinants and Impact of Property Rights."

17. Fogel, Robert W. 1994. "Economic Growth, Population Theory, and Physiology." North, Douglass C. 1994. "Economic Performance Through Time."

18. David, Paul A. 1985. "Clio and the Economics of QWERTY." Arthur, Brian W. 1994. *Increasing Returns and Path Dependence.* Liebowitz, Stan and Stephen Margolis. 1995. "Path Dependence, Lock-In, and History." Roe, Mark J. 1996. "Chaos and Evolution in Law and Economics." Bebchuk, Arye and Mark Roe. 1999. "Path Dependence in Corporate Ownership."

19. Bebchuk, Arye and Mark Roe. 1999. "Path Dependence in Corporate Ownership."

20. North, Douglass C. 1997. "Institutions, Transaction Costs, and the Rise of Merchant Empires."

21. Carlos, Ann and Stephen Nicholas. 1988. "Giants of an Earlier Capitalism." Carlos, Ann and Stephen Nicholas. 1996. "Theory and History." Jones, S.R.H. and Simon Ville. 1996. "Efficient Transactors or Rent-Seeking Monopolists?"

22. Carlos, Ann M. and Stephen Nicholas. 1988. "Giants of an Earlier Capitalism." Carlos, Ann M. and Stephen Nicholas. 1996. "Theory and History." Jones, S.R.H. and Simon Ville P. 1996. "Efficient Transactors or Rent-Seeking Monopolists?"

23. Greif, Avner. 2006. *Lessons from Medieval Trade*. Greif, Avner, et al. 1994. "The Case of the Merchant Guild." Milgrom, Paul R., et al. 1990. "The Role of Institutions in the Revival of Trade." Cizakca, Murat. 2010. "Was Shari'ah Indeed the Culprit?" Ekelund, Robert B. and Robert D. Tollison. 1980. "Mercantilist Origins of the Corporation." Ekelund, Robert B. and Robert D. Tollison. 1997. *Politicized Economies*. Gelderblom, Oscar and Joost Jonker. 2004. "Completing a Financial Revolution." North, Douglass C., et al. 2009. *Violence and Social Order*.

24. Greif, Avner. 1998. "Historical and Comparative Institutional Analysis."

25. Kuran, Timur. 2005. "The Absence of the Corporation in Islamic Law."

26. Greif, Avner. 2006. *Lessons from Medieval Trade*. Greif, Avner. 2006. "Family Structure, Institutions, and Growth."

27. Rubin, Jared. 2017. *Rulers, Religion, and Riches*.

28. Pomeranz, Kenneth. 2000. *The Great Divergence*.

29. Rosenthal, Jean-Laurent and R. Bin Wong. 2011. *Before and Beyond Divergence*.

30. Zhang, Taisu. 2017. *The Laws and Economics of Confucianism*.

31. The literature in different disciplines uses a variety of terms: *transplantation, transfer, copying, mimicking, circulation, importation, migration, diffusion*, etc. Each has different connotations. For example, some terms denote that the process is voluntary, while some denote coercion. Some terms suggest that the sending end has the agency, while some suggest that the receiving end has the agency. None of them is fully suitable for my purposes. This book uses, in most instances, for terminological consistency, the term *migration* to denote the spatial movement of institutions from one location to another, but in a few appropriate cases deviates from it.

32. La Porta, Rafael, et al. 1998. "Law and Finance." pp. 1115–1516.

33. Glaeser, Edward L. and Andrei Shleifer. 2002. "Legal Origins." La Porta, Rafael, et al. 2008. "The Economic Consequences of Legal Origins." For an explanation based on colonial policy rather than legal origins see Klerman, Daniel M., et al. 2011. "Legal Origin or Colonial History?" pp. 379–409.

34. Acemoglu, Daron, et al. 2001. "The Colonial Origins of Comparative Development." Acemoglu, Daron, et al. 2002. "Reversal of Fortune." Acemoglu, Daron and James A. Robinson. 2012. *Why Nations Fail*.

35. Watson, Alan. 1974. *Legal Transplants*.

36. Berkowitz, Daniel, et al. 2003. "Economic Development, Legality, and the Transplant Effect." Graziadei, Michele. 2006. "The Study of Transplants and Receptions." Whitman, James O. 2009. "Western Legal Imperialism."

37. Kahn-Freund, Otto. 1974. "On Uses and Misuses of Comparative Law." Teubner, Gunther. 1998. "Legal Irritants." Harris, Ron and Assaf Likhovski. 2009. "Histories of Legal Transplantations."

38. Lieber, Alfred E. 1968. "Eastern Business Practices." Udovitch, Abraham. 1970. *Partnership and Profit in Medieval Islam*.

CHAPTER 3. UNIVERSAL BUILDING BLOCKS

1. Hansen, Valerie. 2012. *The Silk Road: A New History*. p. 139.

2. For example, Marco Polo stated that at least two hundred mariners (and sometimes as many as three hundred) boarded a single large Chinese ship (junk). According to Polo,

Chinese merchants used junks for sailing to India. Polo, Marco. 1903 [ca. 1300]. *The Venetian*. Vol. 2. pp. 249–251.

3. van Leur, Jacob. 1967. *Indonesian Trade and Society*. p. 98 ("The majority of the traders in the peddling trade belonged to the lower social groups").

4. Meilink-Roelofsz, Marie. 1962. *Asian Trade and European Influence*. pp. 14–15, 21–22.

5. Fontaine, Laurence. 1996. *History of Pedlars in Europe*. See also van Leur, J. 1967. *Indonesian Trade and Society*. p. 197.

6. Hajnal, J. 1965. "European Marriage Patterns in Perspective." Wall, Richard, et al. 1983. *Family Forms*.

7. Laslett, Peter. 1988. "Family, Kinship and Collectivity." De Moor, Tine and Jan Luiten Van Zanden. 2009. "Girl Power."

8. See, for example: Bullard, Melissa Meriam. 1979. "Marriage Politics and the Family."

9. See also Greif, Avner and Guido Tabellini. 2017. "The Clan and the Corporation."

10. Harris, Ron. Forthcoming. "The Organization of Rome to India Trade."

11. Young, Gary Y. 2001. *Rome's Eastern Trade*. pp. 19–20, 28.

12. Ibid. pp. 28–29.

13. Ibid. pp. 14–15.

14. Casson, Lionel. 1980. "Rome's Trade with the East." Casson, Lionel. 1989. *The Periplus Maris Erythraei*.

15. Rathbone, Dominic. 2000. "The 'Muziris' Papyrus (SB XVIII)." pp. 39–41.

16. For an analysis of the reverse side of the papryraus that attempts to reconstruct the cargo of the *Hermapollon*, see De Romanis, Frederico. 2012. "Playing Sudoku on the Verso of the 'Muziris Papyrus.'"

17. Casson, Lionel. 1990. "New Light on Maritime Loans." p. 200.

18. Harrauer, Hermann and Pieter Sijpesteijn. 1986. *Ein neues Dokument zu Roms Indienhandel P. Vindob. G 40822*. Thür, Gerhard. 1987. "Hypotheken-Urkunde eines Seedarlehens für eine Reise nach Muziris." Casson, Lionel. 1986. "P. Vindob G 40822 and the Shipping of Goods from India." Casson, Lionel. 1990. "New Light on Maritime Loans." Rathbone, Dominic. 2000. "The 'Muziris' Papyrus (SB XVIII)." pp. 39–41. Morelli, Federico. 2011. "Dal Mar Rosso ad Alessandria." De Romanis, Frederico. 2012. "Playing Sudoku on the Verso of the 'Muziris Papyrus.'" Evers, Kasper Grønlund. 2016. *Worlds Apart Trading Together*.

19. Several scholars have identified additional organizational forms that have equity investment features. Malmendier identified the Roman *societas publicanorum*, namely the "society of government leaseholders." Abatino, Dari-Mattiacci, and Perotti identified the peculium as a slave-run company. Other equity-based investments such as the commenda and the joint-stock company had not yet been invented. Malmendier, Ulrike. 2009. "Law and Finance 'at the Origin.'" Abatino, Barbara, et al. 2011. "Depersonalization of Business."

20. Watson, Alan. 1961. *Contract of Mandate in Roman Law*.

21. Knopf, Ellen. 2005. "Contracts in Athenian Law." p. 3.

22. Ibid. p. 138. Riggsby, Andrew M. 2010. *Roman Law and the Legal World of the Romans*. pp. 121–134. Schulz, Fritz. 1951. *Classical Roman Law*. pp. 400–401. Zimmermann, Reinhard. 1996 [1990]. *The Law of Obligations*. pp. 47–58.

23. Cohen, Edward E. 1992. *Athenian Economy and Society*. pp. 160–171. Millett,

Paul. 2002. *Lending and Borrowing in Ancient Athens*. pp. 188–196. Andreau, Jean. "Maritime Loans."

24. Poitras, Geoffrey. 2016. *Equity Capital*. p. 48. Rawson, Stuart. 2012. "How Far Were the Commercial Arrangements for Maritime Loans in Fourth Century BC Athens Dictated by the Legal Framework Available?" pp. 34, 39.

25. Cohen, Edward E. 1992. *Athenian Economy and Society*.

26. Muziris Papyrus. Casson, Lionel. 1990. "New Light on Maritime Loans." p. 200.

27. Randazzo, Salvo. 2005. "The Nature of Partnership in Roman Law."

28. Young, Gary Y. 2001. *Rome's Eastern Trade*. p. 55. McLaughlin, Raoul. 2010. *Rome and the Distant East*. p. 157.

29. Rathbone, Dominic. 2000. "The 'Muziris' Papyrus (SB XVIII)."

30. Casson, Lionel. 1989. *The Periplus Maris Erythraei*. pp. 7–10. Young, Gary Y. 2001. *Rome's Eastern Trade*. p. 54.

31. Young, Gary Y. 2001. *Rome's Eastern Trade*. pp. 54–60.

32. Fitzpatrick, Matthew. 2011. "Provincializing Rome." p. 40.

33. Rathbone, Dominic. 2007. "Merchant Networks in the Greek World."

34. Ruffing, Kai. 2013. "The Trade with India and the Problem of Agency in the Economy of the Roman Empire."

35. Jongman, Willem M. 2014. "Re-Constructing the Roman Economy." pp. 75–100.

36. Meyer, Carol. 1992. *Glass from Quseir al-Qadim*. pp. 105–110.

37. Several scholars have identified additional organizational forms that have equity-investment features. Ulrike Malmendier identified the Roman *societas publicanorum*, namely the "society of government leaseholders." Malmendier, Ulrike. 2009. "Law and Finance 'at the Origin.'" Barbara Abatino and colleagues identified the peculium as the funds of a slave-run company. Abatino, Barbara, et al. 2011. "Depersonalization of Business."

38. Yamamoto, Tatsuro and On Ikeda. 1986. *Contracts*.

39. Turfan is a city on the northern branch of the Silk Route, north of the Taklamakan Desert. It is located in the east of Xinjiang region, northwestern China, and is about 2,000 km east of Samarkand (then at the heartland of Sogdiana, now in Uzbekistan). Rossabi, Morris. 1972. "Ming China and Turfan." p. 206.

40. Hansen, Valerie. 2005. "The Turfan Oasis, 500–800." pp. 283, 289.

41. Dunhuang (also known as Shazhou and Dukhan) is a city in northwestern Gansu Province, western China.

42. Yamamoto, Tatsuro and On Ikeda. 1986. *Contracts*. pp. 18–30.

43. For example, transactions between Sogdians from the homeland and Sogdians from the diaspora could end up elsewhere—if they were recorded at all.

44. Yamamoto, Tatsuro and On Ikeda. 1986. *Contracts*. pp. 18–30.

45. Skaff, Jonathan Karam. 2003. "The Sogdian Trade Diaspora."

46. de la Vaissière, Étienne. 2005. *Sogdian Taders*.

47. Samarkand was a city at the heartland of Sogdiana, now in Uzbekistan. The distance between Samarkand and modern-day X'ian (Chang'an) is about 3,750 km.

48. Skaff, Jonathan Karam. 2003. "The Sogdian Trade Diaspora." pp. 505–510.

49. de la Vaissière, Étienne. 2005. *Sogdian Traders*. p. 194.

50. Hansen, Valerie. 2005. "How Business Was Conducted on the Chinese Silk Road during the Tang Dynasty."

51. The view of Asian trade as based on peddlers was formulated by van Leur. The peddler thesis was then criticized by Meilink-Roelofsz. See p. 66. van Leur, J. C. 1967. *Indonesian Trade and Society.* Meilink-Roelofsz, Marie. 1962. *Asian Trade and European Influence.*

52. One recently discovered starting point could be the so-called Afghan Geniza. This collection is dated to the eleventh to thirteenth centuries and is attributed to a cave found near the site of a small, ancient Jewish community that lived along one of the Silk Route segments in modern-day Afghanistan. The collection includes, in addition to prayer and religious books, a trader's notebook and some agreements. See http://web.nli .org.il/sites/nli/english/library/news/pages/afghan-geniza.aspx. Flecker, Michael. 2011. "A Ninth-Century Arab or Indian Shipwreck in Indonesia."

53. Flecker, Michael. 2011. "A Ninth-Century Arab or Indian Shipwreck in Indonesia."

54. Friedman, Mordechai. 2006. "Quṣayr and Geniza Documents."

55. Guo, Li. 2004. *The Arabic Documents from Quseir.*

56. Das Gupta, Ashin. 2001. *The World of the Indian Ocean Merchant.* For the history and organization of the VOC, see chap. 10, p. 275.

57. Flecker, Michael. 2011. "A Ninth-Century Arab or Indian Shipwreck in Indonesia." p. 101.

58. Burger, Pauline, et al. 2010. "The 9th-Century-AD Belitung Wreck." p. 383.

59. Flecker, Michael. 2011. "A Ninth-Century Arab or Indian Shipwreck in Indonesia." pp. 102, 119.

60. Ibid. pp. 101, 118.

61. Burger, Pauline, et al. 2010. "The 9th-Century-AD Belitung Wreck." p. 384.

62. Flecker, Michael. 2011. "A Ninth-Century Arab or Indian Shipwreck in Indonesia." p. 106.

63. Ibid. p. 107.

64. Ibid. p. 107.

65. Ibid. pp. 118–119.

66. Ibid. p. 111. Guy, John. 2010. "Rare and Strange Goods."

67. Flecker, Michael. 2011. "A Ninth-Century Arab or Indian Shipwreck in Indonesia." p. 118.

68. Goitein, S. D. and Mordechai A. Friedman. 2007. *India Traders of the Middle Ages.* p. 371. Letter from Madmun b. Hasan to Abu Zikri Kohen.

69. See chap. 10 for the use of part-ownership in Europe and its role in the organization of Dutch trade.

70. Goitein, S. D. and Mordechai A. Friedman. 2007. *India Traders of the Middle Ages.* pp. 121, 125.

71. Ibid. p. 125. See also Chakravarti, Ranabir. 2000. "Nakhudas and Nauvittakas." Margariti, Roxani Eleni. 2007. *Aden and the Indian Ocean Trade.* For more about the maritime merchant in the Indian Ocean, see Das Gupta, Ashin. 2001. *The World of the Indian Ocean Merchant.*

72. Gotein, S. D. and Mordechai A. Friedman. 2007. *India Traders of the Middle Ages.*

73. Ibid. pp. 594–599.

74. Ibid. p. 131.

75. According to the findings from the excavations, the two main periods of occu-

pation and use of the port are the Roman (first century BCE to third century CE) and the late Ayyubid to Mamluk (thirteenth–fifteenth century CE). Quseir is connected to the Nile Valley through a well-traveled desert road. See Burke, Katherine Strange. 2004. "Quseir Al-Qadim." Burke, Katherine Strange. 2007. "The Sheikh's House."

76. Guo, Li. 2004. *The Arabic Documents from Quseir.* p. 4.

77. Ibid.

78. The lengthy account (RN 1023*) translation is a good example for the nature of the trade. Ibid.

79. Ibid. See also Guo, Li. 1999. "Business Letters."

80. Friedman, Mordechai A. 2006. "Quṣayr and Geniza Documents."

81. Guo, Li. 2004. *The Arabic Documents from Quseir.* pp. 156, 157. (document RN 1063b). Line numbers are omitted. Verso and retro appear in a sequence.

82. Ibid.

83. Das Gupta, Ashin. 1987. "Ship owning Merchants of Surat." pp. 113. Reprinted in Das Gupta, Ashin. 1994. *Merchants of Maritime India.* chap. 12.

84. Das Gupta, Ashin. 1987. "Ship owning Merchants of Surat." p. 113.

CHAPTER 4. VARYING ORGANIZATIONAL BUILDING BLOCKS

1. Harvey, Peter. 2012. *An Introduction to Buddhism.* pp. 194–235.

2. Lapidus, Ira M. 2014. *A History of Islamic Societies.* pp. 46–50. Morgan, David and A. Reid. 2010. "Islam in a Plural Asia." p. 9.

3. Toma, Marina. 2008. "A History of Zero." Al-Hassani, Salim T. S., et al. 2006. *1001 Inventions.* pp. 84–87.

4. Glassner, Jean-Jacques. 2003. *The Invention of Cuneiform.* p. 2. Fischer, Steven Roger. 2001. *A History of Writing.* pp. 37, 166–168. Diamond, Jared. 1999. *Guns, Germs, and Steel.* pp. 218–220, 231–232.

5. Boruchoff, David A. 2012. "The Three Greatest Inventions." p. 138.

6. For some of the attempts to develop theories of cultural migration, see DiMaggio, Paul J. and Walter W. Powell. 1983. "The Iron Cage Revisited." Strang, David and John W. Meyer. 1993. "Institutional Conditions for Diffusion." Kapchan, Deborah A. and Pauline Strong. 1999. "Theorizing the Hybrid." Even-Zohar, Itamar. 1981. "Translation Theory Today." Girard, René. 1996. *The Girard Reader.*

7. Crosby, Alfred W. 1972. *The Columbian Exchange.*

8. Nunn, Nathan and Nancy Qian. 2010. "History of Disease, Food, and Ideas."

9. Fischer, Steven Roger. 2001. *A History of Writing.* pp. 166–211. Diamond, Jared. 1999. *Guns, Germs, and Steel.* pp. 228–231.

10. Diamond, Jared. 1999. *Guns, Germs, and Steel.* pp. 231–232.

11. MacHugh, David E., et al. 1997. "Microsatellite DNA Variation and the Evolution." Beja-Pereira, Albano, et al. 2006. "Origin of European Cattle." Rowley-Conwy, Peter, et al. 2012. "Distinguishing Wild Boar from Domestic Pigs in Prehistory." Larson, Greger. 2011. "Genetics and Domestication."

12. Wenke, Robert J. 1990. *Patterns in Prehistory.* p. 277. Cohen, Mark Nathan. 1977. *The Food Crisis in Prehistory.* p. 18. Diamond, Jared. 1999. *Guns, Germs, and Steel.* pp. 93–104.

13. Fischer, Steven Roger. 2001. *A History of Writing*. p. 37.

14. Needham, Joseph. 1971. *Science and Civilisation in China*. Smith, Julian A. 1992. "Precursors to Peregrinus." White, Lynn. 1964 [1962]. *Medieval Technology and Social Change*. pp. 132–133.

15. Atwood, Christopher P. 2004. "Mongol Empire." p. 365. Atwood, Christopher P. 2004. "Chronology." pp. 630–631.

16. Allsen, Thomas T. 2004. *Culture and Conquest*. Amitai, Reuven and Michal Biran. 2014. *Nomads as Agents of Cultural Change*. Biran, Michal. 2015. "The Mongols and the Inter-Civilizational Exchange." pp. 534–558. Biran, Michal. 2008. "Culture and Cross-Cultural Contacts." pp. 26–43.

17. For a mitochondrial DNA map of human migrations see "Human mtDNA Migrations." 2013. http://www.mitomap.org/pub/MITOMAP/MitomapFigures/World Migrations2013.pdf.

18. Parker, Charles H. 2010. *Global Interactions in the Early Modern Age*. Brook, Timothy. 2010. *Vermeer's Hat*. Arasaratnam, Sinnappah. 1999. "India and the Indian Ocean." pp. 110–130. Das Gupta, Ashin. 1999. "India and the Indian Ocean in the Eighteenth Century." pp. 131–145.

19. Polo, Marco. 1903 [ca. 1300]. *The Venetian*. Vols. 1 and 2.

20. For example, the first book introducing Western mechanical knowledge into China was *Diagrams and Explanations of the Wonderful Machines of the Far West*, an encyclopedia of Western mechanical devices written by Jesuit Johann Schreck (1576–1630) and translated into Chinese by the scholar Wang Zheng (1571–1644). Amelung, Iwo. 2001. "Weights and Forces." p. 198. Jesuits in Japan taught European navigational and surgical techniques. In the early seventeenth century, Catholic missionaries were expelled from Japan, and Jesuit works in Chinese were banned. Consequently, Japan was only minimally open to new scientific ideas at that time. Burns, William E. 2001. "East Asian Science."

21. Liu, Xinru and Lynda Shaffer. 2007. *Connections across Eurasia*. pp. 107–129.

22. Bentley, Jerry H. 1993. *Old World Encounters*. p. 105.

23. Sen, Tansen. 2003. *Buddhism, Diplomacy, and Trade*.

24. Lapidus, Ira M. 2014. *A History of Islamic Societies*. p. 46. Cobb, Paul M. 2010. "The Empire in Syria." Wink, André. 2010. "The Early Expansion of Islam in India." pp. 99, 266.

25. Lockard, Craig A. 2010. "The Sea Common to All." p. 228.

26. Ibid. p. 230.

27. In 1296, Hormuz prince Baha al-Din Ayaz moved the entire population and its possessions to Jarun, a small nearby island. The new town and its harbor were named New Hormuz. Over time, the epithet "new" was dropped, and the town and the island became known as Hormuz. Floor, Willem. 2012. "Hormuz." http://www.iranicaonline .org/articles/hormuz-ii. Vosoughi, Mohammad. 2009. "The Kings of Hormuz." pp. 89, 92–93.

28. Ibn Batuta, Muhammad. 1829 [ca. 1355]. *The Travels of Ibn Batuta*. p. 63. Polo, Marco. 1903 [ca. 1300]. *The Venetian*. Vol. 1. pp. 107–122.

29. Dreyer, Edward L. 2007. *Zheng He: China and the Oceans*. Levathes, Louise. 1997. *When China Ruled the Seas*.

30. Floor, Willem. 2012. "Hormuz." http://www.iranicaonline.org/articles/hormuz

-ii. Samarqandī, Abd-al-Razzāq. 1857 [ca. 1445]. "India in the Fifteenth Century." pp. 5–7.

31. Floor, Willem. 2006. *The Persian Gulf.* pp. 17–19, 64. See also Vosoughi, Mohammad. 2009. "The Kings of Hormuz." pp. 93–99.

32. In 1515, a Portuguese general, Alfonso de Albuquerque (ca. 1453–December 16, 1515), conquered Hormuz and established Portuguese rule there. Hormuz enjoyed economic, military, and religious importance, and became the launching pad for Portuguese missionary activities in Persia and the Middle East. Floor, Willem. 2012. "Hormuz." http://www.iranicaonline.org/articles/hormuz-ii.

33. Floor, Willem. 2006. *The Persian Gulf.* p. 88.

34. Steensgaard, Niels. 1974. *The Asian Trade Revolution of the Seventeenth Century.* pp. 194–200.

35. The EIC provided naval help to the Persian general Emāmqoli Khan. Floor, Willem. 2012. "Hormuz." http://www.iranicaonline.org/articles/hormuz-ii.

36. Margariti, Roxani. 2007. *Aden and the Indian Ocean Trade.* Gotein, S. D. and Mordechai Akiva Friedman. 2010. *"India Book" Part Two.*

37. Shihab, Saleh Hassan. 1997. "Aden in Pre-Turkish Times." pp. 17–22.

38. For further discussion on Zheng He's voyages, see chap. 1, p. 15. Hui, Deng and Li Xin. 2011. "The Asian Monsoons and Zheng He's Voyages." pp. 210–211, 216.

39. Bouchon, Genevieve and Denys Lombard. 1999. "The Indian Ocean in the Fifteenth Century." pp. 55–56.

40. In the eleventh century, commerce in the seaport of Siraf, Oman, declined. Therefore, Siraf's merchants and residents migrated to Hormuz, which subsequently became cosmopolitan. Vosoughi, Mohammad. 2009. "The Kings of Hormuz." p. 90.

41. Clark, Hugh R. 1995. "Muslims and Hindus."

42. Guy, John. 2001. "Tamil Merchants Guild." pp. 282–302.

43. Chaffee, John. 2006. "Diasporic Identities." p. 3.

44. Nabhan, Gary. 2014. *Cumin, Camels, and Caravans.* So, Billy K. L. 2000. *Prosperity, Region, and Institutions in Maritime China.* pp. 122–125. For further discussion, see chap. 6, p. 178.

45. These are not the only three examples for migratory trade institutions.

46. Cordes, Albrecht. 1997. "Gewinnteilungprinzipien im Hansischen." Aslanian, Sebouh David. 2011. *From the Indian Ocean to the Mediterranean.* Çizakça, Murat. 1996. *A Comparative Evolution of Business Partnerships.* Udovitch, Abraham. 1962. "At the Origins of the Western Commenda."

47. The Athenian form may have been based on even earlier Phoenician merchant practices. Ziskind, Jonathan. 1974. "Sea Loans at Ugarit." Cohen, Edward E. 1992. *Athenian Economy and Society.* Millett, Paul. 2002. *Lending and Borrowing in Ancient Athens.*

48. Ashburner, Walter. 1909. *The Rhodian Sea-Law.* Hoover, Calvin B. 1926. "The Sea Loan in Genoa."

49. Ziskind, Jonathan. 1974. "Sea Loans at Ugarit."

50. Cohen, Edward E. 1992. *Athenian Economy and Society.*

51. Young, Gary Y. 2001. *Rome's Eastern Trade.* p. 55, n. 165. McLaughlin, Raoul. 2010. *Rome and the Distant East.*

52. Harris, Ron. Forthcoming. "The Organization of Rome to India Trade."

53. Ashburner, Walter. 1909. *The Rhodian Sea-Law.* Hoover, Calvin B. 1926. "The Sea

Loan in Genoa." Laiou, Angeliki E. 2002. *The Economic History of Byzantium.* Green, Tom. 2010. *From Rome to Byzantium.*

54. González de Lara, Yadira. 2000. "Enforceability and Risk-Sharing in Financial Contracts."

55. Byrne, Eugene Hugh. 1916. "Commercial Contracts of the Genoese. "Kittell, Ellen E. and Thomas F. Madden, eds. 1999. *Medieval and Renaissance Venice.* pp. 49–68.

56. Hoover, Calvin B. 1926. "The Sea Loan in Genoa." Lopez, Robert S. 1959. "The Role of Trade in the Economic Readjustment of Byzantium."

57. de Roover, Raymond. 1963. "The Organization of Trade." pp. 54–55.

58. Udovitch, Abraham. 1993. "An Eleventh Century Islamic Treatise."

59. Khalilieh, Hassan S. 1998. *Islamic Maritime Law.*

60. Subrahmanyam, Sanjay. 2012. *The Portuguese Empire in Asia.*

61. Oka, Mihoko and François Gipouloux. 2013. "Pooling Capital and Spreading Risk." Oka, Mihoko. 2013. "A Comparative Analysis on the Capital Investment into Portuguese Traders in the XVII Century Asian Port Cities: Case of Japan, Manila and Siam."

62. Al Zuhayli, Wahba. 2006. "The Juridical Meaning of Riba." p. 25. Khalil, Emad H. 2006. "The Shari'a Prohibition of Riba." p. 53. Khadduri, Majid. 1987. *Al-Shafi'i's Risala.* pp. 211–212.

63. Quranic verses were interpreted as prohibiting any loan contract that specified a fixed return to the lender, an increase over the principal, or an increase of the debt amount in compensation for deferring the payment date. Esposito, John. 2014. "Riba". http://www.oxfordreference.com/view/10.1093/acref/9780195125580.001.0001/acref-9780195125580-e-2013?rskey=YRBdc0&result=2013. Al-Zuhayli, Wahbah. 2001. *Financial Transactions in Islamic Jurisprudence.* pp. 312, 329. Khadduri, Majid. 1987. *Al-Shafi'i's Risala.* p. 191.

64. Rubin, Jared. 2017. *Rulers, Religion, and Riches.* pp. 75–98.

65. For example, the Council of Elvira (ca. 306 CE) and the First Ecumenical Council of Nicaea (325) and local synods in Elvira (306), Arles (314), Carthage (345–48), Laodicea (372), Hippo (393), Arles (443), and Tarragona (516). See Gofas, Demetrios. 2007. "The Byzantine Law of Interest." p. 1096. Khalilieh, Hassan S. 2006. *Admiralty and Maritime Laws in the Mediterranean Sea.* p. 229. Geisst, Charles R. 2013. *Beggar Thy Neighbor.* p. 20.

66. Blume, Fred H. and Timothy Kearley. 2014 [540]. "Novel 106." http://www.uwyo.edu/lawlib/blume-justinian/ajc-edition-2/novels/101-120/novel%20106_replacement.pdf.

67. Laiou, Angeliki E. 1991. "God and Mammon." Green, Tom. 2010. *From Rome to Byzantium.* pp. 25, 46, 51–52.

68. Friedberg, Aemilius. 1879. "Decretum magistri Gratiani." http://geschichte.digitale-sammlungen.de/decretum-gratiani/online/angebot. Distinctio 47. Moser, Thomas. 2000. "The Idea of Usury in Patriastic Literature." pp. 40–41.

69. McLaughlin, Terence Patrick. 1939. "The Teaching of the Canonists on Usury." p. 104.

70. Noonan, John T. 1957. *The Scholastic Analysis of Usury.* pp. 16–44.

71. Munro, John H. 2003. "The Medieval Origins of the Financial Revolution." p. 510.

72. For the contacts between Islamic law and the other legal systems of the Middle East, see Salaymeh, Lena. 2013. "Between Scholarship and Polemic." Simonsohn, Uriel. 2008. "Overlapping Jurisdictions: Confessional Boundaries and Judicial Choice Among

Christians and Jews Under Early Muslim Rule." Libson, Gideon. 2003. *Jewish and Islamic Law.* Cohen, Mark R. 2014. *Jewish Self-Government in Medieval Egypt.*

73. Khalilieh, Hassan S. 2006. *Admiralty and Maritime Laws in the Mediterranean Sea.* p. 230. Lopez, Robert S. and Irving W. Raymond. 2001 [1955]. *Medieval Trade in the Mediterranean World.* pp. 170–171.

74. Tan, Elaine. 2002. "An Empty Shell?"

75. Hunt, Edwin S. and James M. Murray. 1999. *Business in Medieval Europe.* See also www.helsinki.fi/iehc2006/papers3/BriysJoos.pdf.

76. Hunt, Edwin and James Murray. 1999. *Business in Medieval Europe.* See also www .helsinki.fi/iehc2006/papers3/BriysJoos.pdf

77. Passamaneck, Stephen M. 1974. *Insurance in Rabbinic Law.* pp. 13, 25.

78. Ibid. p. 21.

79. Slae, Menachem. 1980. *Insurance in Halachah.* pp. 25–26, 83–84.

80. Ibid. p. 26.

81. Passamaneck, Stephen M. 1974. *Insurance in Rabbinic Law.* pp. 33–35.

82. Ibid. p.184.

83. Constable, Olivia Remie. 2003. *Housing the Stranger.*

84. Ibid.

85. Koehler, Benedikt. 2014. *Early Islam and the Birth of Capitalism.*

86. Constable, Olivia Remie. 2003. *Housing the Stranger.*

87. For more information, see note on city names, page xiii.

88. Constable, Olivia Remie. 2003. *Housing the Stranger.*

89. Cytryn-Silverman, Katia. 2010. *Road Inns.*

90. Ibn Ḥawqal, Muhammad Abu al-Kasim. 2014 [originally translated 1938–1939, written 977]. *Kitāb Ṣūrat al-arḍ.* Constable, Olivia Remie. 2003. *Housing the Stranger.*

91. Ibn Ḥawqal, Muhammad Abu al-Kasim. 2014 [originally translated in 1938–1939, written in 977]. *Kitāb Ṣūrat al-arḍ.* Constable, Olivia Remie. 2003. *Housing the Stranger.* p. 73.

92. Hillenbrand, Robert. 1994. *Islamic Architecture.*

93. Ibid.

94. Önge, Mustafa. 2007. "Caravanserais as Symbols of Power."

95. Quintern, Detlev. 2011. "The Role of Samarkand and Bukhara." Gurani, Yesim F. and Tulay Ozdemir Canbolat. 2012. "Aksaray Sultanhan Caravanserai: A Study of Cultural Interactions and Sustainability Along the Silk Road." pp. 277–279 in *Archi-Cultural Translations through the Silk Road.* Mukogawa Women's Univ., Nishinomiya, Japan.

96. Khyade, Vitthalrao B. 2012. "The UNESCO World Heritage." p. 24

97. Gurani, Yesim F. and Tulay Ozdemir Canbolat. 2012. "Aksaray Sultanhan Caravanserai."

98. Önge, Mustafa. 2007. "Caravanserais as Symbols of Power."

99. Thareani-Sussely, Yifat. 2007. "Ancient Caravanserais." pp. 123–128.

100. Hillenbrand, Robert. 1994. *Islamic Architecture.* p. 355.

101. Constable, Olivia Remie. 2003. *Housing the Stranger.*

102. Bryce, Derek, et al. 2013. "The Caravanserai of Isfahan." pp. 205–209. Hillenbrand, Robert. 1994. *Islamic Architecture.* pp. 331, 374–375. Constable, Olivia Remie. 2003. *Housing the Stranger.* pp. 7, 42, 48.

103. Perdue, Peter C. 2005. *China Marches West.* Dale, Stephen Frederic. 2002. *Indian*

Merchants and Eurasian Trade. An ongoing project is forming an inventory of caravan-serais. See UNESCO. "The UNESCO Website on Caravanserais." http://www.unesco.org /culture/dialogue/eastwest/caravan/page1.htm. A recent satelite data based analysis iden-tified 119 caravanserais from the late sixteenth and early seventeenth centuries spaced approximately every 20 kilometers—roughly a day's journey with a large caravan—across Afghanistan's southern deserts alone. See Lawler, Andrew. 2017. "Afghanistan's Lost Empires."

104. Constable, Olivia Remie. 2003. *Housing the Stranger.*

105. Ibid.

106. Koehler, Benedikt. 2014. *Early Islam and the Birth of Capitalism.*

107. Constable, Olivia Remie. 2003. *Housing the Stranger.* pp. 202–207.

108. Ibid. pp. 306–311.

109. Ibid. pp. 349–353.

110. Ibid. pp. 306–310.

111. Ibid. pp. 315–326.

CHAPTER 5. THE COMMENDA

1. Weber, Max. 2003 [1889]. *The history of commercial partnerships.* North, Douglass C. and Robert Paul Thomas. 1973. *The Rise of the Western World.* de Roover, Raymond. 1963. "The Organization of Trade." Lopez, Robert S. and Irving W. Raymond. 2001 [1955]. *Medieval Trade in the Mediterranean World.* Braudel, Fernand. 1982. *The Wheels of Commerce.*

2. Throughout this book, I will use the more familiar term *commenda* when referring to this institution in all civilizations, localities, and periods, including the Arab-Muslim.

3. Udovitch, Abraham. 1970. *Partnership and Profit in Medieval Islam.* pp. 10–16.

4. Goitein, S. D. 1967. *Economic Foundations.*

5. van Doosselaere, Quentin. 2009. *Commercial Agreements and Social Dynamics.* González de Lara, Yadira. 2000. "Enforceability and Risk-Sharing in Financial Contracts." González de Lara, Yadira. 2008. "The Secret of Venetian Success." Williamson, Dean. 2003. "Transparency and Contract Selection."

6. Lopez, Robert S. and Irving W. Raymond. 2001 [1955]. *Medieval Trade in the Mediterranean World.*

7. Weber, Max. 2003 [1889]. *The History of Commercial Partnerships.*

8. Udovitch, Abraham. 1970. *Partnership and Profit in Medieval Islam.*

9. This analysis is based on Hansmann, Henry, et al. 2006. "Law and the Rise of the Firm."

10. Udovitch, Abraham. 1970. *Partnership and Profit in Medieval Islam.*

11. Lopez, Robert S. and Irving W. Raymond. 2001 [1955]. *Medieval Trade in the Mediterranean World.*

12. Udovitch, Abraham. 1970. *Partnership and Profit in Medieval Islam.*

13. Lopez, Robert S. and Irving W. Raymond. 2001 [1955]. *Medieval Trade in the Mediterranean World.*

14. For example, the estate of the Venetian Doge Renieri Zeno, upon his death in 1268, included investment in 132 *colleganze* (the Venetian term for *commenda*) to the

sum of ITL 22,935. The value of his real estate was only ITL 10,000. See Lane, Frederic C. 1973. *Venice, a Maritime Republic.*

15. The best available documentation on the multilateral use of the commenda is that of the contracts made in connection to the sailing of the *Saint Esprit* from Marseille to Acre in 1248. Of 150 contracts connected to that voyage, 132 were commenda contracts. This is the largest depository of commenda contracts referring to a single voyage. For example, a single merchant on board had thirteen commenda contracts with eleven different investing parties. For a fascinating study of these contracts, see Berlow, Rosalind Kent. 1979. "Saint Esprit."

16. The emergence of the limited partnership out of the commenda occurred in Europe after the time period covered here. The *commandite,* the French limited partnership, was recognized by Colbert's 1673 Ordinance. The history of the transformation of the commenda into the limited partnership deserves further research.

17. Udovitch, Abraham. 1970. *Partnership and Profit in Medieval Islam.*

18. Initially the first two terms were used in the Arab peninsula and the third in Iraq, but eventually all three became interchangeable.

19. Çizakça, Murat. 1996. *A Comparative Evolution of Business Partnerships.*

20. Udovitch, Abraham. 1970. *Partnership and Profit in Medieval Islam.* Nyazee, Imran Ashan Khan. 1999. *Islamic Law of Business Organization.*

21. Nyazee, Imran Ashan Khan. 1999. *Islamic Law of Business Organization.*

22. See also Udovitch, Abraham. 1970. *Partnership and Profit in Medieval Islam.* Pryor, John H. 1977. "The Origins of the Commenda Contract." Pryor speculates that the Italian commenda may have had its origins in Roman and Byzantine institutions, but he does not reject Udovitch's conclusion. See ibid.

23. Udovitch, Abraham. 1970. *Partnership and Profit in Medieval Islam.* Bin Haji Hasan, Abdullah Alwi. 1989. "Al-Mudarabah."

24. Udovitch, Abraham. 1962. "At the Origins of the Western Commenda."

25. Hitti, Philip K. 1970. *History of the Arabs.* Hennigan, Peter C. 2004. *The Birth of a Legal Institution.*

26. Crone, Patricia. 1987. *Meccan Trade and the Rise of Islam.*

27. Bulliet, Richard W. 1975. *The Camel and the Wheel.*

28. Crone, Patricia. 1987. *Meccan Trade and the Rise of Islam.*

29. Donner, Fred M. 1981. *The Early Islamic Conquests.* Donner, Fred M. 2010. *Muhammad and the Believers.* See also Serjeant, Robert. 1990. "Meccan Trade and the Rise of Islam."

30. Kister, M. J. 1965. "Mecca and Tamim." Peters, Francis. 1988. "The Commerce of Mecca Before Islam."

31. Erickson-Gini, Tali. 2010. *Nabataean Settlement and Self-Organized Economy.* Johnson, David. 1987. "Nabataean Trade." See also Negev, Avraham. 1977. "The Nabateans and the Provincia Arabia."

32. Gibb, Hamilton and J. H. Kramers. 1961. *Shorter Encyclopaedia of Islam.* 340–341. Erickson-Gini, Tali. 2010. *Nabataean Settlement and Self-Organized Economy.*

33. Crone, Patricia. 1987. *Roman, Provincial, and Islamic Law.* Secunda, Shai. 2014. *The Iranian Talmud.* Monnickendam, Yifat. 2012. "The Kiss and the Earnest."

34. Udovitch, Abraham. 1962. "At the Origins of the Western Commenda."

35. Weber, Max. 2003 [1889]. *The history of commercial partnerships.*

36. Pryor, John H. 1977. "The Origins of the Commenda Contract."

37. Lopez, Robert S. and Irving W. Raymond. 2001 [1955]. *Medieval Trade in the Mediterranean World.*

38. Weber, Max. 2003 [1889]. *The history of Commercial Partnerships.* Pryor, John H. 1983. "Mediterranean Commerce in the Middle Ages."

39. González de Lara, Yadira. 2008. "The Secret of Venetian Success."

40. Williamson, Dean. 2010. "The Financial Structure of Commercial Revolution: Financing Long-distance Trade in Venice 1190–1220 and Venetian Crete 1278–1400."

41. van Doosselaere, Quentin. 2009. *Commercial Agreements and Social Dynamics.*

42. Çizakça, Murat. 2007. "Cross-cultural Borrowing." There is considerable evidence of the importation of Arab business institutions to Europe. It is possible that the commenda was also imported through Spain or Sicily. For the purposes of this chapter, it is not necessary to reach a conclusion.

43. For further discussion on the migration of the funduq, see chap. 4, p. 118.

44. Lieber, Alfred. 1968. "Eastern Business Practices." Panzac, Daniel. 2002. "Le Contrat d'affrètement maritime en Méditerranée."

45. Hobson, John M. 2004. *The Eastern Origins of Western Civilization.* pp. 119–121. See chap. 2, p. 48.

46. They refer to *The Beauties of Commerce* by Abu al-Fadl Jafar ibn Ali. There is, however, a controversy over the dating of the book. Udovitch, following Ritter, dates it to the eleventh century. See Lopez, Robert S. and Irving W. Raymond. 2001 [1955]. *Medieval Trade in the Mediterranean World.* See also Udovitch, Abraham. 1970. *Partnership and Profit in Medieval Islam.*

47. Pryor, John. 1977. "The Origins of the Commenda Contract."

48. Ibid.

49. Favali, Lyda. 2004. *Qirad Islamico.* pp. 110–116.

50. Mignone, Gianni. 2005. *Un contratto per i mercanti del Mediterraneo.* pp. 83–89. Favali agrees with this interpretation as well. See Favali, Lyda. 2004. *Qirad islamico.* pp. 139–141, 233–237, 246–249.

51. Pryor, John H. 1974. "The Commenda in Mediterranean Maritime Commerce."

52. Cordes, Albrecht. 1997. "Gewinnteilungprinzipien im Hansischen."

53. Ibid.

54. Ibid.

55. Cordes, Albrecht. 1998. *Spätmittelalterlicher Gesellschaftshandel im Hanseraum.* Cordes also comments on the validity of the method by which Goldschmidt reached such a conclusion.

56. Cordes, Albrecht. 1997. "Gewinnteilungprinzipien im Hansischen." Whereas Goldschmidt talked about "similar" contract types, Silberschmidt talks about an exact equivalent between *sendeve* and commenda, and *societas maris* and *wedderlegginge*, respectively.

57. Cordes, Albrecht. 1998. *Spätmittelalterlicher Gesellschaftshandel im Hanseraum.* p. 137.

58. Cordes, Albrecht. 1997. "Gewinnteilungprinzipien im Hansischen." p. 136. The first source Cordes cites in his article is an entry in the *Imbreviaturbuch* by the Genoan notary Giovanni Scriba from the mid-twelfth century. In the oldest preserved volume of the debt register of Lübeck, the famous *Niederstadtbuch,* a separate register for trade businesses was managed between 1311 and 1361; the second source comes from this register's early period.

59. Ibid. p. 142. Cordes gives an example of a commenda-type contract in his article, cited from Scriba's *Imbreviaturbuch*: "I, [the capital-bearer] received from you [the investor] 50 Pfund. You want me to take it with me on a business trip to Messina and from there to wherever I want. I will keep a quarter of the profit and the expenses shall be proportionately put on the capital."

60. Gonzalez De Lara, Yadira. 2003. "Commercial Partnerships."

61. Cordes, Albrecht. 1997. "Gewinnteilungprinzipien im Hansischen."

62. Ibid. p. 143.

63. Ibid.

64. Ibid. pp. 140–144. Cordes cites an example from the Lübeck *Niederstadtbuch*: "[The capital-bearer] had 27 Pfennig Marks to which the investor had given him 72 silver Marks from her money. What was achieved with the money by the capital-bearer was divided in two between them. And each of them bore with his money half of the risk." The exchange rate between the silver Marks and the Pfennig Marks was at that time 3:1. The investor, a widow, had therefore invested about eight times more than the capital-bearer, but nevertheless had to be content with only half of the profit! This is an extreme example of the Lübeck custom.

65. Ibid. pp. 145–147. Cordes also mentions the influence of the Nordic merchants and pirates—who also shared the profit according to headcount—on the Hanseatic merchants.

66. Cordes, Albrecht. 1998. *Spätmittelalterlicher Gesellschaftshandel im Hanseraum.* p. 321.

67. Cordes, Albrecht. 1997. "Gewinnteilungprinzipien im Hansischen." pp. 46–145.

68. Cordes, Albrecht. 1998. *Spätmittelalterlicher Gesellschaftshandel im Hanseraum.* p. 322. In this respect, Cordes also comments that, in the revised Lübeck city-law of 1586, a short but significant final sentence was added: "The other [i.e. the capital-bearer] performed the work for free." This was no longer self-explanatory in 1586 and needed special clarification. Cordes, Albrecht. 1997. "Gewinnteilungprinzipien im Hansischen." p. 145.

69. Cordes, Albrecht. 1997. "Gewinnteilungprinzipien im Hansischen." pp. 46–145.

70. Elsewhere, when talking about "the nature of the matter," Cordes gives examples of common interests of merchants, such as demands by merchants from the ruler and types of contracts that were ubiquitous among merchants. Cordes, Albrecht. 2003. "The Search for a Medieval Lex Mercatoria." in *5th Oxford University Comparative Law Forum.*

71. Cordes, Albrecht. 1997. "Gewinnteilungprinzipien im Hansischen." pp. 147–148.

72. Cordes, Albrecht. 1998. *Spätmittelalterlicher Gesellschaftshandel im Hanseraum.* p. 32. Cordes explains: "the early fifteenth century is characterized as a period in which the Hanseatic company-trade—now under clear and verifiable foreign influences, namely Dutch and Italian—became modernized. After 150 years of experience with merchants writing (*Schriftlichkeit*) the ongoing contracts, freedom ruled in the practice of the company-trade in 1420."

73. Cordes, Albrecht. 1997. "Gewinnteilungprinzipien im Hansischen." p. 147. Current writing on the Medieval *lex mercatoria* doubts its existence as a fully autonomous legal system: "Lex mercatoria was not non-state law–it was an amalgam of state and non-state

rules and procedures, kept together by its subject: the merchants." Michaels, Ralf. 2007. "The True Lex Mercatoria."

74. Postan, Michael. 1973. "Partnership in English Medieval Commerce."

75. Ibid. Holdsworth, William. 1931. *A History of English Law*. Plucknett, Theodore F. T. 1956. *A Concise History of the Common Law*. Rogers, James Steven. 1995. *The Early History of the Law of Bills and Notes*.

76. It is impossible to reach a conclusive assessment as to whether the common law recognized the limited liability of the investing partner or subjected him to a full joint and several liability toward creditors, similar to the case of partners in general partnerships. *Odi v. Aringi* (1321). *Coleman v. Marham* (1321). *Septvaux v. Marchaunt* (1377). *Selby v. Palfrayman* (1389).

77. Goitein, S. D. 1967. *Economic Foundations*. Goldberg, Jessica L. 2012. *Trade and Institutions in the Medieval Mediterranean*. Ackerman-Lieberman, Phillip I. 2014. *The Business of Identity*.

78. Libson, Gideon. 2003. *Jewish and Islamic Law*. p. 101.

79. Ibid.

80. Cohen, Mark R. 2013. "A Partnership Gone Bad."

81. See chap. 1, p. 15. See also Goitein, S. D. and Mordechai A. Friedman. 2007. *India Traders of the Middle Ages*.

82. Aslanian, Sebouh David. 2011. *From the Indian Ocean to the Mediterranean*. pp. 124–125.

83. Ibid. p. 128. Baghdiantz McCabe, Ina. 1999. *The Shah's Silk for Europe's Silver*. pp. 84–89.

84. Aslanian, Sebouh David. 2011. *From the Indian Ocean to the Mediterranean*. Baghdiantz McCabe, Ina. 1999. *The Shah's Silk for Europe's Silver*. p. 90.

85. Khachikian, Shushanik. 1998. "Typology of the Trading Companies."

86. Herzig, Edmund M. 1991. "The Armenian merchants of New Julfa, Isfahan." pp. 122–123.

87. Aslanian, Sebouh David. 2007. "Circulation and the Global Trade Networks of Armenian Merchants." Aslanian, Sebouh David. 2011. *From the Indian Ocean to the Mediterranean*. pp. 124–127.

88. Atwood, Christopher P. 2004. "Ortoq." pp. 429–430.

89. Allsen, Thomas. 1989. "Mongolian Princes and Their Merchant Partners." pp. 117–119. Allsen discusses in greater detail the question of whether the ortoy business arrangements can be equated with the commenda.

90. de la Vaissière, Étienne. 2005. *Sogdian Traders*. pp. 107–109.

91. Ibid. p. 107.

92. Petrushevsky, Il'ia. 1968. "The Socio-economic Condition of Iran Under the Īl-Khāns."

93. Atwood, Christopher P. 2004. "Ortoq." pp. 429–430.

94. Allsen, Thomas. 1989. "Mongolian Princes and Their Merchant Partners."

95. de la Vaissière, Étienne. 2014. "Silk Road Deconstructed."

96. Poppe, Nicholas. 1955. "The Turkic Loan Words in Middle Mongolian." Özyetgin, Ayşe. 2007. "On the Term Ortuq."

97. Gibb, Hamilton and Charles Beckingham. 2010 [1994]. "The Travels of Ibn Battuta."

98. Das Gupta, Ashin. 1982. "Indian Merchants and the Trade in the Indian Ocean." pp. 418–419. Das Gupta, Ashin. 1994. *Merchants of Maritime India*. Jan Qaisar, Ahsan. 1999. "From Port to Port." pp. 332, 345–347. Das Gupta, Ashin. 1991. "The Changing Face of the Indian Maritime Merchant." pp. 354–355.

99. Chaudhuri, K. N. 1985. *Trade and Civilisation in the Indian Ocean*. p. 210.

100. Aslanian, Sebouh David. 2011. *From the Indian Ocean to the Mediterranean*. p. 138.

101. Dale, Stephen Frederic. 2002. *Indian Merchants and Eurasian Trade*. pp. 64–65, 119–120, 126–127. Markovits, Claude. 2000. *The Global World of Indian Merchants*. pp. 157–163.

102. Prakash, Om. 2006. "International Consortiums, Merchant Networks and Portuguese Trade with Asia in the Early Modern Period."

103. Pires, Tomé. 1944 [1512–1515]. *The Suma Oriental of Tomé Pires*.

104. van Leur, J. C. 1967. *Indonesian Trade and Society*. Meilink-Roelofsz, Marie. 1962. *Asian Trade and European Influence*.

105. Shiba, Yoshinobu. 1970. *Commerce and Society in Sung China*. pp. 31–33. So, Billy K. L. 2000. *Prosperity, Region, and Institutions in Maritime China*. pp. 211–217, 267–268.

106. Park, Hyunhee. 2012. *Mapping the Chinese and Islamic Worlds*. Hourani, George F. 1995. *Arab Seafaring in the Indian Ocean*. Risso, Patricia. 1995. *Merchants and Faith*.

107. Mukai, Masaki. 2011. "Contacts between Empires and Entrepots and the Role of Supra-regional Network: Song-Yuan-Ming Transition of the Maritime Asia, 960–1405 / Empires, Systems, and Maritime Networks."

108. Endicott-West, Elizabeth. 1989. "The 'Ortoy.'"

109. Allsen, Thomas. 1989. "Mongolian Princes and Their Merchant Partners." p. 118. Atwood, Christopher P. 2004. "Ortoq." pp. 429–430.

110. This term represents the Mongolian pronunciation *orto[y]*. It derives from the Turkic word *ortaq*, meaning *partner*. (129) Thus Endicott-West and Allsen use the Mongol reading of the term (*ortoy*) while others such as de la Vaissière use the Turkic pronunciation (*ortaq*). Endicott-West, Elizabeth. 1989. "The 'Ortoy.'" Allsen, Thomas. 1989. "Mongolian Princes and Their Merchant Partners." de la Vaissière, Étienne. 2014. "Silk Road Deconstructed."

111. A Yuan source from 1301 defines *wotuo* as "the name for [the practice whereby] government funds used for trade were distributed as capital to earn interest." Endicott-West, Elizabeth. 1989. "The 'Ortoy.'" p. 130.

112. de la Vaissière, Étienne. 2014. "Silk Road Deconstructed." p. 107.

113. Endicott-West, Elizabeth. 1989. "The 'Ortoy.'" p. 128.

114. Ibid. p. 130. The sources for information on ortoy activities are scattered and rather limited. Official sources describing the Yuan pay very little attention to the government agencies that regulated ortoy activities.

115. Ibid. pp 127–154. Yasuhiro, Yokkaichi. 2008. "Chinese and Muslim Diasporas." pp. 89–90. Chaffee, John. 2008. "Muslim Merchants and Quanzhou in the Late Yuan." p. 118. Rossabi, Morris. 1981. "The Muslims in the Early Yuan Dynasty." pp. 274–275.

116. Schurmann, Herbert Franz. 1956. *Economic Structure of the Yüan Dynasty*. p. 224.

117. Endicott-West, Elizabeth. 1989. "The 'Ortoy.'" pp. 138–139.

118. Mukai, Masaki. 2010. "The Interests of the Rulers, Agents and Merchants."

119. Endicott-West, Elizabeth. 1989. "The 'Ortoy.'" pp. 140, 152.

120. González de Lara, Yadira. 2008. "The Secret of Venetian Success." Williamson, Dean. 2003. "Transparency and Contract Selection."

121. van Doosselaere, Quentin. 2009. *Commercial Agreements and Social Dynamics.*

122. Hock, Hans Henrich and Joseph D. Brian. 2009. *Language History, Language change, and Language Relationship.* pp. 241–263.

123. Ibid. p. 262.

124. Thomas, George. 1991. *Linguistic Purism.* p. 11.

125. Hall, Robert A. 1974. *External History of the Romance Languages.* pp. 94–96.

126. Gialdroni, Stefania. 2016. "'Propter Conversationem Diversarum Gentium': Migrating Words and Merchants in Medieval Pisa." p. 5.

CHAPTER 6. FAMILY FIRMS IN THREE REGIONS

1. van Leur, J. C. 1967. *Indonesian Trade and Society.*

2. The nature of the sources does not allow the reconstruction of pre-European Indian merchants, and leaves us with seventeenth- and mostly eighteenth-century histories.

3. Varadarajan, Lotika. 1976. "The Brothers Boras and Virji Vora."

4. Mehta, Makrand. 1991. *Indian Merchants and Entrepreneurs in Historical Perspective.* pp. 53–54.

5. Kamdar, Keshavlal H. 1968. "Virji Vorah."

6. Mehta, Makrand. 1991. *Indian Merchants and Entrepreneurs in Historical Perspective.* pp. 53–60.

7. Ibid. pp. 33–52.

8. Ibid. pp. 53–60.

9. Das Gupta, Ashin. 1967. "Malabar in 1740." Reprinted in Das Gupta, Ashin. 1994. *Merchants of Maritime India.*

10. Sarkar, Jagadish Narayan. 1991. *Private Traders in Medieval India.* p. 203. On Coromandel, see Subrahmanyam, Sanjay. 1986. *The Coromandel-Malacca Trade in the 16th Century.* pp. 195–196. On Gujarat, see Mehta, Makrand. 1991. *Indian Merchants and Entrepreneurs in Historical Perspective.* p. 203ff.

11. Varadarajan, Lotika. 1976. "The Brothers Boras and Virji Vora." p. 224–227.

12. Nadri, Ghulam. 2007. "The Maritime Merchants of Surat."

13. Das Gupta, Ashin. 2001. *The World of the Indian Ocean Merchant.* pp. 344–348. Nadri, Ghulam. 2007. "The Maritime Merchants of Surat."

14. Das Gupta, Ashin. 2001. *The World of the Indian Ocean Merchant.* pp. 370–376.

15. Ibid. pp. 346–348.

16. Ibid. p. 98.

17. Ibid. pp. 320–322.

18. This case study relies in full on the research of Oded Abt. Abt served in the capacity of research assistant for this project, with permission to publish findings also in his own articles. His work here partly relied on his earlier work: Abt, Oded. 2012. "Muslim Ancestry and Chinese Identity." Abt, Oded. 2014. "Locking and Unlocking the City Gates: Muslim Memories of Song-Yuan-Ming Transition in Southeast China." Abt, Oded. 2014.

"Muslim Memories of Yuan-Ming." As I did the final selection, drafting and editing the responsibility for any errors is mine alone.

19. However, recent works question this assumption. For the Pu lineage and the debates over its origins, see Abt, Oded. 2014. "Locking and Unlocking the City Gates: Muslim Memories of Song-Yuan-Ming Transition in Southeast China." Abt, Oded. 2014. "Muslim Memories of Yuan-Ming." For this discussion it is sufficient to note that the Pu were deeply involved in Quanzhou's foreign milieu. Whether false or authentic, their Muslim identity or their affinity with the merchant community of Quanzhou are echoed in numerous traditions and family accounts of descendants of Muslims in the region to this day.

20. Huang, Zhongzhao. 2006 [1490]. *Bamin Tongzhi.* Vol. 73. Kuwabara, Jitsuzo. 1935. *On P'u Shou-keng.* Vol. 2. pp. 37–38, 52–55.

21. Mukai, Masaki. 2014. "Transforming Dashi Shippers: The Tributary System and the Trans-national Network during the Song Period." pp. 12–13.

22. Abt, Oded. 2012. "Muslim Ancestry and Chinese Identity." pp. 37–39.

23. Toqto'a. 1977 [1343]. *Song History.* Kuwabara, Jitsuzo. 1935. *On P'u Shou-keng.* Vol. 2. pp. 39, 57–59.

24. Abt, Oded. 2014. "Locking and Unlocking the City Gates: Muslim Memories of Song-Yuan-Ming Transition in Southeast China." The following are sources dealing with the life and deeds of Pu Shougeng and his kinsmen. Kuwabara, Jitsuzo. 1928. *On P'u Shou-keng.* Kuwabara, Jitsuzo. 1935. *On P'u Shou-keng.* Vol. 2. Xianglin, Luo. 1959. *A New Study of Pu Shougeng.* So, Billy Kee-Long. 2000. *Prosperity, Region, and Institutions in Maritime China.* pp. 303–305. Pu, Faren. 1988. *Pu Shougeng Family Line and Ancestors Birthplace.* Li, Yukun. 2001. "20 shiji Pu Shougeng yanjiu shuping."

25. Song, Lian. 1976 [circa 1370]. *Yuan History.* Vol. 10. translated in Kuwabara, Jitsuzo. 1935. *On P'u Shou-keng.* Vol. 2. p. 80.

26. The ortoy was a trade partnership, typically between an investor from the Mongol elite and a traveling foreign merchant. It will be discussed in detail in chap. 5, see p. 155. Mukai, Masaki. 2011. "Contacts between Empires and Entrepots and the Role of Supra-regional Network: Song-Yuan-Ming Transition of the Maritime Asia, 960–1405 /Empires, Systems, and Maritime Networks."

27. Kuwabara, Jitsuzo. 1935. *On P'u Shou-keng.* Vol. 2. pp. 66, 80–87.

28. Of which only 50 were eventually built. Song, Lian. 1976 [circa 1370]. *Yuan History.* Vol. 11. translated in Kuwabara, Jitsuzo. 1935. *On P'u Shou-keng.* Vol. 2. p. 87.

29. So, Billy K. L. 2000. *Prosperity, Region, and Institutions in Maritime China.* pp. 303–305.

30. Xianglin, Luo. 1959. *A New Study of Pu Shougeng.* pp. 71–72, 89. According to So, Pu Shougeng served as the vice-governor of Fujian.

31. Yuguang, Zhang and Jin Debao. 1983. "An Account of Discovering Pu Shougeng's Genealogy." pp. 224–225

32. Abt, Oded. 2014. "Muslim Memories of Yuan-Ming." p. 153. Xianglin, Luo. 1959. *A New Study of Pu Shougeng.* pp. 73–74, 90.

33. Kuwabara, Jitsuzo. 1935. *On P'u Shou-keng.* Vol. 2. pp. 67–68, 92–96, nn. 14–17. So, Billy Kee-Long. 2000. *Prosperity, Region, and Institutions in Maritime China.* pp. 107–114.

34. Abt, Oded. 2012. "Muslim Ancestry and Chinese Identity." pp. 41–42, 333.

35. So, Billy K. L. 2000. *Prosperity, Region, and Institutions in Maritime China.* pp. 114–117. Su, Yanming. 2002. "Marking the 500th Anniversary of Initiating the Compilation of the 'Yanzhi Su Family Genealogy.'" Unpublished article written by the head of the Su family in Quanzhou, and based on the genealogy of the Su family.

36. Abt, Oded. 2014. "Locking and Unlocking the City Gates: Muslim Memories of Song-Yuan-Ming Transition in Southeast China." Abt, Oded. 2012. "Muslim Ancestry and Chinese Identity." pp. 255–309. Abt, Oded. 2014. "Muslim Memories of Yuan-Ming."

37. So, Billy K. L. 2000. *Prosperity, Region, and Institutions in Maritime China.* pp. 122, 348, n. 77. Maejima, Shinji. 1974. "The Muslims in Ch'uan-chou." p. 50.

38. So, Billy K. L. 2000. *Prosperity, Region, and Institutions in Maritime China.* pp. 122–125.

39. Zhixing, Jin. 1555. "Li Shi." p. 52b. Chaffee, John. 2008. "At the Intersection of Empire and World Trade." p. 22. Abt, Oded. 2014. "Locking and Unlocking the City Gates: Muslim Memories of Song-Yuan-Ming Transition in Southeast China." pp. 23–24.

40. See chap 12, p. 357.

41. See Yokkaichi's discussion on similar cases in Jiangnan: Yasuhiro, Yokkaichi. 2006. "The Structure of Political Power and the Nanhai Trade from the Perspective of Local Elites in Zhejiang in the Yuan Period."

42. So, Billy K. L. 2000. *Prosperity, Region, and Institutions in Maritime China.* pp. 206–208. Chaffee does not accept all aspects of So's theory. He prefers to describe members of the Muslim merchant elite as a Sino-Muslim elite consisting of wealthy and long-resident Muslim families in Southern Song Quanzhou, who at the same time remained connected to the broader Muslim trade diaspora. Chaffee, John. 2006. "Diasporic Identities." p. 417. Abt, Oded. 2012. "Muslim Ancestry and Chinese Identity." pp. 40–44.

43. Häberlein, Mark. 2012. *The Fuggers of Augsburg.*

44. Mathew, K. S. 1997. *Indo-Portuguese trade and the Fuggers.* pp. 103–114.

45. Ibid. pp. 157–161. Malekandathil, Pius. 1999. *The Germans, the Portuguese and India.* pp. 47–54. For further discussion on German merchants' trade with India, see chap. 8, p. 236.

46. Malekandathil, Pius. 1999. *The Germans, the Portuguese and India.* pp. 54–60.

47. Schick, Léon. 1957. *Jacob Fugger.*

48. Enigk, Karl. 1989. "History of Veterinary Parasitology." Blendinger, Friedrich. "Fugger Family." https://www.britannica.com/topic/Fugger-family.

49. Mathew, Kuzhippalli. 1997. *Indo-Portuguese trade and the Fuggers.* pp. 117–119, 169–188. Malekandathil, Pius. 1999. *The Germans, the Portuguese and India.* pp. 83–95. Hildebrandt, Reinhard. 1966. *Die "George Fuggerischen Erben."* pp. 146–148. For further discussion, see chap. 8, p. 236.

50. Hunt, Edwin. 1994. *The Medieval Super-Companies.* p. 94.

51. Sapori, Armando. 1926. *La crisi delle compagnie mercantili.*

52. Spufford, Peter. 2002. *Power and Profit.* pp. 22–25.

53. de Roover, Raymond. 1948. *The Medici Bank.* pp. 1–30.

54. Padgett, John F. 2012. "The Emergence of Corporate Merchant-Banks." Padgett, John F. 2012. "Transposition and Refunctionality."

55. Hunt, Edwin S. 1994. *The Medieval Super-Companies.* p. 76.

56. The organizational details of this episode were studied in Schick, Léon. 1957. *Jacob Fugger.*

57. Hildebrandt, Reinhard. 1966. *Die "George Fuggerischen Erben."*

58. Since agreements and wills are mostly unavailable for the period of the second episode, account books are the main available source. Yet not much can be learned from them regarding management. However, more can be learned from them about questions of asset partitioning between business and private assets.

59. Hildebrandt, Reinhard. 1966. *Die "George Fuggerischen Erben".* p. 81.

60. Ibid. p. 86.

61. Ibid. pp. 82–87.

62. Mathew, K. S. 1997. *Indo-Portuguese Trade and the Fuggers.* pp. 226–236.

63. Safley, Thomas Max. 2009. "Business Failure and Civil Scandal." pp. 37–42.

CHAPTER 7. MERCHANT NETWORKS

1. Goitein, S. D. and Mordechai A. Friedman. 2007. *India Traders of the Middle Ages.* pp. 3–9. See also Gotein, S. D. and Mordechai Avika Friedman. 2009. *"India Book" Part One.* pp. 3–8.

2. Goitein, S. D. and Mordechai A. Friedman. 2007. *India Traders of the Middle Ages.* Gotein, S. D. and Mordechai Avika Friedman. *"India Book" Part One.* Gotein, S. D. and Mordechai Avika Friedman. 2010. *"India Book" Part Two.* Gotein, S. D. and Mordechai Avika Friedman. 2010. *"India Book" Part Three.* Friedman, Mordechai Avika. 2013. *"India Book" Part Four (1).* Friedman, Mordechai Akiva. 2013. *"India Book" Part Four (2).*

3. Gotein, S. D. and Mordechai Avika Friedman. 2009. *"India Book" Part One.* pp. 3–8. Goitein, S. D. and Mordechai A. Friedman. 2007. *India Traders of the Middle Ages.* pp. 5–6.

4. Goitein, S. D. and Mordechai A. Friedman. 2007. *India Traders of the Middle Ages.* pp. 8–24. See also Gotein, S. D. and Mordechai Avika Friedman. 2009. *"India Book" Part One.* pp. 5–18.

5. Greif, Avner. 1989. "Evidence on the Maghribi Traders."

6. Cohen, Mark R. 2013. "A Partnership Gone Bad."

7. Goitein, S. D. and Mordechai A. Friedman. 2007. *India Traders of the Middle Ages.* Margariti, Roxani. 2007. *Aden and the Indian Ocean Trade.* pp. 150–153. See also Gotein, S. D. and Mordechai Avika Friedman. 2009. *"India Book" Part One.*

8. Margariti, Roxani. 2007. *Aden and the Indian Ocean Trade.* pp. 150–154.

9. Ibid. pp. 177–205.

10. Benedict, Robert D. 1909. "Historical Position of the Rhodian Law."

11. Goitein, S. D. 1999. *A Mediterranean Society.* pp. 344–349. Goitein, S. D. 1978. *The Family.* pp. 33–47.

12. Goitein, S. D. 1967. *Economic Foundations.* pp. 149–164, 169–180. Margariti, Roxani. 2007. *Aden and the Indian Ocean Trade.* pp. 148–150.

13. Goitein, S. D. 1967. *Economic Foundations.* pp. 164–169. Udovitch, Abraham. 1977. "Formalism and Informalism."

14. Greif, Avner. 1989. "Evidence on the Maghribi Traders." pp. 857–882. Goldberg, Jessica L. 2012. "Reassessing the 'Maghribī Traders.'" Ackerman-Lieberman, Phillip I. 2007. "A Partnership Culture."

15. Greif, Avner. 2012. "The Maghribi Traders: a Reappraisal?"

16. Goldberg, Jessica L. 2012. "Reassessing the 'Maghribī Traders.'" pp. 17–22.

17. Ibid. p. 17

18. Goitein, S. D. and Mordechai A. Friedman. 2007. *India Traders of the Middle Ages.* pp. 13–14.

19. Aslanian, Sebouh David. 2008. "Aden, Geniza, and the Indian Ocean."

20. Goitein, S. D. and Mordechai A. Friedman. 2007. *India Traders of the Middle Ages.* pp. 27–35.

21. Gotein, S. D. and Mordechai Avika Friedman. 2010. *"India Book" Part Three.* pp. 3–34. Goitein, S. D. and Mordechai A. Friedman. 2007. *India Traders of the Middle Ages.* pp. 52–69.

22. Goitein, S. D. and Mordechai A. Friedman. 2007. *India Traders of the Middle Ages.* pp. 52–66.

23. Margariti, Roxani. 2007. *Aden and the Indian Ocean Trade.* pp. 177–188.

24. Chakravarti, Ranabir. 2015. "Indian Trade Through Jewish Geniza Letters." Goitein, S. D. and Mordechai A. Friedman. 2007. *India Traders of the Middle Ages.* pp. 37–47.

25. Goitein, S. D. and Mordechai A. Friedman. 2007. *India Traders of the Middle Ages.* pp. 37–48.

26. See chap. 3, p. 65.

27. See Chakravarti, Ranabir. 2000. "Nakhudas and Nauvittakas."

28. General description: Goitein, S. D. and Mordechai A. Friedman. 2007. *India Traders of the Middle Ages.* pp. 288–299. A verbatim text in Hebrew: Gotein, S. D. and Mordechai Avika Friedman. 2010. *"India Book" Part Two.* pp. 73–112, esp. 80.

29. For further discussion on peddlers, see chap. 3, p. 65.

30. Goitein, S. D. and Mordechai A. Friedman. 2007. *India Traders of the Middle Ages.* p. 575. A verbatim text in Hebrew can be found in Gotein, S. D. and Mordechai Avika Friedman. 2010. *"India Book" Part Three.*

31. Goitein, S. D. and Mordechai A. Friedman. 2007. *India Traders of the Middle Ages.* pp. 52, 54–57.

32. General description: Goitein, S. D. and Mordechai A. Friedman. 2007. *India Traders of the Middle Ages.* p. 251. A verbatim text in Hebrew: Gotein, S. D. and Mordechai Avika Friedman. 2009. *"India Book" Part One.* pp. 222–223.

33. There are other references to commendas in correspondence, but no other contracts were published in the book.

34. al-Mahdiyya is a town in Tunisia.

35. Goitein, S. D. and Mordechai A. Friedman. 2007. *India Traders of the Middle Ages.* pp. 222–223. A verbatim text in Hebrew: Gotein, S. D. and Mordechai Avika Friedman. 2009. *"India Book" Part One.*

36. Goitein, S. D. and Mordechai A. Friedman. 2007. *India Traders of the Middle Ages.* p.226–227. A verbatim text in Hebrew: Gotein, S. D. and Mordechai Avika Friedman. 2009. *"India Book" Part One.*

37. See also Aslanian, Sebouh David. 2011. *From the Indian Ocean to the Mediterranean.* pp. 1–5, 36–40.

38. Aslanian, Sebouh David. 2007. "Circulation and the Global Trade Networks of Armenian Merchants."

39. The abundance may result from the fact that these merchants were active until relatively recently, from the coherency of the ethnic group, from its success, from the intense interest of historians, and probably from a combination of these factors.

40. Sanjian, Avedis K. 1999. "Medieval Armenian Manuscripts at the University of California, Los Angeles."

41. Herzig, Edmund M. 1991. "The Armenian merchants of New Julfa, Isfahan."

42. Aslanian, Sebouh David. 2007. "Circulation and the Global Trade Networks of Armenian Merchants." Aslanian, Sebouh David. 2011. *From the Indian Ocean to the Mediterranean.*

43. Aslanian, Sebouh David. 2007. "Circulation and the Global Trade Networks of Armenian Merchants." A small subset of the collection, about 330 documents, was separated and held as part of the Lansdowne Manuscripts in the British Library. These documents had been known to historians, including Herzig, for some time.

44. Their main shortfall, from our perspective, is their late time coverage. Only very few documents survived from the period before the establishment of New Julfa in 1604–5 and the construction of the Holy Savior Cathedral shortly thereafter. Some documents are available for the late seventeenth and early eighteenth centuries. Most Santa Catharina documents are from the 1740s. Another limitation is that the Armenian case study, though relating to merchants and agents throughout Eurasia, does not necessarily represent organizational practices of other Asians, because the Armenian merchants were Christian with historical connections in the Caucasus and Western Asia. Their institutional knowledge and practices could have originated there and not been representative of other merchants in India and Southeast Asia. This shortcoming is similar to that relating to the Geniza records, namely that they originated from one ethnic-religious group—Jews—which does not necessarily represent the practice of Muslim merchants.

45. See also Aslanian, Sebouh David. 2007. "Circulation of Men and Credit." p. 144.

46. Aslanian, Sebouh David. 2011. *From the Indian Ocean to the Mediterranean.* pp. 144–149. Herzig, Edmund. 1991. "The Armenian merchants of New Julfa, Isfahan." p. 156–82.

47. Aslanian, Sebouh David. 2011. *From the Indian Ocean to the Mediterranean.* pp. 156–165. Herzig, Edmund M. 1991. "The Armenian merchants of New Julfa, Isfahan." pp. 174–179.

48. Aslanian, Sebouh David. 2011. *From the Indian Ocean to the Mediterranean.* pp. 149–158.

49. Herzig identifies four types of relationships: commenda partnerships, true partnerships, commission agency, and representation. Aslanian concludes that the commenda dominated among New Julfa Armenians. Apparently, unlike commenda contracts, of which many survived, no true (general) partnership contracts survived, and only indirect evidence indicates their use by Armenians. This suggests their use was less common.

50. Khachikian, Shushanik. 1998. "Typology of the Trading Companies."

51. Aslanian, Sebouh David. 2007. "Circulation and the Global Trade Networks of Armenian Merchants." p. 494.

52. The commenda was the most widespread form of partnership in the Mediterranean, but only one of several forms of partnership that combined credit and labor in medieval European trade. See also Aslanian, Sebouh David. 2007. "Circulation of Men and Credit." Lopez, Robert S. 1971. *The Commercial Revolution of the Middle Ages.* pp. 74–76. Lane, Frederic C. 1944. "Family Partnerships and Joint Ventures. "

53. Aslanian, Sebouh David. 2007. "Circulation and the Global Trade Networks of Armenian Merchants." p. 513.

54. Bilateral contracts may have been perceived as too complex financially for more than two parties to be involved in them.

55. The claim that the New Julfa Assembly of Merchants was a corporation was first made in the 1940s. It was argued that a treaty between the Russian tsar and the merchants was signed in 1673 by the "Julfa Trading Company." Later historians dismissed this view. They argued that the treaty was mistranslated into Russian and misunderstood. They argued further that the company was not mentioned in other eighteenth-century documents. The defenders of the company view claimed that the company was, in fact, the Assembly of Merchants or, alternatively, that the leading merchants acted together as a quasi company. But this weaker claim was also dismissed. The treaty was signed by a group of individuals. There were several assemblies of individuals performing various political and judicial functions in New Julfa but none of them was involved in trade or in other profit-maximizing activities. The assemblies did not have corporate attributes. I am convinced by the scholars who dismiss the corporate entity claim. While family firms were common, though not dominant, and corporations were absent, commenda were very common. See Baghdiantz McCabe, Ina. 1999. *The Shah's Silk for Europe's Silver.* Baghdiantz McCabe, Ina, et al. 2005. *Diaspora Entrepreneurial Networks.*

56. Aslanian, Sebouh David. 2011. *From the Indian Ocean to the Mediterranean.* pp. 188–197. Yet, according to a new study, from the perspective of Madras and other cities further away in the network, things did not seem to be as centralized. Disputes among Armenians were also taken to the local non-Armenian courts. See Bhattacharya, Bhaswati. 2008. "The 'Book of Will' of Petrus Woskan."

57. Bhattacharya, Bhaswati. 2008. "The 'Book of Will' of Petrus Woskan." p. 72. Greif, Avner. 2006. *Lessons from Medieval Trade.* pp. 86–87.

58. Trivellato, Francesca. 2009. *The Familiarity of Strangers.* pp. 107–108.

59. Ibid. pp. 50–58.

60. Ibid. pp. 21–42.

61. Ibid. pp. 201–205.

62. Epstein, Louis M. 1942. *Marriage Laws in the Bible and the Talmud.* Ray, Jonathan. 2013. *After Expulsion.* pp. 94–98. Davidoff, Leonore and Catherine Hall. 1987. *Family Fortunes.*

63. Trivellato, Francesca. 2009. *The Familiarity of Strangers.* pp. 23–42.

64. Ibid. pp. 139–141.

65. Ibid. p. 111.

66. Ibid. pp. 142–143.

67. Ibid. p. 329.

68. Ibid. pp. 160–161.

69. Ibid. pp. 148–149.

70. Ibid. pp. 145–146.

71. Ibid.

CHAPTER 8. TRADE BY RULERS AND STATES

1. Hansen, Valerie. 2000. *The Open Empire.* pp. 376–387.

2. Dreyer, Edward L. 2007. *Zheng He: China and the Oceans.*

3. The sources used in the microstudy are: Foccardi, Gabriele. 1986. *The Chinese Travelers.* Dreyer, Edward L. 2007. *Zheng He: China and the Oceans.* Ma, Huan. 1970 [1433]. *Ying-Yai Sheng-Lan.* Levathes, Louise. 1997. *When China Ruled the Seas.* Duyven-

dak, J.J.L. 1939. "The True Dates of the Chinese Maritime Expeditions." Ptak, Roderich. 1989. "China and Calicut in the Early Ming Period."

4. Church, Sally K. 2010. "Two Ming Dynasty Shipyards."

5. Chang, Kuei-Sheng. 1974. "Maritime Scene in China at the Dawn of Great European Discoveries."

6. Some of the later voyages had fewer ships and men. Some scholars question the reliability of these extraordinary figures. Church, Sally K. 2005. "Zheng He."

7. The seventh voyage is also reported in detail by more than once source, which can serve as check on the magnitude of the first voyage. According to Zhu Yun Ming, whose *Xia Xiyang* is an important source of detail for the seventh voyage, the number of ships in that voyage totaled more than three hundred, carrying 27,550 personnel, including the officers. His categories are: officers, regular soldiers, foremen or mess leaders, rudder operators, anchor-men, interpreters, business managers, clerks and accountants, doctors, blacksmiths for the anchors, caulkers for the hull, sail makers, other craftsmen, sailors, and civilian boatmen.

8. Ding, J., et al. 2007. "Zheng He's Sailing to West Ocean."

9. Reddick, Zachary. 2014. "The Zheng He Voyages Reconsidered."

10. Kang, David. 2010. *East Asia Before the West Five Centuries of Trade and Tribute.* pp. 54–81, 107–138.

11. Levathes, Louise. 1997. *When China Ruled the Seas.*

12. Ibid.

13. Finlay, Robert. 2008. "The Voyages of Zheng He." pp. 330–31, 336, 339.

14. Stent, Carter G. 1877. "Chinese Eunuchs."

15. Manz, Beatrice. 2007. *Power, Politics and Religion in Timurid Iran.* p. 16.

16. See also Levathes, Louise. 1997. *When China Ruled the Seas.* pp. 173–181.

17. Subrahmanyam, Sanjay. 1997. *The Career and Legend of Vasco da Gama.* pp. 18, 68.

18. Souza, George. 1986. *The Survival of Empire.* pp. 12–15.

19. It appears in accounts such as Chaudhuri, K. N. 1985. *Trade and Civilisation in the Indian Ocean.* pp. 63–79. Abu-Lughod, Janet. 1991. *Before European Hegemony.* pp. 19–20.

20. Steensgaard, Niels. 1974. *The Asian Trade Revolution of the Seventeenth Century.*

21. Subrahmanyam, Sanjay. 2012. *The Portuguese Empire in Asia.* Subrahmanyam, Sanjay and Luís Filipe Thomaz. 1991. "Evolution of Empire."

22. Mathew, K. S. 1997. *Indo-Portuguese trade and the Fuggers.* Malekandathil, Pius. 1999. *The Germans, the Portuguese and India.*

23. Curtin mentions that "the fiscal balance for the Portuguese government over the long run was negative." See Curtin, Philip D. 1984. *Cross-Cultural Trade.* pp. 141–143.

24. Mathew, K. S. 1983. *Portuguese Trade with India.* Kellenbenz notes that, as early as 1493, Diogo Fernandes, a Portuguese diplomat, tried to secure the Fuggers' participation in an expedition to Cathay, but it did not happen. Kellenbenz, Hermann. 1999. *Die Fugger in Spanien und Portugal bis 1560.* p. 49.

25. Prakash, Om. 2006. "International Consortiums, Merchant Networks and Portuguese Trade with Asia in the Early Modern Period." p. 6.

26. Mathew, K. S. 1983. *Portuguese Trade with India.* p. 84.

27. Ibid. p. 84. It should be mentioned that, prior to the involvement of the big mer-

cantile houses, there were other attempts to participate in the pepper trade. For instance, the Ravensburger society bought ginger and cloves that were sent to Genoa from Antwerp (brought there by Vasco da Gama in October 1503) for distribution in Germany. However, in 1503 it was the German Nikolaus de Rechterghem who, for the first time, bought spices directly from Antwerp for sale in Germany. At first he worked independently, but later was employed by the Fuggers. Malekandathil, Pius. 1999. *The Germans, the Portuguese and India.* pp. 54–55. Kellenbenz, Hermann. 1999. *Die Fugger in Spanien und Portugal bis 1560.* p. 437.

28. Mathew, K. S. 1983. *Portuguese Trade with India.* p. 84.

29. Cotta do Amaral, Maria. 1965. "Privilegios do mercadores estrangeiros."

30. Kellenbenz, Hermann. 1999. *Die Fugger in Spanien und Portugal bis 1560.* p. 50. Malekandathil, Pius. 1999. *The Germans, the Portuguese and India.* pp. 43–44. Hümmerich, Franz. 1922. "Die Erste Deutsche Handelsfahrt Nach Indien 1505/06." pp. 10–11. Mathew, K. S. 1983. *Portuguese Trade with India.* p. 163.

31. For further discussion on the Fuggers, see chap. 6, p. 185.

32. Kellenbenz, Hermann. 1999. *Die Fugger in Spanien und Portugal bis 1560.* p. 50.

33. Hümmerich, Franz. 1922. "Die Erste Deutsche Handelsfahrt Nach Indien" p. 11.

34. Ibid. p. 17.

35. See also Walter, Rolf. 2006. "High-Finance Interrelated—International Consortiums in the Commercial World of the 16th Century." pp. 5–6.

36. Mathew, K. S. 1983. *Portuguese Trade with India.* p. 85.

37. Walter, Rolf. 2006. "High-Finance Interrelated—International Consortiums in the Commercial World of the 16th Century." p. 6.

38. Hümmerich, Franz. 1922. "Die Erste Deutsche Handelsfahrt Nach Indien " p. 16. Kellenbenz, Hermann. 1999. *Die Fugger in Spanien und Portugal bis 1560.* p. 50.

39. Mathew, K. S. 1983. *Portuguese Trade with India.* p. 84.

40. Ibid. p. 85.

41. Ibid. pp. 98–99.

42. Subrahmanyam, Sanjay and Luís Filipe Thomaz. 1991. "Evolution of Empire." p. 310.

43. Mathew, K. S. 1983. *Portuguese Trade with India.* pp. 98–99.

44. Ibid. pp. 85–86.

45. Ibid. p. 86.

46. Prakash, Om. 2006. "International Consortiums, Merchant Networks and Portuguese Trade with Asia in the Early Modern Period." p. 6.

47. Ibid. p. 17.

48. Ibid. pp. 18–19. Subrahmanyam, Sanjay. 1986. *The Coromandel-Malacca Trade in the 16th Century.* p. 60.

49. Walter, Rolf. 2006. "High-Finance Interrelated—International Consortiums in the Commercial World of the 16th Century." p. 9.

50. Ibid.

51. Haebler, Konrad. 1895. "Konrad Rott und die Thüringische Gesellschaft."

52. Malekandathil, Pius. 1999. *The Germans, the Portuguese and India.* p. 77.

53. Ibid. pp. 77–78. According to Boyajian, this contract was divided into twelve shares, distributed among: Rott (with five shares); Rovallesca and Giovanni Battista Lisa (together, three and a half); and a group of Portuguese merchants (three and a half shares). Boyajian, James C. 1993. *Portuguese Trade in Asia under the Habsburgs.* p. 18. It is not

clear how this coincides with the apparent sale of 3/8 cited by Malekandathil; perhaps these were sold out of Rott's share.

54. Kalus, Maximilian. 2006. "Tracing Business Patterns in Sixteenth Century European–Asian Trade. New Methods Using Semantic Networking Models." Malekandathil, Pius. 1999. *The Germans, the Portuguese and India.* pp. 77–90.

55. It was a gradual process. See Boyajian, James C. 1993. *Portuguese Trade in Asia under the Habsburgs.* pp. 18–22.

56. Malekandathil, Pius. 1999. *The Germans, the Portuguese and India.* p. 82.

57. Ibid. p. 83.

58. The king needed funds to cover the cost of his wars with the Netherlands and later on with England. Ibid. p. 83.

59. Ibid. p. 84.

60. Ibid. pp. 84–87.

61. Ibid. p. 84.

62. Boyajian, James C. 1993. *Portuguese Trade in Asia under the Habsburgs.* pp. 20–22.

63. Ibid. pp. 19–20.

64. It was bought for the Georg Fuggerische Erben in 1587.

65. Malekandathil, Pius. 1999. *The Germans, the Portuguese and India.* p. 84.

66. Ibid. p. 83.

67. Ibid. pp. 87–88.

68. Ibid. pp. 91–92.

69. Boyajian, James C. 1993. *Portuguese Trade in Asia under the Habsburgs.* p. 12.

CHAPTER 9. THE ORIGINS OF THE BUSINESS CORPORATION

1. Paraphrased based on *Black's Law Dictionary Free Online Legal Dictionary.* 2nd ed. Black, Henry. "Black's Law Dictionary." https://thelawdictionary.org/corporation/.

2. These characteristics are an adaptation on the "Kintner regulations" which were applied in the US in the period 1960–1997 in order to determine whether an entity would be taxed for federal income tax purposes as a corporation (taxable entity) or as a partnership (tax-through entity). United States v. Kintner (1954). http://msi.nga.mil /NGAPortal/MSI.portal?_nfpb=true&_st=&_pageLabel=msi_portal_page_62& pubCode=0005. The Kitner regulations included six characteristics: (i) associates, (ii) an objective to carry on a business and divide the gains therefrom, (iii) continuity of life, (iv) centralization of management, (v) liability for corporate debts limited to corporate property, and (vi) free transferability of interests.

3. Coke, Edward. 1853 [1628]. *A Commentarie upon Littleton.*

4. Duff, P. W. 1938. *Personality in Roman Private Law.*

5. Malmendier, Ulrike. 2009. "Law and Finance 'at the Origin.'"

6. Abatino, Barbara, et al. 2011. "Depersonalization of Business."

7. Avi-Yonah, Reuven S. 2005. "The Cyclical Transformations of the Corporate Form."

8. von Gierke, Otto. 1900 [1881]. *Political Theories of the Middle Age.*

9. The four views of the origins of the European corporation are not necessarily excluding each other. It is feasible that corporate ideas that were nascent in Roman or-

ganizations and Roman law were further developed by Church officials and canon law jurists in the Medieval Roman Catholic Church.

10. Berman, Harold. 1983. *Law and Revolution.* See also ibid. Grant, Edward. 2001. *God and Reason in the Middle Ages.*

11. Tierney, Brian. 1955. *Foundations of the Conciliar Theory.* pp. 96–131. Berman and Tierney base their analysis on earlier work such as: Vauchez, André. 1971. "Michaud-Quantin (Pierre) Universitas." Gillet, Pierre. 1927. *La personnalité juridique en droit ecclésiastique.* For a more recent of the papal legal revolution, the birth of the corporation and the implication of this to the organization of universities and to the emergence of European science see Huff, Toby E. 2017. *The Rise of Early Modern Science.*

12. Ekelund, Robert B., et al. 1996. *Sacred Trust.*

13. Harris, Steven J. 1996. "Confession-Building." pp. 287–318

14. Corporate notions played some role, a different and more limited role, in the conceptualization of rulers and states as well. This role is beyond the scope of the current book. See Maitland, Frederic W. 1900. "Corporation Sole." Maitland, Frederic W. 1901. "Crown as Corporation."Kantorowicz, Ernst H. 1970. *The King's Two Bodies.*

15. See also Feldman, Stephen M. 1997. *Please Don't Wish Me a Merry Christmas.*

16. See also Black, Antony. 2003. *Guild and State.* pp. 12–32. Epstein, S. R. 1998. "Technological Change in Preindustrial Europe." Ogilvie, Sheilagh. 2011. *Institutions and European Trade.*

17. For the legal definition of the corporation in England of the seventeenth century see *The Case of Sutton's Hospital* (1610). Coke, Edward. 1853 [1628]. *A Commentarie upon Littleton.* Sheppard, William. 1659. *Of Corporations, Fraternities and Guilds.* For eighteenth century definitions see Blackstone, William. 1890. *Commentaries on the Laws of England.* pp. 462–467. Kyd, Stewart. 1793. *A Treatise on the Law of Corporations.* pp. 69–70. Harris, Ron. 2000. *Industrializing English Law.* chap. 1.

18. Ogilvie, Sheilagh. 2011. *Institutions and European Trade.* pp. 172, 205.

19. Cawston, George and A. H. Keane. 1896. *The Early Chartered Companies.* pp. 60–66.

20. Braudel, Fernand. 1982. *The Wheels of Commerce.* pp. 433–452.

21. Scott, William. 1912. *The General Development of the Joint-Stock System.* p. 22

22. Felloni, Giuseppe. 2014. *Amministrazione ed etica.* Schmitthoff, Clive M. 1939. "The Origin of the Joint-Stock Company."

23. Headed by Pauw, Hudde, and Karel. Fouché, Leo. 1936. "The Origins and Early History of the Dutch East India Company." pp. 444–448.

24. Bruijn, J. R., et al. 1979. *Dutch-Asiatic Shipping.* Some of the sources count fourteen voyages and sixty-five ships.

25. In the Netherlands, as elsewhere in Europe, one could also be a partner in a trading partnership. Such partnerships involved investment in goods or combined investment in goods and ships. They were often joint ventures formed for a single voyage, at the end of which profits were distributed. Occasionally they were partnerships for the long term.

26. For more information on the secondary market, see Gelderblom, Oscar and Joost Jonker. 2004. "Completing a Financial Revolution."

27. Riemersma, Jelle. 1952. "Trading and Shipping Associations." Mansvelt, William. 1922. *Rechtsvorm en Geldelijk Beheer bij de Oost-Indische Compagnie.*

28. Andrews, Kenneth R. 1964. *Elizabethan Privateering.* p. 46.

29. Scott, William. 1910. *Companies for Foreign Trade, Colonization, Fishing and*

Mining. Andrews, Kenneth R. 1985. *Trade, Plunder, and Settlement.* pp. 101–115. Unlike the Dutch model of two distinct classes of investors, that was used both in the precompanies and the VOC, that seems to me to be based on the asymmetric model of the commenda, this English joint venture model is of syndics in which all investors are of the same class and are different only in their shares. The syndic model in which members of the syndicate sold part of their share could also be found in the Portuguese Asia contracts.

30. Scott, William. 1910. *Companies for Foreign Trade, Colonization, Fishing and Mining.* pp. 76–78.

31. Sicard, Germain. 2015. *The Origins of Corporations.* p. 240. The book was originally published as Sicard, Germain and Georges Boyer. 1953. *Aux origines des sociétés anonymes.*

32. The number of shareholders in Bazacle mills ranged between 63 and 79, and in Château Narbonnais mills indirect evidence suggests numbers between 24 and 63. Almost all shareholders lived in and around Toulouse. It seems as though initially most shareholders were fullers but with time other craftsmen, merchants and landowners became shareholders. Sicard, Germain. 2015. *The Origins of Corporations.* pp. 166–189.

33. Ibid. pp. 199–218.

34. Harris, Ron. 2000. *Industrializing English Law.* pp. 190–193. The New River Company that supplied London with water was divided to 36 shares called moieties. This governance structure is property law based and has resemblance to that of the mills and the mines. See Rudden, Bernard. 1985. "The New River."

35. Willan, T. S. 1956. *The Early History of the Russia Company.*

36. Wood, Alfred C. 1964. *A History of the Levant Company.* Epstein, M. 1908. *The Early History of the Levant Company.* Braudel, Fernand. 1982. *The Wheels of Commerce.* pp. 447–452.

37. Willan, T. S. 1956. *The Early History of the Russia Company.* pp. 41–47, 211–216.

38. Ibid. p. 273.

39. Wood, Alfred C. 1964. *A History of the Levant Company.* pp. 16–23.

40. These abortive, short-lived, or otherwise minor companies include: The Merchant Adventures for Guinea; the Senegal Adventures; the Gynney and Bynney Company; the Greenland Company; the Barbary (or Morocco) Company; the Canary Company; the Cathay Company; and the North West Company. See Scott, William. 1912. *The General Development of the Joint-Stock System.* pp. 105–129. For the history of the North East Company, which is typical of this category of minor companies, see Shammas, Carole. 1975. "The Invisible Merchant and Property Rights."

41. See also chap. 8, p. 233. Chaudhuri, K. N. 1965. *The English East India Company.* Aghassian, Michel and Kéram Kévonian. 1999. "The Armenian Merchant Network." Scott, William. 1912. *The General Development of the Joint-Stock System.* Scott, William. 1910. *Companies for Foreign Trade, Colonization, Fishing and Mining.* Furber, Holden. 1976. *Rival Empires of Trade in the Orient.*

42. Brenner, Robert. 1993. *Merchants and Revolution.*

43. Prakash, Omar Chouhan. 1985. *The Dutch East India Company and the Economy of Bengal.* Chaudhuri, K. N. 1965. *The English East India Company.* pp. 1–14, Braudel, Fernand. 1982. *The Wheels of Commerce.* pp. 445–453. Gelderblom, Oscar, et al. 2013. "The Formative Years of the Modern Corporation."

44. See the discussion of contemporary usury laws and insurance in Malynes, Gerard.

1622. *The Ancient Law-Merchant.* pp. 329–336. For the development of insurance in the major European cities see Leonard, A. B. (Ed.). 2016. *Marine Insurance.*

CHAPTER 10. THE DUTCH EAST INDIA COMPANY

1. de Vries, Jan and Adrianus van der Woude. 1997. *The First Modern Economy.* Israel, Jonathan I. 1989. *Dutch Primacy in World Trade.* Furber, Holden. 1976. *Rival Empires of Trade in the Orient.* Adams, Julia. 2005. *The Familial State.* Gelderblom, Oscar. 2013. *Cities of Commerce.*

2. de Vries, Jan and Adrianus van der Woude. 1997. *The First Modern Economy.* Prakash, Omar Chouhan. 1985. *The Dutch East India Company and the Economy of Bengal.* Steensgaard, Niels. 1977. "Dutch East India Company as an Institutional Innovation."

3. Gepken-Jager, Ella, et al. 2005. *VOC 1602–2002.* pp. 17–38. Dutch transcript pp. 17–28, English translation pp. 29–38. For another English translation, see Reynders, Peter. 2009. "A Translation of the Charter of the Dutch East India Company." http://www .australiaonthemap.org.au/voc-charter/.

4. Gepken-Jager, Ella, et al. 2005. *VOC 1602–2002.* pp. 17–38. Dutch transcript pp. 17–28, English translation pp. 29–38. For another English translation, see Reynders, Peter. 2009. "A Translation of the Charter of the Dutch East India Company." http://www .australiaonthemap.org.au/voc-charter/.

5. The question of whether the incorporation also entailed limitation of liability is debated among scholars. See, for example: de Jongh, Johan Matthijs. 2009. "Shareholder Activists Avant la Lettre: The Complaining Shareholders in the Dutch East India Company." More generally, see de Jongh, Johan Matthijs. 2014. *Tussen Societas en Universitas.*

6. Gepken-Jager, Ella, et al. 2005. *VOC 1602–2002.* pp. 17–38. Dutch transcript pp. 17–28. English translation pp. 29–38. For another English translation, see Reynders, Peter. 2009. "A Translation of the Charter of the Dutch East India Company." http://www .australiaonthemap.org.au/voc-charter/.

7. Subscription books for the other chambers did not survive.

8. den Heijer, Hendrik. 2005. *De geoctrooieerde compagnie.* pp. 70–80. van Dillen, Johannes. 1958. *Het oudste Aandeelhoudersregister van de Kamer Amsterdam.* pp. 42–59.

9. den Heijer, Hendrik. 2005. *De geoctrooieerde compagnie.*

10. More accurately, *bewindhebbers* were required to hold a minimum amount of shares—1,000 Flemish pounds' worth (500 for Hoorn and Enkhuizen)—to qualify for their status. They could not sell their status as *bewindhebbers* in the market. That status was hereditary. They were allowed to buy a larger share in the profits but they could not, by this, gain more voting power.

11. Gaastra, F. S. 2007. "The Organization of the VOC."

12. Gepken-Jager, Ella, et al. 2005. *VOC 1602–2002.* pp. 17–38. Dutch transcript pp. 17–28. English translation pp. 29–38. For another English translation, see Reynders, Peter. 2009. "A Translation of the Charter of the Dutch East India Company." http://www .australiaonthemap.org.au/voc-charter/.

13. Ibid.

14. Ibid.

15. North, Douglass C. and Barry R. Weingast. 1989. "Constitutions and Commitment."

16. Israel, Jonathan I. 1989. *Dutch Primacy in World Trade.*

17. Adams, Julia. 2005. *The Familial State.* pp. 38–74.

18. Weingast, Barry R. 1995. "The Economic Role of Political Institutions."

19. Mansvelt, William. 1922. *Rechtsvorm en Geldelijk Beheer bij de Oost-Indische Compagnie.* p. 54.

20. den Heijer, Hendrik. 2005. *De geoctrooieerde compagnie.* pp. 66–68.

21. Harris, Ron. 2010. "Law, Finance and the First Corporations."

22. Adams, Julia. 2005. *The Familial State.* pp. 52–61.

23. van Dillen, Johannes. 2006 [1935]. "Isaac Le Maire and the Early Trading in Dutch East India Company Shares." Gelderblom, Oscar, et al. 2016. "An Admiralty for Asia."

24. Gepken-Jager, Ella. 2005. "The Dutch East India Company (VOC)." den Heijer, Hendrik. 2005. *De geoctrooieerde compagnie.*

25. The tax burden had to be increased and wartime gaps in tax collection had to be filled by borrowing. As the federal government did not have the administrative apparatus or the political power to collect taxes, the seven provincial states that comprised the United Provinces had to carry the burden. They negotiated a formula to split this burden between them through a quota system. Each of the provinces, in turn, allocated part of the burden to the city magistrates and tax farmers within its territory. de Vries, Jan and Adrianus van der Woude. 1997. *The First Modern Economy.* pp. 91–129

26. Tracy, James D. 1985. *A Financial Revolution in the Habsburg Netherlands.* 't Hart, Marjolein C. 1993. *Making of a Bourgeois State.*

27. Some scholars place its timing in the 1570s, and others around 1600. Some call attention to the fact that municipal borrowing began in the fifteenth century. Some stress the introduction of public borrowing, while others view the reorganization of taxation as equally important. Some argue that the fundamental change was achieved by a shift to the level of the province while others believe that it was accomplished on the city level. Several scholars argue that, on the debt side, it was the shift from short-term debt to long-term debt in the form of annuities that allowed more creditworthiness and increased borrowing, while others argue that transferable short-term obligations were in higher demand. Some argue that the liquidity of the market was limited due to the variation in bond types among various issuers and the resulting lack of standardization. Some argue that the suppliers of credit were mostly *rentiers*, while others claim they were primarily merchants in search of liquid investment. See Tracy, James D. 1985. *A Financial Revolution in the Habsburg Netherlands.* 't Hart, Marjolein C. 1993. *Making of a Bourgeois State.* Fritschy, W. 2003. "A Financial Revolution Reconsidered."

28. Braudel, Fernand. 1982. *The Wheels of Commerce.*

29. van Dillen, Johannes. 1958. *Het oudste Aandeelhoudersregister van de Kamer Amsterdam.* pp. 32–34.

30. de Vries, Jan and Adrianus van der Woude. 1997. *The First Modern Economy.* pp. 147–158. Garber, Peter M. 2000. *Famous First Bubbles.* pp. 15–83. For the Amsterdam stock market of the late seventeenth century, see Neal, Larry. 1990. *The Rise of Financial Capitalism.*

31. Gelderblom, Oscar and Joost Jonker. 2004. "Completing a Financial Revolution."

32. Ibid. Gelderblom, Oscar and Joost Jonker. 2005. "Amsterdam as the Cradle of Modern Futures."

33. Gaastra, F S. 2007. "The Organization of the VOC." p. 16.

34. de Vries, Jan and Adrianus van der Woude. 1997. *The First Modern Economy.*

35. Parthesius, Robert. 2010. *Dutch Ships in Tropical Waters.* pp. 113–117.

36. Findlay, Ronald and Kevin H. O'Rourke. 2007. *Power and Plenty.* pp. 175–187.

CHAPTER 11. THE ENGLISH EAST INDIA COMPANY

1. Thus, the explanations for the design of the EIC and the reasons for that design are somewhat speculative. They are based on an analysis of the available organizational options in 1600 England, on those of the postformation concerns and discussions preserved on record, and on theoretical insights as to the advantages and shortcomings of each of these.

2. Harris, Ron. 2005. "The Formation of the East India Company as a Cooperation-Enhancing Institution."

3. See Stevens, Henry. 1967. *The Dawn of British Trade to the East Indies.* Harris, Ron. 2005. "The English East India Company and the History of Company Law." pp. 224–234.

4. Shaw, John. 1887 [1774]. *Charters relating to the East India Company.* pp. 1–15.

5. Hale, Matthew. 1976. *The Prerogatives of the King.* Maitland, Frederic. 1908. *The Constitutional History of England.*

6. Shaw, John. 1887 [1774]. *Charters Relating to the East India Company.* p. 16. See The Charter Granted by James I, 31 May 1609.

7. Ibid. See The Charter of 1600.

8. In the contemporary Julian calendar, the year began on March 25, thus the voyage left fourteen months after chartering.

9. Scott, William. 1910. *Companies for Foreign Trade, Colonization, Fishing and Mining.* pp. 91–95. Harris, Ron. 2005. "The Formation of the East India Company."

10. Compare to VOC. Sum in today's currency or in silver.

11. Database held with the author. For further information about the database, see Harris, Ron. 2005. "The Formation of the East India Company." pp. 6–7.

12. Rabb, Theodore. 1967. *Enterprise and Empire.*

13. Chaudhuri, Kirti. 1965. *The English East India Company.* p. 33.

14. To simplify future discussion and adapt it to modern theoretical analysis, I will group the various investors in the EIC into *insiders* and *outsiders.* The insiders—the group of entrepreneurs who promoted the EIC—enjoyed superior information about Asian goods, Asian markets, and the state of the routes to Asia.

15. Brenner, Robert. 1993. *Merchants and Revolution.* pp. 21–22. There are no investment records for the second voyage. The database constructed for the present work, based on Rabb's memberships in the Levant Company, holds slightly different numbers: nineteen of those present in the first meeting, five of those appointed directors there, and eight of the committee members identified as Levant members.

16. In a study covering the period 1575–1630, Rabb identified almost 43 percent of Levant Company members (157 altogether) also as EIC members, and about 19 percent of EIC members (230 altogether) also as Levant Company members. Rabb, Theodore. 1967. *Enterprise and Empire.* p. 108 (see table 11.5). The percentage of overlap from the Levant side decreases as it covers members for the period from 1581 to 1630, but the EIC was formed only nineteen years into that period.

17. See ibid. For studies emphasizing the three groups, see Brenner, Robert. 1993. *Merchants and Revolution.* Grassby, Richard. 1995. *The Business Community of Seventeenth-*

Century England. A new comprehensive analysis of the investors in EIC 1599–1625 and their networks was published shortly before this book went to the press. It could not be fully integrated into my analysis. Generally speaking, its findings are in line with this analysis. It shows a wide circle of investors involved in Atlantic trade. While it downplays the significance of Levant merchants among EIC investors, it does not disprove their role in the initial design of the EIC. See Smith, Edmond. 2018. "The Global Interests of London's Commercial Community." pp. 1118–1146.

18. Chaudhuri, Kirti. 1965. *The English East India Company.* pp. 207–224. Scott, William. 1910. *Companies for Foreign Trade, Colonization, Fishing and Mining.* Scott, William. 1911. *Water Supply, Postal, Street-Lighting, Manufacturing, Banking, Finance and Insurance Companies.* pp. 464–467.

19. Scott, William. 1912. *The General Development of the Joint-Stock System.* Harris, Ron. 2005. "The English East India Company and the History of Company Law." pp. 233–234.

20. Shaw, John. 1887 [1774]. *Charters Relating to the East India Company.* See the EIC Charter in this chapter, p. 292.

21. For discussion on the governance structure of the VOC, see chap. 10, p. 287.

22. Shaw, John. 1887 [1774]. *Charters Relating to the East India Company.* p. 16. See Tthe Charter Granted by James I, 31 May 1609.

23. This arrangement was retained in the 1661 charter. Ibid. p. 32. See The Charter Granted by Charles II on April 3, 1661.

24. Ibid.

25. Ibid. See Charter of 1600, Charter of 1609, The Charter Granted by Charles II on April 3, 1661, Charter of 1693, and Charter of 1698.

26. See Harris, Ron. 2005. "The English East India Company and the History of Company Law."

27. The East India Company. 1621. *The Lawes or Standing Orders of the East India Company.* p. 2. The printed version of the bylaws was published in 1621. To the best of my knowledge, no earlier version has survived. I surmise that this publication reflects, at least partly, the bylaws as they existed in the early 1600s.

28. Ibid. pp. 4, 7.

29. For simplification I create a binary distinction between insiders (members of Levant and Russia Companies) and outsiders (the rest), though the actual distinction in availability of information was graduated.

30. EIC. 1621. *The Lawes or Standing Orders of the East India Company.* Clauses 297–319.

31. Harris, Ron. 2000. *Industrializing English Law.*

32. Carruthers, Bruce. 1999. *City of Capital.* p. 167.

33. Chancellor, Edward. 2000. *Devil Take the Hindmost.* p. 34.

34. Braudel, Fernand. 1982. *The Wheels of Commerce.* pp. 97–100, 106–110. Morgan, Edward and William Thomas. 1969. *The Stock Exchange.*

35. Neal, Larry. 1990. *The Rise of Financial Capitalism.* Chancellor, Edward. 2000. *Devil Take the Hindmost.* Harris, Ron. 2000. *Industrializing English Law.* Michie, Ranald. 1999. *The London Stock Exchange.* Morgan, Edward and William Thomas. 1969. *The Stock Exchange.*

36. See the debate between Carlos & Nicholas and Jones & Ville in which there is an assumption that the need for fixed capital investment can explain the formation of chartered corporations. See Jones, S.R.H. and Simon Ville. 1996. "Efficient Transactors or

Rent-Seeking Monopolists?" Jones, S.R.H. and Simon Ville. 1996. "Theory and Evidence." Carlos, Ann and Stephen Nicholas. 1988. "Giants of an Earlier Capitalism." Carlos, Ann and Stephen Nicholas. 1996. "Theory and History." Carlos, Ann and Stephen Nicholas. 1990. "Agency Problems in Early Chartered Companies." That debate focused its attention on later companies, such as the Royal African, that functioned in a different environment. See Carlos, Ann and Jamie Kruse. 1996. "The Decline of the Royal African Company."

37. Harris, Ron. 2005. "The Formation of the East India Company."

38. Ekelund, Robert and Robert Tollison. 1980. "Mercantilist Origins of the Corporation."

39. North, Douglass C. and Barry R. Weingast. 1989. "Constitutions and Commitment."

40. This section is based on Harris, Ron. 2013. "Could the Crown Credibly Commit to Respect its Charters?"

41. Ibid. For the role of the independence of the judiciary as a commitment device see Klerman, Daniel M. 2005. "The Value of Judicial Independence."

42. Erikson, Emily. 2014. *Between Monopoly and Free Trade.*

43. Chaudhuri, Kirti. 1965. *The English East India Company.* p. 74.

44. Stern, Philip. 2011. *The Company-State.* pp. 19–40.

45. Smith, Edmond. "The Global Interests of London's Commercial Community, 1599–1625: Investment in the East India Company."

46. The guilder equivalent of the pound was calculated based on the average guilder-to-pound exchange rate between 1603 and 1610, taken from Denzel, Markus. 2010. *Handbook of World Exchange Rates.* The lowest exchange rate in this period was 10.232 guilders for one pound and the highest was 10.875 guilders for one pound, while the calculated average was 10.553. This was compared to a calculation in a memo prepared by Marcel van der Beek for Oscar Gelderblom (on file with the author). I thank both of them. Van der Beek checked the amount of gold in the coins representing the value of one pound of coins, converted it from English to Dutch weight, checked the amount of Dutch gold ducats that could be manufactured from this amount of gold, and finally calculated the value of this amount of ducats in Dutch guilders and pennies. The exchange rate for 1610 based on this calculation was 10.36, within the range of the previous calculation and thus confirming it.

47. Ehrenberg, Richard. 1928. *A Study of the Fuggers, and Their Connections.* p. 87. Häberlein, Mark. 2012. *The Fuggers of Augsburg.*

48. These data are based on: Allen, Robert. "Consumer Price Indices." http://www.iisg.nl/hpw/allen.rar. and van Zanden, Jan Luiten. "The Prices of the Most Important Consumer Goods." http://www.iisg.nl/scripts/print.php?language=en&url=www.iisg.nl%2Fhpw%2Fbrenv.php.http://www.iisg.nl/hpw/allen.rar. de Vries, Jan and Adrianus van der Woude. 1997. *The First Modern Economy.* p. 85. Posthumus, Nicolaas. 1964. *Prices in Holland.* Vol. 2. pp. 46–48. Posthumus, Nicolaas. 1964. *Prices in Holland.* Vol. 1. p. 107.

49. This is an estimate of the purchasing power of the Fugger family firm in 1610, based on silver prices in 1610: 10.71 g of silver from the Netherlands per guilder.

50. Pfister, Ulrich. 2010. "Consumer Prices and Wages in Germany." https://www.wiwi.uni-muenster.de/cqe/de/publikationen/cqe-working-papers. p. 11.

51. See Allen, Robert. 2001. "The Great Divergence in European Wages." p. 426. Brown, Henry and Sheila Hopkins. 1957. "Wage-Rates and Prices."

52. Country of origin does not denote the organizational form used, but it is a good proxy. Indeed, the late-sixteenth-century English companies were operated by groups of

merchants, and the early Dutch ships by precompanies. However, from the early 1600s, English and Dutch companies were corporate-operated. The vast majority of Portuguese ships were not. A few between 1628–33 were operated by the Portuguese East India Company (Companhia do commércio da Índia). Ships of other European nations were few in numbers and mostly company-operated. See de Vries, Jan. 2003. "Connecting Europe and Asia."

53. Furber, Holden. 2001. "East India Companies." Prakash, Om. 1998. *European Commercial Enterprise in Pre-Colonial India.* pp. 72–83.

54. Conac, Pierre-Henri. 2005. "The French and Dutch East India Companies."

55. Sørensen, Karsten. 2005. "The Danish East India Company."

56. Amend—Traut, Anja. 2012. "The Aulic Council and Incorporated Companies."

57. Bergfeld, Christoph. 2005. "Trade Companies in Brandenburg."

58. Mokyr, Joel. 1993. "The New Economic History and the Industrial Revolution."

59. Weber, Max. 1930 [1905]. *The Protestant Ethic.*

CHAPTER 12. WHY DID THE CORPORATION ONLY EVOLVE IN EUROPE?

1. Most human societies domesticated not only cereals but also pulses, fibers, roots, and melons. For example, peas and chickpeas were domesticated in the Fertile Crescent, soybeans in China, and lima beans in the Andes, all providing protein. Flax in the Fertile Crescent, hemp in China, cotton in India, and yucca in Mesoamerica all provided fiber. Diamond, Jared. 1999. *Guns, Germs, and Steel.* pp. 123–130.

2. Hooker, James. 1990. *Reading the Past.*

3. Nabhan, Gary. 2014. *Cumin, Camels, and Caravans.*

4. Davies, Glyn. 2002. *A History of Money.* pp. 181–182.

5. Ibid. p. 183. Allsen, Thomas T. 2004. *Culture and Conquest.* pp. 177–178.

6. Polo, Marco. 1903 [ca. 1300]. *The Book of Ser Marco Polo, the Venetian.* Vols. 1 and 2.

7. Rashid-al-Din Hamadani (1247–1318) was a Persian statesman, historian, and physician. His book *Jamiʿ al-Tawarikh* (translated as *Compendium of Chronicles* or *History of the World*) describes cultures and major events in world history from China to Europe, especially Mongol history. Melville, Charles. 2012. "Jāmeʿ al-Tawārik." http://www.iranicaonline.org/articles/jame-al-tawarik. Davies, Glyn. 2002. *A History of Money.* p. 183.

8. Davies, Glyn. 2002. *A History of Money.* pp. 178–180.

9. Ibid. p. 552.

10. Ibid. p. 462. Goldberg, Dror. 2009. "The Massachusetts Paper Money."

11. Buringh, Eltjo and Jan Luiten van Zanden. 2009. "Charting the 'Rise of the West.'" More generally, see Eisenstein, Elizabeth. 2005. *The Printing Revolution.*

12. For the independent development of Chinese and Middle Eastern-European writing systems see Fischer, Steven. 2001. *A History of Writing.* pp. 166–211. Diamond, Jared. 1999. *Guns, Germs, and Steel.* pp. 218–231.

13. Angeles, Luis. 2014. "The Economics of Printing." Unpublished. Chow, Kai-wing. 2004. *Publishing, Culture, and Power in Early Modern China.*

14. Bulliet, Richard. 1987. "Medieval Arabic Tarsh."

15. Aslanian, Sebouh D. 2014. "The Early Arrival of Print in Safavid Iran." pp. 1636–1650, 1686–1693.

16. Ayalon, Ami. 2016. *The Arabic Print Revolution*. Robinson, Francis. 1993. "Technology and Religious Change." Coşgel, Metin, et al. 2012. "The Political Economy of Mass Printing." Rubin, Jared. 2017. *Rulers, Religion, and Riches*. pp. 99–118.

17. Abu-Lughod, Janet. 1991. *Before European Hegemony*. pp. 186–209.

18. See also Peacock, Andrew. 2015. *The Great Seljuk Empire*.

19. Abu-Lughod, Janet. 1991. *Before European Hegemony*. Hourani, George. 1995. *Arab Seafaring in the Indian Ocean*. Risso, Patricia. 1995. *Merchants and Faith*.

20. Cansdale, Lena. 1996. "The Radhanites." Gil, Moshe. 1974. "The Rādhānite Merchants." Lopez, Robert S. and Irving W. Raymond. 2001 [1955]. *Medieval Trade in the Mediterranean World*. Thomas, Nigel. 1991. "The Silk Road of the Steppes."

21. Ashtor, Eliyahu. 1956. "The Kārimī Merchants." Fischel, Walter. 1958. "The Spice Trade in Mamluk Egypt." Goitein, Shelomo. 1958. "The Beginnings of the Kārim Merchants." Labib, Subhi. 1969. "Capitalism in Medieval Islam." Tsugitaka, Sato. 2006 "Slave Traders and Karimi Merchants."

22. Fischel, Walter. 1958. "The Spice Trade in Mamluk Egypt." p. 170. Labib, Subhi. 1969. "Capitalism in Medieval Islam." p. 83.

23. Casale, Giancarlo. 2010. *The Ottoman Age of Exploration*.

24. See also Özbaran, Salih. 1994. *The Ottoman Response to European Expansion*.

25. Stern, Samuel. 1970. "The Constitution of the Islamic City." pp. 25–36. Johansen, Baber. 1981. "The All-Embracing Town and its Mosques." Raymond, André. 1994. "Islamic City, Arab City." Sevket, Pamuk. 2014. "Institutional Change and Economic Development in the Middle East."

26. Stern, Samuel. 1970. "The Constitution of the Islamic City." pp. 36–47.

27. Makdisi, George. 1970. "Madrasa and University in the Middle Ages." Arjomand, Said. 1999. "The Law, Agency, and Policy in Medieval Islamic Society."

28. Zahraa, Mahdi. 1995. "Legal Personality in Islamic Law." Nyazee, Imran. 1999. *Islamic Law of Business Organization*. pp. 75–108. Çizakça, Murat. 1996. *A Comparative Evolution of Business Partnerships*. Cizakca, Murat. 2010. "Was Shari'ah Indeed the Culprit?" Kuran, Timur. 2005. "The Absence of the Corporation in Islamic Law."

29. Kuran, Timur. 2001. "The Provision of Public Goods Under Islamic Law." Kuran, Timur. 2011. *The Long Divergence*. pp. 110–115.

30. Hennigan, Peter. 2004. *The Birth of a Legal Institution*. Powers, David. 1999. "The Islamic Family Endowment." Powers, David. 1993. "The Maliki Family Endowment." Schacht, Joseph. 1982. *An Introduction to Islamic Law*.

31. Zahraa, Mahdi. 1995. "Legal Personality in Islamic Law."

32. Heyneman, Stephen. 2004. *Islam and Social Policy*. p. 18.

33. Çizakça, Murat. 1996. *A Comparative Evolution of Business Partnerships*. p. 131.

34. Çizakça, Murat. 2000. *A History of Philanthropic Foundations*. p. 10. Verbit, Gilbert. 2002. *The Origins of the Trust*. pp. 250–273.

35. Avini, Avishe. 1996. "Origins of the Modern English Trust Revisited." p. 1155.

36. Çizakça, Murat. 2000. *A History of Philanthropic Foundations*. p. 10.

37. Shatzmiller, Maya. 2001. "Islamic Institutions and Property Rights." p. 48. Kuran, Timur. 2001. "The Provision of Public Goods Under Islamic Law."

38. See chap. 4, p. 118.

39. Lambton, Ann. 1997. "Economy."

40. Çizakça, Murat. 2000. *A History of Philanthropic Foundations.* p. 97.

41. See Bean, John. 1968. *The Decline of English Feudalism.* Barton, John. 1965. "The Medieval Use." Milsom, Stroud. 1981. *Historical Foundation of the Common Law.* pp. 166–239. Simpson, Alfred. 1986. *A History of the Land Law.* pp. 173–192. Baker, John. 1979. *Introduction to English Legal History.* pp. 283–295, 318–336.

42. Verbit, Gilbert. 2002. *The Origins of the Trust.* Avini, Avishe. 1996. "Origins of the Modern English Trust Revisited."

43. An interesting piece of evidence for the Islamic origins is offered by the 1264 statute of Merton College, Oxford, thought to be one of the earliest colleges in England. According to one study, had it been written in Arabic, it would have been considered a valid waqf-creating document due to the stark similarities. See Gaudiosi, Monica. 1988. "The Case of Merton College."

44. See chap. 5, p. 140.

45. Cohen, Mark. 2013. "A Partnership Gone Bad." Ackerman-Lieberman, Phillip. 2007. "A Partnership Culture."

46. Kuran, Timur. 2011. *The Long Divergence.* pp. 45–96.

47. Kuran, Timur. 2005. "The Absence of the Corporation in Islamic Law." pp. 815–820.

48. Ibid. Kuran, Timur. 2011. *The Long Divergence.* pp. 25–29.

49. Kuran, Timur. 2001. "The Provision of Public Goods Under Islamic Law." Kuran, Timur. 2011. *The Long Divergence.* pp. 110–114.

50. See Harris, Ron. 2000. *Industrializing English Law.*

51. Kuran, Timur. 2011. *The Long Divergence.* p. 97.

52. The first Indian Companies Act was legislated in 1866. See also Rungta, Shyam. 1970. *The Rise of Business Corporations in India.* pp. 109–135.

53. Abu-Lughod, Janet. 1991. *Before European Hegemony.* p. 261.

54. Findlay, Ronald and Kevin O'Rourke. 2007. *Power and Plenty.* pp. 67–71, 98–108, 133–142.

55. Abu-Lughod, Janet. 1991. *Before European Hegemony.* p. 285.

56. Das Gupta, Ashin. 2001. *The World of the Indian Ocean Merchant.*

57. Schimmel, Annemarie and Burzine Waghmar. 2004. *The Empire of the Great Mughals.* pp. 101–102. Levi, Scott. 2002. *The Indian Diaspora in Central Asia and Its Trade.*

58. Some scholars view them as political-military expeditions that derived from the interference in Chinese trade by other countries. See Sen, Tansen. 2009. "The Military Campaigns of Rajendra Chola."

59. Kulke, Hermann. 2009. "The Navel Expeditions of the Cholas."

60. See chap. 6, p. 173.

61. Weber, Max. 1919. *Politics as a Vocation.* pp. 26–27.

62. Abraham, Meera. 1988. *Two Medieval Merchant Guilds.*

63. Roy, Tirthankar. 2008. "The Guild in Modern South Asia." Bayly, Christopher. 1983. *Rulers, Townsmen and Bazaars.* pp. 163–196.

64. Davis, Donald. 2005. "Intermediate Realms of Law."

65. Khanna, Vikramaditya. 2005. "The Economic History of the Corporate Form."

66. Khanna, Vikramaditya. 2005. "The Economic History of the Corporate Form."

67. Arasaratnam, Sinnappah. 1966. "Indian Merchants and Their Trading Methods." p. 86.

68. Ibid. p. 85.

69. Brennig, Joseph. 1979. "Joint-Stock Companies of Coromandel." p. 71.

70. Lucassen, Jan, et al. 2008. "The Return of the Guilds." p. 6.

71. See chap. 1, p. 15.

72. Kang, David. 2010. *East Asia Before the West Five Centuries of Trade and Tribute.*

73. Ibid. pp. 42–44, 46–47. So, Billy Kee-Long. 2000. *Prosperity, Region, and Institutions in Maritime China.* pp. 33–37. Chaffee, John. 2006. "Diasporic Identities." pp. 403–404. Chaffee, John. 2008. "At the Intersection of Empire and World Trade." Clark, Hugh. 1991. *Community, Trade, and Networks.* pp. 121–127. Clark, Hugh. 2001. "Overseas Trade and Social Change in Quanzhou." pp. 50–52.

74. See chap. 8, p. 226.

75. Maddison, Angus. 2001. *The World Economy.* p. 35.

76. Morris, Terence. 1998. *Europe and England in the Sixteenth Century.* p. 9.

77. Chang, Chiung-Fang. 2012. *Population Policy in China.* p. 2.

78. Huang, Ray. 1974. *Taxation and Governmental Finance.*

79. See chap. 8, p. 226.

80. See chap. 6, p. 178.

81. For example, Ruskola, Teemu. 2000. "Conceptualizing Corporations and Kinship."

82. Freedman, Maurice. 1965. *Lineage Organization in Southeastern China.* This book gave rise to an extensive literature, debating issues of typology, periodization, methodology, regional variations, and more. For a glimpse of the literature, see Ebrey, Patricia and James Watson. 1986. *Kinship Organization in Late Imperial China.* See also Goody, Jack. 1996. *The East in the West.* Gates, Hill. 1996. *China's Motor.*

83. Ebrey, Patricia and James Watson. 1986. *Kinship Organization in Late Imperial China.*

84. One has to be aware of regional differences and differences between periods, which cannot be discussed here. For general discussions of the lineage, see Zhenman, Zheng. 2001. *Family Lineage Organization.* Cohen, Myron. 2005. *Kinship, Contract, Community, and State.* Sangren, Steven. 1984. "Traditional Chinese Corporations."

85. Cohen, Myron. 2004. "Writs of Passage in Late Imperial China."

86. Gates, Hill. 1996. *China's Motor.*

87. Zelin, Madeleine. 1990. "The Rise and Fall of the Fu-Rong Salt-Yard Elite." Zelin, Madeleine. 2004. "Managing Multiple Ownership." Zelin, Madeleine. 2005. *The Merchants of Zigong.* Zelin, Madeleine. 2006. "Eastern Sichuan Coal Mines in the Late Qing." Zelin, Madeleine. 2009. "The Firm in Early Modern China."

88. Pomeranz, Kenneth. 1997. "Traditional Chinese Business Forms Revisited."

89. So, Billy Kee-Long. 2000. *Prosperity, Region, and Institutions in Maritime China.*

90. Faure, David. 2007. *Emperor and Ancestor.* pp. 218–232. See also Faure, David. 1986. *The Structure of Chinese Rural Society.*

91. McDermott, Joseph P. Forthcoming (2020). *The Making of a New Rural Order in South China.*

92. Rosenthal, Jean-Laurent and R. Bin Wong. 2011. *Before and Beyond Divergence.* pp. 63–66. Wong, R. Bin. 2014. "China before Capitalism." For a parallel comparison of China and Europe that compares the lineage and the city as organizational frameworks, see Greif, Avner and Guido Tabellini. 2010. "Cultural and Institutional Bifurcation." Greif, Avner and Guido Tabellini. 2012. *The Clan and the City.*

93. Zhenman, Zheng. 2001. *Family Lineage Organization.*

94. Goetzmann, William and Elisabeth Koll. 2007. "The History of Corporate Ownership in China." Interestingly, by then it was based on Japanese law, which was, in turn, recently influenced by German law, and only marginally by English law. See Harris, Ron. 2014. "Spread of Legal Innovations."

95. To wit, I do not argue here that impersonal cooperation was required for China to be able to expand its overseas trade.

CONCLUSION

1. Rosenthal, Jean-Laurent and R. Bin Wong. 2011. *Before and Beyond Divergence.* pp. 67–98.

2. Greif, Avner and Guido Tabellini. 2017. "The Clan and The Corporation."

3. Masten, Scott and Jens Prüfer. 2014. "On the Evolution of Collective Enforcement Institutions."

4. Harris, Ron. 2000. *Industrializing English Law.* pp. 168–198, 218–223.

5. Grafe, Regina and Alejandra Irigoin. 2012. "A Stakeholder Empire." Grafe, Regina. 2014. "On the Spatial Nature of Institutions."

6. Scott, William. 1910. *Companies for Foreign Trade, Colonization, Fishing and Mining.* pp. 241–337. Rose-Troup, Frances. 1930. *The Massachusetts Bay Company.* Craven, Wesley. 1957. "The Virginia Company of London."

7. Bjork, Katharine. 1998. "The Link That Kept the Philippines Spanish." Tremml, Birgit. 2012. "The Global and the Local." Garcia, Rolando, et al. 2001. "Atmospheric Circulation Changes." pp. 2436–2437.

BIBLIOGRAPHY

~ ~ ~

Abatino, Barbara, Giuseppe Dari-Mattiacci, and Enrico C. Perotti. 2011. "Depersonalization of Business in Ancient Rome." *Oxford Journal of Legal Studies* 31(2):365–89.

Abraham, Meera. 1988. *Two Medieval Merchant Guilds of South India.* New Delhi: Manohar.

Abt, Oded. 2012. "Muslim Ancestry and Chinese Identity in Southeast China." PhD dissertation, Tel Aviv University.

Abt, Oded. 2014. "Locking and Unlocking the City Gates: Muslim Memories of Song-Yuan-Ming Transition in Southeast China." Paper presented at the Conference on Middle Period China, 800–1400, Harvard University.

Abt, Oded. 2014. "Muslim Memories of Yuan-Ming Transition in Southeast China." Pp. 147–170 in *Political Strategies of Identity Building in Non-Han Empires in China*, edited by F. Fiaschetti and J. Schneider. Wiesbaden: Harrassowitz.

Abu-Lughod, Janet L. 1991. *Before European Hegemony: The World System A.D. 1250–1350.* New York: Oxford University Press.

Acemoglu, Daron, Simon Johnson, and James A. Robinson. 2001. "The Colonial Origins of Comparative Development: An Empirical Investigation." *American Economic Review* 91(5):1369–1401.

Acemoglu, Daron, Simon Johnson, and James A. Robinson. 2002. "Reversal of Fortune: Geography and Institutions in the Making of the Modern World Income Distribution." *Quarterly Journal of Economics* 117(4):1231–1294.

Acemoglu, Daron and James A. Robinson. 2012. *Why Nations Fail: The Origins of Power, Prosperity, and Poverty.* New York: Crown Business.

Ackerman-Lieberman, Phillip I. 2007. "A Partnership Culture: Jewish Economic and Social Life Viewed through the Documents of the Cairo Geniza." PhD dissertation, Princeton University.

Ackerman-Lieberman, Phillip I. 2014. *The Business of Identity: Jews, Muslims, and Economic Life in Medieval Egypt.* Stanford: Stanford University Press.

Adams, Julia. 2005. *The Familial State: Ruling Families and Merchant Capitalism in Early Modern Europe.* Ithaca: Cornell University Press.

Aghassian, Michel and Kéram Kévonian. 1999. "The Armenian Merchant Network: Overall Autonomy and Local Integration." Pp. 74–94 in *Merchants, Companies and Trade Europe and Asia in the Early Modern Era*, edited by S. Chaudhury and M. Morineau. Cambridge: Cambridge University Press.

Agius, Dionisius Albertus. 2002. "Classifying Vessel Types in Ibn Baṭūṭa's Riḥla." Pp. 174–208 in *Ships and the Development of Maritime Technology on the Indian Ocean*, edited by D. Parkin and R. Barnes. London: Routledge-Curzon.

Agius, Dionisius A. 2005. *Seafaring in the Arabian Gulf and Oman: People of the Dhow.* London: Routledge.

Akerlof, George A. 1970. "The Market for Lemons: Quality Uncertainty and the Market Mechanism." *Quarterly Journal of Economics* 84(3):488–500.

Al-Hassani, Salim T. S., Elizabeth Woodcock, and Rabah Saoud, eds. 2006. *1001 Inventions: Muslim Heritage in Our World*. Manchester: Foundation for Science Technology and Civilization.

Al-Zuhayli, Wahbah. 2001. *Financial Transactions in Islamic Jurisprudence*, Vol. 1. Translated by M. A. El-Gamal. Damascus: Dar Al-Fikr.

Al-Zuhayli, Wahba. 2006. "The Juridical Meaning of Riba." Pp. 25–53 in *Interest in Islamic Economics: Understanding Riba*, edited by A. Thomas. New York: Routledge.

Alchian, Armen A. and Harold Demsetz. 1973. "The Property Right Paradigm." *Journal of Economic History* 33(1):16–27.

Allen, Robert C. "Consumer Price Indices, Nominal/Real Wages and Welfare Ratios of Building Craftsmen and Labourers, 1260–1913." http://www.iisg.nl/hpw/allen.rar.

Allen, Robert C. 2001. "The Great Divergence in European Wages and Prices from the Middle Ages to the First World War." *Explorations in Economic History* 38(4):411–447.

Allsen, Thomas T. 1989. "Mongolian Princes and Their Merchant Partners, 1200–1260." *Asia Major* 2(2):86–126.

Allsen, Thomas T. 2004. *Culture and Conquest in Mongol Eurasia*. Cambridge: Cambridge University Press.

Alpers, Edward A. 2014. *The Indian Ocean in World History*. New York: Oxford University Press.

Alston, Lee J., Gary D. Libecap, and Robert Schneider. 1996. "The Determinants and Impact of Property Rights: Land Titles on the Brazilian Frontier." *Journal of Law, Economics, and Organization* 12(1):25–61.

Amelung, Iwo. 2001. "Weights and Forces: The Introduction of Western Mechanics into Late Qing China." Pp. 197–234 in *New Terms for New Ideas: Western Knowledge and Lexical Change in Late Imperial China*, edited by M. Lackner, I. Amelung, and J. Kurtz. Leiden: Brill.

Amend-Traut, Anja. 2012. "The Aulic Council and Incorporated Companies: Efforts to Establish a Trading Company between the Hanseatic Cities and Spain." *Annales Universitatis Scientiarum Budapestinensis de Rolando Eötvös Nominatae. Sectio juridica* 53:203–238.

Amitai, Reuven and Michal Biran. 2014. *Nomads as Agents of Cultural Change: The Mongols and Their Eurasian Predecessors*. Honolulu: University of Hawai'i Press.

Amrith, Sunil S. 2013. *Crossing the Bay of Bengal: The Furies of Nature and the Fortunes of Migrants*. Cambridge, MA: Harvard University Press.

Anand, R. P. 1983. *Origin and Development of the Law of the Sea: History of International Law Revisited*. The Hague: Martinus Nijhoff.

Andrade, Tonio. 2011. *Lost Colony: The Untold Story of China's First Great Victory Over the West*. Princeton: Princeton University Press.

Andreau, Jean. 2006. "Maritime Loans." *Brill's New Pauly, Antiquity Volumes*. Leiden: Brill. http://dx.doi.org.rproxy.tau.ac.il/10.1163/1574–9347_bnp_e1106380.

Andrews, Kenneth R. 1985. *Trade, Plunder, and Settlement: Maritime Enterprise and the Genesis of the British Empire, 1480–1630*. Cambridge: Cambridge University Press.

Andrews, Kenneth R. 1964. *Elizabethan Privateering: English Privateering During the Spanish War, 1585–1603*. Cambridge: Cambridge University Press.

Angeles, Luis. 2014. "The Economics of Printing in Early Modern China and Europe." London School of Economics.

Arasaratnam, S. 1966. "Indian Merchants and Their Trading Methods (circa 1700)." *Indian Economic and Social History Review* 3(1):85–95.

Arasaratnam, Sinnappah. 1994. *Maritime India in the Seventeenth Century*. New York: Oxford University Press.

Arasaratnam, Sinnappah. 1999. "India and the Indian Ocean in the Seventeenth Century." Pp. 94–130 in *India and the Indian Ocean, 1500–1800*, edited by M. N. Pearson and A. Das Gupta. New Delhi: Oxford University Press.

Arjomand, Said Amir. 1999. "The Law, Agency, and Policy in Medieval Islamic Society: Development of the Institutions of Learning from the Tenth to the Fifteenth Century." *Comparative Studies in Society and History* 41(2):263–93.

Arnold, Guy. 2000. *World Strategic Highways*. London: Fitzroy Dearborn.

Arthur, Brian W. 1994. *Increasing Returns and Path Dependence in the Economy*. Ann Arbor: University of Michigan Press.

Ashburner, Walter. 1909. *The Rhodian Sea-Law*. Oxford: Clarendon.

Ashtor, Eliyahu. 1956. "The Kārimī Merchants." *Journal of the Royal Asiatic Society of Great Britain and Ireland* 88(1–2):45–56.

Aslanian, Sebouh David. 2007. "From the Indian Ocean to the Mediterranean: Circulation and the Global Trade Networks of Armenian Merchants from New Julfa/Isfahan, 1605–1747." PhD dissertation, Columbia University.

Aslanian, Sebouh David. 2007. "The Circulation of Men and Credit: The Role of the Commenda and the Family Firm in Julfan Society." *Journal of the Economic and Social History of the Orient* 50(2–3):124–170.

Aslanian, Sebouh David. 2008. "Aden, Geniza, and the Indian Ocean During the Middle Ages." *Journal of Global History* 3(3):451–457.

Aslanian, Sebouh David. 2011. *From the Indian Ocean to the Mediterranean: The Global Trade Networks of Armenian Merchants from New Julfa*. Berkeley: University of California Press.

Aslanian, Sebouh David. 2014. "The Early Arrival of Print in Safavid Iran: New Light on the First Armenian Printing Press in New Julfa, Isfahan (1636–1650, 1686–1693)." Pp. 381–468 in *Handes Amsorya* (Vienna/Yerevan).

Atwood, Christopher P. 2004. "Ortoq (partners)." Pp. 429–430 in *Encyclopedia of Mongolia and the Mongol Empire*, edited by C. Atwood. New York: Facts on File.

Atwood, Christopher P. 2004. "Chronology." Pp. 630–631 in *Encyclopedia of Mongolia and the Mongol Empire*, edited by C. Atwood. New York: Facts on File.

Atwood, Christopher P. 2004. "Mongol Empire." P. 365 in *Encyclopedia of Mongolia and the Mongol Empire*, edited by C. Atwood. New York: Facts on File.

Avi-Yonah, Reuven S. 2005. "The Cyclical Transformations of the Corporate Form: A Historical Perspective on Corporate Social Responsibility." *Delaware Journal of Corporate Law* 30(3):767–818.

Avini, Avishe. 1996. "The Origins of the Modern English Trust Revisited." *Tulane Law Review* 70(4):1139–1164.

Ayalon, Ami. 2016. *The Arabic Print Revolution*. Cambridge: Cambridge University Press.

Ayres, Ian and Robert Gertner. 1989. "Filling Gaps in Incomplete Contracts: An Economic Theory of Default Rules." *Yale Law Journal* 99(1):87–130.

Baghdiantz McCabe, Ina. 1999. *The Shah's Silk for Europe's Silver: The Eurasian Trade of the Julfa Armenians in Safavid Iran and India (1530–1750)*. Atlanta: Scholar's Press.

Baghdiantz McCabe, Ina, Gelina Hariaftis, and Ioanna Pepelasis Minoglou, eds. 2005. *Diaspora Entrepreneurial Networks: Four Centuries of History*. Oxford: Berg.

Baker, J. H. 1979. *An Introduction to English Legal History*. London: Butterworths.

Barton, John. 1965. "The Medieval Use." *Law Quarterly Review* 81:562–577.

Barzel, Yoram. 1997. *Economic Analysis of Property Rights*. New York: Cambridge University Press.

Bayly, C. A. 1983. *Rulers, Townsmen and Bazaars: North Indian Society in the Age of British Expansion, 1770–1870*. London: Cambridge University Press.

Bean, J. M. W. 1968. *The Decline of English Feudalism, 1215–1540*. Manchester: Manchester University Press.

Bebchuk, Arye Lucian and Mark J. Roe. 1999. "A Theory of Path Dependence in Corporate Ownership and Governance." *Stanford Law Review* 52(1):127–170.

Beckwith, Christopher I. 2009. *Empires of the Silk Road: A History of Central Eurasia from the Bronze Age to the Present*. Princeton: Princeton University Press.

Beja-Pereira, Albano et al. 2006. "The Origin of European Cattle: Evidence from Modern and Ancient DNA." *Proceedings of the National Academy of Sciences* 103(21):8113–118.

Benedict, Robert D. 1909. "The Historical Position of the Rhodian Law." *Yale Law Journal* 18(4):223–242.

Bentley, Jerry H. 1993. *Old World Encounters: Cross-Cultural Contacts and Exchanges in Pre-Modern Times*. New York: Oxford University Press.

Benton, Lauren. 2010. *A Search for Sovereignty: Law and Geography in European Empires, 1400–1900*. New York: Cambridge University Press.

Bergfeld, Christoph. 2005. "Trade Companies in Brandenburg." Pp. 251–261 in *VOC 1602–2002: 400 Years of Company Law*, Vol. 6, edited by E. Gepken-Jager, G. van Solinge, and L. Timmerman. Deventer: Kluwer.

Berkowitz, Daniel, Katharina Pistor, and Jean-Francois Richard. 2003. "Economic Development, Legality, and the Transplant Effect." *European Economic Review* 47(1):165–95.

Berlow, Rosalind Kent. 1979. "The Sailing of the 'Saint Esprit.'" *Journal of Economic History* 39(2):345–362.

Berman, Harold J. 1983. *Law and Revolution: The Formation of the Western Legal Tradition*. Cambridge, MA: Harvard University Press.

Bhattacharya, Bhaswati. 2008. "The 'Book of Will' of Petrus Woskan (1680–1751): Some Insights into the Global Commercial Network of the Armenians in the Indian Ocean." *Journal of the Economic and Social History of the Orient* 51(1):67–98.

Bin Haji Hasan, Abdullah Alwi. 1989. "Al-Mudarabah (Dormant Partnership) and Its Identical Islamic Partnership in Early Islam." *Hamdard Islamicus* 12(2):11–38.

Biran, Michal. 2008. "Culture and Cross-Cultural Contacts in the Chaghadaid Realm (1220–1370): Some Preliminary Notes." *Chronica* 7:26–43.

Biran, Michal. 2015. "The Mongols and the Inter-Civilizational Exchange." Pp. 534–558 in *Expanding Webs of Exchange and Conflict, 500 CE–1500 CE*, edited by B. Kedar and M. Wiesner-Hanks. Cambridge: Cambridge University Press.

Bjork, Katharine. 1998. "The Link that Kept the Philippines Spanish: Mexican Merchant Interests and the Manila Trade, 1571–1815." *Journal of World History* 9(1):25–50.

Black, Antony. 2003. *Guild and State: European Political Thought from the Twelfth Century to the Present*. New Brunswick: Transaction.

Black, Henry. "Black's Law Dictionary Free Online Legal Dictionary." https://thelaw dictionary.org/corporation/.

Blackstone, William. 1890. *Commentaries on the Laws of England*, Vol. 1. San Francisco: Bancroft-Whitney.

Blendinger, Friedrich. 2009. "Fugger Family." Encyclopedia Britannica website. https://www.britannica.com/topic/Fugger-family.

Blume, Fred H. and Timothy Kearley. 2014 [540]. "Novel 106: Concerning Interest on Maritime Loans (De nautico fenore)." *Annotated Justinian Code*, 2. http://www.uwyo .edu/lawlib/blume-justinian/ajc-edition-2/novels/101–120/novel%20106_replace ment.pdf.

Borschberg, Peter. 2011. *Hugo Grotius, the Portuguese, and Free Trade in the East Indies.* Singapore: NUS Press.

Boruchoff, David A. 2012. "The Three Greatest Inventions of Modern Times: An Idea and Its Public." Pp. 133–163 in *Entangled Knowledge: Scientific Discourses and Cultural Difference*, edited by K. Hock and G. Mackenthun. Münster: Waxmann.

Bouchon, Genevieve and Denys Lombard. 1999. "The Indian Ocean in the Fifteenth Century." Pp. 46–70 in *India and the Indian Ocean, 1500–1800*, edited by A. Das Gupta and M. N. Pearson. New Delhi: Oxford University Press.

Boyajian, James C. 1993. *Portuguese Trade in Asia under the Habsburgs, 1580–1640.* Baltimore: Johns Hopkins University Press.

Braudel, Fernand. 1981–1985. *Civilization and Capitalism, 15th–18th Century.* 3 vols. London: Collins.

Brenner, Robert. 1993. *Merchants and Revolution: Commercial Change, Political Conflict, and London's Overseas Traders, 1550–1653.* Princeton: Princeton University Press.

Brennig, Joseph. 1979. "Joint-Stock Companies of Coromandel." Pp. 71–96 in *The Age of Partnership: Europeans in Asia before Dominion*, edited by B. Kling and M. Pearson. Honolulu: University Press of Hawaii.

Brewer, John. 1989. *The Sinews of Power: War, Money and the English State, 1688–1783.* London: Routledge.

Brook, Timothy. 2010. *Vermeer's Hat: The Seventeenth Century and the Dawn of the Global World.* London: Profile.

Brown, E. H. and Sheila V. Hopkins. 1957, "Wage-Rates and Prices: Evidence for Population Pressure in the Sixteenth Century." *Economica* 24(96):289–306.

Bruijn, J. R., F. S. Gaastra, and I. Schöffer, eds. 1979. *Dutch-Asiatic Shipping in the 17th and 18th Centuries*, Vol. 3: *Homeward-bound Voyages from Asia and the Cape to the Netherlands, 1597–1795.* The Hague: Martinus Nijhoff.

Bryce, Derek, Kevin D. O'Gorman, and Ian W. F. Baxter. 2013. "Commerce, Empire and Faith in Safavid Iran: The Caravanserai of Isfahan." *International Journal of Contemporary Hospitality Management* 25(2):204–226.

Bullard, Melissa Meriam. 1979. "Marriage Politics and the Family in Florence: The Strozzi-Medici Alliance of 1508." *American Historical Review* 84(3):668–687.

Bulliet, Richard W. 1975. *The Camel and the Wheel.* Cambridge, MA: Harvard University Press.

Bulliet, Richard W. 1987. "Medieval Arabic Ṭarsh: A Forgotten Chapter in the History of Printing." *Journal of the American Oriental Society* 107(3):427–438.

Bulliet, Richard W., Pamela Crossley, and Daniel Headrick. 2015. *The Earth and Its Peoples: A Global History.* Stamford: Cengage Learning.

Burger, Pauline, Armelle Charrié-Duhaut, Jacques Connan, and Pierre Albrecht. 2010. "The 9th-Century-AD Belitung Wreck, Indonesia: Analysis of a Resin Lump." *International Journal of Nautical Archaeology* 39(2):383–386.

Buringh, Eltjo and Jan Luiten van Zanden. 2009. "Charting the 'Rise of the West': Manuscripts and Printed Books in Europe—a Long-Term Perspective from the Sixth through Eighteenth Centuries." *Journal of Economic History* 69(2):409–445.

Burke, Katherine Strange. 2004. "Quseir Al-Qadim." Pp. 125–132 in *The Oriental Institute Annual Report 2003–2004*, edited by G. J. Stein. Chicago: University of Chicago Oriental Institute.

Burke, Katherine Strange. 2007. "Archaeological Texts and Contexts on the Red Sea: The Sheikh's House at Quseir Al-Qadim." PhD dissertation, Department of Near Eastern Languages and Civilizations, University of Chicago.

Burns, William E. 2001. "East Asian Science." Pp. 89–90 in *The Scientific Revolution: An Encyclopedia*. Santa Barbara: ABC-CLIO.

Byrne, Eugene Hugh. 1916. "Commercial Contracts of the Genoese in the Syrian Trade of the Twelfth Century." *Quarterly Journal of Economics* 31(1):128–170.

Cansdale, Lena. 1996. "The Radhanites: Ninth Century Jewish International Traders." *Australian Journal of Jewish Studies* 10(1/2):65–77.

Carlos, Ann M. 1992. "Principal-Agent Problems in Early Trading Companies: A Tale of Two Firms." *American Economic Review* 82(2):140–45.

Carlos, Ann M. and Santhi Hejeebu. 2007. "The Timing and Quality of Information: The Case of the Long-Distance Trading Companies, 1650–1750." Pp. 139–168 in *Information Flows: New Approaches in the Historical Study of Business Information*, edited by L. Müller and J. Ojala. Helsinki: Finnish Literature Society.

Carlos, Ann M. and Jamie Kruse Brown. 1996. "The Decline of the Royal African Company: Fringe Firms and the Role of the Charter." *Economic History Review* 49(2):291–313.

Carlos, Ann M. and Stephen Nicholas. 1988. "Giants of an Earlier Capitalism: The Chartered Trading Companies as Modern Multinationals." *Business History Review* 62(3):398–419.

Carlos, Ann M. and Stephen Nicholas. 1990. "Agency Problems in Early Chartered Companies: The Case of the Hudson's Bay Company." *Journal of Economic History* 50(4):853–875.

Carlos, Ann M. and Stephen Nicholas. 1996. "Theory and History: Seventeenth-Century Joint-Stock Chartered Trading Companies." *Journal of Economic History* 56(4):916–924.

Carruthers, Bruce G. 1999. *City of Capital: Politics and Markets in the English Financial Revolution*. Princeton: Princeton University Press.

Casale, Giancarlo. 2010. *The Ottoman Age of Exploration*. New York: Oxford University Press.

The Case of Sutton's Hospital. 1612. 77 Eng Rep 960 (Court of Exchequer Chamber).

Casson, Lionel. 1980. "Rome's Trade with the East: The Sea Voyage to Africa and India." *Transactions of the American Philological Association* 110:21–36.

Casson, Lionel. 1986. "P. Vindob G 40822 and the Shipping of Goods from India." *Bulletin of the American Society of Papyrologists* 23(3/4):73–79.

Casson, Lionel. 1989. *The Periplus Maris Erythraei: Text with Introduction, Translation, and Commentary*. Princeton: Princeton University Press.

Casson, Lionel. 1990. "New Light on Maritime Loans: P. Vindob G 40822." *Zeitschrift für Papyrologie und Epigraphik* 84:195–206.

Cawston, George and A. H. Keane. 1896. *The Early Chartered Companies (A.D. 1296–1858)*. London: Edward Arnold.

Chaffee, John. 2006. "Diasporic Identities in the Historical Development of the Maritime Muslim Communities of Song-Yuan China." *Journal of the Economic and Social History of the Orient* 49(4):395–420.

Chaffee, John. 2008. "At the Intersection of Empire and World Trade: The Chinese Port City of Quanzhou (Zaitun), Eleventh–Fifteenth Centuries." Pp. 99–122 in *Secondary Cities and Urban Networking in the Indian Ocean Realm, c. 1400–1800 (2008)*, edited by K. R. Hall. Lanham: Lexington.

Chaffee, John. 2008. "Muslim Merchants and Quanzhou in the Late Yuan-Early Ming: Conjectures on the Ending of the Medieval Muslim Trade Diaspora." Pp. 115–132 in *The East Asian "Mediterranean,"* Vol. 6: *Maritime Crossroads of Culture, Commerce and Human Migration*, edited by A. Schottenhammer. Wiesbaden: Harrassowitz.

Chakravarti, Ranabir. 2000. "Nakhudas and Nauvittakas: Ship-Owning Merchants in the West Coast of India (c. AD 1000–1500)." *Journal of the Economic and Social History of the Orient* 41(3):34–64.

Chakravarti, Ranabir. 2015. "Indian Trade Through Jewish Geniza Letters (1000–1300)." *Studies in Peoples History* 2(1):27–40.

Chancellor, Edward. 2000. *Devil Take the Hindmost: A History of Financial Speculation*. New York: Plume.

Chandler, Tertius. 1987. *Four Thousand Years of Urban Growth: An Historical Census*. Lewiston: St. David's University Press.

Chang, Chiung-Fang. 2012. *Fertility, Family Planning and Population Policy in China*. London: Routledge.

Chang, Kuei-Sheng. 1974. "The Maritime Scene in China at the Dawn of Great European Discoveries." *Journal of the American Oriental Society* 94(3):347–359.

Chaudhuri, K. N. 1965. *The English East India Company: The Study of an Early Joint-Stock Company 1600–1640*, Vol. 4. London: Cass.

Chaudhuri, K. N. 1985. *Trade and Civilisation in the Indian Ocean: An Economic History from the Rise of Islam to 1750*. Cambridge: Cambridge University Press.

Chow, Kai-wing. 2004. *Publishing, Culture, and Power in Early Modern China*. Stanford: Stanford University Press.

Church, Sally K. 2005. "Zheng He: An Investigation into the Plausibility of 450-ft Treasures Ships." *Monumenta Serica* 53(1):1–43.

Church, Sally K. 2010. "Two Ming Dynasty Shipyards in Nanjing and their Infrastructure." Pp. 32–49 in *Shipwreck Asia: Thematic Studies in East Asian Maritime Archaeology*, edited by J. Kimura. Adelaide: Maritime Archaeology Program.

Cipolla, Carlo M. 1965. *Guns, Sails, and Empires: Technological Innovation and the Early Phases of European Expansion, 1400–1700*. New York: Pantheon.

Çizakça, Murat. 1996. *A Comparative Evolution of Business Partnerships: The Islamic World and Europe, with Specific Reference to the Ottoman Archives*. Leiden: Brill.

Çizakça, Murat. 2000. *A History of Philanthropic Foundations: The Islamic World from the Seventh Century to the Present*. Istanbul: Boğaziçi University Press.

Çizakça, Murat. 2007. "Cross-cultural Borrowing and Comparative Evolution of Institutions Between Islamic World and the West." Pp. 671–718 in *Relazioni economiche tra*

Europa e mondo Islamico, Secc. XIII–XVIII, edited by S. Cavaciochi. Florence: Le Monnier.

Çizakça, Murat. 2010. "Was Shari'ah Indeed the Culprit?" Pp. 97–116 in *The Long Divergence: How Islamic Law Held Back the Middle East*, edited by T. Kuran. Princeton: Princeton University Press.

Clark, Hugh R. 1991. *Community, Trade, and Networks: Southern Fujian Province from the Third to the Thirteenth Century.* Cambridge: Cambridge University Press.

Clark, Hugh R. 1995. "Muslims and Hindus in the Culture and Morphology of Quanzhou from the Tenth to the Thirteenth Century." *Journal of World History* 6(1):49–74.

Clark, Hugh R. 2001. "Overseas Trade and Social Change in Quanzhou Through the Sung." Pp. 47–94 in *The Emporium of the World: Maritime Quanzhou, 1000–1400*, edited by A. Schottenhammer. Leiden: Brill.

Coase, R. H. 1937. "The Nature of the Firm." *Economica* 4(16):386–405.

Coase, R. H. 1960. "The Problem of Social Cost." *Journal of Law and Economics* 3:1–44.

Cobb, Paul M. 2010. "The Empire in Syria, 705–763." Pp. 226–268 in *The Formation of the Islamic World, Sixth to Eleventh Centuries*, edited by C. F. Robinson. Cambridge: Cambridge University Press.

Cohen, Edward E. 1992. *Athenian Economy and Society: A Banking Perspective.* Princeton: Princeton University Press.

Cohen, Mark Nathan. 1977. *The Food Crisis in Prehistory: Overpopulation and the Origins of Agriculture.* New Haven: Yale University Press.

Cohen, Mark R. 2013. "A Partnership Gone Bad: Business Relationships and the Evolving Law of the Cairo Geniza Period." *Journal of the Economic and Social History of the Orient* 56(2):218–263.

Cohen, Mark R. 2014. *Jewish Self-Government in Medieval Egypt: The Origins of the Office of the Head of the Jews, ca. 1065–1126.* Princeton: Princeton University Press.

Cohen, Myron L. 2004. "Writs of Passage in Late Imperial China: The Documentation of Practical Understandings in Minong, Taiwan." Pp. 39–93 in *Contract and Property in Early Modern China: Rational Choice in Political Science*, edited by M. Zelin, J. Ocko, and R. Gardella. Stanford: Stanford University Press.

Cohen, Myron L. 2005. *Kinship, Contract, Community, and State: Anthropological Perspectives on China.* Stanford: Stanford University Press.

Cohen, Saul B. 2008. "Sarai." In *The Columbia Gazetteer of the World*, Vol. 3: *P to Z*, edited by S. B. Cohen. New York: Columbia University Press.

Coke, Edward. 1853 [1628]. *The First Part of the Institutes of the Laws of England, Or a Commentarie upon Littleton*, Vol. 1. Philadelphia: Robert H. Small.

Coleman v. Marham. 1321. Y.B 14 Edw. II 353.

Columbus, Christopher. 1906 [1492–1493]. "Journal of the First Voyage of Columbus." Pp. 87–258 in *The Northmen, Columbus and Cabot, 985–1503: Original Narratives of Early American History*, edited by J. Olson and E. Bourne. New York: Scribner.

Conac, Pierre-Henri. 2005. "The French and Dutch East India Companies in Comparative Legal Perspective." Pp. 131–158 in *VOC 1602–2002: 400 Years of Company Law*, edited by E. Gepken-Jager, G. van Solinge and L. Timmerman. Deventer: Kluwer.

Constable, Olivia Remie. 2003. *Housing the Stranger in the Mediterranean World: Lodging, Trade, and Travel in Late Antiquity and the Middle Ages.* New York: Cambridge University Press.

Cordes, Albrecht. 1997. "Gewinnteilungprinzipien im Hansischen und Oberitalienischen

Gesellschaftshandel des Spätmittelalters." In *Wirkungen europäischer Rechtskultur,* edited by K. Kroeschell, G. Köbler, and H. Nehlsen. Munich: Beck'sche Verlagsbuchhandlung.

Cordes, Albrecht. 1998. *Spätmittelalterlicher Gesellschaftshandel im Hanseraum Quellen und Darstellungen zur hansischen Geschichte.* Cologne: Bohlau.

Cordes, Albrecht. 2003. "The Search for a Medieval Lex Mercatoria." In *5th Oxford University Comparative Law Forum.*

Coşgel, Metin, Thomas J. Miceli, and Jared Rubin. 2012. "The Political Economy of Mass Printing: Legitimacy and Technological Change in the Ottoman Empire." *Journal of Comparative Economics* 40(3):357–371.

Cotta do Amaral, Maria. 1965. "Privilegios do mercadores estrangeiros no reinado de D. João III." Lisbon: Instituto de Alta Cultura, Centro de Estudos Históricos.

Craven, Wesley. 1957. "The Virginia Company of London, 1606–1624." Pp. 57–117 in *Jamestown 350th Anniversary Historical Booklets,* edited by E. G. Swem. Richmond: Virginia 350th Anniversary Celebration Corporation.

Crone, Patricia. 1987. *Meccan Trade and the Rise of Islam.* Princeton: Princeton University Press.

Crone, Patricia. 1987. *Roman, Provincial, and Islamic Law: The Origins of the Islamic Patronate.* Cambridge: Cambridge University Press.

Crosby, Alfred W. 1972. *The Columbian Exchange: Biological and Cultural Consequences of 1492.* Westport: Greenwood Press.

Cunliffe, Barry. 2015. *By Steppe, Desert, and Ocean: The Birth of Eurasia.* Oxford: Oxford University Press.

Curtin, Philip D. 1984. *Cross-Cultural Trade in World History.* Cambridge: Cambridge University Press.

Cytryn-Silverman, Katia. 2010. *The Road Inns (Khāns) in Bilād al-Shām.* Oxford: Archaeopress.

da Gama, Vasco. 1989 [1497–1499]. *A Journal of the First Voyage of Vasco da Gama, 1497–1499.* Translated by E. G. Ravenstein. London: Hakluyt Society.

Dale, Stephen Frederic. 2002. *Indian Merchants and Eurasian Trade, 1600–1750.* Cambridge: Cambridge University Press.

Das Gupta, Ashin. 1967. "Malabar in 1740." *Bengal: Past and Present* 86:90–117.

Das Gupta, Ashin. 1982. "Indian Merchants and the Trade in the Indian Ocean c. 1500–1750." Pp. 407–433 in *The Cambridge Economic History of India,* Vol. 1, edited by T. Raychaudhuri and I. Habib. Cambridge: Cambridge University Press.

Das Gupta, Ashin. 1987. "A Note on the Ship-Owning Merchants of Surat, c. 1700." Pp. 109–115 in *Marchands et hommes d'affaires asiatiques dans l'Océan Indien et la mer de Chine, 13–20 siècles,* edited by D. Lombard and J. Aubin. Paris: Editions de l'Ecole des Hautes Etudes en Sciences Sociales (EHESS).

Das Gupta, Ashin. 1991. "The Changing Face of the Indian Maritime Merchant." Pp. 353–362 in *Emporia, Commodities, and Entrepreneurs in Asian Maritime Trade, C. 1400–1750,* edited by R. Ptak and D. Rothermund: Steiner.

Das Gupta, Ashin. 1994. *Merchants of Maritime India, 1500–1800.* Aldershot: Variorum.

Das Gupta, Ashin. 1999. "India and the Indian Ocean in the Eighteenth Century." Pp. 131–161 in *India and the Indian Ocean, 1500–1800,* edited by M. N. Pearson and A. Das Gupta. New Delhi: Oxford University Press.

Das Gupta, Ashin. 2001. *The World of the Indian Ocean Merchant, 1500–1800: Collected Essays of Ashin Das Gupta*. New Delhi: Oxford University Press.

David, Paul A. 1985. "Clio and the Economics of QWERTY." *American Economic Review* 75(2):332–337.

Davidoff, Leonore and Catherine Hall. 1987. *Family Fortunes: Men and Women of the English Middle Class, 1780–1850*. Chicago: University of Chicago Press.

Davies, Glyn. 2002. *A History of Money from Ancient Times to the Present Day*. Cardiff: University of Wales Press.

Davis, Donald R. 2005. "Intermediate Realms of Law: Corporate Groups and Rulers in Medieval India." *Journal of the Economic and Social History of the Orient* 48(1):92–117.

de Jongh, Johan Matthijs. 2009. "Shareholder Activists Avant La Lettre: The Complaining Shareholders in the Dutch East India Company." In *Welberade (Festscrift of the Research Department of the Supreme Court of The Netherlands)*, edited by M. Duker, R. Pieterse, and A. J. P. Schild.

de Jongh, Johan Matthijs. 2014. *Tussen Societas en Universitas: de Beursvennootschap en Haar Aandeelhouders in Historisch Perspectief*. Deventer: Kluwer.

de la Vaissière, Étienne. 2005. *Sogdian Traders: A History*. Translated by J. Ward. Leiden: Brill.

de la Vaissière, Étienne. 2014. "Trans-Asian Trade, or Silk Road Deconstructed (Antiquity, Middle Ages)." Pp. 101–124 in *The Cambridge History of Capitalism*, Vol. 1: *The Rise of Capitalism: From Ancient Origins to 1848*, edited by L. Neal and J. G. Williamson. Cambridge: Cambridge University Press.

De Moor, Tine and Jan Luiten Van Zanden. 2009. "Girl Power: The European Marriage Pattern and Labour Markets in the North Sea Region in the Late Medieval and Early Modern Period." *Economic History Review* 63(1):1–33.

den Heijer, Hendrik. 2005. *De geoctrooieerde compagnie: De VOC en de WIC als voorlopers van de naamloze vennootschap*. Deventer: Kluwer.

Denzel, Markus A. 2010. *Handbook of World Exchange Rates, 1590–1914*. Burlington: Ashgate.

De Romanis, Frederico. 2012. "Playing Sudoku on the Verso of the 'Muziris Papyrus': Pepper, Malabathron and Tortoise Shell in the Cargo of the Hermapollon." *Journal of Ancient Indian History* 27:75–101.

de Roover, Raymond. 1948. *The Medici Bank: Its Organization, Management, Operations and Decline*. New York: New York University Press.

de Roover, Raymond. 1963. "The Organization of Trade." Pp. 42–118 in *Economic Organization and Policies in the Middle Ages*, edited by M. Postan, E. E. Rich, and E. Miller. Cambridge: Cambridge University Press.

Devendra, Somasiri. 2002. "Pre-Modern Sri Lankan Ships." Pp. 128–173 in *Ships and the Development of Maritime Technology on the Indian Ocean*, edited by D. Parkin and R. Barnes. London: Routledge-Curzon.

de Vries, Jan. 2003. "Connecting Europe and Asia: A Quantitative Analysis of the Cape-route Trade, 1497–1795." Pp. 35–106 in *Global Connections and Monetary History, 1470–1800*, edited by D. O. Flynn, A. Giráldez and R. von Glahn. London: Ashgate.

de Vries, Jan and Adrianus van der Woude. 1997. *The First Modern Economy: Success, Failure, and Perseverance of the Dutch Economy, 1500–1815*. Cambridge: Cambridge University Press.

De Zwart, Pim. 2016. *Globalization and the Colonial Origins of the Great Divergence: Intercontinental Trade and Living Standards in the Dutch East India Company's Commercial Empire, c. 1600–1800*. Leiden: Brill.

Diamond, Jared. 1999. *Guns, Germs, and Steel: The Fates of Human Societies*. London: Norton.

Dickson, P. G. M. 1967. *The Financial Revolution in England: A Study in the Development of Public Credit 1688–1756*. London: Macmillan.

DiMaggio, Paul J. and Walter W. Powell. 1983. "The Iron Cage Revisited: Institutional Isomorphism and Collective Rationality in Organizational Fields." *American Sociological Review* 48(2):147–160.

Ding, J., C. J. Shi, and A. Weintrit. 2007. "An Important Waypoint on Passage of Navigation History: Zheng He's Sailing to West Ocean." *TransNav: International Journal on Marine Navigation and Safety of Sea Transportation* 1(3):285–293.

Donner, Fred M. 1981. *The Early Islamic Conquests*. Princeton: Princeton University Press.

Donner, Fred M. 2010. *Muhammad and the Believers: At the Origins of Islam*. Cambridge, MA: Harvard University Press.

Dreyer, Edward L. 2007. *Zheng He: China and the Oceans in the Early Ming Dynasty, 1405–1433*. New York: Pearson-Longman.

Duff, P. W. 1938. *Personality in Roman Private Law*. Cambridge: Cambridge University Press.

Duyvendak, J. J. L. 1939. "The True Dates of the Chinese Maritime Expeditions in the Early Fifteenth Century." *T'oung Pao* 34(5):341–413.

Dworkin, Ronald. 1977. *Taking Rights Seriously*. Cambridge, MA: Harvard University Press.

The East India Company. 1621. *The Lawes or Standing Orders of the East India Company*. London.

Easterbrook, Frank H. and Daniel R. Fischel. 1996. *The Economic Structure of Corporate Law*. Cambridge: Harvard University Press.

Ebrey, Patricia Ebrey and James L. Watson. 1986. *Kinship Organization in Late Imperial China, 1000–1940*. Berkeley: University of California Press.

Eggertsson, Thráinn. 1990. *Economic Behavior and Institutions: Principles of Neoinstitutional Economics*. Cambridge: Cambridge University Press.

Ehrenberg, Richard. 1928. *Capital and Finance in the Age of the Renaissance: A Study of the Fuggers, and Their Connections*. Translated by H. M. Lucas. New York: Harcourt Brace.

Einaudi, Luca. 2013 "Florins and Ducats: The Return of Gold to Europe in the late Middle Ages." *Coins of the Month*, Joint Centre for History and Economics, Magdalene College and King's College, University of Cambridge. http://www.histecon.magd.cam.ac.uk/coins_april2013.html.

Eisenstein, Elizabeth L. 2005. *The Printing Revolution in Early Modern Europe*. Cambridge: Cambridge University Press.

Ekelund, Robert B., Jr., Robert F. Hébert, Robert D. Tollison, Garmy M. Anderson, and Audrey B. Davidson. 1996. *Sacred Trust: The Medieval Church as an Economic Firm*. Oxford: Oxford University Press.

Ekelund, Robert B. and Robert D. Tollison. 1980. "Mercantilist Origins of the Corporation." *Bell Journal of Economics* 11(2):715–720.

Ekelund, Robert B. and Robert D. Tollison. 1997. *Politicized Economies: Monarchy, Monopoly, & Mercantilism*. College Station: Texas A&M University Press.

Ellacott, Samuel. 1954. *The Story of Ships.* New York: Roy.

Elliott, J. H. 2006. *Empires of the Atlantic World: Britain and Spain in America, 1492–1830.* New Haven: Yale University Press.

Endicott-West, Elizabeth. 1989. "Merchant Associations in Yüan China: The 'Ortoy'." *Asia Major* 2(2):127–154.

Enigk, K. and H. C. Habil. 1989. "History of Veterinary Parasitology in Germany and Scandinavia." *Veterinary Parasitology* 33(1):65–91.

Epstein, Louis M. 1942. *Marriage Laws in the Bible and the Talmud.* Cambridge, MA: Harvard University Press.

Epstein, M. 1908. *The Early History of the Levant Company.* London: G. Routledge.

Epstein, S. R. 1998. "Craft Guilds, Apprenticeship, and Technological Change in Preindustrial Europe." *Journal of Economic History* 58(3):684–713.

Erickson-Gini, Tali. 2010. *Nabataean Settlement and Self-Organized Economy in the Central Negev: Crisis and Renewal.* Oxford: Archaeopress.

Erikson, Emily. 2014. *Between Monopoly and Free Trade: The English East India Company, 1600–1757.* Princeton: Princeton University Press.

Esposito, John L. 2014. "Riba." *The Oxford Dictionary of Islam.* Oxford University Press. http://www.oxfordreference.com/view/10.1093/acref/9780195125580.001.0001/acref -9780195125580-e-2013?rskey=YRBdc0&result=2013.

Even-Zohar, Itamar. 1981. "Translation Theory Today: A Call for Transfer Theory." *Poetics Today* 2(4):1–7.

Evers, Kasper Grønlund. 2016. *Worlds Apart Trading Together: The Organization of Long-Distance Trade Between the Mediterranean and the Indian Ocean, 1st–6th Cen. CE:* Oxford: Archaeopress.

Fama, Eugene F. and Michael C. Jensen. 1983. "Agency Problems and Residual Claims." *Journal of Law and Economics* 26(2):327–349.

Faure, David. 1986. *The Structure of Chinese Rural Society: Lineage Organization and Village in the Eastern New Territories.* Hong Kong: Oxford University Press.

Faure, David. 2007. *Emperor and Ancestor: State and Lineage in South China.* Stanford: Stanford University Press.

Favali, Lyda. 2004. *Qirad islamico, commenda medievale e strategie culturali dell'Occidente.* Turin: Giappichelli.

"Fedosiya." 2014. Encyclopedia Britannica website. http://www.britannica.com/place /Feodosiya.

Feldman, Stephen M. 1997. *Please Don't Wish Me a Merry Christmas: A Critical History of the Separation of Church and State.* New York: New York University Press.

Felloni, Giuseppe. 2014. *Amministrazione ed etica nella casa di San Giorgio (1407–1805): Lo Statuto del 1568.* Florence: Olschk.

Ferguson, Niall. 2001. *The Cash Nexus: Money and Power in the Modern World, 1700–2000.* London: Allen Lane.

Findlay, Ronald and Kevin H. O'Rourke. 2007. *Power and Plenty: Trade, War, and the World Economy in the Second Millennium.* Princeton: Princeton University Press.

Finlay, Robert. 2004. "How Not to (Re)Write World History: Gavin Menzies and the Chinese Discovery of America." *Journal of World History* 15(2):229–242.

Finlay, Robert. 2008. "The Voyages of Zheng He: Ideology, State Power, and Maritime Trade in Ming China." *Journal of the Historical Society* 8(3):327–347.

Fischel, Walter J. 1958. "The Spice Trade in Mamluk Egypt: A Contribution to the Economic History of Medieval Islam." *Journal of the Economic and Social History of the Orient* 1(2):157–174.

Fischer, Steven Roger. 2001. *A History of Writing*. London: Reaktion.

Fitzpatrick, Matthew P. 2011. "Provincializing Rome: The Indian Ocean Trade Network and Roman Imperialism." *Journal of World History* 22(1):27–54.

Flecker, Michael. 2011. "A Ninth-Century Arab or Indian Shipwreck in Indonesia: The First Archaeological Evidence of Direct Trade with China." Pp. 101–119 in *Shipwrecked: Tang Treasures and Monsoon Winds*, edited by R. Krahl and A. Effeny. Washington, DC: Arthur M. Sackler Gallery (Smithsonian Institution), the National Heritage Board of Singapore, and the Singapore Tourism Board.

Floor, Willem. 2006. *The Persian Gulf: A Political and Economic History of Five Port Cities, 1500–1730*. Washington, DC: Mage.

Floor, Willem. 2012 "Hormuz (Section 2: Islamic Period)": Encyclopædia Iranica website. http://www.iranicaonline.org/articles/hormuz-ii.

Foccardi, Gabriele. 1986. *The Chinese Travelers of the Ming Period*. Wiesbaden: Harrassowitz.

Fogel, Robert W. 1994. "Economic Growth, Population Theory, and Physiology: The Bearing of Long-Term Processes on the Making of Economic Policy." *American Economic Review* 84(3):369–395.

Fontaine, Laurence. 1996. *History of Pedlars in Europe*. Translated by V. Whittaker. Durham: Duke University Press.

Fouché, Leo. 1936. "The Origins and Early History of the Dutch East India Company (1602–1652)." *South African Journal of Economics* 4(4):444–59.

Freedman, Maurice. 1965. *Lineage Organization in Southeastern China*. London: Athlone.

Freedman, Paul. 2008. *Out of the East: Spices and the Medieval Imagination*: New Haven: Yale University Press.

Friedberg, Aemilius. 1879 "Decretum magistri Gratiani" *Corpus iuris canonici*, Leipzig. http://geschichte.digitale-sammlungen.de/decretum-gratiani/online/angebot.

Friedman, Mordechai A. 2006. "Quṣayr and Geniza Documents on the Indian Ocean Trade." *Journal of the American Oriental Society* 126(3):401–409.

Friedman, Mordechai Akiva. 2013. *Sefer Hodu Dalet(Alef)—Halfon veYehuda Halevi: Al-Pi Teudot Genizat Kahir* ["India Book" part four(1)—Halfon and Judah Halevi: According to the Cairo Genizah documents]. Jerusalem: Ben Zvi Institute.

Friedman, Mordechai Akiva. 2013. *Sefer Hodu Dalet(Beth)—Halfon haSoher haMaskill vehaNosea haGadol: Teudot meGenizat Kahir* ["India Book" part four(2)—Halfon the educated merchant and great traveler: Documents from the Cairo Geniza]. Jerusalem: Ben Zvi Institute.

Fritschy, W. 2003. "A Financial Revolution Reconsidered: Public Finance in Holland During the Dutch Revolt, 1568–1648." *Economic History Review* 6(1):57–89.

Furber, Holden. 1976. *Rival Empires of Trade in the Orient, 1600–1800*. Minneapolis: University of Minnesota Press.

Furber, Holden. 2001. "East India Companies." Pp. 269–314 in *South East Asia: Colonial History*, Vol. 1: *Imperialism Before 1800*, edited by P. Kratoska and P. Borschberg. London: Routledge.

Gaastra, F. S. 2007. "The Organization of the VOC." Pp. 13–27 in *Archives of the Dutch*

East India Company (VOC) and the Local Institutions in Batavia (Jakarta), edited by L. Balk, F. van Dijk, and D. Kortlang. Leiden: Brill.

Garber, Peter M. 2000. *Famous First Bubbles: The Fundamentals of Early Manias*. Cambridge, MA: MIT Press.

Garcia, Rolando R., Henry F. Díaz, Ricardo García Herrera, Jon Eischeid, María del Rosario Prieto, Emiliano Hernández, Luis Gimeno, Francisco Rubio Durán, and Ana María Bascary. 2001. "Atmospheric Circulation Changes in the Tropical Pacific Inferred from the Voyages of the Manila Galleons in the Sixteenth–Eighteenth Centuries." *Bulletin of the American Meteorological Society* 82(11):2435–2455.

Gat, Azar. 2006. *War in Human Civilization*. New York: Oxford University Press.

Gates, Hill. 1996. *China's Motor: A Thousand Years of Petty Capitalism*. Ithaca: Cornell University Press.

Gaudiosi, Monica M. 1988. "The Influence of the Islamic Law of Waqf on the Development of the Trust in England: The Case of Merton College." *University of Pennsylvania Law Review* 136(4):1231–1261.

Geisst, Charles R. 2013. *Beggar Thy Neighbor: A History of Usury and Debt*. Philadelphia: University of Pennsylvania Press.

Gelderblom, Oscar. 2013. *Cities of Commerce: The Institutional Foundations of International Trade in the Low Countries, 1250–1650*. Princeton: Princeton University Press.

Gelderblom, Oscar, Abe de Jong, and Joost Jonker. 2013. "The Formative Years of the Modern Corporation: The Dutch East India Company VOC, 1602–1623." *Journal of Economic History* 73(4):1050–76.

Gelderblom, Oscar, Abe de Jong, and Joost Jonker. 2016. "An Admiralty for Asia: Isaac le Maire and Conflicting Conceptions about the Corporate Governance of the VOC." Pp. 29–60 in *Origins of Shareholder Advocacy*, edited by J. G. Koppell. New York: Palgrave Macmillan.

Gelderblom, Oscar and Joost Jonker. 2004. "Completing a Financial Revolution: The Finance of the Dutch East India Trade and the Rise of the Amsterdam Capital Market, 1595–1612." *Journal of Economic History* 64(3):641–672.

Gelderblom, Oscar and Joost Jonker. 2005. "Amsterdam as the Cradle of Modern Futures and Options Trading, 1550–1650." Pp. 189–206 in *The Origins of Value*, edited by W. Gotezmann and G. Rouwenhorst. Oxford: Oxford University Press.

Gepken-Jager, Ella. 2005. "The Dutch East India Company (VOC)." Pp. 41–82 in *VOC 1602–2002: 400 Years of Company Law*, edited by E. Gepken-Jager, G. Van Solinge, and L. Timmerman. Deventer: Kluwer.

Gepken-Jager, Ella, Gerard van Solinge, and Levinus Timmerman, eds. 2005. *VOC 1602–2002: 400 Years of Company Law*. Deventer: Kluwer.

Gialdroni, Stefania. 2016. "'Propter Conversationem Diversarum Gentium': Migrating Words and Merchants in Medieval Pisa." Paper presented at the Migrating Words, Migrating Merchants, Migrating Law, Frankfurt.

Gibb, Hamilton and Charles Beckingham. 2010 [1994]. *The Travels of Ibn Battuta, AD 1325–1354*. Vol. 4. Farnham: Ashgate.

Gibb, Hamilton and J. H. Kramers. 1961. *Shorter Encyclopaedia of Islam*. Leiden: Brill.

Gil, Moshe. 1974. "The Rādhānite Merchants and the Land of Rādhān." *Journal of the Economic and Social History of the Orient* 17(3):299–328.

Gillet, Pierre. 1927. *La Personnalité juridique en droit ecclésiastique: Spécialement chez les décrétistes et les décrétalistes et dans le code de droit canonique*. Malines: W. Godenne.

Gilson, Ronald J. and Bernard S. Black. 1995. *The Law and Finance of Corporate Acqui-sitions*. Westbury: Foundation.

Gilson, Ronald J. and Bernard S. Black. 2003. *The Law and Finance of Corporate Acqui-sitions: 2003–2004 Supplement*. Westbury: Foundation.

Girard, René. 1996. *The Girard Reader*. New York: Crossroad Herder.

Glaeser, Edward L. and Andrei Shleifer. 2002. "Legal Origins." *Quarterly Journal of Eco-nomics* 117(4):1193–1229.

Glassner, Jean-Jacques. 2003. *The Invention of Cuneiform: Writing in Sumer*. Translated by Z. Bahrani and M. Van de Mieroop. Baltimore: Johns Hopkins University Press.

Glick, Thomas F. 2014. "Ibn Majid, Ahmad." Pp. 252 in *Medieval Science, Technology, and Medicine: An Encyclopedia*, edited by T. Glick, S. Livesey, and F. Wallis. New York: Routledge.

Goetzmann, William and Elisabeth Koll. 2007. "The History of Corporate Ownership in China." Pp. 149–184 in *A History of Corporate Governance around the World: Family Business Groups to Professional Managers*, edited by R. Morck. Chicago: University of Chicago Press.

Gofas, Demetrios. 2007. "The Byzantine Law of Interest." Pp. 1095–1104 in *The Economic History of Byzantium from the Seventh Through the Fifteenth Century*, Vol. 3, edited by A. Laiou. Washington, DC: Dumbarton Oaks Research Library and Collection.

Goitein, S. D. 1958. "New Light on the Beginnings of the Kārim Merchants." *Journal of the Economic and Social History of the Orient* 1(2):175–184.

Goitein, S. D. 1967–1999. *A Mediterranean Society: The Jewish Communities of the World as Portrayed in the Documents of the Cairo Geniza*. 3 vols. Berkeley: University of California Press.

Gotein, S. D. and Mordechai A. Friedman. 2007. *India Traders of the Middle Ages: Doc-uments from the Cairo Geniza, India Book*. Leiden: Brill.

Gotein, S. D. and Mordechai Akiva Friedman. 2009. *Sefer Hodu Alef—Yosef Al-Lebdi, Soher-Hodu Hagadol: Teudot meGenizat Kahir* ["India Book" part one—Joseph Al-Lebdi, the great Indian trader: Documents from the Cairo Geniza]. Jerusalem: Ben Zvi Institute.

Gotein, S. D. and Mordechai Akiva Friedman. 2010. *Sefer Hodu Beth—Madmūn Nagid Eretz Teiman veSahar Hodu: Teudot meGenizat Kahir* ["India Book" part two—Madmūn, governor of Yemen and India trade: Documents from the Cairo Geniza]. Jerusalem: Ben Zvi Institute.

Gotein, S. D. and Mordechai Akiva Friedman. 2010. *Sefer Hodu Gimmel—Avraham Ben Yijū, Soher veYatzran beHodu: Teudot meGenizat Kahir* ["India Book" part three—Avraham Ben Yijū, trader and manufacturer in India: Documents from the Cairo Geniza]. Jerusalem: Ben Zvi Institute.

Goldberg, Dror. 2009. "The Massachusetts Paper Money of 1690." *Journal of Economic History* 69(04):1092–1106.

Goldberg, Jessica L. 2012. "Choosing and Enforcing Business Relationships in the Eleventh-Century Mediterranean: Reassessing the 'Maghribī Traders.'" *Past & Present* 216(1):3–40.

Goldberg, Jessica L. 2012. *Trade and Institutions in the Medieval Mediterranean*. New York: Cambridge University Press.

González de Lara, Yadira. 2000. "Enforceability and Risk-Sharing in Financial Contracts:

From the Sea Loan to the Commenda in Late Medieval Venice." PhD dissertation, Department of Economics, European University Institute, Florence.

Gonzalez de Lara, Yadira. 2003. "Commercial Partnerships." Pp. 480–483 in *The Oxford Encyclopedia of Economic History*, Vol. 1, edited by J. Mokyr. Oxford: Oxford University Press.

González de Lara, Yadira. 2008. "The Secret of Venetian Success: A Public-Order, Reputation-Based Institution." *European Review of Economic History* 12(3):247–285.

Goody, Jack. 1996. *The East in the West*. Cambridge: Cambridge University Press.

Grafe, Regina and Alejandra Irigoin. 2012. "A Stakeholder Empire: The Political Economy of Spanish Imperial Rule in America." *Economic History Review* 65(2):609–651.

Grafe, Regina. 2014. "On the Spatial Nature of Institutions and the Institutional Nature of Personal Networks in the Spanish Atlantic." *Culture and History Digital Journal* 3(1):e006.

Granovetter, Mark. 1985. "Economic Action and Social Structure: The Problem of Embeddedness." *American Journal of Sociology* 91(3):481–510.

Grant, Edward. 2001. *God and Reason in the Middle Ages*. Cambridge: Cambridge University Press.

Grassby, Richard. 1995. *The Business Community of Seventeenth-Century England*. Cambridge: Cambridge University Press.

Graziadei, Michele. 2006. "Comparative Law as the Study of Transplants and Receptions." Pp. 441–475 in *The Oxford Handbook of Comparative Law*, edited by M. Reimann and R. Zimmermann. Oxford: Oxford University Press.

Green, Tom. 2010. *From Rome to Byzantium: Trade and Continuity in the First Millennium AD*. Bristol: Werburgh.

Greif, Avner. 1989. "Reputation and Coalitions in Medieval Trade: Evidence on the Maghribi Traders." *Journal of Economic History* 49(4):857–882.

Greif, Avner. 1998. "Historical and Comparative Institutional Analysis." *American Economic Review* 88(2):80–84.

Greif, Avner. 2000. "The Fundamental Problem of Exchange: A Research Agenda in Historical Institutional Analysis." *European Review of Economic History* 4(3):251–284.

Greif, Avner. 2006. "Family Structure, Institutions, and Growth: The Origins and Implications of Western Corporations." *American Economic Review* 96(2):308–312.

Greif, Avner. 2006. *Institutions and the Path to the Modern Economy: Lessons from Medieval Trade*. Cambridge: Cambridge University Press.

Greif, Avner. 2008. "Commitment, Coercion and Markets: The Nature and Dynamics of Institutions Supporting Exchange." Pp. 727–786 in *Handbook of New Institutional Economics*, edited by C. Ménard and M. Shirley. Dordrecht: Springer.

Greif, Avner. 2012. "The Maghribi Traders: A Reappraisal?" *Economic History Review* 65(2):445–469.

Greif, Avner, Paul Milgrom, and Barry R. Weingast. 1994. "Coordination, Commitment, and Enforcement: The Case of the Merchant Guild." *Journal of Political Economy* 102(4):745–776.

Greif, Avner and Guido Tabellini. 2010. "Cultural and Institutional Bifurcation: China and Europe Compared." *American Economic Review* 100(2):135–140.

Greif, Avner and Guido Tabellini. 2012. "The Clan and the City: Sustaining Cooperation in China and Europe." Working paper. Centre for Economic Policy Research, London.

Greif, Avner and Guido Tabellini. 2017. "The Clan and The Corporation: Sustaining Cooperation in China and Europe." *Journal of Comparative Economics* 45(1):1–35.

Gunaratne, Shelton A. 2001. "Paper, Printing and the Printing Press: A Horizontally Integrative Macrohistory Analysis." *International Communication Gazette* 63(6):459–479.

Guo, Li. 1999. "Arabic Documents from the Red Sea Port of Quseir in the Seventh/Thirteenth Century, Part 1: Business Letters." *Journal of Near Eastern Studies* 58(3):161–190.

Guo, Li. 2004. *Commerce, Culture, and Community in a Red Sea Port in the Thirteenth Century: The Arabic Documents from Quseir*. Leiden: Brill.

Gurani, Yesim F. and Tulay Ozdemir Canbolat. 2012. "Aksaray Sultanhan Caravanserai: A Study of Cultural Interactions and Sustainability Along the Silk Road." Pp. 277–279 in *Archi-Cultural Translations through the Silk Road*. Mukogawa Women's University, Nishinomiya, Japan.

Guy, John. 2001. "Tamil Merchants Guild and the Quanzhou Trade." Pp. 283–308 in *The Emporium of the World: Maritime Quanzhou, 1000–1400*, edited by A. Schottenhammer. Leiden: Brill.

Guy, John. 2010. "Rare and Strange Goods: International Trade in Ninth-Century Asia." Pp. 19–28 in *Shipwrecked: Tang Treasures and Monsoon Winds*, edited by R. Krahl and A. Effeny. Washington, DC: Smithsonian Institute Press.

Häberlein, Mark. 2012. *The Fuggers of Augsburg: Pursuing Wealth and Honor in Renaissance Germany*. Charlottesville: University of Virginia Press.

Haebler, Konrad. 1895. "Konrad Rott und die Thüringische Gesellschaft." Pp. 180–181 in *Neues Archiv für Sächsische Geschichte und Alterumskunde*, Vol. 16, edited by H. Ermisch.

Hajnal, J. 1965. "European Marriage Patterns in Perspective." Pp. 101–143 in *Population in History: Essays in Historical Demography*, edited by D. V. Glass and D. Eversley. Chicago: Aldine.

Hale, Matthew. 1976. *The Prerogatives of the King*. London: Selden Society.

Hall, Robert A. 1974. *External History of the Romance Languages*. New York: Elsevier.

Hang, Xing. 2016. *Conflict and Commerce in Maritime East Asia: The Zheng Family and the Shaping of the Modern World, c. 1620–1720*. Cambridge: Cambridge University Press.

Hansen, Valerie. 2000. *The Open Empire: A History of China to 1600*. New York: Norton.

Hansen, Valerie. 2005. "How Business Was Conducted on the Chinese Silk Road during the Tang Dynasty, 618–907." Pp. 43–64 in *The Origins of Value: The Financial Innovations that Created Modern Capital Markets*, edited by W. M. Goetzmann and G. K. Rouwenhorst. New York: Oxford University Press.

Hansen, Valerie. 2005. "The Impact of the Silk Road Trade on a Local Community: The Turfan Oasis, 500–800." Pp. 283–310 in *Les Sogdiens en Chine*, edited by E. de la Vaissiere and E. Trombert. Paris: Ecole Française d'Extreme Orient.

Hansen, Valerie. 2012. *The Silk Road: A New History*. New York: Oxford University Press.

Hansmann, Henry; Reinier Kraakman, and Richard Squire. 2006. "Law and the Rise of the Firm." *Harvard Law Review* 119(5):1333–1403.

Harrauer, Hermann and Pieter Sijpesteijn. 1986. *Ein neues Dokument zu Roms Indienhandel P. Vindob. G 40822*. Anzeiger der österreichischen Akademie der Wissenschaften.

Harris, Ron. 2000. *Industrializing English Law Entrepreneurship and Business Organization, 1720–1844*. Cambridge: Cambridge University Press.

Harris, Ron. 2003. "The Encounters of Economic History and Legal History." *Law and History Review* 21(2):297–346.

Harris, Ron. 2005. "The English East India Company and the History of Company Law." Pp. 217–248 in *VOC 1602–2002: 400 Years of Company Law*, edited by E. Gepken-Jager, G. van Solinge, and L. Timmerman. Deventer: Kluwer.

Harris, Ron. 2005. "The Formation of the East India Company as a Cooperation-Enhancing Institution." SSRN (Social Science Research Network) working paper. Available at http://ssrn.com/abstract=874406.

Harris, Ron. 2010. "Law, Finance and the First Corporations." Pp. 145–172 in *Global Perspectives on the Rule of Law*, edited by J. Heckman, R. Nelson, and L. Cabatingan. Abingdon: Routledge.

Harris, Ron. 2013. "Could the Crown Credibly Commit to Respect its Charters? England 1558–1640." Pp. 21–47 in *Questioning Credible Commitment: Perspectives on the Rise of Financial Capitalism*, edited by D. M. Coffman, A. Leonard, and L. Neal. Cambridge: Cambridge University Press.

Harris, Ron. 2014. "Spread of Legal Innovations Defining Private and Public Domains." Pp. 127–168 in *The Cambridge History of Capitalism*, Vol. 2: *The Spread of Capitalism: From 1848 to the Present*, edited by L. Neal and J. G. Williamson. Cambridge: Cambridge University Press.

Harris, Ron. Forthcoming. "The Organization of Rome to India Trade: Loans and Agents in the Muziris Papyrus." Vol. 2: *Roman Law & Economics*, edited by G. Dari-Mattiacci and D. P. Kehoe. Oxford: Oxford University Press.

Harris, Ron and Assaf Likhovski. 2009. "Histories of Legal Transplantations." *Histories of Legal Transplantations*, special issue of *Theoretical Inquiries in Law* 10(2):299–743.

Harris, Steven J. 1996. "Confession-Building, Long-Distance Networks, and the Organization of Jesuit Science." *Early Science and Medicine* 1(3):287–318.

Hart, H. L. A. 1961. *The Concept of Law*. Oxford: Oxford University Press.

Hart, Oliver. 1989. "An Economist's Perspective on the Theory of the Firm." *Columbia Law Review* 89(7):1757–1774.

Harvey, Peter. 2012. *An Introduction to Buddhism: Teachings, History and Practices*. Cambridge: Cambridge University Press.

Headrick, Daniel R. 2010. *Power over Peoples Technology, Environments, and Western Imperialism, 1400 to the Present*. Princeton: Princeton University Press.

Hejeebu, Santhi. 2005. "Contract Enforcement in the English East India Company." *Journal of Economic History* 65(2):496–523.

Hennigan, Peter C. 2004. *The Birth of a Legal Institution: The Formation of the Waqf in Third-Century AH Hanafi Legal Discourse*. Leiden: Brill.

Herzig, Edmund M. 1991. "The Armenian Merchants of New Julfa, Isfahan: A Study in Pre-Modern Asian Trade." PhD dissertation, Oxford University.

Heyneman, Stephen P. 2004. *Islam and Social Policy*. Nashville: Vanderbilt University Press.

Hildebrandt, Reinhard. 1966. *Die "George Fuggerischen Erben."* Berlin: Duncker & Humblot.

Hillenbrand, Robert. 1994. *Islamic Architecture: Form, Function, and Meaning*. New York: Columbia University Press.

Hitti, Philip K. 1970. *History of the Arabs: From the Earliest Times to the Present.* New York: St. Martin's Press.

Hobson, John M. 2004. *The Eastern Origins of Western Civilization.* Cambridge: Cambridge University Press.

Hock, Hans Henrich and Joseph D. Brian. 2009. *Language History, Language Change, and Language Relationship: An Introduction to Historical and Comparative Linguistics.* Berlin: Mouton de Gruyter.

Hodgson, Geoffrey M. 2006. "What Are Institutions?" *Journal of Economic Issues* 40(1): 1–25.

Hoffman, Philip T. 2012. "Why Was It Europeans Who Conquered the World?" *Journal of Economic History* 72(3):601–633.

Hoffman, Philip T. 2015. *Why Did Europe Conquer the World?* Princeton: Princeton University Press.

Holdsworth, William. 1931. *A History of English Law,* Vol. 8. Boston: Little, Brown.

Hooker, J. T. 1990. *Reading the Past: Ancient Writing from Cuneiform to the Alphabet.* Berkeley: University of California Press.

Hoover, Calvin B. 1926. "The Sea Loan in Genoa in the Twelfth Century." *Quarterly Journal of Economics* 40(3):495–529.

Hourani, George F. 1995. *Arab Seafaring in the Indian Ocean in Ancient and Early Medieval Times.* Princeton: Princeton University Press.

Huang, Ray. 1974. *Taxation and Governmental Finance in Sixteenth-Century Ming China.* Cambridge: Cambridge University Press.

Huang, Zhongzhao. 2006 [1490]. *Bamin Tongzhi* [Comprehensive gazetteer of the eight Min prefectures]. Fuzhou: Fujian Renmin Chubanshe.

Huff, Toby E. 2017. *The Rise of Early Modern Science: Islam, China, and the West.* Cambridge: Cambridge University Press.

Hui, Deng and Li Xin. 2011. "The Asian Monsoons and Zheng He's Voyages to the Western Ocean." *Journal of Navigation* 64(2):207–218.

"Human mtDNA Migrations." 2013. MITOMAP: A Human Mitochondrial Genome Database. http://www.mitomap.org/pub/MITOMAP/MitomapFigures/World Migrations2013.pdf.

Hümmerich, Franz. 1922. "Die Erste Deutsche Handelsfahrt Nach Indien 1505/06." In *Ein Unternehmen der Welser, Fugger und anderer Augsbutger sowie Nürnberger Häuser.* Munich: R. Oldenbourg.

Hunt, Edwin S. 1994. *The Medieval Super-Companies: A Study of the Peruzzi Company of Florence.* Cambridge: Cambridge University Press.

Hunt, Edwin S. and James M. Murray. 1999. *A History of Business in Medieval Europe, 1200–1550.* New York: Cambridge University Press.

Ibn Batuta, Muhammad. 1829 [ca. 1355]. *The Travels of Ibn Batuta.* Translated by S. Lee. London: Oriental Translation Committee.

Ibn Ḥawqal, Muhammad Abu al-Kasim. 2014 [977, originally translated 1938–1939]. *Kitāb Ṣūrat al-arḍ.* Translated by J. H. Kramers. Leiden: Brill.

Israel, Jonathan I. 1989. *Dutch Primacy in World Trade, 1585–1740.* Oxford: Clarendon.

Israel, Jonathan I. 1998. *The Dutch Republic: Its Rise, Greatness, and Fall, 1477–1806.* New York: Clarendon.

Jan Qaisar, Ahsan. 1999. "From Port to Port: Life on Indian Ships in the Sixteenth and

Seventeenth Centuries." Pp. 331–350 in *India and the Indian Ocean, 1500–1800,* edited by A. Das Gupta and M. N. Pearson. New Delhi: Oxford University Press.

Jensen, Michael C. and William H. Meckling. 1976. "Theory of the Firm: Managerial Behavior, Agency Costs and Ownership Structure." *Journal of Financial Economics* 3(4):305–360.

Johansen, Baber. 1981. "The All-Embracing Town and Its Mosques: Al-Misr Al-Gâmiʿ." *Revue de l'Occident Musulman et de la Méditerranée* 32(1):139–161.

Johnson, David. 1987. "Nabataean Trade: Intensification and Culture Change." PhD dissertation, Department of Anthropology, University of Utah.

Jones, Eric. 2003. *The European Miracle: Environments, Economies and Geopolitics in the History of Europe and Asia.* New York: Cambridge University Press.

Jones, S.R.H. and Simon P. Ville. 1996. "Efficient Transactors or Rent-Seeking Monopolists? The Rationale for Early Chartered Trading Companies." *Journal of Economic History* 56(4):898–915.

Jones, S.R.H. and Simon P. Ville. 1996. "Theory and Evidence: Understanding Chartered Trading Companies." *Journal of Economic History* 56(4):925–926.

Jongman, Willem M. 2014. "Re-Constructing the Roman Economy." Pp. 75–100 in *The Cambridge History of Capitalism,* Vol. 1: *The Rise of Capitalism: From Ancient Origins to 1848,* edited by L. Neal and J. Williamson. Cambridge: Cambridge University Press.

Kahan, Marcel and Edward B. Rock. 2007. "Hedge Funds in Corporate Governance and Corporate Control." *University of Pennsylvania Law Review* 155(5):1021–1093.

Kahn-Freund, Otto. 1974. "On Uses and Misuses of Comparative Law." *Modern Law Review* 37(1):1–27.

Kalus, Maximilian. 2006. "Tracing Business Patterns in Sixteenth Century European-Asian Trade. New Methods Using Semantic Networking Models." Paper presented at the Fourteenth International Economic History Congress, Helsinki.

Kamdar, Keshavlal H. 1968. "Virji Vorah, Surat Millionaire Mahajan (in Gujarati)." *Journal of the Gujarat Research Society* 30(4):277–279.

Kang, David. 2010. *East Asia Before the West Five Centuries of Trade and Tribute.* New York: Columbia University Press.

Kantorowicz, Ernst H. 1970. *The King's Two Bodies: A Study in Mediaeval Theology.* Princeton University Press.

Kapchan, Deborah A. and Pauline Strong. 1999. "Theorizing the Hybrid." *Journal of American Folklore* 112(445):239–253.

Kaw, Mushtaq. 2011. "Restoring India's Links with Central Asia across Kashmir: Challenges and Opportunities." Pp. 179–196 in *Mapping Central Asia: Indian Perceptions and Strategies,* edited by S. Peyrouse and M. Laruelle. Farnham: Ashgate.

Kellenbenz, Hermann. 1999. *Die Fugger in Spanien und Portugal bis 1560: Ein Grossunternehmen des 16 Jahrhunderts.* Munich: Vogel.

Kennedy, Paul. 1987. *The Rise and Fall of the Great Powers: Economic Change and Military Conflict from 1500 to 2000.* New York: Random House.

Khachikian, Shushanik. 1998. "Typology of the Trading Companies Owned by the Merchants of New Julfa." *Iran and the Caucasus* 2(1):1–4.

Khadduri, Majid. 1987. *Al-Shafiʿiʾs Risala: Treatise on the Foundation of Islamic Jurisprudence.* Cambridge: Islamic Texts Society.

Khalil, Emad H. 2006. "An Overview of the Shariaʾa Prohibition of Riba." Pp. 53–68 in

Interest in Islamic Economics: Understanding Riba, edited by A. Thomas. New York: Routledge.

Khalilieh, Hassan S. 1998. *Islamic Maritime Law: An Introduction*. Leiden: Brill.

Khalilieh, Hassan S. 2006. *Admiralty and Maritime Laws in the Mediterranean Sea (ca. 800–1050): The "Kitāb Akriyat al-Sufun" vis-à-vis the "Nomos Rhodion Nautikos."* Leiden: Brill.

Khanna, Vikramaditya S. 2005 "The Economic History of the Corporate Form in Ancient India." Social Science Research Network. http://papers.ssrn.com/sol3/papers.cfm?abstract_id=796464.

Khyade, Vitthalrao B. 2012. "Silk Route: The UNESCO World Heritage." *International Academic Journal of Science and Engineering* 3(12):20–27.

Kister, M. J. 1965. "Mecca and Tamim (Aspects of Their Relations)." *Journal of the Economic and Social History of the Orient* 8(2):113–163.

Kittell, Ellen E. and Thomas F. Madden, eds. 1999. *Medieval and Renaissance Venice*. Urbana: University of Illinois Press.

Klerman, Daniel M. 2005. "The Value of Judicial Independence: Evidence from Eighteenth Century England." *American Law and Economics Review* 7(1):1–27. doi: 10.1093/aler/ahi005.

Klerman, Daniel M. 2018. "Quantitative Legal History." P. 343 in *The Oxford Handbook of Legal History*. Oxford: Oxford University Press.

Klerman, Daniel M., Paul G. Mahoney, Holger Spamann, and Mark I. Weinstein. 2011. "Legal Origin or Colonial History?" *Journal of Legal Analysis* 3:379–539.

Knopf, Ellen. 2005. "Contracts in Athenian Law." PhD dissertation, Classics, City University of New York.

Koehler, Benedikt. 2014. *Early Islam and the Birth of Capitalism*. Lanham: Lexington.

Kulke, Hermann. 2009. "The Naval Expeditions of the Cholas in the Context of Asian History." Pp. 1–19 in *Nagapattinam to Suvarnadwipa: Reflections on the Chola Naval Expeditions to Southeast Asia*, edited by H. Kulke, K. Kesavapany and V. Sakhuja. Singapore: Institute of Southeast Asian Studies.

Kuran, Timur. 2001. "The Provision of Public Goods Under Islamic Law: Origins, Impact, and Limitations of the Waqf System." *Law & Society Review* 35(4):841–898.

Kuran, Timur. 2005. "The Absence of the Corporation in Islamic Law: Origins and Persistence." *American Journal of Comparative Law* 53(4):785–834.

Kuran, Timur. 2011. *The Long Divergence: How Islamic Law Held Back the Middle East*. Princeton: Princeton University Press.

Kuwabara, Jitsuzo. 1928–1935. *On P'u Shou-keng*, 2 vols. Tokyo: Memoirs of the Research Department of the Toyo Bunko. Oriental Library.

Kyd, Stewart. 1793. *A Treatise on the Law of Corporations*, Vol. 1. London: J. Butterworth.

La Porta, Rafael, Florencio Lopez-de-Silanes, Andrei Shleifer, and Robert W. Vishny. 1998. "Law and Finance." *Journal of Political Economy* 106(6):1113–1155.

La Porta, Rafael, Florencio Lopez-de-Silanes, and Andrei Shleifer. 2008. "The Economic Consequences of Legal Origins." *Journal of Economic Literature* 46(2):285–332.

Labib, Subhi Y. 1969. "Capitalism in Medieval Islam." *Journal of Economic History* 29(1):79–96.

Laiou, Angeliki E. 1991. "God and Mammon: Credit, Trade, Profit and the Canonists." Pp. 261–300 in *Byzantium in the 12th Century: Canon Law, State and Society*, edited by N. Oikonomides. Athens: Etareia Byzantinon kai Metabyzantinon Meleton.

Laiou, Angeliki E. 2002. *The Economic History of Byzantium from the Seventh Through the Fifteenth Century*, Vol. 1. Washington, DC: Dumbarton Oaks Research Library and Collection.

Lambton, Ann. 1997. "Economy (Section 5: From the Arab Conquest to the End of the Il-Khanids)." Pp. 107–132 in *Encyclopaedia Iranica*, Vol. 8, edited by E. Yarshater. Encyclopaedia Iranica Foundation.

Landes, David S. 1998. *The Wealth and Poverty of Nations: Why Some Are So Rich and Some So Poor*. New York: Norton.

Lane, Frederic C. 1944. "Family Partnerships and Joint Ventures in the Venetian Republic." *Journal of Economic History* 4(2):178–196.

Lane, Frederic C. 1973. *Venice, a Maritime Republic*. Baltimore: Johns Hopkins University Press.

Lapidus, Ira M. 2014. *A History of Islamic Societies*. New York: Cambridge University Press.

Larson, Greger. 2011. "Genetics and Domestication: Important Questions for New Answers." *Current Anthropology* 52(4):485–495.

Laslett, Peter. 1988. "Family, Kinship and Collectivity as Systems of Support in Pre-Industrial Europe: A Consideration of the 'Nuclear-Hardship' Hypothesis." *Continuity and Change* 3(2):153–175.

Lawler, Andrew. 2017. "Satellites Trace Afghanistan's Lost Empires." *Science* 358(6369):1364–1365.

Leonard, A. B. (Ed.). 2016. *Marine Insurance: Origins and Institutions, 1300–1850*. London: Palgrave Macmillan.

Levathes, Louise. 1997. *When China Ruled the Seas: The Treasure Fleet of the Dragon Throne, 1405–1433*. New York: Oxford University Press.

Levi, Scott C. 2002. *The Indian Diaspora in Central Asia and Its Trade, 1550–1900*, Vol. 3. Leiden: Brill.

Li, Yukun. 2001. "20 shiji Pu Shougeng yanjiu shuping" [Review of twentieth-century research about Pu Shougeng]. *Zhongguo shi yanjiu dongtai* 8:16–23.

Libecap, Gary. 1978. "Economic Variables and the Development of the Law: The Case of Western Mineral Rights." *Journal of Economic History* 38(2):338–362.

Libecap, Gary. 1989. *Contracting for Property Rights*. Cambridge: Cambridge University Press.

Libson, Gideon. 2003. *Jewish and Islamic Law: A Comparative Study of Custom During the Geonic Period*. Cambridge: Islamic Legal Studies Program, Harvard Law School.

Lieber, Alfred E. 1968. "Eastern Business Practices and Medieval European Commerce." *Economic History Review* 21(2):230–243.

Liebowitz, Stan and Stephen Margolis. 1995. "Path Dependence, Lock-In, and History." *Journal of Law, Economics, and Organization* 11(1):205–226.

Liu, Xinru and Lynda Shaffer. 2007. *Connections Across Eurasia: Transportation, Communication, and Cultural Exchange on the Silk Roads*. Boston: McGraw-Hill.

Liu, Xinru. 2010. *The Silk Road in World History*. New York: Oxford University Press.

Lockard, Craig A. 2010. "The Sea Common to All: Maritime Frontiers, Port Cities, and Chinese Traders in the Southeast Asian Age of Commerce, ca. 1400–1750." *Journal of World History* 21(2):219–247.

Lopez, Robert Sabatino. 1952. "China Silk in Europe in the Yuan Period." *Journal of the American Oriental Society* 72(2):72–76.

Lopez, Robert S. 1959. "The Role of Trade in the Economic Readjustment of Byzantium in the Seventh Century." *Dumbarton Oaks Papers* 13:67–85.

Lopez, Robert S. 1971. *The Commercial Revolution of the Middle Ages, 950–1350*. Englewood Cliffs: Prentice-Hall.

Lopez, Robert S. and Irving W. Raymond. 2001 [1955]. *Medieval Trade in the Mediterranean World: Illustrative Documents*. New York: Columbia University Press.

Lucassen, Jan, Tine De Moor, and Jan Luiten van Zanden. 2008. "The Return of the Guilds: Towards a Global History of the Guilds in Pre-Industrial Times." *International Review of Social History* 53(S16):5–18.

Ma, Huan. 1970 [1433]. *Ying-Yai Sheng-Lan* [The overall survey of the ocean's shores]. Translated by J. V. G. Mills. Cambridge: Cambridge University Press for the Hakluyt Society.

Macaulay, Stewart. 1963. "Non-Contractual Relations in Business: A Preliminary Study." *American Sociological Review* 28(1):55–67.

MacHugh, David E., et al. 1997. "Microsatellite DNA Variation and the Evolution, Domestication and Phylogeography of Taurine and Zebu Cattle (Bos Taurus and Bos Indicus)." *Genetics* 146(3):1071–1086.

MacNeil, Ian R. 1978. "Contracts: Adjustment of Long-Term Economic Relations under Classical, Neoclassical and Relational Contract Law." *Northwestern University Law Review* 72(6):854–905.

Maddison, Angus. 2001. *The World Economy: A Millennial Perspective*. France: Development Center of Organization for Economic Cooperation and Development (OECD).

Maejima, Shinji. 1974. "The Muslims in Ch'uan-chou at the End of the Yuan Dynasty—Part 2." *Memoirs of the Research Department of the Toyo Bunko* 32:47–71.

Maitland, Frederic W. 1900. "Corporation Sole." *Law Quarterly Review* 16:335.

Maitland, Frederic W. 1901. "Crown as Corporation." *Law Quarterly Review* 17:131.

Maitland, Frederic W. 1908. *The Constitutional History of England: A Course of Lectures*. Cambridge: Cambridge University Press.

Makdisi, George. 1970. "Madrasa and University in the Middle Ages." *Studia Islamica* 32:255–264.

Malekandathil, Pius. 1999. *The Germans, the Portuguese and India*. Münster: Lit Verlag.

Malmendier, Ulrike. 2009. "Law and Finance 'at the Origin.'" *Journal of Economic Literature* 47(4):1076–1108.

Malynes, Gerard. 1622. *Consuetudo, Vel Lex Mercatoria, or the Ancient Law Merchant*. London: Adam Islip.

Manguin, Pierre-Yves. 1993. "Trading ships of the South China Sea. Shipbuilding Techniques and Their Role in the History of the Development of Asian Trade Networks." *Journal of the Economic and Social History of the Orient* 36(3):253–280.

Mansvelt, William. 1922. *Rechtsvorm en Geldelijk Beheer bij de Oost-Indische Compagnie*. Amsterdam: Swets & Zeitlinger.

Manz, Beatrice. 2007. *Power, Politics and Religion in Timurid Iran*. Cambridge: Cambridge University Press.

Maqbul Sayyid, Ahmad. 2008. "Ibn Mājid." Pp. 35–37 in *Complete Dictionary of Scientific Biography*, Vol. 9. Detroit: Scribner.

Margariti, Roxani Eleni. 2007. *Aden and the Indian Ocean Trade: 150 Years in the Life of a Medieval Arabian Port*. Chapel Hill: University of North Carolina Press.

Markovits, Claude. 2000. *The Global World of Indian Merchants, 1750–1947: Taders of Sind from Bukhara to Panama*. Cambridge: Cambridge University Press.

Masten, Scott E. and Jens Prüfer. 2014. "On the Evolution of Collective Enforcement Institutions: Communities and Courts." *Journal of Legal Studies* 43(2):359–400.

Mathew, K. S. 1983. *Portuguese Trade with India in the Sixteenth Century*. New Delhi: Manohar.

Mathew, K. S. 1997. *Indo-Portuguese trade and the Fuggers of Germany*. New Delhi: Manohar.

McDermott, Joseph P. Forthcoming (2020). *The Making of a New Rural Order in South China*. Vol. 2: *Merchants, Markets, and Lineages, 1500–1700*. Cambridge: Cambridge University Press.

McEvedy, Colin and Richard Jones. 1978. *Atlas of World Population History*. New York: Penguin.

McLaughlin, Raoul. 2010. *Rome and the Distant East: Trade Routes to the Ancient Lands of Arabia, India and China*. New York: Continuum.

McLaughlin, Terence Patrick. 1939. "The Teaching of the Canonists on Usury, XII, XIII and XIV Centuries." *Mediaeval Studies* 1:81–147.

McNeill, William H. 1991. *The Rise of the West: A History of the Human Community*. Chicago: University of Chicago Press.

Mehta, Makrand. 1991. *Indian Merchants and Entrepreneurs in Historical Perspective: With a Special Reference to Shroffs of Gujarat, 17th to 19th Centuries*. Delhi: Academic Foundation.

Meilink-Roelofsz, Marie. 1962. *Asian Trade and European Influence in the Indonesian Archipelago Between 1500 and About 1630*. The Hague: Martinus Nijhoff.

Melville, Charles. 2012. "Jāmeʿ al-Tawārīḵ." Encyclopedia Iranica website. http://www.iranicaonline.org/articles/jame-al-tawarik.

Menzies, Gavin. 2002. *1421: The Year China Discovered the World*. London: Bantam.

Meyer, Carol. 1992. *Glass from Quseir al-Qadim and the Indian Ocean Trade*. Chicago: Oriental Institute, University of Chicago.

Michaels, Ralf. 2007. "The True Lex Mercatoria: Law Beyond the State." *Indiana Journal of Global Legal Studies* 14(2):447–468.

Michie, Ranald. 1999. *The London Stock Exchange: A History*. Oxford: Oxford University Press.

Mignone, Gianni. 2005. *Un contratto per i mercanti del Mediterraneo: L'evoluzione del rapporto partecipativo*. Naples: Jovene.

Milgrom, Paul R., Douglass C. North, and Barry R. Weingast. 1990. "The Role of Institutions in the Revival of Trade: The Law Merchant, Private Judges, and the Champagne Fairs." *Economics & Politics* 2(1):1–23.

Millett, Paul. 2002. *Lending and Borrowing in Ancient Athens*. Cambridge: Cambridge University Press.

Millward, James A. 2013. *The Silk Road: A Very Short Introduction*. New York: Oxford University Press.

Milsom, S.F.C. 1981. *Historical Foundation of the Common Law*. London: Butterworths.

Mokyr, Joel. 1993. "Editor's Introduction: The New Economic History and the Industrial Revolution." Pp. 1–131 in *The British Industrial Revolution: An Economic Perspective*, edited by J. Mokyr. Boulder: Westview.

Mokyr, Joel. 2005. *Gifts of Athena: Historical Origins of the Knowledge Economy*. Princeton: Princeton University Press.

Mokyr, Joel. 2009. *The Enlightened Economy: An Economic History of Britain 1700–1850.* New Haven: Yale University Press.

Monnickendam, Yifat. 2012. "The Kiss and the Earnest: Early Roman Influences on Syriac Matrimonial Law." *Le Muséon* 125(3–4):307–334.

Morelli, Federico. 2011. "Dal Mar Rosso ad Alessandria. Il verso (ma anche il recto) del 'papiro di Muziris' (SB 18, 13167)." *TYCHE–Contributions to Ancient History, Papyrology and Epigraphy* 26:41–41.

Morgan, David and A. Reid. 2010. "Introduction: Islam in a Plural Asia." Pp. 1–17 in *The Eastern Islamic World, Eleventh to Eighteenth Centuries*, edited by D. Morgan and A. Reid. Cambridge: Cambridge University Press.

Morgan, E. Victor and W. A. Thomas. 1969. *The Stock Exchange: Its History and Functions.* London: Elek.

Morris, T. A. 1998. *Europe and England in the Sixteenth Century.* London: Routledge.

Moser, Thomas. 2000. "The Idea of Usury in Patristic Literature." Pp. 24–44 in *The Canon in the History of Economics: Critical Essays*, edited by M. Psalidopoulos. New York: Routledge.

Mukai, Masaki. 2010. "The Interests of the Rulers, Agents and Merchants behind the Southward Expansion of the Yuan Dynasty." Pp. 428–445 in *Journal of the Turfan Studies: Essays on the Third International Conference on Turfan Studies: The Origin and Migration of Eurasian Nomadic Peoples.* Shanghai: Shanghai Guji Chubanshe.

Mukai, Masaki. 2011. "Contacts between Empires and Entrepots and the Role of Supra-regional Network: Song-Yuan-Ming Transition of the Maritime Asia, 960–1405 / Empires, Systems, and Maritime Networks." Paper presented at the Workshop on Empires and Networks: Maritime Asian Experiences, 9th to 19th Centuries, Institute of Southeast Asian Studies, Singapore.

Mukai, Masaki. 2014. "Transforming Dashi Shippers: The Tributary System and the Trans-National Network during the Song Period." Paper presented at the Conference on Middle Period China, 800–1400, Harvard University.

Munro, John H. 2003. "The Medieval Origins of the Financial Revolution: Usury, Rentes, and Negotiability." *The International History Review* 25(3):505–562.

Nabhan, Gary Paul. 2014. *Cumin, Camels, and Caravans: A Spice Odyssey.* Berkeley: University of California Press.

Nadri, Ghulam. 2007. "The Maritime Merchants of Surat: A Long-Term Perspective." *Journal of the Economic and Social History of the Orient* 50(2/3):235–258.

Neal, Larry. 1990. *The Rise of Financial Capitalism: International Capital Markets in the Age of Reason.* New York: Cambridge University Press.

Needham, Joseph. 1971. *Science and Civilisation in China*, Vol. 4: *Physics and Physical Technology*, Part 3: *Civil Engineering and Nautics.* Cambridge: Cambridge University Press.

Negev, Avraham. 1977. "The Nabateans and the Provincia Arabia." Pp. 520–586 in *Politische Geschichte (Provinzen und Randvölker: Syrien, Palästina, Arabien)*, Vol. 8, edited by W. Haase and H. Temporini. Berlin: De Gruyter.

Noonan, John T. 1957. *The Scholastic Analysis of Usury.* Cambridge, MA: Harvard University Press.

North, Douglass C. 1990. *Institutions, Institutional Change and Economic Performance.* Cambridge: Cambridge University Press.

North, Douglass C. 1994. "Economic Performance Through Time." *American Economic Review* 84(3):359–368.

North, Douglass C. 1997. "Institutions, Transaction Costs, and the Rise of Merchant Empires." Pp. 22–40 in *The Political Economy of Merchant Empires: State Power and World Trade, 1350–1750*, edited by J. Tracy. Cambridge: Cambridge University Press.

North, Douglass C. and Robert Paul Thomas. 1973. *The Rise of the Western World: A New Economic History*. New York: Cambridge University Press.

North, Douglass C., John Joseph Wallis, and Barry R. Weingast. 2009. *Violence and Social Order: A Conceptual Framework for Interpreting Recorded Human History*. Cambridge: Cambridge University Press.

North, Douglass C. and Barry R. Weingast. 1989. "Constitutions and Commitment: The Evolution of Institutions Governing Public Choice in Seventeenth-Century England." *Journal of Economic History* 49(4):803–832.

Nunn, Nathan and Nancy Qian. 2010. "The Columbian Exchange: A History of Disease, Food, and Ideas." *Journal of Economic Perspectives* 24(2):163–188.

Nyazee, Imran Ashan Khan. 1999. *Islamic Law of Business Organization: Partnerships*. Islamabad: International Institute of Islamic Thought, Islamic Research Institute.

O'Brien, Patrick K. 1988. "The Political Economy of British Taxation, 1660–1815." *Economic History Review* 41(1):1–32.

Ogilvie, Sheilagh. 2011. *Institutions and European Trade: Merchant Guilds, 1000–1800*. Cambridge Cambridge University Press.

Oka, Mihoko. 2013. "A Comparative Analysis on the Capital Investment into Portuguese Traders in the XVII Century Asian Port Cities: Case of Japan, Manila and Siam." Paper presented at the First International Conference: Globalisation's Origins and the Great Divergence: Trading Networks and the Trajectory of Economic Institutions, Europe-Asia, 1500–2000, Paris. https://f.hypotheses.org/wp-content/blogs.dir/158/files/2013/11/Non-commentateurs_-Tentative-Programme-26–11.2013–1st-GDRI-conference.pdf.

Oka, Mihoko and François Gipouloux. 2013. "Pooling Capital and Spreading Risk: Maritime Investment in East Asia at the Beginning of the Seventeenth Century." *Itinerario* *Itinerario* 37(3):75–91.

Önge, Mustafa. 2007. "Caravanserais as Symbols of Power in Seljuk Anatolia." Pp. 49–69 in *Power and Culture: Identity, Ideology, Representation*, edited by J. Osmond and A. Cimdina. Pisa: Pisa University Press.

Ostrom, Elinor. 2005. *Understanding Institutional Diversity*. Princeton: Princeton University Press.

Özbaran, Salih. 1994. *The Ottoman Response to European Expansion: Studies on Ottoman-Portuguese Relations in the Indian Ocean and Ottoman Administration in the Arab Lands During the Sixteenth Century*. Istanbul: Isis.

Özyetgin, Ayşe. 2007. "On the Term Ortuq (~ Ortaq) "Merchant" among the Old Turks." *International Journal of Central Asian Studies* 1(11):1–17.

Padgett, John F. 2012. "The Emergence of Corporate Merchant-Banks in Dugento Tuscany" and "Transposition and Refunctionality: The Birth of Partnership Systems in Renaissance Florence. Pp. 121–167 and 168–207 in *The Emergence of Organizations and Markets*, edited by J. Padgett and W. Powell. Princeton: Princeton University Press.

Pamuk, Sevket. 2014. "Institutional Change and Economic Development in the Middle East, 700–1800." Pp. 193–224 in *The Cambridge History of Capitalism*, Vol. 1: *The Rise of Capitalism: From Ancient Origins to 1848*, edited by L. Neal and J. G. Williamson. Cambridge: Cambridge University Press.

Panzac, Daniel. 2002. "Le Contrat d'affrètement maritime en Méditerranée: Droit maritime et pratique commerciale entre Islam et Chrétienté (XVIIe–XVIIIe siècles)." *Journal of the Economic and Social History of the Orient* 45(3):342–362.

Park, Hyunhee. 2012. *Mapping the Chinese and Islamic Worlds: Cross-Cultural Exchange in Pre-Modern Asia*. New York: Cambridge University Press.

Parker, Charles H. 2010. *Global Interactions in the Early Modern Age, 1400–1800*. New York: Cambridge University Press.

Parthesius, Robert. 2010. *Dutch Ships in Tropical Waters: The Development of the Dutch East India Company (VOC) Shipping Network in Asia 1595–1660*. Amsterdam: Amsterdam University Press.

Passamaneck, Stephen M. 1974. *Insurance in Rabbinic Law*. Edinburgh: Edinburgh University Press.

Peacock, A. C. S. 2015. *The Great Seljuk Empire*. Edinburgh: Edinburgh University Press

Pegolotti, Francesco. 1936 [ca. 1340]. "La Pratica della mercature." Edited by A. Evans. Cambridge: Medieval Academy of America.

Pegolotti, Francesco. 2010 [ca. 1340]. "Notices of the Land Route to Cathay and of Asiatic Trade in the First Half of the Fourteenth Century." Pp. 277–308 in *Cathay and the Way Thither: Being a Collection of Medieval Notices of China*, edited by H. Yule. New York: Cambridge University Press.

Perdue, Peter C. 2005. *China Marches West: The Qing Conquest of Central Eurasia*. Cambridge, MA: Belknap, Harvard University Press.

Peters, Francis. 1988. "The Commerce of Mecca Before Islam." Pp. 3–26 in *A Way Prepared: Essays on Islamic Culture in Honor of Richard Bayly Winder*, edited by F. Kazemi and R. D. McChesney. New York: New York University Press.

Petrushevsky, Il'ia. 1968. "The Socio-Economic Condition of Iran Under the Īl-Khāns." Pp. 483–537 in *The Saljuq and Mongol Periods*, edited by J. A. Boyle. Cambridge: Cambridge University Press.

Pfister, Ulrich. 2010 "Consumer Prices and Wages in Germany, 1500–1850." University of Münster, Center for Quantitative Economics (CQE). https://www.wiwi.uni-muenster.de/cqe/de/publikationen/cqe-working-papers.

Pires, Tomé. 1944 [1512–1515]. *The Suma Oriental of Tomé Pires*. Vols. 1 and 2. Translated by A. Cortesão. London: Hakluyt Society.

Plucknett, Theodore F. T. 1956. *A Concise History of the Common Law*. Boston: Little, Brown.

Poitras, Geoffrey. 2016. *Equity Capital: From Ancient Partnerships to Modern Exchange Traded Funds*. New York: Routledge.

Polo, Marco. 1903 [ca. 1300]. *The Book of Ser Marco Polo, the Venetian*. Vols. 1 and 2. Translated by H. Yule. London: John Murray.

Pomeranz, Kenneth. 1997. "Traditional Chinese Business Forms Revisited: Family, Firm, and Financing in the History of the Yutang Company of Jining, 1779–1956." *Late Imperial China* 18(1): 1–38.

Pomeranz, Kenneth. 2000. *The Great Divergence: China, Europe, and the Making of the Modern World Economy*. Princeton: Princeton University Press.

Poppe, Nicholas. 1955. "The Turkic Loan Words in Middle Mongolian." *Central Asiatic Journal* 1(1):36–42.

Postan, Michael. 1973. "Partnership in English Medieval Commerce." Pp. 65–71 in *Medieval Trade and Finance*. Cambridge: Cambridge University Press.

Posthumus, Nicolaas W. 1964. *Inquiry into the History of Prices in Holland*, Vol. 1. Leiden: E. J. Brill.

Powers, David S. 1993. "The Maliki Family Endowment: Legal Norms and Social Practices." *International Journal of Middle East Studies* 25(3):379–406.

Powers, David S. 1999. "The Islamic Family Endowment (Waqf)." *Vanderbilt Journal of Transnational Law* 32(4):1167–1190.

Prakash, Omar Chouhan. 1985. *The Dutch East India Company and the Economy of Bengal, 1630–1720*. Princeton: Princeton University Press.

Prakash, Om. 1998. *European Commercial Enterprise in Pre-Colonial India*. Cambridge: Cambridge University Press.

Prakash, Om. 2006. "International Consortiums, Merchant Networks and Portuguese Trade with Asia in the Early Modern Period." Paper presented at Session 37 of the Fourteenth International Economic History Congress, Helsinki.

Pryor, John H. 1974. "The Commenda in Mediterranean Maritime Commerce During the Thirteenth Century: A Study Based on Marseilles." PhD dissertation, University of Toronto.

Pryor, John H. 1977. "The Origins of the Commenda Contract." *Speculum: A Journal of Medieval Studies* 52(1):5–37.

Pryor, John H. 1983. "Mediterranean Commerce in the Middle Ages: A Voyage under Contract of Commenda." *Viator* 14(1):133–194.

Ptak, Roderich. 1989. "China and Calicut in the Early Ming Period: Envoys and Tribute Embassies." *Journal of the Royal Asiatic Society of Great Britain & Ireland* 121(1):81–111.

Pu, Faren. 1988. *Pu Shougeng xingyi yu xianshi jiguan* [Pu Shougeng family line and ancestors' birthplace]. Tainan: Shijie Puxing zongqin zonghui.

"Pub. 151: Distance Between Ports." 2001. 11th ed. Bethesda: National Geospatial Intelligence Agency. http://msi.nga.mil/NGAPortal/MSI.portal?_nfpb=true&_st=&_pageLabel=msi_portal_page_62&pubCode=0005.

"Pub. 161: Sailing Directions (Enroute)—South China Sea and the Gulf of Thailand." 2011. 13th ed. Bethesda: National Geospatial Intelligence Agency. https://msi.nga.mil/MSISiteContent/StaticFiles/NAV_PUBS/SD/Pub161/Pub161bk.pdf.

Quintern, Detlev. 2011. "Cosmopolitism, Scientific Discoveries, and Technological Inventions along the Ancient Silk Road: The Role of Samarkand and Bukhara." In *Annual Report of the Institute for Transport and Development*, Vol. 1, edited by Hans-Heinrich Bass and Hans-Martin Niemeier.

Rabb, Theodore F. 1967. *Enterprise and Empire: Merchant and Gentry Investment in the Expansion of England, 1575–1630*. Cambridge, MA: Harvard University Press.

Randazzo, Salvo. 2005. "The Nature of Partnership in Roman Law." *Australian Journal of Legal History* 9(1):119–130.

Rathbone, Dominic. 2000. "The 'Muziris' Papyrus (SB XVIII): Financing Roman Trade with India." *Bulletin de la Société archéologique d'Alexandrie (The Archaeological Society of Alexandria-Bulletin, Alexandrian Studies II in Honour of Mostafa el Abbadi)*. Vol. 46.

Rathbone, Dominic. 2007. "Merchant Networks in the Greek World: The Impact of Rome." *Mediterranean Historical Review* 22(2):309–320.

Rawson, Stuart. 2012. "How Far Were the Commercial Arrangements for Maritime Loans in Fourth Century BC Athens Dictated by the Legal Framework Available?" *Student Researcher* 2(1):33–44.

Ray, Jonathan. 2013. *After Expulsion: 1492 and the Making of Sephardic Jewry*. New York: New York University Press.

Raymond, André. 1994. "Islamic City, Arab City: Orientalist Myths and Recent Views." *British Journal of Middle Eastern Studies* 21(1):3–18.

Reddick, Zachary. 2014. "The Zheng He Voyages Reconsidered: A Means of Imperial Power Projection." *Quarterly Journal of Chinese Studies* 3(1):55–65.

Reynders, Peter. 2009 "A Translation of the Charter of the Dutch East India Company (Verenidge Ostiindische Compagnie or VOC)." Australasian Hydrographic Society. http://www.australiaonthemap.org.au/voc-charter/.

Riemersma, Jelle. 1952. "Trading and Shipping Associations in 16th Century Holland." *Tijdschrift voor geschiedenis* 65:330–338.

Riggsby, Andrew M. 2010. *Roman Law and the Legal World of the Romans*. Cambridge: Cambridge University Press.

Risso, Patricia. 1995. *Merchants and Faith: Muslim Commerce and Culture in the Indian Ocean*. Boulder: Westview.

Robinson, Francis. 1993. "Technology and Religious Change: Islam and the Impact of Print." *Modern Asian Studies* 27(1):229–251.

Rodger, N.A.M. 2001. "Guns and Sails in the First Phase of English Colonization: 1500–1650." Pp. 79–98 in *The Origins of Empire: British Overseas Enterprise to the Close of the Seventeenth Century*, Vol. 1, edited by N. Canny and A. Low. Oxford: Oxford University Press.

Roe, Mark J. 1996. "Chaos and Evolution in Law and Economics." *Harvard Law Review* 109(3):641–668.

Rogers, James Steven. 1995. *The Early History of the Law of Bills and Notes: A Study of the Origins of Anglo-American Commercial Law*. Cambridge: Cambridge University Press.

Rose-Troup, Frances. 1930. *The Massachusetts Bay Company and Its Predecessors*. New York: Grafton.

Rosenthal, Jean-Laurent and R. Bin Wong. 2011. *Before and Beyond Divergence: The Politics of Economic Change in China and Europe*. Cambridge, MA: Harvard University Press.

Rossabi, Morris. 1972. "Ming China and Turfan, 1406–1517." *Central Asiatic Journal* 16(3):206–225.

Rossabi, Morris. 1981. "The Muslims in the Early Yuan Dynasty." Pp. 257–295 in *China Under Mongol Rule*, edited by J. Langlois. Princeton: Princeton University Press.

Rossabi, Morris. 1993. "The Decline of the Central Asian Caravan Trade." Pp. 351–370 in *The Rise of Merchant Empires: Long Distance Trade in the Early Modern World 1350–1750*, edited by J. Tracy. Cambridge: Cambridge University Press.

Rowley-Conwy, Peter, Umberto Albarella, and Keith Dobney. 2012. "Distinguishing Wild Boar from Domestic Pigs in Prehistory: A Review of Approaches and Recent Results." *Journal of World Prehistory* 25(1):1–44.

Roy, Tirthankar. 2008. "The Guild in Modern South Asia." *International Review of Social History* 53(S16):95–120.

Rubin, Jared. 2017. *Rulers, Religion, and Riches: Why the West Got Rich and the Middle East Did Not*. New York: Cambridge University Press.

Rudden, Bernard. 1985. *The New River: A Legal History*. Oxford: Oxford University Press.

Ruffing, Kai. 2013. "The Trade with India and the Problem of Agency in the Economy of the Roman Empire." Pp. 199–210 in *Egitto dai Faraoni agli Arabi*, edited by S. Bussi. Pisa, Rome: Fabrizio Serra.

Rungta, Shyam Radhe. 1970. *The Rise of Business Corporations in India, 1851–1900*. Cambridge: Cambridge University Press.

Ruskola, Teemu. 2000. "Conceptualizing Corporations and Kinship: Comparative Law and Development Theory in a Chinese Perspective." *Stanford Law Review* 52(6):1599–1729.

Safley, Thomas Max. 2009. "Business Failure and Civil Scandal in Early Modern Europe." *Business History Review* 83(1):35–60.

Salaymeh, Lena. 2013. "Between Scholarship and Polemic in Judeo-Islamic Studies." *Islam and Christian-Muslim Relations* 24(3):407–418.

Slae, Menachem. 1980. *HaBituach BaHalachah* [Insurance in Halachah]. Tel Aviv: Israel Insurance Association.

Samarqandī, Abd-al-Razzāq. 1857 [ca. 1442]. *India in the Fifteenth Century: Being a Collection of Narratives of Voyages to India, in the Century Preceding the Portuguese Discovery of the Cape of Good Hope; From Latin, Persian, Russian, and Italian Sources*. Edited by R. H. Major. London: Hakluyt Society.

Sangren, Steven P. 1984. "Traditional Chinese Corporations: Beyond Kinship." *Journal of Asian Studies* 43(3):391–415.

Sanjian, Avedis K. 1999. "Medieval Armenian Manuscripts at the University of California, Los Angeles." Berkeley: University of California Press.

Sapori, Armando. 1926. *La Crisi delle compagnie mercantili dei Bardi e dei Peruzzi*. Florence: Olschki.

Sarkar, Jagadish Narayan. 1991. *Private Traders in Medieval India*. Calcutta: Naya Prokash.

Scammell, G. V. 1981. *The World Encompassed: The First European Maritime Empires, c. 800–1650*. Berkeley: University of California Press.

Schacht, Joseph. 1982. *An Introduction to Islamic Law*. Oxford: Clarendon.

Schick, Léon. 1957. *Un grand homme d'affaires au début du XVIe siècle, Jacob Fugger*. Paris: S.E.V.P.E.N.

Schimmel, Annemarie. 2004. *The Empire of the Great Mughals: History, Art and Culture*. London: Reaktion.

Schmitthoff, Clive M. 1939. "The Origin of the Joint-Stock Company." *University of Toronto Law Journal* 3(1):74–96.

Schulz, Fritz. 1951. *Classical Roman Law*. Oxford: Clarendon.

Schurmann, Herbert Franz. 1956. *Economic Structure of the Yüan Dynasty*. Cambridge, MA: Harvard University Press.

Scott, William. 1910–1912. *The Constitution and Finance of English, Scottish and Irish Joint-Stock Companies to 1720*. 3 vols. Cambridge: Cambridge University Press.

Secunda, Shai. 2014. *The Iranian Talmud: Reading the Bavli in Its Sasanian Context*. Philadelphia: University of Pennsylvania Press.

Sen, Tansen. 2003. *Buddhism, Diplomacy, and Trade: The Realignment of Sino-Indian Relations, 600–1400*. Honolulu: Association for Asian Studies and University of Hawaii Press.

Sen, Tansen. 2009. "The Military Campaigns of Rajendra Chola and the Chola-Sri Vijaya-China Triangle." Pp. 61–75 in *Nagapattinam to Suvarnadwipa: Reflections on the Chola*

Naval Expeditions to Southeast Asia, edited by H. Kulke, K. Kesavapany, and V. Sakhuja. Singapore: Institute of Southeast Asian Studies.

Septvaux v. Marchaunt. 1377. Y.B. 8–10 Rich II 187.

Serjeant, Robert. 1990. "Meccan Trade and the Rise of Islam: Misconceptions and Flawed Polemics." Book review. *Journal of the American Oriental Society* 110(3):472–486.

Shammas, Carole. 1975. "The Invisible Merchant and Property Rights." *Business History* 17(2):95–108.

Shankar, D., P. N. Vinayachandran, and A. S. Unnikrishnan. 2002. "The Monsoon Currents in the North Indian Ocean." *Progress in Oceanography* 52(1):63–120.

Shapiro, Scott J. 2007. "The Hart-Dworkin Debate: A Short Guide for the Perplexed." Pp. 22–55 in *Ronald Dworkin*, edited by A. Ripstein. New York: Cambridge University Press.

Shatzmiller, Maya. 2001. "Islamic Institutions and Property Rights: The Case of the 'Public Good' Waqf." *Journal of the Economic and Social History of the Orient* 44(1):44–74.

Shaw, John. 1887 [1774]. *Charters Relating to the East India Company from 1600 to 1761.* Reprint. Madras: Government Press.

Sheppard, William. 1659. *Of Corporations, Fraternities and Guilds.* London: H. Twyford, T. Dring, and J. Place.

Shiba, Yoshinobu. 1970. *Commerce and Society in Sung China.* Translated by M. Elvin. Ann Arbor: University of Michigan Center for Chinese Studies.

Shihab, Saleh Hassan. 1997. "Aden in Pre-Turkish Times (1232–1538): The Arabian Entrepot of the Western Asian." Pp. 17–32 in *Gateways of Asia: Port Cities of Asia in the 13th–20th Centuries*, edited by F. Broeze. London: Kegan Paul.

Sicard, Germain. 2015 [1953]. *The Origins of Corporations: The Mills of Toulouse in the Middle Ages.* Translated by Matthew Landry. New Haven: Yale University Press.

Simkin, Colin. 1968. *The Traditional Trade of Asia.* London: Oxford University Press.

Simonsohn, Uriel. 2008. "Overlapping Jurisdictions: Confessional Boundaries and Judicial Choice Among Christians and Jews under Early Muslim Rule." PhD dissertation, Princeton University.

Simpson, A.W.B. 1986. *A History of the Land Law.* Oxford: Oxford University Press.

Skaff, Jonathan Karam. 2003. "The Sogdian Trade Diaspora in East Turkestan during the Seventh and Eighth Centuries." *Journal of the Economic and Social History of the Orient* 46(4):475–524.

Smith, Edmond. 2018. "The Global Interests of London's Commercial Community, 1599–1625: Investment in the East India Company." *Economic History Review* 71(4):1118–1146. doi: 10.1111/ehr.12665.

Smith, Julian A. 1992. "Precursors to Peregrinus: The Early History of Magnetism and the Mariner's Compass in Europe." *Journal of Medieval History* 18(1):21–74.

So, Billy Kee-Long. 2000. *Prosperity, Region, and Institutions in Maritime China: The South Fukien Pattern, 946–1368.* Cambridge: Harvard University Asia Center.

Song, Lian. 1976 [ca. 1370]. *Yuanshi Juan* [Yuan history]. Beijing: Zhonghua Shuju.

Sørensen, Karsten Engsig. 2005. "The Danish East India Company." Pp. 107–130 in *VOC 1602–2002: 400 Years of Company Law*, edited by E. Gepken-Jager, G. van Solinge, and L. Timmerman. Deventer: Kluwer.

Souza, George. 1986. *The Survival of Empire: Portuguese Trade and Society in China and the South China Sea, 1630–1754.* Cambridge: Cambridge University Press.

Spence, Michael. 1973. "Job Market Signaling." *Quarterly Journal of Economics* 87(3):355–374.

Spufford, Peter. 2002. *Power and Profit: The Merchant in Medieval Europe*. London: Thames & Hudson.

Starr, Frederick S. 2013. *Lost Enlightenment: Central Asia's Golden Age from the Arab Conquest to Tamerlane*. Princeton: Princeton University Press.

Steensgaard, Niels. 1974. *The Asian Trade Revolution of the Seventeenth Century: The East India Companies and the Decline of the Caravan Trade*. Chicago: University of Chicago Press.

Steensgaard, Niels. 1977. "Dutch East India Company as an Institutional Innovation." Pp. 235–257 in *Dutch Capitalism and World Capitalism*, edited by M. Aymard. Cambridge: Cambridge University Press.

Stent, Carter G. 1877. "Chinese Eunuchs." *Journal of the North China Branch of the Royal Asiatic Society* 11:143–84.

Stern, Philip J. 2011. *The Company-State: Corporate Sovereignty and the Early Modern Foundations of the British Empire in India*. New York: Oxford University Press.

Stern, Samuel. 1970. "The Constitution of the Islamic City." Pp. 25–50 in *The Islamic City: A Colloquium*, edited by A. Hourani and S. Stern. Oxford: Cassirer.

Stevens, Henry. 1967. *The Dawn of British Trade to the East Indies as Recorded in the Court Minutes of the East India Company, 1599–1603*. London: Cass.

Stiglitz, Joseph and Bruce Greenwald. 1986. "Externalities in Economies with Imperfect Information and Incomplete Markets." *Quarterly Journal of Economics* 101(2):229–264.

Strang, David and John W. Meyer. 1993. "Institutional Conditions for Diffusion." *Theory and Society* 22(4):487–511.

Su, Yanming. 2002. "Jiuzhuan Wenwu Hui Quan Sheng—Jinian Shichuang 'Yanzhi Sushi Zupu' 500 Zhou Nian" [A marvelous ancient relic of historical records—marking the 500th anniversary of initiating the compilation of the 'Yanzhi Su family genealogy']."

Subrahmanyam, Sanjay. 1986. "The Coromandel-Malacca Trade in the 16th Century: A Study of Its Evolving Structure." *Moyen Orient et Océan Indien* 3: 55–80.

Subrahmanyam, Sanjay. 1997. *The Career and Legend of Vasco da Gama*. New York: Cambridge University Press.

Subrahmanyam, Sanjay. 2012. *The Portuguese Empire in Asia, 1500–1700: A Political and Economic History*. Chichester: Wiley.

Subrahmanyam, Sanjay and Luís Filipe Thomaz. 1991. "Evolution of Empire: The Portuguese in the Indian Ocean During the Sixteenth Century." Pp. 298–331 in *The Political Economy of Merchant Empires: State Power and World Trade, 1350–1750*, edited by J. Tracy. Cambridge: Cambridge University Press.

Tan, Elaine. 2002. "An Empty Shell? Rethinking the Usury Laws in Medieval Europe." *Journal of Legal History* 23(3):177–196.

Teubner, Gunther. 1998. "Legal Irritants: Good Faith in British Law, or How Unifying Law Ends Up in New Divergencies." *Modern Law Review* 61(1):11–32.

Thareani-Sussely, Yifat. 2007. "Ancient Caravanserais: An Archaeological View from Aroer." *Levant* 39(1):123–141.

't Hart, Marjolein C. 1993. *Making of a Bourgeois State: War, Politics and Finance During the Dutch Revolt*. Manchester: Manchester University Press.

Thomas, George. 1991. *Linguistic Purism*. London: Longman.

Thomas, Nigel. 1991. "Râdhânites, Chinese Jews, and the Silk Road of the Steppes." *Sino-Judaica* 1:1–25.

Thür, Gerhard. 1987. "Hypotheken-Urkunde eines Seedarlehens für eine Reise nach Muziris und Apographe für die Tetarte in Alexandria (zu P. Vindob. G. 40.822)." *Tyche* (2):229–245.

Tibbetts, G. R. 1971. *Arab Navigation in the Indian Ocean Before the Coming of the Portuguese*. London: Royal Asiatic Society of Great Britain and Ireland.

Tierney, Brian. 1955. *Foundations of the Conciliar Theory: The Contribution of the Medieval Canonists from Gratian to the Great Schism*. Cambridge: Cambridge University Press.

Toma, Marina. 2008. "A History of Zero." *Journal of Science and Arts* 8(1):117–122.

Toqto'a. 1977 [1343]. *Songshi juan* [Song history], Vol. 47. Beijing: Zhonghua Shuju.

Tracy, James D. 1985. *A Financial Revolution in the Habsburg Netherlands: Renten and Renteniers in the County of Holland, 1515–1565*. Los Angeles: University of California Press.

Tremml-Werner, Birgit. 2012. "The Global and the Local: Problematic Dynamics of the Triangular Trade in Early Modern Manila." *Journal of World History* 23(3):555–586.

Trivellato, Francesca. 2009. *The Familiarity of Strangers: The Sephardic Diaspora, Livorno, and Cross-Cultural Trade in the Early Modern Period*. New Haven: Yale University Press.

Tsugitaka, Sato. 2006 "Slave Traders and Karimi Merchants during the Mamluk Period: A Comparative Study." *Mamluk Studies Review* 10(1):141–155.

Udovitch, Abraham. 1962. "At the Origins of the Western Commenda: Islam, Israel, Byzantium?" *Speculum* 37(2):198–207.

Udovitch, Abraham. 1970. *Partnership and Profit in Medieval Islam*. Princeton: Princeton University Press.

Udovitch, Abraham. 1977. "Formalism and Informalism in the Social and Economic Institutions of the Medieval Islamic World." Pp. 61–81 in *Individualism and Conformity in Classical Islam*, edited by A. Banani. Wiesbaden: O. Harrassowitz.

Udovitch, Abraham. 1993. "An Eleventh Century Islamic Treatise on the Law of the Sea." *Annales islamologiques* 27:37–54.

UNESCO. n.d. "The UNESCO Website on Caravanserais." http://www.unesco.org/culture/dialogue/eastwest/caravan/page1.htm.

United States v. Kintner. 1954. 216 F.2d 418 (9th Cir.).

van Dillen, Johannes. 1958. *Het oudste Aandeelhoudersregister van de Kamer Amsterdam der Oost-Indische Compagnie*. Leiden: Martinus Nijhoff.

van Dillen, Johannes. 2006 [1935]. "Isaac Le Maire and the Early Trading in Dutch East India Company Shares." Pp. 45–63 in *Pioneers of Financial Economics* 1, translated by Asha Majithia.

van Doosselaere, Quentin. 2009. *Commercial Agreements and Social Dynamics in Medieval Genoa*. Cambridge: Cambridge University Press.

van Leur, J. C. 1967. *Indonesian Trade and Society: Essays in Asian Social and Economic History*. The Hague: W. van Hoeve.

van Zanden, Jan Luiten. "The Prices of the Most Important Consumer Goods, and Indices of Wages and the Cost of Living in the Western Part of the Netherlands, 1450–1800." http://www.iisg.nl/scripts/print.php?language=en&url=www.iisg.nl%2Fhpw%2Fbrenv.php.

Varadarajan, Lotika. 1976. "The Brothers Boras and Virji Vora." *Journal of the Economic and Social History of the Orient* 19(1):224–227.

Vaucher, Jean. 2014 "(Brief) History of European-Asian Trade." http://www.iro.umontreal
.ca/~vaucher/Genealogy/Documents/Asia/EuropeanExploration.html.

Vauchez, André. 1971. "Michaud-Quantin (Pierre) Universitas. Expressions du mouve-
ment communautaire dans le Moyen Age latin." *Archives de Sciences Sociales des Religions* 31(1):225–226.

Verbit, Gilbert. 2002. *The Origins of the Trust*. Philadelphia: Xlibris.

von-Gierke, Otto. 1900 [1881]. *Political Theories of the Middle Age*. Translated by F. W.
Maitland. Cambridge: Cambridge University Press.

Vosoughi, Mohammad. 2009. "The Kings of Hormuz: From the Beginning until the
Arrival of the Portuguese." Pp. 89–104 in *The Persian Gulf in History*, edited by L. G.
Potter. New York: Palgrave Macmillan.

Wall, Richard, Jean Robin, and Peter Laslett, eds. 1983. *Family Forms in Historic Europe*.
Cambridge: Cambridge University Press.

Wallerstein, Immanuel. 2011 [1974, 1980, 1989, 2011]. *The Modern World-System*. 4 vols.
Berkeley: University of California Press.

Walter, Rolf. 2006. "High-Finance Interrelated: International Consortiums in the Commercial World of the 16th Century." Paper presented at Session 37 of the Fourteenth
International Economic History Congress, Helsinki. http://www.helsinki.fi/iehc2006
/papers1/Walter.pdf.

Watson, Alan. 1961. *Contract of Mandate in Roman Law*. Oxford: Clarendon.

Watson, Alan. 1974. *Legal Transplants: An Approach to Comparative Law*. Athens: University of Georgia Press.

Weber, Max. 1919. *Politics as a Vocation*. Munich: Duncker & Humblodt.

Weber, Max. 1930 [1905]. *The Protestant Ethic and the Spirit of Capitalism*. Translated by
T. Parsons. London: George Allen & Unwina.

Weber, Max. 2003 [1889]. *The History of Commercial Partnerships in the Middle Ages*.
Translated by L. Kaelber. Lanham: Rowman & Littlefield.

Weingast, Barry R. 1995. "The Economic Role of Political Institutions: Market-Preserving
Federalism and Economic Development." *Journal of Law, Economics and Organization*
11(1):1–31.

Wenke, Robert J. 1990. *Patterns in Prehistory: Humankind's First Three Million Years*. New
York: Oxford University Press.

White, Lynn. 1964. *Medieval Technology and Social Change*. London: Oxford University
Press.

Whitman, James Q. 2009. "Western Legal Imperialism: Thinking About the Deep Historical Roots." *Theoretical Inquiries in Law* 10(2):305–332.

Wild, Oliver. 1992 "The Silk Road." University of California, Irvine, Department of Earth
System Science. http://www.ess.uci.edu/~oliver/silk.html.

Willan, T. S. 1956. *The Early History of the Russia Company, 1553–1603*. Manchester:
Manchester University Press.

Willetts, William. 1964. "The Maritime Adventures of Grand Eunuch Ho." *Journal of
Southeast Asian History* 5(2):25–42.

Williamson, Dean. 2003. "Transparency and Contract Selection: Evidence from the Financing of Trade in Venetian Crete, 1303–1351." *Journal of Economic History*
63(2):555–557.

Williamson, Dean. 2010. "The Financial Structure of Commercial Revolution: Financing
Long-Distance Trade in Venice 1190–1220 and Venetian Crete 1278–1400." Paper

presented at the Fifteenth Annual Conference of the International Society for New Institutional Economics, Stanford.

Williamson, Oliver E. 1979. "Transaction-Cost Economics: The Governance of Contractual Relations." *Journal of Law and Economics* 22(2):233–261.

Williamson, Oliver E. 1985. *The Economic Institutions of Capitalism: Firms, Markets, Relational Contracting*. New York: Free Press.

Wink, André. 2010. "The Early Expansion of Islam in India." Pp. 78–99 in *The Eastern Islamic World, Eleventh to Eighteenth Centuries*, edited by D. Morgan and A. Reid. Cambridge: Cambridge University Press.

Wong, R. Bin. 2014. "China before Capitalism." Pp. 125–164 in *The Cambridge History of Capitalism*, Vol. 1: *The Rise of Capitalism: From Ancient Origins to 1848*, edited by L. Neal and J. Williamson. Cambridge: Cambridge University Press.

Wood, Alfred C. 1964. *A History of the Levant Company*. London: Cass.

Xianglin, Luo. 1959. *Pu Shougeng Yanjiu* [A new study of Pu Shougeng and his times]. Hong Kong: Institute of Chinese Culture.

Yamamoto, Tatsuro and On Ikeda. 1986. *Tun-Huang and Turfan Documents: Concerning Social and Economic History*, Vol. 3: *Contracts*. Tokyo: Committee for the Studies of the Tun-Huang Manuscripts; the Toyo Bunko.

Yasuhiro, Yokkaichi. 2006. "The Structure of Political Power and the Nanhai Trade from the Perspective of Local Elites in Zhejiang in the Yuan Period." Paper presented at the Association for Asian Studies Annual Conference. San Francisco. http://aas2.asian -studies.org/absts/2006abst/Interarea/I-27.htm.

Yasuhiro, Yokkaichi. 2008. "Chinese and Muslim Diasporas and the Indian Ocean Trade Network under Mongol Hegemony." Pp. 73–102 in *The East Asian Mediterranean*, Vol. 6: *Maritime Crossroads of Culture, Commerce and Human Migration*, edited by A. Schottenhammer. Wiesbaden: Harrassowitz.

Young, Gary Y. 2001. *Rome's Eastern Trade: International Commerce and Imperial Policy, 31 BC—305 AD*. London: Routledge.

Yuguang, Zhang and Jin Debao. 1983. "Baogao fajian Pu Shougeng jiapu jingguo" [An account of discovering Pu Shougeng's genealogy]." In *yanjiu lunwen xuan* [Symposium on Quanzhou Islam], edited by the Q. F. M. Museum. Quanzhou: Fujian People's Publishing Society.

Zahraa, Mahdi. 1995. "Legal Personality in Islamic Law." *Arab Law Quarterly* 10(3):193–206.

Zelin, Madeleine. 1990. "The Rise and Fall of the Fu-Rong Salt-Yard Elite: Merchant Domi Nance in Late Qing China." Pp. 82–109 in *Chinese Local Elites and Patterns of Dominance*, edited by J. Esherick and M. Rankin. Berkeley: University of California Press.

Zelin, Madeleine. 2004. "Managing Multiple Ownership at the Zigong Saltyards." Pp. 230–268 in *Contract and Property in Early Modern China*, edited by M. Zelin, J. Ocko and R. Gardella. Stanford: Stanford University Press.

Zelin, Madeleine. 2005. *The Merchants of Zigong: Industrial Entrepreneurship in Early Modern China*. New York: Columbia University Press.

Zelin, Madeleine. 2006. "Eastern Sichuan Coal Mines in the Late Qing." Pp. 102–122 in *Empire, Nation, and Beyond: Chinese History in Late Imperial and Modern Times*, edited by F. Wakeman, J. Esherick, W. H. Yeh, and M. Zelin. Berkeley: Institute of East Asian Studies.

Zelin, Madeleine. 2009. "The Firm in Early Modern China." *Journal of Economic Behavior & Organization* 71(3):623–637.

Zhang, Taisu. 2017. *The Laws and Economics of Confucianism: Kinship and Property in Preindustrial China and England*. New York: Cambridge University Press.

Zhenman, Zheng. 2001. *Family Lineage Organization and Social Changein Ming and Qing Fujian*. Honolulu: University of Hawai'i Press.

Zhixing, Jin. 1555. "Li Shi." Pp. 52a-53a in *Qingyuan Jin Shi Zupu*. [Genealogy of the Qingyuan Jin family], edited by J. Zhixing.

Zimmermann, Reinhard. 1996. *The Law of Obligations: Roman Foundations of the Civilian Tradition*. New York: Oxford University Press.

Ziskind, Jonathan. 1974. "Sea Loans at Ugarit." *Journal of the American Oriental Society* 94(1):134–137.

INDEX

~ ~ ~